Studies of Language, Thought and Verbal Communication

Studies of Language, Thought and Verbal Communication

Edited by

R. ROMMETVEIT *and* R. M. BLAKAR

Institute of Psychology,
University of Oslo, Oslo, Norway

1979

ACADEMIC PRESS

LONDON   NEW YORK   SAN FRANCISCO

A Subsidiary of Harcourt Brace Jovanovich, Publishers

ACADEMIC PRESS INC. (LONDON) LTD.
24/28 Oval Road
London NW1

United States Edition published by
ACADEMIC PRESS INC.
111 Fifth Avenue
New York, New York 10003

Library of Congress Catalog Card Number: 78–18030
ISBN: 0–12–594660–0

Printed and bound in Great Britain by
Morrison & Gibb Ltd, London and Edinburgh

Contributors

Berkley, M. *Department of Psychology, Cornell University, Ithaca, New York 14853, U.S.A.*

Blakar, R. M. *Institute of Psychology, University of Oslo, Box 1094 Blindern, Oslo 3, Norway*

Brøgger, J. *Institute of Social Science, University of Trondheim, Trondheim, Norway*

Hundeide, V. *Institute of Psychology, University of Oslo, Box 1094 Blindern, Oslo 3, Norway*

Kleiven, J. *Oppland Distriktshøgskole, Box 193, 2601 Lillehammer, Norway*

Kvale, S. *Institute of Psychology, University of Århus, Århus, Denmark*

Lagerløv, T. *Voldsveien 170, 1343 Eiksmarka, Norway*

Rommetveit, R. *Institute of Psychology, University of Oslo, Box 1094 Blindern, Oslo 3, Norway*

Sølvberg, H. A. *Eg Sykehus, 4600 Kristiansand, Norway*

Stokstad, S. J. *Stallerudveien 95, Oslo 6, Norway*

Strømnes, F. *Institute of Psychology, University of Tromsø, Norway*

Svendsen, D. *Institute of Psychology, University of Bergen, 5000 Bergen, Norway*

Toch, H. *State University New York (SUNY) at Albany, 1700 Washington Avenue, Albany, New York 12222, U.S.A.*

Turner, E. A.* *Medical Research Council, Speech and Communication Research Unit, 31 Buccleuch Place, Edinburgh 8, U.K.*

Wold, A. H. *Institute of Psychology, University of Oslo, Box 1094 Blindern, Oslo 3, Norway*

*The author's name is now Carswell, E. A.

Preface

Traditionally, language, thought and communication have been among the most thoroughly investigated and most intensively debated topics within the field of general psychology. Inspired by and organized around Professor Ragnar Rommetveit, a research milieu devoted to these issues has existed for more than 20 years at the University of Oslo. Over the years many empirical research reports and theoretical papers from this research group have appeared in different books and journals. The aim of the present book is to collect and bring together in one volume a selective sample of what we consider representative and significant papers written within this research tradition. In his various monographs Rommetveit has presented the conceptual and theoretical framework of this "social-cognitive" approach towards language, thought and communication. In particular, "On Message Structure" gives an integrated account of this theoretical position. During the last years we have noticed a steadily increasing interest in the theoretical-empirical studies upon which the development of this conceptual framework is based. "Studies of Language, Thought and Verbal Communication" thus collects and makes available studies conducted within this particular conceptual framework. Within the general frame given by the title, the 35 papers in the present volume cover a wide range of issues (*from* micro-analysis of the process of reading *to* patterns of communication in families containing schizophrenic members; *from* word processing *to* construction of social realities; *from* associative networks *to* contractual aspects of communication, etc.). Moreover, a considerable period of time is covered (*from* 1960 *to* a paper prepared for this volume). In his introduction, Rommetveit briefly outlines how the various studies constitute parts of an integrated research programme.

The Editors want to acknowledge the permissions given by the previous publishers to reprint the various articles and papers.

NOVEMBER, 1978   ROLV MIKKEL BLAKAR

Introduction

That this anthology came into being is largely due to the initiative and efforts of my co-editor, Rolv Mikkel Blakar. He made the observation that students and researchers from different fields who knew part of our work and were interested in learning more about it, had difficulties because the written contributions brought together in this book have appeared in journals and books covering topics ranging all the way from experimental psychology via sociology, linguistics and psychiatry to philosophy of social science. This anthology contains contributions across the entire range and covers nearly two decades of theoretical and empirical enquiries into language, thought and human communication.

What I feel has emerged out of these enquiries is, first of all, a growing and increasingly reflectively elaborated sensitivity toward the complexity and multifaceted nature of Man's symbolic and communicative achievements. My own enquiries have been steps along a very long and cumbersome path in the hope that—some blessed day—I might reach the mountain from where all only fragmentarily known parts of a vast and intriguing land would become visible and the interrelationships among them revealed. We all know that this is a futile hope. It is hardly ever entirely abandoned, though, and hence possibly one of the futile necessities of research.

A reading of the more programmatically flavoured essays in Part 1 in the order in which they were written will reveal a persistent and growing concern with the—possibly Utopian—prospect of a shared conceptual basis for inter-disciplinary ventures. Constructive efforts in that direction grew mainly out of critique of dominant research traditions (Chapters 2, 3, 7 and 35) and attempts at a synthesis of "positivistic" and "hermeneutic-dialectic" approaches (Chapters 4 and 5). More specific implications of an alternative approach, however, could only be spelled out in empirical research (cf., e.g. Chapters 19, 20, 23, 27, 28, 32, 33, 34 and 35). This does not imply that insight into the riddles of human thought and communication has been attained in a firmly empirically founded and strictly cumulative fashion. However, the sensitive reader will hopefully be able to relate what is programmatically preached in Part 1 to some of the findings reported in Part 2 and—at least—appreciate our willingness to subject theoretical notions to empirical tests.

Many of the experimental reports on word perception and aspects of word meaning (Chapters 3–20) may thus be read as empirical corroborations and elaborations of the theoretical micro-analysis of language processing in Chapter 1. The essentials of this analysis, moreover, constituted points of departure for subsequent experiments on intra- and extralinguistic context (Chapters 21–28) and were—as the scope of our enquiries was extended so as to cope more explicitly and systematically with interactional aspects—incorporated in a macro-analysis of message structure (Chapters 2 and 4). This macro-analysis was extended to communication patterns in fairly complex yet experimentally controlled, situations (Chapters 33 and 34). Issues concerning power and control were made foci of conceptual analysis as well (Chapters 6 and 7), and illuminated in enquiries into socially important issues such as potentially ideological components in public education on drug abuse and the way in which sex roles are reflected and possibly conserved in ordinary language (Chapters 29 and 32). What is meant by semantic potentialities (as opposed to "semantic markers" or "lexical meaning", see Chapters 5 and 7), moreover, is hopefully further explicated in experimental studies of the interdependence of language and thought in specific cases of child-adult communication (Chapter 35).

Conceptual progress, however, may also lead to some re-evaluation and even re-interpretation of experimental "facts". The impact of verbalization upon otherwise "intuitive" cognition first observed nearly two decades ago (Chapters 9–12) may thus today in retrospect, in view of recent sociolinguistic concepts of speech acts discussed in Chapter 7, serve primarily as a warning against over-simplification. There is within current sociolinguistics a definite tendency to reduce the semantic aspects of verbal communication to "actions performed by words". What is easily overlooked in such an analysis, however, is the "innocence of silence" and the subtle transformation of knowledge which at times seems to be part and parcel of the very act of verbalization. An old lady I knew used to talk about "the mercy to be able to keep silent". What she had in mind, I think, was that quite a few things may as well remain unspoken because putting them into words will somehow alter the status of the potential topic from that of innocent, not yet socially confirmed intuitions to that of "public", embarrassing knowledge. This subtle transformation—or construction —of knowledge is in retrospect the most significant issue in our experiments on concept formation. More recent reflections on the boundaries between semantic competence and intuitive knowledge of the world (Chapter 7) are thus in part further elaborations of ideas that were subject to preliminary experimental explorations a long time ago (Chapters 9–12).

The connection between experimental evidence and philosophical considerations may in such a case appear tenuous, and one may also wonder how, e.g. micro-analysis of reading under conditions of binocular rivalry of letters (Chapters 16–20) fits into a more general and abstract explication of message structure and prerequisites for human intersubjectivity (Chapters 2 and 5). Why do fluent readers under certain experimental conditions spontaneously read a particular pair of competing letters such as r/p as only p, as only r, as pr or as rp, depending upon which resolution of the rivalry conflict yields a word, and what do such perceptual strategies reveal about general pre-requisites for linguistically mediated meaning and intersubjectivity?

My tentative answers are as follows: The reader sees words because the rivalling letters are encountered in a socially constructed, tacitly and firmly taken-for-granted, habitat of human meaning. The genuinely social nature of language is thus revealed even in highly automatized linguistic skill displayed in solitary performance under artificially created laboratory conditions, since such performance becomes comprehensible only when explicitly recognized as embedded in a social game. Our more general claim that intersubjectivity has in some sense to be taken for granted in order to be achieved (Chapter 5) is thus corroborated even in micro-analysis of language processing. A very general theoretical assumption is thus in this case further explicated by reference to specific experimental findings, and the latter are made more intelligible in view of precisely that assumption.

This is not merely a matter of logical necessity and strict deduction, however, and the reader may perhaps often find it difficult to follow our attempts at integrating empirical evidence from micro- and macro-analysis of language, thought and human communication into a co-herent conceptual framework. Verbal communication is, as Wittgenstein claimed, embedded in "the stream of life", and many of the empirical studies reported in Part 2 may indeed be interpreted as attempts at pursuing various implications of that very general claim.

There are, in my opinion, no God-given boundaries between social science on the one hand and epistemological and ontological enquiries on the other. Our mastery of symbolic interaction with fellow men borders on our general and partially shared knowledge of the world. Our insight into that mastery, moreover, borders on only partially explicated presuppositions of an epistemological and ontological nature.

NOVEMBER, 1978   RAGNAR ROMMETVEIT

Contents

Part 1
Theoretical Perspectives

Part 2
Empirical Research

Part 1
Theoretical Perspectives

1. Words, Contexts and Verbal Message Transmission*

R. ROMMETVEIT

Modern psycholinguistics is a very heterogeneous and rapidly expanding field of research, and psycholinguists who are currently engaged in psycholinguistic studies came there from very different theroretical backgrounds. They have very little in common, therefore, apart from a research interest in those very aspects of language which Ebbinghaus struggled to get rid of when he first introduced linguistic stimuli into the laboratories of a young scientific psychology. Ebbinghaus' nonsense syllables and Shakespeare's words were in certain significant respects considered as belonging to entirely different domains. Only recently have experimental psychologists ventured to expand their enquiries into the latter sphere of words, meaning and verbal message transmission.

The riddles of human language are manifold and subtle, however, and current psycholinguistic research resembles a guerrilla warfare in a vast and largely unknown territory. Experimental psychologists detach words from utterances and utterances from their proper communication settings in order to gain knowledge concerning different aspects of language processing. Some of us do experiments on speech discrimination, some are engaged in measurement of so-called affective word meaning, others employ psychological research methods to investigate semantic relationships, still others use word association tasks in order to map associative networks, and quite a few psychologists have joined structural linguists in a search for so-called surface and deep sentence structures. As a consequence, we are left with very scattered, very fragmentary and very tentative insights only, and with a challenge to bring such fragments of exploratory knowledge together into a coherent psychological picture of human language in action.

* Expanded version of paper presented at the psycholinguistic seminar in Oslo, May, 1968. Published in "Social Contexts of Messages" (1971). (A. E. Carswell and R. Rommetveit, Eds). Academic Press, London and New York.

The present paper is, in a way, a response to such a challenge. We shall not even try to survey the various "schools" of psycholinguistics, let alone try to reconcile them into an eclectic psycholinguistic theory. Some rather important clues to the riddles of human language, however, may possibly be discovered in psychological studies of words. Words are tools for message transmission in a shared human world of objects and events. We shall try to examine them as they emerge in acts of decoding and encoding, and we shall explore sensori-perceptual processes as well as higher-order cognitive aspects of such acts. After a psychological micro-analysis of the word in isolation, we shall briefly explore what happens when it appears in its natural habitat, i.e. when it constitutes an integral part of an utterance embedded in a context of human communication.

The Word as a Hierarchically Organized Psychological Process

Consider, first, a person from an entirely different community listening to your own language. Such a person who does not know any English at all might be asked to parse the preceding spoken utterance into "words" or word-like segments. He will, in all likelihood, end up with an incorrect segmentation: the whole sequence "to-your-own" might be judged to be one word only, whereas "listening" might be conceived of as two separate words (*"liste"* and *"ning"*). Failures like these show that purely acoustic-articulatory features of speech such as pause and intonation are insufficient cues for appropriate perceptual organization of speech. A listener who masters the language, however, has apparently additional internally provided resources at his disposal. Segments of speech acquire the status of words by a process of "active hearing": temporal strings of speech sounds are chunked in accordance with morphological and semantic rules of the language.

It seems safe to conclude, therefore, that words emerge in acts of decoding if and only if appropriate cognitive-perceptual operations are performed upon temporal strings of speech sounds or, in the case of written speech, upon particular visual forms. These cognitive-perceptual operations must somehow involve a process of recognition, i.e. a checking of the acoustic or visual stimulas input against an acquired vocabulary. Recognition of perceptual form, however, does not necessarily imply comprehension of meaning. Sometimes, I may recognize a pattern of speech sounds as an empty perceptual form only, as "a word I have heard before, but do not understand". And in the case of homonyms, perceptual forms that convey two or more very different word meanings, recognition of phonetic or visual form alone leaves me in a state of indecision.

Let us consider for a moment the sequence of letters STRENG, the common mediator of two very different Norwegian words. When it is used as a stimulus in a word association list and preceded by nouns referring to cords, ribbons, etc., it generates a noun meaning "string". In a word association list of Norwegian adjectives for personal attributes, on the other hand, it is usually experienced as an adjective corresponding to the English word "severe". Entirely different word association responses to the very same letter sequence in the two different settings provide evidence that different words emerged in decoding of the same visual stimulus input (Rommetveit and Strømnes, 1965). A spontaneous choice among different semantic alternatives is also required whenever we encounter words with multiple but related meanings, such as the English words "play" and "board".

Recognition and choice are not unique to speech perception. Some more subtle and possibly unique aspects of the word, however, may perhaps be brought to our attention when particular tricks are played upon linguistic stimulus input in the laboratory. In one series of experiments, a stereo-tachistoscope was used to introduce binocular rivalry of letters (Rommetveit *et al.*, 1968; Rommetveit and Kleiven, 1968). Short strings of typewritten or typed letters were exposed for periods of 170 or 200 ms, and subjects were asked to report as accurately as possible what they saw. The stereograms contained strings of letters such as *sog/sor* and *sug/sur*, and the letters g and r would then compete for the same position in the subject's visual field.

What was seen under such conditions of brief exposure and binocular rivalry was, to a large extent, determined by purely linguistic properties of the two monocular images and their possible combinations. This was the case with the two rivals g and r. They were seen as g only, as r only, as *gr* and as *rg*, depending upon which resolution of the rivalry conflict yielded a word. *Sug/sur* was thus seen by nearly everybody as either the Norwegian word "sug" or the Norwegian word "sur", and most subjects were highly confident that there were only those three letters "out there". *Sog/sor*, on the other hand, was by many subjects clearly seen as *sorg*. Whether both or only one of the two competing letters were seen, was thus obviously not a matter of rivalling visual forms only. The experience of the word "sorg" in response to the two non-word images *sog* and *sor* testifies to a process of word formation in which the perceiver intuitively betrays his mastery of morphological rules.

These and a number of other experimental studies provide us with a psychological picture of the word as a very complex and hierarchically organized *process*. Sequences of speech sounds and written strings of letters are as such devoid of meaning, but words emerge in acts of decoding when such stimuli are met with an internally provided request for some meaningful message element. The process by which words emerge out of acoustic or visual stimulus input may therefore be schematically visualized as a complex test-operate-text-exit mechanism (a TOTE mechanism, see Miller *et al.*, 1960). When the input (I) is tested against a request for some appropriate message element (T_x), a state of incongruity will necessarily arise (Fig. 1). Hence, a very complex operate (O_x) is initiated, the final outcome of which is again tested against the superordinate request for meaning. Congruity between test and outcome will lead to exit (E), i.e. to the execution of the entire programme for message reception for that particular input. This means simply that comprehension has taken place, and that the TOTE mechanism is available for novel stimulus input.

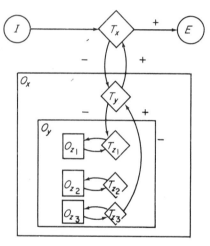

FIG. 1. A TOTE hierarchical model for generation of words from strings of letters: (I) input, (O) operate, (T) test, (E) exit and $(+, -)$ outcome of test. O_{z1-3}: generation of word form; T_{z1-3}: test for word form; O_y: search for semantic correlate (s); O_x: choice of specific semantic correlate and T_x: test for specific semantic correlate as part of message.

The operate (O_x), however, must be conceived of as some sort of a Chinese box, with subordinate TOTE units embedded in it. The test at the immediately subordinate level may be thought of as a matching of an already identified *word form* against admissible semantic correlates or "meanings". A negative outcome at this level yields the experience of "a word I have heard before, but do not understand". Tests at the lowest level (T_z), finally, involve a matching of stimulus input against familiar perceptual forms.

The *operations* required at this lowest level (O_z) under conditions of tachistoscopic word recognition are, in very simple cases, a position-by-position reading of letters from left to right (O_{z1}). This is prohibited under conditions of binocular rivalry of letters, however, since there are two different letters occupying one and the same position in the visual field. Therefore, a second operation (O_{z2}) is initiated, by which first one and then the other of the two competing letters is simply ignored. This operation yields a positive outcome when both images are word strings of letters such as *sug/sur*. It fails for non-word images such as *sog/sor*, however, and a third operation (O_{z3}) is then required. The two rivals are then both registered and re-arranged in space, first in one order and then in the opposite. *R* and *g*, for instance, occur always in the order *rg* in endings, whereas they can only appear as *gr* in beginnings of Norwegian words. And this is exactly what happens to them when they are rivals in stereograms such as *sog/sor* and *gøt/røt*: the former is seen as *sorg*, the latter as *grøt*.

The main lesson to be learned from these experiments on binocular rivalry of letters, perhaps, is a suspicion that words can only be explored psychologically as very complex *processes*, that subordinate perceptual operations are embedded as "sub-routines" in higher-order mental operations, and that entirely novel perceptual tactics may develop when such tactics are required in order for a perceiver to generate meaning. The perceived word is thus as much a product of efferent processes as of afferent processes, and strictly analogous considerations can be brought to bear upon the spoken word. *Homonymy* is thus most appropriately described as a purely incidental convergence of entirely different higher-order processes. It so happens that Norwegians have to produce the same sound pattern ("streng") when talking about severity and strings, i.e. the same sensori-motoric "subroutines" serve entirely different higher-order purposes of message transmission.

The hierarchical structure of the word may also be explored in terms of which part processes are "attended to" and "accessible to awareness". In general, we would expect residuals of lower level operations to fade away once they have provided appropriate input for higher levels; we attend to the message conveyed by linguistic stimuli rather than to the perceptual tactics by which messages are generated. The dominance of *meaning* over *perceptual form* is experienced as a serious obstacle by the proof reader. A content-orientated reader experiences a dilemma; his duty is to check for typographical errors and deviations from appropriate perceptual forms, but his interest is geared toward meaning. His dilemma seems to arise from a lack of capacity to attend to more than one level of the hierarchy at a time. Typographical errors tend to go unnoticed if he attends to meaning, whereas a careful attention to perceptual form prohibits comprehension of meaning.

A somewhat similar state of incompatibility may possibly occur under conditions of semantic satiation of words. Continued fixation of a written word form or repeated exposure to a spoken word form allow for a prolonged period of low level processing, far beyond the very minimal time required in order for semantic attribution to occur. Once the subordinate operations have served to "excess" their function of providing input to the highest level, we may expect a detachment to occur. Mere repetition of them as autonomous perceptual activities may then attract the attention that ordinarily is focused upon the highest level only. This shift of attention from higher to lower levels of the hierarchy may possibly account for the experienced "loss of meaning" and the concomitant strange experience of empty perceptual form.

The perceptual forms (whether acoustic or graphic) under ordinary conditions of verbal communication thus have apparently hardly any function other than that of providing appropriate input to higher-order semantic and cognitive processes. We comprehend, and may even remember, ideas and messages, but we do not ordinarily store the acoustic or visual images by which ideas and messages were conveyed. This has also been experimentally confirmed in a study by Kolers (1965). Kolers had French-English bilinguals learn mixed lists of French and English words. The clearly subordinate status of perceptual form was then reflected in recall, in the high frequency with which a French word was given back in terms of its English equivalent and vice versa. What appears to be attended to, accessible in immediate memory and stored even in word recall tasks, thus is the highest level apparently, that of semantic attribution.

Semantic Attribution and Assessment of Word Meaning Potentialities

What, then, have psycholinguists to say about semantic attribution and word meaning? First of all, perhaps, some words of caution concerning search for word meanings. Words differ markedly with respect to their functions in message transmission. Some words have hardly any independent functions at all, but may nevertheless contribute to message transmission when they appear in particular linguistic contexts. The definite article, for example, may be said to have a dependent semantic value (Reichling, 1963), although it conveys nothing in itself. When I am visiting a friend, however, and he says: "The dog has disappeared", I most likely assume that *his* dog has been lost. What is achieved, therefore, is what Reichling has labelled "eine Als-bekannt-Setzung". Other words serve purely *deictic* or *pointing* functions. Demonstrative pronouns such as *"this"* and *"that"* refer to whatever the speaker and the listener temporarily attend to or have in mind, be it a delicious dish of food or a very sophisticated psychological theory. Psychological studies of word meaning, however, have dealt almost exclusively with words that are said to have some autonomous, inherent signification, with so-called content words or designators such as "silly", "beautiful", "rat", "poison", "beg", "capitalism" and "vacation". And let us now see how the meaning of such content words may be assessed in terms of psychological processes.

We have to assume, first of all, an initial *process of reference* (R_1). Somehow, the word *form* must activate conceptual or representational processes. In the case of homonyms, distinctively different processes of reference are involved. If STRENG triggers a reference to a particular kind of cord, we shall expect one pattern of subsequent associative processes; if it triggers a process of reference to some personal attribute, on the other hand, we expect entirely different associations and concomitant affective processes. An initial process of reference is thus a prerequisite for subsequent associative and potential affective part processes.

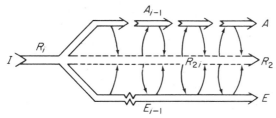

FIG. 2. The word as a three-component temporal pattern. (I): input (word form); (R_1): act of reference, choice of specific semantic correlate; (R_2): process of representation (sustained); (A): associative process and (E): emotive process.

Somehow, however, some process of representation (R_2) must be sustained over time beyond the stage of initiating associations and affective processes, and the sustained representation is then very likely affected by concomitant associations (A) and emotive processes (E). Consider, for instance, the processes triggered by the word form *"horse"* in two situations in which I have nothing else to do than to ponder its meaning. On one occasion, it may remind me of one particular horse, the delight I experienced when riding that horse, etc. On the other occasion, residuals of my zoological school training may dominate my associative chain. The initial process of reference is assumed to be the same in the two cases. A magic cross-cut into subsequent processes $(R_2, A$ and $E)$, however, would probably reveal somewhat different "horses". The sustained representation is most likely enriched by somewhat different concomitant associative and emotive processes on the two occasions.

What we propose is thus a very crude and schematic three-component model of word meaning: an initial process of reference is assumed to branch off into sustained representation, affecting and affected by an associative and an affective activity. The relative contributions of the assumed three components, however, may vary from one communication setting to the other. Consider the word *"democracy"* in the following three contexts:

(1) I am listening to a lecture on modern history, and the lecturer says: "Democracy, however, presupposes very specific economic and educational conditions".

(2) I am listening to an actor reading a poem: "Democracy . . . (long pause), "battles were fought for ideas . . .".

(3) I am listening to a speech on our National Independence Day: ". . . and as good Norwegians, we shall always remain devoted to democracy!".

It seems reasonable to assume that conceptual-representational processes (R^2) are fairly dominant component of the entire meaning pattern in the lecture context whereas associative processes (A) are relatively more dominant in the context of the poem, and that purely emotive processes (E) constitute a very significant component when the word appears in the patriotic speech. It seems reasonable to expect, moreover, that abstract representational-conceptual processes become an increasingly salient and dominant component of word meaning with age, as the child's general intellectual capacity develops. The predominance of the emotive component in younger children has been demonstrated in word sorting tasks. Rommetveit and Hundeide (1967) asked children at different age levels to sort sets of familiar words. Each set had been selected so that it fitted into a fourfold table: they were either "good" or "bad" words, and half of all good and bad words referred to one class of objects whereas the other half referred to a different class. Thus, one set contained the Norwegian words for hospital, squirrel, cottage, wolf, crocodile, castle, rat, villa, hovel, butterfly, pussycat and prison. With the latter two words ("pussycat", a *good animal*, and "prison", a *bad building*) given as cue words, the set could now be split into two halves in two different ways. The child either sorts out as similar to "pussycat" all *good* words, irrespective of reference ("squirrel," "cottage", "castle", "villa" and "butterfly"), or he could pick all *animal* words irrespective of their emotive loadings ("squirrel', "wolf", "crocodile", "rat", "butterfly").

Young children adopted a purely emotive strategy of sorting (good versus bad words) significantly more frequently than older ones. In addition, a correspondence was revealed between word sorting and subsequent recall. Again, a diagonal pair (like "pussycat" and "prison") were provided as cues, and the child was asked to try to reproduce the entire list. Emotive sorters then introduced significantly more novel words which were emotively in agreement with the cue word only (i.e. "candy" being introduced below "pussycat"). Children who had sorted on the basis of reference, on the other hand, introduced more novel words resembling the cue word with respect to reference only (i.e. "snake" being reproduced below "pussycat").

In addition to situational and developmental factors determining word meaning patterns, we encounter considerable differences between different sets of content words. Some words, such as "*nigger*" in the American language, have a very significant and well-defined emotive function. In addition to its reference, the word "nigger" conveys a hostile attitude toward coloured people. Other words, such as "democracy", "crime" and "communism", appear to have ambiguous and dual functions of reference and signalling of affect. Still others, such as "rectilinear", "vertical" and "transform", are nearly devoid of emotive loading. The interrelationships between the various assumed part processes of word meaning appear to be very subtle, however, and have hardly been systematically investigated at all.

The Assessment of Meaning Potentialities of the Isolated Word and the Activation of Such Potentialities in Particular Contexts

Our tentative evidence concerning components of word meaning stems mainly from studies of the isolated word in the psychological laboratory. Such settings allow us to enquire into meaning *potentialities*, but very little has been said so far about the ways in which such potentialities are brought into action in natural contexts of verbal communication.

When the word occurs in an utterance, there is first of all a drastic reduction of the time available for its processing. For example, consider the following excerpt from a discourse: "The distance from the last cottage on your right to the intersection where you take a left turn is approximately two miles. From that intersection you can see a red barn . . ." If I pursued associative pathways of "cottage" into remote parts of its associative networks while listening to such an utterance, I would probably be entirely lost in associative thought at the moment the speaker has come to "a left turn". Even lakes and fishing and mountains that constitute very central elements of its associative network are probably left out when the word "cottage" appears in such an utterance. The most obvious effect of context is thus a process of elimination (Fig. 3 (A)); only a fraction of those meaning potentialities which are assessed by requests for definition, word association tasks and semantic differential measurements appears to be operant in any particular context. A skeleton of a process of reference only, and no associative fringe or emotive meaning, is required in response to "cottage" in the utterance conveying driving instructions. The initial process of reference, however, appears to be a *sine qua non* for comprehension of the message, and hence it may be said to constitute the "core meaning" of content words.

An elimination of associative fringe and secondary affective processes, however, is by no means the whole story. A careful examination of the dictionary will convince us that almost every word has a whole sphere of referential and related associative possibilities. The "water" I en-

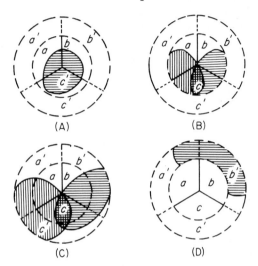

(A)   (B)

(C)   (D)

Fig. 3. Different patterns of activation of word meaning potentialities. Sectors *a*, *b* and *c* represent major features of the core meaning, whereas *a′*, *b′* and *c′* represent fringe features connected to those areas. Shaded regions represent meaning components operant in the actual setting. (A) instances 1–4, (B) instances 5a–8b, (C) instances 9a and 9b and (D) instances 10a and 10b.

counter in a poem about a thirsty and nostalgic Norwegian sailor in Hong Kong is thus distinctively different from the "water" in the chemistry book. In the context of the poem, "drinkability" will very likely be a dominant feature of reference, and the associative fringe may be one of "glasses" and "beverage". In the other context, fragments of chemical knowledge will probably enter the sustained representation.

Like most other words, "water" seems to encompass an abundance of referential-associative-emotive potentialities. Both drinkability and chemical formulae may thus appear in my response to the word in a word-association task, when I have ample time to ponder its meaning via multiple strategies of reference and related associative pathways. In a particular linguistic context, however, there is very often a pro-active constraint upon processing; only very selected features of reference and association will fit the frame provided by what has already been said.

What is brought into action then sometimes is only a particular part of "the core meaning" such as the feature *"maleness"* or *"adulthood"* of the word "man" (Fig. 3 (B)), for instance. This will be the case when the word appears in questions such as:

"Who opened the door, a woman or a man?"
"Who opened the door, a boy or a man?"

In other cases, entirely different potentialities such as an associative fringe of masculinity and courage are brought into action. This is probably what happens when I read the following about a soldier: "He had really shown that he was a man" (Fig. 3 (D)). Information concerning humanness, adulthood and maleness in the latter case has been amply provided by the preceding text, and the word form is thus free to convey fringe meaning related to, e.g. the maleness feature. A contextually induced semantic state will thus, in all cases, interfere at the superordinate level of the word process, and in such a way that only particular contextually appropriate parts of the entire pattern of meaning potentialities are activated.

In other cases, some retroactive process is obviously required. When polysemous word forms appear as initial elements of utterances, for instance, decoding must be postponed. Consider the following examples:

"The ball I went to buy yesterday was expensive."
"The ball I went to yesterday was boring."

The inherent ambiguity of "ball" cannot be resolved immediately. The word form is hence probably processed only at a lower level and kept in storage until subsequent information allows for an unequivocal semantic attribution. In still other cases, an initial process of reference may be retroactively *enriched* by particular associative and emotive fringe processes. Consider, again, an example:

"Only a man and two women were at the station."
"Only a man would be able to endure the hardships of the coal mine."

Identical processes should be triggered by "man" at the moment the words "Only a man" and nothing more has been heard. Any additional features (e.g. of masculinity) which differentiate the man in the coal mine from the man at the station, therefore, must derive from a retroactive process.

Speech comprehension then may be analysed as semantic decision-making along the temporal axis of the utterance and some of the decisions have to do with deciding which of a variety of meaning potentialities were encoded in a given form. Disambiguation, i.e. selection of a particular and contextually appropriate subregion of the area of meaning potentialities in Fig. 3, is sometimes instantaneous. Extralinguistic context or preceding speech has then induced a superordinate semantic state (T_x in Fig. 1) which controls the cognitive output of the word process at the moment of perception. For instance, consider the word "craft" and its entire domain of referential possibilities (Weinrich, 1966). On one occasion, I am sitting with a friend on a shore watching the boats passing by, and my friend says: "*Which craft would you prefer?*" The meaning of "craft" is then immediately restricted to "watercraft" (e.g. the horizontally shaded subregion in Fig. 3 (B)). Precisely the same selective activation is achieved when I encounter the word in a linguistic context such as "*I should like to sail a craft some day*".

When clarification is achieved retroactively, on the other hand, the hearer is sometimes temporarily left in a state of uncertainty equal to the entire domain of meaning potentialities. Final semantic attribution must then be postponed until some subsequent linguistic or extra-linguistic input allows the hearer to decide which subregion of poten-tialities has been encoded. In the meantime, the semantically ambiguous element must be kept in storage in immediate memory in some form. Some reports (Jaspars *et al.*, 1971; Kvale, 1971; Wold, 1971) deal with the impact of such retroactive mechanisms of decoding upon storage and retrieval.

The notion of a sphere of referential and associative potentialities allows for systematic investigations of the impact of extralinguistic and intralinguistic contexts upon reference. What constitutes so-called "free" (i.e. assumed) information in a given discourse, for instance, may often be determined by a tacit contract between participants, by virtue of convergence of assumptions and/or their loci within a social structure. The referent of "water" in the context of the textbook of chemistry is thus obviously determined by the institutional frame of scientific education in which it is embedded. Such social determinants of referents of messages are explored by Paul Henry (1971).

The discreteness and strict temporal segmentation of speech thus are clearly at variance with the processing of word meaning when words are embedded in spoken utterances. The articulatory-acoustic channel of speech sound transmission does not allow for more than one sound to get across at any given time. This universal and severe constraint upon human languages, however, is very efficiently counteracted. Long strings of speech are chunked into segments such as word forms, and identical perceptual forms mediate different meaning potentialities in different communication settings. Psychological studies of words *qua* complex cognitive-perceptual-motor processes may therefore be said to provide us with some tentative, yet very important clues to some of the riddles of human languages. They may help us understand how an infinite variety of messages can be transmitted by temporal chains of a very limited number of speech sounds.

References

Henry, P. (1971). On processing of message referents in contexts. *In* "Social Contexts of Messages". (E. A. Carswell and R. Rommetveit, Eds) pp. 77–95. Academic Press, London and New York.

Jaspars, J., Rommetveit, R., Cook, M., Havelka, N., Henry, P., Herkner, W., Pêcheux, M. and Peeters, G. (1971). Order effects in impression formation. *In* "Social Contexts of Messages". (E. A. Carswell and R. Rommetveit, Eds) pp. 109–125. Academic Press, London and New York.

Kolers, P. (1965). Bilingual facilitation of short term memory words remembered with respect to semantic rather than morphemic properties. Paper presented at the Eastern Psychological Association Meeting in Atlantic City, New Jersey.

Kvale, S. (1971). The temporal perspective of remembering. *In* "Social Contexts of Messages". (E. A. Carswell and R. Rommetveit, Eds) pp. 143–158. Academic Press, London and New York.

Miller, G. A., Galanter, E. and Pribram, K. H. (1960). "Plans and the Structure of Behavior." Holt, Rinehart and Winston, New York.

Reichling, A. (1963). Das problem der bedeutung in der sprachwissenschaft. *Innsbrucker Beiträge zur Kulturwissenschaft* Sonderheft 19.

Rommetveit, R. (1968). "Words, Meanings and Messages." Academic Press and Universitetsforlaget, New York, London and Oslo.

Rommetveit, R. and Hundeide, V. (1967). Emotive and representational components of meaning in word sorting and recall. *Pedagogisk Forskning* **11**, 47–59.

Rommetveit, R. and Kleiven, J. (1968). Word generation, A replication. *Scandinavian J. Psychology* **9**, 277–281.

Rommetveit, R. and Strømnes, F. (1965). Determinants of interpretation of homonyms in a word association context. *Pedagogisk Forskning* **9**, 179–184.

Rommetveit, R., Berkley, M. and Brøgger, J. (1968). Generation of words from stereoscopically presented non-word strings of letters. *Scandinavian J. Psychology* **9**, 150–156.

Weinreich, U. (1966). Explorations in semantic theory. *In* "Current Trends in Linguistics. Theoretical Foundations". (T. A. Sebeok, Ed.) Vol. 3, pp. 395–477. Mouton, The Hague.

Wold, A. H. (1971). Impression formation. A psycholinguistic approach. *In* "Social Contexts of Messages". (E. A. Carswell and R. Rommetveit, Eds) pp. 127–138. Academic Press, London and New York.

2. Deep Structure of Sentences versus Message Structure

Some critical remarks on current paradigms, and suggestions for an alternative approach *

R. ROMMETVEIT

Quo Vadis, Psycholinguistics?

Psycholinguistics is the child of structural linguistics and individual (as contrasted to *social*) cognitive psychology, and it was baptized in an atmosphere of optimism at a time when the relationship between its parents was still that of a hectic love affair. The roles of the two parents in nurturing the child during its first happy decade at Harvard and M.I.T. were prescribed in such a way that little doubt was left with respect to authority pattern. Structural linguistics—and that meant *transformational grammar*—was supposed to assume responsibility for its ideology and theoretical development. What this implied for the other parent was aptly formulated by Ervin-Tripp and Slobin (1966): "To psychologists remains the challenge of finding the processes by which the competence described by the linguists is acquired by children and is reflected in performance under a variety of conditions" (p. 436).

Since then, however, we have witnessed symptoms of controversies and bewilderment which—if they had occurred within a less optimistic and consolidated family—might easily lead to internal quarrel and even divorce. In 1968, Chomsky suggested that linguistics actually should be considered *a branch of cognitive psychology*. At the same time, he made some remarkable statements concerning that *linguistic competence* or *"knowledge of language"* whose manifestations psychologists until then

* Read as a paper for Colloque international du C.N.R.S., "Problèmes actuels en Psycholinguistique", Paris, December 13–17, 1971. Published in *Norwegian J. Linguistics* (1972) **26**, 3–22.

so eagerly had investigated (Chomsky, 1968):

> "We observe . . . that knowledge of language . . . is to a large extent independent of intelligence . . ." (p. 53).
>
> "They offer no way to describe or account for the most characteristic and normal constructions of human intelligence, such as linguistic competence." (p. 53, referring to empirist assumptions concerning language acquisition.) (My italics.)
>
> "What initial structure must be attributed to the mind . . .? . . . it appears to be a species-specific capacity that is essentially independent of intelligence." (p. 68, in connection with the prospect of the generative grammar for some language as a clue to the origin of knowledge.)

Katz and Fodor (1963, p. 200) once performed a careful semantic analysis of the words "*spinster*" and "*infant*" in order to show that the sentence "*My spinster aunt is an infant*" is anomalous. Time seems now ripe for expanding such an analysis, from incidental complaints about aunts to authoritative statements concerning psycholinguistic theory and research strategy, and in particular to expressions such as "*knowledge of language*", "*linguistic competence*", "*independent of*", "*normal and characteristic construction of*" and "*intelligence*" in the quotations above. It is well known that psychologists fear shallowness and feel attracted to depth, and one of the most fascinating aspects of the concept of competence provided by the transformational grammarian is indeed that it is so extremely far removed from the surface of linguistic performance. A competence that is at the same time supposed to be *independent of* and *a normal and characteristic construction of* human intelligence, however, may become the source of even more serious worries than an infantile aunt. This may explain why the psychologist's faith in linguistically defined deep language structures seems to waver. Miller and McNeill, for instance, have in a recent programmatic presentation of the field of psycholinguistics far more problems with defining the psychologist's role in psycholinguistic research than was the case with Ervin-Tripp and Slobin three years earlier. Miller and McNeill write (1969):

> As Katz and Postal (1964) have pointed out, only the surface structure is in any sense observable . . .
>
> . . . problems relating to meaning cannot be treated adequately within the framework of strict stimulus-response theories . . . Faced with this difficulty, a *conditioning theorist* . . . can supplement his discussion of surface appearances with a cognitive theory sufficiently rich to account for the deeper semantic aspects of language; which is the approach adopted in this chapter. (My italics.) (p. 675.)

It seems quite clear that the hope to account for *deep* aspects of language is sustained, and equally clear that the challenge to the psychologist today differs from that formulated by Ervin-Tripp and Slobin seven years ago. But what does the novel programme imply in terms of theoretical perspectives and paradigms for research? In what sense— and by whom—is surface structure supposed to be *observed*? And what will be the future of a psycholinguistics within which the psychologist adopts the position of a *conditioning theorist* who makes use of cognitive theory only in order to *supplement* his discussion of surface appearances?

Such questions indicate that the crisis psycholinguistics is encountering as a teenager is to a large extent a reflection of parental identity problems. Chomsky's syntactic structures (1957) were initially in some important respects a foreign body within psychology, in themselves entirely devoid of psychological content. And as the psychologist became engaged in search for manifestations of such structures, he seemed to lose some of his professional autonomy and self-confidence. Hoping to understand language the way Chomsky attempts to do, he also adapted his traditionally *linguistic* strategy of examining *sentences in vacuo* instead of *utterances in communication settings*. Chomsky maintains: "If we hope to understand human language and the psychological capacities on which it rests, we must first ask what *it is*, not *how or for what purposes it is used*". (My italics.) But how is it possible, in view of Wittgenstein's thorough analysis of these issues (1968), to disentangle *meaning* from *use*? Will not any statement pretending to maintain something about what language *is* include *concealed assumptions concerning use*? And which such assumptions are embedded in current psycholinguistic descriptions of *deep sentence structures*?

This last issue will be a minor, though recurrent, theme in the remaining part of this paper. My major task will be to outline a tentative alternative framework for psycholinguistic research, an approach which has been elaborated in far more detail elsewhere (Rommetveit, 1972a, b). By doing so, I shall try to suggest a prospect for psycholinguistics in which it is offered a fair chance of achieving autonomy and emancipation from its dominant transformational parents.

Psycholinguistics, Message Transmission and Social Realities: Suggestions for a novel terminology and research strategy

Message Structure versus Deep Sentence Structure

Message Transmission and Nesting of Information

Consider, first, a very simple game which is often used in order to explain the essentials of information theory: An object is located in the upper left corner cell of a square with 16 cells, and your task is to find out in which of the 16 cells it is located by asking me questions that can be answered by either "Yes" or "No". The dialogue may then proceed as follows:

(1) *"Is it in the right half?"*—*"No."*
(2) *"Is it in the upper half of the left half?"*—*"Yes."*
(3) *"Is it in the right half of the upper half?"*—*"No."*
(4) *"Is it in the upper half of the left half?"*—*"Yes."*

The word *"square"* does not enter this dialogue at all, despite the fact that message transmission at every stage of the game presupposes that the two of us have the same particular square in mind. We assume (correctly, and by a tacit contract) that we are talking about the same square. This is the initial shared, unquestioned, or *free information* onto which your first question is nested or *tied*. Notice, moreover, how my answer at each stage is nested onto *what already has been established* as free information, and how my answer at stage *n* is being *tacitly presupposed* in your question at stage *n + 2*. What has been achieved successively during the question-and-answer game can thus be assessed as the *message structure* of question (4) in its fully expanded version:

(4′) *"Is it in the upper half of the left half of the upper half of the left half of the square?"*

Embedded Propositions versus Presuppositions as Nesting of Temporarily Shared Social Realities

Psychologists, being professionally obliged to try to understand human beings and human interaction, ought to be primarily concerned with issues such as *what is being made known* and *how it is made known* when something is said. And the question-and-answer game above shows how verbal message transmission under specific and systematically arranged conditions can be described as a progressive nesting of information onto what the speaker and listener (in that particular case veridically) assume to be the case.

Let us now try to adopt a similar approach to a far more complex instance of verbal communication. Two men who live in an apartment house meet in front of the entrance of the house. So far, all flats have been occupied by young couples. The day before, however, they had both watched a man, appearing to be in his 60s, move into a vacant flat. And one of the two men now says to the other:

(5) *"The old man is poor."*

In this case, the fragment *"The . . . man"* seems to function as *"eine Als-bekannt-Setzung"* (Reichling, 1963), as an anchorage in a shared social reality of what is mediated by the remaining parts of the utterance. It thus plays a role analogous to that of "the square" in (4′). The word *"old"* is nested onto *"The . . . man"* as an additional, further specification, and *"is poor"* is tied to the whole phrase *"The old man"*.

Of course, message structure cannot in this case be explicated in terms of progressive reduction of a specified initial state of uncertainty in the same strict fashion as in (4′). Notice, however, the resemblance between the two utterances with respect to *nesting pattern*: what is mediated by "*old*" cannot be determined unless "*man*" is assumed and *age is attributed to man*. And whatever the speaker wants to *make known* or assert by "*is poor*", will not be transmitted unless "*The old man*" is tagged by speaker and listener onto the same person in their shared social world.

Let us now compare the above analysis to a traditional explication of *deep sentence structure*. I have elsewhere (Rommetveit, 1972a) tried to disclose the *ad hoc* nature of such explications. As we shall see later on (in connection with "*eager to . . .*" and "*easy to . . .*"), depth is sometimes explicated in terms of "logical subject" and "logical object", i.e. in terms of *agens* and *patiens* from the good old-fashioned categorial grammar. On other occasions, relationships between parts of the assumed deep structure are described in terms developed (in transformational grammar) for description of *surface structure*. Thus, the sentence "*I expected John to be examined by a specialist*" is said to have a deep structure in which one constituent sentence S_2 ("*A specialist will examine John*") is included as the grammatical direct object in another sentence S_1 (i.e. in "I expected S_2", see Chomsky, 1965, p. 22). On still other occasions, there is a resort to paradigms and terminology from *the calculus of propositions*. This seems to be the case, for instance, when "*John*" is said to be the subject of "*stupid*" in the deep structure of "*What disturbed John was being regarded as stupid*" (see Chomsky, 1965, p. 70). And such attempts at dissolving the sentence into a set of constituent propositions or assertions from which it may be derived are, of course, in perfect agreement with traditional *linguistic* definitions of *presuppositions*: Presuppositions are assertions that remain unquestioned across negation.

The deep structure of (5) should, according to what has been said so far, emerge as we dissolve it into the two constituent assertions:

(6) "*The man is old*," and
(7) "*The man is poor*."

And the very same underlying constituent assertions should hence be embedded in the deep structures of

(8) "*The poor man is old*," and
(9) "*The man is old and poor*."

Such explications should perhaps be interpreted as systematic surveys of *message potentials*, i.e. of *the entire range of assertions that can be mediated by the sentence across the entire range of possible and plausible communication settings*. If that is the purpose, however, it is obviously not achieved. The dissolution of (5) into (6) and (7), for instance, fails to cover the potentialities of assertions concerning species, sex and age ("*man*"), and concerning time (*"is"*), for instance the message structures of (5) when *"man"* is stressed in response to a question (or extralinguistically mediated symptoms of doubt) *whether the woman or the man is poor* and when *"is"* is stressed in response to a question *whether the man's poverty pertains to his past, only.*

The transformation of *"The old man"* to the quasi-propositional form "The man is old", moreover, seems to imply *assumptions about usage* which are at best very dubious and—in view of the message structure of utterance (5)—*false.* Nothing is being asserted about age (nor about *sex* and *species* aspects of *"man"*) in utterance (5) above. Propositions as defined within propositional calculus are statements which can be assigned a truth value, and it is quite clear that *"The old man"* cannot be said to be true or false in the same way as *"is poor".* It serves its function if and only if the two participants in the communicative act tag it onto the same person in a shared social world, and it fails if the listener has one particular person X in mind whereas the listener thinks of some other person Y. The fact that X and Y both happen to be *old men* does not help at all on such an occasion.

What is lost in the analysis of deep sentence structure is thus a crucial distinction between what is being assumed as *a shared social reality* and *what is being asserted* or *made known.* Resort to shared social realities is necessary in order to establish a common topic of discourse. The word "old", for instance, may be required because the speaker otherwise would engage the listener in a conversation about *a young man passing by during the act of speech.* The old age of the new tenant is assumed to be agreed upon and hence used (*as if it were* a fact) *in order to establish convergence with respect to topic.* The whole phrase *"The old man"* might thus under slightly different conditions be replaced by the single deictic word *"He".* This would be the case if both speaker and listener were watching the new tenant during the act of speech, or if, for instance, the listener had just mentioned his name.

Let us now examine what happens when (5) is negated, i.e. when the listener replies:

(5N): *"The old man is not poor."*

Since the scope of negation is *"poor"*, only, it may at first seem reasonable to believe that an assertion such as (6) or (6'), *"There exists a man who is old"*, is left unchanged. The plausibility of such a belief, however, appears upon closer examination to stem from irrelevant assumptions concerning *extralinguistic states of affairs* rather than from *what is being said.* This is brought into the open as soon as we engage in the same kind of search for underlying presuppositions in utterances such as:

(10) *"Flying saucers are hallucinations."*

What remains unchanged across (5) and (5N) is thus "*The old man*" as explicated in our analysis of the message structure, i.e. as *a pattern of nesting of social realities*. The dissolution of (5) into (6) and (7), however, is as unwarranted as the blunder of reading into (10) an assertion that flying saucers exist. Such an *ad hoc* procedure for inferring deep sentence structure has hence embedded in it *an implausible assumption concerning language use*, namely that *acceptance of something* (e.g. of deep sentence structure) *as a topic of discourse implies an assertion that such an entity exists*.

Other serious complications concerning paradigms from the calculus of propositions in analysis of natural language were encountered when a long time ago (as an exercise in symbolic logic) I tried to recode detective stories into propositional language, and some of the problems were once more brought to my attention in recent analysis of individual performances in Shannon-type guessing games. Identification of segments of natural language mediating something equivalent to the *logical predicate* in the calculus requires a careful analysis of what is presented as *novel information* or *made known* as distinguished from what is *already assumed to be known, accepted as a social reality*, or as *a topic of discourse*. Suppose, then, that we make up a complete survey of message potentials of sentence (5). The outcome of such a survey will be that each of the words "*old*", "*man*", '*is*" and "*poor*" (as well as some combinations of them) may mediate novel information. Let us now consider two cases, only, namely *the new tenant setting* described above and a communication situation in which there is already consensus that *only one out of two particular persons, either the old woman or the old man, is poor*.

Notice how in the latter case both age and the species of "*man*" are already known. What corresponds to the logical predicate is thus not all of "*man*", but rather *what is left when we subtract species and age aspects from its entire meaning potential*. A careful psycholinguistic analysis of what is being made known via particular content words under different conditions thus requires a systematic analysis of *decoding of content words across varying contexts* (see Rommetveit, 1968, pp. 172–180, 1972b). And such an analysis will be of great comfort to people who complain about infantile aunts. The infantile nature of such creatures is hardly ever more successfully made known by the word "infant" than in situations in which the word's irrelevant and trivial age component is subtracted— for instance due to decoding of "*spinster*" in the apparently contradictory utterance "*My spinster aunt is an infant*".

Consider, next, "poor" as a candidate for the logical predicate of (5) in the new tenant setting. It is well known from Shannon-type guessing games that words positioned toward the end of normal right-branching sentences are highly redundant. It is equally obvious from my own recent analysis of individual guessing performances (Rommetveit, 1971) that observed redundancy in such cases has nothing to do with knowledge of letter sequences *as such*. The subject is *requested* to guess letter by letter. If we examine his *strategy* toward the end of a particular game, however, we find that *correct letter sequences* emerge in acts of encoding *appropriate words*, and that appropriate words are hit upon in a deliberate attempt at completing some *plausible message* (or *message potential*). There are thus in "*The old man is* . . ." considerable constraints upon what is supposed to appear in the next word slot.

These constraints may partly be explicated in terms of *selection restrictions* (what *can* and what *cannot* be attributed to *living creatures, to men, to old men*), partly in terms of assumed semantic-associative networks, which in turn to some extent mirror beliefs about states of affairs in the real world (such as contiguities of, e.g. *old age* and respectively *death, sickness* and *poverty*). The important issue in the present context, however, is *the relationship between such constraints and the novelty aspect of what is being made known. Discourse* has an extension in *real time*, whereas *propositions* and *deep sentence structures* are abstractions in which language *has been deprived of its temporal dimension*. The novel information in an utterance is hence never *entirely novel*, but comprehensible only against the background of *what has already been understood* or *assumed to be the case*. Observed patterns of redundancy in different types of target sentences under systematically varied conditions of extralinguistic context may thus yield insight into important aspects of the decoding process, i.e. into what hermeneutic-dialectic philosophers of language (see Apel, 1965, 1966) have labelled "*Vorverständigung*". Such pre-knowledge is not *magic*. Nor is it *noise* which should be looked into only at that prospective later stage at which the psycholinguist's understanding of pure competence and a-temporal deep structures is supposed to be so complete that he finally can afford to tackle theoretically insignificant pragmatic issues. On the contrary: it appears to be *a universal and essential feature of language in action*, but one we can hope to explore with some success only if search for manifestations of deep structures in hypothetical supra-human speakers-hearers is replaced by systematic investigation of message structures in verbal communication between mortal men.

Contracts and Message Structure

The Dialogue and the Temporarily Shared Social World

Vygotsky (1962) has quoted a passage from Tolstoy in which two people in love engaged in a dialogue of one-word-utterances only "and understood each other perfectly". Equally cryptic conversations may take place between persons watching a football game together.

Such instances are interesting, not because lovers (or football fans) are of any particular concern to psycholinguists, but because their cryptic dialogues under those particular conditions may shed some light upon subtle (and hopefully: general) relationships between what is *made known*, what is *verbally mediated as free information for what is made known*, and *what is tacitly assumed as a shared social reality*. If we have full confidence in Tolstoy's intuition, we may even reverse the traditional linguistic approach to the issue of ellipsis: *ellipsis*, we may claim, *is the normal case under conditions of love, trust and a shared social world. A request for full sentences stems from linguists and pedantic schoolmasters who believe that man is alienated from his fellow man.*

I have elsewhere (Rommetveit, 1972b) in great detail tried to show *in what sense* and *how* encoding and decoding are complementary processes. Encoding contains always a component of anticipatory decoding, and decoding takes the form of reconstructing fragments of an intended message. These features are revealed in a great variety of experimental investigations of language processing and at every level of analysis, e.g. in a person's strategy in *a Shannon-type of guessing game* as well as when in *experiments on phoneme discrimination* he seems to use ". . . the inconstant sound as a basis for finding his way back to the articulatory gestures that produced it and thence, as it were, to the speaker's intent" (Liberman *et al.*, 1967, p. 453).

We may thus actually consider *verbally mediated free information as a means of establishing a temporarily shared world in cases when there is at the moment of speech a less than perfect pre-established complementarity*. Returning to the question-and-answer game, for instance, we notice how my answer at stage *n* is included as free information in your question at stage *n + 1*. A contract of convergence has then been *established and confirmed*—and is *therefore tacitly assumed from then on*. And we have already shown how the whole phrase *"The old man"* in (5) may be replaced by *"He"* when the new tenant constitutes the shared focus of attention. When as a natural next step we omit *"He is"* as well, we arrive at the cryptic dialogue under the conditions of perfect complementarity and synchronization of intention and thought of Tolstoy's lovers.

Different Kinds of Contracts

What can be *made known* under conditions of nearly complete ignorance with respect to encoder and encoding situation, for instance when a sentence such as (5) is heard from a tape (or seen in the slot of a memory drum) in a psycholinguistic experiment on sentence recall?

The subject is then, in a way, encountering *an arbitrary segment of discourse in a vacuum*. In contrast to Tolstoy's lovers, he has hardly any extralinguistic anchorage for what he hears—apart from whatever plausible communication setting he may dream up himself. Suppose, for instance, that he listens as if he were listening to the opening sentence of a short story by an unknown author, but with no expectation of continuation and hence with the additional intention to comprehend and remember what he hears as *an autonomous entity*. The sentence may then be interpreted as depicting a composite state of affairs, or an event, *the cognitive representation of which is assumed to serve as the input to sentence encoding and the output of sentence decoding*. A decomposition of (5) into (6) and (7), moreover, may be accepted as a tentative procedure for identifying the constituents of that cognitive representation.

By accepting such an *ad hoc* deep structure as a tentative description of what the sentence in some more profound sense *is*, we are actually endorsing *a false picture theory of language use*. Assertions (6) and (7) may be said to describe plausible extralinguistic conditions for uttering (5), i.e. conditions under which (5) may be said to convey a *true statement*. The problem is, however, that *they are equally appropriate for* (8) *and* (9). There is thus something more in (5) than a Cartesian individual cognitive representation of what is asserted about states of affairs in (6) and (7), something which can be understood only if we explore the sentence as contained within an *act of communication* and keep in mind the complementary relationship between encoding and decoding. The contracts established between the anonymous encoder and the subject in the psycholinguistic experiment have to do with *which aspects of the composite state of affairs should be considered an unquestioned background relative to other aspects*. These contracts commit the decoder to a *particular pattern of nesting of novelties* corresponding to the message structure described on p. 20: Comprehending the sentence in this somewhat atypical setting implies playing the game of presupposing that some man *has already been identified* and that *his old age is assumed to be a fact when it is made known that he is poor as well*.

The dissolution of (5) into (6) and (7) has been discussed at such length because it is symptomatic of a general trend within psycholinguistics, namely a preoccupation with resemblance between sentences that are synonymous *salva veritate* and a primary concern with individual cognitive representations and processes rather than with shared social worlds and communication. This trend was particularly transparent in the search for *"kernel forms"* and *"syntactic footnotes"*. Thus, since there appears to be no difference between them with respect to what is made known *within the sentence*, an active, declarative sentence and its equivalent in the passive voice were compared with respect to potential differential strains on *individual information storage capacity*.

As we expand the scope of enquiry to the utterance in the communication setting, however, entirely different aspects of the active-passive option are brought into focus. Once more, it seems plausible to explore potential *contracts of communication*. The contracts we encounter in sentence voice within the context of the dialogue, however, cannot be explicated as patterns of nesting such as those we have described above, but rather in terms of *foregrounding* and *what is being proposed as the topic for the sustained discourse*. The issues are thus very similar to those encountered in recent research on *negation* (Clark, 1970, Just and Carpenter, 1971).

Just and Carpenter examined the expressions *"few of"* and *"a minority of"* under experimental conditions in which the two expressions were clearly synonymous *salva veritate*, each of them being used to refer to two out of sixteen dots. Observed reaction times in true-false judgments, however, provided unequivocal evidence that *"few of"* made the subject attend to *all sixteen* (or the majority), whereas *"a minority of"* focused his attention on *the two* dots. And the resemblance between these findings and *observations on use of active and passive voice* is perhaps best brought out by expanding the discourse by anaphorical deixis. We have then:

(10)   *"A minority of the dots are red. They . . ."*
(10N) *"Few of the dots are red. They . . ."*
(11)   *"Bill hits John. He . . ."*
(11P) *"John is hit by Bill. He . . ."*

Contracts concerning the sustained topic are revealed in the linkage of *"They"* to *"A minority"* in (10) versus that of *"They"* to *"the dots"* in (10N); and in the linkage of *"He"* to *"Bill"* in (11) versus that of *"He"* to *"John"* in (11P).

What is achieved, then, by examining, e.g. sentence voice as involving *contracts* of communication?

Notice, first of all, that the rules of anaphorical deixis in (11) and (11P) apply *whether the discourse is continued by the speaker himself or by his partner in the dialogue*. Consider, next, the relationship between *a particular event* and *what is veridically said about that event* in (11) and (11P). How can anything at all be made known by verbal means if not against the background of something that is already assumed to be known, and without any foregrounding or commitment concerning a sustained topic? What could be the differential roles of forms (11) and (11P) in a truly Cartesian monologue?

Such issues have been thoroughly explored by Wittgenstein (1968), and by outstanding representatives of a cognitive *social* psychology such as Mead (1950), Piaget (1926) and Heider (1958). Linguists like Reichling (1963) and Uhlenbeck (1963), moreover, have in their exploration of linguistic rules been far less removed from a psychology of communication than was the case with Chomsky in his first explication of deep syntactic structures (Chomsky, 1957). A notion of *contract* as tentatively elaborated above may hence serve to bring together in a systematic fashion what is known about *linguistically defined rules* and social psychological explorations of respectively *attribution, decentration*, and what Mead referred to as *"taking the role of the other"*.

The social world explored by Mead, Piaget and Heider is a world of a great variety of social realities and potential perspectives. In the particular event made known in (11) and (11P), for instance, there seems to be *an immediately experienced causal-temporal structure* corresponding to *the word order of* (11). A certain capacity for decentration, i.e. for emancipation from the immediately experienced event structure, is hence required in (11P). And insufficient decentration may therefore explain why children do not master the passive voice at an age when they are supposed to have acquired full linguistic competence—at all events if they were good children, making efficient use of Miller and McNeill's LAD (see Miller and McNeill, 1969, p. 715).

Different perspectives are clearly also involved in one of the classical cases of evidence for the existence and utility of deep structure, namely in the sentences:

(12) "*John is easy to please,*" and
(13) "*John is eager to please.*"

Miller and McNeill (1969, p. 675) maintain: "The surface structure of these two sentences is the same . . . In the deep structure, however, we recognize that in the sentence *John is easy to please, John* is the object of the verb, whereas in *John is eager to please, John* is the subject".

However, what can Miller and McNeill have in mind when they claim that *John is the subject of the verb in one case and the object in the other?*

As previously shown, any relationships to the calculus of propositions (on other occasions indicated by the strange terminology: "logical subject" and "logical object") are illegitimate and at best very dubious. And if they refer to *the grammatical subject* (NP_1 in formation rule $I:S\rightarrow NP_1 + VP$) and *grammatical object* (NP_2 in rule $II: VP\rightarrow V + NP_2$), we are faced with the danger of circularity or *infinite regression*. What is left as the only plausible alternative are then the old notions of *agens* and *patiens*. The reason for Miller and McNeill's detour into deep structure is thus clearly *their definition of surface structure as devoid of semantics*, and *what is achieved* is nothing more than *a retrieval of semantics in terms of awkward notions from categorial grammar*.

With some *more* confidence in what pychologists have to say about attribution, decentration and perspectives and *less* confidence in the psychological realities of linguistically defined cognitive structures, however, we may adopt an entirely different approach. Consider, for a moment, what is achieved by each of the two expressions "*John is easy to . . .*" and "*John is eager to . . .*" under conditions *when the rest of each utterance is lost in noise*. The listener has then comprehended what has been said if in the first case he has *adopted the perspective of considering John (aspect of) a task*, whereas in the other case he has adopted *the perspective of considering John a potential source of action*. Comprehension must hence be explored in terms of *semantic competence*, and, more specifically, in mastery of the words *"easy"* and *"eager"*. What is explicated as the semantic rules of *"easy"* (in contexts such as (12)) must therefore bear some systematic relationships to cognitive capacities such as (a) *attributing easiness and difficulties to tasks* and (b) *capacity for decentered shifts of perspectives on people* such that, e.g. a person can on one occasion be considered *a source of action*, on another occasion (aspect of) *a task*.

This Columbus's egg solution to the classical "easy/eager case" thus indicates a general paradigm for psycholinguistic research in which the psychologist is assigned a far more important task than those suggested by Ervin-Tripp and Slobin (see p. 17) and Miller and McNeill (see p. 18). He can, among other things, help linguists understand more about *what semantic rules are* by exploring such rules as *contracts concerning perspectives*.

Language Games and "Meta-contracts"

A resort to *cognitive perspectives, shared social worlds* and *contracts of communication* is in many respects a frightening prospect. It is particularly frightening to those who hope *that transformational grammar*—re-baptized as cognitive psychology, but nevertheless with a very impressive linguistic heritage of apparently stringent explications of relationships between deep structures and surface appearances—*may ultimately provide us with an orderly picture of mind*. The prospect of a social psychological reorientation has at the same time a strong appeal to those of us who, *inspired and provoked by the achievements of transformational grammar*, argue that we can only hope to learn more about what language is if we explicitly and systematically explore it in the more comprehensive framework of *human communication*.

This implies, in my opinion, even systematic attempts at exploring interrelationships between *extralinguistically provided* and *verbally mediated free information*. Consider, for instance, sentence (5) in the *new tenant setting* as compared to the situation in which it serves as *the opening sentence in a short story*. Resorting to Wittgenstein's terminology, we may describe comprehension on those two occasions as *moves within somewhat different language games*. In one case, comprehension implies a very safe move from an experientially established and confirmed social reality to a position at which that shared social reality is slightly expanded. We assume, in such a description, *credibility* and *mastery of communication contracts* as suggested on p. 25 (including, of course, agreement concerning the reference of "poor"). The move is also safe in the sense that *very little is required in terms of capacity for decentration, imagination and adoption of abstract "as if"-perspectives on the part of the listener*.

Considerably more is obviously required in the other case, even though the abstract message structure appears to be the same. The listener to the short story must, in a way, endorse a "meta-contract". He must be willing (and have the capacity) to cope with abstract novelties *as if* they were already familiar, on the assumption that what is initially abstract and unknown will become more familiar as he continues listening. Comprehension is thus an adventurous move into an imagined social world, and *far beyond the capacity of many mentally retarded people who have no problems in comprehending the same sentence in the new tenant setting*.

It is tempting, therefore, to relate performances in the two different communication settings to what Chomsky said about knowledge of language, inborn capacities and intelligence (see p. 18). How can linguistic competence be defined *without any reference to communication settings*: And *if* no such specification is included, how can psychologists ever hope to be able to relate such a competence to performance?

Wittgenstein's analogy of games is intimately related to his analysis of the ways in which utterances are embedded in more inclusive patterns of human interaction and may also be brought to bear upon *institutional and ritual frames serving as free information for what is being said and understood*. I have elsewhere (Rommetveit, 1968, p. 50, pp. 62–63, pp. 111–112) discussed a number of such cases. A politician says to the janitor at the beginning of a campaign meeting, when the room is getting crowded: "*Here are two few chairs*", and it is immediately comprehended as a *request for more chairs* and may, moreover, even later on be *recalled and re-encoded in an imperative version*. A "meta-contract" of master-to-servant communication must hence have been endorsed by both participants in the act of communication.

An entirely different contract (namely, that the main topic of discourse is supposed to be the husband's success in the campaign) is very likely endorsed when the politician's wife listens to her husband saying over the telephone: "Here are two few chairs". Whether primarily *referential* or *emotive* components of the entire meaning potential will be involved in decoding of the word "*democracy*", moreover, is dependent upon whether the word is embedded in *a lecture on governmental forms* or in *a patriotic speech* on the Day of National Independence. Discourse is in the one case partly determined by a "meta-contract" of mediation of knowledge, whereas in the latter case it is part of a ritual game of celebration and consolidation of patriotic feelings.

It is interesting to notice what happens when such "meta-contracts" are broken, for instance when a student is listening to the serious lecture *as if it were a patriotic speech* and when a member of the joyful audience of the patriotic speaker starts listening to what he says about democracy *as if it were intended to convey scientific information*. The resultant *state of alienation* in the latter case clearly indicates how under normal conditions a given ritual or institutional frame may serve as *free*, i.e. *not-*

reflected-upon, unquestioned, information at the level of meta-communication. And we may thus conceive of *free information* as *incorporated in tests at different levels in a hierarchically organized decoding process.*

This implies, among other things, also a novel approach to the issue of "disambiguation". Consider, for instance, the classical case:

(14)   *"They are flying planes."*

A complete analysis of the processes involved in comprehending such an utterance will reveal *many potential ambiguities.* The last phoneme, for instance, mediates the *plurality morpheme,* but might *in principle* be mistaken for the *third-person-present-tense morpheme* as, e.g. manifested in *"He explains".* Its identity is unknown *in vacuo,* but spontaneously identified (as if by a trivial, subordinate sub-routine in a decoding programme) as it is *bound* to the *free* morpheme/plane/. The word *"are",* moreover, may be the *copula* or *part of the progressive construction "are flying",* and the utterance may *eo ipso* be assigned two different sentence structures.

But neither plurality morphemes, copulas, nor sentences are *decoded in vacuo.* They may, of course, be *inspected* and *reflected upon,* and inferences concerning syntactic structure and message potentials may then be made by comparing a given sentence to other sentences, and by embedding it in a variety of imagined communication settings. The ambiguities detected by the linguist in his armchair, however, are non-existent in the normal communication setting: a person listening to (14) while wondering what (one or more) dot(s) over the horizon *are,* experiences no more ambiguity in *the whole utterance* than in *the /s/ of "planes".* The spontaneous "disambiguation", moreover, seems in both cases to occur according to a general formula of nesting of *tied* to *free* information.

Experimental Evidence on Message Structure, Temporal Organization and Recall

In the present paper I have deliberately tried to play the role of the naive child in H. C. Andersen's tale about the emperor's new clothes, insisting that presumably carefully explicated and very deep *linguistic structures* are devoid of *psychological reality.* And I do not believe that non-existent clothes can be brought into existence by re-cutting them, i.e. by moving the scissors as if what was not there in the first place is being made more fashionable and in line with what we now increasingly feel *ought to be there.* The only alternative left for psycholinguistics in its teenage crisis is hence to reject basic parental ideology imposed upon it and engage in a search for a far more autonomous and independent future. This revolutionary attitude implies, of course, that purely destructive efforts are out of proportion to the vagueness and very exploratory character of *constructive alternatives*. I have tried to show, however, how an alternative conceptual framework can be adopted when approaching old issues as well as in systematic accounts for some more recent experimental findings. And evidence bearing more directly upon the proposed novel framework is now being collected. *Message structure* is still an infant, but an infant whose psychological reality hopefully can be clearly revealed in performance.

Some relevant evidence has thus been established in experiments by Heen Wold, whose findings on *word order and recall* have only in part been presented in a progress report (Wold, 1971). A series of descriptions (of persons and things) were tape-recorded and presented in a recall task. The same set of words (one noun and five descriptive adjectives) was arranged in different orders, e.g. as:

(15A) *"A secretary who is severe, cool, extraordinary, beautiful, pleasant,"* or
(15B) *"A severe, cool, extraordinary, beautiful, pleasant secretary."*

All descriptions were in one condition presented in an order of type (A), in another condition in type (B), and *the noun* was in several conditions used as a prompt word in the subsequent retrieval task. *Nearly twice as many adjectives were then retrieved under the condition of post-position of adjectives.* And similar results, though less striking, were found in recall of adjectives inserted in full sentences under systematic variation of word order such as:

(16A) *"That the examinations went well, was pleasant, noteworthy, and encouraging,"* and
(16B) *"It was pleasant, noteworthy, and encouraging that the examinations went well."*

Notice that versions A and B are identical as far as any plausible explication of *deep structure* is concerned. What serves as free information for decoding of adjectives, however, is not made known in versions B until the subject has heard all the adjectives. This implies that cumulative decoding is prohibited: *final decoding* and *nesting onto the free information* provided by respectively the noun (in 15B) and the clause (in 16B) must all be performed at the final "decoding station". The clearly inferior recall of versions B must hence be attributed to *discrepancy between message structure and temporal organization*.

Similar results were obtained in recall experiments in which pictures were presented as ready signals for the utterances to be recalled (Rommetveit *et al.*, 1971). Every picture was supposed to portray a plausible extralinguistic condition for uttering what immediately followed. The linkages between picture and utterance, however, were of two kinds. Half of them resembled:

(17A) Picture of hand knocking at a door, followed by:
"It is a pity she was not at home."

The other half were similar to:

(17B) Picture of a fading flower, followed by:
"There were insufficient light and heat."

The difference can thus be described as a difference with respect to pattern of nesting. What is conveyed by the picture was in (17A) supposed to serve as *free information for what is said*, whereas the opposite was supposed to be the case for (17B). The impact of pictures on recall was assessed by including a condition in which ready signals were not meaningfully related to utterances. And a comparison of recall performances showed that there was *no impact of picture context at all* upon recall of the utterance when the linkage was of *type B*, but *a very strong impact* when the linkage was of *type A*.

The findings of Rommetveit *et al.* were only partly replicated in a later experiment (Blakar and Rommetveit, 1971). These experiments are all of a very exploratory nature, however, serving primarily as first steps in an attempt at *assessing message structure across extralinguistically mediated and verbal components of communication.*

References

Apel, K. O. (1965). Die entfaltung der "sprachanalytischen" philosophie und das problem der "Geisteswissenschaften". *Philosophisches Jahrbuch* **72**, 239–289.

Apel, K. O. (1966). Wittgenstein und das problem des hermeneutischen Verstehens. *Zeitschrift Theologie Kirche* **63**, 49–87.

Blakar, R. M. and Rommetveit, R. (1971). Processing of utterances in contexts versus rote learning of sentences. *In* "Social Contexts of Messages". (E. A. Carswell and R. Rommetveit, Eds) Academic Press, London and New York.

Chomsky, N. (1957). "Syntactic Structures." Mouton, The Hague.

Chomsky, N. (1965). "Aspects of a Theory of Syntax." M.I.T. Press, Cambridge, Massachusetts.

Chomsky, N. (1968). "Language and Mind." Harcourt Brace Jovanovich, New York.

Clark, H. H. (1970). How we understand negation. Paper presented at Workshop at University of California, Irvine.

Ervin-Tripp, S. M. and Slobin, D. (1966). Psycholinguistics. *Annual Review Psychol.* **17**, 435–474.

Heider, F. (1958). "The Psychology of Interpersonal Relations." John Wiley and Sons, New York.

Just, M. and Carpenter, P. (1971). Comprehension of negation with quantification. *J. Verbal Learning Verbal Behavior* **10,** 244–253.

Katz, J. J. and Fodor, F. A. (1963). The structure of a semantic theory. *Language* **39,** 170–210.

Liberman, A. M., Cooper, T. S., Shankweiler, D. P. and Studdert-Kennedy, M. (1967). Perception of the speech code. *Psychological Review* **74,** 431–461.

Mead, G. H. (1950). "Mind, Self and Society from the Standpoint of a Behaviorist." University of Chicago Press, Chicago.

Miller, G. A. and McNeill, D. (1969). Psycholinguistics. *In* "Handbook of Social Psychology." (G. Lindzey and E. Aronson, Eds) Vol. III. Academic Press, New York and London.

Piaget, J. (1926). "The Language and Thought of the Child." Harcourt Brace Jovanovich, New York.

Reichling, A. (1963). Das problem der bedeutung in der sprachwissenschaft. *Innsbrucker Beiträge zur Kulturwissenschaft* Sonderheft 19.

Rommetveit, R. (1968). "Words, Meanings and Messages." Academic Press, New York and London.

Rommetveit, R. (1971). On concepts of hierarchical structures and microanalysis of language and thought. *In* "Hierarchical Models in the Study of Cognition." (G. Eckblad, Ed.) Mimeograph, University of Bergen.

Rommetveit, R. (1972a). Language games, deep syntactic structures, and hermeneutic circles. *In* "The Context of Social Psychology: A Critical Assessment." (J. Israel and H. Tajfel, Eds) Academic Press, London and New York.

Rommetveit, R. (1972b). "Språk, tanke og kommunikasjon." Universitetsforlaget, Oslo.

Rommetveit, R., Cook, M., Havelka, N., Henry, P., Herkner, W., Pêcheux, M. and Peters, G. (1971). Processing of utterances in context. *In* "Social Contexts of Messages." (E. A. Carswell and R. Rommetveit, Eds) Academic Press, London and New York.

Uhlenbeck, E. M. (1963). An appraisal of transformation theory. *Lingua* **12,** 1–18.

Vygotsky, L. S. (1962). "Thought and Language." John Wiley and Sons, New York.

Wittgenstein, L. (1968). "Philosophische Untersuchungen—Philosophical Investigations." (G. E. M. Anscombe, Ed.) Blackwell, Oxford.

Wold, A. H. (1971). Impression formation: A psycholinguistic approach. *In* "Social Contexts of Messages." (A. E. Carswell and R. Rommetveit, Eds) Academic Press, London and New York.

3. Language Games, Syntactic Structures and Hermeneutics

In search of a preface to a conceptual framework for research on language and human communication*

R. ROMMETVEIT

Introduction

Just as formerly there existed a movement for the physicalistic unity of science, so today we witness a legitimate request by the advocates of hermeneutic and dialectic positions for a more thorough explication of basic presuppositions underlying social scientific research. Such requests are usually accompanied by an appeal for subscription to some unitary philosophy of science, which may be a particular epistemology with its prescriptions concerning scientific methodology, or a "tradition of thought" with its unique set of ontological assumptions and definitions of knowledge. The novel hermeneutic-dialectic philosophy thus sets out to examine the social sciences in the broader context of an "anthropology of knowledge" (Apel, 1968), searching for the synthesis of *geisteswissen-schaftliches Verstehen* and *naturwissenschaftliche Erklärung* ("understanding" and "explanation") by which social scientific research is to acquire its unique *emancipatory* function.

This chapter may be viewed as an empirically oriented psychologist's protest against the philosopher's persistent attempt to lure him into various traps inherent in monistic systems and views of the world. Such traps may be differently baited—by promises of an ultimate communion with the nuclear physicist in a future land of unity of science, or by the prospect of playing a significant political role in saving the world. An apparent intellectual simplicity and elegance of approach is

* Published in "The Context of Social Psychology: A Critical Assessment" (1972). (J. Israel and H. Tajfel, Eds) Academic Press, London and New York.

usually achieved by singling out as *the* paradigm for social scientific research and mediation of knowledge, *particular* paradigms of research practice and knowledge mediation, such as the worshipped hypothetico-deductive method of the physicist or the psychoanalyst's "dialectic mediation of explanation and understanding". However, the philosophy-of-science version of how the physicist achieves his success may at times be so remote from his everyday professional experience that he himself refuses to subscribe to it; similarly, the psychoanalyst may well find himself unable to subscribe to the novel general paradigm of "dialectic mediation". Strangely enough, this does not appear to reduce the probability of support from researchers who are neither physicists nor psychoanalysts. We have witnessed psychologists confessing their faith in a hypothetico-deductive reductionism at a time when most physicists either ignored or rejected it; we may yet see sociologists subscribing to a "dialectic mediation of explanation and understanding" while psychoanalysts reject Apel's (1968) and Habermas' (1968) exegesis of their trade. It is tempting, therefore, to view the various unitary philosophy-of-science programmes as ideological superstructures or "false ideologies", i.e. as sets of ideas which primarily serve purposes other than explicating ontological premises, the essence of methods, and the ultimate goals of social scientific research. The gospel of an ultimate communion with the physicist, with its basis in the resemblance between social and natural sciences, had a particularly strong appeal for social scientists struggling for academic recognition and status to their young disciplines in a Western world committed to the blind pursuit of technological progress. The image of the social scientist as a therapist, which has its basis in humanistic understanding and engagement, helps us convey a *raison d'être* to a world in despair at the fruits of blind technological progress.

However, it is not my intention to attempt to refute Habermas' general theory of "objective interests" or his specific hypotheses concerning the relationship between capitalism and positivistic social science. Nor shall I argue that his novel hermeneutic-dialectic approach has its origins in an abrupt change in public relations programme in response to rapid changes in the world situation. I want to voice the suspicion, though, that we have little understanding of the relationship between largely inductively elaborated concepts of cognition, meaning and communication *within* social science and those apparently related philosophical concepts in which some of us are seeking support for a radical reorientation of our research. It thus seems probable that this reorientation may—like the presumably dominant positivistic orientation—merely serve to voice an ideology whose immediate emotive appeal contrasts strangely with its lack of unequivocal implications for our conceptualization of substantive issues and reflections on methodology. The lip service which psychologists pay to particular positivistic concepts has at times taken the form of puritan declarations of independence from "meaning". Skinner's programme for research on verbal behaviour (1957), for instance, represents an attempt at detaching himself as a scientist from his role as a participant in the games of everyday language. The futility of such an attempt has been cogently and eloquently demonstrated by Chomsky (1959) in his critique of Skinner. A tacit reliance upon "meaning" is also easily discovered as we examine behaviourist-associationist approaches to concept learning within the American tradition of research on verbal learning (Underwood and Richardson, 1956). Ease of learning is, for instance, in some experiments predicted as "response dominance" which is expressed in terms of the average frequency with which the "concept word" (e.g. "round") has been elicited in response to each of the "stimulus words" (e.g. "apple", "tomato", "collar", etc.). It is worth noticing, however, that a word such as "angular" is not included in the stimulus lists when the concept desired happens to be "round", even though the observed association linkage "angular-round" is very strong. Such *ad hoc* restrictions on choice of stimulus words for the concept reveal, of course, an exploitation of one's intuitive mastery of the language as a participant in language games, and *Vorverständigung* (presuppositions) of a nature quite different from the reported measures of associative strength. It is equally obvious, moreover, that such restrictions are a *sine qua non* for prediction of ease of learning from measures of associative strength (see Rommetveit, 1968a, p. 126). The *necessity* to transcend the role of the participant, however, is also pointed out with no less cogency, in a later work by Chomsky (1968, pp. 21–22 and 52). Referring to Wittgenstein's observations that the most important aspects of things are hidden because of their simplicity and familiarity, he states (ibid., p. 22): "We tend too easily to assume that explanations must be transparent and close to the surface. The greatest defect of classical philosophy of mind, both rationalist and empiricist, seems to me to be its unquestioned assumption that the properties and the content of the mind are accessible to introspection . . ." Despite his rejection of Skinner's particular strategy of *Verfremdung* (estrangement), Chomsky (ibid., p. 52) is thus clearly in agreement with Skinner concerning the necessity "to establish the appropriate physical distance (from the relevant phenomena) and to make them strange to ourselves . . ."

This paradox of futile necessity (or necessary futility) is a recurrent theme in social scientific and philosophical enquiries into language and human communication. Wittgenstein felt trapped inside the realm of what could be said because its premises could not be expressed. He insisted on silence rather than any metaphysical explication, however, arguing: "(All models or schemes of interpretation) will have a bottom level and there will be no such thing as an interpretation of that". (Wittgenstein, 1962, p. 739.)

Wittgenstein's attitude of resignation can thus be reconciled with the hermeneutic position that scientific knowledge presupposes "a certain understanding of the world publicly tested through interaction"* (Apel, 1965, p. 247), that acquisition of novel knowledge is preceded by *Vorverständnis* (agreement), and that "all objective knowledge presupposes intersubjective understanding" (Apel, 1968, p. 169). Wittgenstein might even have endorsed the assertion that "the constitution of every meaning refers back to a perspective which corresponds to a standpoint, i.e. a bodily engagement of the cognizing mind" (Apel, 1968, p. 39). He once remarked: "An utterance has meaning only in the stream of life". This comment struck Malcolm (1967, p. 93) as being especially noteworthy and as summing up a good deal of his philosophy.

The peculiar appeal of Apel's and Habermas' philosophy of social science seems to reside in their suggestions concerning the way in which the social scientist—once he has realized his imprisonment—can *achieve freedom*. It seems to be the case, moreover, that their proposed road to freedom is paved with insights into "dialectic" and "complementary" relationships between "causes" and "rational reasons" (Apel, 1968, p. 46), between "analytic insight" and "misguided cultural process", and between presumably different modes of acquisition of knowledge such as "understanding" and "explaining". The famous "hermeneutic cycle" was described by Dilthey as a spiral, i.e. "(a structure) in which a rule which prompted the expression of another rule in an 'utterance' (*Ausdrück*) may itself be corrected by that subsequent rule . . ." (Apel, 1966, p. 86). Apel and Habermas appear to promise an expansion of the spiral from the realm of knowledge to that of human conduct:

> (The prospect that) by reflecting about himself, Man can transform the language of psychological and sociological "explanations" into the language of a deepened self-understanding . . . (and) . . . through self-consciousness he can transform into understandable actions those modes of behaviour which are amenable to causal explanation. (Apel, 1968, pp. 59 and 60.)

It is clearly the case, moreover, that the struggle towards emancipatory self-understanding is viewed as a continuous effort to understand the rules of the language games in which we participate. Habermas (1968, p. 237) speaks about "a grammar of language games", about "a world constituted by everyday language" (ibid., p. 239), and about "the grammar of the apprehension of the world and of action" (ibid., p. 241). And he states: "The grammar of everyday language regulates not only

---

* This, and other original quotations in the text, have been translated by the editors.

the context of symbols but also the intersection of the elements of language, of patterns of actions and of expressions". (Ibid., pp. 266–267.) Apel is equally seriously concerned with a grammar which is fundamental enough to cope with language as well as non-linguistic modes of human interaction. He writes:

> . . . it is the mode of the sentence which expresses in the language game the interweaving between the way the language is used and the situational reference of the mode of life (*Lebensform*). Because of this, the "deep grammar" of sentence modes cannot be restricted to those typical forms which are usually differentiated in the traditional grammar. Such a restriction is invalid, since it is contradicted by the fact that a sentence is initially endowed with meaning because it is placed in the context of a wider meaning which is composed of language and of the practice of living—i.e. precisely in the context of the "language game". (1966, p. 72.)

Those of us who are engaged in empirical enquiries into language and human communication are continually trapped within the games of our own everyday language, yet professionally obliged to disclose their mysteries by transcending them. And, being attracted to depth and fearing shallowness, we are also naturally attracted by the prospect of disclosing a grammar "deep" enough to account for verbal as well as non-verbal human interaction, and even for "schemata for the understanding of the world" (*Schemata der Wertauffassung*, Habermas, 1968, p. 237). I have argued elsewhere (Rommetveit, 1968a, pp. 217–218 and 1968b) that psycholinguists seeking depth only in "deep sentence structures" are bound to fail, and I shall try to demonstrate how Chomsky (1968), whose support they claim, is on the verge of expanding the scope of his search for deep syntactic structures beyond the utterance *in vacuo* and into complex patterns of communication.

A major object of this chapter is the examination of potentially fruitful novel orientations and paradigms for research on human communication across traditional academic boundaries. In surveying recent contributions in the fields of linguistics, psycholinguistics, cognitive psychology and social psychology, I shall attempt to explore underlying *philosophies of language* and positivistic or "hermeneutic-dialectic" *philosophies of science*. My attitude towards philosophical texts, however, is very different from that of the hermeneutic theologians towards the Bible at the time when the first version of the hermeneutic cycle was formulated in the context of "the authority of the Holy Scriptures". Even the fundamental notions of the novel hermeneutic-dialectic philosophy will be considered as symptoms of "false ideology" or, at best, suggestive metaphors, until their content can be elaborated in terms of precise relationships to current psychological concepts of cognition and communication and the particular implications (of rejection or acceptance) for the specific methods by which the empirically oriented social scientist of today tries to deepen his understanding of human cognition, communication and interaction.

The relationship between the philosopher (particularly the philosopher of science) and the social scientist is too often accepted as a relationship between master and servant: the social scientist is requested to clarify his tacit philosophical assumptions in a terminology dictated by the philosopher. My deliberate attempt at reversing this relationship is provoked by the suspicion that the proponent of novel hermeneutic-dialectic ideas may easily become insulated in a vicious hermeneutic triangle consisting of famous and "deep" philosophical forefathers, a straw-man of positivistic social science, and himself. I shall not try to refute the suggestion of Apel (1966) that Wittgenstein, by virtue of his later notions about "language games", may be counted among those famous forefathers; nor' shall I question the potential depth of these notions. It is worth remembering, however, that the idea of language as *games with words* struck Wittgenstein one day as he was passing a field where a game of football was in progress (Malcolm, 1967, p. 65). The potential depth of the idea, moreover, will hardly ever be reached if we consider the incident of its genesis as an instance of revelation.

What characterized Wittgenstein's own philosophy as *Praxis* was a programmatic disrespect for vague and indirect philosophical metaphors, not excluding those he had used himself. The best way of achieving further clarification of the ideas that occurred to Wittgenstein as a result of watching the football game is hence to attempt to relate them to notions emerging from our own research. The same applies to the main concepts of the novel hermeneutic-dialectic philosophy of social science. Their content and their relevance to social scientific research cannot be brought out by *werkimmanente Interpretation* of philosophical works only, but must be examined in the context of, for example, the recent linguistic search for universals of natural languages, reflections by sociologists and psychologists in connection with their empirical investigations of human cognition and communication, and even ideas which have been developed by psycholinguists while planning and watching the games known as psycholinguistic experiments.

Reference and Deixis

The point of departure for any analysis of verbal communication is what might be called the *temporal-spatial-directional co-ordinates* of the act of communication. In the case of spoken language, these co-ordinates are defined in terms of the *time* at which the act of speech takes place, its *location*, and the reciprocal identification of *speaker* and *listener*. A social scientific analysis of the communication process, however, has to transcend the precise assessment of the *now*, and *here* and the *I-you* of the act of speech in terms of a physicalistically defined point-in-space and the proper names of speaker and listener. The intersubjectively established *now*, for instance, will have very different denotative extensions depending upon whether we are timing a sprinter at an athletic competition or engaged in a discussion of the history of Western philosophy. The *here* of the act of speech, moreover, may be tagged onto continental Europe or a particular corner of the conference room, depending upon whether we are oriented towards the issue of the relationship between American pragmatism and European hermeneutics or the issue of where coffee is going to be served. And the *I* of the act of speech has served as a pivot for perpetual philosophical and psychological disputes—including the issues of subjective experience versus public knowledge and the nature of and boundaries for Man's knowledge of Man.

All natural languages contain elements by which particulars of an intersubjectively presupposed and/or temporarily established shared and immediate *Lebenswelt* (life space) can be introduced into the process of verbal communication. They are the so-called *deictic* ("pointing") linguistic tools ("indicators") such as demonstratives, time and place pronouns, tense of verbs, etc. and deictic aspects of language may hence serve as an initial point of departure for a further clarification of the hermeneutic cycle. Apel states:

> In order to achieve a constitution of meaning the mind must be fully engaged; that is, it must be genuinely engaged in the here-and-now. Every constitution of meaning refers back to an individual perspective, to a standpoint, or in other words to a bodily engagement (*Leibengagement*) of the cognizing mind. (1968, p. 39.)

The role of bodily engagement and the dependence upon an individual perspective are revealed in a literal fashion in space and time deixis: the *here* versus *there* and the *now* versus *past* and *future* can play no role at all in the language game unless they are attached to an *I* as the centre of a *Lebenswelt*. That active, subjective agent of speech and action, the *I*, which Mead (1950) considers inaccessible to introspection, has been described in subjective spatial-temporal terms as that which connects *behind* with *in front*, *to the left* with *to the right*, and *what has been* with *what is going to be* (Chein, 1944). The breakdown of such a basic spatial-temporal structuring of experience is, according to Koffka (1935, p. 323), the very clue to the understanding of his interesting case of "a behavioural world without an ego".

I shall return later to the issue of person deixis and the *I* as a "boundary of the world" (Wittgenstein, 1922, p. 631). What is suggested by the term *Leibengagement* (bodily engagement)—in addition to purely bodily position—is some sort of a vested interest, a state of drive or an intention on the part of any person seeking knowledge and participating in a communication process. Such a suggestion may be interpreted in different ways: as a claim that entirely disinterested cognition is as absurd a notion as subjective human experience without anchorage in a bodily defined here-and-now, as a recognition of hereditary sin, or as an insistence that human experience is pervaded by intentionality.

The first two interpretations are closely related. Both imply that human cognition is inherently constrained by subjective perspectives and somehow guided or affected by subjective desires. The latter may be described in existential terms, in terms of instinctive forces, or in terms of the necessarily instrumental nature of cognition by virtue of its intimate relationship to (technical) mastery of the world or of fellow human beings. What is required in order to attribute such an assumed state of affairs to hereditary sin is the postulate of one "good" or omniscient perspective and a notion of absolute unselfishness against which the individual's (and humanity's) shortcomings can be viewed.*

Leaving the issue of human intentionality for the moment, we are at this stage left with an apparent contradiction between *Leibengagement* and *intersubjektive Verständigung* ("intersubjective agreement"). Deictic words seem to be firmly anchored in a subjective perceptual-motivational perspective and bodily engagement in the world; yet they are entirely useless in the language game unless the participants in the communicative act are able to transcend their *Leibengagement* and establish a shared world. The deepest semantic content of *Leibengagement* thus implies an essential feature of *egocentrism* (Piaget, 1926). It is most clearly reflected in the child's incapacity to take the role of the other. Words such as *he* and *that* are often used by the small child in such a way that the listener is incapable of tagging them onto previously mentioned entities. Objects which are visible only to the child himself are talked about as if they belonged in a shared visual world. Erroneous inference concerning another child's preference ordering of toys, moreover, is diagnosed as a breakdown of a principle of transitivity due to a *breakthrough* of the egocentric child's own likes and dislikes (Smedslund, 1967). Furthermore, Werner and Kaplan state: ". . . early objects are defined almost entirely in conative-pragmatic terms, formed through the changing affective-sensory-motor patterns of the individual." (1963, p. 44.)

The child's mastery of deixis, however, is dependent upon aspects

---

* I have elsewhere (Rommetveit, 1960) discussed sin and potential criteria for rationality. Human irrationality, according to the criteria discussed in that essay, can be broken down into three S's: Sin, Stupidity and Sociability.

of cognitive growth which have been labelled *decentration* (Piaget, 1926) and *distancing* or *polarization* (Werner and Kaplan, 1963). The hermeneutic emphasis upon *Leibengagement* must hence, when extended beyond the egocentric child, be explained with reference to psychological observations and theories of cognitive development. It is a very important aspect of human existence that any effort to understand the world, oneself, and one's fellow human beings is embedded in a temporal-spatial-personal deictic frame. It is equally obvious, however, that the issue of imprisonment of thought in a bodily perceptual-motivational perspective represents very different issues, depending upon whether we study the inferences that Piaget made when he was four years old about another child's preference ordering of toys, or whether we consider his reflections, fifty years later, on the protocols derivable from such observations of egocentrism under carefully controlled conditions. Thus a strong and categorical denial of *Wert-freiheit* ("value-freedom") in social scientific research is, to a psychologist, entirely devoid of content unless such terms as *Leibengagement* and *Interesse* (Apel, 1968, p. 51; Habermas, 1968, p. 242) are clarified with reference to psychological observations and theories concerning decentration in the ontogenesis of human cognition.

Neither cognitive psychologists nor their physicalistic colleagues (if such creatures exist) can deny the fact that Piaget was "engaged in the world" in both instances referred to above. But some cognitive psychologists—among them, Piaget—have adopted the attitude that the issues of the nature and potential transcendence of bodily engagement and individual perspectives cannot be adequately explored within the framework of a traditional philosophical dialogue about *a priori* boundaries of human cognition; and this is clearly reflected in their *Praxis* as researchers. Piaget's reflections have become a psychological contribution not because he has rejected the general philosophical topic of basic human conditions of knowledge, but because of his decision to invite fellow human beings who are *not* professional philosophers to enter the dialogue, his deliberate attempt to break well-established hermeneutic cycles by exploring human cognition at such an early stage of ontogenetic development that the transcendence of the *Interpretations-gemeinschaft* ("community of interpretation") of philosophers becomes essential, and so does his strategy of systematic experimental variations of *conditions of cognition*. Despite the "prediction and control" implicit in them, experiments on cognition are primarily means of expanding the observational basis for reflection beyond the speculative philosopher's restricted reserve of pertinent incidents from everyday life and his unlimited, but somewhat more dubious, collection of imagined states of affairs. It is puzzling, therefore, that a theory of science which is explicitly formulated within the context of an anthropology of knowledge as opposed to a "logic of science" (Apel, 1968, p. 37) should be outlined in the terminology of Kant, Fichte, Hegel, Marx and Dilthey, as if psychological enquiries during the last fifty years into the acquisition of knowledge and ontogenetic development had added nothing to our insight into the anthropological problems raised by Kant.*

Let us return briefly to the problem of *Wertfreiheit* and Habermas' notion of *Erkenntnisinteresse*.† Habermas writes:

> Interests which guide knowledge (*Erkenntnisleitende Interessen*) mediate between the natural history of the human species and the logic of its process of creation. By interests I mean the basic orientations which relate to the fundamental conditions that enable Mankind to reproduce and organize itself. These conditions are work and interaction. (1968, p. 242.)

He also claims:

> . . . knowledge is not purely an instrument for the adaptation of the organism to changing environment; nor is it an act of a purely rational being, a contemplation divorced from the context of life. (Ibid., p. 242.)

It is difficult to decide what is implied by "the logic of the process of creation of the human species" in this context—unless one is willing to subscribe to Hegel's metaphysics. If we try to relate "interests which guide knowledge" to the notion of the "bodily engagement of the apprehending mind", however, we are immediately faced with the issue of emancipation of thought from perceptual-motivational imprisonment which Piaget, as a professor of child psychology *and* of the history of scientific thought, has discussed in his genetic epistemology (Piaget, 1950). The constructive and adjustive aspects of cognition

* Kant's programme for a philosophy *in sensu cosmico* was characterized by four fundamental questions: (1) What can I know? (2) What ought I to do? (3) What may I hope? (4) What is Man? He considered the fourth question *the anthropological problem*, and, since the first three questions are intimately related to the last, all four problem areas are "anthropological". The first question, however, was considered the basis for metaphysics, the second one the core of ethics, whereas the answer to the third question was to be sought in religion (cf. Buber, 1962, p. 689).

† It is interesting to notice how an *evolutionary perspective* pervades Habermas' reflections on *Interessen*. His assertion that such interests *bemessen sich allein an jenen objektiv gestellten Problemen des Lebenserhaltung* (1968, p. 242) reminds one of the basic evolutionary perspective on human cognition adopted by the prominent American behaviourist Clark L. Hull, whose "Principles of Behaviour" (1943) is replete with references to survival and whose hypothetico-deductive style bears the unequivocal marks of "Principia Mathematica" on the writing desk of the author. Habermas' *Lebenserhaltung* is clearly expanded so as to comprise *continuation of cultural life*. However, this does not relieve him from making very difficult decisions concerning two types of knowledge, namely knowledge about what cannot be changed and "emancipatory knowledge".

have been thoroughly discussed in connection with his concepts of "assimilation" and "accommodation". Also, his empirical enquiries into cognitive achievement at successive age levels have been summarized in an elaborate theory of (dialectic?) stages of egocentrism, pre-operational and concrete operational thinking, and genuinely abstract thought, a theory according to which decentred scientific reflection about the world and the conditions and potentialities of human knowledge emerges as the negation of—and final emancipation from—the stage of entirely drive-and-stimulus bound *Leibengagement* of the newborn child.

The capacity for decentering implies, amongst other things, that a scientist or a philosopher can reflectively and systematically counteract any vested interest in the outcome of his research and reflection *once such an interest has been diagnosed and clearly identified*. And the most complete emancipation of acquisition of knowledge from "world and interaction" and immediate *Leibengagement* is encountered in the role of the professional truth-seeker, e.g. in Wittgenstein's philosophy and reflection and Piaget's enquiries as a professor of child psychology and of the history of scientific thought. It is hence very difficult to refute a weak thesis of *Wertfreiheit* of social science, i.e. that the social scientist is able to take presumably efficient precautions against potential "sources of errors" ranging from self-fulfilling prophesies in experimentation (Rosenthal, 1966) to ideological compliance with the demands of a capitalistic society (Habermas, 1968). A strong thesis of *Wertfreiheit*, on the other hand, would imply that the social scientist should be able to counteract constraining and biasing conditions *before such conditions are identified*, and such a thesis is therefore meaningful if and only if we dare at this stage to claim revelation of an omniscient perspective and absolute truth.

Consider, for instance, Habermas' hypothesis concerning the relationship between capitalism and positivism in social science. The image of the positivistic psychologist and sociologist emerging from his analysis (Habermas, 1968) and from Skjervheim's discussion (Skjervheim, 1959) is a horror image of a person eagerly trying to manipulate, control and predict his fellow human beings as "objects", taking care to write down what he finds out in terms of causal laws which are *comprehensible* only within the *Interpretations-gemeinschaft* ("community of interpretation") of his positivistic colleagues and *useful* only to those who have power to exploit others. What has been omitted from this image is, among other things, the basic epistemological and methodological rationale for Man's dependence upon other fellow human beings in his struggle towards self-understanding. Malcolm (1964, p. 154) has aptly summed up behaviourism's shortcoming as a philosophy of psychology (*not* as a theory of evidence) by saying that it regards Man as *solely* an *object*. The other horn of the dilemma is to regard Man *solely* as a *subject*, implying an imprisonment of Man's knowledge of Man inside the active *I* which constitutes the *origo* of the deictic temporal-spatial-personal co-ordinates of individual human experience and action. This *I* is "a boundary of the world" because it is in principle inaccessible to introspection. I have argued elsewhere (Rommetveit, 1960), partly on the basis of experiments on cognitive achievement, that the "double intentionality" of cognizing and reflecting upon the act of cognizing (Husserl, 1964, p. 157) is bound to result in an oscillation between an active *I* of immediate cognition followed by another active *I* reflecting upon the first *I as a passive "me"*, *in retrospect*; there is then a third active *I* engaged in a cognitive activity *which has been modified* by the intervening activity of retrospection and reflection, and so on. Resort to other human beings as subjects in experiments* is hence a *sine qua non* when one wishes to acquire knowledge about one's own cognition under conditions in which it is not being self-supervised and guided by the characteristic double intentionality of the introspective philosopher and psychologist.

Embedded in empirical psychological research as *Praxis* are thus various detour strategies of getting at the active *I* of actions, cognitions and acts of speech. What is known as "deception" in social psychological experiments, for instance, must be interpreted as an antidote against the self-deception inherent in introspection. Treating fellow human beings as "objects" in an experiment and either withholding from them completely the purpose of the experiment or giving them distorted information about it, cannot truly be regarded as an instance of tacit positivistic metaphysics of causation and denial of human intentionality. On the contrary, such detour strategies testify to a clear recognition of the crucial role of human intentionality and of Man's capacity for self-reflection and self-control. Thus they should be viewed and evaluated as serious attempts at transcending a *Verstehen* constrained by the tradition of an aristocracy of philosophers whose empirical basis for insight into conditions of human knowledge has consisted of their own reflections, introspection (sometimes raised to the second and even third power) and selected an anecdotes.

It must immediately be admitted that the social psychological experiment is a very dubious antidote for self-deception when ingenuity of experimental design is combined with a behaviouristic attempt at emancipation from "meaning". What in published form takes on the appearance of tests of "behavioural laws", phrased in terms of concepts equally applicable to Man and to the rat in the Skinner box, may, upon a closer examination, turn out to be something else. Success at pre-

* This implies, according to the terminology of Skjervheim (1959), treating them as "objects".

dicting behaviour in the experimental situation may be shown to be intimately related to the experimenter's familiarity with the subject's *Lebenswelt* and his interpretation of the experimental situation. Failure to replicate the outcome in different cultural settings indicates that the "variables" or "laws" may have been strongly infected by tacit surplus meaning of the kind hermeneutic philosophers emphasize. Successful prediction in the familiar setting may thus actually reveal more about the extent to which the experimenter and his subject share a *Lebenswelt* than about the "laws" as formulated in published papers. A programmatic declaration of independence from meaning prohibits the experimenter from exploiting such failures of replication for the purpose of gaining deeper insight into the processes he wants to understand. It is possible, however, to subject this issue of subject-experimenter relationship to theoretical and empirical investigations. (See Israel and Tajfel, 1972.) I shall thus not for a moment deny that some psychologists—and in particular those who have openly confessed to a behaviouristic philosophy—have at times been so absorbed in the study of Man as a *He* that their efforts can hardly be defended as methodologically sophisticated detours aiming at an *I*. However, a careful analysis of particular contributions, from the inception of the main ideas to the publication of the findings, very often reveals quite intriguing relationships, such as those existing between the researcher's own *Lebenswelt* and subjective reflections on basic human condition and *the published reports* which lead a hermeneutic philosopher of science to assign the researcher to the class of predicting (and predictable), controlling (and controlled), manipulating (and manipulated) social scientists. For instance, published "quasi-causal" theories of affiliation motives may, upon closer examination, turn out to be more appropriately interpreted as a social psychologist's reflections about his own loneliness and about Man's dependence upon others as part of the "basic human condition". The reason why an underlying humanistic orientation is concealed in the published report may in such cases often be sought in an imitation of natural scientific style and terminology (Koch, 1959). There is always the temptation in a novel field of empirical enquiry to establish some contact with the ideas developed within different and more highly advanced fields by means of analogies. Psychologists will thus sometimes feel that talking about "valences" may promote their insight into interpersonal relationships, whereas the chemist feels that little is gained by talking about love between atoms. The psychologist studying affiliation will also, of course, try to transcend his subjective and idiosyncratic notions by anchoring his concepts in observations accessible to a more inclusive "community of interpretation". The necessary resort to other human beings as subjects in his experiments, *and*, possibly, the positivistic ideological superstructure to which he has been exposed in his experience with editors of journals, may at the same time seem to promote communication of results, and serve to conceal underlying existential and humanistic orientations.

Suppose that Habermas' description of American society were essentially correct and even confirmed by thorough empirical studies and critical theoretical analysis. If Skjervheim and Habermas examined modern American social science with less of an attitude of estrangement (and more "hermeneutic understanding"), they might even encounter latent patterns of subtle protection beneath the surface of historical co-occurrence of capitalism and positivism. A positivistic superstructure may at times serve as a camouflage and protective device which allows the "egghead"—the sensitive intellectual who feels alienated in a society presumably pervaded by competition and a striving towards technical mastery of the world and fellow human beings—to be paid by that society for pursuing his explorations of those very issues which Kant tried to formulate as "the anthropological problem". And a psychology of Man in the third person would not be abolished once and for all the moment the inadequacy of a physicalistic philosophy of psychology had been proved. The issues of understanding "the mind of the other person" and the futility of self-observation as the only avenue towards understanding the self must reappear in terms of intricate problems of epistemology, methodology and ethics in any serious novel philosophy of social science.

Let us at this stage comment briefly upon some ethical issues. The goal of deepened and emancipatory self-understanding and the paradigm of "dialectic mediation of explanation and understanding" seem to imply an oscillation between Man as subject and object, between the *I* and a *He* of person deixis. The request for emancipatory self-understanding, however, may be translated in terms of more specific and quite severe constraints upon social scientific research. There is first a potential constraint upon choice of problem area and conceptualization which may be expressed in the novel commandment: *Thou shalt not seek knowledge about thine Brother that cannot be converted into self-insight in Him.* This means, more specifically, that some pre-knowledge concerning possible implementation via communication of the researcher's insight into the "naive" fellow human being must be available in advance: we should thus pursue issues which allow for such implementation and abstain from pursuing those whose solutions are unlikely ever to be converted into genuine self-insight. Practical application of social scientific knowledge in pursuance of issues in this forbidden latter category might imply circumvention of the other person's self-reflection and control and hence *manipulation* of some sort.

It is worth noticing that ethical issues such as those suggested above seem to be very salient in current theoretical and methodological reflections upon research on decision-making and management. Soelberg (1970), for instance, wants to elaborate a model of decision-making with a one-to-one correspondence (if not *identity*) between model constructs and the symbolic entities used by subjects in their own thinking. This request is in part based upon an explicitly stated programme of establishing the necessary conditions for a dialogue between the social scientists studying decision-making and those who are continually and professionally engaged in making decisions without any professional obligation to reflect upon intuitive strategies and tacit presuppositions inherent in their choice behaviour. Choice of empirical approach and conceptualization (such as inviting the "naive" decision-maker to "think aloud" and trying to capture what is happening in concepts fitting the perspective of the decision-maker as an *I*, or observing specific conditions and outcomes of decisions in order to test "quasi-casual" hypotheses derived from simple hedonistic or utilitarian models of Man) may thus affect the prospect of potential emancipatory self-understanding in crucial ways.

Neither of these approaches seems to possess any inherent emancipatory political value, *irrespective of potential practical implementations*. A well-fitting quasi-causal model, for example, might very well become useful to workers trying to predict the behaviour of a powerful management; it would be especially useful if they were to have a long-range perspective of taking over the management of the firm. The "thinking-aloud" approach may, on the other hand, be successfully exploited by a powerful management trying to improve its control and exploitation of the workers.

It is nevertheless important to keep in mind, as Israel points out in this book, that the social scientist is able to transcend what appears to be given and present novel potential alternatives of action and future outcomes. However, none of those imagined states of affairs may be real alternatives in the sense that they would be chosen, assuming specific criteria for rational choice. If the "naive" person includes them in his visualization of futures in the form of a regret matrix, his rational choice among "real" alternatives may still be affected: his visualization of imagined (including unrealistic) futures will thus, under some conditions, affect the course of action which *determines* his future (see Rommetveit, 1960). On the other hand, whether subsequent plans of action are going to be successful may in turn be highly dependent upon knowledge of biological constraints (see Israel and Tajfel, 1972). Hence, in "action research" we are often forced to adopt an eclectic position of "combined voluntarism and determinism" (see Israel and Tajfel, 1972).

The psychologist's services to his fellow human beings are very often called upon when these fellow human beings have already been defined by society as outside the "community of communication" of ordinary social life. His attempts at understanding mental retardation and behavioural disorders of various varieties and degrees start, as a rule, at that very locus of interpersonal intercourse at which a hermeneutic cycle has been broken. The possibility of being able to convert his insight into his fellow human being into emancipatory self-insight *in the other*, moreover, may be very slim in many such cases.

Consider, for example, the diagnosis of various cognitive disorders such as failure to cope with abstract ideas, or speech and reading disorders varying from severe aphasia to various forms of dyslexia. Faced with such problems, we are immediately forced to realize that we are on our own. Our philosophical forefathers—however profound their ideas might have been—were reflecting upon the human mind within hermeneutic cycles of "normal" (and even particularly gifted) human beings. Their understanding of the world, tacitly preserved within their own community, did not imply being with others whose individual human conditions were, in some important respects, at variance with those of the philosophizing *I*. Their *Verstehen* of cognition and speech, for instance, was therefore never seriously challenged beyond its plausibility as a description of presumed universals or culturally defined "normal" or "ideal" models of functioning.

The challenge of cognitive dysfunctions to psychology may illuminate some of the ambiguities inherent in the novel hermeneutic-dialectic programme for social scientific research. The request for conversion of knowledge of "the other" into emancipatory self-insight in him appears palpably absurd in research on mental retardation. What may be achieved, however, on certain occasions, is a somewhat different and more thorough self-insight *on the part of the researcher*, a self-insight which in turn may contribute to empathy with the deviant. This may possibly be accomplished by a systematic oscillation between the attitudes of estrangement and empathy. The aphasic's strange behaviour is "explained" by careful experimental analysis of perceptual and ideational achievements in a variety of specific conditions, and his globally perceived acts of cognition and communication are broken down into hypothetical, interrelated functions and sub-functions. The purpose of such a procedure is to try to identify the locus (or loci) of the dysfunction within a complex architecture of cognitive and sensory-motor activities. An unequivocal identification, moreover, paves the way for a more appropriate empathic understanding. The psychologist can now ponder: "How would I experience the world if I were not capable of performing that particular function?" However, he is most likely to achieve through this reflection an expansion of knowledge which is purely unilateral and not of a kind that can be converted into self-insight in the handicapped person. It may nevertheless enable the handicapped person to see ways in which particular rearrangements of immediate material conditions may help him circumvent his handicap in everyday life, and may indirectly improve his condition by unilateral dissemination of the psychological knowledge to "significant others" surrounding him.

In what sense, then, is such a case* an instance of "dialectic mediation of explanation and understanding"?

Apel may be interpreted as claiming that a functional analysis of the other person is necessarily "causal" (or "quasi-causal"), whereas self-insight is devoid of such "casual" or "quasi-causal" components. Such a claim may appear plausible against the intangible background of physicalistic psychologists, but blatantly implausible against the more real background of modern cognitive psychology. A survey of important psychological contributions within the latter field, across subfields as diverse as Piaget's early developmental psychology (1926), Heider's psychology of interpersonal relations (1958) and Miller's enquiries into hierarchically organized processes (Miller *et al.*, 1960), leaves us with an unequivocal impression of a common acceptance of, and concern with, the fact of human intentionality. The various proponents of this quite complex and very heterogeneous psychological research tradition might indeed express an essential aspect of their underlying philosophy of science by a collective endorsement of Brentano's definition of psychological phenomena as "those phenomena which contain within themselves an intentional object"† (Brentano, 1874, p. 116).

This implies that cognitive dysfunctions in the other person are always explored as contained in a matrix of intentionality and more or less successful self-control. It implies *eo ipso* that the cognitive psychologist is entirely—and reflectively—unwilling to alternate between a "causal" analysis of "the other" and a "non-causal" analysis of self. According to this basic outlook on the historical origin of the discipline and the legitimate practical demands upon it, psychology must develop as an expansion of that "understanding in the human sciences" (and,

---

* An abundance of specific cases conforming to this general paradigm are available in research on aphasia, and on schizophrenic thought and speech, etc.

† Strangely enough, some of the most interesting explications of this definition are currently being formulated in connection with laboratory experiments on the role of efference in perception (Festinger and Canon, 1965). Philosophers who fight against physicalism and *for* explicit recognition of human intentionality in social scientific research may thus stumble upon their most powerful evidence in psychological laboratories which they enter with the expectation of finding psychologists studying persons solely as objects with instruments resembling those of the well-equipped laboratory of natural science. Such visits, combined with, perhaps, a careful study of Michotte's (1954) experimental analysis of perception of causation, may open their eyes to some very thought-provoking *empirical* games with human conditions and potentialities beyond the conditions of everyday life.

of course, as the correction of "misunderstanding") that philosophers established before the first psychological laboratory was built. A functional analysis of the other person is an absolutely necessary detour, however, if we are ever going to transcend the self-insight into cognition and speech of that stage of knowledge. And one test of transcendence is encountered when we are called upon to deal with dysfunctions.

My thesis is that Apel's paradigm of "dialectic mediation of explanation and understanding" is not applicable in such a situation. The paradigm presupposes, amongst other things, a kind of psychological knowledge of causal or quasi-causal textures of cognition and speech which does not exist.* Even Skinner, the lonely defender of a behaviouristic philosophy of psychology, appears to withdraw—or at least qualify —his declaration of independence from "meaning" (Skinner, 1964). And some sort of a synthesis of *naturwissenschaftliche Erklärung* and *geisteswissenschaftliches Verstehen* appears already to be a characteristic feature of an empirical cognitive psychology of language, thought and communication, including the novel and rapidly expanding field of psycho- and sociolinguistics. The salient feature of this synthesis is *not* an amalgamation of two distinctively different modes of acquiring knowledge, but rather an adaptation and application of some abstract rules for documentation of knowledge, developed within natural sciences, to problem areas in which progress has been hampered because of an unfortunate tradition of heavy reliance upon subjective and intuitive verification procedures.†

To clarify this issue let us examine in detail some acts of speech. We may then, with Merleau-Ponty (1962, pp. 174–199), reflect upon the intentionality of the body, the *Leibengagement* of the *I* of the act of speech, the perceived unity of thought and word, and the immediate expression and comprehension of "meanings" which appear and exist externally as segments of speech. Merleau-Ponty's insistence that acts of speech and comprehension are rooted in social action and social life, moreover, is in agreement with Wittgenstein's notion of language games and emphasis upon the *use* as opposed to the *meaning* of words. Merleau-Ponty's unique perspective, however, is consistently and solely that of *Man as a subject*, the *I* of speaking and listening. His phenomenology of speech and speech perception is thus in a way an attempt at explicating

* My subsidiary thesis, which will be elaborated in somewhat more detail later, is that research on "causal connections" with no recognition of intentionality would be bound to fail.

† The intersubjective agreement achieved under such conditions may, of course, in turn, be partly due to ideological uniformity within the *Interpretationsgemeinschaft*, and hence serve to sustain prejudices against, for example, racial and ethnic groups whose access to higher education has been prohibited by economic and political barriers.

what Wittgenstein left undefined but called "a boundary of the world".*

I shall not try to refute Merleau-Ponty's phenomenology,† but shall attempt to show that there is no such thing as a plausible anti-thesis of causal explanation, which, in conjunction with Merleau-Ponty's thesis, provides the required conditions for a synthesis of "explanation" and "understanding". My thesis is that the essential components of Merleau-Ponty's subjectivistic philosophy of language—inherent intentionality, some sort of unity or complementarity of thought and speech, and the idea that speech has its origin in social action and life—are (and have to be) preserved even when attempting to expand our enquiries (by detour to other speakers and hearers) into those automatized and intuitive aspects we have to understand in order to diagnose and eventually cure speech disorders.

Some details of the proof of this thesis have been presented elsewhere (Rommetveit, 1971). We will now consider briefly the issue of subcomponents of speech, for example, words, morphemes, phonemes and single speech sounds. A physicalistic definition of such entities would have to resort to articulatory motor activities and acoustic sound patterns. Merleau-Ponty seems to deny the psychological existence of such entities. Suppose, however, that we follow a natural scientific approach and try to interpret them by adopting an attitude of "estrangement", that is by listening to (and "measuring") speech sounds as if they were not phases of acts of speech, in the way in which we might study an entirely unknown and esoteric spoken language. Such a physicalistic description would, if feasible, in turn serve as an anti-

* This is clearly the case in his analysis of authentic speech and speech comprehension, when he refers to comprehension as "a synchronizing change of my own existence, a transformation of my being" (Merleau-Ponty, 1962, p. 184). Authentic speech appears by definition to be unitary, devoid of the duality of "symbolic activity" and "natural sign". The discovery of such a duality in ordinary verbal communication cannot be made by the engaged speaker or listener as an active I. A third person is required in order to disentangle what is intentionally made known from what is (involuntarily) mediated by, for example, paralinguistic means. The significance of the distinction, however, is often clearly revealed when the speaker is called upon to assume (public) responsibility for what has been said. He will then (hopefully) assume responsibility for the message conveyed by the narrowly defined linguistic medium, but hardly for subtle "surplus" aspects mediated by the shifts of tone of voice, concomitant facial expressions, etc. Authenticity can then be re-established as a normative notion. We may publicly subscribe to an ethical code according to which perfect unity of (or harmony between) linguistic and concomitant paralinguistic aspects is considered good and desirable.

† Thorough phenomenological enquiries into the "tip of the tongue" phenomenon and experience of groping for appropriate words, as well as experimental studies of "coding stations" along the temporal axis of an utterance (Rommetveit, 1968a, p. 218), however, seem to call for important modifications of his metaphors dealing with thought and speech and his approach to temporal organization.

thesis to Merleau-Ponty's humanistic and phenomenological approach.

The identification of segments of speech *qua* sound, with no reference to its *embeddedness* in acts of communication and its *subordination* to the intentions of communication is, according to the central ideas of modern linguistics and psycholinguistics, an utterly futile task. It contradicts an idea which serves as a common denominator for all varieties of structuralism, namely the assumption that "a structure is sufficient unto itself and does not require that, in order to grasp it, one resorts to all kinds of elements which are alien to its nature" (Piaget, 1968, p. 6). This implies, in the case of speech, that a purely physicalistic description of the speech sound is blatantly inadequate, and even if it were *possible* for some classes of speech sounds it would be extraneous to any structuralistic description of acts of speech and speech comprehension.

What, then, is implied by the relationship between embeddedness and subordination suggested above? Let us, first of all, make an excursion into the laboratory studies of the psychophysics of speech sounds. A reasonable minimal requirement for a physicalistic anti-thesis to Merleau-Ponty's thesis seems to be a rough one-to-one correspondence between the acoustic shape of the speech sound (defined in terms of a spectrographic pattern) and experienced quality. This means, more specifically, that a given acoustic pattern such as the one that is experienced as the phoneme /d/ in the acoustic context /di/ should preserve its experienced quality of /d/ across different contexts such as /de/, /du/ and /da/. Liberman and his co-workers at the Haskins laboratories (Liberman *et al.*, 1967) have shown that this is definitely not the case. The same acoustic pattern is experienced as distinctly different speech sound categories (phonemes) in different contexts. Continuous variation of one sound pattern along a given acoustic dimension, moreover, is responded to by discontinuous experience (e.g. from /b/ via /d/ to /g/).

An impressive series of experimental studies of the psychophysics of speech sounds has thus provided conclusive evidence that there can never be such a thing as simple psychophysics of speech sound in terms of specific invariant relationships between physically defined sound patterns on the one hand and experienced qualities (or categorization) on the other. The investigators have suggested, however, that invariance is reached as we go beyond the acoustic shape, via the act of articulation, and towards the "neural signals" by which the speaker initiates and controls his articulation. And, translated in more mentalistic terms, this means an approximation to a one-to-one correspondence between the quality experienced by the hearer and the articulatory intention of the speaker.

I have argued elsewhere (Rommetveit, 1968a, p. 43) that encoding implies anticipatory decoding, and that decoding implies a retrieval of the intention inherent in the act of encoding. The Haskins studies may be interpreted as a literal confirmation of such a thesis of complementarity; they indicate that we do not hear the sound pattern produced by the speaker but his "intention to speak".* The highly automatized component of anticipatory decoding in speech, moreover, is revealed in the unreflected and spontaneous switch from one language to another of the multi-lingual person in accordance with the requirements of the "you" of the deictic frame in which his speech is contained. We can thus consider the minimal segments of speech as Chinese boxes contained within successively larger boxes until we reach the utterance contained within the more inclusive pattern of interpersonal interaction; ultimately we find patterns of interactions that are embedded in a *Kommunikationsgemeinschaft.*

What is entirely lost in such an analogy is the dynamic aspect of subordination, i.e. the fact that the very identity of any such "box" is determined by the box in which it is contained.† This may be exemplified by one of Chomsky's instances of syntactic ambiguities (Rommetveit, 1968a, p. 77). The "are" in the utterance "They are flying planes" is either the copula (i.e. a mode of assertion) or a constituent of the progressive form ("are flying"), depending upon whether something is being said about pilots or about not-yet-identified objects appearing in the clouds. What is being said is, in turn, determined by the situation in which it is said (including such things as a convergence of attention or intention on pilots or objects in the air on the part of the speaker and the hearer).

The phenomenon of subordination has also been explored under highly artificial experimental conditions of reading (Rommetveit *et al.*, 1968; Rommetveit and Kleiven, 1968; Kleiven, 1969; Kleiven and Rommetveit, 1970). Two letters may compete for the same position in the visual field. The two letters *r* and *g*, for instance, may be binocular rivals in non-word strings of letters such as *sog* (to the left eye) or *sor* (to the right eye), or they may compete for the last position in two Norwegian words such as *sug* ("suck") and *sur* ("sour"). What is seen under such conditions of brief exposure to binocular rivalry depends to a significant extent upon which solution of the conflict yields a word.

---

* All these studies may hence be viewed as empirical explications and confirmations of the basic ideas of symbolic interactionism (see chapter by Asplund, in Israel and Tajfel, 1972).

† Simon's (1962) "architecture of complexity" is thus, as far as I can see, hardly appropriate as a description of the patterns of part–whole relationships and the interdependences involved. All instances he refers to as examples of "nearly decomposable systems" (p. 99), seem to consist of sub-systems whose identity is preserved across inclusion in different more inclusive systems. The notion of embeddedness as used in the present context is thus clearly something other than *membership* in the logic of classes and *inclusion* in set theory.

The rivals *sog* and *sor* are thus often seen as the Norwegian word *sorg* (meaning "grief"), whereas *sug* and *sur* are seen as either *sug* or *sur*. These studies are only a few of numerous similar investigations demonstrating how sensory-motor processes in the acts of speaking, writing, listening and reading are intrinsically controlled by more inclusive and at the same time *higher-order* processes in which they are embedded.

The intuitive, spontaneous and automatized nature of speech and speech comprehension prohibits conversion of such insights into emancipatory self-understanding of the kind Habermas refers to in his resort to psychoanalytic therapy as a model for applied social research. Speech therapy and educational programmes for the teaching of reading must as a rule be based upon quite different principles. The vicious circle in stammering, for instance, will become only more vicious if the therapist forces his patient to reflect even more than before, and in psycholinguistic terms, upon his speech disorder. According to many researchers it is precisely a reflective interference in acts of speech that keeps the stammerer imprisoned in a vicious circle: his situation resembles that of the centipede who started reflecting upon which foot to put forward first.

Very similar difficulties arose in connection with other problems of speech and communication. Hardly anyone—unless he is programmatically committed to protest against analytic thinking and empirical research—would deny that speech often has the dual character of behaviour (or "natural sign") *and* symbolic activity. My voice may on one occasion involuntarily betray my state of depression while conveying a message that is entirely unrelated to my mood; on another occasion it may reveal engagement and devotion to the cause I am talking about. Enquiries into such subtle interrelationships between linguistic and paralinguistic aspects of speech have already yielded insight transcending our present intuitive knowledge; such insight, moreover, may be (and has been) converted to self-insight and implemented in rhetoric.

This insight itself is, in some important respects, "value-free". It can be deliberately disregarded on the ethical grounds that we do not want to add any more faked components to our verbal communication than those which have already been involved. It can even—at least temporarily and in some cases—make for a reflective interference producing centipedian speechlessness. It can, on the other hand, be used in a deliberately manipulatory fashion to promote causes which themselves may be subject to ethical judgement. It may, finally, also help members of the audience to discover the manipulatory manoeuvres of the person promoting a good or a bad cause, and thus serve as an antidote against demagogic persuasion of any kind. It is difficult to see, however, which *Interesse* is involved in such psycholinguistic research in the first place, and which particular emancipatory power is contained in the resultant knowledge—beyond the potentialities of increased self-control and control of others which are embedded in any novel insight into conditions of human existence and interaction.

These excursions have led us far away from the problem of deixis in the more restricted, purely linguistic sense. We have discussed *Leib-engagement* as related to the *I* of the act of speech, the various detours that psychologists resort to in order to capture that *I* when it is not in a state of self-supervision, Merleau-Ponty's phenomenological reflections on the inherent intentionality of speech, and the futility of a dialectically opposed physicalistic approach. Most of these issues, and in particular the recurrent themes of *Vorverständnis* and the fact that the act of speech has its basis in social interaction, are bound to arise once we expand our enquiries into deixis beyond the strictly linguistic domain; they are at the same time central issues in a hermeneutic analysis of language. The point of departure for such analysis is, according to Apel (1968a, p. 47), that "it is only those human behaviour patterns (*Verhaltensreaktionen*) which can be made understandable as intentional structures related to speech which are endowed with the property of 'understanding' ".

It is not very easy to decide precisely what is implied by "the property of understanding" when attributed to *Verhaltensreaktionen*. It is quite obvious, though, that an act of pointing cannot serve a deictic function unless it is being performed *and* perceived as a gesture of communication. The entity pointed to, moreover, is by no means automatically identified immediately the gesture is understood by both participants in the act of communication.* Successful deixis presupposes both a "grammar of pointing" and *Vorverständnis* (presuppositions) with respect to the target of the gesture. Acts of pointing or purely deictic words such as "this" and "that" cannot, therefore, via ostensible definitions, serve as the pivot for linguistic reference. This is clearly demonstrated in the *Philosophische Untersuchungen* of Wittgenstein and constitutes one of the most significant points of convergence between his late philosophy and a hermeneutic philosophy of language.

A researcher approaching these issues from recent studies of linguistics and psychological enquiries into verbal communication would find it particularly interesting to examine how different monistic philosophies of language have achieved their unitary nature by elevating different universal functions or aspects of usage to the status of the primary or

---

* I have elsewhere (Rommetveit, 1968a, pp. 188–190) tried to clarify this issue by the example of two persons watching a football game. One of them is thoroughly familiar with the rules and all the subtleties of the game, but the other has never watched a football game before. A "that" uttered by the former in the sense of "that pass" or "that tackling" is hardly intelligible at all to the person beside him who is watching football for the first time in his life.

essential function. A consistent hermeneutic philosophy is, by virtue of its foregrounding of *Liebengagement, Vorverständnis* and embeddedness of speech in social life and action, primarily a philosophy of deixis. The picture theory of Russell and Wittgenstein's *Tractatus*, on the other hand, make predication and reference the essence of language. Wittgenstein's later refutation of the theory and his insistence upon investigations of use instead of search for meaning should hence be interpreted as a plea for careful social scientific studies of the ways in which deictic, referential and as yet not appropriately identified aspects of use are called into action as language enters into different and sometimes quite complex and composite games of human interaction.

In every natural language reference is achieved by some linkage between linguistic signs and non-linguistic events. This linkage allows the *I* of the act of speech to transcend the *here* and *now* of the immediate deictic frame. One can inform the hearer about past events and state one's beliefs about states of affairs beyond that shared perceptual world which constitutes the immediate matrix for deictic functions. Reference is thus a prerequisite for deception, and hence a *sine qua non* for so-called empirical verification of statements. Utterances may accordingly be viewed not only as further explications of a pre-linguistically established *Vorverständingung*, but as devices depicting "facts" or as "elementary sentences" which in turn can be checked against observation or "sense data". As we then focus upon problems of predication and representation as *the* issues of human language, we leave the grammar of deixis in favour of *the syntax of assertion and the semantics of the content word*.

The more complex issue of predication will be discussed in the next section; I shall therefore restrict my present exploration of reference to a few comments about the role of content words or "designators" ("general terms") in predication. It is obvious that we need linguistic signs which have reference when we use language in games of seeking or giving information; and it is equally obvious that the process of reference is very subtle, and that a linkage between given signs and corresponding classes of objects or events in itself does not provide the necessary condition for predication. Take any psychological theory of reference: a theory of representation of the object via the word which triggers "the idea" of it; an orthodox behaviouristic theory of object-word substitution;* a neo-behaviourist theory of covert and mediating stimulus-response patterns;† or a cognitive-psychological approach emphasizing active categorization.‡ What any such theory can account for—if successful—is the process by which (or the conditions under

* See, for instance, Russell (1940, p. 82).
† See Morris (1946 and 1964); Osgood (1952).
‡ See Rommetveit (1968a, pp. 112–127).

which) some non-linguistic entity may be made psychologically salient to a hearer via the utterance of the word for that entity. Combination of such content words may in turn account via endocentric linguistic constructions (Miller and Ervin, 1964) for "representation" of more complex entities. The noun "triangle" and the adjective "equi-angular", for example, may, in the combination "equi-angular triangle", provide the basis for reference to a class of geometrical entities denotatively defined as the intersection of all triangles and all equi-angular subsets of planes. Such a reference is then extensionally defined in terms of a subset of the extension of each of the designators entering the construction.

Any assertion, however, transcends the purely combinatorial reference of the content elements that enter into it. A search for the "composite reference" of utterances such as "Man is mortal", "the triangle is equi-angular" in terms of the intersection of all men and all mortal beings, and the intersection of a given triangle and all equiangular entities, is thus utterly futile. What is achieved by such linguistic constructions appears to be a description of particular states of affairs (*Tatsachen*) which is exocentric in relation to the reference of constituent words. The reference of content words is thus a necessary, but insufficient, condition for predication. The inadequacy of a purely extensional approach to reference of content words, moreover, is clearly illustrated by the example of Husserl's "equi-angular triangle" and "equilateral triangle".* What is easily lost sight of as we switch from deixis to reference, however, is the subtle interplay of deictic linguistic elements and content elements in natural language. Consider once again the sentence "The triangle is equi-angular". The definite article serves as *eine Als-bekannt-setzung* (Reichling, 1963): the attribute of equi-angularity is ascribed to some entity towards which the speaker and hearer are already oriented during the act of speech, or an entity which the speaker *is going to* make known to the hearer. Alternatively, consider the simple utterance: "He went home". "He" is in this case— apart from the sex content—entirely dependent upon a temporarily established deictic frame; "home" is in turn dependent upon "He", and "went" contains, in addition to its reference to an act of going, a temporal determination relative to the "now" of the act of speech. Articles and mixed deictic-designative elements thus ordinarily work jointly when language is used in games of exchange of information as well as for other purposes. Pure content words, moreover, will vary with respect to reference, depending upon their linguistic and extra-linguistic context.†

* See Rommetveit (1968a, p. 121).

† Systematic variations have been dealt with by linguists in terms of "selection restrictions". The impact of extralinguistic factors upon reference of content words has been discussed elsewhere (Rommetveit, 1968a, pp. 185–193).

This subtle interplay of tacit presuppositions, deixis and reference in verbal communication prohits the invention of any simple formula by which the reference of complex utterances can be assessed. Wittgenstein's picture theory of language, which he refuted in *Philosophische Untersuchungen*, has therefore very little to offer in terms of specific rules for verification. The validity of his *Tatsache* is, by definition, assessable by observation (Wittgenstein, 1922, 4.024). The proposition and the state of affairs it depicts are said to have a common form. Also, utterances conveying false beliefs do so because they arrange "names" in ways in which objects are *not* arranged. Wittgenstein's and Russell's philosophy of reference is thus geared away from the issue of reference of content words and endocentric constructions towards isomorphy between complex assertions and composite states of affairs.

Towards a Grammar of Human Communication

The search for *forms* common to complex sentences and composite states of affairs has been pursued relatively independently by logicians developing calculi of propositions and relations and by linguists explicating syntactic relationships within the framework of categorial grammar. The confounding of symbolic logic and structural linguistics will be discussed later on: here we will comment briefly upon the ways in which *sentences* may be said to depict *events* according to the traditional categorial definitions of constituents of sentences.

The basic principle may be illuminated by considering simple active, declarative sentences such as "John hit the ball". "John" is the *subject*, "hit" the *predicate*, and "the ball" the *direct object*; and the sentence may be said to depict an event which may be appropriately described as an agent acting upon some (acted-upon) element. There is thus a one-to-one correspondence between constituents of the sentence and components (or aspects) of the event. The *agent* of the event enters the slot of the *subject*, the *activity* that of the *predicate*, and the *acted-upon element* that of the *direct object*. There is even, in this case, a temporal or quasi-logical isomorphy: an agent exists prior to the activity he engages in, and that activity is required in order that some object can be acted upon. This order reappears in the left-to-right concatenation of subject-predicate-direct object.

Chomsky's redefinition of syntactic surface structure (Chomsky, 1957) represents an entirely different principle of sentence decomposition. Constituents are, in his generative grammar, defined in terms of the sequence of decomposition (or, if we adopt the point of view of sentence formation, in terms of the sequence of sentence derivation). What in categorial grammar was labelled *subject* appears as the *main noun phrase* of the sentence, defined as NP in the formation rule (1) S→

NP + VP. The predicate, moreover, appears as the *main verb*, defined as V in (2) VP→V + NP. The direct object finally reappears as the NP in (2). What remains of syntactic categories must hence, in addition to their loci in a process of derivation, be explicated in terms of *parts of speech* ("word classes") now devoid of the semantic constraints imposed upon them by a one-to-one correspondence to agents, action and acted-upon elements of non-linguistic states of affairs. The numerous exceptions to the simple rules of categorial grammar therefore constitute no problem at all when constituents are defined in terms of their loci in a sequential derivation. The verb "ignored" in "John ignored the ball" is clearly *the main verb* of that sentence and "the ball" is the direct object (as NP in VP→V + NP), despite the fact that we would hesitate to consider "ignored" a name of activity and "the ball" the name of the acted-upon element of the event. Chomsky's description of syntactic surface structure may hence, for the lack of a more appropriate label, be described as a *technical-derivational approach* to grammar.

The issue of isomorphy between sentence and event structures reappears, however, in Chomsky's search for deep syntactic structures. Consider, for instance, his analysis of the sentence: "What disturbed John was being regarded as stupid." (Chomsky, 1965, p. 70). "John" is in this case said to be the object of "disturbed" and "regarded" but the subject of "stupid". This inference concerning deep structure is arrived at via a two-step procedure of (1) breaking down the complex sentence into more atomic sentences contained within it, and (2) analysing the resultant, more atomic sentences in terms of their structure according to the principles of categorial grammar *and* the logic of predication. The constituent more "atomic" sentences must be of the form (A) "X disturbed John", (B) "Y regarded John" and (C) "John . . . stupid". "John" is then clearly the acted-upon element of (A) and (B); and "John" is *the subject of a proposition* in (C).

Another example is provided by the following sentences: (1) "I expected John to be examined by a specialist."* (2) "I persuaded John

---

* It is interesting to observe that Chomsky, in his preliminary explication of the deep structure of this sentence, does not even mention the *normative expectation* interpretation of the verb "expected". Notice, moreover, that the "descriptive expectation" interpretation can be fairly easily fitted into a model for depicting future states of affairs, whereas the "normative expectation" alternative requires some explication of impact of present language use upon those future states of affairs. The more complex alternative of a dual intention of conveying a belief about the future *and* contributing to its verification can hardly be explicated at all within the framework of an underlying picture theory of language. The issue of normative aspects of descriptive sentences, however, is a central problem in enquiries into social norms and roles (Rommetveit, 1969, p. 22) as well as in current discussions of self-fulfilling "prognoses" concerning future social conditions.

to be examined by a specialist." The deep structure of sentence (1) is explicated in terms of *a derivational history* as follows:

$$S_1 \longrightarrow NP_1 + VP_1 \qquad\qquad S_2 \longrightarrow NP_2 + VP_2$$
$$\longrightarrow NP_1 + V_1 + S_2 \qquad\qquad \longrightarrow NP_2 + V_2 + NP_3$$

S_1 is then to be interpreted as "I expected S_2" and S_2 as "a specialist will examine John". (Chomsky, 1965, p. 221.)

The derivational history of (2), on the other hand, is portrayed in the following way:

$$S_1 \longrightarrow NP_1 + VP_1 \qquad\qquad S_2 \longrightarrow NP_3 + VP_2$$
$$\longrightarrow NP_1 + V_1 + NP_2 \qquad\qquad \longrightarrow NP_3 + V + NP_2$$

S_1 is to be interpreted as "I persuaded John" and S_2 as "a specialist will examine John". "John" appears therefore in the deep syntactic structure in two separate capacities, as the direct object of "persuaded" and as the direct object of "examine".

Similar procedures have repeatedly been applied by psycholinguists who have tried to explore how deep syntactic structure affects learning and mnemonic organization of sentences. Blumenthal (1967) and Blumenthal and Boakes (1967) have studied prompted recall of superficially similar sentences such as "John is eager to please" versus "John is easy to please" in which "John" is said to be *the logical subject* of the former and *the logical object* of the latter sentence. The finding that "John" serves as a better prompt word for recall of sentences in which it is *the logical subject* is then interpreted as evidence for the "psychological reality" of deep structure relationships as operationally defined by Chomsky's procedures for assessment of such structures.

A closer examination of these procedures reveals considerable ambiguity with respect to underlying principles. The procedures are, in some respects, *ad hoc* procedures for assessing "event structures" encoded in the complex utterance, and may accordingly be interpreted as evidence for an underlying picture theory of language like that put forward in Wittgenstein's earlier works. The decomposition of the composite sentence into more simple sentences resembles the decomposition of complex propositional expressions into simple propositions. The interrelationships between the inferred more simple sentences, however, are left largely unexplored by Chomsky. Nothing is said, for instance, about the way in which the two constituent sentences "I persuaded John" and "a specialist will examine John" are related in the deep structure of "I persuaded John to be examined by a specialist".*

* More detailed comments on this particular sentence have been presented elsewhere (Rommetveit, 1968, p. 213 and pp. 216–217). There is nothing in Chomsky's tenta-

The structure of the constituent sentences, moreover, is described in a terminology which testifies to a confounding of the logic of propositions and categorial grammar. This seems definitely to be the case in the analysis of "What distrubed John was being regarded as stupid". The inferred sentence "John . . . stupid" is analysed as a proposition, and "stupid" is obviously interpreted as *a logical predicate*. When "John" is considered the object of "disturbed" and "regarded", on the other hand, we are apparently dealing with the direct object of categorial grammar. The confounding of logic and categorial grammar is also revealed in terms like *logical subject* and *logical object* (for "John" in "John is eager to deceive" and "John is easy to deceive").*

Even if we move slightly from Chomsky's linguistic procedures for assessing deep sentence structures towards the cognitive capacity for comprehending such structures we will find that the clue to the depth in some cases must be sought in the individual's capacity for "polarization" of composite non-linguistic events into, for example, attributes of *persons* and *tasks*. The difference (with respect to deep structure) between "John is easy to deceive" and "John is eager to deceive" is unintelligible until the child has learned to attribute *easiness* to *tasks*, but *capacity* and *eagerness* to *persons*. Mastery of the deep grammar of sentences about interpersonal relations presupposes therefore mastery of a "grammar" of interpersonal relations such as that of Fritz Heider (1958).† The linguistic competence revealed in the comprehension of some deep syntactic structures can hardly be disentangled from general cognitive compentence, a competence which Habermas seems to have in mind when he talks about *eine umgangssprachlich konstituierte Welt* and *grammatische Regeln der Konstituierung dieser Welt*.

Let us now return to the issue of the confounding of logic and

---

tive explications corresponding to the operators of the propositional calculus. Empirical investigations of children's mastery of English words such as "and", "or", "if-then", etc. indicate a strong interrelationship between use of such words and a variety of other cognitive achievements. The syntactic competence required in dealing with syllogisms can thus hardly be disentangled from mastery of particular *abstract operations* as defined by Piaget (Gardiner, 1965).

* A logistic frame of reference with an implicit underlying picture theory of language is particularly transparent in Katz and Fodor's early attempts at developing a semantic theory as an expansion of Chomsky's first version of his theory of syntax. Their relegation of sentences such as "my spinster aunt is an infant" from the set of ordinary, legitimate English sentences can only be defended by reference to combinatorial rules prohibiting arrangements of words which are at variance with the arrangements of objects (or states of affairs) depicted by those arrangements of words (Katz and Fodor, 1963, p. 200). The prohibition is made possible only by very strict conventions concerning the reference of such words as "spinster" and "infant".

† One interesting expansion of Heider's approach, of particular relevance to psycholinguistics, is Abelson and Reich's attempt at extracting "implicational molecules" from discourse (Abelson and Reich, 1969).

linguistics in recent structural linguistics and the ambiguities inherent in Chomsky's structural analysis. Summarizing what has been said so far, we may roughly distinguish between three different approaches to the problem of the form of sentences. The first approach is what has been labelled the technical-derivational approach. This approach is adopted in the assessment of *surface structure*: it defines constituents of sentences in terms of their roles and loci in some inferred process of *sentence formation*, and it is devoid of assumptions concerning isomorphy between sentences on the one hand and states of affairs to be depicted by those sentences on the other.

Secondly, we have the approach adopted in identification of deep syntactic structures of sentences. This approach is, as indicated above, very similar to that of traditional categorial gammar. Constituents are *not* defined in terms of their loci in the process of sentence formation but rather by a matching of the sentence against some state of affairs it is assumed to portray. Let us therefore label it *the picture approach*.

Finally, we encounter an attempt to identify which tacit assertions are conveyed by *the sentence*. This approach may in many cases be impossible to distinguish from the picture approach, since the latter also may be interpreted as portraying beliefs concerning possible states of affairs. The underlying principles, however, are in one case inherited from categorial grammar, whereas in the other case they are borrowed from the logic of predication. The inferred "John . . . stupid" in "What disturbed John was being regarded as stupid", for instance, must be interpreted as *a proposition*, i.e. "stupid" is being considered the *logical predicate* of "John" (as distinguished from the *activity predicate status* of "regarded" and "disturbed" according to which "John" becomes the acted-upon element of those two verbs in the deep structure of the composite sentence). We may label this attempt—which in Chomsky's analysis is adopted in combination with the picture approach—as *the communication approach*.

Let us approach the sentences "John is easy to deceive" and "John is eager to deceive" from all three, presumably different, angles. The *technical derivational procedure* yields identical structures in the two cases: "John" is clearly the main noun phrase in both sentences. *The picture approach*, however, reveals an underlying structure according to which "John" is the victim of an act of deception in the first sentence and the agent of deception in the second.

The communication approach, on the other hand, does not allow for any unequivocal solution in the present case. We may, arbitrarily, decide to consider the phrases "easy to deceive" and "eager to deceive" as composite logical predicates. But in doing so we would ignore the fact that predication is a *semiotic*, and not a narrowly defined linguistic form, or, as Wittgenstein describes it, "a form complete in itself" (1961,

p. 18). What is required, in order to borrow principles from the logic of predication, is hence an expansion of the scope of the analysis from the sentence *in vacuo* to the utterance in its specific setting of interpersonal communication.

What should be considered the logical predicate in the sentence "John is easy to deceive" will obviously vary across different communication settings, depending upon what is already known or presupposed and which novel elements are conveyed by the utterance. The topic of deception may already be presupposed, and the utterance may then be made in response to the question: "Is John difficult or easy to deceive?" If so, we may perhaps consider "easy" as conveying the logical predicate. What is known beforehand may in another situation be that somebody is easy to deceive, and the question then becomes "Who is that person?"

I do not claim that "logical predicates" can be determined by any simple formula such as inferring *the question* which the utterance is an answer.* However, I do claim that the only plausible expansion of the logic of predication to verbal communication appears to be an exploration of what is being asserted, claimed or made known when something is said, and that such an exploration is entirely futile unless we transcend the utterance as such and examine it "in the stream of life", i.e. in the more inclusive semiotic matrix of human interaction. If we want to study language employed in games of information exchange, construction and modification of social realities, and social influence, we must—as Habermas and Apel seem to suggest—start searching for a grammar of communication deep and comprehensive enough to cope with deictic aspects of speech and tacit presuppositions involved in the act of communication as well as those aspects of message transmission which are mediated by speech sounds. The line of demarcation between what is being transmitted via intentional acts of communication and via "natural signs" does not coincide with that between *speech* and *non-verbal behaviour*. The current tendency of specialization in terms of, for example, studies of non-verbal communication and searching for the deep structures of sentences *in vacuo* as entirely separate autonomous social scientific fields of research are, viewed in such a perspective,

---

* One of the many intricate problems we encounter as we proceed from a logic of predication to a grammar of communication has to do with modes and gradation of novelty, that is, with which beliefs, categorizations or states of uncertainty exist in the hearer *before* something ("the logical predicate") is made known by the act of speech. Some of these problems can be illuminated by case analysis of "redundancy", using the Shannon guessing game techniques (see Rommetveit, 1968a, pp. 66–70, and 1971). Achievement in the guessing game may, from one point of view, be interpreted as a measure of *Vorverstandigung*. Another related problem has to do with subtle mixtures and gradations of *assertive and interrogative communications* (Rommetveit, 1968a, pp. 62–64).

entirely irrational and only comprehensible as symptoms of the modern academician's need for personal security within a narrow field of personal competence and his institution's docile acceptance and encouragement of such needs.

There are, however, some definite symptoms of expansion of scope and co-operation across traditional boundaries between academic disciplines: Chomsky's structural analysis has thus had a peculiar appeal to cognitive psychologists. What will emerge out of the resultant psycholinguistic research tradition once—and if—the scope is expanded from *individual cognitive structures* to *communication*, is yet to be seen. There are signs in Chomsky's more recent work (1968) that his own search for depth may take the direction of a grammar of communication.

His recent work on linguistic transformations is clearly geared towards disclosure of principles of universal grammar, and his examples from English phonology and syntax are introduced in order to illuminate such potentially universal principles. The specific rules for formation of wh-questions (and also relative clauses) in English are thus tentatively explicated as manifestations of a general "A-over-A principle", which states: ". . . if a transformation applies to a structure of the form (S . . . (A . .)A) . . .) S for any category A, then it must be so interpreted as to apply to the maximal phrase of type A." (1968, p. 43).

The sentence:

(1A) "He saw the picture of Bill",

will thus in interrogative form appear as:

(1B) "What did he see?"

whereas the form:

(1C) "Whom did he see the picture of?"

is prohibited by the A-over-A principle (1968, p. 46).

The sentence:

(2A) "John kept the car in *the garage*",

on the other hand, is ambiguous. It can mean "the car in the garage was kept by John", or "the car was kept in the garage by John" (1968, p. 43). In the first case, the italicized phrase is part of a noun phrase, "the car in the garage", in the latter case it is not.

The interrogative:

(2B) "What (garage) did John keep the car in?"

presupposes an interpretation in which the italicized phrase is not part of a noun phrase.

There are, however, numerous violations of the A-over-A principle.

The sentence:

(1A′) "He saw a picture of Bill"

can thus be transformed into the question:

(1C′) "Whom did he see a picture of?"

In order to account for the cases in which the transformation can be applied to a noun phrase which itself is a part of a noun phrase, Chomsky is hence led to suggest a rule stating the conditions under which the maximal noun phrase is *transparent*:

> It seems that what is involved is indefiniteness of the dominating noun phrase; if so, then for certain dialects there is a rule assigning transparency to a noun phrase of the form
>
> $$\left[_{NP} \text{indefinite} \ldots \text{NP}\right] \text{NP} \quad (1968, \text{p. } 416).$$

What is implied by "indefiniteness of the dominating noun phrase" in the above context seems to be something more than strictly linguistic indefiniteness (as defined by the English indefinite article). Consider, for instance, the following sentences:

(1A″) "He saw the picture of that man"
(1A‴) "He saw the picture of that particular man"

The dominating noun phrase ("the *picture*") is in each of these cases definite, but the corresponding wh-question may still be:

(1C″) "Whom did he see the picture of?"

This is definitely the case with the Norwegian equivalents:

(for 1A″) "*Han såg biletet av den mannen*" and
(for 1A‴) "*Han såg biletet av den spesielle mannen*".

The grammatically fully acceptable—and even most plausible— "kv-question" for those sentences in Norwegian is:

(equivalent to 1C) "*Kven såg han biletet av?*"

Transparency is thus assigned in spite of the fact that the dominating noun phrase ("*the* picture", "bilet*et*") is definite. The rule assigning transparency may hence have to be rephrased in terms of *which entity* (*picture* or *man*) is most unequivocally identified. The deictic identification ("that man") and the strengthened deictic identification ("that particular man") override, in a way, the *Als-bekannt-setzung* mediated by the definite article of the dominating noun phrase. The issue of indefiniteness versus definiteness thus becomes an issue of nesting of interrelated elements of the message, that is, *which entity is presupposed when the other is mentioned*. The constructions "that picture of something" and "a picture of that" represent very different patterns of nesting as far as "picture" is concerned. What has already been unequivocally identified in the first case is *a particular picture*, and information concerning its content is dependent upon a joint attention or intention toward that picture on the part of the speaker and the hearer. What is presupposed in the other case is some deictically identified entity ("that") which is "transparent" or "free" (Henry, 1971). It is *not* contained within the preceding "a picture" and can hence freely appear in the wh-slot of the interrogative form. Chomsky's "A-over-A principle" may thus be interpreted as an attempt at analysing how the speaker himself imposes a particular structure upon the event the moment he had to make that event known to others (and himself?) by means of verbalization; this is an instance of transition to a "communication approach" to grammar.

The more subtle aspects of such an analysis, which are potentially very significant, may perhaps become more clear if we reflect upon the notion of nesting of message elements as compared to a simple picture theory of language. The latter approach puts the speaker, in a sense, in the role of a photographer. The notion of nesting, on the other hand, provides him with considerable freedom and opportunity for productivity, even in a situation in which he uses language to inform another person "truthfully" about events and states of affairs which he did not know about before. In addition to the productivity inherent in the openness of the semantic system,* he has the freedom of choosing what to presuppose as "background information", which aspects of the complex states of affairs to introduce as *fait accompli* and, in a way, prerequisites for other aspects. Two persons observing exactly the same sequence of events may thus structure their "true" stories about that sequence in such a way that quite different *social* realities are mediated in the two cases.†

* This has been discussed elsewhere (see footnote, p. 59). The freedom to describe a given complex event by words contained within entirely different semantic-associative networks *and*, at the same time, within socially defined very different deictic frames, is exercised intentionally and successfully in political mass media. The strike of miners in Kiruna in Sweden, for instance, may be described in terms of the traditional terminology of trade union negotiations, salaries and productivity, or in terms of alienation and the imprisonment of underprivileged human beings in a capitalist society. I have elsewhere (Rommetveit, 1970) tried to show how institutions planning information campaigns on drug and drug abuse even in their choice of vocabulary to be used are forced to clarify their position with respect to ideologically controversial issues, such as drug and alcoholism legislation.

† This, by the way, is involved in the very definition of "social" as opposed to "physical reality" (Festinger, 1954). Whether a belief is anchored primarily in a social reality or not is thus determined not by the topic, that is by the issue of whether

A consistent communication approach also implies a somewhat different attitude towards problems of structural ambiguity. Sentences such as "I disapprove of John's drinking" (Chomsky, 1968, p. 27) may be *genuinely ambiguous* in the sense that the speaker is encoding a diffuse approval whose target has not yet been unequivocally identified. His omission of disambiguating elements (such as either "excessive" in front of or "beer" immediately after "drinking") may even be deliberate, serving as a provocation and an introduction to a discussion of the issue of whether John should stop drinking altogether or merely should be advised to reduce his consumption considerably. The ambiguity may hence reveal a *shallow intention* on the part of the speaker (Naess, 1953) or an intended duality of the assertion conveyed by his utterance.

Chomsky's attitude toward Wittgenstein's *Philosophische Untersuchungen* may indeed be interpreted as revealing either some shallowness of intention or a deliberate ambiguity. He claims: "If we hope to understand human language and the psychological capacities on which it rests, we must first ask what it is, not how or for what purposes it is used" (1968, p. 62). It is very difficult, however, to see how he can define "indefiniteness" in connection with the A-over-A principle and transparency of embedded noun phrases without resorting to language use and, more specifically, to nesting of message elements as related to an extralinguistic matrix of shared presuppositions on the part of the speaker and the hearer. The linguistic competence required in such nesting, moreover, has to be of the kind Chomsky has in mind as an instance of "the most characteristic and normal constructions of human intelligence" (1968, p. 53), and *not* the innate structure which "appears to be a species-specific capacity that is essentially independent of intelligence" (1968, p. 68). The latter notion is more consistent with what has previously been referred to as "a technical-derivational approach" to grammar, and to psychological enquiries into the sense (and ways) in which Man can be said to be "pre-programmed for language" (Lenneberg, 1967).

The programmatic decision to find out what language *is* before raising questions of purpose and use is thus very problematic. The transition from surface to deep structures is clearly not only character-ized by increased depth, but also, as suggested above, by resort to an underlying picture theory of language use. Also, the principles adopted in recent analysis (as exemplified by the A-over-A principle) seem to

---

the belief concerns such things as interpersonal relations or astronomy. Anchorage in social reality is defined in terms of dependence upon other human beings (*eine Interpretationsgemeinschaft*).

indicate a necessary modification of assumptions concerning use—in the direction of the philosophy of the late Wittgenstein.

The problems of nesting, of patterns of dependency between what is *seen* and what is said, of "free" and "tied" information, etc. have been pursued in recent psychological investigations.* The shared perceptual world which constitutes the stage for an utterance may sometimes provide specific presuppositions without which comprehension of what is said appears to be impossible. What is being said, may, on the other hand, at times impose a definite structure upon *what is seen* or upon *the situation in which it is being said* (Rommetveit *et al.*, 1971). I may be told, for instance, as I am watching a large and derelict building: "There was not enough profit from the production". What I am not told at all—but yet am forced to assume in order to make sense of what I hear—is that the building in front of me is a factory or a business building of some sort.

The interdependence between parts of messages has also been studied in connection with intralinguistic contextual arrangements such as *pre*-versus *post-position of adjectives* in noun + adjective combinations (Wold, 1971; Jaspars *et al.*, 1971; Skjerve, 1971). The nesting of the adjective (as attribute) and the noun is revealed in retrieval of such adjective + noun combinations: the recall is approximately twice as good when the adjective *follows* the noun (post position), i.e. the condition under which the contextually appropriate reference of the adjective can be determined immediately because the noun to which it refers is already known. The problem of nesting has been explored, moreover, in attempts at assessing the syntax of connected discourse and its "conditions of production" (Pêcheux, 1969), and in enquiries into the ways in which referents are *constructed* and imposed upon *eine Interpretationsgemeinschaft* in ideologically loaded discourse (Henry, 1971).

* A number of such rather exploratory experimental and theoretical enquiries have been published in "Social Contexts of Messages" (Carswell and Rommetveit, 1971). The notion of nesting may be illuminated by comparing the two sentences: (A) "The old professor is stupid" and (B) "The professor is old and stupid". Chomsky's analysis of deep syntactic structures, which has also been adopted by Osgood (1963), leads to the conclusion that both sentences contain the following assertions ("propositions"): (1) "The professor is old", and (2) "The professor is stupid". The word "old" in sentence (A), however, may most often provide *specification* or *identification*, i.e. contribute to a convergence of orientations onto the same person in a deictically structured and shared world. Stupidity is, by sentence (A), attributed by the speaker to the "free" (i.e. presupposed) entity "the old professor". "Old" in sentence (A) has hence *not* the status of "logical predicate", irrespective of the situational frame of the utterance. If the two participants in the discourse share the beliefs that there are two professors, one being young and the other old, and that only one of them is stupid, then, of course, "old" will convey the only element of novel information. Which elements are "free" (presupposed) and which are "tied" (i.e. belonging to presupposed elements) can hence never be determined for the utterance *in vacuo*.

What is emerging as the common denominator of these studies is not yet sufficient for the formulation of a theory; but it provides the beginning of a preface to a theory in which irrational and traditional boundaries between linguistics and a social psychology of communication tend to disappear. There is already considerable evidence indicating that utterances are decoded, stored and retrieved in markedly different ways, depending upon whether they are experienced in experimental contexts resembling natural communication settings or *in vacuo*, i.e. as stimuli for rote learning only. The problem of what language *processing* is can hence no longer be safely approached with the underlying assumption that modes of comprehension, retention and retrieval remain essentially invariant across the whole range of possible conditions of use. What language is in a typical laboratory rote learning situation may actually bear a rather moderate resemblance to what it may be in some other laboratory situations and in games of communication in everyday life.*

Hermeneutic-dialectic philosophers seem to emphasize that speech has its origin in human action and interaction, the subtle interplay between *Vorverständigung* (presuppositions) and what is being said; and this has thus already been made the topic of theoretical and experimental enquiries. Meanwhile we are becoming more and more convinced that metaphors and armchair philosophies are at best only first approximations to an understanding of some aspects of language. What Wittgenstein had in mind when talking about language games may possibly be somewhat further clarified as we examine in an exploratory, yet systematic, way the very complex patterns of articulation between linguistic and non-linguistic aspects of human interaction. Acts of human communication may—in accordance with Wittgenstein's outlook in "Philosophische Untersuchungen"—be explored as extremely intricate equations. The loci of the unknown entities may vary, depending upon which kind of game is being played.

Even if, in our analysis of verbal communication, we remain within the present, very restricted frame of games of information exchange, we have to engage in an extremely intricate analysis. For example, what is being said may sometimes reveal significant and previously unknown aspects of the speaker's social identity (see Uhlenbeck, 1967) —his identification with some collectivity on whose behalf he is acting in the given situation, his assumed power or authority relative to the "you" toward which his speech is being addressed, etc. Such (and other) important aspects may be revealed by a variety of different and ordinarily intimately interacting means. We may have to identify

* Exploratory studies by Rommetveit *et al.* (1971) have thus been replicated and expanded (Blakar and Rommetveit, 1971), and results not yet published reveal very interesting differences with respect to *mode of recall* in the two types of situations.

particular tacit presuppositions underlying what is being said, notice
which segments of speech have their basis in, for example, stress and
intonation, examine which aspects of composite events are being
encoded as "free information" and dealt with as pre-conditions for
other aspects, etc.

Whatever "grammar of communication" will emerge from such
analysis will put a very heavy strain upon our reflective capacities.
Whether emancipatory implementation is within the realm of possibility or beyond it will depend upon our interpretation *and* how far
we pursue our enquiries. If we demand implementation in the form of
reflective choice of tacit presuppositions, deliberate planning of nesting
of information, etc. *during discourse*, we are clearly once more up
against the problems of the inaccessibility of the "active I" and there is
a very high risk of centipedian speechlessness. But if our emancipatory
efforts are focused solely on ourselves and our fellow human beings as
listeners, we are faced with at least two problems. The first concerns
the feasibility of converting our wisdom to "school grammars of
communication" which might enable the man in the street to achieve
a deeper reflective understanding (of, for example, tacit presuppositions)
when listening to others. This may turn out to be primarily an issue
of overloading public programmes of general education. The other
problem has to do with potentially undesirable components of *reflective
interference* and *psychologizing* in the trained and reflective listener; it
would arise if dissemination of such insight into language games became
possible on a large scale.

It is hard to see, therefore, in what sense the problem of emancipatory
application in such cases can be clarified in terms of the substantive
issues, conceptual framework, and research paradigms involved; that
is, in terms of inherent value orientations rather than policies of
technical implementation and dissemination of knowledge, which, in
certain important respects, in itself must be considered "value-free".
The commandment prohibiting knowledge about our brothers that
cannot be converted into emancipatory self-insight in them may then
perhaps be rephrased in rules by which the investment in the seeking
of new knowledge is proportioned and paced in accordance with
estimates of immediate and large-scale dissemination of emancipatory
results.

A categorical request for emancipatory and *only* emancipatory
goals may thus very easily lead to the conclusion that social scientists
should not use too much of their current talents and resources in a
search for a grammar of communication of the kind suggested above.
From all reports it seems that what has been achieved so far by experimental studies may not be worthy of *werkimmanente Interpretation*; *at
best* it has provided tentative insights which may serve to encourage

and guide future dialectic efforts to deepen our understanding of human communication. Nevertheless these efforts will continue through reflections upon everyday experience and attempts at expanding our observational basis for self-understanding by playing the games of psychological experiments. The prospects of progress may be slim. However, it is hard to see how they can be improved by adopting a philosophy of social science prohibiting penetration of the rules of language games beyond the point at which knowledge no longer can be mediated as emancipatory self-insight via "school grammars of communication".

References

Abelson, R. P. and Reich, C. M. (1969). Implicational molecules: a method for extracting meaning from input sentences. Paper read at International Joint Conference on Artificial Intelligence, Washington, D.C.

Apel, K. O. (1965). Die entfaltung der "sprachanalytischen" philosophie und das problem der "Geisteswissenschaften". *Philosophisches Jahrbuch* **72**, 239–289.

Apel, K. O. (1966). Wittgenstein und das problem des hermeneutische verstehen. *Zeitschrift Theologie Kirche* **63**, 49–87.

Apel, K. O. (1968). Die erkenntnisanthropologische funktion der kommunikationsgemeinschaft und die grundlagen der hermeneutik. *In* "Information und Kommunikation". (S. Moser, Ed.) pp. 163–171. R. Oldenburg, München, Wien.

Apel, K. O. (1968a). Szientifik, hermeneutik, ideologie-kritik: Entwurf einer wissenschaftslehre in erkenntnisanthropologischer sicht. *Man and the World*, **1**, 37–63.

Blakar, R. M. and Rommetveit, R. (1971). Processing of utterances in contexts versus rote learning of sentences: some pilot studies and a design for an experiment. *In* "Social Contexts of Messages". (E. A. Carswell and R. Rommetveit, Eds) Academic Press, London and New York.

Blumenthal, A. L. (1967). Prompted recall of sentences. *J. Verbal Learning and Verbal Behavior* **6**, 203–206.

Blumenthal, A. L. and Boakes, R. (1967). Prompted recall of sentences. *J. Verbal Learning and Verbal Behavior* **6**, 674–676.

Brentano, F. (1874). "Psychologie vom Empirischen Standpunkte." Duncker and Humbolt, Leipzig.

Buber, M. (1962). What is Man? *In* "Philosophy in the Twentieth Century". (W. Barrett and H. E. Aiken, Eds) Vol. 4, pp. 688–719. Random House, New York.

Carswell, E. A. and Rommetveit, R. (Eds) (1971). "Social Contexts of Messages." Academic Press, London and New York.

Chein, I. (1944). The awareness of the self and the structure of the ego. *Psychological Review* **51**, 5.

Chomsky, N. (1957). "Syntactic Structures." Mouton, The Hague.

Chomsky, N. (1959). A review of *Verbal Behavior* by B. F. Skinner. *Language* **35**, 26–58.

Chomsky, N. (1965). "Aspects of a Theory of Syntax." M.I.T. Press, Cambridge, Massachusetts.

Chomsky, N. (1968). "Language and Mind." Harcourt Brace Jovanovich, New York.

Festinger, L. (1954). A theory of social comparison processes. *Human Relations* **7**, 117–140.

Festinger, L. and Canon, L. K. (1965). Information about spatial location based on knowledge about efference. *Psychological Review* **72**, 373–384.

Gardiner, W. L. (1965). An investigation of understanding the meaning of the logical operators in propositional reasoning. Unpublished doctoral dissertation, Cornell University.

Habermas, J. (1963). "Erkenntnis und Interesse." Suhrkamp, Frankfurt.

Heider, F. (1958). "The Psychology of Interpersonal Relations." John Wiley and Sons, New York.

Henry, P. (1971). On processing of language in context and referents of messages. *In* "Social Contexts of Messages." (E. A. Carswell and R. Rommetveit, Eds) Academic Press, London and New York.

Hull, C. L. (1943). "Principles of Behaviour." Appleton-Century-Crofts, New York.

Husserl, E. (1964). "The Phenomenology of Internal Time Consciousness." Martinus Nijhoff, The Hague.

Israel, J. and Tajfel, H. (Eds) (1972). "The Context of Social Psychology: A Critical Assessment." Academic Press, London and New York.

Jaspars, J., Rommetveit, R., Cook, M., Havelka, N., Henry, P., Herkner, W., Pêcheux, M. and Peters, G. (1971). Order effects in impression formation. A psycholinguistic approach. *In* "Social Contexts of Messages." (E. A. Carswell and R. Rommetveit, Eds) Academic Press, London and New York.

Katz, J. J. and Fodor, F. A. (1963). The structure of a semantic theory. *Language* **39**, 170–210.

Kleiven, J. (1969). Om frekvens og mening ved binokular rivalisering. Unpublished thesis. Institute of Psychology, University of Oslo.

Kleiven, J. and Rommetveit, R. (1970). Meaning and frequency in a binocular rivalry situation. *Scandinavian Journal of Psychology* **11**, 17–20.

Koch, S. (1959). Epilogue. *In* "Psychology: A Study of a Science." (S. Koch, Ed.), pp. 729–788. McGraw-Hill, New York.

Koffa, K. (1935). "Principles of Gestalt Psychology." Harcourt Brace Jovanovich, New York.

Lenneberg, E. H. (1967). "Biological Foundations of Language." John Wiley and Sons, New York.

Liberman, A. M., Cooper, F. S., Shankweiler, D. P. and Studdert-Kennedy, M. (1967). Perception of the speech code. *Psychological Review* **74**, 431–461.

Malcolm, N. (1965). Behaviourism as a philosophy of psychology. *In* "Behaviourism and Phenomenology". (T. W. Wann, Ed.), pp. 141–154. University of Chicago Press, Chicago.

Malcolm, N. (1967). "Ludwig Wittgenstein. A Memoir." Oxford University Press, Oxford.

Mead, G. H. (1950). "Mind, Self and Society from the Standpoint of a Behaviourist." (C. W. Morris, Ed.) University of Chicago Press, Chicago.

Merleau-Ponty, M. (1962). "Phenomenology of Perception." Routledge and Kegan Paul, London.

Michotte, A. (1954). "La Perception de la Causalité." 2nd edn. Publications Universitaires de Louvain, Louvain.

Miller, G. A., Galanter, E. and Pribram, K. H. (1906). "Plans and the Structure of Behaviour." Holt, Rinehart and Winston, New York.

Miller, W. and Ervin, S. M. (1964). The development of grammar in child language. *Monographs of the Society Research Child Development* **29,** 9–34.

Morris, C. (1946). "Signs, Language and Behavior." Prentice-Hall, New York.

Morris, C. (1964). "Signification and Significance." M.I.T. Press, Cambridge, Massachusetts.

Naess, A. (1953). "Interpretation and Preciseness." Jacob Dybwad, Oslo.

Osgood, C. E. (1952). The nature and measurement of meaning. *Psychological Bulletin* **49,** 197–237.

Osgood, C. E. (1963). On understanding and creating sentences. *American Psychologist* **18,** 735–751.

Pêcheux, M. (1969). "Vers L'Analyse Automatique du Discours." Dunod, Paris.

Piaget, J. (1926). "The Language and Thought of the Child." Harcourt Brace Jovanovich, New York.

Piaget, J. (1950). "Introduction à L'Epistémologie Génétique." Presses Universitaires de France, Paris.

Piaget, J. (1968). "Le Structuralisme." Presses Universitaires de France, Paris.

Reichling, A. (1963). Das problem der Bedeutung in der Sprachwissenschaft. *Innsbrucker Beiträge zur Kulturwissenschaft.* Sonderheft 19.

Rommetveit, R. (1960). "Action and Ideation." Munkgaard, Kobenhavn.

Rommetveit, R. (1968a). "Words, Meanings and Messages." Academic Press and Universitetsforlaget, New York, London and Oslo.

Rommetveit, R. (1968b). Review of J. Lyons and R. J. Wales (Eds). Psycholinguistic Papers. *Lingua* **19,** 305–311.

Rommetveit, R. (1969). "Social Norms and Roles." 2nd edn. Universitetsforlaget, Oslo.

Rommetveit, R. (1970). Verbal communication and social influence. *In* "Communication and Drug Abuse." (R. J. Wittenborn, J. P. Smith and S. A. Wittenborn, Eds) Charles C. Thomas, Springfield, Massachusetts.

Rommetveit, R. (1971). On concepts of hierarchical structures and micro-analysis of language and thought. *In* "Hierarchical Models in the Study of Cognition." (G. Eckblad, Ed.). University of Bergen, Bergen.

Rommetveit, R. and Kleiven, J. (1968). Word generation: a replication. *Scandinavian Journal of Psychology* **9,** 277–281.

Rommetveit, R., Berkley, M. and Brøgger, J. (1968). Generation of words from stereoscopically presented non-word strings of letters. *Scandinavian Journal of Psychology* **9,** 150–156.

Rommetveit, R., Cook, M., Havelka, N., Henry, P., Herkner, W., Pêcheux, M. and Peters, G. (1971). Processing of utterances in context. *In* "Social

Contexts of Messages." (E. A. Carswell and R. Rommetveit, Eds) Academic Press, London and New York.

Rosenthal, R. (1966). "Experimenter Effects in Behavioural Research." Appleton-Century-Crofts, New York.

Russell, B. (1940). "Inquiry into Meaning and Truth." Allen and Unwin, London.

Shannon, C. E. (1951). Prediction and entropy of printed English. *Bell System Technical Journal* **30**, 50–64.

Simon, H. (1962). The architecture of complicity. *Proceedings American Philosophical Society* **106**, 467–482.

Skinner, B. F. (1957). "Verbal Behaviour." Appleton-Century-Crofts, New York.

Skinner, B. F. (1964). Behaviourism at fifty. *In* "Behaviourism and Phenomenology." (T. W. Wann, Ed.) pp. 79–96. University of Chicago Press, Chicago and London.

Skjerve, J. (1971). Word sequence and recall. *In* "Social Contexts of Messages." (E. A. Carswell and R. Rommetveit, Eds) Academic Press, London and New York.

Skjervheim, H. (1959). "Objectivism and the Study of Man." Universitetsforlaget, Oslo.

Smedslund, J. (1967). "Psykologi." Universitetsforlaget, Oslo.

Soelberg, P. (1970). "A Study of Decision Making: Job Choice." M.I.T. Press, Cambridge, Massachusetts.

Uhlenbeck, E. M. (1967). Language in action. *In* "To Honour Roman Jakobson." Janua Linguarium Series. pp. 2060–2066. Mouton, The Hague.

Underwood, B. J. and Richardson, J. (1956). Verbal concept learning as a function of instructions and dominance level. *Journal Experimental Psychology* **51**, 229–238.

Weinreich, U. (1963). On the semantic structure of language. *In* "Universals of Language". (J. H. Greenberg, Ed.) M.I.T. Press, Cambridge, Massachusetts.

Weinrich, U. (1966). Explorations in semantic theory. *In* "Theoretical Foundations". (T. A. Sebeok, Ed.) pp. 395–477. Vol. 3 of "Current Trends in Linguistics". Mouton, The Hague.

Werner, H. and Kaplan, B. (1963). "Symbol Formation." John Wiley and Sons, New York.

Wittgenstein, L. (1922). "Tractatus Logico-Philosophicus." Routledge and Kegan Paul, London.

Wittgenstein, L. (1961). "Note Books." (G. H. von Wright and G. E. M. Anscombe, Eds) Harper and Row, New York.

Wittgenstein, L. (1962). The Blue Book. *In* "Philosophy in the Twentieth Century". (W. Barrett and H. D. Aiken, Eds) Vol. 2, pp. 710–774. Random House, New York.

Wittgenstein, L. (1968). "Philosophische Untersuchungen—Philosophical Investigations." (G. E. M. Anscombe, Ed.) Blackwell, Oxford.

Wold, A. H. (1971). Impression formation. A psycholinguistic approach. *In* "Social Contexts of Messages". (E. A. Carswell and R. Rommetveit, Eds) Academic Press, London and New York.

4. On "Emancipatory" Social Psychology*

R. ROMMETVEIT

Introduction

The aim of the present paper is not to contribute toward increased social psychological knowledge, but rather to increase our uncertainty with respect to the nature of such knowledge. There seems to be among us an almost unanimous discontent with current "minitheories"; yet at the same time there appears a surprising complacency with respect to tradition-bound philosophical premises for research and theory construction. The novelty of presumedly novel paradigms is hence largely restricted to proposals for improvements and/or eclectic integration of already established theoretical models, and partial empirical corroboration of such minimodels is interpreted as evidence that we are, after all, on the right track. Why shouldn't we, then, continue our trade along the paths we have pursued so far, with sharpened methodological tools and refined theories, yet with an attitude of agnostic innocence or proud independence toward rebels who question its philosophical foundation?

I do not share this complacency, and my faith cannot even be restored by prospects of novel, eclectic, cross-cultural studies accounting for nearly 100% of people's helping-another-person behaviours (see Triandis, 1976, pp. 223). Nor do I believe that hermeneutic-dialectic philosophers of science have provided us with a ready-made novel foundation for our trade. I would feel very pessimistic, however, if even the younger rebels among us soon join the establishment of tradition-bound researchers, because they are offered more advanced mathematics and "have experimentation in their bones". Their discontent testifies to a genuine feeling of homelessness and an unwillingness to seek safety

---

* Published in "Social Psychology in Transition" (1976). (L. H. Strickland, K. J. Gergen and F. J. Aboud, Eds) Plenum Press, New York.

within narrowly defined fields of academic expertise. And such a feeling of homelessness does not necessarily lead to irrationality and anti-scientific attitudes. Epochs of homelessness may also—as suggested by Kuhn (1970) in his analysis of "revolutions" in the history of natural sciences, and by Buber (1962) in his account of Western philosophy—bring about sound and stringent re-evaluation of axiomatic components of theories and increased depth and independence of "anthropological thought".

The unique characteristic of anthropological thought is in Buber's opinion its serious concern with Kant's basic question: What is man? Such thought is suppressed during periods of "normal", tradition-bound research and during "epochs of habitation" in philosophy. Its core question is then considered futile or even nonsensical because *some preliminary answer to it is embedded in the prevailing mode of thought and tacitly taken for granted*. Thus, man becomes a comprehensible species along with other species in Aristotle's image of a self-contained and geocentric world of "things", whereas he is made "the horizon and the dividing line of spiritual and physical nature" in the philosophy of Acquinas and Dante's "Divina comedia". Complacency with such solutions does not last long, however, and various ramifications of the Kantian problem are pursued in novel ways by ardent and genuinely "homeless" thinkers such as Augustine, Pascal, Kierkegaard and Wittgenstein.

The relevance of Kant's basic philosophical question to humanistic scholars and social scientists—including social psychologists—is brought to the foreground by considering each discipline's contribution toward an understanding of man as a whole. Popper (1974), referring to our increased insight into matter and the merging theoretical unity of physics and chemistry, maintains:

> . . . pure knowledge (or "fundamental research" as it is sometimes called) grows . . . almost in the opposite direction to . . . increasing specialization and differentiation. As Herbert Spencer noticed, it is largely dominated by a tendency towards increasing integration towards unified theories (p. 262).

Our insight into man appears, in comparison, to be of an extremely fragmentary nature. Novel academic disciplines and subdisciplines such as psychology and social psychology have, indeed, been awarded scientific status only insofar as they could proclaim and legitimize their lack of concern with the Kantian question. They may thus, when considered within Buber's (1962) more inclusive perspective on human self-knowledge, even be interpreted as symptoms of evasion:

> From time immemorial man has known that he is the subject most deserving of his own study, but he has also fought shy of treating this subject as a whole, that is, in accordance with its total character.

Sometimes he takes a run at it, but the difficulty of this concern with his own being soon overpowers and exhausts him, and in silent resignation he withdraws—either to consider all things in heaven and earth save man, or to divide man into departments which can be treated singly, in a less problematic, less powerful and less binding way (p. 688).

The ramification of what at one time constituted a global and vaguely defined topic for philosophical discourse into conceptually and methodologically encapsulated scientific subdisciplines has within psychology reached its peak in specialties such as measurement of affective word meaning, studies of non-verbal communication, and analysis of deep sentence structure. "Experts" from such subdisciplines, while proudly proclaiming their emancipation from speculative philosophy, have hardly any shared conceptual basis for dialogues across the boundaries between their specialties. Nor can any of them engage in any kind of scientifically meaningful discourse with a friend whose academic expertise pertains, for example, to literary analysis.

This is indeed a rather sad state of affairs, in particular if we keep in mind how the expert on sentence structure and his friend, the expert on poetry, prior to their academic specialization actually may have entered the same university with very similar, though only vaguely apprehended, objectives of deepening their understanding of man and human communication. *Divide et impera* seems to be an essential aspect of scientific knowledge: ignorance can hardly be defeated at all until it can be split up and attacked by research workers who come to know more and more about successively more and more restricted parts or aspects of the entire, initially only vaguely defined field. It is doubtful, however, whether genuine insight follows from such victories unless the resultant fragments of knowledge can be integrated into a coherent picture of the entire field.

A renewed concern with Kant's "anthropological question" implies serious search for a common axiomatic foundation across encapsulated fields of academic expertise. And such a concern is not only expressed by philosophers in search of a novel foundation for social scientific research, but also by the politically engaged and impatient sophomore who feels that we feed him stones instead of bread, and even by the wise layman who—totally unimpressed by our particular professional jargons—asks us *what we have found out* and *how it can be used*. Academic boundaries, as they exist today in the humanities and social sciences, are certainly *not* God-given barriers between mutually exclusive avenues for knowledge. Some of them may upon closer examination actually betray symptoms of a deplorably secular origin, such as the modern academician's needs for professional security and personal achievement within a narrowly defined field of expertise and his institution's docile acceptance and even encouragement of those needs.

On Positivism, Hermeneutic–Dialectic Positions and Agnostic Innocence with Respect to Philosophies of Social Science

American and Western European social psychology are today accused of being dominated by a positivistic bias, and proponents of a hermenneutic–dialectic philosophy such as Apel (1968) argue that positivistic social science is characterized by its technical-manipulatory aim. Progress is assessed in terms of increased control of segments of behaviour rather than more profound understanding. Man is made an object of enquiry on a par with matter; his subjectivity is conceived of as an obstacle to "objective knowledge" rather than a phenomenon of significant and legitimate scientific concern; basic epistemological issues such as the reflexivity inherent in man's knowledge of man are evaded or dealt with as embarassing methodological difficulties only. Thus, Feigl (1953) maintains:

> The one remarkable feature in which social-science predictions differ from those in the natural sciences is the well-known fact that once these predictions have been divulged, their very existence (i.e., their being taken cognizance of) may upset the original prediction. It seems at present problematic as to whether it is possible to devise something like a method of convergent successive approximations, in order to take account of the effect of divulged predictions and thus to obviate the notorious difficulty (p. 418).

The unique characteristics of social scientific research are thus often described in terms of deviance from (ideal) strategies by which the experimental physicist gains knowledge and control of matter. The philosophically agnostic but methodologically conscientious social scientist feels obliged to reduce that deviance to a minimum, and his imitation of the natural scientist makes for a science of man "in the third person". His subjectivity is for artists rather than social scientists to explore, the task of "understanding himself and the environment" in such a way as to affect man's self-image and fate is assigned to "the creators" rather than to social psychologists. The denial of the possibility of a humanistic social science thus often goes together with a faith in two mutually exclusive avenues to knowledge and an admiration of artistic intuition. This is particularly transparent in Hebb's rejection of the very idea of a humanistic psychology. He maintains (1974):

> Humanistic psychology, I think, confuses two very different ways of knowing human beings and knowing how to live with self-respect. One is science, the other is literature. A science imposes limits on itself and makes its progress by attacking only those problems that it is fitted to attack by existing knowledge and methods . . . The other way of knowing about human beings is the intuitive artistic insight of the

poet, novelist, historian, dramatist, and biographer. This alternative to psychology is a valid and deeply penetrating source of light on man, going directly to the heart of the matter (p. 74).

The same faith in mutually exclusive avenues to knowledge is also expressed by outstanding humanistic scholars. Thus, Wellek (1966) maintains about literary analysis:

> In reading with a sense for continuity, for contextual coherence, for wholeness, there comes a moment when we feel that we have "understood," that we have seized on the right interpretation, the real meaning. The psychologists might say that this is a mere hunch, a mere intuition. But it is the main source of knowledge in all humanistic branches of learning, from theology to jurisprudence, from philology to the history of literature. It is a process that has been called "the circle of understanding." It proceeds from attention to a detail to an anticipation of the whole and back again to an interpretation of that detail. It is a circle that is not vicious, but a fruitful circle. It has been described and defended by the great theorists of hermeneutics, by Schleiermacher and Dilthey, and recently by one of the best living practitioners of stylistics, Leo Spitzer (p. 419).

The point of departure for some novel programmes for an emancipatory and hermeneutic–dialectic social science is precisely this dichotomy between natural scientific explanation and humanistic understanding. Thus, Apel sets out to outline a general theory of science within the context of "an anthropology of knowledge". And some of his central theses may be summarized as follows (see Apel, 1968, p. 38): Natural sciences originate from subject–object relations and describe or "explain" events according to laws. "Sciences of the mind", on the other hand, stem from an interest in understanding (communication) within the intersubjective dimension of the human "community of interpretation". The latter is also presupposed in our constitution of objects, and the problem of understanding can for that reason not even in principle be reduced to a problem of objective "explanation". The two methods of knowledge are in fact complementary, the one (intersubjectivity and "understanding" within the human community of interpretation) being a *sine qua non* for the other. The methods of modern social science cannot, according to Apel, be reduced to either those of the explaining natural sciences or those of the understanding sciences of the mind. The aim is a synthesis: the explaining social sciences of human beings. The results of the latter, which as objects are also potentially the subjects of these sciences, can be transformed into deepened self-understanding. This appears to be the goal in psychoanalysis: The patient's symptoms are made the object of causal explanation, made intelligible to him—and overcome. Both Apel and Habermas (1968) hence refer to successful psychoanalytic therapy as a paradigm case of "dialectic mediation of explanation and under-standing". A distinctive and basic difference between positivistic social science on the one hand and hermeneutic–dialectic social science on the other is thus revealed in their approaches to the issue of reflexivity: What from one perspective is encountered as a notorious difficulty is from the other conceived of as an asset and a prerequisite for emanci-patory effects. Apel and Habermas are accordingly both very much concerned with the possibilities of changing human conditions and conduct by unraveling "quasi-causal" relationships. The unique characteristic of such regularities is that they resemble "laws of nature" only *as long as they remain unknown*, since taking cognizance of them may in principle be conducive to their negation as laws of nature.

Apel and Habermas are thus modern proponents of the gospel of enlightenment. Implicit in their recipe for emancipation is the assump-tion that man is rational and that his domain of rational choice can be expanded by increased self-knowledge. Aspects of his conduct that must be conceived of as embedded in a causal texture and therefore "part of nature" as long as he remains ignorant about them may, once that causal texture is revealed and transformed into self-insight, become accessible to self-control. The notion of an emancipatory social science is for that reason in accordance with Nietzche's answer to the Kantian question (see Buber, 1962, p. 713): Man is "the animal that is not yet established", he "suffers from himself and the problem of what life means". This is also a central theme in a dialectic philosophy of *becoming* with its origin in existentialistic thought. Laing and Cooper (1971, pp. 50, 130) speak of prerequisites for human choice of fate in terms of "becoming conscious of oneself" and "becoming a historical subject", and reality is from such an existentialistic-dialectic position conceived of as a "coefficient of resistance to my practicee". Such ideas are mediated primarily via works of fiction and only partially compre-hensible philosophical essays, however, works whose ethical pathos and appeal are at variance with, or even inversely related to, their contribu-tions toward sober elucidation of biological and social constraints pertaining to change of man's conduct and social conditions. The existentialists are, unlike the positivistic social scientists, submerged in speculations concerning man's subjectivity, so much so that Lévi-Strauss (1971, p. 164) accuses them of preferring a subject devoid of rationality to a rationality that leaves out the subject. They are, therefore, if we endorse the proposal concerning boundaries suggested by Hebb, "creators" or "intuitive artists" rather than social scientists. It is surprising, however, how psychologists subscribing to different philosophies tend to converge when issues of rationality and self-control are discussed within more narrowly and pragmatically defined contexts. Consider, for instance, Carl Rogers and Donald Hebb, who recently have announced very different positions with respect to humanistic psychology. Hebb (1974) maintains:

> Mind . . . is the capacity for thought, and thought is the integrative activity of the brain—that activity in the control tower that . . . overrides reflex response and frees behavior from sense dominance . . . Free will is not a violation of scientific law; it doesn't mean indeterminism, it's not mystical. What it is, simply, is a control of behavior by thought process (p. 75).

And Rogers (1974) approaching closely related issues in a retrospective account of his experiences from non-directive counselling, concludes:

> the individual has within himself vast resources for self-understanding, for altering his self-concept, his attitudes, and his self-directed behavior —and . . . these resources can be tapped if only a definable climate of facilitative psychological attitudes can be provided (p. 116).

Both Rogers and Hebb are thus proponents of emancipatory social science in the sense that they assume that *the domain of man's self-control and rational choice can be expanded*. Rogers is also in agreement with the Frankfurt philosophers with respect to the role of communication and increased self-understanding. Insight in the other is to be achieved by "emphatic listening"; the dialogue between the psychotherapist and his client presupposes some commonality with respect to interpretation; psychological knowledge is in part conceived of as an explication of meaning of a kind resembling the "circle of understanding" in hermeneutic analysis of texts.

I have argued elsewhere, in a critical analysis of parts of the programme advocated by Apel and Habermas, that their request for emancipatory and *only* emancipatory knowledge may possibly be rephrased in terms of a novel, anti-positivistic commandment (Rommetveit, 1972) "Thou shalt not seek knowledge about thine Brother that cannot be converted into self-insight in Him" (p. 227). Rogers may possibly even agree to such a directive, at least as a recommendation for social psychological and personality research geared toward improved counselling and individual and group therapy. Hebb, on the other hand, will probably strongly object to such constraints. He may argue that they confuse two very different ways of knowing human beings, that psychological knowledge about man's self-control is achieved by imagination and strict experimentation rather than by emphatic listening; and that such knowledge, in order to be scientific, must be formulated in terms of abstract models of brain activity rather than in concepts intelligible to his lay brother by virtue of their firm foundation in that shared and only intuitively accessible *Lebenswelt* which constitutes the basis for humanistic enquiries. Hebb's rejection (Hebb, 1974) of the idea of a humanistic psychology is based upon the conviction that "Science is the servant of humanism, not part of it" (p. 74). Apel (1968), on the other hand warns against the danger that a science of man "in the third person" may be applied as fragmentary expert knowledge in such a way that man and society are degraded into something that can be manipulated. And this is precisely what most likely will happen according to the prognosis of many futurists. Geneticists will in the future be serving mankind by breeding an intellectual elite; man's personality will be reshaped by means of the technological fruits of psychopharmacological research; scientific knowledge of brain activity will have reached a stage that allows for an extension of human intelligence via symbiosis of brain and computer. In other words, man will have drastically changed his own "nature" and existential conditions via implementation of expert biological and social scientific knowledge without ever having pondered the Kantian question of what he is or wants to be. Some of our colleagues seem to adopt the position that we as social psychologists are and should be primarily observers of such large-scale social change and innovation. From this point of view, social change (rather than, e.g. novel and philosophically significant social insight into human conditions) will generate philosophical change, and finding order in chaos will be a task for "creators" (artists and intellectuals) rather than for social scientists. We shall thus as professional social psychologists, if we have faith that affairs will turn out as predicted by the futurists, dedicate our improved mathematical and statistical sophistication to the preparation of "social indicators", scales for assessing "happiness" and "quality of life". We shall feel that it is by no means our duty to provide man with self-understanding of a kind that may significantly affect his future. Such a fatalistic outlook, when considered from the perspective of Apel's "anthropology of knowledge", is based upon agnostic innocence with respect to some of the central themes within his philosophy of emancipatory social science. Quantification is always based upon a qualitative foundation: "facts" about man and society can be converted to numbers only via interpretation; and options of interpretation have in turn to do with man's "understanding himself and the environment" and hence with *explicitly stated or tacitly and unreflectively endorsed assumptions of a philosophical nature*. The professional social psychologist who claims independence from philosophy and denies co-responsibility for large-scale social change is accordingly a blindfolded "creator" from the point of view of Apel's philosophy. He may justly, and with the appropriate scientific modesty, insist that *his* particular minitheory is hardly of any significance whatsoever to humanity at large, and he may conceive of practical implementations of that fragment of novel knowledge which constitutes *his* particular contribution as a minor technological affair. The combined net results of all such minor implementations of social psychological knowledge may, however, nevertheless contribute more to the states of affairs in the year 2000 than the combined efforts of all presumedly far more influential "creators".

On Kantian Themes in Social Psychological Research and Potential and Indirect Emancipatory Effects

The formula of "dialectic mediation of explanation and understanding" with its reference to classical psychoanalytic therapy may appear somewhat esoteric to non-directive counsellors as well as to social psychologists. Neither Rogerian therapists nor applied social psychologists are very much concerned with expansion of "ego control" to domains ruled by "the id". Options with respect to interpretation of human conduct and social conditions are revealed in alternative conceptual models and coding systems, however, and eating the fruits of knowledge from some psychological tree implies adopting *schemata for categorization* characteristic of that particular theory. Conversion of such knowledge to self-understanding, moreover, implies that the informed layman comes *to size up his own social situation and action alternatives in accordance with those schemata*. Impact of social psychological knowledge upon action via revised self-understanding, including potential "emancipatory" effects, may hence possibly be further illuminated by an excursion into decision theory.

Consider the following case: An individual is faced with a choice between three actions, a_1–a_3. Whatever he does, he runs the risk of losing some money. The magnitude of his loss, however, is dependent upon his choice and a future state of nature. He knows that one of two different states of nature S_1 and S_2 may occur, but he is entirely ignorant with respect to the probabilities of S_1 and S_2. Let us assume then that he is faced with the loss matrix below. If he chooses action a_1 and S_1 occurs, he will lose \$200. If a_1 is chosen and S_2 occurs, he will lose nothing at all, etc:

	S_1	S_2
a_1	200	0
a_2	168	48
a_3	120	120
(a_4)	(0)	(300)

Let us assume, furthermore, that the individual's major aim is simply to safeguard himself against regret afterward. In other words, he wants to choose a mode of behaviour "minimizing maximal regret". For that purpose, the loss matrix is transformed into a regret matrix. If he chooses a_1 and S_1 occurs, the regret will be $80, i.e. his regret will then be that of having lost $80 more than if he had chosen a_3, which is the optimal behavioural choice provided S_1 occurs. The regret matrix under conditions of these behavioural choices will therefore be as described below, and his aim of safeguarding himself against great regret is securely achieved by choosing action a_2. By that choice he does not risk a regret greater than $48 at all, whereas a_1 and a_2 imply risks of regrets of $80 and $120, respectively:

	S_1	S_2
a_1	80	0
a_2	48	48
a_3	0	120

If now our individual has been misinformed in the sense that he believes that a fourth behavioural choice (a_4 in the loss matrix) is available, his regret matrix will be significantly changed. The amounts of post-decision regret he is now faced with will be as shown in the following regret matrix:

	S_1	S_2
a_1	200	0
a_2	168	48
a_3	120	120
a_4	0	300

Under these conditions, therefore, a_3 will be his logical choice. In other words, his choice among three possible actions has been influenced by the introduction of an additional irrelevant alternative, even though the latter is not chosen at all.

This paradigm may serve to explain the intentionally creative impact of some forms of science fiction: the socially engaged writer may affect our choice between alternative realistic action programmes by visualizing some particular combination of an additional irrelevant alternative and a future state of nature he knows that we want to avoid. And formally analogous situations may arise in counselling and social psychological action research, even though the creative or conserving impact in the latter case often is camouflaged by quantification and for that reason very seldom recognized. Options with respect to interpretation and categorization of alternative courses of action are in action research revealed in *alternative models of social realities*, however. This has recently been cogently pointed out by Campbell (1974), who maintains "record-ing of responses and the coding of free response answers achieve quantification only as the end product of a qualitative judgmental process . . ." (p. 13). "If we are truly scientific, we must re-establish . . . qualitative grounding of the quantitative in action research" (p. 30). Let us at this stage leave problems of applied social psychology, however, and consider potentially "creative" or "emancipatory" effects inherent in dissemination of social psychological theory. What kind of an image of man and his action alternatives is conveyed to people via popularization of social psychology, and in what manner may such large-scale dissemination affect social planning, policy making and legislation?

Apel and Habermas argue that dissemination of positivistic minitheories makes for alienation and apathy because such theories, unlike dialectic approaches, deal with reflective self-control and self-initiated change as "notorious difficulties" rather than basic human phenomena of legitimate scientific concern. Social psychological theory is today a collection of partially competing theoretical paradigms with hardly any shared axiomatic foundation. The common denominator of the positivistic part of that collection, moreover, is, according to hermeneutic–dialectic philosophers, its imitation of natural sciences and programmatic evasion of issues having to do with meaning and human subjectivity. The popularized version of such a science makes for a peculiar "self-understanding" that, in caricature, resembles an enlightened state of paralysis: the "well-informed" layman feels relieved from assuming responsibility and offering reasons for his conduct because the latter is "explained" as a necessary consequence of antecedent conditions. This is the kind of opportunistic determinism advocated by the young people in "West Side Story", and different versions of such a vulgar social scientific fatalism are exploited by "creators" of social satire. The invariant and central theme, though, appears to be the dilemma of perfect self-knowledge versus freedom of will. We may therefore cautiously conclude that social psychological theory has at least an indirectly creative impact by providing themes for creators of satire. This would hardly be the case, however, unless it were misunderstood by the satirist and his audience in terms of some absurd form of determinism. The immediate effect of dissipation of social psychological knowledge formulated in terms of "laws" and deterministic models on the layman is a feeling of being imprisoned within some causal texture rather than an experience of being offered an enriched menu of action alternatives. Russell (1953) warns against the very terminology of causation, in natural as well as in social sciences: "The reason why physics has ceased to look for causes is that, in fact, there are no such things. The law of causality, I believe, like much that passes muster among philosophers, is a relic of a bygone age, surviving, like the monarchy, only because it is erroneously supposed to do no harm" (p. 387). Further, "what science does, in fact, is to select the *simplest* formula that will fit the facts. But this, quite obviously, is merely a methodological precept, not a Law of Nature" (p. 401). Popper (1974) claims: "In my view, aiming at simplicity and lucidity is a moral duty of all intellectuals: lack of clarity is a sin, and pretentiousness is a crime" (p. 44).

A methodological precept in natural science does not necessarily preserve its epistemological innocence when adopted by social scientists, however, and it is easily interpreted as something else by those who are concerned with implementation of the results rather than with the methods of enquiry. Simplicity, moreover, may sometimes border on simplemindedness, and our urge for lucidity may at times become so strong that it makes us search only in well-illuminated areas for something we know we lost where it is dark. The simplicity of the "behavioural laws" from the "age of theory" within psychology may thus in view of recent open systems approaches appear as simple-mindedness. And systematic evasion of problems of meaning, *even in psychological research on language and communication*, indicates that we often prefer elucidating trivialities to groping for significance in the dark (see Rommetveit, 1972, p. 214; 1974, pp. 95–101).

The notion of *causal explanation* is intimately related to that of *prediction*, but scientific explanation is nevertheless perfectly possible even when prediction is precluded. Scriven (1969, p. 118) therefore advises us social scientists to replace our favourite myth of the Second Coming (of Newton) with the recognition of the reality of the Already Arrived (Darwin). Life may be understood—and explained—*backward*, and its continuation may also be affected by such understanding. Moreover, experimentation within the social sciences may serve the purpose of explanation even when its immediate goal is purely diagnostic. Psychologists like Michotte and Piaget may thus actually be conceived of as true descendants from Kant. A major aim of their experimentation is to reveal *what man is*—how he reasons and experiences events—under conditions transcending both everyday life situations and those imagined by the speculative philosopher.

The idealized paradigm of the "hard" natural sciences is the hypothetic-deductive method, whereas that of the "soft" humanities is the hermeneutic circle. The former aims at knowledge of nature in terms of an axiomatically organized set of "laws"; the latter aims at explication of human meaning. Many social scientific enquiries, however, appear to be characterized by some mixture of the two. Sociological and social psychological "explanation" of some social reality, for instance, is in part a matter of defining that reality in terms of its locus within some more inclusive network of social institutions and human attribution. *Crime* is thus in part "explained" by comparing it to *sickness*, and a careful analysis of borderline cases shows that *attribution of personal responsibility* is crucial for the decision as to whether some deviant conduct is to be handled by the legal or the medical institution (Aubert, 1958). Such a systematic explication may even become part of a revised public notion of what crime is. This in turn implies an enriched rational basis for decisions concerning institutional reactions to social deviance.

Aubert's analysis of the criminal and the sick is thus in a way a Kantian analysis: Some state of affairs which traditionally has been conceived of as a reality is explicated in such a way that its *social* reality component is clearly revealed. Revised "self-understanding" implies, therefore, recognition of novel action alternatives which, even if they turn out to be unrealistic, may affect political decisions and be conducive to institutional innovation. The same general formula seems to apply to dissemination of sociological and social psychological role theory: the latter provides for a novel perspective on well-known "facts", and inherent in that perspective are possibilities of change that were not clearly recognized before. A "scientifically founded" programme for women's emancipation may thus be formulated as a deliberately planned transcendence of a formerly taken-for-granted "female nature" via removal of man-made constraints and self-fulfilling prophecies inherent in pre-scientific notions.

Kantian themes in social psychology have to do with the social nature of man and the subtle interrelationships between man and man-made social realities. They are particularly visible in enquiries into symbolic interaction, cognitive dissonance and attributions. They may be pursued in macro- as well as in micro-analysis of social behaviour, and by scholars with definite philosophical orientations as well as by experimentalists whom hardly anybody would accuse of criminal philosophical pretentiousness. Significant aspects of man's social nature are thus elucidated in small group experiments on social comparison processes (Festinger, 1954) and studies of social determinants of emotive states showing how individuals tend to seek company with others who are assumed to resemble them or to have suffered a similar fate (Schachter and Singer, 1962). Conditions of subjective uncertainty may then be transformed to self-knowledge anchored in a social reality. What seems to emerge from experimental analysis of verbal communication, moreover, is hopefully a more and more intelligible picture of man as a creature capable of transforming part of his subjectivity into states of intersubjectivity (Rommetveit, 1976).

Polanyi (1968) has analysed various kinds of indeterminacy of scientific knowledge, and in particular its dependence upon pre-scientific "tacit knowledge". Positivistic social psychology tries to eliminate such indeterminacy by systematic evasion of human meaning. Explication of personal versus impersonal causality, of crime versus sickness, and of the nature of social reality is on the other hand bound to contain some residual indeterminacy. And such a residual is possibly the price we have to pay if we want to preserve some sort of bridge between our scientific knowledge and what we "tacitly knew" prior to our professional training. It may hence provide a basis for emancipatory self-understanding, and possibly also for rewarding dialogues with philosophers concerned with ontological and epistemological issues.

References

Apel, K. O. (1968). Scientifik, hermeneutik, ideologie—kritick: Entwurf einer wissenschaftslehre in erkenntnisanthropologischer sicht. *Man and the World* 1, 37–63.

Aubert, V. (1958). Legal justice and mental health. *Psychiatry* 21, 101–113.

Buber, M. (1962). What is man? *In* "Philosophy in the twentieth century". (W. Barrett and H. E. Aiken, Eds) Vol. 4, pp. 688–719. Random House, New York.

Campbell, D. T. (1974). Qualitative knowing in action research. Kurt Lewin Award Address at A.A. meeting in New Orleans, September.

Feigl, H. (1953). Notes on causality. *In* "Readings in the philosophy of science". (H. Feigl and M. Brodbeck, Eds) pp. 408–418. Appleton-Century-Crofts, New York.

Festinger, L. (1954). A theory of social comparison processes. *Human Relations* 7, 117–140.

Habermas, J. (1968). "Erkenntnis und Interesse." Suhrkamp, Frankfurt.

Hebb, D. O. What psychology is about. *American Psychologist* 29, 71–79.

Kuhn, T. S. (1970). "The structure of scientific revolutions." University of Chicago Press, Chicago.

Laing, R. D. and Cooper, D. G. (1971). "Reason and violence. A decade of Sartre's philosophy 1950–1960." Random House, New York.

Lévi-Strauss, C. (1971). "L'homme nu." Plon, Paris.

Polanyi, M. (1968). Logic and psychology. *American Psychologist* 23, 27–43.

Popper, K. R. (1974). "Objective knowledge. An evolutionary approach." Clarendon Press, Oxford.

Rogers, C. R. (1974). In retrospect. Forty-six years. *American Psychologist* 29, 115–129.

Rommetveit, R. (1972). Language games, deep syntactic structures, and hermeneutic circles. *In* "The Context of Social Psychology: A critical assessment." (J. Israel and H. Tajfel, Eds) Academic Press, London and New York.

Rommetveit, R. (1974). "On message structure. A conceptual framework for the study of language and communication." John Wiley and Sons, New York.

Rommetveit, R. (1976). On the architecture of intersubjectivity. *In* "Social Psychology in Transition." (L. H. Strickland, K. J. Gergen and F. J. Aboud, Eds) pp. 201–214. Plenum Press, New York.

Russell, B. (1953). On the notion of cause, with application to the free-will problem. *In* "Readings in the Philosophy of Science". (H. Feigl and M. Brodbeck, Eds) pp. 387–407. Appleton-Century-Crofts, New York.

Schachter, S. and Singer, J. E. (1962). Cognitive, social and physiological determinants of emotive state. *Psychology Reviews* **69,** 379–399.

Scriven, M. (1969). Explanation and prediction as non-symmetrical. *In* "The Nature and Scope of Social Science: A Critical Anthology". (L. I. Krimerman, Ed.) Appleton-Century-Crofts, New York.

Triandis, H. (1976). Social psychology and cultural analysis. *In* "Social Psychology in Transition". (L. H. Strickland, K. J. Gergen and F. J. Abond, Eds) Plenum Press, New York.

Wellek, R. (1966). From the point of view of literary criticism. Closing statement. *In* "Style in Language". (A. Sebeok, Ed.) M.I.T. Press, Cambridge, Massachusetts.

5. On the Architecture of Intersubjectivity*

R. ROMMETVEIT

Introduction

The Harvard-M.I.T. brand of psycholinguistics came into being as the love child of generative grammar and *individual* (as opposed to *social*) cognitive psychology. And transformational-generative linguistics, it was argued, represented a return to a pre-positivistic view of science (Fodor and Garrett, 1966). Based on this philosophy, the idea of linguistic competence came to resemble the idea of ideal physical (e.g. bodies falling freely through perfect vacua).

Fodor and Garrett's reference to perfect vacua is very deceptive, however. It is certainly true that Newton was concerned with ideal physical events, but his most impressive insight was that gravity is based on an attraction between bodies, that is, an *interaction*. A science of psycholinguistics based on the utterance *in vacuo* represents, therefore, actually a return to a pre-positivistic, pre-Newtonian, and scholastic approach. Its obvious shortcomings cannot be remedied by additional scholastics, such as adding a set of increasingly complicated auxiliary hypotheses concerning contexts onto an explication of "deep structures" or "propositional form and content" of sentences *in vacuo* (see Chomsky, 1972; Fillmore, 1972; Lakoff, 1972).

The conceptual framework suggested in the present paper is based upon the assumption that language is a thoroughly and genuinely social phenomenon. The notion of an utterance deprived of its context of human interaction is as absurd as the notion of a fall deprived of the gravitational field within which it takes place. *What is made known* in an act of verbal communications can therefore be properly assessed only if we venture to explore the architecture of intersubjectivity within which it is embedded.

* Published in "Social Psychology in Transition" (1976). (L. H. Strickland, K. J. Gergen and F. J. Aboud, Eds) Plenum Press, New York.

The Skeleton of Intersubjectivity

Communication aims at transcendence of the "private" worlds of the participants. It sets up what we might call "states of intersubjectivity". In order to explore such states, we need to start with the a system of co-ordinates such as the one indicated in Fig. 1. These co-ordinates may be defined in terms of three dimensions: the time at which the act of communication takes place, its location, and (in the case of spoken language) the identification of listener by speaker and vice versa. The I and YOU constitute the two poles of potential states of intersubjectivity, and they are immediately given in terms of an unequivocal *direction of communication*. Whatever is shared, presupposed, or assumed to be known already is hence shared, presupposed, or assumed by the I and the YOU within a temporarily shared HERE and NOW.

The intersubjectivity established HERE and NOW of a dialogue will take on very different denotative extensions depending on what constitutes the topic of discourse. The spatial-temporal-social co-ordinates of states of intersubjectivity can therefore not be assessed independently of each other, nor—as we shall see—independently of *meta-contracts* of communication endorsed by the participants in the communicative act.

On Complementarity of Intentions and Control of the Temporarily Shared Social World

In order to explore some of the basic prerequisites for intersubjectivity, let us now briefly examine what happens under certain conditions of serious communication disorders. Consider, for instance, the so-called *homonym symptom* of the schizophrenic. The patient may start out talking about a grand party, and he says:

(I) I too was invited, I went to the ball . . . and it rolled and rolled away. . . .

His intention in this case is to make known something about a ball to which he was invited and what happened at that ball. We, the listeners, immediately comprehend what is said because we are spontaneously decoding it in accordance with the speaker's intention and *on his, the speaker's, premises*. At the moment of his pause, we thus very likely expect him to continue with "and then . . ." or some such expression: We know he has been invited to that ball, he is going there, and we expect him to make known what happens next.

It is precisely at this moment, however, that our firmly rooted, though entirely intuitive and unreflective, assumption concerning complementarity between *the act of speaking and that of listening* is disconfirmed.

Having uttered *"the ball . . ."* the schizophrenic seems to stumble, in a way. His act of speech is disrupted, his story does not continue in accordance with what he initially intended to make known. He pauses, apparently bewildered by what he himself has just uttered.

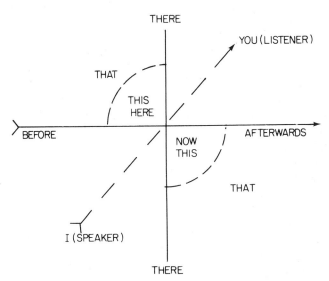

FIG. 1. The spatial-temporal-interpersonal co-ordinates of the act of speech.

His answer represents a perfectly rational solution to this riddle, however, once we endorse *his* basic distrust in intersubjectivity and accept the riddle as such. The spoken form "ball" is, of course, also the word for a very familiar object: It refers to a toy having a spherical shape, which is used in play or athletic games. The word ball is in fact used more to refer to such objects than in the way the schizophrenic had intended to use it initially on this occasion. What he says after the pause about rolling is thus in some respect a "publicly" plausible completion of his act of speech. Instead of finishing what he intended to say, he tries to complete the sentence with a phrase that *may* have made something known to a listener who was not bound to his premises. His pause after having uttered "the ball" thus signals lack of control of the intersubjectively established HERE and NOW.

Such control is under normal conditions unequivocally linked to the *direction of communication*: The speaking "I" has the privilege of pointing out the objects, events and states of affairs to enter the field of shared attention. Which of all possible entities of an experientially shared situation will be introduced and enter the slots of THIS, HERE and THAT, THERE of the formal skeleton of intersubjectivity is thus in principle determined by the speaker. The same holds true for any topic, whether introduced by deixis, by identifying descriptions, or by other means. The listener has to accept and engage in whatever social reality is introduced.

And this is exactly what *we* do when listening to (I). As the speaker is uttering ". . . it", we spontaneously make sense of what he is saying in terms of the ball to which he has been invited. The full-fledged act of verbal communication is thus, under normal conditions, based upon a reciprocally endorsed and spontaneously fulfilled contract of complementarity: *Encoding* is tacitly assumed to involve *anticipatory decoding*. It is taken for granted that speech is continuously *listener oriented*. The speaker therefore monitors his speech in accordance with his assumptions about the extent of social world and strategies of categorization which are shared by him and his listener. Conversely—and on precisely those premises—*decoding* is tacitly assumed to be *speaker oriented*, aiming at a reconstruction of what the speaker intends to make known.

Intersubjectivity has thus in some sense to be taken for granted in order to be achieved. It is based on mutual faith in a shared social world. Thus decentration in both interactants is a necessary basis for this reciprocally endorsed contract of complementarity. Wittgenstein's comment (1968, p. 108) that language is "habit and institution" certainly holds true for the fundamental complementarity inherent in acts of communication: What George Herbert Mead coined "taking the attitude of the other" (Mead, 1950) constitutes such a basic and pervading feature of normal social interaction that it remains entirely inaccessible to the reflective consciousness of the speaking I and the listening YOU.

On Meta-contracts and Variant Premises for Intersubjectivity

In order to gain some more insight into the subtle interplay between *what is said* and *what is taken for granted* we are therefore forced to transcend the traditional paradigms of substitution within linguistics and literary text analysis. These paradigms are all intralinguistic, in that one segment of discourse is being replaced by another in order to examine similarities and differences between the two. Contractual and partly institutionalized aspects of intersubjectivity are, in such an analysis, of secondary concern if they are of any concern at all. In order to bring such aspects into focus, we have to engage in systematic substitutions of the I-YOU co-ordinate of the act of communication (see Fig. 1).

Let us now transplant the incoherent segment of the schizophrenic's story about the party into an entirely different setting. This time, we are listening to a poet as he is reciting:

> (I')   I too was invited,
> I went to the ball . . .
> and it rolled
> and rolled away . . .

Our immediate reactions on this occasion are entirely devoid of the kind of bewilderment we experienced when listening to the former incoherent story. When asked what is conveyed by (I') as part of a poem, some of us may perhaps answer that we honestly do not quite know. Others may express a feeling of having grasped its meaning intuitively and emotionally, without being able to put it into words. Still others may venture to verbalize the feeling that has been conveyed to them by the poet. They may maintain, for instance, that he has managed to portray conditions of human existence when our grip of "ordinary reality" is wavering because we discover that things are not what we firmly expected them to be.

Consider, next, what may happen when newspaper headlines about, for example, the war in Vietnam, the increase in sales of cosmetics, the famine in India, and the stabilization of the European stock market are brought together in a college poem. Since firmly and unreflectively we assume that the poet wants to convey some things over and beyond what is made known by professional news reporters, our habitual and desensitized orientation toward daily mass media novelties is immediately abolished. To the extent that the author indeed has constructed the college on that assumption, our expectation is institutionally founded and essentially correct. It is, moreover, *eo ipso* self-fulfilling.

Spontaneous and contextually appropriate interpretations in such different settings testify to a capacity to adopt the attitude of different "others". The general paradigm of complementarity thus allows for variant premises for intersubjectivity which can vary according to the institution and situation. Such premises have to do with what is unreflectively taken for granted, with the basic WHY of communication and what Ducrot (1972) has coined "les sous entendus" and "l'implicit d'enoncé". An utterance *in vacuo* can therefore only be examined with respect to its message *potential*. Its potential meaning must be considered by examining these *drafts of contracts concerning shared categorization and attribution*, which are conveyed in the speech act itself.

The significance of variant premises for intersubjectivity is more clearly illustrated if we transplant newspaper headlines into a book of poetry, segments of a patriotic speech into an academic lecture, excerpts from medical reports into a funeral sermon, and fragments of an informal conversation between two friends into an interpersonal setting characterized by an unequivocal master-to-servant relationship. The main lesson to be learned from such transplantations is very simple: What is made known is dependent on what kind of *meta-contract* of communication has been tacitly and reciprocally endorsed in each particular case.

On Anticipatory Comprehension (Vorveständigung)

Hermeneutic philosophers of language (Apel, 1968) and scholars of literature (Wellek, 1966) argue that whatever is made known in acts of verbal communications has to be conceived of as expansions and/or modifications of a pre-established shared *Lebenswelt*. Let us now examine how their concept of *anticipatory comprehension* (Vorverständigung) may be explicated in terms of the logic of information theory.

The main features of the latter can be exhibited by means of a very simple question-and-answer task. An object is located in one of the cells of a square consisting of 16 cells (see Fig. 2). I know where it is, but you do not. Your task is then simply to find out in which of the 16 cells the object is located, and you are requested to do so by means of questions that can be answered by either yes or no. The dialogue may hence proceed as follows:

(1) "Is it in the right half?" "No."
(2) "Is it in the upper half of the left half?" "Yes."
(3) "Is it in the right half of the upper half?" "No."
(4) "Is it in the upper half of the left half?" "No."

What has been made known at this stage is that the object is located in cell X, and the entire dialogue can in this case be described as a sequentially arranged reduction of an initial state of uncertainty on your part. This initial state corresponds to the entire square in Fig. 2: You know at the outset that the object is located in some as yet not identified cell of that square, that it may be located in any one of the 16 cells. My first answer serves to eliminate one-half of that entire area, my second answer eliminates one-half of the remaining half of it, and so on. Let us deliberately ignore these purely quantitative aspects, however, and turn to the dialogue as such.

Notice, first of all, that the word "square" does not enter our dialogue at all, despite the fact that at every single stage the message transmission is based upon the assumption that the two of us have the same particular square in mind. We assume—correctly, and by a tacitly endorsed contract—that we are talking about the same square. This constitutes the *initially shared, unquestioned or free information* onto which your very first question is nested or *bound*. Whether I have shown you a visual display of the square or carefully described it to you in advance is of no particular significance in the present context. It constitutes in either case an initially shared social reality and a *sine qua non* for further meaningful discourse on the location of the object.

This is not only true of the unmentioned square, however, but also of, for example, *the right half of it* introduced in question (1)—or rather *the left half* implied by my answer—when it from stage (3) on is no longer mentioned. Notice, thus, how my answer at every successive stage is

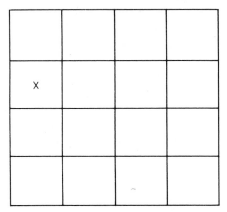

FIG. 2. Square for the question-and-answer game.

nested onto what at that particular stage has already been established as a shared social reality (or unquestioned, *free information*). Notice further how my answer at stage n is tacitly presupposed in your question at stage $n + 2$. Both of us know (and know that the other knows) after stage (1) that the object is located somewhere in the left half of the square in Fig. 2. This shared knowledge is a prerequisite for what is made known at stage (3), even though at that stage it is tacitly taken for granted by both of us.

What is left of sequential structure in our dialogue, when we leave out quantification, is a particular pattern whereby novel information is nested onto what is already assumed to be the case. What is made known at any particular stage is thus not only made part of an expanded shared social reality, but serves at the same time as a prerequisite for making proper sense of what is said next. And this dual function is preserved also when my four successive answers are condensed into one single utterance such as:

(II) It is (in the square), in its left half, in the upper half of that left half, in the left half of that upper half, and in the lower half of that left half.

Analogous patterns of nesting are often encountered in narratives, for instance, when the identity of some person is taken for granted by the narrator—and *eo ipso* intersubjectively established—on the basis of inference from what has been made known at some earlier state. We may, for example, hear about two persons, one old man and one young man. The latter is subsequently referred to as *the son*, although nothing has been *said* about kinship. Only two persons have so far been introduced into our temporarily shared social world. Therefore when "the son" (by virtue of the definite article) is assumed to be known already, he has to be the younger one of those two men and nobody else.

Message Structure: Nesting of bound to free information

What appears from the general perspective of information theory as sequential constraints may, from the perspective of the architecture of intersubjectivity, be assessed as Vorverständigung based upon tacitly endorsed contracts concerning a temporarily shared social world. *Message structure* may accordingly be conceived of as a particular pattern of nesting, generated in an interplay of tacit and verbally induced presuppositions on the one hand and semantic potentialities on the other.

Consider, for instance, what may be made known by a sentence such as:

(III) My spinster aunt is an infant.

The sentence is one of the many so-called *semantic* anomalies so eagerly documented by semanticists of the Harvard-M.I.T. school at an early stage: It has to be relegated to the abyss of unreason by scholars who believe in invariant semantic features rather than in semantic potentialities bound to variant premises for intersubjectivity (see Katz and Fodor, 1963, p. 200).

A great many things may be known by such an utterance, however, depending on which meta-contracts of communication have been endorsed and what is jointly and tacitly presupposed at the moment of speech. Its *message potential* may then, within each type of setting, be explored by examining possible questions to which (III) provides the answer. These may ask, for example, *how* the speaker's aunt is, *who* is an infant, *which of his aunts* is an infant.

Let us briefly consider two contextual variants. Consider, first, a conversation between two friends. The listener knows already the speaker's aunt by sight, and *an infant* is stressed in response to his question as to how that lady is. Message transmission must then be conceived of in terms of a pattern of nesting of information analogous to that of the question-and-answer game: What is made known by "an infant" is bound to "My spinster aunt", and the latter is in turn bound to an already intersubjectively identified entity within the temporarily shared social world at the moment of the act of speech. What is intended by the speaker and presupposed to be intended by him on the part of the listener is hence neither the early stage of life cycle nor the incapacity to speak, but rather only partially determined potentialities such as immaturity and dependency.

Let us next examine a case when (III) is uttered in response to *who* is an infant. The latter question may for instance be raised in an informal and noisy discussion about candidates for political offices, one of whom happens to be the spinster aunt. The conversation is in such a situation by a tacitly endorsed meta-contract restricted to adult persons only. What is said about them, moreover, has to do with their potential capacities as politicians rather than as artists or athletes.

Even an overheard fragment of an utterance such as ". . . is an infant" is for that reason immediately understood in terms of the general abstract potentialities suggested above, but on this occasion constrained by *le sous entendu* that someone is claimed to be an infant when viewed as a politician. And (III) uttered in response to the question "Who is an infant?" is hence, by anticipatory comprehension, "perfectly understood": It makes known *whom* the speaker declares immature with respect to political insight and skill.

The meaning potentialities *intended* and *understood as intended* in the phrase "an infant" can thus only be revealed by assessing the message structure. We must therefore first examine how the phrase is bound to other segments of the utterance and to tacitly endorsed presuppositions. Its entire set of semantic potentialities must subsequently be matched against all presuppositions to which the phrase is bound. We must also examine *if* and eventually *how* what is already taken for granted overlaps with what otherwise (in other contexts) might be made known by the expression.

We find then that some potentialities have to be disregarded on the ground that what would be made known by them is already presupposed. Such potentialities are therefore redundant. This is the case with a semantic potentiality such as *animate* of the phrase "an infant" in the settings we have analysed above. Certain other potentialities are over-ruled by what in that particular act of communication is taken for granted. This applies to age or stage of life cycle potentialities: Stage of life cycle is unequivocally conveyed by "spinster" and constitutes part of the unquestioned, free information to which "an infant" is bound. Such overruling is by no means an arbitrary or magic affair: The outcome is strictly determined by nesting of bound to free information. This precise phenomenon has for ages been explored in the literary analyses of metaphors.

An elimination of redundant and overruled semantic potentialities, however, yields only a partial determination of what is made known. We have thus so far only restricted what is made known in the expression "an infant" to a subset of its meaning potentialities defined by the elimination of animate and early stage of life cycle. What is left may therefore be described in terms of abstract, but largely open potentialities, such as dependency and immaturity. Such a description may in fact represent a very plausible account of what is conveyed by the expression in the conversation between the two friends: The listener may not be any more informed at all at that stage, and the innocent dependency and/or immaturity of that spinster aunt is possibly going to be a central theme as the conversation continues.

What is left open and largely undetermined after our procedure of elimination, however, may in other cases be further specified in view of additional presuppositions to which the expression is bound. This is clearly the case in the noisy and informal discussion of political candidates: Whatever is made known by "an infant" when said about some such candidate is by a tacit meta-contract bound to refer to him in his capacity as a politician. This does not by any means imply that the expression has been fully and finally determined with respect to propositional content. On the contrary, the remark may very likely initiate a lengthy dialogue concerning what, more precisely, has been asserted by "an infant". What has been "perfectly understood", however, is that neither status as animate nor stage of life cycle nor immaturity in general has been asserted. Further clarification of the phrase may from now on be safely restricted to dealing with political immaturity and, possibly, of semantically mediated emotive and attitudinal contagion.

This is indeed a deplorably poor achievement when gauged against criteria developed within formal logic, yet not so poor when we keep in mind that it is achieved in and about a multifaceted, only partially shared, and only fragmentarily known world. Even such a partial determination of what is made known is in certain respects quite an impressive performance, definitely beyond the capacity of a person in a schizophrenic or autistic state of mind, and also, I believe, beyond what can be accounted for by the expanded versions of propositional analysis proposed by semanticists of the Harvard-M.I.T. school. It presupposes complementarity and reciprocal role taking. The speaker must monitor what he says on the premises of the listener, and the listener must listen on the premises of the speaker. Both of them, moreover, must continually relate what is said at any particular stage of their dialogue to whatever at that stage has been jointly presupposed.

On Commonality with Respect to Interpretation (Interpretationsgemeinschaft) and Shared Strategies of Attribution

Rossi (1973) maintains about Lévi-Strauss and the emphasis upon "l'inconscient" in structural analysis:

The preoccupation with the unconscious is a preoccupation with dis-
covering the basic structures which are common to the mental mold
of the sender of the receiver of the message, and which enable a genuine
intersection of two intentionalities (p. 43).

Critics have accused Lévi-Strauss of having elevated the unconscious
and irrational to a position of dominance and control in human and
social life (see Corvez, 1969), but he may with equal right be praised for
having brought to our attention basic taken-for-granted and not-
reflected-upon cognitive pre-conditions for human interaction. Such
pre-conditions, moreover, constitute a very intricate problem area in
which a variety of philosophical, humanistic and social scientific
inquiries seem to converge. Wittgenstein (1962) claims that any scheme
of interpretation ". . . will have a bottom level and there will be no
such thing as an interpretation of that" (p. 739). Hermeneutic philosophers of language are concerned with such a bottom level in terms of
an unreflectively taken-for-granted commonality with respect to interpretation, *eine Interpretationsgemeinschaft* (Apel, 1965, 1968). Merleau-
Ponty (1962) conceives of situationally and interpersonally established
premises for a given dialogue as "a certain kind of silence" (p. 184).
And Lévi-Strauss' search for *l'inconscient* may indeed, as suggested by
Rossi, be interpreted as an attempt to explicate a widely shared aspect
of "silence", in other words, the common denominators of a whole
range of situational variants.

Let us now ponder what, more specifically and from a social psychological point of view, is implied by such tacit pre-conditions for intersubjectivity. Imagine, for instance, a situation in which you are asked
how a particular person is. And let us assume that you have never
verbalized your impressions of that person until the very moment you
are asked about it. Suppose, moreover, that your partner in the
dialogue is considering the person he is enquiring about for a particular
job. Being aware of that and knowing that the job is neither well paid
nor particularly interesting, you may perhaps answer:

(IV) He is easy to please.

Imagine, on the other hand, a situation in which you know that the
person you are asked about has decided to start out on a long and
solitary expedition that in all likelihood will be monotonous and devoid
of exciting events. Assuming that your interrogator is worried about the
person's capacity to endure months of solitary and uneventful travelling,
you may very well answer:

(V) Oh, he can gain pleasure from small things.

Making known your impression of a particular person in situations
such as those described above is clearly something more than converting

a ready-made cartesian cognitive representation into a temporally extended sequence of speech sounds. It is a social activity in the sense that you spontaneously monitor what you say in accordance with tacit assumptions concerning what both of you already know and what more your listener wants to know. You may thus induce a shared perspective by which the person you are talking about is considered a potential manipulandum, or you may engage your listener in a verbally induced strategy of attributing talents to him.

What is made known by words such as "easy" in (IV) and "can" in (V), moreover, is clearly bound to a more comprehensive scheme for attribution (Heider, 1958). The latter is in some respects analogous to the square in Fig. 1: It is taken for granted as a shared frame of reference for making sense of what is said. And this may hopefully be demonstrated in Fig. 3 as we ponder what is made known by cryptic expression such as:

(VI) John is easy;
(VII) John can; and
(VIII) John is eager.

Some composite state of affairs of the general form (X(do)Y) is evidently taken for granted in all three expressions. The two poles of the composite state of affairs, moreover, make for a subdivision analogous to that by which the square is divided into the right and the left half, since what is made known about John is dependent on which

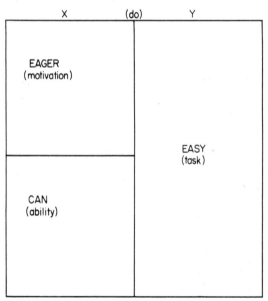

Fig. 3. Tacit presuppositions inherent in EASY, EAGER and CAN.

of two distinctively different capacities he is talked about in. The word "easy" in (VI) is thus comprehensible if and only if he is considered as part or aspect of some action or task ((do)Y). What is conveyed by either "eager" or "can", on the other hand, can only be made known if John is attended to as a potential actor; as X is in (X(do)). The word "eager", moreover, makes sense if and only if said about motivational aspects rather than his ability as a potential actor.

Heider's enquiries into attribution are investigations of behaviourally revealed inference rules rather than explications of interrelationships between words. They may hence, like the enquiries of Lévi-Strauss, be said to aim at discovery of ". . . basic structures which are common to the mental mold of the sender and the receiver of the message, and which enable a genuine intersection of the two intentionalities". Sharing rules of attribution is indeed a basis for enabling us to transcend our initial imprisonment in a private and egocentric world. These rules are, in fact, also prerequisites for obtaining consensus with respect to verification: What is made known by "John can" is proved true if he tries and succeeds.

The message potentials of expressions such as (VI), (VII) and (VIII) are thus bound to a particular commonality with respect to interpretation (eine Interpretationsgemeinschaft). None of them makes sense in acts of verbal communication unless some scheme for attribution such as the one suggested in Fig. 3 is tacitly presupposed and mastered by both participants in the act. Each expression is of course incomplete when gauged against criteria for fully determined "propositional content", yet comprehensible and partially determined by aspects of the scheme about which nothing is said. Some task or intended action is thus always taken for granted, even though the particular nature of (do) in (X (do) Y) may remain unknown. A prerequisite for a temporarily shared social world in the case of (VI), moreover, is a capacity for decentered shifts of perspective on people such that a particular person can on one occasion be attended to as a source of action and on another occasion as (aspect of) a task. Figure 3 may thus be said to portray features of a culturally shared "kind of silence" out of which adult discourse about ease, eagerness and ability is generated.

On Message Structure and Residuals in Acts of Verbal Communication

Irrational compartmentalization of knowledge is sustained by vicious circles. The raison d'etre of an encapsulated expertise on sous entendus and literary exceptions must thus in part be sought in a general semantics concerned with "literal" readings and "propositional content". The hermeneutic scholar thus often deals with residuals from the general semanticist's analysis, and his own exegesis is addressed to us as insiders of a presumably universal, though entirely open and undefined *Interpretationsgemeinschaft*.

I have in the present paper examined basic premises for inter-subjectivity such as complementarity of intentions, capacities for decentred categorization and attribution, and a capacity to adopt the perspective of different others. An analysis of message structure will thus—unlike assessment of propositional form and content—have to deal with residuals in terms of tacitly taken for granted shared social realities and/or presupposed commonality with respect to interpretation. Such residuals, however, are *not* to be conceived of as *ad hoc* manifestations of some undifferentiated and only intuitively revealed *Interpretationsgemeinschaft*, but must in each case be specified by a systematic analysis of nesting of *bound* to *free* information.

The residual may in some cases be conceived of as analogous to the axiomatic foundation for interpretation of particular scientific statements. What is made known by EASY, EAGER and CAN in expressions such as (VI), (VII) and (VIII) thus appears to be bound to a tacitly and reciprocally taken for granted "space of action" in a fashion resembling that by which particular geometrically defined terms for distances, areas, and volumes are bound to axiomatically defined Euclidian space.

Partial determination implies on other occasions simply optional elaborations of some general draft of a contract. What is conveyed by the word INFANT in a particular situation may thus, by tacitly endorsed meta-contracts, be intended and understood in terms of political immaturity, but such consensus may in turn serve as a point of departure for negotiations concerning specific criteria for verification. Moreover, what is made known by POOR may on two different occasions be un-equivocally determined in a general fashion as the opposite of WEALTHY, yet in a conversation about inhabitants of the third world be specified as living conditions below the subsistence level and in a dialogue about neighbours as dependence upon public financial support. Full mastery of the general poverty-wealth potentiality of POOR is thus revealed in contextually appropriate optional elaborations—and so contingent upon the generalized capacity to adopt the perspective of different others.

Semantic competence can therefore only be appropriately understood as an integral component of *communicative competence*. Semantic potentialities inherent in ordinary language must be conceived of as drafts of contracts concerning categorization and attribution, bound to more comprehensive schemes, yet to a considerable degree negotiable and contingent upon meta-contracts in the form of actively induced or pre-established *sous entendus*.

References

Apel, K. O. (1965). Die entfaltung der "sprachanalytischen" philosophie und das problem der "Geisteswissenschaft". *Philosophisches Jahrbuch* **72,** 239–289.

Apel, K. O. (1968). Szientifik, hermeneutik, ideologie-kritik: Entwurf einer wissenschaftslehre in erkenntnis-anthropologischen sicht. *Man and the World* **1,** 37–68.

Chomsky, N. (1972). "Studies on Semantics in Generative Grammar." Mouton, The Hague.

Corvéz, M. (1969). "Les Structuralists." Aubier-Montaigne, Paris.

Ducrot, O. (1972). "Dire et ne pas dire. Principes de semantique linguistique." Hermann, Paris.

Fillmore, C. J. (1972). Subjects, speakers and roles. *In* "Semantics of Natural Language". (D. Davidson and G. Harman, Eds) pp. 1–24. Reidal, Dordrecht.

Fodor, J. and Garrett, M. (1966). Some reflections on competence and performance. *In* "Psycholinguistic Papers". (J. Lyons and R. J. Wales, Eds) pp. 133–154. Edinburgh University Press, Edinburgh.

Heider, F. (1955). "The Psychology of Interpersonal Relations." John Wiley and Sons, New York.

Katz, J. J. and Fodor, J. A. (1963). The structure of a semantic theory. *Language* **39,** 170–210.

Lakoff, G. (1972). Linguistics and natural logic. *In* "Semantics of Natural Language". (D. Davidson and G. Harman, Eds) pp. 545–665. Reidal, Dordrecht.

Mead, G. H. (1950). "Mind, self, and society from the standpoint of a behaviorist." University of Chicago Press, Chicago.

Merleau-Ponty, M. (1962). "Phenomenology of perception." Routledge and Kegan Paul, London.

Rommetveit, R. (Ed.) (1974). On message structure. "A conceptual framework for the study of language and communication." John Wiley and Sons, Chichester.

Rossi, I. (1973). The unconscious in the anthropology of Claude Lévi-Strauss. *American Anthropologist* **75,** 20–48.

Wellek, R. (1966). From the point of view of literary criticism. Closing statement. *In* "Style in Language". (T. A. Sebeok, Ed.) M.I.T. Press, Cambridge, Massachusetts.

Wittgenstein, L. (1962). The blue book. *In* "Philosophy in the twentieth century". (W. Barret and D. H. Aiken, Eds) Vol. 2, pp. 710–774. Random House, New York.

Wittgenstein, L. (1968). "Philosophical Investigations." (G. E. Anscombe, Ed.) Blackwell, Oxford.

6. Language as a Means of Social Power

Theoretical-empirical explorations of language and language use as embedded in a social matrix*

R. M. BLAKAR

Introduction

Almost irrespective of which aspect of man one is interested in, one sooner or later finds oneself probing into problems connected with "language and communication". This is not at all remarkable, since it is exclusively through communication—mainly verbal communication—that we can announce ourselves (*Mitteilung*) and get into contact with other human beings. (In analysing the problems involved in being a psychologist, Smedslund maintains: "The only bridge crossing the gap between the psychologist and the subjective world of his subject or client is that of communication" (Smedslund, 1972). Smedslund's telling "gap-and-bridge" terminology describes, I feel, every human being's relationship to his fellow human beings.) Furthermore, it is via language that the reality is grasped and conceptualized as well as "inherited" from generation to generation (Berger and Luckmann, 1967). To a large extent do we actually live and behave *within* a "world of language". Ernst Cassirer (1944) nicely expressed this when he labelled man as the "symbol animal".

Realizing this, one is not surprised by the fact that so many have tried to explore and inquire into language and language processing. It is more of a paradox that relatively few academic disciplines seem

* The author wants to express his thanks to the people who read the manuscript and provided help and advice, especially Colin Fraser, Ivana Markova, Jo Kleiven, Hilde Eileen Nafstaad, Ragnar Rommetveit and Astri Heen Wold. The studies upon which this paper is based, have been supported by the Norwegian Research Council for Science and the Humanities. This paper was prepared in 1973/77 to appear in "Pragmalinguistics: Theory and Practice" (J. L. Mey, Ed.) Peter de Ridder Press. However for various reasons this book is still in press.

traditionally to have had almost a monopoly on studying language; mainly different philosophical and linguistic traditions. However, recently other disciplines—such as *biology* and *mathematics*, but primarily *the social sciences*, and among them, especially, *psychology*—have defined language as a legitimate area of research. Labels such as "psycholinguistics" and "sociolinguistics" reflect this new involvement. A most convincing expression of the strong position already won by psychology is that the dominant linguist of our time, Noam Chomsky, subsumes linguistics "as a branch of cognitive psychology" (Chomsky, 1968).

As the social scientist approaches language, he will naturally be rather critical toward different aspects of the dominant approaches. In particular he will be opposed to the dominant strategy of research that language is explored (a) *in vacuo* or out of relevant contexts, and (b) without taking an explicit communication perspective (Rommetveit, 1968, 1972a, 1972b; Uhlenbeck, 1967; Kleiven, 1970; Blakar, 1973a, 1973b; Blakar and Rommetveit, 1971, 1975). Moreover, the social scientist has started asking questions which have so far been totally neglected. Primarily the social scientist has tried to explore language and the processing of language *as embedded in a social matrix or context*. (The picture is actually more complicated in that (1) some linguists (e.g. Uhlenbeck, 1967) have seriously criticized the study of language *in vacuo*, while (2) too many psycholinguists seem to have inherited the linguists' tendency to study language out of contexts. In defining their task the psycholinguists have been too eager to buy whatever the linguists had to offer, including the non-social approach (cf., e.g. Ervin-Tripp and Slobin's definition of psycholinguistics, 1966.))—In their theoretical as well as empirical work Rommetveit and his colleagues have tried to launch an alternative programme, where language and language use is explicitly studied from a communication perspective and as embedded or integrated in more comprehensive social contexts. (The theoretical foundations of this group are elaborated in Rommetveit's two books "Words, Meanings and Message" (1968) and "Språk, tanke og kommunikasjon" (1972a) and in two papers (Rommetveit, 1972b, 1972c). Furthermore, a collection of theoretical-empirical papers are presented in Carswell and Rommetveit (1971), and Eckblad (1971). The following references should give a representative picture of the empirical work done according to this programme: Rommetveit *et al.*, 1968; Rommetveit and Blakar, 1973; Rommetveit and Kleiven, 1968; Rommetveit *et al.*, 1968a, 1968b; Rommetveit and Turner, 1967; Kleiven, 1973; Blakar, 1973a, 1973b, 1973d; Blakar and Rommetveit, 1975.)

The purpose of the present paper is to explore language as embedded in a social frame or matrix. Actually we will try to analyse language and the processing of language as an integrated aspect of the social and political activities or behaviour structuring and controlling our everyday life. This will be done by presenting and discussing the results from a series of theoretical-empirical analyses we have conducted on "language and language use as a means of social power" (Blakar, 1971, 1972a, 1972b, 1973a).

Some Examples and a Comment on the Concept of Power*

Example I. Some friends are drinking together. There is a bottle on the table. Exactly half its content has been consumed. Almost simultaneously John and Peter remark:

Peter: "The bottle's half empty."
John: "The bottle's half full."

Both are correct, or, to put it another way—logically—, if one is right the other must also be right. As far as the outer, extentional reference is concerned, the two expressions are synonymous. A listener would obtain information about "the same state" whether he had heard Peter or John. Nevertheless, there is good reason to assume that the two expressions may have quite different effects on the atmosphere. We see this more clearly if we expand the expressions a bit:

Peter: The bottle's *already* half empty.
John: The bottle's *still* half full.

Peter, with his choice of phrasing, could take the life out of the liveliest party, while John's choice of words could liven up a party even if it was on its way to dying out.

Example II. Two journalists A and B were sent out to cover the Vietnam war. We take the following extracts from their reports: A writes about "the American engagement in Vietnam", while B writes about "the American aggression in Vietnam". Again A writes "Vietcong", where B writes "the People's Liberation Army".

It is obvious that readers, i.e. receivers in this particular act of communication, will come to a very different understanding of the events in Vietnam according to whether they read A's or B's report. The expression "the American engagement in Vietnam" creates a very

* A particular problem in writing this paper was that my analyses had been conducted on Norwegian, and all my examples, illustrations, etc. were thus in Norwegian. And to translate examples of "pragmatic effects of language" is almost impossible. One has to find analogous examples in English. However, this requires a very good knowledge about English—and again and again my knowledge was shown to be insufficient. Some examples from Norwegian will be used therefore, and merely be explained in English. I am also very grateful to Christine Seim and Maureen Hultberg for their help in finding analogous examples in English.

different impression of the U.S.A. and the American activities in Vietnam than the expression "the American aggression in Vietnam". Similarly, the alternative labels "Vietcong" or "the Peoples' Liberation Army" give a very different impression of the other side.

Here it must be added that the latter communication situation is obviously much more complex than the previous one. This is mainly because it is far more difficult to decide *what* the different expressions refer to. In the example referring to the amount in the bottle, it was much simpler "to see" exactly what was referred to. It was thus much easier to consider the expressions and, for example, to judge whether they were true or false.

From these examples from everyday communication we can see *how* the sender's choice of expression affects the receiver's understanding. Even if the sender tries "to express himself objectively", we see that his choice of expression will structure and influence the impression the recipient receives. This structuring and influencing capacity of language and the language user is exactly what we have in mind when we maintain that "language is a means of social power". We have deliberately chosen to use the concept of *power* in order to emphasize an aspect of communication and language use which is often neglected. Among those interested in language (especially philologists) one has often heard discussions about which expression is the most correct in the purely linguistic or stylistic sense. One hardly ever is witness to discussions about which *interests* or *perspectives* lie behind a particular verbal expression. However, for a social scientist and psychologist it is—or should be—difficult to avoid asking questions such as: What sort of interests underly this or that way of expression? Apart from the purely stylistic or linguistic, what sort of effect does one expression convey which another does not?, etc. An attempt to inquire into the structuring and shaping functions of language and its user was thus to be performed, and the concept of *power* was felt to be appropriate regarding this analysis. It is obvious that the possibility of structuring and influencing another individual's experience of something, whether it occurs via language or by other means, is in effect to exert (social) power over those others. The concept of power has been chosen irrespective of the fact that within the social sciences the concept has been applied in many different ways, technical as well as non-technical. The concept is here used in its broad everyday sense, implying that everybody being in a position of influencing somebody, exerts power.*

It is generally accepted that through language power *can* be exerted. We are familiar with the idea that some people have "the gift of the gab", this usually referring to people who are clever and persuasive in

* An introduction to the concept of "power" is given in "The Encyclopaedia of Philosophy".

argument and discussion. Others have previously pointed out how the manipulatory capacities of language have been exploited by advertising people (cf. Hansen, 1965) and in political propaganda (ideology) (see Marcuse, 1968, 1969). Poets and authors too have always been aware of the power of words, in which lie their own possibility of influence (cf. Carling, 1970).

However, the idea that our—your and my—ordinary everyday use of language, our neutral relaxed conversation, implies the exertion of power, i.e. an influencing and structuring of anothers experience, this can seem both surprising and provocative. One reason for this may be that our possible scope of influence by means of language is fairly restricted. Other language users—on the radio, on television, in the press, in advertising, etc. have a very different scope (*position of power*), so that the effect of their language use (*means of power*) is much greater (see p. 135 and Blakar, 1972a). Still, as we could see in the two examples—and, as we will try to clarify more thoroughly later in the article, it would seem that all language use implies such structuring and influencing effects. In other words, it would appear to be impossible to express oneself "neutrally". Even apparently synonymous expressions such as "It's half full" and "It's half empty" *can* affect the receiver quite differently. As soon as one emits a single word one seems to be bound to take a "position" and "exert influence". We are not here concerned by whether the receiver intentionally exerts influence, we will only demonstrate that this is what happens. *The language user's social influence is thus here defined through effect or consequence, completely disregarding whether the effect is intended or not* (Blakar, 1973a).

The Basis of Language as a Means of Social Power

Before we start to explore more systematically the basis which makes language and its use a means of social power, we want to mention briefly the different levels on which language actually may involve exertion of power. Through our empirical-theoretical studies (Blakar, 1971, 1972a, 1972b, 1973a) three distinct levels were identified and explored. First we have the single act of communication, where the transmitter's particular use of language structures and influences the receiver's experience of whatever the communication is about. (The influencing and structuring on this "level" was explored by theoretical-empirical studies of the type which will be presented in Part II of this paper. Moreover, systematic analyses of the language use in newspapers with divergent political perspectives as well as more experimental approaches were conducted (Blakar, 1973a).) Second, the language system by its way of conceptualizing "the reality" represents particular perspectives or interests, thereby giving those perspectives a pervasive influence on everybody learning and using that language. How the language system itself represents particular perspectives (not being "neutral") was dramatically revealed by an analysis of *how* the sex roles were represented, reflected, preserved and conveyed in Norwegian. (A theoretical-empirical analysis of *how* the Norwegian language represents, reflects, preserves and conveys our sex-role pattern gave a striking indication of how the language itself expresses particular interests of a male dominated society (Blakar, 1971, 1975). Furthermore, politically and ideologically loaded words—such as *arbeidsgjevar* "employer"—were analysed, to see if and whose perspectives and interests the verbal label represented.) Thirdly, different languages and dialects—even mixed in the same area—may have varying status. Knowing the intimate relationship between language and identity, one can easily imagine the controlling and oppressive effect of downgrading a people's or group's language or dialect.*, † In this paper we will mainly concentrate upon the first level, merely briefly comment upon the second, and totally neglect the third level.

Taking the examples presented above as a point of departure, we will now inquire more systematically into the basis which makes "language a means of social power". Through our analyses, four such basic factors or characteristics of language have been identified.

Choices in Encoding and Decoding

A communication situation is one in which a sender has "something" (a message) he wants (intention) to convey to a receiver. Such conveying can occur in many different ways and through many different media (Hockett, 1963). However, among human beings language is the most usual medium. When the sender has an idea or a message he wants to convey, this can be coded in many alternate but functionally equivalent codes, i.e. the same meaning or message can be expressed through several different expressions. The meaning content that "X is late" can be conveyed both through "X came late" and through "X did not come in time". Similarly, all three statements "not enough", "insufficient" and "too little" may convey the idea that something is lacking. Diction-

---

* A variety of the recent sociolinguistic studies illustrate this; take, e.g. how the so-called "matched-guise" technique has revealed how even a minor change in dialect/ language may almost totally change the social attitudes expressed toward the language user (Lambert *et al.*, 1960, Lambert, 1972). And the report (Holmestad and Lade, 1969) from a conference held in Oslo for "lingual minorities in Europe" testifies to the social power expressed on this "level".

† Some classic works, such as Brown and Gilman's (1960) "The pronouns of power and solidarity" and Ferguson's (1959) "Diglossia", which in different ways show how language reflects the social structure of the community, seem to involve aspects from all the three "levels".

aries of synonyms exist exactly for this purpose—a lexicon where one can look up *different* words and expressions for the *same* idea or meaning content.

Everytime we want to express "something" we have to *choose* among several alternative possible ways in which this "something" can be expressed. The receiver is confronted with a similar problem. He hears the sounds (or reads the letters) which the sender emits, he decodes (takes out, grasps) the content or meaning which has been conveyed. However, many (all?) sounds or written sequences can convey several differing meaning contents. Homonym in speech and graphonym in writing are the clearest examples. The word *ball* may elicit two quite separate meanings, *a ball* which we can kick or *a ball* at which we dance. And when we hear *in vacuo* the utterance "Peter beat John", it is impossible to know whether Peter won a race they both ran or, alternatively, that he hit John with a stick.

When the receiver hears or reads something he must *choose* one of several possible meanings as he decodes. In this the receiver is helped by the context; the situation itself, what has been said previously, as well as what was said later.* If we accept that the act of communication has these characteristics, then we can really begin to wonder if it is ever possible for the receiver to "pluck" out of the verbal utterance exactly the thoughts and feelings which the sender intended to communicate? As we have seen, communication can easily be misleading both during encoding at the sender end if the sender *chooses* verbal expressions which do not adequately cover what he wants to convey, as well as if the receiver decodes something other than the sender intended.

It is, however, *in exactly these choices* which both sender and receiver *must* make—and especially in relation to the sender's choice—that we find the basis for asserting that "use of language implies exertion of power". (Here we have used "choice" and "choosing" without considering whether the choice is conscious and intentional or not.) As we learned from the examples, even so-called synonymous expressions may function quite differently; they can emphasize or focus on different aspects of a situation as well as convey or indicate different actions or attitudes toward what is referred to. Here it is important to remember that we can only transmit one sound or element at a time. We cannot send complete thought or meaning contents *directly* from one human brain to another—we are obliged to unfold our thought and meaning content in sounds over time (Lashley, 1951; Rommetveit, 1968, 1971).

* In a series of experiments we have tried to explore such contextual influences in the processing of language (Rommetveit, 1968, 1972a, Rommetveit and Blakar, 1973, Rommetveit *et al.*, 1968a, 1968b, Rommetveit and Turner, 1967, Carswell and Rommetveit, 1971, Blakar, 1970, 1972d, 1973b, 1973d, Blakar and Rommetveit, 1975).

Neither is it possible for us to use two or more mutually modifying statements *simultaneously*. We are obliged *to choose* and "put all our money on one horse".

David's mother has discovered that there are less cakes in the cake tin than expected. Suspicion immediately falls on David. She can express her suspicion in many different ways, e.g:

(1) Have you taken the cookies David?
(2) Have you pinched the cookies David?
(3) Have you snitched the cookies David?
(4) Have you lifted the cookies David?
(5) Have you removed the cookies David?
(6) Have you stolen the cookies David?

In using these six different utterances, the mother signals very different attitudes to David and his "criminal behaviour". David's mother had probably a complex of feelings and attitudes toward David and his behaviour. Thus, though all six utterances contain some element of truth, none of them alone is entirely adequate in covering the mother's *total experience*. In order to communicate to the "sinner", she must choose one of the expressions from among all the potential. In her choice she emphasizes a particular aspect of her experience, and by this choice probably implies some hint as to what punishment David can expect. (This analysis has been restricted to the verbal expression only. In a real situation, however, this verbal utterance would be embedded in a *total* communication situation with non-verbal cues, facial expressions, etc.) Similarly, we can expect that the emotional sanctions from listeners to the radio news will vary greatly according to whether they hear that (1) "The Americans are intensifying their air combat strength in Vietnam", (2) "The Americans are expanding the air battles in Vietnam", (3) "The Americans are increasing bombing over Vietnam". While (1) can perhaps lead one to think of a strong opponent whose existence makes this "intensification" necessary, and (2) may give associations toward a give and take air battle, (3) much more easily reminds one of villages with children and old people being hit by the bombs.

The fact that the relationship between language and reality is so complex is one of the reasons why the sender's choices during the encoding are so decisive for structuring by language. The relationship between language and reality has concerned philosophers as well as poets and authors (Næss, 1961). The language-reality relationship will not be discussed in any detail here. We will merely show how it partly is the complexity of this relation which gives the sender's choices in the phase of encoding such strong a structuring or influencing effect. For a lot of verbal statements it is quite simple to answer questions such as "It is true?", "Is it right?", "Does it correspond to reality?", etc. If we go back to the example about the bottle, it is quite easy to find out if the statement "The bottle is half full" (half empty) is in accordance with the facts. If the answer is in the affirmative we can be sure that statements such as "The bottle is empty" or "The bottle is full" are *not* in accordance with reality. In the case of other statements it is sometimes possible in principle, though practically more or less impossible to answer questions of this type. Take for instance the statement, "In the Sahara there are 7.753.538.421 grains of sand".

However, for a great many of the verbal statements by which we are surrounded, and which create the basis for our insight and understanding, it is not possible to answer questions in a comparable manner to those mentioned above. For example, which of the following statements is in accordance with the facts: (1) "David has taken the cakes", (2) "David has pinched the cakes", (3) "David has stolen the cakes"? These statements can only partially be tested as being true or false against the "reality criterion". It can be tested whether it was David, John, or anybody else who "took/pinched/stole" the cakes, *if* it is true that any cakes are lost at all. However, there gives no such criterion against which it can be tested whether the cakes were "taken", "pinched" or "stolen". Nevertheless, it is *not* a matter of indifference for David and his mother which one of the expressions is chosen. This is also the case with a great deal of the statements communicated through the press and the radio, etc. (cf. the examples from Vietnam).

The Complexity of the Single Verbal Unit

In addition to the fact that the sender *must* always choose between many potential means of expressions, language itself is a compound and complex instrument on which the user plays. Let us clarify this by examining the word. Rommetveit (1968, 1972), both in his theoretical analyses and in his empirical studies, has shown that at least three different processes or components of experience are elicited when a word is processed. The first one is the referential function; second, an associative component is released; and thirdly each word has an emotive aspect. (Most studies on words and the processing of words have focused upon only one of these aspects, and the different aspects have been explored within different theoretical and empirical frameworks. The referential component has mainly been explored by philosophers (e.g. Næss, 1953). The associative component has been explored in philosophy as far back as Aristotle, and for a variety of reasons psychologists have explored and used word-associations (cf. the Kent-Rosanoff standard list of stimulus words as from 1910). And the emotive component has been most systematically studied by means of the semantic differential (Osgood *et al.*, 1957.))

Let us make this more tangible by using some examples. The referential function can most easily be demonstrated by a homonym, i.e. a word form (a letter or sound sequence) which can release two quite separate meanings. Take the word *ball*, which can release two quite different references; "something we kick" and "somewhere to dance".

The associative component is clearly illustrated with words such as *cottage*. For many of us this word brings to mind pictures of mountains, snow, ski-ing, logfires, etc. All this has nothing to do with the interpretation of the word *cottage* in the narrow sense, but represents an associative network which is activated by the word.

We are also familiar with the idea that feelings or emotions can be triggered off by a word. The associations activated by the word *cottage* above are mostly of a positive kind. However, we see the emotive component more clearly if we take two or more words referring to the same thing, but activating more or less totally different emotions. A typical example of this is the use of *coloured, black, negro* and *nigger*, which all stands for "one with a dark skin pigment", but which activates very different feelings and betray very different attitudes toward the person(s) in focus on the part of the speaker.

When we hear or understand a word, we obviously are not aware of all these separate factors. Under ordinary circumstances the three parts of the process occur together and have mutual influences on each other, thus creating *the total experience* which is elicited in the receiver. And even if a verbal unit is usually experienced as a totality, it is nevertheless important to realize that the word is a complex instrument composed of separate components, because the language user can use or emphasize the different components in different ways. To illustrate how a user can more or less systematically exploit these different components of language, we can take the word *democracy*. In common with most content words, the word *democracy* activates all the three part-processes mentioned above. The language user can, however, exploit the three in different ways, as is exemplified in the following descriptions—exaggerated as they may be: What the word *democracy* really means or what it refers to is often difficult to discern; still, in discussions between professional social scientists, the reference component will be emphasized. In a discussion of this type the emotional and associative components will (ought to) stay in the background. Alternatively in an Independence day speech it is likely that the emotive component, especially the positive emotions, will be almost totally dominant. Whether *democracy* really implies among other things "fair distribution of all property" or not, will not be salient in an Independence day speech. And, for example, in a poem the poet may rely more or less exclusively upon the associative component (cf. the associations to *cottage* above).

The point to note here is that each verbal element is a complex and sensitive instrument on which the language user plays when using language. Thus the experience and comprehension awakened in the receiver is dependent on the use the sender is able to make of this delicate instrument. It is in fact exactly this play with the different components and processes of the word which has always been exploited in rhetoric, by political demagogues as well as in poetry. Advertising language is an example where the referent component is diffuse and kept in the background, but where the emotive aspect, especially positive emotions, are actively exploited (Hansen, 1965). However, in our ordinary everyday conversations we also use these very same mechanisms whether we are aware of it or not.

If words are multifactoral and complex, phrases and sentences are obviously even more so. Sentences do not evolve as the sum of a string of words (word + word + word, etc.). Sentences and phrases are in their turn a product of a subtle interplay between the various constituents. Miller (1965) has nicely expressed this when he says that "the words in a sentence interact". To demonstrate that the meaning in sentences *cannot* be created by a word + word + word model we can compare the sentences: *"Peter beat John* at chess" with *"Peter beat John* with a stick" and *"At last the spring came* to Paris" and *"At last the spring came* from the manufacturer". (Such retro-active contextual influences have been used to illustrate different aspects of the processing of language (Lashley, 1951, Rommetveit and Turner, 1967; Kvale, 1971; Blakar, 1970, 1973b.))

Language as an "Open" and Generative System

A third characteristic of language constituting the basis for "language use implying the exertion of power" is that language is an "open" and generative system. By this we mean that for instance by means of the English vocabulary one can create an infinite number of sentences, and constantly new sentences and phrases which never have been used before (and still they are understood) (cf. Chomsky, 1964). And the words used can themselves partially change their meaning and content as they are applied in everchanging combinations and contexts. Such changes may occur in all the three component processes of the word which we have explored above.

However, the most important thing to notice in this connection is that as users of language we are continually creating new words and expressions. And these new labels are, of course, not neutral. An example will illustrate: Up till now we have had in towns what we call garbage or trash collectors. These "garbage men", instead of going round with their own carts, are now often employed by the local authorities or "Cleansing

Departments" and in some places their official title is now "cleansing officer". Behind changes of labels of this type may lie economic and political factors as well as prestige. Changes in nomenclature can thus reflect conflicts of interests and changing spheres of influence and prestige. Actual changes in the town garbage collection and in the type of work the men do, *is not in itself* likely to be enough to push through such changes in verbal labelling. (An illustrative example is a political party in Norway which changed its name from *Bondepartiet*, "The Farmer's Party", to *Senterpartiet*, "The Centre Party".) On other occasions it is not a case of familiar phenomena receiving new verbal labels, but new phenomena appear, thereby requiring to be named. In this way expressions like "regional development" appear. It is nonetheless clear to everyone in the outlying regions in Norway and in Europe generally that in this case the creator of the expression (i.e. the politicians) put most emphasis on the word's emotive and associative character, and much less on whether the expression covered the "political reality"; labels such as "regional depopulation" or "regional neglect" might have been more adequate for the actual policy in Europe today. (The corresponding Norwegian example goes: The actual policy is labelled *distriktsutbygging*, "regional development", while *distriktsnedbygging*, "regional dismantling" or *distriktsavfolking*, "regional depopulation", would be at least as appropriate labels.)

Language System Itself as a Mirror and Expression of the Existing Power Constellations

The three basic characteristics of language and communication explored so far have this in common, they oblige each *language user* to structure, influence, and take a point of view, etc. *through* his use of language. The fourth basic characteristic we will examine is unlike these in that it does not in the same way operate *through* the individual language user. Language itself as a system represents only one particular—of all possible—way of conceptualization, only one way to grasp and understand reality. As we shall see the "language itself" more or less clearly reflects the socio-political power structure in a given society and inevitably takes a point of view, i.e. takes sides.

Some examples will illustrate better than any long theoretical explanation. In our western societies the vast majority of people are wage earners. But what do we call those for whom the wage earners work? The language label can tell us a great deal about *how* we experience and understand this role, or rather *how* those who have power to govern the labelling (and thus our understanding) want us to interpret the role. Opposed to the wage earner is the *employer*, i.e. the one who gives people work or employment. This particular term emphasizes certain aspects of the role at the same time as other aspects are kept in the background. "Labour buyer" or "hirer" would after all be just as adequate a name. (The corresponding Norwegian example goes: The label used is *arbeidsgjevar*, "the one who *gives* people work", while logically seen *arbeidskjøpar*, "the one who *buys* people's work", might have been at least as appropriate a label.) These labels would, however, focus on quite different aspects of the role. The picture of the "hard exploitative businessman who buys workers' labour as cheaply as possible" would probably become stronger than the picture of the "charitable employer who gives people a livelihood". The point to be made is that our language by its labelling has taken a position, a point of view, and that this is inevitable. It is impossible to find neutral expressions which catch the full range of our experience. A verbal label like "police" is obviously not neutral. Alternative terms which illustrate this have appeared, e.g. "cops". Let me here mention that a dictionary of synonyms must necessarily choose a position implicitly or explicitly about what sort of comprehension our language should represent. The standard English dictionary* does not mention "cops" as a possible synonym for "police". However, "civil administration", "public order", "Civil force responsible for maintaining public order", "police officer", etc. are all given as synonyms. Dictionaries, as language in general, are not unbiased. They hold a particular point of view and represent a particular understanding.

The simplest way to get an idea of the social power and influence exerted by a language system is to analyse an area where the constellation of power is relatively clear. An example of this is the sex role division in our male-dominated society. Through a fairly comprehensive analysis of Norwegian, it was demonstrated how language in different ways (a) *reflects* and (b) *conserves* the existing sex role pattern, even to the extent that language can be said to (c) *counteract change*. Further it was shown (d) how boys and girls, both directly and indirectly, learn their traditional sex roles as they learn and understand their mother tongue (Blakar, 1971, 1975).

Against this background it is not surprising that it is in times of crisis and swift change that one becomes clear about *how* language exerts power over us. In an essay by Enzensberger in 1963, "In search of the lost language", it is shown how the collapse of the German Reich in 1945 also led to a collapse in the language. And Hinton remarks: "Every revolution creates new words. The Chinese Revolution created a whole new vocabulary" (1968, VII). The last two examples should illustrate the intimate connection between language and its use on the one hand, and social power and its exertion on the other.

When each language actually *is* obliged to choose *how* to label every-

* "The Concise Oxford Dictionary."

thing, this is because the relation existing between the verbal label and the phenomenon labelled is arbitrary (digital). There is nothing about the sun which in itself necessitates that it must be called the "sun". Similarly there is nothing special about the moon which makes us call it the "moon". The language labels which have been given the planets are only expressions of *social conventions* or *contracts of language use*. We could just as easily have called the moon "sun", and the other way round.

We will see the implications of this more clearly when we have considered some examples showing that signs *can* bear lawful relationships to that to which they refer. As far as traffic signals are concerned, the signs are related to that which they stand for mainly by analogy (Z means a dangerous corner, ∼ means a rough road, etc.). In baby language a sheep is often referred to as *ba-ba*, a dog as a *bow-wow*, a cat as *puss-puss*, etc. Here it is obvious that there is *something* about the labelled phenomenon itself which gives it one label and not the other. In our language code we could easily call the dog for "cat" and the opposite, if only we were agreed upon this, i.e. established another social contract. However, if we employ a system such as the child language described above, a cat could not be called a *bow-wow*, nor a dog a *puss-puss*.

The type of relationship which exists in the ordinary language code between the language labels and that which they refer to, make it possible for us to choose what sort of label we will attach to a particular phenomenon, just as long as we only are agreed about this. Since, as we have seen, the verbal label may have profound implications for our conception of the phenomenon labelled, then getting one's labels accepted represents quite an important act of social power. In a democracy it might be worth studying whether in fact everybody and every group has equal opportunity to have his language label suggestions accepted in the on-going social contract for language use. (The concept of contract has been elaborated by Rommetveit (1972a, 1972b), and an experimental situation in which such contracts can be empirically explored has been developed (Blakar, 1973d).)

Exertion of Power in the Act of Communication

A Critical Examination of the Model of Communication

The above analysis gives at least some of the reasons why language and the use of language implies structuring and influencing. A natural next step should be to analyse in some more detail an act of communication, and try to identify and systematize the different *tools* which the language user has at his disposal or actually is bound to exploit (the first of the three levels).

This analysis will take as its point of departure a thorough criticism of the following, still dominant model of communication: A (transmitter) experiences or observes *something* he thinks or has reason (intention) to inform B (receiver) about. For this—that is, the submitting of information about this "something"—A often uses language. A encodes that which he will relay through language. B listens to it and decodes; B takes out the thought or meaning content that A put into the expression. In such a way B receives information about the "something" *without* having experienced it himself. In such a—here somewhat caricatured—model of communication there is implied a definite point of view as to what language is and its relation to the non-linguistic. That is, that language *depicts* observations, events and the consequences of events in the outside world. With the help of language, we can give a "parallel account" of that which happened (is happening) in the outside world.

It is unlikely that any theoretician of communication would subscribe to such a model of communication. Nevertheless, the models of communication applied more or less implicitly have a good deal in common with that caricature. At any rate, the model can, caricature or not, serve as a starting point for our attempt to demonstrate *the transmitter as an active creator*, actively *constructing* as regards the "something" he speaks about, as regards language or medium, as regards himself (as sender), and as regards the social situation in which the communication takes place.

The caricature model is inadequate in a number of points. Here we will especially take up the implied notion of the transmitter as a "passive relayer" of information. Let us take the following situation as a starting point. A man walking along the streets in Oslo hears a terrible uproar from the American Embassy. He asks what is happening. Imagine that the informer (sender) is a young radical who has just taken part in a demonstration from which the noise has come. Or, imagine that the informer (sender) is a conservative who has by chance observed the demonstration. It is reasonable to expect that the political demonstration about which the person concerned receives verbal information and, thus, insight into, will appear to have been quite different in these two instances.

When the transmitter tells about something he has experienced to one who has not experienced it, creating, structuring or modification can enter in three separate phases: During *the perception phase*,* during *the*

---

* "The central assertion is that seeing, hearing, and remembering are all acts of *construction*, which may make more or less use of stimulus information depending on circumstances" (Neisser, 1967). Particularly the Gestalt Psychologists have stressed the active and creative aspect of perception, and studies on influences from motivation (e.g. Bruner and Goodman, 1947) and emotion (e.g. McGinnies, 1948) upon perception testifies to the active structuring in perception.

recall phase,* and, last but not least, during *the verbalizing or encoding phase.* Perhaps the most thorough going restructuring occurs during the verbalizing or encoding phase. It is the structuring during this phase that we shall consider here. We get a first impression of the structuring which occurs during this phase when we try to place ourselves in the transmitter's place. The transmitter has a thought or meaning content which he wants to communicate. The thought or meaning content is atemporal, but as he begins to speak (write) he only gets out one sound, one element at a time. In a way the content must be "unfolded over a period of time" (Lashley, 1951; Rommetveit, 1968, 1971, 1972a). (When Watts compares our written language with Chinese, the problems of "unfolding" become evident: "In this respect, the Chinese written language has a slight advantage over our own, and is perhaps symptomatic of a different way of thinking. It is still linear, still a series of abstractions taken in one at a time. But its written signs are a little closer to life than spelled words because they are essentially pictures, and as a Chinese proverb puts it: One showing is worth a hundred sayings" (Watts, 1957).) In doing this the transmitter must make a number of choices. He must choose a sequence, what he wants to begin with and what he wants to end with. He must choose words and expressions, syntax, etc. For each of these varied choices or selections we can imagine that there are *tests* which the transmitter can use to test for adequate means of expression (Miller *et al.*, 1961; Rommetveit, 1968; Blakar, 1973b.).

Before we identify and analyse the linguistic tools which the transmitter has at his disposition—and is actually *forced* to choose among— during the verbalization, we shall briefly show why it is so important to point out the inadequacies of the caricaturistic model of communication which we have presented. This is first of all because to a large extent we "live in a linguistic world". In a great number of areas we only know the "map", and have no direct access to the "territory", to say it in Korzybski's (1945) terms. In an increasing number of situations we must take a stand and act on the basis of verbal information alone. There is a steadily decreasing part of our "knowledge" for which we have the opportunity to "check the terrain" ourselves. And perhaps the most common, though often implicit, model of communication is the one about "the passive referrer who merely relays information". Some examples will illustrate what I mean.

Only rarely do we meet the idea that the news broadcasts represent a

---

* Except for the so-called "passive decay theory", all theories of memory implicate activity or restructuring in one form or another (Hilgard, 1962). Bartlett (1932) has probably more than any other emphasized the changes going on in memory. A series of experiments of the type which Carmichael *et al.* (1932) conducted has attempted to describe the changes in memory.

suggestion as to what is important at the current time and what is less important. More commonly we have the impression that one is told what has happened around the world. In spite of all the modern "psychology of the witness", the common underlying conception seems to be that the witness really *can* tell what happened. And take for example a report of a track-race. Presumably in such a case, most people experience the broadast as an extension of their own sensory equipment all the way to the stadium. But even here the reporter's selection and structuring enter the picture. "Ben Jipcho takes the lead from Jim Ruyan" and "Jim Ruyan is staying behind Ben Jipcho" have different implications for what the listener imagines is happening in the track.

However, a model of communication of the type sketched above is not implicit only in daily life. It has been dominant, though in somewhat more refined form, in both philosophy and psychology.* Let me immediately add that this model could have survived *because so few have taken an explicitly communication perspective* in the study of language. As Rommetveit (1968, 1972a, 1972c, and particularly 1972b) points out, many linguistic, philosophical as well as psychological studies of language have been carried out where one has *not* taken the perspective of communication. In psychology this is perhaps primarily true of the learning oriented psychologists, but it also holds with those who have been inspired by Chomsky. Both in the mapping of the surface structure (e.g. Garrett *et al.*, 1966; Johnson, 1965), and in attempts at studying deep structure (e.g. Chomsky, 1968; Blumenthal, 1967) *one has taken language out of the context of communication.* The semantic analysis of Katz and Fodor (1963) illustrates that it is difficult to go back to natural communication from analyses and studies where the perspective of communication has *not* been taken into consideration. They claim for example that the sentence, "My spinster aunt is an infant", is an anomaly or contradiction since "spinster aunt" and "infant" imply different ages (Katz and Fodor, 1963).† When one analyses language independently of the active, creative relation one has to language in the communication situation such conclusions may perhaps seem reasonable, but as soon as one takes the perspective of communication it is easy to imagine situations where the sentence in question communicates significant messages (for example, that "my spinster aunt" must be taken care of as "an infant").

In the dispute on the complicated relationship between language and thought, the perspective of communcation has been particularly noticeable by its absence. We can see that this perspective can introduce

---

* Wittgenstein (1968) and Heidegger (cf. Fløistad, 1968) represent rare exceptions.
† Uhlenbeck (1967) and Rommetveit (1968) have seriously criticized Katz and Fodor's position.

significant correctives here too if, for example, we consider Whorf's hypothesis. In their critical discussion of this hypothesis, Miller and McNeill (1969) examine three different versions "differing on the presumed locale of linguistic influence on cognition. Whereas the strong version deals with thought and the weak version deals with perception, the weakest version deals with memory" (Miller and McNeill, 1969). If we compare this with our schematic approach to the different phases during which structuring can occur, we see that the last, namely the encoding or verbalizing phase, is missing. Were we to formulate "the weakest version" of Whorf's hypothesis it would be that the linguistic medium, with its implicit structuring, limits *that which we can communicate*. (An example would be that we can easily imagine a society where there is genuine equality between the sexes, but in Norwegian (and in English) it is difficult, if not impossible, to *communicate* the ideas about such a society. Among other things, this is so because the words *mann* "man" and *kvinne* "woman" have such unequal status and are integrated in such different semantic-associative networks (Blakar, 1971, 1973a, 1972c).) It is tempting to underline the fact that even in their critical review of psycholinguistics Miller and McNeill "forget" to bring the perspective of communication into this discussion. Against this background it is important to see the user of language as structuring, constructive and creative, in other words, to see language as a tool or instrument of power in this process.

The Transmitter's Different Power Tools

The following more detailed analysis and exemplification of some of the transmitter's "instruments of power" will hopefully testify to the relevance of the more theoretical points made above. Furthermore, it is our hope that the following more "empirical" analysis will demonstrate the need of studying language as embedded in a social context or matrix. The following list of "power instruments" does not claim to be complete, and it has to be supplemented by further analyses, theoretical as well as empirical. The following six "power instruments" on behalf of the transmitter will be explored: (1) Choice of words and expressions; (2) creation of (new) words and expressions; (3) choice of grammatical form; (4) choice of sequence; (5) use of suprasegmental features; (6) choice of implicit or tacit premises.

Choice of Words and Expressions

The reason that choice of word or phrase (expression) represents a tool or instrument of power lies in the fact that one and the same phenomenon can be expressed in several synonymous ways. "There may be one meaning and different referents, or different meanings and one referent", to quote Vygotsky (1963). As we know it is almost impossible to find synonyms in the strict sense (Blakar, 1972a), and it is precisely here, in the often subtle differences between so-called synonymous expressions, that the transmitter has one of his most important tools. A saying has it that "a beloved child has many names". We shall see that the transmitter communicates varying attitudes to, and emphasizes different aspects or characteristics of the "beloved child" depending on which name he chooses.

Let us take Husserl's example of "equal sided" and "equal angled" triangles. A triangle which is "equal sided" is also "equal angled" and vice versa. Nevertheless, the receiver will probably respond with different behaviour depending on whether he is asked to inspect if a triangle is "equal sided" or "equal angled" (see Rommetveit, 1972b). According to Vygotsky (1963) there are two words for "moon" in Russian: "the changing form" and "the measurer, measurer of time". As we see each of these two names brings forth entirely different aspects of the moon. In fact, there seem to be different thought processes behind the etymologically different names.

On choosing from among "synonymous" expressions, one can signal his attitude toward that which is referred to (pragmatic aspects of language, Rommetveit, 1968, 1972a). When an American chooses among "black", "coloured", "negro" and "nigger", he simultaneously expresses his attitude. And behind "poor box" and "social welfare" we encounter different attitudes.

"The bottle is half empty" and "the bottle is half full" are extentionally synonymous. Nevertheless, there is reason to believe that they influence the mood of a joyful gathering differently. Perhaps the expression here says something about the transmitter himself; thus, he creates the impression the others receive. He who speaks of the "half full" bottle is perhaps more optimistic.

Let us now take two phrases from current political debate: (1) "The demonstrators were arrested by the police", (2) "The demonstrators were arrested by the cops". "The police" and "the cops" refer to the same persons (at least extentionally, "in the physical sense"). Nevertheless, the two expressions will, because of these two words, *be referred to and understood within two fundamentally different ideological frameworks*. This can in part be explained by the fact that the two words have and elicit fundamentally different semantic-associative networks (Blakar, 1972a; Rommetveit and Blakar, 1973). In ideological and political debate the choice of words and expressions is an extremely important instrument of power in the structuring of that "reality" over which the debate rages (cf. the reporter in Vietnam). (In political and ideological contexts discussions about the use of language are not rare. There may be arguments about which use of language is "veiling" or which "reveals the objective realities". Here we are examining the linguistic mechanisms, and it is of no interest whether the examples we present illustrate "veiling" or "revealing".)

Sociologists, for example Aubert (1965), have considered how the powerplay within the social system make it possible for the same person to be called "criminal" or "alcoholic", "prisoner" or "patient", according to "the eyes or experts who see". It is obvious that this leads to quite different consequences for the person in question (cf. David, mother and the cakes).

Here it is tempting to mention a Norwegian proverb which says that "The name harms no one". That saying seems to imply "a passive relationship" between the label and they or those who bear it. That the language user influences by his label giving (cf. the creation of new words), and use of names seems obvious. Names such as "light fingered Larry" or "little John" give a preconception of the one who bears the name. Vygotsky (1963) points out that the same person can be referred to as "The Victor of Jena" and "The Looser of Waterloo". These two labels give different impressions of the military leader. And there is an implied difference in talking about "police" or "cops". This demonstrates how words or names influence that to which the name refers. By using a word or concept which is usually used in connection with people, a thing can acquire the status of a person, or vice versa (cf. for example, language use in fairy tales). "The moon" shifts from the status of a thing and acquires more of the status of a person through: (1) "The moon reflects light from the sun", (2) "The moon shines clearly", (3) "The moon smiles". Certain scholars (Marcuse, 1968 and 1969; Steiner, 1969) have suggested that "alienation" among other things is caused by people being described with words originally used in connection with things. Here it is worth remembering Buber's (1937) clear distinction between "it" and "thou".

A party game introduced by Bertrand Russell in the BBC illustrates a number of the aspects about the choice of words analysed up to now. In addition, we understand even better *how* the choice of words and expressions is influenced by the social context (who we are speaking with, who we are talking about, etc.). This party game is called "emotive conjugation" according to the pattern: I stick to principles—You are insistent—He is stubborn. Here the choice of word reflects "a social game" in which we undoubtedly all recognize ourselves.

This brings us back to the individual act of communication where the choice of words—"fortunate or unfortunate choice"—can result in determining the development. An example will illustrate this: Two people were enthusiastically occupied in a discussion on photography and photo-technical details. In his irritation over the fact that a particular brand name was unable to use a specific technical detail because of the patent situation, one of them, almost paranthetically, asserted that the patent system served the capitalists and not the consumers. Someone who had been sitting by passively *now* entered the discussion and asked whether the previous speaker also had become an anti-capitalist radical. The conversation, thereby, turned to a political discussion. If the speaker had said that the patent system served "the inventors" or perhaps "the factories" and had not used the word "capitalist", it is less likely that the conversation would have taken the described course. Here, in the middle of the actual act of communication, we see *both* (1) how the choice of words and expressions is a product of the social context, *and* (2) how these choices in turn influence and structure the social context (Blakar, 1970). A more direct confrontation with the psychological and social forces involved in interpersonal communication is difficult to get.

The Creation of New Words and Expressions

There are two main reasons for "making up" new names, words and expressions. First of all, new phenomena pop up which need names. How new things are received are not least of all dependent upon how successful the "baptismal" process is. Secondly, there can be a reason for changing the name of an already existing phenomenon. Behind such changes of names can lie questions of politics, economics, prestige, communication, etc.

The creation of words and expressions illustrates perhaps even more clearly than the choice of words how the language enters in a structuring way. The political policy which we are witness to in Norway and Europe today can just as well be called "regional neglect" or "district depopulation" as the positively loaded and newly created "regional development".

Particularly in advertising and ideological use of the language there is a tendency to create words with a positive colouring. With the help of positively loaded words plus the language's veiling effect, a politician in *the same speech* can be *for* full energy development (or, perhaps, road development) and *for* ecology, without giving any priority.

How a phenomenon is received can, as previously mentioned, be dependent upon how the name catches on. One of the few arguments that has been used against ecology in Norway is that it is too expensive. Would the same arguments have been used if one had originally called this work *menneskevern* "protection of people" and not *naturvern* "protection of nature". Here one can mention that the word *naturvern* "protection of nature" is receding in use. Now one says *miljøvern* "environmental protection".

Marcuse asserts that those who have power in the society use language to define and veil "the real situation", but, he also points out how one who desires to expose the existing system can use the language in active re-creation, essentially by "re-naming" the existing institutions. One can, for example, call President X and Governor Y "Pig X" and "Pig Y" and refer to their speeches as "oink, oink" (Marcuse, 1969).

He who desires re-creation and reform of society has an effective tool in linguistic reform, but here it is a difficult problem of balance. On the one hand, if one accepts the existing use of language "one is trapped" and gets the existing social system in the bargin. On the other hand, if one creates too many new words and concepts, this hinders communication and makes contact difficult. A variety of philosophic, political, as well as religious movements have become isolated small sects because of a much too original use of language.

Tied to creation is the misuse of words, and the use of "empty words". We also find this most clearly illustrated in advertising and politics. . . . "the only detergent with blue power pearls", ". . . the only soap with bacteria killing X". Political speeches and slogans such as "man in the centre" are also entirely empty of content. Marcuse (1968) gives examples of some new word combinations which when one looks more closely at them seem completely absurd. For example, there have been advertisements for "luxurious bomb shelters". That is to say, shelters with TV and carpeting on the floor. The new creation of "luxurious bomb shelters" takes the fear of war and the awfulness away from the experience of a "bomb shelter". Another example is "harmless fallout" in connection with atom bomb tests. These are only extreme examples of a relatively common linguistic tool, namely, the use of language to create distance from that which is frightening, such as the phenomena "fallout" and "bomb shelters".

On a Norwegian detergent package it says that "X kills up to 99 per cent of all bacteria". This type of advertising claim is an excellent example of language's creating effect. First of all, the use of "up to" will have little effect next to the exact "99 per cent" (instead of "up to 100 per cent"). It would be interesting to see how many would forget "up to" in a recall test. For another thing, let us consider the sentence's truth value. The assertion is "true" if the detergent kills more than zero per cent (pure water does that), but less than 99 per cent of all bacteria. Nonetheless, the sentence gives the impression that X is very effective. (On the background of the above analysis Moscovici's (1967) criticism of traditional content analyses of the mass media is understandable: "Content analyses applied to the mass media most often consist of a count of themes or of key words (such as democracy or bolshevism); they rarely constitute an examination of the semantic field, the syntactic organization of the message".)

The Choice of Grammatical Form

It is not irrelevant whether the race-track reporter says (1) "Ben Jipcho beat Jim Ruyan" or (2) "Jim Ruyan was beaten by Ben Jipcho". Perhaps the reporter from Kenya, with a joyous voice, will choose (1), while the American reporter, resigned, informs his listeners with the help of (2).

The structuring effect of grammatical form becomes even more clear through the comparison between (1) "The police took the demonstrators" and (2) "The demonstrators were taken by the police". Here the grammatical forms actually indicate vaguely, but subtly, the separate contexts. In (1) the police, more or less actively, take the action (the police took action, the police struck). In (2), on the other hand, it seems implicit that the demonstrators carried on in such a way that the police were forced to take action (the demonstrators did, the demonstrators provoked). The different points of view expressed as regards causality becomes much clearer in (1) "Police took action" (2) "The police had to take action". Nevertheless, the listener in an ordinary communication situation must be quite observant to realize that the two expressions actually imply entirely different causative relationships.

The choice between active and passive sentence form not only has implications for the receiver's experience of the causative context, perhaps even more important is the possibility that this change actually appears to involve a shift in who the "main person" is, who it is we are speaking about. If we consider a fight between John and Jack it can seem equivalent whether we say (1) "John beat Jack" or (2) "Jack was beaten by John". However, the fact that these two sentence forms actually lead us to focus on different persons, can be seen if we, immediately after having said (1) or (2), only say "He . . .". After (1) the word "he" points back to John, and the receiver may expect to hear that, "He is tough and hits hard", or the like. After (2) the word "he", on the other hand, seems to point back to Jack, and the receiver perhaps expects to hear something along the lines of "He began to cry". Rommetveit (1972b) discusses how sentences of this type (1 versus 2) seem to imply different *contracts* about what will be the theme for the continuing conversation. Since a change in grammatical form actually can determine "who it is about" and can indicate causative relationships, it is naturally not surprising that the choice of forms also can reflect the transmitter's perspective and interests. This becomes more obvious if we, for example let John's mother or Jack's mother watch the fight. Whether John's mother will use (1) or (2) will naturally depend upon whether she thinks it is good that John learns to fight and defend his interests, or whether she is opposed to fighting.

We have considered the active and passive sentence form in quite some detail as an example of the choice of grammatical form. This we

have done because we have a strong feeling that many experience the
shift between active and passive as a shift "merely of form". Whether
one uses the active or passive form represents only question of form, style,
a variation in means of expression, etc. This analysis should make it
clear enough that the "bending of grammatical forms", for example
from active to passive, can have other and much more profound
consequences. (In recent years a variety of work has been done to
examine what the change from active to passive implies: cf., e.g.
Johnson-Laird, 1968a, 1968b.)

The Choice of Sequence

Even the sequence between otherwise equal elements (for example,
adjectives) as, for instance, in a list has an influence upon the impression
which is created (Asch, 1946; Wold, 1971; Jaspars *et al.*, 1971). If one
characterizes a politician with a number of adjectives, such that one
who studies the description carefully finds it to be balanced, one can, by
changing the sequence, vary the impression which is created. Perhaps
even more significant is the fact that the placement in a list has an
influence on memory (Wold, 1971; Jaspars *et al.*, 1971). In such a way
the transmitter actually can assure himself that the receiver is presented
a balanced characterization, but remembers the different characteristics
unequally.

Suprasegmental Characteristics such as Emphasis, Tone of Voice, etc.

With emphasis the transmitter indicates, among other things, what he
considers to be essential. The statements (1) "*He* beat me", (2) "He *beat*
me" and (3) "He beat *me*" (emphasis on the italicized word) transmit
messages about one single event which are in part quite different, one
from the other. This comes forth clearly if we imagine a pupil saying,
"He struck me", to the teacher. In (1) the essential point seems to be
that it was precisely he, "that bully", who struck. In (2) the event is
essentially "Look, teacher, he struck, even though you have forbidden
fighting". And in (3) the essential element is that the event "injured me"
(Blakar, 1972b).

Emphasis will also indicate and determine that which is new information. This also may be clearly seen in the fact that "He beat me"
actually can be the answer to three entirely different questions, and the
emphasis here will be an important indicator (Blakar, 1972b). Here are
examples: (1) Who was it that struck you? *He* struck me. (2) What has
he done to you? He *struck* me. (3) Who was it that he struck? He
struck *me*.

The tone of voice can determine whether a sentence is intended as a
question, an explanation, a denial, an acceptance, etc. Emphasis and
tone of voice can be particularly effective in structuring *because* no one

can assert, for example in a court of law, that you said ". . .", and then repeat anything but the words (the content). The tone of voice is lost forever, but it has had its effect. Take, for example, the impression which is created about "the sick one" when "Now he is sick again" is said with sympathy as opposed to irony.

The Choice of Implicit or Tacit Premises

Up to now we have concentrated on purely linguistic tools, but the distinction between the linguistic and non-linguistic, between that which is said and left unsaid in an act of communication, is extremely complicated. Often (always?) that which is said can only be understood when one knows the implicit and tacit premises. (In a series of experiments Rommetveit and his group (Rommetveit et al., 1971; Blakar and Rommetveit, 1971, 1975) studied the interrelationships between what is heard (utterance) and what is seen or imagined (picture).) This becomes obvious when we overhear conversations on the train or bus, and understand every single word but, nonetheless, do not really understand anything from the conversation.

We are seldom aware of the implicit premises, because all who take part in the communication usually share these. Something almost special must happen—a misunderstanding, a meeting with people of very different backgrounds—before we discover everything we normally take for granted.

In the interview situation, for example, the interviewer through his questions and formulations suggests which premises are fundamental. Usually the person interviewed is captivated and tries to answer according to the premises implied by the interviewer. However, occasionally, we find that the person interviewed takes up "the battle about the assumptions". With the help of the tacit premises one can say a lot "without saying it". In an article about "Nordic TV" * it was asserted that "The background for this is the indisputable fact that progress requires . . .". Without saying it explicitly, the author manages to tell those of us who might be "naïve", and believe something different, that progress cannot be stopped (or steered).

In the so-called "latest news" in radio and TV we meet the implicit, but actively structuring premises in the interpretation, understanding and transmission of the actual situations. Take, for example, the sensational reports connected with My-Laï in Vietnam on the background of the daily reports of so-and-so many killed, civilians as well as soldiers.

Several of the linguistic tools which we have discussed above reflect just this choice of implicit assumptions. The choice between "synonomous expressions" is typical. Whether the transmitter says "He is drunk" or "He is not sober" can demonstrate his insight or lack of

* R. Broby-Johansen in "Dagbladet", October 29, 1970.

insight into the receiver's expectations about the person's condition. When mother says "Johnny" and the teacher "John Christian Johnson" this says something about the relationship between those involved. If mother should say "John Christian" or even "John Christian Johnson" this would implicitly communicate a great deal. Use of single words can also indicate different implicit assumptions. The word "politics" in the two statements "everything is *politics*" and "I refuse to discuss this, because it is *politics*", illustrates this.

Henry (1971) has introduced a fruitful distinction between what he calls "free" and "tied" information to distinguish between that which must be taken as given and that information which is tied to this in the linguistically mediated message. We can illustrate with one of Henry's own examples. In a speech to the Congress before a tax debate, President Johnson said something like "It is not the regular increase in administration charges that calls for an increase of income taxes, but the Vietnam war" (Henry, 1971). As we can see Johnson *did not invite* discussion on whether or not the taxes should be increased. The tax increase was taken as *given* ("free information"), while Congress was invited to discuss the different causes (presented as "tied information") which necessitated the tax increase.

Rommetveit (1972b) starts more directly from the communication situation itself and separates out those parts of the linguistic statement which primarily serves a deictic function. Rommetveit illustrates with the sentence (1) "The old man is poor". This can, in the same way as (2) "The man is old and poor", be split into "The man is old" and "The man is poor". Nevertheless, (1) and (2) function entirely differently in the communication. In (1) the phrase "the old man" is used to point out who is being spoken about. It is asserted about this person that "he is poor". In (2) "the man" has this deictic function, and it is said that he "is old and poor".

This distinction represents a mechanism which the transmitter can take advantage of in creating, structuring and transmitting. With the help of this mechanism the transmitter makes suggestions about the structuring of "that which we are talking about". In "The old man is poor" it is taken as given that he is old—no discussion is invited about this—while the receiver can much more easily take up the question as to whether or not the man is poor.

This mechanism can actually be used to "smuggle in" information which the receiver does not readily have an opportunity to take a stand about. Let us imagine two students discussing the election in the student council. The first asks, (1) "Do you think the moderate candidates have any chance?". He might just as well have asked, (2) "Do you think the conservative candidates have any chance?", or (3) "Do you think the reactionary candidates have any chance?". In each case the receiver is asked about "the chances of one of the possible groups of candidates". The transmitter is inviting discussion about the chances of winning. Nevertheless, *at the same time* he creates and transmits a definite impression about this group of candidates. The receiver must break out, change perspective and restructure the entire conversation situation if he wants to question whether the characterization (moderate, conservative, reactionary) is adequate. The phrase "the . . . group of candidates" serves the transmitter primarily in a purely deictic function in the communication, and is not put forth for discussion or evaluation.

These different tools are naturally related to the basic properties of language and communication which we analysed, each one in different ways. For example, if we consider the first of the tools analysed, namely the choice of words and expressions, we see that to a certain extent this is related to all the four basic properties. First of all, the choice of words and expressions is naturally an indication of the transmitter's *choices in the encoding phase*. Further, the different choices of words get different implications *because* the individual words (elements) represent such a complicated and composite instrument. And, since the language is open and productive, the user of language can use individual words and expressions in new ways and in new contexts. Last, but not least, the language system itself, with its specific reflections of the social reality, creates the basis for those choices which the individual language user can make, but also puts boundaries or limits around these choices.

If we should try tentatively to point out what is common among the different linguistic tools which the transmitter has at his disposal for structuring or creating, we could say that most of the mechanisms play on the different context effects (see Blakar, 1970). Paradoxically, we can say that *we choose words and expressions which create or generate that context within which we want our statements to be taken.*

The Transmitter with Different Positions (of Power)

We have now considered some of the linguistic tools (instruments of power, if one will) which the transmitter has at his disposal. A fruitful supplement is to see how different transmitters (with different positions of power) can use the tools. (When speaking about power, there is a significant distinction between *instruments of power* and *positions of power*. Instruments of power in this context are the different linguistic tools. The position of power is determined primarily by factors such as range, relationship to the receiver, etc. A tool, such as a linguistic tool, represents an instrument of power *only* when the user (here the transmitter) has a position of power.) We see that the different tools can be used with varying effectiveness by comparing (a) how the transmitter in a normal conversation manages to structure the universe for the receiver as opposed to (b) how one generation (transmitter) structures the universe for the next (receiver) through language. The mass media, press, radio, TV, advertising, etc. represent an intermediary situation.

Whether the TV and radio use "police" or "class-fuzz" and reports about "the American engagement" or "American aggression" in Vietnam, etc. has a great deal of influence on the picture of the world which we establish. When new phenomena are introduced it is of great importance which labels are chosen by the mass media. Even more important are those implicit premises which lie beneath the "reports" which the mass media communicate. All of these are extremely important tools and instruments of power also in ordinary conversation situations, but because of the transmitter's much weaker position of power, the effect is so very much smaller.

However, the interplay between linguistic instruments of power and the position of power is more complicated than that *all* senders have the same tools of power, but not the same position of power. (1) First of all, people with different positions of power have different opportunities to learn the more advanced linguistic tools. (2) He who has most power (position) can decide, at any given time, which linguistic tool is most advantageous. We can, for example, see this clearly in how different dialects and minority languages are evaluated (Blakar, 1972b, Holmestad and Lade, 1969). (3) He who has power (position) determines, to a large extent, the use and meaning of words and expressions (instruments of power). In the U.S.A. a "negro" is one who has the slightest amount of "negro blood" in his veins. An analogous definition would be that a "white" is one who has . . . (Hayakawa, 1963). We see clearly who has interest in maintaining the current definition. (4) Finally, the linguistic tool is important in the battle for a position of power. We see this in ordinary discussion, but it comes forth especially clearly in therapeutic situations where linguistic tools are used in a pure power struggle between the therapist and the patient (Watzlawick *et al.*, 1967; Haley, 1963).

What Is It That Is Structured?

Through our explorations and examples so far, it has naturally been illustrated *what* it is that language and language use influences and structures. This has been done somewhat unsystematically, however, and will therefore be briefly systematized here:

First of all, this "something" about which we are speaking is influenced to a large extent through our use of language, and may even partly be created or established through our particular use of language. As should be evident from the examples given above, a name or linguistic label can to a large extent constitute and influence our understanding of and attitudes toward the *this* or *that* which is referred to. Politicians and advertising people seem always to have been very much aware of this. They compete in the launching of their newest ideas and goods wrapped in positive, well sounding and, most important of all, sale-enhancing linguistic labels.

Our *social reality* is to a large extent linguistically structured and mediated. That the English language lacks many expressions such as "masculinist", "charman", "houseman", but has "feminist", "char-woman", "housewife", is of course quite decisive as to what sort of social reality we can conceive of, understand and convey further with the help of the English language. (These few examples from English are illustra-tive as regards what we found in our systematic analysis of how the sex roles were represented in Norwegian (Blakar, 1971, 1975.) What will generally be accepted as the contemporary social reality will *not* be independent of whether the radio or television uses "Vietcong" or "The Peoples Liberation Army", "the American aggression in Vietnam" or "the American engagement in Vietnam", "police" or "cops", etc.

In addition we create and present a picture of ourselves through our language use. If we return to the introductory example, there is every reason to believe that he who remarks "The bottle is half empty" creates a more pessimistic impression than he who says "The bottle is half full". Through our use of language we indicate our attitudes and feelings towards that which we talk about, and this is again *reflected back* upon us and tells about ourselves. The two reporters in Vietnam do not only structure and communicaté their impressions from Vietnam, but through their respective choice of, e.g. "Vietcong" versus "The peoples Liberation Army" they convey their own attitude. In a similar manner our language use signalizes and reflects our conception of as well as our attitudes toward those we are addressing.

Thirdly, the use of language may affect or influence the community feeling (or possibly lack of such a feeling) which is created between those who are involved in an act of communication. The ability of language to establish social bonds as well as its potential as an isolator, are easy to illustrate. Just think of two persons who are talking in dialect to each other, or in some technical or professional lingo that outsiders do not understand, and thus are feeling excluded. A typical example of this can be found among young people where whole subcultures are strengthened and identified by means of their own slang, thus emphasizing the strong internal solidarity existing within the group, while at the same time excluding non-members, i.e. adults. Through choice of language and by using various degrees of formality in address we can regulate our interpersonal relationships and our social attachments to groups. Most languages have for instance varying forms of address which clearly indicate or invite various reactions, e.g. the *Vous* and *tu* from the French (cf. Roger Brown's comprehensive analysis of the social implications of varying systems of address, Brown and Gilman, 1960; Brown, 1966). The use of swearing, coarse or vulgar expressions, are also sensitive linguistic means of creating intimacy and contact *vs* aloof distance.

Limitations on the Transmitter's "Freedom to Structure"

This analysis of the transmitter's linguistic power tools cannot be finished without the factors *restricting* his "power" have been mentioned. What is it thus which limits creative freedom? First of all, it is reality itself, *that* which is being talked about. The transmitter is bound by the fact that he must try to communicate his experiences and thoughts about reality (otherwise he will be stamped as one who does not have contact with reality). However, our perception is active conception. And, our contact with "reality" is mainly socially mediated, in other words, to a significant degree mediated through language. Those restrictions placed by "reality" are, thus, difficult to delineate. Artists (cf. Carling, 1970) often move the boundaries, so one does not always "know what is reality". Korzybski's (1945) distinction between "map" and "territory" is an attempt to tackle these problems.

In discussions about what is "true" we meet a particular version of these problems. It is easy to determine that the statement "Oslo is the capital of England" is not true. However, it is much more difficult to decide which of the following statements are "true" and "false": (1) "Newspaper X is moderate", (2) "Newspaper X is conservative", (3) "Newspaper X is reactionary". The relationship between the true-false distinction is once again complicated. "The old man is poor" and "The man is old and poor" are either both true or both false. Nonetheless, they communicate different assertions.

Furthermore, the language itself, as a system, sets limits on the transmitter. As mentioned it is difficult, even if one wants to, to communicate the concepts about or sketch a society with full equality between the sexes using the Norwegian language, because, among other things, the words for man and woman have such different status. And, as has been pointed out, in its way of conceptualizing reality each language represents a particular perspective.

Thirdly, the transmitter, and particularly the receiver's conception of and attitude toward the transmitter, places certain limits. In particular it is important how much faith the receiver has in the transmitter (credibility). However, it is, in any case, more complicated than merely a question of faith or trust, because, as Asch (1952) points out, the transmitter is actually "a part of the message". A statement such as "A little rebellion is a good thing" is thus interpreted altogether differently depending on whether the receiver is told that it was said by Jefferson or Lenin.

The fourth and perhaps most important limitation on the transmitter's power to structure and influence the receiver's experience, is the receiver's own "freedom" to interpret and take a stand toward that which he hears himself. When above we analysed the bases of "language being a means of social power", we pointed especially to the potential freedom of choice which lies in both the encoding phase (by the transmitter) and in the decoding (by the receiver). This freedom of choice in the decoding implies that the receiver is by no means helplessly trapped by the transmitter's linguistic power tools, and that he must accept the transmitter's structuring suggestions. Let us, therefore, take a couple of those examples which we used to illustrate the transmitter's different tools and see how the receiver actually can refuse both the transmitter's explicit and implicit structuring suggestions.

We remember that President Johnson, in his speech during the tax debate, through his particular use of language implied that the tax increase should be taken as *given*, while Congress was invited to argue about the reasons why taxes had to be increased. Johnson here used a relatively subtle linguistic or communicational tool to structure the debate in his preferred way. *But*, there is every reason to believe that at least some of his opponents among the listeners would refuse to accept his structuring suggestion. Some of the receivers presumably would *not* let themselves be trapped by Johnson's implicit structuring, but would change perspective and "take up the battle about the premises". They would, thus, try to make the debate into a discussion for and against the tax increase. However, it is obvious that linguistic structuring of this type *can* succeed relatively easily, such that the receiver "bites the hook" and accepts the implicit structuring. In any case, the receiver must be continually observant in order *not* to enter a discussion on those premises which the transmitter introduces (cf. all of the transmitter's linguistic tools exemplified above).

If we consider the two reports on Vietnam, where one speaks about (1) "The American engagement in Vietnam" and the other about (2) "The American aggression in Vietnam", the receiver has the *choice* as to how these shall be interpreted. He can attribute (cf. Heider, 1958) the message he receives *either* to fact, in other words, to the situation in Vietnam, *or* to the person, in other words, the reporter. In the first case the reporter's structuring suggestion will perhaps be accepted and the choice between (1) and (2) will thus be able to structure and influence the receiver's understanding of what is going on in Vietnam. In the second case, on the other hand, the receiver will hold onto the interpretation he has about Vietnam, and whether the reporter uses (1) or (2) will merely influence his conception of what kind of political view the reporter seems to represent.

We thus see that we face a complicated and intriguing interaction between transmitter and receiver. At this point we have two comments on this interaction. First of all, the transmitter and receiver will, in an ordinary conversation, continually *shift* between being transmitter and receiver. Thus, they will alternatively have at their disposition the tools and instruments of power which the transmitter and receiver respectively have access to. (Exceptions here are members of the mass media such as the press, radio, TV, etc., and it is not the least this *one-way* structuring and influencing which makes the mass media into such a tremendously power factor.) Secondly, the transmitter must—in order to assure himself that he has been understood, and is not expressing himself completely autistically—"anticipate the receiver's decoding" (Rommetveit, 1968). That is to say, the transmitter in his encoding must try to anticipate and determine how the receiver, based on *his* background and *his* perspective, will interpret and understand the message. Through this the receiver *indirectly* influences the transmitter's linguistic and communicational structuring. We see precisely in this alternation, or this interaction between transmitter and receiver, that there is the basis for a "power struggle", that is to say a battle about which (whose) premises, which (whose) perspective, which (whose) use of language and, thus, which (whose) structuring of social reality shall be taken for granted.

Concluding Remarks

This paper does not claim to represent a complete analysis of what might be called "the power aspects of symbolic interaction". (Among other things, a more complete analysis will have to be more explicitly related to general theory of psychology—*cognitive* (individual) as well as *social* psychology (cf. Allport, 1962; Blakar, 1972c). Relevant theories of social psychology are Mead, 1934; Heider, 1958; and Goffman, e.g. 1967; and Neisser's (1967) theory of cognition fits this analysis very well.) The purpose of the present paper has been two-sided: (1) to identify and explore in some detail what has been usually called "the pragmatic aspects or functions of language" and (2) to try in a more systematic manner to relate these pragmatic aspects to a more general concept, namely "social power". The concept of power was chosen because (a) it is a central variable in everyday life, which at the same time (b) has been almost totally neglected in the study of language and communication.

Since research on language and communication at the moment seems to be characterized by (a) an overwhelming amount of detailed facts, and at the same time by (b) an almost total lack of agreement upon basic paradigms, we feel that we cannot bring this paper to an end without briefly commenting upon the eventual implications of the above analysis for the more basic paradigms. Our analyses of "language as a means of social power" (Blakar, 1971, 1972a, 1972b, 1973a) have convinced us that Rommetveit is right as regards the three main points in his basic criticism of the dominant traditions within modern psycholinguistics (Rommetveit, 1972b). First, he opposes Chomsky's (1957) claim that we have to study what language *is* before we can study language *use*. It is most unlikely that all these structuring aspects involved in the processing of language (actually aspects of the essence of language) could ever be revealed *without* exploring the use of language. Secondly, he opposes the widely accepted position, clearly expressed by Ervin-Tripp and Slobin (1966), that the psychologist's task is to identify "the processes by which the competence described by the linguists is acquired by children and is reflected in performance under a variety of conditions". Again, it is unlikely that social variables such as "power" would be given any central place in the linguists' description of "competence". Thirdly, Rommetveit vigorously criticized the dominant linguistic and psycho-linguistic traditions for exploring language *in vacuo* and out of relevant social contexts. It has only been by overlooking the contextual influences that it has been possible to almost totally neglect the power aspects of language and language use.

All these empirical-theoretical analyses of "language as a means of social power", furthermore, were conducted under the "naïve" hope that they might have *an emancipatory function*. For example, analyses of the type presented above might make us more on our guard against the structuring and influencing effects of the linguistic tools exploited in advertising, by the mass media, as well as in everyday conversations.

References

Allport, F. H. (1962). A structuronomic conception of behavior: Individual and collective. *J. Abnormal Social Psychology* **64**, 3–30.
Asch, S. E. (1946). Forming impression of personality. *J. Abnormal Social Psychology* **41**, 258–290.
Asch, S. E. (1952). "Social Psychology." Prentice-Hall, New York.
Aubert, W. (1965). "The Hidden Society." Totowa, New York.
Bartlett, F. C. (1932). "Remembering." Cambridge University Press, Cambridge.
Berger, P. L. and Luckmann, T. (1967). "The Social Construction of Reality." Anchor Books, Doubleday, New York.
Blakar, R. M. (1970). Konteksteffektar i språkleg kommunikasjon. Unpublished thesis, University of Oslo.
Blakar, R. M. (1971). "Kan mannssamfunnet sprengast utan språkrevolusjon?" *Syn og Segn* **77**, 550–561.

Blakar, R. M. (1972a). Språket som maktmiddel eller avsendaren som aktiv skapar. *Tidsskrift for samfunnsforskning* 13, 199–222.

Blakar, R. M. (1972b). "Det voldtatte 'fjøsspråket' eller jenta som kom 'fra Benklærnes i Lobenet'." *Mål og Makt* 2/3-4, 2–13.

Blakar, R. M. (1972c). Om ordassosiasjons-forsøk som metode og infallsport til språkpsykologisk innsikt. *Working Papers in Linguistics from Oslo* 1/3, 65–92.

Blakar, R. M. (1972d). "Språk—kontekst og kommunikasjon. Kvifor det er nødvendig å ta eit eksplisitt kommunikasjonsperspektiv i studiet av språkprosessar." Stencilled report, Institute of Psychology, University of Oslo.

Blakar, R. M. (1972e). "The impossibility of a social psychology proper: Some ruminations about conceptual and methodological problems connected to disentangling social and individual psychology." Stencilled report, Institute of Psychology, University of Oslo.

Blakar, R. M. (1973a). "Språk er makt." Pax forlag, Oslo.

Blakar, R. M. (1973b). Context effects and coding stations in sentence processing. *Scandinavian J. Psychology* 14, 103–105.

Blakar, R. M. (1973c). Unrepresentativeness of current studies on memory of verbal material. *Scandinavian J. Psychology* 14, 9–11.

Blakar, R. M. (1973d). An experimental method for inquiring into communication. *European J. Social Psychology* 3, 715–725.

Blakar, R. M. (1975). How the sex roles are represented, reflected and conserved in the Norwegian language. *Acta Sociologica* 18, 162–173.

Blakar, R. M. and Rommetveit, R. (1971). Processing of utterances in contexts versus rote learning of sentences: Some pilot studies and a design for an experiment. In "Social Contexts of Messages". (E. A. Carswell and R. Rommetveit, Eds) Academic Press, London and New York.

Blakar, R. M. and Rommetveit, R. (1975). Utterances *in vacuo* and in contexts: An experimental and theoretical exploration of some inter-relationships between what is heard and what is seen or imagined. *International J. Psycholinguistics* 4, 5–32.

Blumenthal, A. L. (1967). Prompted recall of sentences. *J. Verbal Learning Verbal Behavior* 6, 203–206.

Brown, R. (1966). "Social Psychology." The Free Press, New York.

Brown, R. and Gilman, A. (1960). The pronouns of power and solidarity. In "Style in Language". (T. A. Sebeok, Ed.) M.I.T. Press, Cambridge, Massachusetts.

Bruner, J. S. and Goodman, C. C. (1947). Value and need as organizing factors in perception. *J. Abnormal Social Psychology* 42, 33–44.

Buber, M. (1937). "I and Thou." T. and T. Clark, Edinburgh.

Carling, F. (1970). "Skapende sinn: En skisse av forfatteres selvopplevelse." Gyldendal, Oslo.

Carmichael, L., Hogan, P. H. and Walter, A. A. (1932). An experimental study of the effect of language on the reproduction of visually perceived form. *J. Experimental Psychology* 15, 72–86.

Carswell, E. A. and Rommetveit, R. (Eds) (1971). "Social Contexts of Messages." Academic Press, London and New York.

Cassirer, E. (1944). "An Essay on Man." Yale University Press, New Haven.

Chomsky, N. (1957). "Syntactic Structures." Mouton, The Hague.

Chomsky, N. (1964). Current issues in linguistic theory. *In* "The Structure of Language: Readings in the Philosophy of Language". (F. A. Fodor and J. J. Katz, Eds) Prentice-Hall, Englewood Cliffs, New Jersey.

Chomsky, N. (1968). "Language and Mind." Harcourt Brace Jovanovich, New York.

Eckblad, G. (Ed.) (1971). "Hierarchical Models in the Study of Cognition." Institute of Psychology, Bergen.

Enzensberger, H. M. (1963). In search of the lost language. *Encounter* **XXI** (September), 44–51.

Ervin-Tripp, S. and Slobin, D. (1966). Psycholinguistics. *Annual review Psychology* **17**, 435–474.

Ferguson, C. A. (1959). Diglossia. *Word* **15**, 325–340.

Fløistad, G. (1968). "Heidegger." Pax forlag, Oslo.

Garrett, M., Bever, T. and Fodor, J. A. (1966). The active use of grammar in speech perception. *Perception and Psycho-physics* **1**, 30–32.

Goffmann, E. (1967). "Interactional Ritual. Essays on Face-to-Face Behavior." Doubleday, Anchor books, New York.

Haley, J. (1963). "Strategies in Psychotherapy." Grune and Stratton, New York.

Hansen, E. (1965). "Reklamesprog." Hans Reitzels forlag, København.

Hayakawa, S. I. (1963). "Language in Thought and Action." Harcourt Brace Jovanovich, New York.

Heider, F. (1958). "The Psychology of Interpersonal Relations." John Wiley and Sons, New York.

Henry, P. (1971). On processing of language in contexts and referents of message. *In* "Social Contexts of Messages". (E. A. Carswell and R. Rommetveit, Eds) Academic Press, London and New York.

Hilgard, E. R. (1962). "Introduction to Psychology." Harcourt Brace Jovanovich, New York.

Hinton, W. (1968). "Fanshen: A Documentary of Revolution in a Chinese Village." Vintage books, New York.

Hockett, C. F. (1963). The problem of universals in the language. *In* "Universals of Language". (J. F. Greenburg, Ed.) M.I.T. Press, Cambridge, Massachusetts.

Holmestad, E. and Lade, A. J. (Eds) (1969). "Lingual Minorities in Europa." Det Norske Samlaget, Oslo.

Jaspars, J., Rommetveit, R., Cook, M., Havelka, N., Henry P., Pêcheux, M. and Peters, G. (1971). Order effects in impression formation: A psycholinguistic approach. *In* "Social Contexts of Messages". (E. A. Carswell and R. Rommetveit, Eds) Academic Press, London and New York.

Johnson, N. F. (1965). The psychological reality of phrase structure rules. *J. Verbal Learning Verbal Behavior* **4**, 469–475.

Johnson-Laird, P. N. (1968a). The interpretation of the passive voice. *J. Experimental Psychology* **20**, 69–73.

Johnson-Laird, P. N. (1968b). The choice of the passive voice in a communicative task. *British J. Psychology* **59**, 7–15.

Katz, J. J. and Fodor, F. A. (1963). The structure of a semantic theory. *Language* **39**, 170–210.

Kleiven, J. (1970). Om språklige ytringer og deres kontekst. *Forskning fra Psykologisk Institutt i Bergen* 1/2.

Kleiven, J. (1973). Verbal communication and intensity of delivery. *Scandinavian J. Psychology* **14**, 111–113.

Kleiven, J. and Rommetveit, R. (1970). Meaning and frequency in a binocular rivalry situation. *Scandinavian J. Psychology* **11**, 17–20.

Korzybski, A. (1945). "Science and Sanity." The Science Press Printing Co., Lancaster, Pennsylvania.

Kvale, S. (1971). The temporal perspective of remembering. *In* "Social Contexts of Messages". (E. A. Carswell and R. Rommetveit, Eds) Academic Press, London and New York.

Lambert, W. E. (1972). "Language, Psychology, and Culture." Stanford University Press, Stanford.

Lambert, W. E., Hodgson, R. C., Gardner, R. C. and Fillenbaum, S. (1960). Evaluational reactions to spoken languages. *J. Abnormal Social Psychology* **60**, 44–51.

Lashley, K. S. (1951). The problem of serial order in behavior. *In* "Cerebral Mechanism sin Behavior". (L. A. Jeffries, Ed.) John Wiley and Sons, New York.

Marcuse, H. (1968). "One Dimentional Man." Routledge and Kegan Paul, London.

Marcuse, H. (1969). "An Essay on Liberation." Bacon Press, New York.

McGinnies, E. (1948). Emotionally and perceptual defence. *Psychological Review* **56**, 244–251.

Mead, G. H. (1934). "Mind, Self and Society." University of Chicago Press, Chicago.

Miller, G. A. (1965). Some preliminaries to psycholinguistics. *American Psychologist* **20**, 15–20.

Miller, G. A., Galanter, E. and Pribram, K. H. (1960). "Plans and the Structure of Behavior." Holt, Rinehart and Winston, New York.

Miller, G. A. and McNeill, D. (1969). Psycholinguistics. *In* "Handbook of Social Psychology III". (G. Lindzey and E. Aronsen, Eds) Academic Press, New York and London.

Moscovici, S. (1967). "Communication processing and the properties of language." *In* "Advances in Experimental Social Psychology". (L. Berkowitz, Ed.) Vol. III. Academic Press, London and New York.

Neisser, U. (1967). "Cognitive Psychology." Appelton-Century-Crofts, New York.

Næss, A. (1953): "Interpretation and Preciseness." Jacob Dybvad, Oslo.

Næss, A. (1961). "Filosofiens historie." Universitetsforlaget, Oslo.

Osgood, C. E., Suci, G. J. and Tannenbaum, P. H. (1957). "The Measurement of Meaning." University of Illinois Press, Urbana.

Rommesveit, R. (1968). "Words, Meanings, and Messages." Academic Press and Universitetsforlaget, New York, London and Oslo.

Rommetveit, R. (1971). On concepts of hierarchical structures and micro-analysis of language and thought. *In* "Hierarchical Models in the Study of Cognition". (G. Eckblad, Ed.) Institute of Psychology, Bergen.

Rommetveit, R. (1972a). "Språk, tanke og kommunikasjon." Universitetsforlaget, Oslo.

Rommetveit, R. (1972b). Deep structure of sentences versus message structure: Some critical remarks to current paradigms, and suggestions for an alternative approach. *Norwegian J. Linguistics* **26**, 3–22.

Rommetveit, R. (1972c). Language games, deep syntactic structures, and hermeneutic circles. *In* "The Context of Social Psychology: A Critical Assessment". (J. Israel and H. Tajfel, Eds) Academic Press, London and New York.

Rommetveit, R., Berkley, M. and Brøgger, J. (1968). Generation of words from stereoscopically presented non-word strings of letters. *Scandinavian J. Psychology* **9**, 150–156.

Rommetveit, R. and Blakar, R. M. (1973). Induced semantic-associative states and resolution of binocular rivalry conflicts between letters. *Scandinavian J. Psychology* **14**, 185–194.

Rommetveit, R., Cook, M., Havelka, N., Henry, P., Herkner, W., Pêcheux, M. and Peters, G. (1971). Processing of utterances in context. *In* "Social Contexts of Messages". (E. A. Carswell and R. Rommetveit, Eds) Academic Press, London and New York.

Rommetveit, R. and Kleiven, J. (1968). Word generation: A replication. *Scandinavian J. Psychology* **9**, 277–281.

Rommetveit, R., Toch, H. and Svendsen, D. (1968a). Effects of "contingency" and "contrast" contexts on the cognition of words: A study of stereoscopic rivalry. *Scandinavian J. Psychology* **9**, 138–144.

Rommetveit, R., Toch, H. and Svendsen, D. (1968b). Semantic, syntactic and associative context effects in a stereoscopic rivalry situation. *Scandinavian J. Psychology* **9**, 145–149.

Rommetveit, R. and Turner, E. A. (1967). A study of "chunking" in transmission of messages. *Lingua* **18**, 337–351.

Smedslund, J. (1972). "Becoming a Psychologist." Universitetsforlaget, Oslo.

Steiner, J. (1969). The language animal. *Encounter* **XXXIII** (August), 7–24.

Vygotsky, L. S. (1963). "Thought and Language." M.I.T. Press, Cambridge, Massachusetts.

Watts, A. W. (1957). "The Way of Zen." Penguin, Harmondsworth.

Watzlawick, P., Beavin, J. H. and Jackson, D. D. (1967). "Pragmatics of Human Communication." Norton, New York.

Wittgenstein, L. (1968). "Philosophical Investigations." (G. E. Anscombe, Ed.) Blackwell, Oxford.

Wold, A. H. (1971). Impression formation: A psycholinguistic study. *In* "Social Contexts of Messages". (E. A. Carswell and R. Rommetveit, Eds) Academic Press, London and New York.

7. On Negative Rationalism in Scholarly Studies of Verbal Communication and Dynamic Residuals in the Construction of Human Intersubjectivity*

R. ROMMETVEIT

An enlightened layman who tries to assess what linguists, psycholinguists and sociolinguists have achieved since he left school twenty years ago will very likely—as was the case with Molière's Jourdain—take a novel pride in his own mastery of prose. A joint scholarly explication of his communicative competence in terms of some appropriate collection of general syntactic, semantic and pragmatic rules may indeed be read as a scientifically established passport for entry into a strictly and rationally ordered semiotic universe in which whatever can be *meant* can also be *said* and *understood*. Thus, Searle (1974, p. 20) takes it to be an analytic truth about language that ". . . for any speaker S whenever S means (intends to convey, wishes to communicate in an utterance, etc.) X then it is possible that there is some E such that E is an exact expression of or formulation of X". "What is meant", moreover, may be further explicated in terms of rules that connect *what is said* to "*actions being performed with words*". These are rules of interpretation (and their *inverse*: rules of production). In addition, there are rules of sequencing which connect "actions being performed with words" in everyday discourse. The major task of sociolinguistic discourse analysis is to analyse all such rules and ". . . thus to show that one sentence follows another in a coherent way" (see Labov, 1972, pp. 121–123). In order to hit upon the exact expression of what he intends to convey in any particular context of social interaction, the speaker must hence also have the ability ". . . to select from the totality of grammatically correct expressions . . . forms which appropriately reflect the social norms

* Published in "The Social Contexts of Method" (1978). (M. Brenner, P. Marsh and M. Brenner, Eds) pp. 16–32. Croom Helm, London.

governing behaviour in specific encounters" (Gumperz, 1972, p. 205). His communicative competence must therefore include ". . . knowledge of the different aspects of dialectal and stylistic variation . . ." within the more inclusive speech community of which he is a member (Pride and Holmes, 1972, p. 10). The communicated meanings, however, are according to Habermas identical for all members of such a speech community. And *"pure intersubjectivity"* may hence be attained under conditions of unlimited interchangeability of dialogue roles, i.e. ". . . when there is complete symmetry in the distribution of assertion and disputation, revelation and hiding, prescription and following, among the partners of communication" (Habermas, 1970, p. 143).

However, as our friend the enlightened layman continues his study with the aim of *improving his own capacity to understand and make himself understood*, his initial pride is bound to turn into despair and feelings of alienation. His everyday communication takes place in a pluralistic, multifaceted, only fragmentarily known and only partially shared social world, a word fraught with ideological conflicts, generation gaps, and uneven distribution of power, knowledge and expertise. He may hence often have the feeling that he has hit upon the exact and socially appropriate expression of what he intends to make known, yet fail to make himself understood. And who is to decide on such occasions which expression is "the exact expression" of what is being meant?

I shall in what follows try to argue that our friend the enlightened layman's despair is well founded and that *Habermas' promised land of "pure intersubjectivity" is a convenient fiction which allows scholars of human communication to pursue their trade with scientific rigour, formal elegance, and academic success while evading practically urgent and basic existential issues of human intersubjectivity*. It is certainly true that not only sociolinguists but also "pure" linguists today are far more concerned with what people actually say than was the case twenty years ago. Their theoretical account of what they observe, however, testifies to a confounding of normative linguistics and descriptive social science. The "rules" they reveal are accordingly not easily understood by the enlightened layman: They are in part *by definition* intuitively mastered and hence of no practical value whatsoever in his attempts to improve himself, in part rules by which what is actually said and understood may be gauged against what *should* be said and understood under Utopian conditions of perfect commonality with respect to interpretation and fully shared knowledge of the world. Searle's "principle of expressibility", Labov's notion of production rules as the inverse of rules of interpretation, and Habermas' formulation of prerequisites for "pure intersubjectivity", I shall argue, are thus manifestations of a *"negative rationalism"*. They are *not* axiomatic assumptions capturing basic prerequisites for human intersubjectivity, but normative conditions imposed upon human discourse at variance with the actual conditions under which such discourse takes place.

Acquisition of knowledge entails systematic comparison, and we may often gain knowledge of something initially unknown by examining how it resembles and in which respects it differs from something we assume to be known already. Thus, human thought may be studied and in part made known to us in terms of resemblance to and deviance from the operations of some particular logical calculus. Acquisition of semantic competence within some field, moreover, may be assessed as an approximation to a given, systematically elaborated, scientific framework. These are perfectly legitimate and useful strategies, of immediate diagnostic and evaluative relevance in educational settings aiming precisely and explicitly at mastery of such calculi and scientific frameworks. The resultant knowledge is bound to be of a negative nature, though, in the sense that our initial ignorance is being replaced by knowledge of *shortcomings*. And our interpretation of results is to a large extent contingent upon how we conceive of those formal models against which human performance is being gauged.

I have elsewhere (Rommetveit, 1974, pp. 6–7) questioned the rationale for applying criteria from formal logic in semantic analysis of ordinary language. The calculus of propositions, for instance, was developed for particular purposes and with carefully considered gains and costs: An algorithm for assessing truth values of composite expressions was gained at the cost of the semantic flexibility inherent in everyday discourse. A recourse to criteria from formal propositional logic in analysis of segments of such discourse may hence, of course, serve to reveal those very shortcomings of natural language which motivated the creators of the propositional calculus. We may for instance, as Katz and Fodor (1963, p. 200) have done, claim that a sentence such as "*My spinster aunt is an infant*" is contradictory or even "ungrammatical". What we do then, however, is simply to impose upon an isolated segment of discourse a straightjacket of "propositional content" contrary to the intersubjectivity established premises and presuppositions of the dialogue in which it is embedded.

More subtle forms of negative rationalism are revealed in characteristic sins of omission: What is "meant" by single words is thus often explicated with reference to scholarly taxonomies without any account of the relationship between such taxonomies and lay notions. It is certainly true, for instance, that *butterflies are insects*. Since dictionaries are supposed to contribute to the dissipation of such taxonomic knowledge, it may even be proclaimed part of the "public" meaning of the word BUTTERFLY. This, however, does by no means imply that such knowledge of class membership is entailed in intuitive mastery of the word in everyday discourse. The question of "scientific" versus "lay" anchorage of "public" word meaning has thus been raised by Deese (1962, p. 174) who maintains that ". . . contrary to Zoology, associative BUTTERFLIES are as closely related to the birds as to the moths". This bird-like quality of BUTTERFLY within the "Lebenswelt" of ordinary people, however, is hardly ever considered worthy of serious linguistic enquiries and hence never taken into account in explications of the "public meaning" of the word.

Lay notions at variance with established scientific taxonomies are thus—in dictionaries as well as in theoretical semantic analysis—as a rule relegated from the sphere of "public" and "literal" meaning. They may reappear, though, in attempts to account for "connotative meaning" and "metaphorical use". This is particulary transparent in semantic analysis of kinship when the meaning of words such as UNCLE, BROTHER, etc. are defined in terms of class membership and degree of consanguinity without any reference whatsoever to kinship *roles*.Thus, Chomsky compares the following three expressions:

"John's uncle."

"The person who is the brother of John's mother or father or the husband of the sister of John's mother or father."

"The person who is the son of one of John's grandparents or the husband of a daughter of one of John's grandparents but is not his father."

And he maintains: "If the concept of 'semantic representation' ('reading') is to play any role at all in semantic theory, then these three expressions must have the same semantic representation." (Chomsky, 1972, p. 85.)

I have elsewhere (Rommetveit, 1974, pp. 18–19) explored some rather puzzling implications of such a claim. Of particular interest in the present context, however, is Chomsky's sin of omission: Synonymy salva veritate (and hence: the possibility of "pure intersubjectivity") is achieved by relegating from the "public" meaning of UNCLE those aspects that in ordinary discourse about kinship are subject to modification by evaluative adjectives. "*John's good uncle*", for instance, is thus clearly *not* synonymous with "*the good person who is the brother of John's mother or father or the husband of the sister of John's mother or father*". The particular person referred to by the expression may in fact be a *bad* person whose kinship role relationship to John stands out in marked contrast to his moral in all other interpersonal relations.

Incapacity to cope with relational aspects of kinship is, according to Piaget, characteristic of egocentric thought. The point of departure for some of his enquiries is the "three brothers' problem" from the Binet-Simon test. The child is told about a family consisting of three brothers, and he is requested to place himself at the point of view of one of them so as to count the latter's brothers. Lack of mastery of BROTHER as a relation is then revealed in conclusions such as: "*I have three brothers, Paul, Ernest and myself*". What happens, according to Piaget (1951, p. 88), is thus that ". . . judgments of relations are constantly transformed into judgments of inherence (inclusion or membership)".

This, however, is also precisely what—for entirely different reasons—happens to UNCLE *as a relation* in Chomsky's explication of the meaning of that word and to BROTHER (UNCLE, FATHER, etc.) *as a relation* in conventional dictionary accounts. Let us therefore examine somewhat more closely the relationship between the dictionary meaning we take for granted when we count heads of relatives *and* kinship as a role relation. Consider, for instance, a family consisting of the four brothers Paul, Ernest, Jean and Noam. The BROTHER relations involved are in that case the set of all 12 possible ordered pairs (1) Paul, Ernest; (2) Ernest, Paul; (3) Paul, Jean; (4) Jean, Paul; etc. Each such ordered pair represents one discrete and autonomous BROTHER *relation* in the sense that, e.g. Paul may be a good brother to Ernest even though Ernest is a bad brother to Paul. And such a complete enumeration of relations is of course as "objective" and "referential"—and no more "connotative"—than the counting of heads. The number of BROTHER relations in the family described above is thus increased by four the moment a sister is born.

Such specific relations, moreover, constitute the very matrix of social interaction out of which the child's initial mastery of kinship words develop. As his semantic competence expands so as to encompass knowledge of descent and marital institutions, it may even come to entail semantic potentialities such as Chomsky's "readings" of the word UNCLE. Such "readings" may in fact prove essential in order to establish intersubjectivity when he, being asked *who* are his uncles, engage in a counting of heads. Potentialities mirroring purely relational aspects of kinship, however, may be essential in other contexts. Suppose, for instance, that Jean's relationship to his brother Noam is devoid of that shared dependency upon adult providers, that attitude of solidarity, etc. that may be said to constitute distinctive features of BROTHER as a relation. Noam, moreover, being greatly distressed by such a deplorable state of affairs, may want to make that known to his best friend. And he may in fact succeed in doing so by saying: "Jean and I have the same parents, but he has never been a brother to me".

The use of BROTHER in such a context is according to Chomsky and Searle an illustration of "metaphorical", "parasitic" use. The claim that such use is "parasitic", however, seems in part to be founded on the assumption that a logic of relations is contingent upon class logic. This implies, in the present case, that you have to be able to count the heads of your brothers in order to assess some characteristic quality of their relations to you. The lexigrapher may hence feel justified in his general practice of treating such brotherly qualities as mediated by a connotative fringe contingent upon a "literal" core. He may, in addition, refer to his own role as an educator of the general public: His commitment to a technologically oriented society is such that he should not confuse people who consult him by exposing them to fragments of "soft" social sciences in cases when relevant wisdom from more established academic fields is at his disposal. Role relationships are thus—unlike the biological mechanisms of procreation—subject to cultural variation and social change. Whatever is implied by, e.g. UNCLE and BROTHER as *relations* is hence necessarily *negotiable*. And any armchair inference from *what is said* to *what is meant* and vice versa (and hence also: Searle's "principle of expressibility") is of course jeopardized if a word such as UNCLE (BROTHER, MOTHER, etc.) is allowed to convey class membership and/or some only partially defined and negotiable role relation. The aims of the lexicographer as an educator and the scholar engaged in construction of formally elegant semantic theory are thus different, but convergent. The "public" meanings proposed by the lexicographer are accordingly stripped of residual fringes of lay notions and, with minor modifications, endorsed by the theoretical semanticist—while lip service is being paid to the native speaker-hearer. Possible complaints, moreover, are easily overruled by powerful and compelling scholarly arguments. It is an essential part of the duties of theoretical semanticists and lexicographers to establish *order*, and order is impossible without *internal consistency*. Composite word meanings must hence be explicated in the form of *conjunctions of semantic markers*, not as *veljunctions of only partially determined semantic potentialities*.

The stories about Chomsky's UNCLE and the lexicographer's BROTHER may accordingly be supplemented with similar case studies of INFANT, MAN, DEMOCRACY, SELL, BUY, KILL, DIE, POOR, SHORT, HEAVY, etc. (see Rommetveit, 1974 and 1977). What invariably happens to such words when trapped in scholarly nets of negative rationalism is that very significant—though often negotiable—semantic potentialities get lost. These are potentialities mirroring options with respect categorization and attribution and hence polysemies and genuine ambiguities of discourse in and about a multifaceted, pluralistic, only fragmentarily known and only partially shared "Lebenswelt". And this has to be so because utterances have meanings only in the stream of life and because our mastery of words borders on our imperfect knowledge of the world and only partially explicable ontological assumptions (Wittgenstein, 1962, p. 739). Polysemy due to the manifold of possible social realities and human perspectives can thus never be eliminated by recourse to prestigious, but monistic "conceptual realities" nor by lexicographical legislation. We may of course attempt to disambiguate a word such as

HUMAN by anchoring its interpretation in Zoological taxonomy, and we may even decide to make that interpretation "a semantic marker", i.e. an Archimedian point in our assessment of the "public" meanings of a set of other words. This may indeed seem plausible ". . . after three hundred years of science and criticism of religion . . ." (Habermas, 1970, p. 137). However, it will not prevent religious people engaged in conversations or preaching from exploiting other "lay" (or "theological") potentialities of the word such as those revealed in contrasts like HUMAN/DIVINE, HUMAN/SAINTLY, etc. Archimedian points in assessment of human meaning are hence necessarily provisional and contingent upon some "world view", never entirely neutral with respect to competing ontologies. *And even a Zoologically founded interpretation of* HUMAN *is bound to contain some residual ambiguity.* This may indeed in principle be revealed in lack of referential consensus if we on some planet should happen to encounter entirely novel forms of living beings. Suppose, for instance, that some of them grow like plants. They are in possession of a sign system similar to our languages, however, are clearly extremely intelligent according to earthly criteria, and are also engaged in a variety of creative and communicative activities. Some astronauts may hence maintain that they are human, others may argue that they are not. And how could we, on the basis of *a taxonomy constrained by our earthly experiences* of variants of life, resolve that dispute?

The moral of this excursion into metaphysics and science fiction is very simple: The semantic system inherent in our everyday language is *orderly* and *borders on our knowledge of the world*, yet *ambiguous* and *open*. The order exists in the form of *constraints upon semantic potentialities*, however, and *not* in unequivocal "literal" meanings. Such meanings exist only in dictionaries but are nevertheless, as Wright (1977, p. 56) has observed, a convenient fiction in the British philosophy of ordinary language in the 1950s. This is also Goffman's conclusion. He maintains:

> "Literal" . . . is a wonderfully confusing notion, something that should constitute a topic in linguistic study, not a conceptual tool to use in making studies. Sometimes the dictionary meaning of one or more words of the utterance is meant, although how *that* meaning is arrived at is left an open question. And the underlying, commonsense notion is preserved that the word *in isolation* will have a general, basic, or most down-to-earth meaning, that this meaning is sustained in how the word is commonly used in phrases and clauses, but that in many cases words are used 'metaphorically' to convey something they don't really mean. (Goffman, 1976, p. 303.)

The practice of reading unequivocal *"literal" meanings* into *semantic potentialities*, however, paves the way for the assignment of *"propositional content"* to sentences whose *message potentials* are legio, though constrained by the combinatorial possibilities of semantic potentialities inherent in the words of which they are composed. "John's uncle" is thus doomed the moment Chomsky starts assigning a "reading" to the expression: His kinship *role* is sacrificed with lip service to *John's* intuition, but for *Chomsky's* purpose of securing unequivocal readings of sentences in subsequent analysis of texts containing such kinship words. Issues such as *genuine vagueness and ambiguity, negotiability of meaning,* and *social control of criteria for proper interpretation* are hence evaded. What is meant by what is said is assumed *not* to be subject to negotiation, but fully determined by linguistic *rules.* And this practice of reading *unequivocal "literal" meaning* into mere *semantic potentialities* and assigning *propositional content* to only partially determined *message potentials* seems to pervade semantic analysis by transformational linguists like a hereditary sin, in spite of recent concern with presuppositions and other signs of a pragmatic counter-revolution against Chomsky's Cartezian rationalism (see Rommetveit, 1974, pp. 79–101).

The notion of linguistic competence we encounter in generative-transformational theories of language may be conceived of as a heavenly version of our mastery of a common code, a version devoid of dialectal variations, stripped of ambiguities, and dyed in pure reason. Chomsky's postulation of unequivocal literal meanings and evasion of the issue of negotiable residuals may hence be defended by reference to some of his own Cartezian, explicitly stated, metatheoretical assumptions: His ideal speaker-hearer's communication is *a monologue in disguise* because it is assumed to take place in a society characterized by *perfect commonality with respect to interpretation.* Sociolinguistics, on the other hand, is by definition a study of human discourse under conditions of linguistic and cultural variation, and for that reason, one should expect, precisely of *negotiable residuals in human communication.* It is very strange, therefore, to witness how its theoretical foundation nevertheless is being infiltrated by assumptions about unequivocal literal meanings very similar to those of the transformational-generative semanticists. A Trojan horse in this enterprise seems to be Searle's theory of speech acts and let us therefore return to his basic "principle of expressibility" (see p. 147).

Some of the consequences of this principle are explicated as follows:

> . . . the principle that *whatever can be meant can be said* does not imply that whatever can be said can be understood by others; for that would exclude the possibility of a private language, a language that it was impossible for anyone but the speaker to understand. . . . It has the consequence that cases where the speaker does not say exactly what he means—the principal cases of which are *nonliteralness, vagueness, ambiguity, and incompleteness*—are not theoretically essential to linguistic communication. But most important . . . it enables us to equate rules for performing speech acts with rules for uttering linguistic elements,

since for any possible speech act there is a possible linguistic element the meaning of which (given the context of the utterance) is sufficient to determine that *its literal utterance* is a performance of precisely that speech act (Searle, 1974, pp. 20–21). (My italics.)

Notice, first of all, that the principle as such says nothing about *the hearer*. His interpretation of what is said is assumed to be identical to that of the speaker, however, provided that the latter ". . . is *speaking literally* and that the context is appropriate" (Searle, 1974, p. 18; my italics). Sociolinguistic rules of discourse are accordingly based upon the assumption that rules of interpretation are the inverse of rules of production and ". . . connect what is said to the actions performed with words . . ." (Labov, 1972, p. 121, 123). They are not only supposed to reveal how *what is meant* is converted into *exact expressions* and vice versa, but also to account for what happens when tacit though contextually appropriate and *shared propositional knowledge* merge with literal speech. Thus, Labov maintains:

> *If A makes a request for information Q-S_1, and B makes a statement S_2 in response, that cannot be expanded by rules of ellipsis to the form XS_1Y, then S_2 is heard as an assertion that there exists a proposition P known to both A and B:*
> If S_2, then (E) S_1,
> *where (E) is an existential operator, and from this proposition there is inferred an answer to A's request: $(E)S_1$.*
> This is a rule of interpretation that relates what is said (S_2) to what is done (the assertion of P and the answer to Q-S_1). Note that there is no direct connection between the two utterances Q-S_1 and S_2, and it would be fruitless to search for one (1972, p. 1221).

The rule is then applied in an analysis of the following fragment of a dialogue:

A: Are you going to work tomorrow? (Q-S_1)
B: I am on jury duty. (S_2).

The tacit proposition P assumed to be known to both A and B is in this case that *B cannot go to work the next day if he is going to be on jury duty then*. This appears to be a valid inference since we may safely assume that knowledge about work and jury duties constitutes part of A's and B's shared social reality. B's response entails therefore a "no" to A's question even though no direct semantic connection can be established between Q-S_1 and S_2. Labov can thus by his rule apparently reveal what is meant by what is said solely on the basis of *literal meaning* and *shared propositional knowledge of the world*.

Suppose, however, that A's question is being addressed to B as they are bumping into each other outside the courthouse, and that B responds while hurrying away from B and toward the entrance. Or let us imagine that A and B are friends engaged in an informal conversation.

The latter may then take a variety of different courses, for instance:

(I)   A: *Are you going to work tomorrow?*
      B: *I'm on jury duty.*
      A: Couldn't you get out of it?
      B: We tried everything.
      A: Well, it's a pity you are not free. I hoped we could go fishing together.

(II) A: *Are you going to work tomorrow?*
      B: *I'm on jury duty.*
      A: Lucky you! I wish I too had some legitimate excuse to evade the issue of tomorrow's strike.

(III) A: *Are you going to work tomorrow?*
      B: *I'm on jury duty.*
      A: But the doctor has allowed you to start working again, then?

(IV) A: *Are you going to work tomorrow?*
      B: *I'm on jury duty.*
      A: But you'll be driving to the city then, won't you?
      B: Yes.
      A: Fine. I have some errands there, and I had sort of relied on you for transportation.

(V)   B: You look terrible. For how long do you think you can continue like this without consulting a psychiatrist?
      A: *Are you going to work tomorrow?*
      B: *I'm on jury duty.* Why do you ask, by the way? Why do you always switch to some other silly topic whenever I try to talk some reason into you?

These are all possible—and even plausible—expansions of that very fragment of a dialogue Labov himself has chosen in order to show what can be achieved when his formally very impressive rule is applied in analysis of real-life discourse. I have refrained from potential esoteric and "metaphorical" interpretations of expressions such as, for instance, that of "jury duty" when it is used by teachers as a label for that *part of their work* that consists in oral examinations. What I have done is simply to insert Labov's pair of consecutive utterances into different social encounters and then, *within* the general friendly-conversation-frame, to imagine alternative intersubjectively established HERE-and-NOWS. We may thus explore whether his inference from what is said to "the actions performed with words" is valid across our range of contexts. Labov claims, we remember, that B's response "*I'm on jury duty*" entails a "*no*" to A's question "*Are you going to work tomorrow*" because both of them know that a person on jury duty is relieved of his daily occupational obligations.

The outcome of our enquiries, however, is very depressing as far as the validity of such a claim is concerned. The only case in which it seems entirely plausible is in fact case V, i.e. when A's question appears to be an evasive manoeuvre of "empty talk". And this, I shall argue, is a sad but by no means incidental outcome of our validation study. Case V is namely also the only case in which A's question can be treated as an *"exact expression"* of *a proposition in the interrogative mode*, i.e. as fully determined and (according to Searle's criteria) *"complete"* in the sense that it can be unequivocally answered in terms of *"yes"* or *"no"*. Propositions are namely *by definition* immune against semantic infiltration from "streams of life", and utterances approach the status of propositions (and grow assymptotically empty) the more they are detached from patterns of meaningful human action and interaction. The *"no"* which Labov claims is entailed in B's response is thus a perfectly satisfactory answer in case V because whether B is going to work the next day is a topic of no relevance whatsoever to, e.g. A's recreation plans, his concern with B's health, or any other issue of significance to him.

Let us now return to the cases in which Labov's claim appears to be false or misplaced and keep in mind that *neither of Labov's explicitly stated premises is altered when we do so*. The proposition P (that jury duty implies absence from work) is part of the *sustained* shared social reality of A and B, and the very same pair of consecutive utterances reappears in every case. Why, then, is Labov's conclusion plausible in case V, while absurd in the outside-the-courthouse case and—at best—very questionable in the remaining four cases? Is his rule simply false, or is it correct *in principle* but incomplete with respect to specification of significant dynamic aspects of the dialogue that cannot be captured *either by what "literally" is said or by what is said in conjunction with shared propositional knowledge*? And, if so, what are these residual dynamic aspects?

What happens outside the courthouse seems fairly simple. The very location of the encounter *and* B's hurried locomotion become significant features of an immediately shared HERE-and-NOW in which B's response to A is embedded *as soon as it is uttered and understood*. What is *made known* is thus the simple truth that B is on jury duty *today*, and this also explains why he has no time to engage in a conversation with A. This, I shall argue, is very likely how B's reply is meant and "heard". We have therefore no reason to believe that what both of them know about jury duty and legitimate absence from work (Labov's proposition P) enters their *temporarily shared social reality* at all.

Common to cases I, II, III and IV is that A on every occasion has some particular *reason* for engaging in the dialogue. His introductory question, moreover, is the first move in a game, the rules of which are at that stage yet not fully revealed to B. What he says is accordingly an incomplete expression of what he means. This, however, will in principle always be the case unless *what actually is said* is fully transparent with respect to the underlying WHY of communication (see Ducrot, 1972).

The reason why A asks B whether he is going to work tomorrow is in case I that he wants B's company when going fishing. The alternative prospects entailed in his question are thus whether B will be *tied up (with work)* or *free to engage in recreational activities.* An appropriate "proposition P" can thus in view of these prospects hardly be Labov's P. *The incompatibility between jury duty and recreational activity,* however, may also be said to constitute part of A's and B's sustained shared world knowledge. And this fragment seems also to be made part of *the immediately shared* HERE-*and*-NOW *of their dialogue* as A reveals more of what he meant with his introductory question. Case II, on the other hand, seems at first glance to corroborate Labov's conclusion. What A initially sets out to find out, however, is whether B will *go to work* or *join those who plan to go on strike.* B's response brings into the temporarily shared social reality of possible prospects a third alternative, one that has not been foreseen by A. It entails therefore no unequivocal answer at all to A's question *as it was meant the moment A uttered it.* The same may be said about B's response in case III. The issue presupposed in A's initial question in case IV, finally, is whether B will *go to work tomorrow and hence be able to provide transportation to the city* or *stay at home.* What "actions" A and B perform with words in that situation, moreover, are clearly contingent upon which issues and prospects are proposed and/or presupposed by them in an only partially shared HERE-and-NOW. Labov's conclusion is thus also in this case highly questionable. There is no compelling reason at all why shared propositional knowledge about jury duty and absence from work should enter A's and B's *temporarily shared, dialogically relevant, social reality,* and B's response can hardly be said to entail a "no" to A's intended, though incompletely expressed, question.

Labov maintains (1972, p. 121) that ". . . formalization is a fruitful procedure even when it is wrong . . .". This is true, and his own formalization of rules of discourse may indeed serve to illuminate what is basically wrong with the foundation of current sociolinguistic theory. The assumption that *one can infer what actions are being performed with words on the basis of what is said* is thus, in view of the general outcome of our "validation" study, obviously *false.* Such an assumption may prove valid in accounts of meta-communicative frames, for instance in Labov's account of how members of a youth subculture in Harlem distinguish between personal and ritual insult (Labov, 1972, p. 157). What happens when it is converted into an axiom in general discourse analysis, however, is that sociolinguists need not any longer concern themselves with the very complex issue of *what is made known when something is said and understood*. Which particular fragments of shared world knowledge enter a dialogue may then be inferred from *what is said* without enquiring into *which issues and prospects are taken for granted by the speaker only, the listener only, and both of them at the moment it is said*. Lack of consensus with respect to such prospects as well as with respect to only partially determined semantic potentialities of words is simply pro-hibited because production is assumed to be the mirror image of interpretation. What is meant in a verbal exchange such as *"Are you going to work tomorrow?—I'm on jury duty"* is accordingly supposed to remain the same across variant dialogically established HERE-and-NOWS. Searle's notion of *"what is meant"* in speech acts is thus in current sociolinguistic theory elaborated into a hybrid of Utopian literal meanings and vaguely described *"actions being performed with words"*. The resultant picture is bound to be a masterpiece of negative rationalism, replete with shared world knowledge and literal meanings, but devoid of essential dynamic aspects of human communication. And the dynamics involved in the construction of human intersubjectivity can hardly be captured by adding a few auxiliary rules to a conceptual framework based on erroneous assumptions. Let me therefore, very briefly, suggest some features of an alternative approach.

The futility of postulating "literal meanings" and fully determined propositional content follows from the fact that ordinary language is semantically open and embedded in "the stream of life". We cannot, therefore, attain closure in our theoretical account of verbal com-munication without prejudging a multifaceted, only partially known and opaque reality. What in *normative linguistics* has been labelled a semantic rule may hence from *a sociolinguistic point of view* more appro-priately be conceived of as a linguistically mediated draft of a contract concerning categorization or attribution. The entire set of basic semantic potentialities inherent in ordinary language may be thought of as constituting a common code of such drafts, i.e. of potentially shared strategies of categorization and cognitive-emotive perspectives on what is being talked about. Institutionally, ritually and situationally provided frames for social interaction, moreover, may determine which more restricted subsets of semantic potentialities are intended within different kinds of contexts. A word such as DEMOCRACY may thus be "heard" in very different ways, depending upon whether it is en-countered in a demagogical political speech or in an academic lecture by a political scientist. And what is *made known* by what is said is always in part contingent upon what at that moment is *tacitly taken for granted*.

Transcendence of the "private" worlds of the participants in acts of communication, i.e. states of partial intersubjectivity, presupposes *capacity for decentered categorization and attribution, reciprocal roletaking* and *complementarity of intentions.* Reciprocity and complementarity may indeed be conceived of as generative "pragmatic postulates" in the construction of intersubjectivity. I have, for instance, to *assume that my partner in the dialogue is trying to answer my question in order to make sense of his response to it.* This is also the case when his response sounds odd. My faith in him, however, will make me search for some *by him* potentially taken-for-granted aspect of our only partially shared HERE-and-NOW *which may confirm my faith.* If I succeed, our shared HERE-and-NOW is immediately expanded, and we have an instance of "prolepsis" (Rommetveit, 1974, p. 87). Additional shared presuppositions may then also immediately provide an answer to my question, but this is not necessarily so; and probably very seldom in authoritarian school situations. The participant making the request for information, moreover, is as a rule by firmly established tacit and mutual understanding in control of the criteria by which the odd response is judged to entail an answer or not. *What was meant by his question cannot be decided by the respondent if the two of them happen to disagree.* Assymetry with respect to power and expertise, however, may also override such a rule, and so may a symbiotic relationship between a small child and an adult (Bateson, 1973, p. 185). What is meant with a question from an ignorant pupil may be decided by his teacher, and what kind of information is sought by a small child may under conditions of pathological mother-child relationships rather arbitrarily be decided by the mother. The first case is an instance of a *quasi-dialogue,* the latter very likely part of a pattern leading to *autism.*

The plausible essence of Labov's rule relating some odd response S_2 to a preceding question $Q-S_1$ (see p. 155) may hence be converted into a generative "pragmatic" postulate and embedded in our alternative, more dynamic approach. And so may even Searle's entire *"principle of expressibility"* (see p. 154). The anticipation that persons *will* understand is according to Garfinkel (1972, p. 6) a sanctional property of common discourse, and Schuetz (1945, p. 534) maintains that ". . . the world is from the outset . . . an intersubjective world, common to all of us . . ." Mutual understanding is based upon mutual faith in a shared social world, and the anticipation that others will understand us may be enhanced and in some sense corroborated because we qua *speakers* are in control of the intersubjectively shared HERE-and-NOW. Rules of control constitute part of the basic complementarity of intentions *and control is unequivocally linked to direction of communication*: It is the speaker who (*unless he is responding to a question*) has the privilege of deciding which entities within a sustained shared social reality are going to enter the *temporarily* shared HERE-and-NOW of the dialogue. Searle's assumption that everything that can be meant can also be said may thus be an analytic *fallacy* about ordinary language. That fallacy, however, can be converted into a true, even though semiparadoxical generative "pragmatic" postulate: We must, naïvely and unreflectively, take *the possibility of perfect intersubjectivity* for granted in order to achieve *partial intersubjectivity* in real life discourse with our fellow men.

References

Bateson, G. (1973). "Steps to an Ecology of Mind." Palladin, Suffolk.

Chomsky, N. (1972). "Studies on Semantics in Generative Grammar." Mouton, The Hague.

Deese, J. (1962). The structure of associative meaning. *Psychological Review* **69**, 161–175.

Ducrot, O. (1972). "Dire et ne pas dire. Principes de Semantique Linguistique." Hermann, Paris.

Garfinkel, H. (1972). Studies of the routine grounds of everyday activities. *In* "Studies in Social Interaction." (D. Sudnow, Ed.) The Free Press, New York.

Goffman, E. (1976). Replies and responses. *Language in Society* **5**, 257–313.

Gumperz, J. J. (1972). Sociolinguistics and communication in small groups. *In* "Sociolinguistics." (J. B. Pride and J. Holmes, Eds) Penguin Books, Harmondsworth.

Habermas, J. (1970). Toward a theory of communicative competence. *In* "Recent Sociology". (P. E. Dreitzel, Ed) No. 2. MacMillan, London.

Katz, J. J. and Fodor, J. A. (1963). The structure of a semantic theory. *Language* **39**, 170–210.

Labov, W. (1972). Rules for ritual insults. *In* "Studies in Social Interaction". (D. Sudnow, Ed.) The Free Press, New York.

Piaget, J. (1951). "Judgment and Reasoning in the Child." Routledge and Kegan Paul, London.

Pride, J. B. and Holmes, J. (Eds) (1972). Introduction. *In* "Sociolinguistics". Penguin Books, Harmondsworth.

Rommetveit, R. (1974). "On Message Structure." John Wiley and Sons, London.

Rommetveit, R. (1977). On Piagetian operations, semantic competence, and message structure in adult–child communication. *In* "The Social Context of Language". (I. Markova, Ed.) John Wiley and Sons, Chichester.

Schuetz, A. (1945). On multiple realities *Philosophical and Phenomenological Research* **5**, 533–576.

Searle, J. (1974). "On Speech Acts." Cambridge University Press, Cambridge.

Wright, E. L. (1977). Words and intentions. *Philosophy* **52**, 45–62.

Wittgenstein, L. (1962). The blue book. *In* "Philosophy in the Twentieth Century". (W. Barrett and H. D. Aiken, Eds) Vol. 2. Random House, New York.

8. On Common Codes and Dynamic Residuals in Human Communication*

R. ROMMETVEIT

The notion of linguistic competence we encounter in early generative-transformational theories of language may be conceived of as a heavenly version of a basic common code, a version devoid of dialectical variations, stripped of ambiguities, and dyed in pure Cartezion reason. Sociolinguistics, on the other hand, is by definition a study of human discourse under conditions of social, cultural and linguistic variation. Bernstein's notion of restricted and elaborated codes is thus apparently fully consonant with Wittgenstein's claim that *an utterance has meaning only in the stream of life* (see Malcolm, 1967, p. 93). As Hasan (1973, p. 263) puts it: "Members of different types of societies use different codes; ultimately, the codes differ linguistically in some particular respects only because they reflect the two modes of the living of life".

Bernstein claims, moreover, that the semantic properties of the codes can be predicted from the elements of the social structure which gives rise to them. A restricted code emerges under conditions of *mechanical solidarity*, where the culture or subculture raises the "we" above the "I", where a lot is taken for granted and ambiguity is generally not anticipated. And language controlled by the restricted code is characterized by a predominance of exophoric references. An elaborated code, on the other hand, reflects a social structure integrated by *organic solidarity*, a manner of living in which not much can be taken for granted, and an attitude which is basically analytic. And whereas everybody has access to the restricted code, the elaborated code may become the prerogative of one social class only through the latter's forms of socialization and access to education (see Bernstein, 1967, 1969, 1971; Hasan, 1973).

These notions of codes, however, have in common with many other potentially fruitful social scientific notions a considerable amount of

* Paper presented at the Bernstein Seminar in Oslo, September, 1977.

ambiguity. The purpose of the present paper is to explore that ambiguity and try to relate Bernstein's conceptual framework to some alternative, though possibly supplementary, notions. Let me hence briefly return to Wittgenstein's reflections concerning the embeddedness of language in streams of life and the very intriguing issue of dynamic residuals in human communication.

The general problem of residuals may be formulated as a question about "*the bottom level of interpretation*", i.e. about that base of tacit and *uninterpreted* premises on which our ultimate and explicitly formulated premises for interpretation rest (see Wittgenstein, 1962, p. 247). There is, in principle, no natural end to our explication of linguistically mediated meaning: Whatever is meant and understood has as its prerequisite that something else (by both participants in the act of communication) is taken for granted. A prerequisite for linguistically achieved intersubjectivity is thus a tacitly assumed commonality with respect to interpretation, an "Interpretationsgemeinschaft" (Apel, 1965). This is persistently argued by ethnomethodologists. Thus, Garfinkel maintains (1972, p. 28) that ". . . no matter how specific the terms of common understanding may be—a contract may be considered the prototype—they attain the status of an agreement for persons only in so far as the stipulated conditions carry along an unspoken but understood *et cetera* clause". And Cicourel (1970, p. 34) lists as one of the basic features of social interaction: ". . . an *et cetera* rule and its subroutines . . . permitting temporary, suspended, or 'concrete' linkages with short-term or long-term store of socially distributed knowledge".

Even the most highly elaborated code is thus—if Wittgenstein and the ethnomethodologists are right—contingent upon some residual, tacitly taken for granted commonality with respect to interpretation. And the difference between Bernstein's restricted and elaborated codes may accordingly be described in terms of, e.g. length of chain of reflective explication from surface to bottom level or, more generally, in terms of different modes of coping with residual *et ceteras* in acts of verbal communication.

I have elsewhere (Rommetveit, 1974), in an attempt at explicating some basic prerequisites for human intersubjectivity, tried to explore what, more specifically, may be involved in such residual *et ceteras*. I have tried to show how *message potentials* of particular expressions may in part be explored in terms of *meaning potentials* of constituent words, and how any given such meaning potential can be assessed as a set of *semantic potentialities*. Each such basic semantic potentiality, moreover, may be conceived of as a general *draft of a contract concerning categorization*, ordinarily bound to some more comprehensive scheme of attribution. Our mastery of words such as EASY, EAGER and CAN in particular expressions, for instance, is thus contingent upon attribution of "personal causality" (see Heider, 1958; Rommetveit, 1974, pp. 113–117). And we may claim, more generally, that such general schemes of categorization and attribution constitute *a minimal constant residual of sustained shared world knowledge*, i.e. an axiomatic foundation of shared human experience upon which our semantic competence is built.

Linguistically mediated drafts of contracts concerning categorization, however, are by definition such that they allow for optional elaborations. What is conveyed by a word such as POOR, for instance, may be different things depending upon whether artistic skill or financial issues constitute the topic of discourse. What is intended and understood by POOR in a discourse about financial issues, moreover, may be unequivocally determined as the opposite of WEALTHY, yet in a conversation about the third world specified as *living conditions below the subsistence level* and in a chat about neighbours in our welfare society as *dependency upon public financial support*. Full mastery of the *poverty-wealth* potentiality of POOR is thus revealed in contextually appropriate, though frequently negotiable, optional elaborations—and hence contingent upon a general capacity to adopt the perspective of different "others" across a range of variant social situations.

The entire set of basic semantic potentialities inherent in ordinary language may thus be thought of, *not* as static components of a linguistically mediated shared knowledge of the world, but as constituting a common code of drafts of contracts, i.e. of potentially shared strategies of categorization and cognitive-emotive perspectives on what is being talked about. And only particular fragments of sustained shared world knowledge enter the HERE-and-NOW of any given dialogue. What is attended to and what is tacitly taken for granted in any particular case of social interaction are dependent upon variant background expectancies, and which aspects of a multifaceted social situation are focused upon are in part determined by the explicitly given or tacitly assumed referential domain of discourse *and* the actor's engagement and perspective. Institutionally, ritually and situationally provided frames for social interaction, moreover, will determine which more restricted subsets of semantic potentialities are intended within different kinds of contexts. And some of the optional elaborations are, as already mentioned, *negotiable*. Which one of a set of alternative interpretations is valid may thus at times be a matter of control of the dialogically established HERE-and-NOW (see Rommetveit, 1978).

Human discourse thus takes place in a pluralistic and multifaceted social world. There is, as Schuetz (1951, p. 168) has put it, ". . . a selection of things and aspects of things relevant to me at any given moment whereas other things and other aspects are for the time being of no concern to me or even out of view". How different explicitly introduced referential domains affect linguistic encoding and decoding has been cogently demonstrated in psycholinguistic experiments by Olson (1970), Deutsch (1976) and Rommetveit (1977). Which of a set of possible verbal expressions will be used to refer to any particular object material is determined by *the range of other objects from which the referent must be set apart*. And there is no reason to believe that such referential domains are of less significance when they are tacitly taken for granted, as part of a dialogically established shared HERE-and-NOW.

An encounter between a restricted and an elaborated code may in view of these considerations accordingly in part be described as *a mismatch of presuppositions*: The representative of the restricted code talks about some object or aspect of objects against the tacitly assumed background of a narrow and presumedly familiar referential domain, and from a perspective determined by the immediate instrumental relevance of that object (or aspect of objects) in his life situation. The relative absence of parameters of differentiation (and low frequency of modifiers and qualifiers, see Hasan, 1973, p. 264) is simply due to an *et cetera* of erroneously assumed commonality with respect to scope of referential domain and perspectives on whatever is being talked about. It is erroneously assumed, however, only to the extent that the representative of the elaborated code interprets what is said against the background of a different, more inclusive tacitly taken for granted referential domain and adopts a perspective characterized by "objective" classification, detached from the speaker's engagement in the situation. Lack of intersubjectivity is thus due to failure to adopt the role of the other, i.e. to the "restricted" speaker's failure to engage in the kind of decentered categorization and attribution characteristic of the listener's approach and to the "elaborated" listener's incapacity to share the engagement and more restricted perspective of the speaker.

It is to expect, therefore, that a restricted code is appropriate in a social matrix characterized by "mechanical" solidarity, veridically assumed commonality with respect to perspectives and interests, and intimacy. I have elsewhere argued that Searle's "principle of expressibility" should be conceived of as a basic pragmatic postulate of verbal communication (see Rommetveit, 1978). Searle takes it to be an analytic truth about language that *everything that can be meant can also be said*. This may certainly be questioned. The dynamics of the residual *et cetera* in acts of verbal communication, however, seems to involve a component of self-fulfilling prophecy in the sense that intersubjectivity must in some sense unreflectively be taken for granted in order to be achieved. This implies a basic trust in *shared* residuals of human existential conditions. What happens when there is no such trust is revealed in severe cases of communication breakdown, in autism and schizophrenia. What happens when such trust is met with an attitude of alienation and lack of reciprocity is perhaps most cogently revealed precisely in an encounter between a restricted and an inflexible elaborated code.

Erroneously assumed shared presuppositions may on the other hand, under conditions of reciprocal trust, also be conducive to intimacy and even lead to an expansion of the dialogically established HERE-and-NOW. Such a process of *prolepsis* has been demonstrated experimentally (see Blakar and Rommetveit, 1975), and it is often encountered in fiction when the reader feels (correctly) that he has comprehended something in addition to what he actually has read. What from a strictly "objective" or "public" point of view appears as unwarranted presuppositions on the part of the creative writer may then more appropriately be conceived of as self-fulfilling assumptions by which the reader is made an insider of a tacitly expanded and enriched HERE-and-NOW. He is made an insider—not merely *informed* about it—precisely because that expanded social reality is taken for granted rather than explicitly spelled out. A restricted code may hence, via prolepsis, serve to sustain and perpetuate that particular solidarity of social life out of which it is supposed to emerge.

We may accordingly try to break down Bernstein's dichotomy of a restricted versus an elaborated code into a set of different, though intimately related, components. Linguistic meaning—and even some important sets of basic semantic potentialities inherent in ordinary language—border on a "meaning of life" which to a considerable extent is determined by basic material conditions. Different ecological, economic and social living conditions thus make for significant differences with respect to perspectives and engagement. What is meant by a word such as LABOUR, for instance, must in the mouth of an unskilled worker necessarily carry with it a tacit residual flavoured by his real life experiences of, e.g. toil, wages, strikes and unemployment. This does not imply that he is in principle incapable of mastering particular lexical elaborations such as for instance ergometric or scientifically formulated economic definitions of the word. Such elaborations, however, are hardly of any practical significance to him. What he has been taught about work and finances in social studies at school, moreover, has hardly been tagged onto his early life experience as authentic knowledge. His school experience has namely according to Bernstein most likely taken the form of a "quasi-dialogue", i.e. a discourse controlled by an elaborated code in which criteria for comprehension and intersubjectivity are unilaterally dictated by representatives of a middle class outlook on life. His linguistically mediated categorizations within the entire semantic field of work and economy will therefore—given the class differences in our societies and the semantic openness and polysemies of our ordinary language—border on an experiential residual very different from that of a typical middle class person.

These are the kinds of residuals that Schuetz has dealt with in his analysis of multiple realities (Schuetz, 1945), and they may possibly be conceived of as *basic ideological components of codes*. Such differences with respect to perspective and "world view", however, is hardly revealed linguistically in frequency of exophoric reference and qualifiers. They are neither due to different scope and cognitive organizations of tacitly presupposed referential domains nor merely to immediate versus long-chained connections between what is said and what is taken for granted. We have rather to do with *multiple social realities*, i.e. with different and possibly even conflicting outlooks on a pluralistic, only fragmentarily known, and only partially shared social world. The particular version determined by one's material conditions and social background, moreover, is to the growing individual simply *the* reality, as unreflectively taken for granted as the water by the fish. It is—unless the person is uprooted from his subculture—continually socially confirmed in his transactions with significant others and (Schuetz, 1945, p. 534): ". . . from the outset not the private world of an individual, but an intersubjective world . . . in which we have not a theoretical but an eminently practical interest".

Such different, though intersubjectively taken for granted social realities, I shall argue, constitute at the same time a bottom component in the child's growing mastery of the language and a base for acquisition of further authentic knowledge of the world. They should hence be of focal interest in Bernstein's analysis of the intriguing relationships between class structure and linguistic codes. It is by no means clear, however, whether his implicitly adapted *general* semantic theory is such that it allows him to cope explicitly and systematically with such subtle ideological components. They are apparently *not* taken into account in his notion of "ground rules" (Bernstein, 1977, p. 254). And one may wonder whether he actually—despite his rejection of Chomsky's ideal speaker-listener—considers the semantic components of the two codes as bordering on the same "objective" and ideologically "neutral" knowledge of the world. Different life perspectives and the possible impact of such perspectives on negotiable semantic potentialities are evaded rather than explicitly dealt with in his discussion of cognitive aspects of codes.

We are thus repeatedly told that the two types of code differ with respect to *how much* is tacitly taken for granted in acts of verbal communication, and this is presumedly revealed in fairly easily measurable linguistic indices such as relative frequency of exophoric reference and qualifiers. *How much* is taken for granted, however, is obviously primarily contingent upon variant institutionally and interpersonally established features of the communication setting rather than social background.

Highly educated people may thus efficiently evade numerous qualifiers in discourse about people and modes of life by describing a particular person as a FALSTAFFIAN character and a particular mode of living as DIONYSIAN, and we may under appropriate conditions make known our impression of very complex political states of affairs by labelling them manifestations of DE GAULLISME. Very much is indeed taken for granted in such cases, and we might therefore in accordance with Bernstein's and Hasan's basic substantial and formal criteria argue that communication is being controlled by the restricted code. The tacit residuals involved in such discourse are fragments of a cultural heritage shared by literally and politically educated people rather than fragments of a presumedly taken for granted and immediately shared "Lebenswelt". The cryptic expressions can hence—in view of *what* is tacitly taken for granted—hardly be considered manifestations of a *class determined* restricted code.

The issues of *what* is tacitly taken for granted, *how much*, and *the manner* in which what is said is imbued with meaning from what is presupposed are in Bernstein's analysis of language controlled by the restricted code of working class children not dealt with as separate issues at all. His illustrative examples are mostly cases in which what is said is anchored in some extralinguistic conditions of immediate relevance to the intended message. These conditions are never explicitly spelled out and most often hardly referred to at all, and the general flavour of interaction is one of presupposed intimacy and trust in a shared HERE-and-NOW. The global patterns of communication he describes are hence not easily assessed in terms of formal, purely linguistic criteria only, but some of his illustrations of the restricted code in action seem to conform to a characteristic pattern very similar to that of a typical dialogue between two persons jointly engaged in some *intricically meaningful* manual labour. What is said under such conditions derives its meaning and immediate significance from the ongoing operations of work. It may be exceedingly cryptic, yet immediately and unequivocally understood within the context of those ongoing manual operations; and so thoroughly embedded in that stream of co-operative work that one may even conceive of the entire temporal pattern of interaction as being organized in terms of a mixed linguistic and behavioural syntax (see Slama-Cazacu, 1976). Such an inter-actional setting is thus—unlike many a spiritual conversation between competitive intellectuals on FALSTAFFIAN characters and DIONYSIAN styles of life—characterized by nearly perfect organic complementarity.

It is in that respect also very different from the general pattern of communication in formal educational settings characterized by a traditional, explicitly authoritarian, and "visible pedagogy" (Bernstein, 1977). The latter is also visibly *assymetric* in the sense that the teacher and he alone by virtue of his role is fully in control of the premises for interpretation and the criteria by which comprehension and intersubjectivity are evaluated. He—not the pupil—is assumed to be in possession of the knowledge required in order to fill in the unspoken *et ceteras*. He may for that reason—if he considers a pupil exceedingly ignorant—even decide that a given request for information is *meant* in a way different from that in which it was actually *intended*. And such a violation of a basic rule of normal communication may indeed also be justified in terms of his role as an educator: He serves a system in which the topics of discourse are obligatory. They do not emerge out of problems of immediate significance to the pupil in either his work or daily life, but are dictated by curriculae aiming at skills and knowledge supposed to be of value in themselves or of some practical use in a remote future. Schools of this kind are therefore institutions in which children are supposed to learn a lot of answers to questions they never have asked and where knowledge is sought on premises provided by adult educators in hope of some *deferred gratification*.

Bernstein's analysis of the fate of the British working class child within such an educational system has geared the interests of educators and social scientists all over the world toward issues of utmost practical and theoretical significance. Some of these issues, it seems to me, have more to do with *general dilemmas inherent in our formal systems of education* than with *class determined linguistic codes*. It is certainly true that our educational systems are pervaded by middle class values and that knowledge is being transmitted in an elaborate code. It has also been shown that working class children and children from coloured minority groups feel alienated at school, that many of them perform poorly or drop out, and that some end up in open revolt and try to establish their personal identities in counter-subcultures (Labov, 1972). However, drop-out and revolt have become familiar worries among middle class parents as well. What happens to a majority of "nice and obedient" middle class children, moreover, is apparently that they, by conforming to the norms of the system and accepting information on premises other than their own, *achieve scholarly success at the cost of authenticity and genuine engagement*. These are possibly some of the sour—or dry —fruits of any tree of knowledge uprooted from its natural soil, i.e. of *any formal educational system detached from the living occupational and social world it is supposed to serve*.

Let me, finally, pursue this very abstract and sad theme into some recent investigations of children's verbal communication in situations in which they are faced with some Piagetian type of tasks (see Hundeide, 1977; Rommetveit, 1977). And this excursion may eventually bring us back to our main theme, namely Bernstein's notion of codes and possible components of codes.

One kind of tasks we tried out are indicated in Fig. 1. The referential domain would for instance be six circles, presented in one of the two spatial arrangements shown in Cells 1 and 2, and the child would be asked to point out:

(1) "the one of the WHITE circles that is SECOND LARGEST".

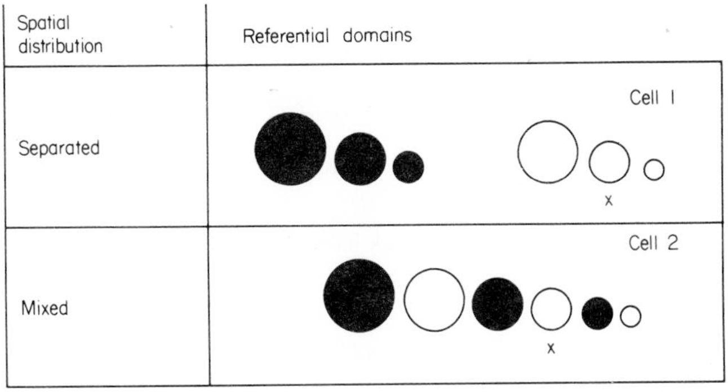

FIG. 1. Target object within referential domain.

Correct identification of the target object presupposes in this case mastery of *cross-classification* and *ordering*. Notice, however, how different purely spatial arrangements of the same six objects may affect ease of identification. There were thus quite a few children at the age of six and seven years who were perfectly capable of pointing out the target object in Cell 1, yet unable to do so when it was encountered in Cell 2. Their errors in the latter case, moreover, were all of the same kind. They pointed out the second largest of ALL circles rather than the second largest one of the WHITE circles only.

This error is thus clearly due to *diffusion of the domain of the ordering operation*. Children who hit the target object in Cell 1 but fail to identify it in Cell 2 will therefore succeed *also in the latter task* if the same target object is verbally described as:

(1') "the one of the WHITE circles that is SECOND SMALLEST".

This identifying description merely implies a reversal of the direction of ordering, starting from the SMALLEST one and proceeding from left to right. The second smallest of ALL circles is BLACK, however. The child will hence—even though initially engaged in ordering ALL six circles—immediately discover the error with respect to colour and proceed one step further to the left.

Let us now briefly reconsider the task of identifying "*the one of the WHITE circles that is* SECOND LARGEST" in Cell 2 of Fig. 1. What is required, in terms of Piagetian cognitive operations, in order to solve it? The child must obviously be able to cross-classify and order objects and, in addition, be capable of restricting his ordering operation to one particular subset of the referential domain while attending to the entire set of objects. Mastery of *cross-classification, ordering* and *class inclusion* is hence apparently required in order for the child to establish inter-subjectivity on adult premises.

Consider, next, an alternative identifying description of the target object in Cell 2. The child is now, immediately before he is shown the drawing of objects, asked to point out:

(1A) "the one of the SNOWBALLS that is SECOND LARGEST".

Some children who failed when the white objects were described as WHITE CIRCLES were now able to solve the task. What is achieved by verbal categorization of the subset as SNOWBALLS is thus an effect comparable to that obtained by spatial separation of the two subsets in Cell 1: The white objects are apparently *mentally set apart* from all others in such a way that ordering of the entire set is prevented. What happens may thus perhaps be transcribed into Bernstein's conceptual framework as follows: The linguistic encoding of the circles as CIRCLES (in Norwegian: RUNDINGER) requires an attitude of abstraction and an elaborated code which the child at that particular stage of language acquisition and cognitive growth does not yet master. The word SNOWBALL however, is part of a more restricted vocabulary firmly anchored in real life experience. By labelling the circles SNOWBALLS, they are hence assimilated by the child into a familiar domain of real life objects.

Some of the tasks described above were first systematically tried out in a pre-school for six to seven year old children in an upper middle class district in the Oslo area and later on—in a more casuistic and exploratory fashion—in a day institution for children of the same age but from very poor social backgrounds. What then became evident was a striking difference in performance between the two groups. Thus, all children from the upper middle class pre-school managed to identify the target object (labelled CIRCLE) in Cell 1, and most of them were even able to single it out in Cell 2. Only one single child from the day institution managed to identify the target circle in Cell 1, however, and none of them succeeded in Cell 2.

It turned out that most of our six to seven year old children from the poor social background did not master the expression SECOND LARGEST at all in these tasks, not even in the context of a referential domain of only three white circles with a simple spatial arrangement as shown in Cell 1. We were convinced, however, that all of them would have been able to do so in a situation in which, e.g. the child had won the second prize in a contest and then was told to pick up the SECOND

LARGEST one from a strictly analogous referential domain of *candies*. How could it be, then, that they failed when the ordering operation had to be performed on *circles*?

Our tentative answer to this riddle—in part corroborated by subsequent enquiries—is as follows: The children from the poor background were perfectly capable of ordering, given a situation of immediate instrumental relevance, but *incapable of attributing sense to such an operation on meaningless geometrical patterns on a paper*. The circles resemble balls, however, even though all of them appear smaller than the kind of real balls they are used to playing with. This latter, real ball is hence spontaneously tacitly introduced into the HERE-and-NOW of the game, the white circles on the paper are assimilated into a context of familiar play objects, and the adult's question becomes meaningful: *She wants to know which one of those round things comes closest to the tacitly introduced real ball with respect to size*! What may be considered *lack of decentration* and total *absence of an analytic attitude* may thus, from a different point of view, be interpreted as *unwillingness to cope with problems detached from all practical significance*. The children from the poor background thus failed because they spontaneously refused to engage in an ordering operation *purely for the sake of ordering*, without any significance to their world of actions upon real objects. The refusal is not reflective, of course, but due to a persistent propensity to assimilate apparently novel and unfamiliar states of affairs into familiar schemata of some real life significance.

Similar reactions have been observed by Hundeide (1977) in small children's performance on class inclusion tasks of the traditional Piagetian type. A child is for instance shown a drawing of, e.g. *five tulips* and *three flowers of some different kind* and then asked what there are most of, TULIPS or FLOWERS. Whatever his answer may be, he is then asked *why* he thinks there are most of X. Some of the children in Hundeide's study who gave the incorrect answer (TULIPS) would, when asked to repeat the question, say: "What are there most of, TULIPS or OTHER FLOWERS?" And their explanations why there were more TULIPS were as a rule very plausible in view of some tacitly introduced real life context such as, e.g. *that the flowers were going to be sold and* TULIPS *brought most profit*.

What in such experiments is considered evidence of incapability to cope simultaneously with super- and subordinate classes may thus apparently often be interpreted as a spontaneous transformation of the task (as intended by the experimenter). What is achieved by that transformation is some real life significance and plausibility for the social transaction: The task is not any longer (as intended by the investigator) a test of pure reasoning, but in fact a reasonable everyday problem. A correct response, on the other hand, implies acceptance of premises imposed by the adult, premises which are entirely detached from plausible real life contexts of practical significance.

The strange ordering performance of our children from a poor social background and the incorrect response patterns in class inclusion tasks observed by Hundeide may thus, in accordance with the Piagetian tradition, be interpreted as evidence of lack of decentration and incapacity to adopt that analytic attitude which is one of the distinctive features of an elaborated linguistic code. Correct responses, on the other hand, should by the same token indicate mastery of an elaborated code. They are at the same time, however, contingent upon a certain readiness to accept alien and externally imposed premises for interpretation, and to engage in a clearly assymetrical social interaction. The transaction with the adult yielding an *incorrect response* is thus characterized by autonomy and independence on the part of the child, whereas *"the right answer"* can only be achieved by submission. The analytic attitude revealed in a correct response is hence *eo ipso* in some respects an *authoritarian* attitude, and we are thus once more faced with one of the dilemmas we touched upon in our general speculations concerning the tree of knowledge. One horn of that dilemma appears to be *naïve spontaneity*, the other *reflective alienation*, and these two horns are also clearly embedded in Bernstein's two codes. It is a blessing, therefore, that he has allowed us to make use of both. If forced to choose, however, I would probably prefer being naïve on premises of my own to being sophisticated on those imposed upon me by others.

References

Apel, K. O. (1965). Die entfaltung der "sprachanalytischen" philosophie und das problem der "Geisteswissenschaft". *Philosophisches Jahrbuch* **72,** 239–289.

Blakar, R. M. and Rommetveit, R. (1975). Utterances *in vacuo* and in contexts. *International J. Psycholinguistics* **4,** 5–32.

Bernstein, B. (1967). Open schools, open societies? *New Society* September.

Bernstein, B. (1969). A sociolinguistic approach to socialization: with some reference to educability, I. "The Human Context" Vol. II. Chancer, London.

Bernstein, B. (1971). Social class, language and socialization. *In* "Current Trends in Linguistics". (A. S. Abraham, Ed.) Vol. 12. The Hague, Mouton.

Bernstein, B. (Ed.) (1974). Postscript. *In* "Class, Codes and Control". Vol. I, 2nd Edn. Routledge and Kegan Paul, London.

Bernstein, B (Ed.) (1977). Class and pedagogics: visible and invisible. *In* "Class, Codes and Control". Vol. III, 2nd Edn. Routledge and Kegan Paul, London.

Cicourel, A. V. (1970). Basic and normative rules in the negotiation of status and role. *In* "Patterns of communicative Behaviour". (H. P. Dreitzel, Ed.) MacMillan, London.

Deutsch, W. (1976). "Sprachliche Redundanz und Objectidentifikation." Lahn, Marburg.

Garfinkel, H. (1972). Studies of the routine grounds of everyday activity. *In* "Studies in Social Interaction". (D. Sudnow, Ed.) Free Press, New York.

Hasan, R. (1973). Code, register and social dialect. *In* "Class, Codes and Control". (B. Bernstein, Ed.) Vol. II. Routledge and Kegan Paul, London.

Heider, F. (1958). "The Psychology of Interpersonal Relations." John Wiley and Sons, New York.

Hundeide, K. (1977). "Piaget i kritisk lys." Cappelen, Oslo.

Labov, W. (1972). Rules for ritual insults. *In* "Studies in Social Interaction". (D. Sudnow, Ed.) Free Press, New York.

Malcolm, N. (1967). "Ludwig Wittgenstein, A Memoir." Oxford University Press, Oxford.

Olson, D. (1970). Language and thought. Aspects of a cognitive theory of semantics. *Psychological Review* **77**, 257–273.

Rommetveit, R. (1974). "On Message Structure " John Wiley and Sons, Chichester.

Rommetveit, R. (1977). On the relationship between children's mastery of Piagetian cognitive operations and their semantic competence. *Nordisk Tidsskrift Logopedi og Foniatri* **2**, 107–117.

Rommetveit, R. (1977). On negative rationalism in scholarly studies of verbal communication and dynamic residuals in the construction of human intersubjectivity. *In* "The Social Contexts of Method". (M. Brenner, P. Marsh and M. Brenner, Eds) Croom Helm, London.

Schuetz, A. (1945). On multiple realities. *Philosophical and Phenomenological Research* **5**, 533–576.

Schuetz, A. (1951). Choosing among projects of action. *Philosophical and Phenomenological Research* **12**, 161–184.

Slama-Cazacu, T. (1976). Nonverbal components in message sequence: "mixed syntax". *In* "Language and Man". (W. McCormick and S. Wurm, Eds) The Hague, Mouton.

Wittgenstein, L. (1962). The blue book. *In* "Philosophy in the Twentieth Century". (W. Barrett and H. D. Aiken, Eds) Vol. 2, pp. 710–774. Random House, New York.

Part 2
Empirical Research

9. Stages in Concept Formation and Levels of Cognitive Functioning

An experiment on intuitive conceptual processes*

R. ROMMETVEIT

Some interesting controversies in research on the formation and use of concepts are reflected in the ways in which different psychologists define a concept. Thus Smoke (1935, p. 277) conceives of a concept as "a symbolic response (usually, but not necessarily linguistic) which is made to the members of a class of stimulus patterns but not to other stimuli". Vinacke (1951, p. 22) also refers to the concept as a symbol representing the common elements in the range of stimuli. Hebb (1949, p. 33), on the other hand, ventures to maintain that "a great deal of conceptual activity is unreportable (and so "unconscious") in human thought", and he does not consider the verbal tag attached to the concept essential.

Theoretical Considerations

Some Basic Findings

Experimental evidence in support of an intuitive conceptual activity has been accumulated ever since the pioneering study by Hull (1920). He found that subjects mastered the concept behaviourally, i.e. they sorted complex stimulus patterns *as if* they were able to abstract and consciously identify the defining properties, even though they were completely unable to describe those very properties. Such behavioural mastery in the absence of any adequate symbolic representation was then referred to as a *functional concept.*

* This study has been financed by the Norwegian Research Council for Science and the Humanities, and was conducted by the author with the assistance of Mr. Roar Svalheim. Published in *Scandinavian J. Psychology* (1960) **1**, 115–124.

In recent experimental studies, apparently intuitive conceptual activity has been re-examined from the point of view of Osgood's mediation theory of meaning (Osgood *et al.*, 1957). Thus, Lipton and Blanton (1957) claim that they have observed the acquisition of a common "meaning" of a set of different stimuli under conditions in which their subjects did not learn a symbol representing the common stimulus elements at all. The common meaning is then defined as identical *response* elements, and symbolic representation of defining properties is actually considered a secondary aspect of the concept. Staats and Staats provide additional evidence in support of such a view, maintaining (1957, p. 79) that "verbal concepts are signs that have been conditioned to the identical response components involved in the total response to each of several objects or signs".

Instances of apparently intuitive conceptual activity have also been repeatedly observed by Rommetveit (1960) in his studies of selective person perception. The stimuli were then "persons", artificially constructed by combining photographs of young men and written accounts of behaviours in such a way as to make up a set of stimulus persons (Sps) systematically distributed in an attribute space as shown in Fig. 1.

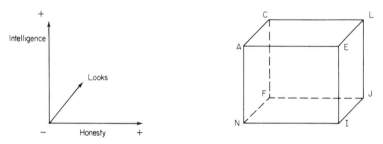

FIG. 1. Distribution of stimulus persons in an attribute space.

When asked to rank such a set of Sps in the order he prefers them as personal friends, a subject may adopt a simple conceptual approach in the sense that his ranking is being based upon one attribute only. He may for instance prefer all honest Sps (E, L, J and I), irrespective of the fact that each Sp's honesty is revealed in unique modes of behaviour, and in spite of the fact that all honest Sps are different with respect to some other personal attribute(s).

Many subjects adopted such a systematic conceptual strategy in their preference ranking, and the intuitive nature of their strategy was corroborated in retrospective accounts and recall tests immediately after the ranking. As a rule, they were apparently not aware of having adopted any systematic strategy at all, and they had even a particularly poor memory of those very stimulus items upon which their conceptual sorting had apparently been based. A person having preferred all honest Sps would thus remember fairly well the items by which level of intelligence was revealed, whereas he would fail to recall correctly a single item of those by which honesty had to be inferred.

Hebb (1946, p. 87) maintains that the essence of intuition seems to be judgements which "follow premises or steps of inference of which the judge is unaware . . .". According to his criterion, we are probably faced with a distinctly intuitive use of a concept. The particularly poor immediate recall of sensory premises for the conceptual sorting of Sps testifies to a lack of awareness and stands out clearly as a contrast against the results obtained under conditions of intentional use of concepts. When subjects were explicitly asked to rank Sps with respect to level of honesty, their retention of "honesty items" turned out to be superior to their memory of other items, such as those, for example, by which intelligence had to be inferred.

The Role of Intention

These findings direct our attention toward the role of *intention* in the use and learning of concepts. Conceptual activity initiated by an intent to sort stimuli into specific categories seems to enhance what Nuttin (1955, p. 352) labels "reflective consciousness", i.e. a recording of and reflection upon the processes of abstraction and inference determining the individual's discriminatory behaviour. When conceptual activity is "incidental" and only indirectly instrumental relative to some salient immediate goal, however, the latter may apparently attract the individual's intention and awareness to such an extent that he will be completely unable to put into words the chain of inference, and even be entirely ignorant of the fact that he is adopting any conceptual strategy in his sorting of stimuli.

Whereas the role of intention has been largely neglected in studies of concept use, it is considered very significant in experiments on concept formation. According to Vinacke (1951) and Podell (1958), an unequivocal intent to form conceptions enhances a process of *active search*. During the learning session, the individual is actively searching for and trying to spell out for himself the common elements of stimulus patterns which represent instances of the concept. If he then has the expectancy that a given specific stimulus property X is a defining characteristic, a single instance contradicting that expectancy leads to a rejection of the hypothesis. The essence of intentional concept formation thus appears to be a deliberate silent formulation and checking of specific hypotheses against instances.

In other studies, however, concept formation is "incidental" in the sense that the subject's task is defined as something other than learning the concept, e.g. as memorizing (Hull, 1920) or esthetic evaluation (Podell, 1958). Learning is then taking place without any particular intent to form conceptions, being only indirectly related to the major experimental task toward which the experimenter wants to gear the subject's intention and reflective consciousness. Under such conditions concept formation is described as a process of *passive summation*. According to Vinacke (1951, p. 7) the subject is then "essentially a passive recipient of sensory impressions which gradually summate in a concept".

Hypotheses Concerning Levels of Cognitive Organization in Concept Formation

As previously mentioned, some learned concepts (such as, for example, a concept of honesty) may apparently function at different levels of cognitive organization, as *intuitive discriminatory mechanisms* under conditions of "incidental" sorting of stimuli and *with awareness and symbolic representation of defining properties* under conditions of intentional conceptual sorting. The intuitive discriminatory mechanism, furthermore, is described as the end product of a passive summation, whereas the reflective symbolic representation is considered an end product of active search. Is it possible that one and the same concept may be learned in two distinctly different ways, both incidentally, by passive summation, and intentionally, by active search? Or do we have reasons to believe that its intuitive and reflective manifestations are learned successively, at different stages of one multi-phasic process of concept formation?

Let us discuss some of the prerequisites for intuitive concept learning somewhat more in detail, and try to elaborate into more specific hypotheses the suggestion offered by Staats and Staats (1957) that the verbal concept may be learned as a superstructure upon an already intuitively established discriminatory mechanism.

In a tentative model of cognitive processes, Osgood (1957) distinguishes between three levels of organization: a projection level, an integration level and a representation level. On the basis of Osgood's model and the suggestions made by Staats and Staats we may thus venture to hypothesize a process of concept formation involving three separate stages:

(a) a *perceptual stage*, at which the aspect(s) of the stimulus patterns corresponding to the defining properties of the concept (S_x) acquires perceptual dominance over other aspects, even though it has as yet not been coupled to a specific category of discriminatory responses (R_y);

(b) an *integration stage*, at which a given response category is associated to the perceptually dominant stimulus aspect(s) (S_x-R_y), even though the individual has as yet not attained a symbolic representation of the stimulus characteristics determining his response; and

(c) a *representational stage*, at which the individual also attains a verbal concept, i.e. a symbolic representation of the already established discriminatory mechanism (R_{Sx-Ry}).

Under what conditions would we then expect concept formation to proceed in such a way—as an intuitive process penetrating into successively higher levels of cognitive organization?

First, what we have already said about the role of intention and reflective consciousness naturally directs our attention toward settings in which concept learning is incidental. If the crucial stimulus aspects are to have a chance to acquire perceptual dominance without the individual's awareness, the latter must be successfully directed toward phenomena other than the discriminatory activity as such.

Secondly, we want to emphasize some significant prerequisites pertaining to the nature of the concept to be learned. If we examine carefully the stimulus patterns used in studies testifying to "functional concepts", "passive summation" and "unconscious meaning", we find that they are all *complex* and *unfamiliar*. Hull's subjects had to identify one entirely unfamiliar geometrical form embedded in patterns of equally unfamiliar irrelevant figures. Podell's subjects were given a number of complex designs including a series of differently located, relevant and irrelevant, free forms, and the subjects in Lipton and Blanton's experiment were exposed to a series of composite and multidimensional geometrical patterns, in which only one crucial figure was systematically varied with respect to some attribute such as, for example, circularity. In short, *behavioural mastery in the absence of symbolic representation of defining properties seems to be the rule when the subject has no previous knowledge of (and therefore no ability to put into words) those defining properties.* When the nature of the discriminatory task is such that the highest level of cognitive functioning—what Osgood describes as "the station for semantic decoding and encoding"—cannot be of any help at all, it seems to us that concept formation *has* to proceed intuitively.

Symbolic representation may then be conceived of as an entirely new task, i.e. as *a task of verbalizing, and thereby co-ordinating into a more inclusive cognitive system, a newly acquired discriminatory mechanism.* Whether symbolic representation will actually be attained or not may depend upon a number of factors. As the discrimination is over-learned, for instance, the individual's attention will probably gradually be directed away from the easily obtainable goal so as to enhance self-insight and verbalization. A symbolic representation may probably also be facilitated if there is a pressure to report and communicate to others what one is doing. Finally, the achievement of the verbal concept will be partly dependent upon the ease with which the newly acquired discrimination can be encoded into familiar linguistic signs.

Some of the main prerequisites for our hypothesized sequence of perceptual selectivity—functional concept—verbal concept may be summarized as follows:

(1) The discriminatory activity must be incidental and subordinate relative to some salient goal.

(2) The task of discrimination must involve unfamiliar stimulus patterns.

(3) The defining properties of the concept to be learned must be related to already acquired concepts in such a way that they can relatively easily be represented by means of familiar linguistic or other symbols.

Experimental Study

The main purpose of the study to be reported below was an examination of concept formation under conditions fulfilling the three main hypothesized prerequisites for the three-stage process listed above.

Stimulus Materials

Our stimulus materials were 81 cards, 75×95 mm, showing a "cup and saucer" pattern in red lines as depicted in Fig. 2. The total pattern thus consists of two stimulus units, *the cup* and *the saucer*, and is always

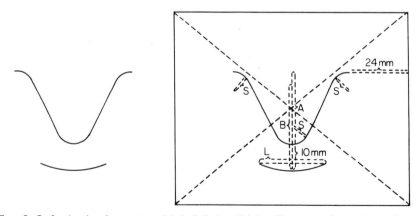

Fig. 2. Left: A stimulus at two-thirds full size. Right: The same figure located on the card with auxiliary lines demonstrating all geometrical characteristics. The measurements are A_2, S_2, L_2 and B_2 (cf. the text).

located in such a way that the diagonals cross in A and divide it into two halves. The cup varies with respect to "height" or amplitude (A) and with respect to "roundness" of the smoothly curved forms at the bottom and top (S). The saucer varies with respect to length (L) and "bowedness" (B). Each of these specific attributes are presented in three values, tentatively chosen in such a way that the extremes (A_1–A_3, S_1–S_3, L_1–L_3, and B_1–B_3, respectively) should be between 1 and 2 jnd's apart (Rommetveit and Svalheim, 1959). The variations were (cf. Fig. 2):

A: $A_1 = 27$ mm $A_2 = 29$ mm $A_3 = 31$ mm
S: $S_1 = 6$ mm $S_2 = 7$ mm $S_3 = 8$ mm
L: $L_1 = 24$ mm $L_2 = 26{\cdot}5$ mm $L_3 = 29$ mm
B: $B_1 = 42$ mm $B_2 = 34$ mm $B_3 = 26$ mm

The 81 cards thus constitute all possible combinations of the three values of the four specific attributes as shown in Table I.

TABLE 1. The 81 stimulus figures, with EC-stimuli marked off by crosses and RC-stimuli by circles.

| | A_1 | | | A_2 | | | A_3 | | |
	L_1	L_2	L_3	L_1	L_2	L_3	L_1	L_2	L_3
B_3	⊗	○	○	○	⊗	○	○	○	⊗
$S_3\,B_2$	×				×				×
B_1	×				×				×
B_3	×				×				×
$S_2\,B_2$	⊗	○	○	○	⊗	○	○	○	⊗
B_1	×				×				×
B_3	×				×				×
$S_1\,B_2$	×				×				×
B_1	⊗	○	○	○	⊗	○	○	○	⊗

A sample of 27 cards only was used in each of our learning conditions. In what may be called the *extent condition* (EC) A and L were strictly covaried by excluding all combinations of geometrical characteristics other than those involving $A_3\,L_3$, $A_2\,L_2$ and $A_1\,L_1$. In the *roundness condition* (RC) only those 27 combinations involving $S_3\,B_3$, $S_2\,B_2$ and $S_1\,B_1$ were used. The EC-cards and the RC-cards were mounted on rotating wheels so as to allow for successive tachistoscopic presentation of the figures.

Experimental Procedures

The learning session was introduced as *playing at a wheel of fortune*. The subject was first given a small amount of money to use for playing, and the experimenter assured him that he would win at least some additional money during the play. He was then seated in front of a screen. By putting a 2 öre coin in a slot in the screen and pushing a button the hidden wheel of fortune would start rotating. When the wheel stopped turning, a figure would appear in the exposure room in front of him. Some such figures were *good*, he was told, and each time a good figure appeared, 7 öre would be immediately released. The coins, which would appear through a slot to the left on the screen, were then to be cashed immediately. Other figures were *bad*, however, and would give no prize at all. Still other figures, he was told, would be neither particularly good nor bad. For each such figure the (automatically released) prize would be 2 öre, i.e. exactly the amount he had to put in each time.

Thus every time the subject had to put a 2 öre coin in the slot in order to get a new figure exposed. By pushing the button he initiated a buzzing tone, sounding as if the hidden wheel were turning. Once the buzzing stopped, the small screen covering the exposure room was withdrawn, the figure appeared, and after an exposure time of approximately three seconds, the appropriate prize was released through the slot. The subject thus believed that the rotation of the wheel of fortune was every time determined by his pushing the button, even though the sequence of figures actually was strictly *a priori* determined. When he did not push "sufficiently hard", he was asked to push once more.

In EC the "good cards" were the nine figures in the right column and the "bad cards" were the nine figures in the left column of Table I. In RC the "good cards" were the nine figures in the top row, whereas the "bad cards" were the nine figures in the bottom row. In EC the strictly covaried aspects *height of cup* and *length of saucer* were the instrumentally relevant aspects of the composite geometrical patterns, i.e. high cups with long saucers consistently signalled luck. In RC *roundness of cup* and the strictly covaried *bowedness of saucer* were instrumentally relevant.

The figures were exposed in a fixed random order, and in such a way that equivalent figures (for instance $S_3 B_3 A_1 L_2$ in RC and $A_3 L_3 S_1 B_2$ in EC) were presented at the same serial position. Each subject went through two learning sessions including in all 648 exposures. The first session lasted for approx. 85 minutes, and the next session (on the following day) lasted for approx. 75 minutes. Rest periods were interspersed at regular intervals, and the subject would then count and exchange the coins he had won so far.

Recognition was tested after presentations nos 27, 72, 144, 247, 396 and 620. Each time, the subject was unexpectedly asked to identify among nine figures, mounted in a random and (positionally) irregular order on a black and round board, the figure that had just disappeared.

After having indicated which of the nine figures he felt was most similar to the one he had just seen, he was asked to tell which of the remaining figures were second and third most similar to the test figure. Test figures were the four corner figures of Table I, and the figures mounted on the round board (the "recognition figures") were all nine figures (with both cross and circle) common to the two conditions.

Each recognition test was followed by a measure of the extent to which the subject had achieved a functional concept. He was then, for each of 12 reward and punishment figures included in the 18 presentations following the recognition test, simply asked to tell whether the figure was good or bad. The prize was then always withheld until he had made his guess. After the session, he was given an extra reward of 2 öre for every correct guess.

When the second learning session was finished, the subject was asked, in the absence of any stimulus material, to give his own free account of "good" and "bad" characteristics. No attempts at probing were made at all until the subject himself indicated that he was not able to give any more detailed account of good and bad properties, and he was also allowed to express his notions of good and bad figures by drawing.

Subjects

Subjects were recruited on a voluntary basis from an elementary school in Oslo. They were 12–13 year old boys, all of whom had normal vision and were considered by their teachers to belong to the upper halves of their classes with respect to intellectual capacity and achievement. The 14 boys were randomly assigned to EC and RC, seven of them to each condition.

Results

Our information on the formation of a concept of "good (and bad) wheel-of-fortune figures" is based upon three main sets of data: (1) the unexpected recognition tests measuring *perceptual selectivity*, (2) the learning tests by which we examined whether a *functional concept* had been achieved, and (3) the post-experimental free description of good and bad figures by which we wanted to get at the subject's *verbal concept*.

In spite of the fact that all systematically varied stimulus aspects had been found to be equally hard to discriminate (Rommetveit and Svalheim, 1959), a considerable difference in learnability between the two composite aspects "roundness" and "extent" was observed. The formation of a concept of a "good wheel-of-fortune figure" turned out to be considerably more difficult in EC, when extent signalled luck.

Three of our seven EC-subjects actually had "roundness hypotheses" during the learning session, i.e. their guesses at good and bad cards were in one or more of the learning-test series significantly related to the irrelevant geometrical attributes S and/or B. For that reason, our presentation of group data will be limited to RC.

The main quantitative aspects of perceptual selectivity and discrimination learning in RC are shown in Fig. 3. The error-of-recognition curves are based upon individual error-of-recognition scores, and the latter are computed as follows. For AL-recognition, the column

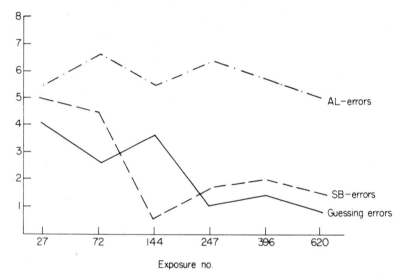

FIG 3. Curves for selective recognition and guessing, RC.

distance between the test figure and the figure recognized as most similar is multiplied by three, the column distance between the test figure and the second most similar figure is multiplied by two, and the column distance between the test figure and the third most similar figure is then added to these two products. Column distance here refers to the three columns $A_1 L_1$, $A_2 L_2$ and $A_3 L_3$ in Table I, and a perfectly correct identification of the extent aspect of the test figure thus yields an AL error score of 0. For SB-recognition, error scores were computed by the formula above on the basis of row distances.

Suppose, then, that the test figure is $S_3 B_3 A_1 L_1$ and the subject picks out as the most, second most and third most similar recognition figures $S_1 B_1 A_1 L_1$, $S_2 B_2 A_1 L_1$ and $S_3 B_3 A_2 L_2$, respectively. He will then get an AL error score of 1 and a SB error score of 8. By computing the expected distribution of all possible error-of-recognition scores under conditions of random choice, we find that an error score of 0 has a probability of 0·01, whereas scores less than 2 (0 and/or 1) have a probability of 0·05.

The guessing curves in Fig. 3 are based upon the average number of errors in a series of 12 guesses at good and bad cards. According to the sign test (Siegel, 1956, p. 250), less than three errors are required in order to infer at a 5% level of confidence that discrimination learning has taken place. Incidentally, and fortunately for diagrammatical purposes, the medians for the expected random distributions of both guessing errors and recognition errors are six.

The combined results obtained from our seven RC-subjects provide us with a fairly clear and unequivocal picture of perceptual selectivity and discrimination learning. In brief, almost perfect identification of the "good" aspect of the wheel-of-fortune figure is on the average achieved at exposure no. 144, even though guesses at good and bad figures throughout the immediately succeeding learning test do not, as a rule, testify with any reasonable degree of confidence to discrimination learning. Recognition of the irrelevant extent aspect (AL), furthermore, does not at any stage surpass the region of random performance.

Owing to the considerable individual variations, however, in particular within EC, the most reliable information is to be achieved by means of an analysis of individual cases. We then find, also among EC-subjects, a recurrent pattern of correct identification of the "good" stimulus aspects in the unexpected recognition test prior to correct guessing at good and bad cards. In all, five of our 14 subjects conform to the pattern presented in Fig. 4. Each of these subjects shows for the first time that he is able to tell which figures are good and bad, a considerable time after having demonstrated an almost perfect recognition of the good-bad aspect of the figure.

Five other subjects have approximately coinciding recognition and guessing curves, i.e. their first correct identification of the instrumentally relevant stimulus aspect comes immediately prior to the learning test in which their guesses at good and bad cards are significantly better than chance. The four remaining subjects represent ambiguous cases. One of them did not learn at all which figures were good, and the remaining three were EC-subjects who oscillated between extent and roundness hypotheses in their guessing at good and bad cards.

Of our 14 subjects, five RC-subjects and two EC-subjects gave adequate accounts of good and bad properties after the learning session. Each of these subjects gave, freely and without any probing, an essentially correct description of the geometrical characteristic(s) that had determined his guessing. The six remaining subjects, who had been guessing significantly better than chance during the last two learning test series, gave vague and partly misleading verbal accounts. One RC-subject said he had the impression that good figures were slightly more heavily drawn than others, the other referred vaguely to good figures as "more smooth" than bad ones. Of the four EC-subjects in this category, three referred primarily to roundness of cup and/or

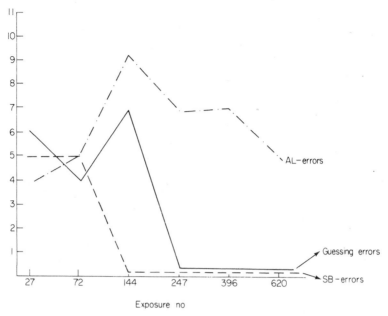

Fig. 4. An individual case of perfect SB-recognition prior to correct guessing (subject no. 7).

bowedness of saucers in their account of good properties. Number four, whose guessing showed that he too distinguished fairly well between good and bad figures, mentioned exclusively other clearly irrelevant properties in his vague and hesitant description of them.

Concluding Comments

It should be kept in mind that the subject was entirely ignorant of the purpose of the experiment. His main activity throughout the two sessions consisted of pushing the button and cashing money. He knew in advance that some figures would signal good luck and others bad luck. He had no previous knowledge of the many subtle differences between figures, however. Nor had he any opportunity for simultaneous comparison. The task of discrimination was thus apparently incidental and subordinate relative to that of winning money, and it involved unfamiliar and complex differences whose unfamiliarity emerged out of a combination of a number of small familiar differences concerning form and extent.

These conditions, we suggest, represent the keys to the understanding of our findings. Perfect recognition of the instrumental aspect of a figure can only occur if that aspect has been dominant at some time during the exposure of the test figure, i.e. at a time when the subject, engaged in his playing and with no expectancy that his recall will be tested, has been looking at it. Some of our unexpected recognition and guessing tests were therefore apparently administered at a stage in the formation of a concept of a "good wheel-of-fortune figure" *after* the initially unfamiliar "good" aspect of the figure had acquired perceptual dominance, but *before* the correct discriminatory behaviour, i.e. the verbal response "good figure", had been attached to it.

In most cases, the learning session continued after the correct discriminatory behaviour had been thoroughly learned and over-learned. As a rule, the subject was then able to describe good and bad figures in a way corresponding to his actual discriminatory behaviour. A tendency to reflect upon and put into words the characteristics of good and bad figures may have increased as the discriminatory task itself required successively less effort and awareness. Such a tendency may also have been reinforced by our request for guessing.

Subjects who had not yet over-learned the correct discriminatory behaviour, however, gave as a rule inadequate and misleading accounts of good and bad figures. In the latter cases our request for a verbal account has apparently been administered at a stage of learning when a newly acquired discriminatory mechanism has not yet been "forced into reflective consciousness".

In brief, then, our findings provide us with some evidence of a process of concept formation, initially intuitive but expanding successively into higher levels of cognitive organization. In similar experimental studies now under way we want to find out how previous *knowledge of stimulus differences* and an *intention to learn the concept* will affect the learning process.

References

Hebb, D. O. (1946). Emotion in man and animal: an analysis of initiative processes of recognition. *Psychological Review* **53,** 88–106.

Hebb, D. O. (1949). "Organization of Behavior." John Wiley and Sons, New York.

Hull, C. L. (1920). Quantitative aspects of the evolution of concepts: an experimental study. *Psychological Monographs* **28,** no. 1 (whole no. 123).

Lipton, L. and Blanton, R. L. (1957). The semantic differential and mediated generalization as measures of meaning. *J. Experimental Psychology* **54,** 431–439.

Nuttin, J. (1955). Consciousness, behavior and personality. *Psychological Review* **62,** 349–355.

Osgood, C. E. (1957). A behavioristic analysis of perception and language as cognitive phenomena. *In* "Contemporary Approaches to Cognition". Harvard University Press, Cambridge, Massachusetts.

Osgood, C. E., Suci, G. J. and Jannebanm, P. H. (1957). "The Measurement of Meaning." University of Illinois Press, Urbana.

Podell, H. M. (1958). Two processes of concept formation. *Psychological Monographs* **72,** no. 15 (whole no. 468).

Rommetveit, R. (1960). "Selectivity, Intuition and Halo Effects in Social Perception." Oslo University Press, Oslo.

Rommetveit, R. and Svalheim, S. (1959). Some halo effects in perception of geometrical patterns. *Acta Psychological* **16,** 11–24. (Also *Nordisk Psykologica* **11,** 11–24.)

Siegel, S. (1956). "Nonparametric Statistics for the Behavioral Sciences." McGraw-Hill, New York.

Smoke, K. L. (1935). The experimental approach to concept learning. *Psychological Review* **42,** 274–279.

Staats, C. K. and Staats, A. W. (1957). Meaning established by classical conditioning. *J. Experimental Psychology* **54,** 74–80.

Vinacke, W. E. (1951). The investigation of concept formation. *Psychological Bulletin* **48,** 1–31.

10. Effects of an Extra Intention to Verbalize the Concept and of Stimulus Pre-differentiation*

R. ROMMETVEIT

In a previous study, a "pre-functional" stage of concept formation was identified. While learning to discriminate between categories of complex geometrical patterns, the relevant attribute (i.e. the geometrical attribute defining the concept to be learned) had acquired distinctiveness at a stage when the subjects were as yet incapable of better-than-chance sorting of patterns into conceptual categories (Rommetveit, 1960).

Every subject was invited to play at a wheel of fortune. The latter was hidden and would start rotating when he put a 2 öre coin in a slot and pushed a button. When it stopped, a geometrical figure resembling a cup-and-saucer pattern would appear in front of him. Some such figures, he had been told, would be "good", some "neither good nor bad" and some "bad". Whenever a "good" pattern appeared, 7 öre would automatically be released immediately afterwards. Every "medium" pattern would release 2 öre, and "bad" patterns would give no money at all.

The geometrical patterns had been selected on the basis of psychophysical judgement (Rommetveit and Svalheim, 1959). Prior to any learning, they would all look very much alike, even though varied systematically with respect to two complex attributes that may be labelled *extent* and *roundness* respectively. A sample of nine such patterns is shown in Fig. 1. In one condition, extent was made instrumentally relevant. Thus, all large patterns like C, F and I in Fig. 1 would signal luck, whereas every small pattern like A, D and G would be followed by no reward at all. In another condition, roundness was rewarded. Then, all maximally roundish patterns like A, B and C would signal maximal

* This study was supported by the Norwegian Research Council for Science and the Humanities. Published in *Scandinavian J. Psychology* (1965) **6**, 59–64.

reward and all extremely angular patterns like G, H and I were
"bad".

Conceptual achievement was assessed in terms of (a) unexpected
recognition tests; (b) sorting behaviour and (c) post-experimental
verbal descriptions of "good" and "bad" patterns. Recognition was
tested at exposures no. 27, 72, 144, 247, 396 and 620. Each time, the

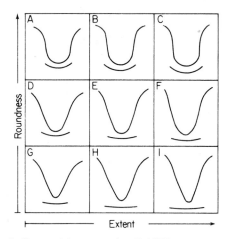

FIG. 1. Recognition test stimuli (differences exaggerated).

subject was asked to identify, among nine different patterns randomly
labelled and mounted in an irregular order on a round board, the
pattern that had just disappeared. After doing so, he was asked to tell
which of the eight remaining patterns were most and second most
similar to the one he had just seen on the wheel of fortune. The patterns
exposed at presentations no. 27, 72, etc. were always chosen from the
four corner positions in Fig. 1, i.e. it would be either A or C or G or I;
and the patterns *mounted on the "recognition board"* were all nine patterns
in Fig. 1. Therefore, recognition could be assessed in terms of error of
roundness- and extent-recognition, i.e. in terms of deviations from the
appropriate row and the appropriate column of Fig. 1, respectively.
Responses were weighted, furthermore. The subject's first choice would
be multiplied by three, his second choice by two, and his third choice
by one. If pattern C had been shown and he afterwards identified B,
C and D as, in order, the pattern itself and the ones most and second-
most similar to it, his recognition-of-roundness error score would be
$0 \times 3 + 0 \times 2 + 1 \times 1 = 1$, and his recognition-of-extent score $1 \times 3 + 0 \times 2$
$+ 2 \times 1 = 5$.

Each such recognition test was followed by a guessing series. For
each of 12 extreme (either "good" or "bad") patterns, the subject was
then asked to tell whether the pattern was good or bad, and the prize

was always withheld until he had made his guess. In this way, a measure of sorting achievement or "functional concept" was assessed.

The results showed that concept learning, as measured both by recognition and sorting, was faster when roundness was rewarded. Furthermore, *a perfect (and selective) recognition of roundness was achieved at a stage of learning when the actual sorting of patterns into "good" and "bad" was still no better than chance.*

It should be kept in mind, however, that these persons had *not* been given the task of "learning a concept". They were just playing at the wheel of fortune, expecting to have a chat with the experimenter afterwards about their interests in such "gambling activities". Nor had they been informed beforehand about systematic geometrical differences between stimulus patterns.

Method

The present study is an expansion of the experiment summarized above. Stimuli and experimental procedures have been described in detail before (Rommetveit, 1960), and part of the data was then included (F, or our $\bar{\text{I}}\bar{\text{P}}$-condition). In short, learning a concept in this experimental context means simply *learning the difference between cup-and-saucer patterns signalling luck and those not signalling luck at a wheel of fortune.*

Subjects were 12–13 year old boys from elementary schools in Oslo. In each case, the boy was given some money and invited to play at the wheel of fortune. In condition $\bar{\text{I}}\bar{\text{P}}$ (neither any extra *intention* to describe the difference nor sensory *predifferentiation*) no further instruction was given. In condition IP (extra *intention* to verbalize and *pre-differentiation*) the following additional treatments were given:

(I) The subject was explicitly told that he would be asked to describe the difference between "good" and "bad" patterns.

(P) He was shown four test patterns by which all the varied geometrical dimensions (*height and roundness of cup* and *length and bowedness of saucer*) were clearly demonstrated. Before starting to play, he was thus taught to point out and label all the geometrical aspects along which the wheel-of-fortune patterns differed.

The two other conditions ($I\bar{\text{P}}$ and $\bar{\text{I}}P$) were simply the remaining combinations of I and P, as will be seen in Table I.

Apart from these differential treatments prior to the playing session, the procedures were identical for all four conditions. *The "good" figures were always the maximally round ones, irrespective of extent.* Thus, ABC in Fig. 1 were good and GHI were bad. Eight subjects were assigned randomly to each condition, and the playing session consisted of 324 trials, with recognition test and subsequent guessing series inserted at exposures no. 27, 72, 144 and 247.

TABLE I. Pre-experimental treatments.

		Taught to notice and label all varied attributes	
		Yes	No
Extra request to describe	Yes	IP	IP̄
good and bad figure	No	ĪP	ĪP̄

Results

The information concerning a concept of good (and bad) wheel-of-fortune pattern stems from two main sets of data: (1) unexpected recognition tests, and (2) guessing at good and bad patterns. Table II shows the number of subjects acquiring the concept with respect to

TABLE II. Number of subjects achieving the concept with respect to each of two criteria.

	Condition			
Task	IP	IP̄	ĪP	ĪP̄
Recognition	6	5	4	7
Guessing	7	7	5	7
N	8	8	8	8

each of the criteria. *Recognition* is here recorded as correct only if the subject on at least one of the tests had a recognition-of-roundness error below two ($p < 0.05$; Rommetveit, 1960, p. 121). For *guessing*, ten or more correct guesses out of 12 are required ($p < 0.05$; ibid., p. 122). It will be seen that most subjects learned to guess correctly at good and bad wheel-of-fortune figures before the playing session came to an end. A more thorough examination of the temporal sequences of recognition and guessing achievements, however, reveals some characteristic differences between conditions.

Table III shows the results of the unexpected recognition test at exposure no. 144, when some learning was first clearly demonstrated. The subject was then, immediately after the exposure of pattern C,

TABLE III. "Hits" of recognition at exposure no. 144.

	Condition			
Location	IP	IP̄	ĪP	ĪP̄
Within BCF	35	30	31	37
Within ABC	36	32	24	43
Within CFI	27	21	25	18

asked to identify it among the nine patterns in Fig. 1 as they appeared randomly labelled and randomly mounted on the round wheel. He was also asked to pick out the pattern most similar and the one second-most similar to the one he had just seen. In Table III, his three choices are weighted. His first choice is considered as three throws, his second choice as two throws, and his third choice as one throw at Fig. 1 with the aim of hitting cell C. Each condition is thus given $8 \times 6 = 48$ throws. For any triad of cells, furthermore, the expected random performance is 16, whereas maximal number of hits is 48.

Observed overall accuracy of recognition (hits within BCF) is fairly stable over conditions, no difference between any pair of conditions reaching the 10% level of significance as estimated by Chi-square tests. If hits in the upper row are counted, however, ĪP̄ is superior to all other conditions. It is as if subjects in ĪP̄ have been aiming exclusively at the appropriate roundness row without concern about the irrelevant attribute (column location of the pattern). When trained to point out and label all stimulus attributes prior to the learning session (conditions ĪP and IP), however, they have clearly been aiming at the appropriate column as well.

The upper row of Table IV gives the number of persons in each condition whose first error-of-recognition score below two was obtained by locating the test figure in the appropriate row. Again ĪP̄ stands out; comparing these subjects with all others, the ratios are 7/1 versus 16/8 ($p < 0.01$ by Fischer's exact probability test).

TABLE IV. Distribution of individual temporal sequences of achievements under the four conditions.

	Condition			
Pattern	IP	IP̄	ĪP	ĪP̄
Hit of row as first significant achievement	3/8	3/8	2/8	7/8
Error-of-roundness-recognition curve passing three before guessing curve	1/6	0/7	3/8	6/7

The relationships between curves for roundness recognition errors and guessing errors for each person (Rommetveit, 1960, p. 122) are recorded in the lower row of Table IV. An error score of three is here chosen as the point of departure, and all subjects whose recognition *and* guessing scores drop below three *simultaneously* are excluded. (The expected distributions of both error scores range from 0 to 12, with $M = 6$.) Once more, $\bar{\text{I}}\bar{\text{P}}$ stands out as clearly different from all other conditions. The selective perceptual focusing upon the relevant roundness aspect of the geometrical patterns at an early stage of learning was thus *not* observed when an extra intention to verbalize the concept had been induced. Nor was it observed under conditions of sensory pre-differentiation prior to the learning session.

Discussion

The purpose of this study was to explore the conditions under which the relevant stimulus aspect acquires distinctiveness prior to any behavioural manifestation of concept learning. The unexpected recognition test is actually nothing more than a request that the subject shall identify a visual pattern which has just disappeared. However, the patterns among which he identifies the test stimulus are so arranged that it can be inferred whether perceptual learning has occurred and which aspect of the two-dimensional geometrical pattern has been focused upon.

As might be expected, pre-differentiation training seems to sensitize subjects to the irrelevant aspect. Table III shows that the number of "hits" in the appropriate column is 27 and 25 for IP and $\bar{\text{I}}$P, respectively. As compared to an expected random performance of 16 hits, these numbers testify to a fairly accurate recognition of "extent". In the I$\bar{\text{P}}$-condition, however, correct column identification is not so good.

The only unequivocal case of perceptual selectivity, though, is I$\bar{\text{P}}$, whose roundness recognition represents only a slight (and statistically insignificant) deviation from perfect hit, and whose extent recognition is almost as close to random performance as possible. Even of greater interest is the distribution of temporal patterns of achievement. As Table IV shows, the rule for I$\bar{\text{P}}$ subjects is a perfect roundness recognition prior to correct guessing. This does not hold when a person anticipates being rehearsed about differences. Nor does it hold when he has been trained to notice and label systematic stimulus differences prior to the playing session.

It must be concluded, therefore, that selective perception of the relevant stimulus attribute occurs only under a very narrow range of conditions. In the next study, a replication of the I$\bar{\text{P}}$-condition will be included in order to decide whether the first results actually can be relied upon. Further theoretical discussion will be postponed until the results from these new experiments are obtained.

References

Rommetveit, R. (1960). Stages in concept formation and levels of cognitive functioning. *Scandinavian J. Psychology* **1,** 115–124.

Rommetveit, R. and Svalheim, S. (1959). Some halo effects in perception of geometrical patterns. *Acta Psychologica* **16,** 11–24. (Also *Nordisk Psykologica* **11,** 11–24.)

11. Further Enquiries into the Effects of an Extra Intention to Verbalize*

R. ROMMETVEIT and S. KVALE

In previous experiments (Rommetveit, 1960, 1965) subjects learned to discriminate between complex geometrical patterns signalling luck and those not signalling luck at a wheel of fortune. It was found that the instrumentally relevant attribute of patterns acquired perceptual distinctiveness at a stage of learning when the subjects were not yet able to sort patterns into appropriate conceptual categories. However, such a "pre-functional" stage of concept formation was *not* identified when the subjects had been told explicitly that they would be asked what "good" and "bad" patterns were like. Nor was it observed when they were trained to observe and label all systematically varied geometrical properties of the patterns before they started playing.

Method

The present experiment is a replication and further extension of the studies mentioned above. The only deviations from the previously reported stimulus presentation are as follows:

(a) The geometrical patterns were drawn in black, not in red.
(b) Exposure time for each pattern was 2·5 s.

The subjects were 12–13 year old boys from elementary schools in Oslo. Each boy was given a small amount of money and invited to play at a wheel of fortune. For half of the subjects no further instructions were given. The other half were also told explicitly that they would be asked to describe the difference between "good" and "bad" patterns afterwards.

"Roundness" of stimulus patterns (the vertical dimension in Fig. 1)

* This study was supported by a grant from the Norwegian Council for Science and the Humanities. Published in *Scandinavian J. Psychology* (1965) **6**, 65–74.

was made the relevant attribute. This time, however, the reward schedule was different for different conditions. Independent studies had provided unequivocal evidence that 12–13 year old boys *a priori* expected maximally roundish patterns to signal luck and the more angular ones to be "bad" (Rommetveit, 1963). For half of the subjects, therefore, GHI in Fig. 1 were reward patterns and ABC were "bad". For the other half the opposite held true.

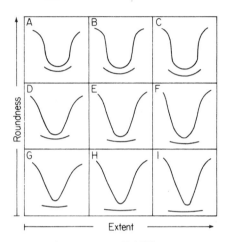

Fig. 1. Recognition test stimuli (differences exaggerated).

The resultant combination of instruction and reward schedule are presented in Table I. Conditions IE (extra *intention* to report difference, reward schedule *expected*) and ĪE (no such extra intention, reward schedule expected) are simply replications of previous conditions (Rommetveit, 1965). Conditions IĒ and ĪĒ aim at exploring the effects of the extra intention to describe the difference when the "good" and "bad" properties to be learned go contrary to pre-established expectations. Eight boys were randomly assigned to each condition.

Recognition tests were inserted in the playing session at exposures no. 27, 54, 81, 108, 135, 162, 189, 216 and 243, and the subject was not asked to guess at "good" and "bad" figures until he had recognized roundness correctly. Once he had achieved a recognition-of-roundness error score below two, a guessing series was introduced instead of the subsequent recognition test. The subject was then asked to tell whether the pattern was good or bad throughout a series of 12 extreme patterns, i.e. only upper and lower row patterns in Fig. 1. Once he had made ten or more correct guesses, the playing was stopped. If this criterion was not reached, playing was stopped (after a final recognition test *and* a guessing series) at exposure no. 270. Then followed: (a) A free verbal description of "good" and "bad" patterns and of the difference between them. (b) Drawing of one "good" and one "bad" pattern, the subject being asked to exaggerate the difference between them. (c) Sorting of a set of ready-made written descriptions of geometrical characteristics into three boxes, i.e. as either "fits the good figure", or "fits the bad figure", or "fits neither the good nor the bad figure".

When comparing the present study with the ones previously reported, the new features (common to all four conditions) can be summarized as follows:

(1) More recognition tests were inserted as interruptions of playing behaviour.

(2) A stop rule was introduced. Guessing was not asked for until unexpected recognition tests showed that the subject recognized the relevant stimulus attribute. Playing was stopped and post-experimental measures obtained immediately after the guessing series in which the subject demonstrated better-than-chance achievement.

(3) Drawings were obtained from all subjects.

(4) Sorting of ready-made verbal descriptions was introduced as a novel post-experimental measure.

TABLE I. Experimental conditions.

| | | Reward schedule consonant with expectation | |
		Yes	No
Extra request to describe "good" and "bad" figure	Yes	I E	I Ē
	No	Ī E	Ī Ē

Results

Gross Findings

A gross picture of findings is provided by Table II, where *recognition* was recorded as correct only when the subject on at least one recognition test had identified the roundness aspect better than chance (Rommetveit, 1960, p. 121). For *guessing*, ten or more correct guesses out of 12 in a series ($p < 0.05$ by the sign test) were required. For the three post-experimental measures, three judges coded each individual response. Thus, all 32 pairs of drawings were scrambled and each judge had to infer, from each pair, whether the subject producing it had been given reward schedule E ("round good") or Ē ("angular good").

If, and only if, all judges independently were able to identify the reward schedule correctly from the two drawings, were the latter coded as correct. Coding of the free descriptions and sorting of written descriptions were done in the same way. Coder reliability as estimated by Hoyt's analysis (1941) varied from 0·73 for drawings to 0·84 for free verbal descriptions.

TABLE II. Number of subjects who achieved the concept according to each of five criteria.

			Condition			
Task	IE	IĒ	ĪE	ĪĒ	I	Ī
Recognition	6	5	8	6	11	14
Guessing	6	5	5	4	11	9
Free verbalization	5	4	6	6	9	12
Drawing	5	4	6	4	9	10
Sorting of descriptions	3	4	6	7	7	13
N	8	8	8	8	16	16

Table II shows that accurate recognition of roundness was particularly frequent when the reward schedule was tacitly expected and the subject did not anticipate being asked to describe the difference between "good" and "bad" figures (condition ĪE). The table also suggests that subjects who did not expect to describe the difference were *superior* to those with an extra intention to describe when all of them were asked to sort ready-made verbal descriptions at the end of the experiment.

Recognition

A more sensitive measure of *recognition performance* is given in Table III. Here, the average of the three first tests is given for each condition, and the numbers should be read as follows: Pattern C in Fig. 1 has just disappeared and the subject is unexpectedly asked to identify it among the nine patterns in Fig. 1. (Actually both C and G and A were used as recognition test stimuli. The three corresponding matrices of hits have here been combined into one.) Each individual recognition test is conceived of as six throws at the target C, giving $6 \times 8 = 48$ throws under each condition. For any triad of cells, maximal number of hits for each condition is thus 48 and expected random performance is 16.

For the subjects who were not asked to verbalize and who got a reward schedule consonant with expectations (the ĪE condition), the results in Table III replicate the previous findings (Rommetveit, 1965).

TABLE III. Average number of "hits" of recognition in three first tests and temporal sequences under different conditions.

Location	Conditions			
	IE	IĒ	ĪE	ĪĒ
Within BCF	20	19	21	23
Within ABC	21	16	26	19
Within CFI	18	25	17	20
Row hit prior to *column*	3/8	3/8	8/8	2/8

Recognition of the relevant roundness aspect at exposures no. 27, 54 and 81 was on the average fairly accurate ($p < 0.01$ by the Chi-square test), whereas identification of the (irrelevant) "extent" of patterns was not better than chance. Under the other conditions, and in particular when the reward schedule went contrary to expectations, extent was recognized as well.

The bottom row of Table III shows the proportion of subjects whose first error-of-recognition score below two was hit of the *appropriate row*. Again, ĪE stands out as different from all other conditions ($p = 0.025$ for ĪE versus IE and for ĪE versus IĒ, and $p = 0.01$ for ĪE versus ĪĒ, according to Fischer's exact test).

Patterns of Achievements

A distribution of *individual patterns of achievements* as assessed at the end of the learning session is given in Table IV. In the Ī-conditions, 13 out of 16 individual patterns conform to a Guttman scale according to which

TABLE IV. Frequencies of different individual patterns of conceptual achievement.

Pattern					Condition					
R	S	F	D	G	IE	IĒ	ĪE	ĪĒ	I	Ī
+	+	+	+	+	3	2	4	2	5	6
+	+	+	+	—	—	—	1	2	—	3
+	+	+	—	—	—	—	—	1	—	1
+	+	—	—	—	—	—	1	—	—	1
+	—	—	—	—	—	1	1	—	1	1
—	—	—	—	—	—	—	—	1	—	1

recognition test (R), sorting of descriptions (S), free verbalization (F), drawing (D) and guessing (G) can be interpreted as measuring the same underlying variable in a descending order of sensitivity. In the I-conditions only six out of 16 individuals fit this structure.

When all possible intercorrelations between pairs of individual achievements were computed by Kendall's tau for Ī and I separately, the results were as follows: For Ī, nine out of ten taus came out above 0·50, whereas for I, only four out of ten exceeded 0·50. With Fischer's exact test of probabilities on these distributions of intercorrelation measures, a p value of 0·05 is obtained. In short, the analysis of individual patterns of achievement reflects a common internal structure among the subjects who did not anticipate being rehearsed about good and bad figures (condition Ī). No such unequivocal common structure was observed among those who anticipated being rehearsed (condition I).

Sorting of Pregnant and Non-pregnant Descriptions

A more thorough analysis of sortings of verbal descriptions was also performed, and the main outcome is presented in Table V. The upper row shows proportions of subjects who sorted the description "rounder" (in Norwegian: "rundere") correctly. This description seems to be a particularly appropriate and pregnant verbalization of the difference between "good" and "bad" wheel-of-fortune figures. It had frequently been emitted spontaneously in pre-test situations in which 13 year old boys were asked to describe the difference *while looking at the figures*. And in a pre-test group of 23 boys who were asked to sort all the ready-made descriptions with the two extreme patterns in front of them, every single subject sorted them correctly. After having played at the wheel-of-fortune with extra intention to verbalize the difference, however, most subjects were unable to do so. The difference between I and Ī with respect to correct sorting of "rounder" yields a p value of 0·001 as estimated by Fischer's exact test.

TABLE V. Proportion of subjects within each condition who achieved correct sorting of verbal descriptions.

Description(s) sorted	Condition					
	IE	IĒ	ĪE	ĪĒ	I	Ī
"Rounder"	3/8	3/8	6/8	7/8	6/16	13/16
All "pregnant"	3/8	3/8	6/8	7/8	6/16	13/16
All "non-pregnant"	4/8	3/8	3/8	3/8	7/16	6/16

In the two lower rows of Table V, all ready-made descriptions of relevant stimulus differences have been divided into a set of "pregnant" and a set of "non-pregnant" descriptions. The pregnant descriptions were: "rounder"; "sharper"; "more V-shaped"; "more U-shaped"; (cup) "wider at the bottom"; and (cup) "more narrow at the bottom". (In Norwegian: "rundere"; "spissere"; "mer V-formet"; "mer U-formet"; "videre i bunnen"; and "spissere i bunnen".) The non-pregnant descriptions were: "more straight-lined"; "less straight-lined"; (cup) "hooks at top larger"; (cup) "hooks at top smaller"; (saucer) "more curved"; and (saucer) "less curved". (In Norwegian: "mer rettlinjet"; "mindre rettlinjet"; "hakene oppe større"; "hakene oppe mindre"; "mer bøyd"; "mindre bøyd".)

The *a priori* rationale for dividing the 12 descriptions into two separate sets is simply that the items belonging to the "pregnant" set refer to salient and global features of the stimuli and were readily emitted by a naïve subject observing one good and one bad pattern in front of him. The "non-pregnant" items refer to less pregnant, more peripheral aspects.

TABLE VI. Reliability and common variance of sorting and guessing achievements for I and Ī as estimated by an extended Hoyt procedure.

Measures	Sorting all pregnant descriptions	Sorting all non-pregnant descriptions	Guessing
Sorting all pregnant descriptions	I = 0·81 Ī = 0·78		
Sorting all non-pregnant descriptions	I = 0·35 Ī = −0·25	I = 0·72 Ī = 0·57	
Guessing	I = 0·24 Ī = 0·49	I = 0·27 Ī = −0·64	I = 0·70 Ī = 0·70

The empirical basis for our split stems from an analysis of variance of sorting and guessing achievements. The results of this analysis are presented in Table VI. Here, the guessing series has been considered a 12-item test. The sortings of pregnant and non-pregnant descriptions have been treated as two separate 6-item tests, and the diagonal cells simply show test reliability as computed by the Hoyt procedure (Hoyt, 1941). The estimation of variance common to any pair of tests is based upon an extension of the Hoyt procedure as described by Rabinowitz and Eikeland (1964).

The results under Ī-conditions may be described as follows. Sorting of pregnant descriptions was fairly reliable, though entirely unrelated to sorting of non-pregnant descriptions. Correct sorting of pregnant descriptions tended to coincide with correct guessing, whereas correct sorting of non-pregnant descriptions was slightly negatively correlated with correct guessing. (The common variance measure of -0.49 corresponds to $r = -0.24$.)

The overall sorting achievement must therefore be broken down into two separate units, i.e. into the pregnant and non-pregnant descriptions as described above. And for the two lower rows of Table V, "correct sorting" means at least four out of six descriptions put in the appropriate box.

Considering, then, the sorting of all six pregnant descriptions, the results come out exactly as those for the single description "rounder". The extra intention to describe good and bad patterns leads to a poorer performance at the sorting-of-verbal-descriptions task. This poorer performance is restricted to the set of pregnant verbal labels only and holds for both reward schedules (conditions IE and IĒ).

Discussion

The present results include an unequivocal replication of previously reported findings (Rommetveit, 1960, 1965) in which a "pre-functional" stage of concept formation was identified. This early stage of learning is inferred from unexpected recognition tests and sequences of guessing tasks as a stage at which the initially unfamiliar, relevant stimulus aspect has acquired distinctiveness even though the subject is as yet unable to sort consecutively presented instances into the appropriate categories "good" and "bad" wheel-of-fortune patterns.

This early perceptual achievement, however, is observed only when the following requirements are fulfilled: (1) The reward schedule is consonant with pre-established expectations, i.e. roundish patterns are good. (2) The subject is given no training in attending to and labelling stimulus differences prior to playing at the wheel of fortune. (3) The subject does not anticipate being asked to describe the difference between good and bad patterns.

It seems reasonable, therefore, to conceive of the pre-established expectation "round figures are good" as an implicit programme for perceptual scanning, i.e. as a primary "hypothesis" (Krechevsky, 1932), or "search plan" (Miller et al., 1960). Attending to the irrelevant aspect "extent" will then occur only when (1) the initial expectation proves wrong, or (2) the subject has been taught to notice and label differences in extent, or (3) he has an extra intention to describe—and therefore search for—stimulus differences.

The observed improved recognition of the irrelevant attribute when the reward schedule goes contrary to expectation is thus in harmony with dissonance theory (Festinger, 1957). The experience that "roundish patterns are *not* good" represents a state of dissonance, out of which search for new information, i.e. scanning of patterns with respect to other attributes, emerges. Such scanning of an irrelevant aspect is also to be expected when the subject has been trained to notice and label it in advance.

The extra request for a description of the difference between good and bad figures resembles instructions by which subjects are required to make use of specific verbal labels during discrimination learning (Kendler and Kendler, 1962; Luria, 1961). In the present case, *the subject himself* must find the appropriate label(s). The anticipation that he will be rehearsed by the experimenter induces *a set to report*. Perceiving proper may then be temporarily interrupted by *a process of retrospective linguistic encoding of the perceived*, which in turn affects subsequent perceptual scanning. If so, his visual exploration of stimuli has the additional purpose of *checking tentative verbal descriptions of differences* (Rommetveit, 1961). This may explain why his exploration extends beyond the otherwise primary scanning of roundness only.

Evidence in support of such an interpretation is found when examining post-experimental verbal descriptions of good and bad patterns. Spontaneous reference to stimulus details like hooks was thus more frequent among the subjects who anticipated being rehearsed. The most convincing evidence, however, stems from the sorting of ready-made verbal descriptions (Tables V and VI). The nearly complete failure of the extra-intention subjects to sort highly pregnant descriptions like "rounder" correctly makes it clear that they had not been attending selectively to roundness in the same way as roundness is attended to by naïve subjects who *form* and *verbalize* first impressions of the differences between a good and a bad pattern. The fact that their sorting of non-pregnant verbal descriptions is *as good* and *as highly related to* correct guessing, furthermore, testifies to a search for stimulus differences over and beyond such a global scanning of the relevant aspect.

The major experimental variable in this study—an extra intention on the part of the subject to describe good and bad patterns—is introduced by a few extra words prior to the playing session. The effect of these words upon subsequent conceptual achievement, however, is dramatic. The modal individual patterns in the two conditions are clearly different, as seen in Table IV.

When subjects have been playing without any extra intention to report differences, conceptual achievement can apparently afterwards be assessed as a unitary and scalable variable. Some subjects are able to recognize the relevant aspect, but fail at all other measures. Others can both recognize roundness correctly and sort pregnant verbal descriptions, but nothing else. Still others master both recognition and sorting and are, in addition, able to describe the difference fairly appropriately in their own words. A still higher level of achievement may be attributed to those who master all the above mentioned tasks plus drawing of good and bad figures so that they can be correctly identified. And finally, correct guessing enters as the highest achievement, attained only by those who master the concept with respect to all the above mentioned criteria.

An extrapolation from this post-experimental pattern of achievement to *a temporal pattern of concept formation* raises almost insurmountable difficulties. It is conceivable that some learning occurs during post-experimental tasks. The temporal sequence of tasks therefore raises problems. One subject may, for instance, become aware of a specific difference between good and bad patterns while trying to draw two such patterns. If so, his subsequent sorting of verbal descriptions may reflect learning over and beyond his level of achievement at the end of the playing session.

Secondly, *base-line probabilities are different for different tests*. For the recognition and guessing tasks, probability of success is very low ($p <$ 0·05). For free verbalization, drawing, and sorting of verbal descriptions, on the other hand, final scoring by the group of judges involve only two categories. For each of these tests, therefore, the most conservative estimate of probability of success will come close to 0·50.

Identical tests and *the same sequence among them* apply to both main conditions, however. Yet, different final patterns of achievement presuppose different geneses. An attempt will now be made to explore into the impact of the extra intention to verbalize upon concept learning by a *post facto* analysis. Consider the common pattern observed under conditions when no extra set to report has been induced. Which temporal pattern of concept formation would generate the post-experimental distribution of achievements presented in Table IV? The proposed answer is as follows.

First, *the relevant stimulus attribute acquires distinctiveness*. As previously reported by Rommetveit (1960), "roundness" is more salient and more easily discriminated than "extent", despite the fact that the two discrimination tasks appear to be equally difficult as estimated in terms of threshold values obtained from psychophysical judgements (Rommetveit and Svalheim,1959).

Independent studies in our laboratory by T. Lund (1964) of paired comparisons with our cup-and-saucer patterns as stimuli, corroborate this finding. When subjects were simply given the task to order patterns with respect to similarity, roundness proved significantly superior to extent. In addition, 12–13 year old boys expect "roundness" to be associated with luck in the playing situation (Rommetveit, 1963). The very first strategy to be adopted will therefore probably be *a scanning of patterns with respect to the relevant stimulus aspect.*, i.e. *roundness*.

If the subject were captured at this early scanning stage and asked to sort *ready-made* verbal descriptions of the difference between good and bad figures, incorrect sorting of very pregnant descriptions would hardly ever occur. Once he is on the right track in his visual exploration of the stimuli, he will also be able to check his impression of good and bad figures against pregnant verbal labels in such a way as to avoid failure. When asked to describe the difference in his own words, furthermore, he would be expected to do so at least slightly better than chance. His description may be highly inadequate in many respects. It may be global and physiognomic ("the good figure smiles, the bad figure is sad") or it may include clearly irrelevant aspects ("the good figure is large, it is more heavily drawn", etc.). Still, his description as a whole may be sufficiently informative for the group of judges to infer whether round or angular figures have been rewarded.

It is important to remember, however, that neither of these "verbal measures" can be interpreted as assessing the formation of a verbal concept. No active verbalization in the form of silent speech during the preceding playing is required prior to successful performance. Optimal performance may indeed occur—and is perhaps even most likely to occur—when the preceding perceptual scanning has been devoid of linguistic encoding, for instance on the part of a subject whose sorting of descriptions was controlled by an eidetic memory of specific good and bad figures. We have no reason to believe that eidetic imagery played any significant role at all. The important point is, however, that success at the two post-experimental verbal tasks may stem from entirely "wordless" impressions.

Such impressions may still prove insufficient when the subject is given the task of communicating them by means of free drawings. The latter implies reproduction of the entire pattern, parts of which may have been largely ignored during the formation of a first global impression. Successful reproduction also requires some motor skill.

The shortcomings of such global impressions are most clearly revealed when the subject is called upon to decide whether specific figures are good or bad. Each instance represents a unique combination of relevant and *irrelevant* attributes. Thus one "good" pattern is roundish and contains a high cup and a short saucer, another contains a low cup and a long saucer, etc. and discriminable differences with respect to extent may therefore serve to mask similarities with respect to curvature. Being on the right track, i.e. proceeding on the tacit assumption that "roundish patterns are good", will then prove insufficient as a basis for judging which specific instances belong to which conceptual category.

The main effect of an extra intention to report on the difference between good and bad patterns may then be conceived of as *a disruption of the intuitive strategy* described above. Subjects in the I-conditions are set to encode impressions of differences in their own words. Their reactions to a given pattern may, therefore, involve an oscillation between two activities, namely perceptual scanning (impression formation) and a checking of tentative verbal labels against as yet non-verbalized impressions. No simple verbal labels (like "rounder") are fully appropriate, however, when their impressions of differences are to be communicated to another person. In order to solve the extra task of verbal communication, therefore, the subjects in the I-conditions probably proceed to *scan and encode parts and aspects of the patterns over and beyond the central parts and relevant aspects captured by the word "rounder"*. As their actual sorting of instances improves, they are more and more inclined to discard as inappropriate the pregnant verbalizations that appear natural to subjects who proceed "privately", i.e. with no extra intention to communicate their impressions of good and bad patterns to the experimenter.

In the next study, we shall try to explore further into this assumed negative interference by assessing effects of verbalization at different stages of learning.

References

Festinger, L. (1957). "A Theory of Cognitive Dissonance." Row, Petersen and Co., Evanstone.

Hoyt, C. (1941). Test reliability obtained by analysis of variance. *Psychometrika* **6**, 153–160.

Kendler, H. H. and Kendler, T. S. (1962). Vertical and horizontal processes in problem solving. *Psychological Review* **69**, 1–14.

Krechevsky, G. (1932). "Hypotheses" in rats. *Psychological Review* **39**, 516–532.

Lund, T. (1964). A psychometric analysis of perceived similarities among multidimensional geometrical patterns. Manuscript of the University of Oslo.

Luria, A. R. (1961). "The role of speech in the regulation of normal and abnormal behavior." Pergamon Press, Oxford.

Miller, G. A., Galanter, E. and Pribram, K. H. (1960). "Plans and the structure of behavior." Holt, Rinehart and Winston, New York.

Rabinowitz, W. and Eikeland, H. M. (1964). Estimating the reliability of tests with clustered items. *Pedagogisk forskning* (Oslo) **1**, 85–106.

Rommetveit, R. (1960). Stages in concept formation and levels of cognitive functioning. *Scandinavian J. Psychology* **1**, 115–124.

Rommetveit, R. (1961). Perceptual behavior and ideational components of discriminatory and conceptual activities. *Acta Psychologica* **18**, 201–215.

Rommetveit, R. (1963). Cognition of expected and unexpected relations. *Perceptual and Motor Skills* **17**, 396.

Rommetveit, R. (1965). Stages in concept formation II. Effects of an extra intention to verbalize the concept and of stimulus pre-differentiation. *Scandinavian J. Psychology* **6**, 59–62.

Rommetveit, R. and Svalheim, R. (1959). Some halo effects in perception of geometrical patterns. *Acta Psychologica* **16**, 11–24. (Also *Nordisk Psykologica* **11**, 11–24.)

12. A Temporal Analysis of Effects of an Extra Intention to Verbalize*

R. ROMMETVEIT and S. KVALE

In a series of studies (Rommetveit, 1960, 1965; Rommetveit and Kvale, 1965) 12–13 year old boys have learned the difference between geometrical patterns that signal luck and those not signalling luck while playing at a wheel of fortune. In the last study, conceptual achievement was assessed by (1) unexpected recognition tests, (2) guessing tasks, (3) free verbal descriptions, (4) drawings and (5) sorting of ready-made verbal descriptions.

In the first studies it was possible to identify an early stage of learning during which a subject has a selective recognition of the relevant geometrical aspect of the pattern but cannot yet tell which patterns are "good" and "bad". The findings were replicated in a later study by Rommetveit and Kvale (1965). This early perceptual stage, however, has been clearly demonstrated only when (1) the reward schedule conforms to a priori expectations, and (2) the subject is not trained to notice and label geometrical differences between the patterns before he starts playing, and (3) the subject does not anticipate being rehearsed about "good" and "bad" patterns afterwards.

In the last study, the most striking finding was a very poor performance on the part of the boys who anticipated being rehearsed, when they were given the tasks of sorting fairly simple and pregnant verbal descriptions of the difference into the three boxes "fits good pattern", "fits bad pattern" and "fits neither good nor bad pattern". They were slightly superior to others at guessing which patterns were good and bad, but clearly inferior with respect to sorting of descriptions, and reflected on the whole a less tightly structured pattern of individual achievement.

The present study is an attempt to explore further into the apparently detrimental effect of an intention to verbalize by measuring conceptual achievements at a very early stage of learning.

* This study was supported by the Norwegian Research Council for Science and the Humanities. Published in Scandinavian J. Psychology (1965) 6, 75–79.

Method

Two experiments were conducted. In both of them the reward schedule was consonant with expectations, i.e. the maximally round patterns signalled luck. In both experiments, furthermore, half of the subjects (12–13 year old boys) were told that they would be asked to describe "good" and "bad" patterns after having played for a while (Condition I), whereas the other half were just invited to play (Condition I). All subjects were playing at the wheel of fortune without interruption for 81 trials. The 18 subjects in the first experiment were then given a recognition test, continued playing throughout a guessing series, and were immediately afterwards asked to describe good and bad figures, to draw a good and a bad figure, and to sort verbal descriptions. The 20 subjects in the second experiment were given the sorting task immediately after exposure no. 81, i.e. without any other task preceding it.

Results

The results from the first experiment are presented in Tables I and II. Scoring and coding criteria have been described before (Rommetveit and Kvale, 1965). It is seen that a majority of the Ī-subjects already at this stage had mastered the *three post-experimental tasks*. They could use their own words to describe the difference, they could draw two extreme patterns, and they could sort ready-made descriptions in such a way that three judges for each such individual achievement as a rule unanimously inferred concept learning. Among the boys who antici-pated being rehearsed, however, guessing achievement was good and verbal descriptions rather poor.

TABLE I. Number of subjects who achieved the concept according to each of five criteria.

Condition	N	Recognition	Guessing	Free verbalization	Drawing	Sorting
I	9	0	5	2	5	7
Ī	9	2	2	7	7	8

The pattern analysis in Table II, furthermore, reflects the same structure as observed in the earlier study. Under the Ī-condition, seven out of nine subjects fit a Guttman scale pattern according to which sorting (S), free verbalization (F), drawing (D), guessing (G) and recognition (R) may be interpreted as measuring the same variable in a descending order of sensitivity.

TABLE II. Distribution of individual patterns of conceptual achievements after 81 trials

Pattern					Condition	
S	F	D	G	R	I	Ī
+	+	+	+	+	—	1
+	+	+	+	—	1	1
+	+	+	—	—	—	4
+	+	—	—	—	1	—
+	—	—	—	—	1	1
—	—	—	—	—	—	—

If recognition is ignored, the pattern of achievements is identical to the one revealed by 13 out of 16 Ī-subjects at the end of a longer playing session (Rommetveit and Kvale, 1965). A similar internal structure cannot be found in the I-condition. When the post-experimental tasks alone are considered, six out of nine Ī-subjects have mastered all of them while only one I-subject has done so. The difference yields a $p < 0.05$ by Fischer's exact probability test.

TABLE III. Proportion of subjects under each condition who achieved correct sorting at stage 1, 2 and 3.[a]

	Descriptions								
	Rounder			All pregnant			All non-pregnant		
Condition	1	2	3	1	2	3	1	2	3
I	7/10	7/9	6/16	7/10	7/9	6/16	8/10	5/9	7/16
Ī	8/10	8/9	13/16	6/10	8/9	13/16	9/10	7/9	6/16

[a] Cf. text.

In Table III, the sorting-of-verbal-descriptions data from the present experiments and the previous study are brought together. *Stage 1* refers to sortings of descriptions immediately after exposure no. 81. *Stage 2* refers to the sortings at exposure no. 108, after recognition test, guessing, free description and drawing. *Stage 3* refers to the sortings performed at the end of the learning session, i.e. after 270 trials at a maximum. Since the subjects are drawn from a homogeneous population of 12–13 year old school boys and randomly assigned to conditions, we may venture to read the table *horizontally* as describing change from stage to stage and *vertically* as describing differences between learning conditions.

The main findings in Table III can then be briefly summarized as follows: (1) The Ī-subjects were clearly superior to I-subjects at sorting "pregnant" verbal descriptions of the geometrical difference between good and bad figures at the end of a long playing session. Fischer's exact probability test for sortings of "rounder" at stage 3 and of all "pregnant" descriptions at stage 3 yields $p < 0.001$ in both cases. (2) No such difference between conditions is found at the early stages of learning. (3) For the I-condition, sorting of pregnant descriptions is fairly good at the beginning of a playing session, but strikingly poor at a later stage. The proportion of correct sortings of the description "rounder" for stages 1 and 2 combined is thus 14/19; for stage 3 it is 6/16. The difference yields a p-value less than 0.01 by the Chi-square test. The corresponding proportions for success at "pregnant" descriptions as a whole are also 14/19 versus 6/16.

Discussion

The major independent variable throughout this series of experimental studies is an intention on the part of the subject to verbalize the concept. This variable is induced by a few extra words of instruction. In one case, the subject is told in advance that the experimenter will ask him to describe good and bad wheel-of-fortune patterns after he has been playing for a while. In the other case, the subject starts playing without the anticipation that he will be rehearsed about stimulus differences.

The impact of this variable—*absence* versus *presence of an extra intention to communicate subjective impressions*—is reflected in clearly different patterns of achievements. When the subject proceeds "privately", without any request to report, unexpected recognition tests shows that he is able to attend selectively to the "roundness" of patterns at a very early stage. He is also able to sort pregnant *ready-made* descriptions of the difference between good and bad patterns (like "rounder") correctly, even at a stage when his actual sorting of specific patterns into appropriate conceptual properties is hardly better than chance. The post-experimental patterns of individual achievements under conditions of *no extra intention to verbalize* thus testify to an intuitive strategy by which *global* and *non-verbalized* impressions of the relevant stimulus attribute are built up and successively differentiated so as to become a sufficient basis for correct sorting of actual instances, i.e. correct guessing. Success at sorting of ready-made verbal descriptions may therefore be conceived of as a checking of *privately* appropriate but non-verbalized impressions against an externally provided grid of words, and can obviously not be interpreted as evidence of an "active" verbal concept at all. If so, the data in Table III would force us to conclude that a majority of subjects in both conditions achieve an appropriate verbal concept at a very early stage of the playing session.

As earlier suggested by Rommetveit and Kvale (1965), the extra request to verbalize seems to interfere in an otherwise intuitive process. The evidence of interference is provided by observed different patterns of achievements as shown in Table II, and in particular in the failure to apply pregnant ready-made verbal descriptions to the appropriate conceptual categories at a stage of learning when the sorting of actual stimulus patterns in appropriate categories is nearly perfect.

The present experiments provide some additional information concerning the temporal sequence of interference. At the very beginning of the playing session, the I-subjects are apparently as good as Ī-subjects at sorting descriptions. It seems reasonable to assume, therefore, that they start out with the same kind of global, non-verbalized first impressions of differences. A checking of such impressions against tentative verbalizations (to be used to communicate impressions to the experimenter), however, must somehow affect subsequent scanning and linguistic encoding of geometrical patterns.

A tentative model for the resultant bi-polar process of *information seeking* and *linguistic encoding* has been suggested by Rommetveit (1961) and Rommetveit and Kvale (1965). A somewhat dramatic case of *interference* was observed during pilot runs of the experiment.

A boy was playing at the wheel of fortune with no extra intention to verbalize. When he had clearly demonstrated his ability to guess which patterns were good and which were bad, he was asked to describe the difference between the two categories. This, he felt, was "impossible", but upon the experimenter's request he made an attempt, and he ended up by giving a positively wrong description. Afterwards, when he continued playing and was asked to guess which patterns were good and which were bad, his performance was no better than chance. Obviously, he now felt committed to guess on the basis of the verbal description he had given, and proved actually unable to recapture the non-verbalized impression upon which his successful guessing had been based before he was asked to put it into words.

In this case, an *unexpected* request for communication appeared to have a disruptive effect upon an intuitively established strategy of discrimination. The request for communication prior to the playing session, however, will probably make for a subtle strategy of *alternation* between receptive processes and linguistic encoding throughout the learning period.

References

Rommetveit, R. (1960) Stages in concept formation and levels of cognitive functioning. *Scandinavian J. Psychology* **1**, 115–124.

Rommetveit, R. (1961). Perceptional, behavioral and ideational components of discriminatory and conceptual activities. *Acta Psychologia* **18**, 201–215.

Rommetveit, R. (1965). Stages in concept formation II. Effects of an extra intention to verbalize the concept and of stimulus predifferentiation. *Scandinavian J. Psychology* **6**, 59–64.

Rommetveit, R. and Kvale, S. (1965). Stages in concept formation III. Further inquiries into an extra intention to verbalize. *Scandinavian J. Psychology* **6**, 65–74.

13. Determinants of Interpretation of Homonyms in Word Association Contexts*

R. ROMMETVEIT and F. STRØMNES

In studies of the associative meaning of words, the assumption is frequently made that the stimulus word "elicits itself as an association" (Deese 1962; Garskof and Houston, 1963). Such an assumption seems plausible and even necessary in view of certain methodological requirements. Its theoretical implications, however, are by no means unequivocal. If the word always elicits "itself", we should actually expect an endless chain of repetitions of the stimulus word. And the ambiguity of the term "itself" in the context above becomes obvious in the case of homonyms, i.e. when a single written or spoken verbal stimulus pattern serves as a potential releasor of two or more distinctively different representational processes.

When homonyms are encountered as subunits of more extensive verbal messages, we usually experience no problem at all—the context informs us which reference is intended. The present study, however, aims at an exploration of the reference of words under conditions when that process can neither be unequivocally predicted on the basis of an *a prior* identification of "the word itself" nor from a more extensive "natural" linguistic sequence in which it is embedded.

Experimental Procedures

Four Norwegian homonyms were chosen as critical stimulus words:

STRENG, meaning either (A) the adjective "severe" or (B) the noun "string";

FÅR, meaning either (A) present tense of the verb "to get" or (B) the noun "sheep";

* The present study is part of a research project on psycholinguistics at the University of Oslo and was supported by the Norwegian Research Council for Science and the Humanities. Published in *Pedagogisk Forskning* (1965) **9**, 179–188.

PIPE, meaning either (A) the sound verb (to) "cheep" or (B) the noun "pipe"; and

RASK, meaning either (A) the noun "rubbish" or (B) the adjective "quick".

Each homonym may thus release either the one or the other of two distinctly different representational processes, either A or B. For every such pair of competing interpretations, furthermore, A and B correspond to words belonging to two distinctly different parts of speech.

The four homonyms were included as stimulus words in word association lists. Each of them appeared in four different contexts: after three words semantically *and* syntactically consonant with interpretation A (Se Sy); after three words semantically related to A but syntactically consonant with B (Se S̄y); after three words semantically related to B but syntactically consonant with A (S̄e Sy); and, finally, after three words semantically *and* syntactically consonant with B (S̄e S̄y).

The different contexts preceding the homonym STRENG, meaning either (A) "severe" or (B) "string", may serve as an illustration. They were:

Se Sy: GLAD ("glad"), SORGFULL ("sorrowful") and SINT ("angry").
Se S̄y: GLEDE ("joy"), SORG ("sorrow") and SINNE ("anger").
S̄e Sy: BUNDET ("bound"), KNYTTET ("tied") and STRAM ("tight").
S̄e S̄y: BAND ("ribbon"), REM ("strap") and HYSSING ("cord").

For group administration, four booklets were prepared according to a Latin square design with 4×4 cells, each of which consisted of a given homonym preceded by one of its four different contexts. Each booklet thus corresponded to a column of the square. Subjects (Ss) were simply asked to write down their very first association to each of the stimulus words as they appeared, one on each page.

The same four booklets were used for individual administration. The Examiner (E) read each word aloud and recorded S's spoken response immediately.

Sixty-four students taking introductory courses in psychology at the University of Oslo volunteered as Ss. Forty Ss participated in the group study, and 24 Ss were given the word association task individually. Under both sets of conditions, Ss were randomly assigned to the four different sequences of contexts.

Interpretation of a given homonym was inferred exclusively from the associative response it elicited. Thus, responses like "mild", "stubborn" and "authority" to STRENG were considered sufficient evidence for the conclusion that STRENG had been comprehended as the adjective "severe", whereas "violin", "rope" and "thread" would be coded as evidence for the alternative reference, i.e. the noun "string".

In the individual tests, ambiguous first responses like clang associations were followed up by probing until reference could be safely inferred. Among our 164 associative responses to homonyms in the group test, however, only four associations had to be discarded as ambiguous.

Results

The frequencies of interpretation A of each homonym, as inferred from associative responses, are presented in Table I. Since cases of unresolved ambiguities were almost non-existent, the frequencies of interpretation B may for all practical purposes be inferred by subtracting each cell entry from the N presented at the top of the column.

TABLE I. Frequencies of interpretations A of the homonyms in different contexts.

Interpretation	Written, group adm.				Oral, ind. adm.			
	Se Sy N=10	Se $\overline{\text{Sy}}$ N=10	$\overline{\text{Se}}$ Sy N=10	$\overline{\text{Se}}$ $\overline{\text{Sy}}$ N=10	Se Sy N=6	Se $\overline{\text{Sy}}$ N=6	$\overline{\text{Se}}$ Sy N=6	$\overline{\text{Se}}$ $\overline{\text{Sy}}$ N=6
STRENG as "severe"	7	4	3	2	3	1	0	0
FÅR as "gets"	8	4	1	0	6	5	0	0
PIPE as "to cheep"	5	3	1	0	4	2	0	0
RASK as "rubbish"	2	0	0	2	1	0	0	0
M	5·5	2·3	1·3	1	3·5	2	0	0

The first part of the upper row therefore reads as follows: STRENG has been comprehended as "severe" in seven out of 10 cases when preceded by adjectives referring to mood, in four out of 10 cases when preceded by nouns referring to mood, in three out of 10 cases when preceded by adjective forms referring to tying, and in only two out of 10 cases when preceded by nouns referring to tying.

In short, then, Table I provides us with a fairly well structured picture of decreasing frequencies of interpretations A as the preceding contexts varies from Se Sy (semantic *and* syntactic consonance with interpretation A) to $\overline{\text{Se}}$ $\overline{\text{Sy}}$ (semantic and syntactic dissonance with respect to A). The prevailing pattern of relative efficiency of the different contexts observed when the group study and the individual tests are examined jointly can thus be expressed as follows:

$$\text{Se Sy} < \text{Se } \overline{\text{Sy}} < \overline{\text{Se}} \text{ Sy} = \overline{\text{Se}} \text{ } \overline{\text{Sy}}.$$

This pattern is observed in six out of eight cases, whereas its expected probability should be less than one out of 16. The only two exceptions to this rule, furthermore, are found in the case of RASK, the homonym representing by far the most unbalanced overall distribution of interpretations.

Discussion

The situation we have explored resembles the stereoscopic rivalry setting in which the two eyes are provided with images of physically very similar but semantically distinctively different words. Under conditions of brief exposure time, only one of the words will then be reported as seen. The S encounters a forced choice, and no fusion nor alternation occurs (Rommetveit et al., 1964).

In the case of our homonym, there is also a forced choice. The choice, e.g. whether STRENG is being spontaneously decoded as "severe" or as "string" can hardly be distinguished from the very act of reference or immediate process of word comprehension and is clearly revealed by subsequent associative processes. In the case of the homonym, we are therefore forced *to infer the stimulus pattern qua word from subsequent responses to it.* Both reference and grammatical status remain unknown to E until S betrays the stimulus pattern's linguistic identity by associative responses.

The homonym appeared in a sequence of other verbal stimuli. Each of them was presented as a discrete stimulus pattern, though, and every preceding sequence of verbal stimuli was certainly devoid of the kind of syntactic and semantic constraints inherent in sentences. Our best predictor of the relative frequencies of competing interpretations might therefore possibly be the experienced frequencies of the corresponding words in written and spoken language.

Unfortunately, no such reliable baseline-data were available. Gross estimates of baseline probabilities, however, may be made on the basis of observed frequencies of interpretations in the group study *over all conditions.* These are: For STRENG $\cdot40/\cdot60$, for FÅR $\cdot33/\cdot67$, for PIPE $\cdot23/\cdot77$ and for RASK $\cdot10/\cdot90$.

If we venture to conceive of these values as gross estimates of relative saliency of the members of each pair of competing interpretations, when no context is at work, two inferences can be explicated. First, the potency of any given context may be measured as a discrepancy from baseline frequency. In the case of the Se Sy context for the "get"–interpretation of FÅR, for instance, context potency would amount to $\cdot80 - \cdot33 = \cdot47$.

Secondly, a ceiling factor has to be taken into account. The baseline dominance of one interpretation may be so strong that even a context representing maximal consonance with the alternative interpretation may prove insufficient. This may possibly pertain to the pattern RASK in our study.

Finally, our findings may be discussed briefly in terms of their relevance to the more general issue of comprehension of apparently isolated and autonomous verbal stimuli. Items entering a word association list are most often tacitly considered as identified qua autonomous entities, whose "associative meanings" can be mapped and described without specification of potential contextual determinants. Many of them, however, still remain ambiguous qua linguistic element. The pattern PLAY, for instance, may be alternately decoded as an adjective, a noun or a verb. Choice among these alternatives may, as was found for our homonyms, be highly dependent upon preceding items. Choice of interpretation, moreover, will in turn affect subsequent associative processes. The resultant quantifications of associative linkages between PLAY and specific other verbal responses will therefore remain at least as ambiguous as the linguistically ambiguous stimulus pattern itself.

Summary

Four Norwegian homonyms were inserted as stimulus words in word association lists, each of which might serve as a releasor of either one of two distinctively different representational processes, either A or B. In each case, interpretations A and B would correspond to two words from different parts of speech.

Context was manipulated by varying content and form of the three stimulus words immediately preceding each homonym. Whether the latter was being comprehended as A or B was inferred on the basis of the associative response it elicited. Sixty-four Norwegian students served as Ss, 40 of them in a group study involving written stimulus material and responses, and 24 Ss participated in individual experiments involving oral stimulus presentation and responses.

The observed distribution of interpretations testifies to a strong preference for that interpretation of the homonym which conforms most closely to preceding context words with respect to sphere of reference *and* grammatical status. The immediately preceding stimulus words thus seem to bring about a temporary restructuring of related internal linguistic elements in terms of their relative saliency or differential state of evocation. Some problems bearing upon identification of the word as an autonomous stimulus unit are discussed briefly in view of our findings.

References

Bousfield, W. A. (1961). The problem of meaning in verbal learning. *In* "Verbal Learning and Verbal Behavior". (C. N. Cofer, Ed.) pp. 87–91. McGraw-Hill, New York.

Deese, F. (1962). On the structure of associative meaning. *Psychological Review* **69**, 161–175.

Garskof, B. E. and Houston, F. P. (1963). Measurement of verbal relatedness: An ideographic approach. *Psychological Review* **70**, 277–288.

Miller, G. A. (1962). Some psychological studies of grammar. *American Psychologist* **17**, 748–762.

Rommetveit, R., Toch, H. and Svendsen, D. (1964). Effects of "contingency" and "contrast" contexts on the cognition of words in a stereoscopic rivalry situation.

14. Emotive and Representational Components of Meaning in Word Sorting and Recall*

R. ROMMETVEIT and V. HUNDEIDE

In recent psychological research on single words, a majority of empirical studies aim at exploring *emotive meaning* and *assocation processes* (Osgood, 1962; Deese, 1962). Considerably less attention has been devoted to that initial phase of word comprehension by which some cognitive representation or process of reference must be achieved.

Consider, for instance, the string of letters RASK, the common typographical mediator of two distinctively different Norwegian words, namely the adjective "quick" and the noun "rubbish". Distinctively different patterns of associations *and* distinctively different semantic differential profiles will emerge in response to this string of letters, depending upon which one of the two mutually exclusive acts of reference has been performed (Rommetveit and Strømnes, 1965). The logical and temporal priority of word reference relative to emotive and associative processes can thus be clearly demonstrated in studies of specific homonyms.

Once we venture to dissect word meaning into different components, however, some very complex problems of relative saliency and inter-dependence among components arise. Thus, predominance of different meaning components will vary from one *category of words* to another. Words belonging to some parts of speech, e.g. conjunctions, may seem to be almost devoid of any kind of autonomous meaning. Within the same part of speech, furthermore, a very different set of meaning patterns may be encountered. In the case of some isolated adjectives, like "GOOD", "MARVELLOUS", etc. genuinely representational processes

* This study constitutes part of a project on psycholinguistics at the University of Oslo, supported by a grant from the Norwegian Research Council for Science and the Humanities and continued at Cornell University 1964–65 by N.S.F. grant 6458. Published in *Pedagogisk Forskning* (1967) **11**, 47–59.

over and beyond an affective pattern may hardly be clearly identified
at all. Others, like "FAT", "TRIANGULAR", etc. may at least in some
cases mediate cognitive representations of fairly well-defined external
states of affairs.

Relative saliency of representational, emotive and associative processes will also to some extent depend upon the *type of communicative
setting* in which a given word occurs. When listening to the word
"DEMOCRACY" as uttered by my political leader at the end of a patriotic
speech, I may be predominantly affectively influenced. When encountering the same word in a typical information-seeking setting like
a lecture on political science, non-emotive representational processes
may be very salient. And when I dwell for some time on the same
word "DEMOCRACY" in a modern poem, associative processes may
very well constitute the most important aspect of my total response
pattern.

In addition, relative saliency and interdependence among meaning
components may change as a function of *continuous language learning and
intellectual growth*. As the child's cognition of *things* reflects emancipation
from egocentric motor and affective patterns of interaction with them,
this emancipation should also be revealed in his language (Piaget,
1932). Therefore, other things being equal, genuinely representational
processes should tend to become more salient than affective decoding
as the child matures.

The purpose of the present studies is to explore hypothesized emotive
and representational coding strategies. In short, we want to enquire
into the relative importance of affective loading versus reference as
criteria for grouping of words in sorting and recall tasks.

Experimental Study

Stimulus Material

Our stimulus words were six sets of 12 Norwegian words each. Each
such set could be grouped into four subsets of three words. The four
subsets would then correspond to the cells of a fourfold Table generated
by one dichotomy with respect to an *evaluative emotive factor*, either
"good" or "bad", and another dichotomy with respect to *reference*,
referring either to some class *x* or to some other class *y*.

The stimulus words were:*

Series I (Vocal versus motor acts): Å KLORE (TO CLAW), Å JUBLE (TO
　　SHOUT IN DELIGHT), Å DANSE (TO DANCE), Å HYLE (TO HOWL), Å

---

* Few of the translations probably attain full equivalence with respect to emotive
meaning. It may be doubtful, for instance, whether the English words JUMP and RUN

LØPE (TO RUN), Å SLÅ (TO BEAT), Å SYNGE (TO SING), Å TRALLE (TO LILT), Å STIKKE (TO STAB).

Series II (Covert versus overt acts): Å ØDELEGGE (TO DESTROY), Å FORSTÅ (TO UNDERSTAND), Å ORDNE (TO ARRANGE), Å SØRGE (TO MOURN), Å BYGGE (TO BUILD), Å MISBRUKE (TO ABUSE), Å HÅPE (TO HOPE), Å TRO (TO BELIEVE), Å HINDRE (TO HINDER).

Series III (Sounds versus categories of human beings): KJELTRING (SCOUNDREL), JUBEL (SHOUT IN DELIGHT), RIDDER (KNIGHT), SKRIK (SCREAM), BRØL (ROAR), KONGE (KING), GRÅT (CRYING), HELT (HERO), RAMP (VILLAIN), LATTER (LAUGHTER), SANG (SONG), TYV (THIEF).

Series IV (Sensory attributes versus inferred traits): SVART (BLACK), SNILL (KIND), RØD (RED), DUM (STUPID), FEIG (COWARDLY), LYS (LIGHT-COLOURED), DOVEN (LAZY), MYK (SOFT), UJEVN (UNEVEN), VENNLIG (FRIENDLY), FLINK (CLEVER), BESK (ACRID).

Series V (Animals versus buildings): SYKEHUS (HOSPITAL), EKORN (SQUIRREL), HYTTE (COTTAGE), ULV (WOLF), KROKODILLE (CROCO-DILE), SLOTT (CASTLE), ROTTE (RAT), VILLA (VILLA), RØNNE (HOVEL), SOMMERFUGL (BUTTERFLY), PUSEKATT (PUSSYCAT), FENGSEL (PRISON).

Series VI (States of mind versus deeds): ANGST (ANXIETY), ROS (PRAISE), LYKKE (HAPPINESS), HEVN (REVENGE), SKADE (DAMAGE), BEGEISTRING (ENTHUSIASM), KRANGEL (QUARREL), GLEDE (DELIGHT), AVSKY (DISGUST), HJELP (ASSISTANCE), REDNING (RESCUE), SINNE (ANGER).

The four subsets of set I would then be *"good"* verbs referring to *vocal activities* (TO SHOUT IN DELIGHT, TO SING, TO LILT); *"bad"* verbs referring to *vocal activities* (TO SCREAM, TO CRY, TO HOWL); *"good"* verbs referring to *non-vocal motor activities* (TO JUMP, TO DANCE, TO RUN), and *"bad"* verbs referring to *non-vocal motor activities* (TO CLAW, TO BEAT, TO STAB).

Sorting tasks

The six sets of word were presented in the order indicated by their Roman numerals, and each set of 12 words was typed on a separate page. The first ten words of each set were typed in one column at the top of the page in the order in which they appear above. The last two

---

would be as unequivocally "good" as their Norwegian translations HOPPE and LØPE in the contexts provided by set I. By the same token, subtle aspects of reference could obviously not be dealt with successfully at all in a word-to-word translation.

words were typed below, one to the left and the other to the right of the column.

Before proceeding to the first sorting task, subjects were given the following instruction:

"At the top of this page are ten different words." (E reads them.) "There are two kinds of words in this list. Five of them resemble the word TO LILT, and five resemble the word TO STAB. Now, your task is to sort out the five words you feel belong together with the word TO LILT and write them here." (E points to the five open lines below TO LILT.) "In the same way, you are supposed to sort out the five words belonging together with TO STAB and write those words here." (E demonstrates.)

All subsequent sorting tasks were introduced by referring to this general procedure, and subjects were allowed to work at their own pace.

Reproduction tasks

Word memory was tested for Sets III and IV only. Moreover, subjects were assigned to the tasks in such a way that *the ratio of emotive to representational sorters remained the same for each age category.* After all response sheets for the sorting tasks had been collected, the two "key words" for set III (SONG and THIEF) were written on the blackboard. Subjects were asked to try to remember and write down as many as possible of the set of words that had been sorted as similar to SONG and THIEF, respectively. After that, they were asked to reproduce as many as possible of the words from set IV. Again the two "key words" (CLEVER and ACRID) were written on the blackboard.

Word Associations

All 6 × 12 words were scrambled and typed, one on each page of a booklet. Subjects were asked to write down, for every stimulus word, the first word that came to their mind.

The association study was administered after the sorting task, with a minimal period of 24 h between tasks.

Subjects

Our subjects were pupils from grades 3, 5 and 7 in the Norwegian school system, averaging approx. 9, 11 and 13 years of age. In each age group, approximately half were girls and half boys. They all attended the elementary schools of a neighbouring city of Oslo and were similar with respect to all background factors other than age.

Results

Sorting

Word sorting was coded into three mutually exclusive categories: (1) as reflecting an emotive strategy (E), (2) a representational strategy (R), or (3) as neither emotive nor representational. A perfectly consistent emotive strategy is inferred when a subject splits the set of words into one set of "good" and another set of "bad" words, irrespective of reference, and the probability of such an achievement under conditions of random sorting is $(1/2)^5 = 0.03$. However, sortings in which only one word was misplaced were also coded as "emotive", since it might be argued that the single exception could be due to an idiosyncratic emotional response to a single word rather than a breakdown of strategy. By the same token, sortings were coded as representational when all words had been split into the two appropriate subsets with respect to reference. In this case also one error was tolerated.

As estimated against an expected frequency of $0.03 \times 2 = 0.06$, a fully consistent strategy (either emotive or representational) stands out as the rule at all age levels (Table I).

Figure 1 shows choice of strategy for each age group and each set of words. We notice marked between-set differences: Set VI (nouns for *deeds* versus nouns for *states of mind*) seems to reach a ceiling of emotive sortings for all age groups. Set V (nouns for *animals* versus nouns for *buildings*), on the other hand, seems to come close to the ceiling for representational sortings for the older groups.

The other general pattern is an increase of representational sortings with age. For each set of words, three age comparisons are possible, respectively, 9 year old with 11 year old; 11 year old with 13 year old; and 9 year old with 13 year old. When these comparisons are made for all sets of words except set VI, we end up with $3 \times 5 = 15$ comparisons altogether. Of these, 14 cases have the outcome that the older group had a higher frequency of representational sortings. Five of the differences reach statistical significance beyond the 5% level as assessed by Chi square tests, namely that between 7 years old and 11 years old, and the one between 7 years old and 13 years old for *set IV*; the difference between 7 years old and 13 years old for *set I*; that between 7 years old and 13 years old for *set III*; and the difference between 7 years old and 13 years old for *set V*.

Finally, an examination of *sex differences* for all age groups and all sets of words revealed a slightly higher frequency of emotive sortings among girls. Only one sex difference yielded $p < .05$, however, namely the sex difference for sorting of *set V* by 9 year old children.

TABLE I. Average frequencies of "pure", "impure" and unsystematic sorting strategies at different age levels for all word sets.

	Age level		
Strategy	9(N=51)	11(N=57)	13(N=59)
Fully consistent	0·45	0·68	0·78
One exception only	0·39	0·27	0·20
Unsystematic	0·16	0·05	0·02

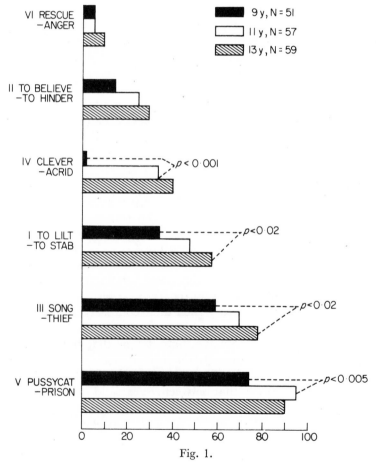

Fig. 1.

Reproduction

Four different measures of reproduction were obtained. First, *correct reproductions* were recorded. Second, *errors*, i.e. words other than those included in the stimulus set, were recorded.

Every such error, however, was examined with respect to *its relationship to the "key word"*. It would be emotively *and* representationally consonant if, for instance, a subject recalled CRIMINAL as belonging to the subset headed by the key word THIEF. Second, it might be dissonant with the key word both emotively and with respect to reference, as when a subject would recall FESTIVAL as belonging to the THIEF set. Thirdly, the incorrect word might be emotively consonant but representationally dissonant with the key word as when for example, GRIEF would be reproduced within the THIEF set. And, finally, the error might be emotively dissonant and representationally consonant with the key word. This would be the case, for instance, when a subject put down, MINISTER as belonging to the THIEF set.

Of all codable errors of reproduction, 36% were of the THIEF-CRIMINAL type, 50% were of the THIEF-GRIEF type; 13% were of the THIEF-MINISTER type, and less than 1% were of the THIEF-FESTIVAL type. In our subsequent analysis, we shall focus only on two of these categories, namely the purely *"emotive"* errors (the THIEF-GRIEF type) and purely *"representational"* errors (the THIEF-MINISTER type).

As for the first two of our reproduction scores (words correctly reproduced *and* errors), we would expect them to be correlated negatively, since the need to introduce novel words would decrease as a function of stimulus words correctly recalled by a subject. When the correlation was computed, an *r* of -0.31 was obtained.

The observed relationship between *sorting strategy* and subsequent *word reproduction* is provided by Table II.

TABLE II. Reproduction performance by "emotive" (E) and "representational" (R) sorters.

Mean no.	Set III		Set IV	
	R(N=45)	E(N=16)	R(N=16)	E(N=38)
Correct responses	5·9	4·2	5·9	4·5
"Emotive" errors[a]	0·6	2·1	0·2	0·9
"Representational" errors[b]	0·5	0·1	0·1	0·1

[a] *"Emotive" error:* SONG–HAPPY, THIEF–POISON, etc.
[b] *"Representational" error:* SONG–HOWL, THIEF–PRESIDENT, etc.

All five differences between emotive and representationally sorters yield $p < 0.001$ when a one-tailed Kolmogorov-Smirnov two-sample test (Siegel, 1956) is applied to the underlying distributions.

Subjects who sorted words with respect to emotive meaning were thus significantly inferior to those who sorted according to reference when both groups were asked to reproduce the two stimulus lists. For both word sets, they wrote down a significantly larger number of novel words that were similar to the key word in terms of emotive meaning but dissimilar as to reference. Subjects who had sorted *set III* words with respect to reference, on the other hand, introduced significantly more novel words that belonged to the same area of reference as that of the key word but were distinctively different from the key word in terms of emotive meaning. For *set IV*, however, such errors were almost entirely absent in all groups of subjects.

Word Associations

First, all instances of associations in which the stimulus word elicited a response belonging to the *same set of words* as the stimulus word were recorded. In all, 11% of all associations were such intra-list pairs. Ninety-five per cent of the latter, however, were also *intra-cell associations*, i.e. stimulus and response words were both emotively similar *and* referred to the same class of referents.

Discussion

The sequence of sorting tasks had been planned so as to counteract *preservation* of strategy over tasks. Sets of words which in pretests had been sorted either almost exclusively emotively or exclusively representationally (sets V and VI) were therefore presented as the last tasks.

Individual pretests had also shown that older children, when requested to do so, might sometimes switch from one stategy to another in sorting the same set of words. After having sorted, for example, the TO LILT–TO STAB set into verbs referring to vocalization and verbs referring to non-vocal motor activities, the children would be asked to "split them into two halves, but in a different way". Some of them would then fairly quickly make a novel, perfectly consistent, sorting of the verbs into "good" and "bad". They would sometimes even spontaneously describe the two bases for their sortings as, for example, "sound words" versus "movement words" and "pleasant words" versus "unpleasant words". Choice of one specific strategy therefore simply indicates that the alternative strategy is less readily available at the moment but *not* necessarily beyond subjects' capacity or potential repertoire.

We notice, furthermore, that the basis for representational sortings hardly ever correspond to natural co-ordinate class dichotomies. This is perhaps most transparent for sets of words like, e.g. verbs for acts of thought versus verbs of action (BELIEVE-HINDER). The dichotomies of reference must therefore be conceived of as *potential, more or less "artificial" bases for representational sortings* rather than "natural" pairs of concepts.

With this very important reservation in mind, we might venture to describe the observed relationship between *kinds of words* and *choice of sorting strategy* as reflecting an increase of emotive strategies as we go from words with a concrete to an abstract reference, e.g. from PUSSYCAT-PRISON to RESCUE-ANGER (Fig. 1). A rigid definition and empirical assessment of level of abstraction, however, is by no means a simple affair. Generalization from our findings concerning dependency of strategy upon kinds of words therefore seems hardly feasible at all.

The differences between age groups, however, do not involve the same kind of ambiguities. In general, frequency of representational sortings tends to increase with age for all kinds of words. The gradients seem to be different, though, for different sets. For the adjectives referring to *sensory attributes* and (inferred) *personal characteristics* (set IV, CLEVER-ACRID), sorting according to the available reference aspect is practically non-existent among 9 year olds but fairly frequent at the age of 11. It seems as though the two different areas of reference, the *sensory-physical* and the *personal-social*, are either not linguistically differentiated or, if so, still subordinate to an affective-meaning component in *younger children*. It also seems reasonable to believe that an expansion of the enquiries so as to include very young children might reveal predominantly emotive strategies even for words with a definitely concrete reference like PUSSYCAT-PRISON.

In order to explore a little further into the two inferred strategies, however, we shall now turn to the observed relationships between sorting and reproduction achievements. Emotive *sorting* presupposes decoding of an emotive "good-bad"-meaning component of the word. When unexpectedly asked to *reproduce* the entire list of stimulus words, a corresponding focus upon affective loading implies an emotive *encoding* as part of the retrieval process. Tagging of the key words as "good" or "bad" may not be very helpful, however, since the two sets of words so tagged each have a tremendously large number of members. The emotive sorter's searching will therefore involve vast areas of uncertainty, *once his effort at reproducing stimulus words proceeds beyond the scope of immediate reminiscence.*

The representational sorter, on the other hand, is presumably guided by some tagging of *reference*. When immediate and "passive" recall fails, his "search in memory" will be constrained to far less extensive segments of his acquired vocabulary. His superior achievement may accordingly be attributed to a superior search strategy in the retrieval situation. Since intra-list *associative* linkage is very infrequent and, when observed, almost exclusively delimited to pairs of words with similar emotive loading *and* same reference category, word associations can be ruled out as an explanation.

Obviously, strong associative linkages cannot explain why emotively *very* dissonant words are grouped in recall, e.g. THIEF and PRESIDENT. Nor can they account for the grouping together of denotatively remote words like THIEF and POISON, as observed so frequently among the emotive sorters. An analysis of associations to all stimulus words using a classification developed by Rommetveit and Brøgger (1965), furthermore, showed no relationship at all between sorting strategy and types of associative responses produced.

Therefore, we have to conclude that two kinds of strategies toward words are revealed both in the sorting and the reproduction task. The *emotive strategy* appears to be essentially a coding of words as belonging to one or the other of two extremely inclusive subsets of the subject's entire vocabulary, e.g. "pleasant" and "unpleasant" words. The *representational strategy*, on the other hand, seems to involve a coding of words as belonging to one or the other of two more restricted areas of reference. This interpretation explains the superiority of the representational sorter in recall, in spite of the fact that he (for set III) made significantly more "representational" errors. Our finding may thus be considered theoretically consonant with the observation made by Miller *et al.* (1951) that ease of word *recognition* seems to be a function of the size of the vocabulary from which the words have to be selected. The very same function seems to obtain for word *reproduction* when the size of relevant vocabularies is determined by two different search strategies.

The most general framework within which our findings can be viewed is possibly one of *"signal"* versus *"symbol"* aspects of single words. The emotive strategy implies *equivalence among words based upon commonality with respect to the pattern of affective responses they elicit, whereas a representational strategy implies equivalence among different words based upon common aspects of reference.* It remains to be explored, however, whether two such strategies can be identified when comprehension and memory involve more extensive linguistic sequences and are not constrained by an experimentally induced search for similarities among isolated words.

Summary

Six sets of 12 words each were used as stimuli. Each set fits into a fourfold Table generated by one dichotomy with respect to emotive meaning ("good" versus "bad" words) and another dichotomy with respect to some aspects of reference (words referring to class *x* versus words referring to class *y*).

In a sorting experiment, two diagonal words were given (a "bad" word with reference *x* and a "good" word with reference *y*); the subject was simply asked to sort the remaining words into two halves on the basis of each word's similarity with one or the other of the diagonal words. Immediately after all sorting tasks, subjects were unexpectedly asked to reproduce two of the sets as accurately as possible. In addition, word associations to all 6×12 words were obtained. Subjects were children at the age of 9, 11 and 13.

When sorting was analysed, two distinctively different strategies were found: Nearly all sortings could be described as either emotive ("good" versus "bad") or representational (class x versus class y). The frequency of the latter strategy, furthermore, was found to increase with age. In addition, a fairly unequivocal relationship was observed between sorting strategy and recall performance. Emotive sorters reproduced significantly fewer of the original stimulus words and introduced significantly more novel words which were emotively, but not representationally, consonant, with the cue word. Representational sorters reproduced significantly more stimulus words, but tended to write down more novel words resembling the original ones with respect to reference only.

An analysis of word associations showed that sorting behaviour and recall could not be accounted for in terms of pre-established intra-set associative linkages.

References

Deese, F. (1962). On the structure of associative meaning. *Psychological Review* **69**, 161–175.

Miller, G. A., Heise, G. H. and Lichten, W (1951). The intelligibility of speech as a function of the test materials. *J. experimental Psychology* **41**, 329–335.

Osgood, C. E. (1962). Studies on the generality of affective meaning systems. *American Psychologist* **17**, 10–28.

Piaget, F. (1932). "The Language and Thought of the Child." Routledge and Kegan Paul, London.

Rommetveit, R. and Brögger, F. (1965). Syntactic stimulus-response concordance in word association. *Pedagogisk Forskning* **9**, 173–178.

Rommetveit, R. and Strömnes, F. (1965). Determinants of interpretation of homonyms in word association contexts. *Pedagogisk Forskning* **9**, 179–188.

Siegel, S. (1956). "Non-Parametric Statistics for the Behavioral Sciences." McGraw-Hill, New York.

15. Syntactic Stimulus-response Concordance in Word Association*

R. ROMMETVEIT and J. BRØGGER

It has been shown by Ervin (1961) that stimulus- and response-words in a free word association test tend to be of the same syntactic category. The aim of this study is to explore further this syntactic concordance between stimulus- and response-word and examine possible inter-relationships between syntactic and semantic determinants.

For that purpose, a word association test of 208 Norwegian words randomly selected from the dictionary was prepared. The words were chosen from all parts of speech and, within each given part of speech, representing different forms (i.e. inflections), and presented orally in a scrambled sequence. The S (subject) was asked to respond by saying the first word that came to his mind, and only his first response to each stimulus-word was included in the analysis. Twenty-eight highly educated Norwegian adults, most of them university students, served as Ss. The test was administered individually. In the following analysis, only the responses to the most frequent categories of stimulus words, i.e. nouns, verbs and adjectives, are included.

Results

The frequency with which a stimulus-word elicited a response-word from the same part of speech† is shown in Table I.

N refers to absolute number of occurrences, and the Table shows relative frequencies of different Stimulus-Response pairs. The upper row thus shows that a noun in 2194 out of 2632 cases, i.e. 83% of the time, elicited another noun as the first association. By examining all the diagonal cells, we find that the average proportion of responses falling within the same part of speech as the stimulus word is 3594/4529, i.e. 79%.

* Published in *Pedagogisk Forskning* (1965), 173–178.
† Whenever S (or R) could not be unequivocally identified with respect to part of speech, the pair was excluded from our analysis.

TABLE I. Gross syntactic stimulus-response concordance.

		Response				
		Nouns	Verbs	Adjectives	Others	N
	Nouns	0·83	0·06	0·07	0·03	2632
Stimulus	Verbs	0·18	0·70	0·06	0·06	1238
	Adjectives	0·15	0·01	0·81	0·02	659
	N	2522	1041	800	166	4529

Secondly, this impressive overall syntactic concordance was analysed and related to type of associative linkage between stimulus- and response-word. All associations were classified into the following eight main categories, similar to those proposed by Karwoski and Schachter (1948):

(1) Sy   — Synonym: QUICK–FAST
(2) Cl   — Class: divided into three subcategories:
   superordinate: HUNDRED–NUMBER
   co-ordinate: WINTER–SPRING
   subordinate: FOOD–BREAD
(3) F   — Function: divided into four subcategories. The index refers to the grammatical category into which the response-word would fall if the function had to be expressed in a sentence:
   F_{subj}:   STRIKE–HAMMER
   F_{pred}:   PENCIL–WRITE
   F_{obj}:   HAMMER–NAIL

A separate, somewhat different subtype was:

   F_{causal}:   LOSE–MISS. The index designates a causal, but not directly instrumental relation between denotation of the stimulus- and response-words.
(4) A   — Attribute: divided into two subcategories:
   A_g: WATER–WET (general attribute)
   A_i: BLUE–SKY (instance of attribute)
(5) Ec   — Ecological contiguity: CHAIR–TABLE
(6) P.W. — Part-whole: WAVE–SEA
(7) Com — Completion: PROBLEM–SOLVING
(8) Con — Contrast: GOOD–BAD

To avoid idiosyncrasies, only responses given by two or more subjects were coded. The coders agreed on 80% of the responses and all responses on which they disagreed were excluded from the following analysis. Thus, Table II includes only associative responses given by two or more of 28 Ss and only those non-idiosyncratic responses which could be unanimously coded as belonging to one of the eight categories. We notice that the syntactic concordance is perfect for synonyms, contrasts, part-whole and contiguity-associations.

TABLE II. Syntactic stimulus-response concordance within each associative category.

	Syn	Cl	Con	P.W.	Ec	F_{causal}	F_{subj}	F_{obj}	Com	A_g	A_i	F_{pred}
N	698	525	339	69	169	165	30	62	103	138	18	50
%	100	100	100	100	100	81	73	71	58	33	0	0

Thirdly, form concordance was examined. For this purpose, only cases of syntactic concordance with respect to part of speech could be used. Thus, all cases of nouns eliciting nouns were examined with respect to concordance of inflection as shown in Table III.

TABLE III. Stimulus-response form concordance of nouns.

			Response				
			Singular		Plural		
			Def.	Indef.	Def.	Indef.	N
	Singular	Def.	0·78	0·20	0·01	0·01	178
		Indef.	0·01	0·97		0·02	1018
Stimulus	Plural	Def.	0·16	0·13	0·23	0·48	31
		Indef.				1·00	30
		N	155	1024	9	67	1257

If we restrict form concordance to the diagonal cells only, the over-all relative frequency is 0·92. The pairs of verb and adjective associations were examined by a strictly analogous procedure. The tense of verbs showed a concordance of 84% and the inflections of adjectives 93%.

Discussion

Our analysis of syntactic concordance in word association strongly confirmed Ervin's earlier findings. The first associative response usually belongs to the same part of speech as the stimulus-word.

The overall concordance, as shown in Table I, might be due to an implicit self-instruction or "plan" (Miller *et al.*, 1960) on the part of the subject. This plan might be thought of as a two-step process. First, the subject discards as potential response-words all words other than those belonging to the same part of speech as the stimulus word. Second, he selects a semantically appropriate member of the latter set. In responding to SEA, for instance, he would then first make the decision to restrict the search for response-words to *nouns* only. After that, he would choose between alternative, semantically appropriate nouns such as BOAT, LAND, SAILOR, etc.

The distribution of cases of stimulus-response concordance over different associative categories shown in Table II, however, indicates that the above interpretation is inadequate. Whether or not the associative response will be the same part of speech as the stimulus-word obviously depends upon the kind of associative chain involved. In the case of synonyms, contrasts, classes, part-whole and contiguity associations, perfect concordance is observed, and this concordance may be conceived of as dictated by and therefore secondary to the semantic processes involved. One could hardly think of synonyms, contrasts, denotations of the same class hierarchy or part of the same substantial unity that would not be symbolized by words of the same parts of speech. And in the case of ecological contiguity, stimulus and response words usually refer to contingent parts *or* attributes *or* processes of the same external environment.

The complete lack of concordance in the case of the F_{pred} and the A_g categories, furthermore, provides strong additional evidence for the temporal priority of semantic factors in the associative process. If a superordinate and strong set for syntactic concordance were at work, concordance would also occur within F_{pred}. In the case of the stimulus-word BLYANT (Pencil) for instance, the verb SKRIVE* (Write) could be replaced by two noun forms, respectively SKRIVING and SKRIFT. Yet, *no such cases were found*. And in the case of attributes, semantic considerations also seem highly relevant. An association pair belonging to this category most often expresses the attribution of a particular quality or property to some object or process. Sometimes a property is described by a noun, e.g. WINTER–SNOW, but more often by a qualifier. Choice of response is thus apparently not restricted by a superordinate set toward syntactic concordance.

So far we have discussed only stimulus-response congruity with respect to parts of speech. As shown in Table III, however, grammatical concordance also extends to inflections, and this concordance, it may be argued, may not be dictated by content. However, inflections also have semantic implications. The definite form of nouns, for instance,

* This was the most frequent response word to BLYANT.

usually directs attention to some particular instance, while the indefinite form may tend to evoke representation of a more abstract, conceptual kind. Synonym and contrast responses to the two different forms may therefore tend to reflect the same values of specificity/universality of reference, *not* because S obeys a rule of syntactic concordance as such, but because form affects associative thinking by determining important aspects of word reference.

Summary

An analysis of grammatical stimulus-response concordance in word associations given by 28 highly educated Norwegian adults strongly confirmed Ervin's (1961) findings that Ss tend to respond with a word belonging to the same part of speech as the stimulus-word. It was found, moreover, that concordance even extends to inflection. Grammatical concordance, however, was found to be highly dependent upon the kind of associative chain involved. The grammatical status of the stimulus-word, therefore, does not seem to affect choice of response directly, in terms of an implicit, superordinate strategy of grammatical sorting prior to concern with content. Syntactic concordance seems rather to follow from some very frequent modes of associative thought.

References

Ervin, S. M. (1961). Changes with age in the verbal determinants of word-associations. *American J. Psychology* **74**, 361–372.

Karowski, T. F. and Schachter, J. (1948). Psychological studies in semantics. III. Reaction times for similarity and difference. *J. Social Psychology* **28**, 103–120.

Miller, G. A., Galanter, E. and Pribram, K. H. (1960). "Plans and the Structure of Behavior." Henry Holt and Co., New York.

Osgood, C. E. (1963). On understanding and creating sentences. *American Psychologist* **18**, 735–751.

16. Effects of Contingency and Contrast Contexts on the Cognition of Words

A study of stereoscopic rivalry*

R. ROMMETVEIT, H. TOCH and D. SVENDSEN

When two very different objects are presented separately to the left and right eye, they are often perceived one after the other. This alternation effect is called stereoscopic rivalry. Stereoscopic rivalry is a "forced choice" situation. If a time limit is imposed, only one of two competing percepts is possible. If one stimulus or category of stimuli consistently dominates when paired with another, it may safely be considered to be more powerful. Stereoscopic rivalry thus allows us to assess the relative strength of competing members of stimulus pairs.

Research on perceptual predominance in stereoscopic rivalry has gone through two stages. Early work focused on *structural* characteristics of stimulus figures. Breese (1899), for example, conducted a series of rivalry studies in which he demonstrated, among other things, that lines predominate over plain fields, and complex figures over lines. He also found that brightness and movement could lead to dominance.

The second research period involved attempts to explore the role of *meaning* in stereoscopic predominance. In these investigations, structural factors were usually controlled or equated. Choice of percept was thus traced to the impact of past experiences and of motivational factors.

This type of research was initiated by Engel (1956). Engel constructed a set of stereograms in each of which the portrait of a young man faced one eye and the *same* portrait *upside down* was presented to the other. He reports that the more familiar "right-side-up" face was almost

* The studies reported were parts of a project on psycholinguistics at the University of Oslo, 1963–64, supported by the Norwegian Research Council for Science and the Humanities. H. Toch participated while on leave of absence from Michigan State University as a Fulbright Scholar. Published in *Scandinavian J. Psychology* (1968) **9**, 138–144.

invariably perceived. Other studies have demonstrated the impact of specific kinds of socio-psychological experiences upon the resolution of binocular conflict involving pictures (Bagby, 1958; Toch and Schulte, 1961). Verbal material has been used by LoSciuto and Hartley (1963). These investigators found that words (and pictures) relating to the religious affiliation of their subjects tended to dominate over material drawn from other religious faiths. In another experiment concerned with language, Davis (1959) observed that high-frequency words tended to dominate over words ranking lower on the Thorndike word count.

The aim of the present study is to explore effects of immediately preceding experience upon resolution of verbal stimulus choices. When the latter are choices between different semantic alternatives, such as "sell" to one eye and "tell" to the other, the outcome should also be affected by temporary semantic or associative states. The test stereograms consisted of such pairs of typographically similar words. When such a pair is presented in isolation, i.e. without any preceding material that relates to it, a "base-line" distribution of responses is obtained, against which effects of experimentally introduced contexts can be estimated.

Experiment I

Apparatus

The apparatus is a version of Engel's (1961) modified stereoscope, enclosed in a light-tight box with a slide holder suspended one inch above the floor. Illumination is provided by 7 W bulbs, set in the front corners of the apparatus. The intensity of the bulbs can be separately controlled by variacs or rheostats.

The visual fields were separated by sliding plastic partitions (instead of black cloth). A timing unit was built into the apparatus to permit reliably timed exposures of the stereograms. The timing device was mechanical, consisting of a small motor with an indented wheel operating a relay. The current for both motor and relays was led through a set of transformers to prevent damage to the equipment. The timer could be disconnected by means of a special switch so as to permit continuous presentation of stimulus material.

Stimulus

Stereograms were prepared, in each of which the text had been so centred that precisely corresponding areas of the two visual fields would be stimulated. The verbal material was typed in small letters, and each slide was partly laminated with scotch tape. Every monocular presentation was a 2 × 2 inch framed square.

The test stereograms consisted of six pairs of Norwegian words, which were structurally identical except for one letter: (1) MANN ("man") and VANN ("water"); (2) FULL ("full") and GULL ("gold"); (3) LANG ("long") and TANG ("tongs"); (4) NORD ("north") and BORD ("table"); (5) FAR ("father") and FAT ("dish"); (6) NATT ("night") and KATT ("cat").

The context stereograms each contained two identical words. Each series of context stereograms contained words related to one of the two words of a test stereogram. Two types of context series were used. (a) *Contingency* contexts consisted of words within the same area of reference as the test word; thus the test word FAT ("dish")—paired with FAR— was preceded by the Norwegian equivalents of "pot", "fork", "spoon", "pitcher" and "cup". (b) *Contrast* contexts were similar to contingency contexts except for the last word in the series, i.e. the stimulus immediately preceding each critical pattern; this word was an *opposite* of the test word. Thus, FAR ("father")—paired with FAT—was preceded by the Norwegian words meaning "uncle", "family", "cousin", "home" and "mother".

Twelve series of context words were prepared, two for each test stereogram. There were six contingency context series, varying from one to six words in length, and six corresponding contrast context series. Each test stereogram was thus preceded either by a contrast context favouring one word, or by a contingency context (of equal word length) favouring the other.

Subjects and Procedure

The first study followed a Latin square design, with contexts subjected to routine rotation and subjects randomly assigned to conditions. Every subject was exposed to all 12 series of context words, each followed by its test stereogram. Twenty-four subjects (12 male and 12 female) participated, one male and one female being assigned to each subcondition. Another group of 24 subjects was exposed to test stereograms alone in order to obtain base-line data. All subjects were students taking introductory psychology at the University of Oslo.

The test words assumed to be evoked by the context were presented alternately to the left and right eye, to control for eye dominance. (Seven subjects were discarded because of the extreme left or right eye dominance.) Exposure time was kept constant at 170 ms, with brightness maintained at 16 lx. These conditions had been found, in pre-tests, to yield a clear percept with moderate reading speed.

The following instructions were used. This is a stereoscope experiment with words. It is important to view the words *very quickly*. You will see each word only for *one brief instant*. As soon as you see a word, report it loudly and distinctly. The slide holder was then focused for the subject, using a stereogram with a monocular circle and a monocular dot, and the instructions stressing accuracy and speed were repeated.

Results

For two pairs (NATT/KATT and NORD/BORD) no contingency effect could be observed, because the contingency member of each pair (KATT and BORD) was reported by every subject even in the no-context condition. The data for the remaining four pairs are presented in Table I. Responses other than choice of either the left-eye or the right-eye image were few. The only clear-cut exception pertains to the pair FAR/FAT in the no-context condition, to which the most frequent response revealed a combination of the two superimposed letters R and T. Such a combination led to the high-frequency Norwegian word FART ("speed"). Hence, the no-context responses can be safely used as base-line data only for the three pairs MANN/VANN, FULL/GULL and

TABLE I. Frequency of responses to four rivalry pairs of words in three different contexts. N = 24.

		Response		
Rivalry pair	Context	Contrast word	Contingency word	Alternation and other
MANN/VANN	Contrast	8	13	3
	None	10	12	2
	Contingency	2	19	3
FULL/GULL	Contrast	16	8	0
	None	12	12	0
	Contingency	3	20	1
LANG/TANG	Contrast	11	7	6
	None	13	11	0
	Contingency	3	20	1
FAR/FAT	Contrast	17	5	2
	None	5	9	10
	Contingency	6	18	0

LANG/TANG. For each of these pairs, the effect of a contrast context can now be assessed by a fourfold table made up of the two upper rows and the two first columns for that pair in Table I (contrast versus contingency choice in contrast context versus in no context). The effect of contingency context is assessed by a fourfold table made up of the two lower rows and the two first columns (contrast versus contingency choice in no context versus in contingency context). Significant deviation from base-line responses are then found only for contingency contexts ($\chi^2 = 6\cdot89$, $p < 0\cdot01$ for MANN/VANN; $\chi^2 = 7\cdot38$, $p < 0\cdot01$ for FULL/ GULL; and $\chi^2 = 8\cdot85$, $p < 0\cdot01$ for LANG/TANG). The response distributions in the contrast context conditions, on the other hand, do not deviate significantly from those observed for the rivalry pairs when no preceding contexts were provided.

The superiority of contingency contexts may conceivably be due to a particularly strong associative linkage. However, word association responses, obtained from 20 subjects drawn from the same student population, showed that this was not the case. For the three test pairs discussed above, the immediately preceding contiguity stimuli were found to elicit their corresponding contiguity test words 30% of the time, on the average. The corresponding measure of average associative strength between preceding stimulus and test word for contrast pairs was 62%. Contingency thus proved superior to contrast in spite of a considerably weaker associative link between pairs of immediately preceding context and test word.

Discussion

The evidence for context effects in the binocular rivalry situation is the subject's choice of image in either the right eye or the left eye. He should most often choose the image whose meaning has been made salient by the preceding context word.

The distinction between contrast and contiguity associations is based upon a system of classification briefly described by Rommetveit and Brøgger (1965) in a study of grammatical stimulus-response consonance in word association. This system resembles that of Karwoski and Schachter (1948). The categories of particular relevance to the present analysis are as follows.

(a) *Ecological contiguity associations*, such as HOUSE–GARDEN, COW–HORSE, MOTHER–FATHER, for all of which it holds that the denotata of stimulus and response words frequently are experienced in spatial-temporal contiguity.

(b) *Contrast associations*, such as SUMMER–WINTER, HELL–HEAVEN, MOTHER–FATHER, for all of which it holds that the denotata of the two words represent opposites, i.e. the two members of each pair constitute together a dichotomy with respect to some attribute.

(c) *Co-ordinate class associations*, such as COW–HORSE, SUMMER–WINTER, MOTHER–FATHER, for all of which it holds that the denotata of the two words represent co-ordinate classes within the same conceptual hierarchy.

According to this classificatory scheme, it may at times happen that a response (like FATHER in response to MOTHER) is a co-ordinate class association and a contingency association as well. Indeed, every contrast response is in certain respects a co-ordinate class association, whereas only a subset of them will be contingency associations as well.

Why, then, did not contrast contexts have any significant effect upon resolution of the binocular rivalry conflicts?

In this first study, context and test stimuli were presented consecutively on separate stereograms and thus separated by intervals ranging from three to four seconds. It is known from word association studies (Karowski and Schachter, 1948) that opposites are emitted significantly faster than contingency associates. Indeed, an evocation of "the opposite" may be conceived of as a semantic analogue to the mechanism of negative after-image in sensation, and the contrast may hence have faded away at a stage when contingency associates still are salient. If the time interval between context and test stimuli is reduced to a minimum, however, contrast context effects should be obtained.

Experiment II

The following innovations in procedure were introduced. (1) The context for each rivalry test was reduced to one word only. (2) The time interval between context and test stimuli was decreased by introducing a condition in which the context and test words followed each other on the same stereogram; these arrangements are called *simultaneous context*. (3) An attempt was made to include only "pure" contrast contexts, leaving out test words that might at the same time be contingency associates of the preceding context words.

Stimuli

All context and test words were nouns. The sample on p. 249 is representative of the stimuli used.

Twenty-four such items were selected and randomly assigned to either the "simultaneous" or the "consecutive" condition. Besides, word associations to all context words, obtained from 24 subjects, showed that the items in the simultaneous and consecutive condition were very similar with respect to associative linkage between context and test words.

Taking one item as illustration, then, the competing stimuli DØD and DÅD would be preceded by either GRAV or LIV, both of which were expected to enhance choice of DØD. The latter would be evoked as a contingency response to GRAV and a contrast response to LIV. Each item

Contexts		Rivalry pair	
Contingency	Contrast	Test word	Control word
GRAV	LIV	DØD	DÅD
(grave)	(life)	(death)	(deed)
SØVN	DAG	NATT	NETT
(sleep)	(day)	(night)	(net)
SELSKAP	FIENDE	VENN	VANN
(party)	(enemy)	(friend)	(water)
RØDME	ÆRE	SKAM	SKUM
(blush)	(honour)	(shame)	(foam)
RYKTE	SANNHET	LØGN	LØNN
(rumour)	(truth)	(lie)	(salary)

of four words was so selected that the test word would be an associative response to both context words, whereas the control word would be elicited as an associative response by neither contingency nor contrast contexts.

Subjects and Procedure

Twelve women and 12 men were included in each group. The instructions for the consecutive condition were identical to those used in Experiment I. The simultaneous condition was preceded by the following instructions. "You will now see two words at a time, with one word above the other. Your task is to perceive both words quickly. You must read the top word first every time." Experimental conditions were the same as before except that exposure time was held constant at 370 m, which proved sufficient to accommodate simultaneous as well as consecutive presentations.

Results

Table II summarizes the main findings. Context appears to have affected the solution of stereoscopic rivalry under all conditions, and contrast contexts were particularly powerful when they appeared simultaneously with (and above) the rivalry pairs. Then, an average of 10·5 (out of maximum 12) test words were reported, as against 7·0 when there was an interval of approx. 3·5 s between exposure of context and rivalry pair. Moreover, decreasing the time interval between context and test pairs tends to increase context effects for contingency contexts as well. Additional evidence for the potency of "simultaneous" as compared with "consecutive" contexts was obtained from subjects who had to be excluded because of extreme eye dominance. Of 13 such subjects who proved completely eye-dominant under the consecutive condition, six lost their eye dominance under the impact of simultaneous contexts.

TABLE II. Mean number of responses to 12 test stereograms under different conditions. N = 24 per condition.

Presentation Context	Simultaneous		Consecutive	
	Contrast	Contingency	Contrast	Contingency
Test word	10·5	9·7	7·0	7·2
Control word	1·0	1·8	4·2	4·1
Alternation and other	0·5	0·5	0·8	0·7

A non-parametric statistical analysis of main findings can be achieved by focusing on the outcome for each item, i.e. on whether contrast context was found to be superior, equal, or inferior to contingency context in bringing about the test word as a response. Table III shows the distribution of outcomes. Fisher's exact probabilities test applied to the fourfold table gives $p < 0.05$ (Siegel, 1965).

TABLE III. Comparison of contrast and contingency context effects in terms of response frequencies from all subjects under consecutive and simultaneous conditions.

Outcome	Condition	
	Consecutive	Simultaneous
Contrast best	5	10
Contingency best	7	1

The findings confirm earlier observations on the relative potency of contrast and contingency contexts in determining the resolution of binocular rivalry when there is a considerable time interval between context and test stimuli. Contingency contexts were then on the average slightly more potent than contrast contexts, in spite of the fact that the latter were found to elicit their respective test words more often in a word association task.

When the interval between context and test word was reduced to a minimum, however, contrast effects were strong. One extreme example pertains to the test pair LOV ("law") and LIV ("life") in the simultaneous condition, preceded by HJERTESLAG ("heartbeat") and DØD ("death"), respectively. In this case, the control word LOV was reported seen in all 24 cases when preceded by HJERTESLAG, whereas LIV was reported in all 24 cases when preceded by DØD.

Considering the latter case in some detail, the subject is exposed to a stereogram with LIV/LOV below DØD/DØD, and he is simply trying to read two words, one above the other. The rivalling letters (i and o) are under this condition competing for the same spatial position in two different words, and this competition takes place while the unequivocal upper string (DØD) is being processed. The very comprehension of "death" must then somehow evoke a semantic state corresponding to its opposite, "life". Hence, i is selected and reported as seen in the middle position of the lower string of letters.

The experimental task is simply to read words, *not* production of associative responses. The "simultaneous" and "consecutive" conditions may therefore be conceived of as tapping different stages of *processing of the context word*. The data seem to confirm the expectation that "the opposite" is evoked at a very early stage. A more stringent and empirically more firmly based analysis of associative connections seems to be required, however, in order to arrive at conclusive results. In addition, greater precision is required in manipulation of time intervals between context and test stimuli. Nevertheless, these first explorations indicate that the binocular rivalry situation may serve as a useful diagnostic tool in attempts at micro-analysis of the processing of written verbal material.

References

Bagby, J. (1957). A cross-cultural study of perceptual predominance in binocular rivalry. *J. Abnormal social Psychology* **54**, 331–334.

Breese, B. B. (1899). On inhibition. *Psychological Review Monograph.* Suppl. 3, No. 1.

Davis, J. M. (1959). Personality, perceptual defense and stereoscopic perception. *J. Abnormal social Psychology* **58**, 389–402.

Engel, E. (1956). The role of content in binocular resolution. *American J. Psychology* **69**, 87–91.

Engel, E. (1961). Binocular methods in psychological research. *In* "Explorations in transactional psychology". (F. P. Kilpatrick, Ed.) pp. 290–305. New York University Press, New York.

Karwoski, T. G. and Schachter, F. (1948). Psychological studies in semantics. III. Reaction times for similarity and differences. *J. Social Psychology* **28**, 103–120.

LoSciuto, L. A. and Hartley, E. L. (1963). Religious affiliation and open-mindedness in binocular resolution. *Perceptual Motor Skills* **17**, 427–430.

Rommetveit, R. and Brøgger, J. (1965). Synactic stimulus-response concordance in word association. *Pedagogisk Forksning* **9**, 173–178.

Siegel, S. (1956). "Non-parametric statistics for the behavioural sciences." McGraw-Hill, New York.

Toch, H. and Schulte, R. (1961). Readiness to perceive violence as a function of police training. *British J. Psychology* **52**, 389–393.

17. Generation of Words from Stereoscopically Presented Non-word Strings of Letters*

R. ROMMETVEIT, M. BERKLEY and J. BRØGGER

In previous studies (Rommetveit *et al.*, 1968a, 1968b) a stereoscopic rivalry situation was used to investigate different types of context effects upon word perception. When very similar typewritten words were presented for 170 ms to the left and the right eye, the subject would as a rule report seeing only one of them. Immediately preceding or simultaneously presented verbal stimuli, furthermore, would partly determine which word would be reported as seen. Incidentally, a strategy other than forced choice was discovered. For one rivalry pair of Norwegian words, a combination of left-eye and right-eye strings of letters also happened to generate a word. For example the two English words "hell" and "sell" may be combined as "shell". When such was the case, some subjects reported seeing the $(n+1)$-letter word rather than one of the other rivalry words of n letters each.

This incidental finding raises a question of some theoretical significance. The two different but superimposed letters (such as h and s in the example above) have obviously been identified as distinct graphic units. Since we were dealing with conditions of illumination and exposure time far above threshold values, this should be the case even when the subject reports seeing only one of them. If, therefore, subjects consistently report seeing e.g. "hell" after the context word "devil", the s in "sell" must have been processed as well. Choice of that alternative which fits the context, presupposes that both alternatives were available to the perceiver at some level and some stage of processing.

It should be kept in mind, moreover, that all but one pair of super-

* This study was conducted while the senior author was a visiting professor of psychology at Cornell University 1964–65. It was supported by National Science Foundation grant 64-58 to Cornell University. Published in *Scandinavian J. Psychology* (1968), **9**, 150–156.

imposed letters in the preceding studies were clear-cut semantic-morphological rivals as well as letter forms competing for the same position in the visual field. This means, more specifically, that the two superimposed letters were competing for the same letter position in two different words. The letters r and p, for instance, would compete for the fourth position in two different words such as "sour" and "soup". Such a semantic-morphological competition would not be the case, however, with a pair such as "shar"/"shap". In the latter case, r and p are acceptable as neighbours in the same word, namely "sharp".

The present study was conducted in order to disentangle *visual* and *semantic-morphological* rivalry. It was hypothesized that the response to strings of letters yielding a visual binocular rivalry pattern, would depend upon which strategy—choice of one rivalling letter or reporting both of them—would generate a word.

Experiment I

Apparatus

The stereoscope resembled in all essential aspects the modified Engel stereoscope previously used (Rommetveit *et al.*, 1968a). Illumination was provided by two 8 W bulbs in the front corners, and exposure time was controlled by an electric timer.

Stimuli

A series of stereograms were prepared, in each of which the text had been typed in small letters and centered so as to cover precisely corresponding areas of the two visual fields. Eight stereograms contained rivalry pairs of typewritten words (for left and right eye): HELL/BELL, ROSE/DOSE, STEP/STOP, BILL/HILL, DAMP/RAMP, BREAD/BROAD, DOPE/ROPE, LEAD/DEAD. Sixteen stereograms contained "fill-in" words, e.g. MINK, STORY, FAIR, HOUND, etc. each word being presented to both eyes. Finally, eight stereograms contained rivalry pairs of non-word strings of letters: SHAR/SHAP, DRIK/DRIN, CAL/CAM, CET/CEN, FAM/FRM, GIT/GIF, CRUL/CREL, SINT/SANT.

For each of the 32 stereograms described above, a corresponding "phrase stereogram" was also prepared; for the rivalry pairs of words: CHURCH HELL/CHURCH BELL, RED ROSE/RED DOSE, FULL STEP/FULL STOP, PHONE BILL/PHONE HILL, PARKING DAMP/PARKING RAMP, BROAD MIND/ BREAD MIND, THICK DOPE/THICK ROPE, and HEAVY LEAD/HEAVY DEAD; for the fill-in items MINK COAT, GOOD STORY, HOUND DOG, etc.; and for the non-word rivalry patterns: SHAR KNIFE/SHAP KNIFE, COOL DRIK/COOL DRIN, CAL REPLY/CAM REPLY, EVERY CET/EVERY CEN, FAM HOUSE/FRM

HOUSE, NICE GIT/NICE GIF, CRUL DEED/CREL DEED, and HOLY SINT/HOLY SANT. In addition, two of the following four patterns were inserted: SOR MIL/SUR MIK, BRAN STRM/BRIN SORM, SOR MIL/SUR MIK, BRAN SORM/BRIN STRM.

Procedure

Each subject was first exposed to all word stereograms and then, after a brief interval, to all phrase stereograms. First, the slide holder was focused, using a stereogram with a monocular circle and a monocular dot. Then the instructions were given: "You will be exposed to each stimulus for a brief moment. As soon as you have recognized it, read it out loudly. Remember to be accurate and distinct in reporting what you see".

Exposures 1 through 8 were rivalry pairs of words, exposures 11, 14, 16, 19, 24, 26, 30 and 32 were non-word rivalry pairs, and the remaining exposures were fill-ins. Exposure time for word stereograms was kept at 170 ms, and phrase stereograms were exposed for 200 ms.

At the end of the word series, two extra stereograms were used. All subjects who read SINT/SANT as "saint" were immediately given the extra stereogram SAINT/SAINT and asked which version of the word, first or second, appeared most clear and easy to perceive. Then followed for all subjects who had responded "farm" the first time a second presentation of FAM/FRM, now *preceded* by FARM/FARM. Again the subject was asked to tell which version had been perceived with least difficulty. After the word series, each word response to a non-word rivalry pair was given back to the subject, paired with its neighbouring fill-in word. For each such pair (e.g. a response "sharp" to SHAR/SHAP and "fair" to FAIR/FAIR) the subject was asked which word had appeared to be more clear of the two. A strictly analogous enquiry was conducted after the phrase series.

Subjects

The subjects were male students taking introductory courses in psychology at Cornell University. If a subject exhibited extreme eye dominance, reporting the image of one of the eyes in response to only one or none of the eight word rivalry pairs, he was left out. Twenty subjects passed this screening, but three of them received only the word stereogram series.

Results

Table I shows the distribution of word responses to all non-word rivalry pairs and should be read as follows. First, each response is assigned a "make-word" index (M-w) reflecting the probability of generating the word response by simply adding the appropriate letter (without having seen it) to either left-eye or right-eye string. Twenty-six

TABLE I. Distribution of word responses by veridical (Ve) and non-veridical (Nv) perceivers in the word and phrase conditions.

Stimuli	Response	M-w	T-L	Word condition Ve($N=11$)	Nv($N=9$)	Phrase condition Ve($N=8$)	Nv($N=9$)
shar/shap	sharp	0·26	A	10	1	7	7
drik/drin	drink	1·00	AA	8	7	6	6
cal/cam	calm	0·00	A	1	0	8	2
cet/cen	cent	0·73	AA	2	2	0	3
fam/frm	farm	0·15	AA	9	1	6	6
git/gif	gift	0·46	A	4	1	3	2
crul/crel	cruel	0·85	46	7	5	5	5
sint/sant	saint	0·66	A	6	5	6	7
% word responses				53	31	56	53

M-w stands for "make-word" index (see text), T-L for Thorndike-Lorge frequency value.

students were given the non-word strings and asked to make a word out of each of them by simply inserting one letter in whatever position they wanted. M—w for SHAR/SHAP $= 0·26$, meaning that 26% of all responses to the two separate non-word strings were the word SHARP. In addition, Thorndike-Lorge frequency values (T-L) are given for all word responses. Accuracy of perception was assessed in terms of errors in response to the fill-in words. Those who made only one or no incorrect response were considered "veridical" subjects; those with two or more errors "non-veridical". Word responses to non-word strings are given separately for these two groups.

The main findings may be summarized as follows. Many subjects reported seeing a word of length n + 1 letters when exposed to two monocular non-word strings of letters, each of length n. Generation of a word was particularly frequent among the veridical perceivers. In the word series, nine out of 11 veridical perceivers gave a word response to four or more rivalry patterns. Only two out of nine non-veridical perceivers gave four or more word responses. (The difference gives $p = 0·025$ by Fischer's exact probability test.) However, the difference stems mainly from two stimulus patterns, SHAR/SHAP ($p < 0·005$) and FAM/FRM ($p = 0·01$), which both have a low M-w index. For the pattern DRIN/DRIK (with M-w $= 1·00$) there is no difference. In the phrase series, non-veridical perceivers gave word responses as often as veridical perceivers. Frequency of word responses also varied from one rivalry pair to another, CAL/CAM, CET/CEN and GIT/GIF generating very few both in the word and phrase series.

Reports of clarity and ease of recognition showed that the word given in response to non-word strings was judged as equally clear or clearer, perceptually, when presented prior to the corresponding word stimulus. Thus, "saint" in response to SINT/SANT was judged as clearer than "saint" in response to SAINT/SAINT by five, as equally clear by two, and as less clear by two subjects. The corresponding judgements for the response "holy saint" were: HOLY SINT/HOLY SANT clearer in two, equally clear in five, and less clear in six cases. Of seven subjects who were given FARM/FARM prior to FAM/FRM, however, six reported either left- or right-eye image to the latter. Only one reported "farm", and he then judged the last version as less clear. In the case of FARM HOUSE/FARM HOUSE-FAM HOUSE/FRM HOUSE, seven subjects gave "farm house" in response to the latter, but reported it to be less clear. The remaining five subjects reported left- or right-eye image to the rivalry pattern.

When asked which had been more difficult to recognize: the word generated from two non-word strings of letters or its fill-in neighbour in the sequence of stereograms, 18 of the 32 subjects judged the former as less clear, 11 as clearer, and three as equal.

Of the 16 subjects exposed to SUR MIL/SOR MIK and BRAN STRM/BRIN SORM, 12 reported seeing "sour milk" and 10 "brain storm". Of 10 subjects exposed to SOR MIL/SUR MIK and BRAN SORM/BRIN STRM, only three reported seeing "sour milk" and six "brain storm".

Discussion

It was found that the binocular rivalry conflicts were resolved in different ways, depending upon whether there was a semantic-morphological rivalry of superimposed letters or not. When neither of two rivalling letters in a given position yields a word, but a combination of them does, the subjects quite frequently reported seeing the word generated by combining the two monocular strings of n letters into a word of length n + 1. The significantly higher frequency of such word responses among particularly veridical perceivers, testifies to a genuinely generative process, rather than to guessing based upon contextual redundancy. In order to make "farm" (and *not* fame, foam, form, from, etc.) out of FAM/FRM, one has to register both A and R and to arrange them in the appropriate sequence. However, correct identification of both the superimposed letters is not a prerequisite for a word response when the remaining letters allow for no alternative words (as in DRIK/DRIN); nor is it essential when a phrase context is added. The phrase context seems to facilitate word generation only when the subject's accuracy of perception is low as measured in terms of correct recognition of fill-in words. Context has hardly an effect on the patterns which fail to yield word responses in isolation, such as CAL/CAM, CET/CEN and GIT/GIF.

The differences between rivalry patterns may be due to various and possibly interacting factors. There may be *masking*, i.e. superimposed letters may be so similar that they hardly can be identified as separate entities at all. This may partly explain why many subjects reported "git" or "gif" in response to GIT/GIF. Secondly, there may be fusing or *mixing*, i.e. pairs of superimposed letters may sometimes yield a pattern similar to a third letter. This seemed to be the case with CAL/CAM, to which the modal response was "can". And, thirdly, some of the non-word trigrams may be almost acceptable as words or abbreviations. This may be true of CET/CEN, for which the modal response strategy was to report one or the other. CET corresponds to a French word, CEN is used as an abbreviation of century.

Whenever a word of $n+1$ letters was generated from two non-word strings of n letters each, it was a rule reported seen as clearly and as much "out there" as any unequivocal fill-in word. The consistent failure to generate the word when the non-word strings appeared immediately after the corresponding "real" word, is a puzzle. Availability of the correct spatial arrangement of letters in short-term memory may possibly explain the absence of word generation in this case.

Finally, observed responses to the four non-word patterns of potential phrases indicate that the generation of the meaningful response does not depend upon displacement of visual fields during exposure of non-word strings. *If* such dependence had been the case, only SOR MIL/SUR MIK and BRAN STRM/BRIN SORM would generate appropriate phrases. SUR MIL/SOR MIK would, by a shift of eye convergence corresponding to one letter position in either direction, yield either SOUR MIKL or SUOR MILK.

A strategy of forced choice in dealing with the initial word rivalry stereograms *and* veridical perception of fill-in stimuli could in the present experiment have built up and sustained the belief that "there are words out there". In a second study, therefore, a condition was set up under which subjects would expect the stimuli to be non-word strings.

Experiment II

Stimuli

Sixteen experimental non-word pairs were used. Five of them were taken from experiment I (e.g. SHAR/SHAP); seven (e.g. TRIL/TRAL) were rivalry pairs, each of which would allow for two or more word responses ("trial" and "trail"); and four (e.g. FCIAND/FRUEMD) were masking pairs which would generate words ("friend") only if subjects picked the appropriate member of each four superimposed pairs of letters. Each experimental stereogram appeared in the same position in the stimulus series under two conditions: subjects being set for words or for non-words.

The remaining stimuli under word set were the same as in experiment I. Eight experimental pairs were interspersed in the first, and the remaining eight in the second run of the same fill-in stimuli.

Under the non-word set every word stimulus was replaced by a corresponding pair of non-word strings. The initial rivalry patterns were thus HELK/BELK, ROQE/DOQE, STER/STOR, BILK/HILK, DARP/RARP, BROAN/BREAN, DOLP/LOLP, and LEAT/DEAT. The fill-ins were MANK, SPORY, FAIP, HOUNZ, etc.

Procedure

Instructions and procedure were essentially the same as in experiment I, with exposure time kept constant at 170 ms. After the experiment, subjects were asked if they remembered any particularly difficult stimuli, and whether they felt that some of them had contained strange arrangements such as superimposed letters.

Only those subjects were excluded who, in responding to all rivalry pairs, made use of one eye only. Twenty-six male students at Cornell University were included in the final analysis, 13 for each condition.

Results

The relative frequencies for the word- and non-word sets were for the SHAR/SHAP type of rivalry pair 0·57 versus 0·22; for the TRIL/TRAL type 0·74 versus 0·41; and for the FCIAND/FRUEMD type 0·35 versus 0·10. Under word set, 11 of the 13 subjects reported words in response to seven or more non-word pairs, whereas only two of the 13 under non-word set did so. (This difference yields $p < 0.005$ according to Fisher's exact probability test.)

TABLE II. Percentage of responses within different veridical strategies for three types of rivalry pairs.

	Word set			Non-word set		
		Combined image			Combined image	
Type of rivalry pair	Left or right image	Non-word	Word	Left or right image	Non-word	Word
hill/bill	69	00	00			
hilk/bilk				58	04	00
shar/shap	08	01	64	35	03	32

Table II gives the percentage of responses within each veridical strategy, the denominator being all responses to all rivalry strings of each type. A *veridical strategy* is defined as a response which shows that the subject has recognized n or n + 1 letters, all of which were presented in one or both of the strings of n letters each. Thus, veridical responses are reports of the image of either the left or the right eye, word responses such as "shapr", "drikn", "fram". The latter, however, were extremely infrequent (see Table II).

For the HELL/BELL and HELK/BELK types, the percentage refers only to the two last appearing pairs of each type. The reason for excluding the first six pairs is simply that subjects under non-word set failed to give veridical reports at the beginning. The percentage of veridical reports increased steadily from four till 62 from the two first to the two last pairs in the initial HELK/BELK series.

Discussion

The observed results provide additional evidence for a process of word generation in response to non-word rivalry pairs. Moreover, word formation appears to be enhanced by a set (built up by fill-in stimuli) that "there are words out there".

What, then, would be the expected distribution of word responses under an assumption of some stochastic, *not* word-directed strategy of processing? Several stochastic models could be proposed.

In the case of the masking pairs (FCIAND/FRUEMD), for instance, it might be assumed that the subject will always respond with n letters and report the first and last letter correctly, whereas his choice for any pair of superimposed different letters will show no left- or right-eye preference. If so, the word would be reported in 6.25% of the cases. Since the obtained value was 10%, there is no evidence for a particular word-directed process when subjects are exposed to masking patterns under non-word set.

For the other rivalry pairs, however, the probability of occurrence of an (n + 1)-letter response must first be estimated. According to Table II, the empirically based estimate would be $p < 0.04$, whereas the obtained frequency for the word-combination responses alone was 0·32. The final proof of a deterministic, word-directed strategy under non-word set is provided by a comparison of word versus non-word combined image. Any stochastic model would predict, for the SHAR/SHAP type, that non-word responses such as "shapr" would be as frequent as word responses ("sharp"). The observed frequencies were 0·05 versus 0·22. Thus, a strategy of word formation is operant even when forming a word stands clearly out, statistically, as a deviant mode of behaviour.

Why is this the case, and what can be stated about the mechanisms involved? Words are generated from graphic patterns by readers *operating upon* strings of letters. The rivalry situation involves a genuine ambiguity with respect to the location of two letters, and this ambiguity is apparently resolved in accordance with overlearned rules of word formation (Gibson *et al.*, 1963; Gibson *er al.*, 1966). Studies at Stanford University by Ruth S. Day (unpublished Ph.D. dissertation) also replicated the findings with acoustic stimuli: The two sound sequences, "roduct" to one ear and "poduct" to the other, were heard as "product".

Concluding Remarks

When trying to assess the theoretical significance of these exploratory studies, two major findings should be kept in mind. First of all, word generation was particularly frequent among accurate perceivers. Secondly, words generated from non-word rivalry pairs were as a rule "seen" as clearly as "real" words. Word perception must therefore under such conditions of sensory input clearly involve efferent processes (Festinger and Canon, 1965); the subject reports seeing *what he has done* to the rivalry strings in order to cognize the word.

A number of problems remain unsolved, however. First of all, purely structural factors should be controlled by employing systematically the very same rivalry pair of letters (e.g. p and r) in different, linguistically defined, rivalry conditions (such as shar/sha*p*; roud/*p*oud; sour/sou*p*; ran/*p*an). Secondly, attempts should be made to separate the role of purely semantic factors ("meaning") from properties of letter sequences, as such.

References

Festinger, L. and Canon, L. K. (1965). Information about spatial location based upon knowledge about efference. *Psychological Review* **72**, 373–384.

Gibson, E. J., Osser, H. and Pick, A. D. (1963). A study in the development of graphemephoneme correspondence. *J. verbal Learning verbal Behavior* **2**, 301–309.

Gibson, E. J., Schurcliff, A. and Yonas, A. (1966). The role of pronounce-ability in perception of pseudo-words by hearing and deaf subjects. *Project Literacy Report* **7**, 62–72.

Rommetveit, R., Toch, H. and Svendsen, D. (1968a). Effects of contingency and contrast contexts on the cognition of words. A study of stereoscopic rivalry. *Scandinavian J. Psychology* **9**, 138–144.

Rommetveit, R., Toch, H. and Svendsen, D. (1968b). Semantic, syntactic and associative context effects in a stereoscopic rivalry situation. *Scandinavian J. Psychology* **9**, 145–149.

18. Word Generation

A replication*

R. ROMMETVEIT and J. KLEIVEN

Two different strategies in resolving binocular rivalry of letters were demonstrated by Rommetveit *et al.* (1968) in a study at Cornell University. The present experiment aims at a replication of that study—with Norwegian stimulus material—under more carefully controlled conditions, since it was not always quite clear what caused the generation of a word. In certain stereograms (such as FRM/FAM, yielding "farm") both semantic factors and certain properties of letter sequences, as such, favoured word generation. Since, in the above example, neither frm nor fam is a word, a semantic explanation of the phenomenon is feasible, but frm is at the same time an unfamiliar and phonologically illegitimate letter sequence.

The present study seeks an answer to the question: How does the word/non-word difference between stimuli affect perception when each of the competing images as well as one combination of them are normal and easily pronounceable letter sequences? A second purpose is to control any structural factors by employing the very same rivalry pair of letters both in word and in non-word stimulus strings.

Method

The stereoscope is the same as used by Rommetveit *et al.* (1968). Exposure time was kept at 200 m by means of an electric timing device. Illumination was not measured, but kept constant throughout the experiment. The stereograms were printed in hand-set type, yielding an accurate correspondence between the two visual fields. The type is

* This study is part of a research programme in psycholinguistics, supported by the Norwegian Research Council for Science and the Humanities. Published in *Scandinavian J. Psychology* (1968) **9**, 277–281.

rather similar to the typewritten letters used in the earlier experiments, and its printer's designation is Gill Sans Light 362 (14 typographical points).

Informal pre-experiments had indicated that certain pairs of rivalling letters elicit combined images more often than others, and the pairs chosen (r/g and ø/y) were among the best in this respect. With the short strings of letters employed in this study, there are only three possible positions of the rivalling letters: at the end, in the middle and at the front of the string. The pair r/g was used both at the front and at the end, while ø/y was used in the middle of the string only. The experimental stimulus items that finally were selected are listed in Table I.

Each stereogram allows for four different veridical responses. The subject may report seeing the left image only, the right image only, or one or the other of two possible combined images. A *legitimate* combined image can be obtained only by a generation response, i.e. by arranging the two rivalling letters in the phonologically appropriate order. Every left-eye, right-eye, and legitimate combined image is thus easy to pronounce, and none of them violates any phonological rule of word formation in Norwegian. The second possible combination of the two

TABLE I. Experimental stimulus items.

Stereogram Left/Right	Possible combined image		Stereogram Left/Right	Possible combined image	
	Legitimate	Reversal		Legitimate	Reversal
SOR/SOG	sorg (sorrow)	sogr	SUR/SUG (sour/suck)	surg	sugr
DVEG/DVER	dverg (dwarf)	dvegr	KLAG/KLAR (complain/clear)	klarg	klagr
RØS/RYS	røys (heap)	ryøs	DØD/DYD (death/virtue)	døyd	dyød
HYDE/HØDE	høyde (hill)	hyøde	RYPE/RØPE (grouse/disclose)	røype	ryøpe
RESK/GESK	gresk (Greek)	rgesk	RIFT/GIFT (scratch/poison)	grift	rgift
GØT/RØT	grøt (porridge)	rgøt	GAP/RAP (gap/belch)	grap	rgap

images is in every case, regardless of item type, phonologically illegitimate, representing a reversal of the appropriate sequence of rivalling letters. There is thus no word in Norwegian with gr as the final letters (such as "sogr" or "sugr"). Nor does any Norwegian word have rg in the beginning.

There are two types of experimental stimuli, generation items and forced-choice items. The difference between them is of a semantic nature. It holds true for every generation stereogram that the subject has to combine the two images by a generation response in order to see a word. Every forced-choice stereogram, on the other hand, yields a word only if either left or right image is chosen.

The subject was seated in a dark room for about 20 min before the apparatus was adjusted to fit his vision. He was told that words would be shown, that he was to read them out aloud, but that many words would be difficult to recognize. Whenever he was not quite sure of a word, he was to say so before making his guess. During the experiment he was asked repeatedly whether words were seen clearly, and all symptoms of hesitation and uncertainty were recorded.

The first series of stereograms contained 10 well-known Norwegian words, such as LITEN/LITEN (little), SÅPE/SÅPE (soap), GATE/GATE (street). Then followed the experimental items, interspersed in random order among 24 stereograms containing short familiar words ("fillers") like the ones in the introductory list. Finally, 10 forced-choice items were presented in order to assess eye dominance. The interval between exposures was kept at a minimum.

Subjects were 30 students at the University of Oslo, 21 male and nine female.

Results

The responses were classified as follows:

Generation	Legitimate combined image (such as "sorg", "surg").
Choice	Only one image (either left or right).
Double	The two rivalling letters seen on top of each other.
Reversal	Rivals seen in phonologically illegitimate sequence (such as "sogr", "sugr").
Other	Other (mostly non-veridical) responses.
None	No response.

For generation and choice responses, level of confidence is indicated by the signs + (confident) and − (uncertain).

Ten subjects proved completely eye-dominant on the final series of forced-choice stereograms, and their responses are presented separately in Tables II and III.

Table II shows that there were relatively few confident generations. Reporting either left or right image was the modal response to forced-choice stereograms, whereas generation occurred almost exclusively in response to generation stereograms. This finding is even more clearly brought out when responses are grouped into three gross categories: generation, choice and all others (Table III). A comparison of responses to generation and forced-choice items by subjects who showed no extreme eye dominance (the upper two rows) yields a highly significant difference ($\chi^2 = 81 \cdot 68$, d.f. $= 2$, $p < 0 \cdot 001$). A similar comparison

TABLE II. Distribution of responses to all experimental items.

Subject	Item type	Genera-tion+	Genera-tion−	Choice +	Choice −	Double	Re-versal	Other	None	Total
Non-dominant	Generation	24	29	22	6	—	1	25	13	120
(n=20)	Forced choice	3	3	68	21	3	1	13	8	120
Dominant	Generation	9	9	16	5	—	—	19	2	60
(n=10)	Forced choice	2	1	42	2	—	1	11	1	60

for eye-dominant subjects (the lower two rows) also brings out a significant difference ($\chi^2 = 21 \cdot 38$, d.f. $= 2$, $p < 0 \cdot 001$). Responses to forced-choice stereograms by dominant and non-dominant subjects (second and fourth row) show no difference between the two groups, but their responses to generation stereograms do yield a significant difference (upper and third row; $\chi^2 = 6 \cdot 49$, d.f. $= 2$, $p < 0 \cdot 05$), non-dominant subjects giving considerably more generation responses.

TABLE III. Responses distributed over three gross categories.

Subject	Item type	Response category		
		Generation	Choice	Other
Non-dominant	Generation	63	28	39
(n=20)	Forced choice	6	89	25
Dominant	Generation	18	21	21
(n=10)	Forced choice	3	46	14

Table IV gives the item-by-item distribution of confident generation responses by all subjects. Every generation item is paired with its corresponding forced-choice item, and Fisher's exact test is applied to each pair. In this table generation responses accompanied by any symptoms of uncertainty are counted as "other". Three of the six comparisons (sorg–surg, dverg–klarg, høyde–røype) yielded differences beyond the 0·01 level of confidence. Moreover, the rivalling letters r/g were seen clearly as rg in 15 cases and as gr in seven cases, depending on which sequence was required for word generation. There were only two generations in response to r/g in forced-choice stereograms.

In the study by Rommetveit et al. (1968) a distinction was made between veridical and non-veridical perceivers, the former giving significantly more generation responses. No such trend was found in the present material.

TABLE IV. Comparison of responses to matched items
($n = 30$). Generation+ responses versus all others.

Item	Generation+	Other	p
		Response	
SOR/SOG	7	23 ⎫	
SUR/SUG	0	30 ⎭	0·005
DVEG/DVER	8	22 ⎫	
KLAG/KLAR	0	30 ⎭	0·002
RØS/RYS	2	28 ⎫	
DØD/DYD	2	28 ⎭	—
HYDE/HØDE	9	21 ⎫	
RYPE/RØPE	1	29 ⎭	0·006
RESK/GESK	4	26 ⎫	
RIFT/GIFT	0	30 ⎭	0·056
GØT/RØT	3	27 ⎫	
GAP/RAP	2	28 ⎭	—

Discussion

The phenomenon of word generation was found with Norwegian stimulus material, but confident generation responses were less frequent. The difference between the present results and those obtained in the previous study may be due to a variety of factors. The stimulus material was structurally different (typed versus printed letters), and neither illumination nor contrast was equated in the two experiments. In addition, degree of phonetic-graphic correspondence in the two languages has to be considered. Written Norwegian is more isomorphic to corresponding spoken sound sequences than in the case of English, and such gross linguistic differences may very likely be reflected in reading habits and in performance in word perception tasks.

Since, in the present study, the same rivalry pairs of letters were employed both in generation and in forced-choice stereograms, purely structural factors can safely be disregarded. The fate of the pair r/g is particularly illuminating in this respect. It was seen as r only, g only, rg, or gr, depending upon which solution yielded a word.

The difference between a generation item and its corresponding forced-choice item does not reside in differential legitimacy of the combined images qua letter sequences. A generation response is equally legitimate in both cases as far as purely phonological rules are concerned. Arranging the rivals in the phonologically appropriate order is in the one case a prerequisite for experiencing a word, whereas such an arrangement prohibits word experience in the other case. Resolution of the rivalry conflict seems therefore to be subordinated to higher-order cognitive processes involving activation of acquired word meanings (Rommetveit, 1968, pp. 97–107).

Binocular rivalry of letters is never encountered under normal reading conditions. The confidence with which most choice responses were given, and the phenomenal reality of words in response to some generation stereograms, indicate that the rivalry most often went entirely unnoticed by the subject. Thus, alternative modes of resolving a rivalry conflict can apparently be embedded as "subroutines" in a reading process, geared toward word meaning.

References

Rommetveit, R. (1968). "Words, meanings and messages." Academic Press and Universitetsforlaget, New York, London and Oslo.

Rommetveit, R., Toch, H. and Svendsen, D. (1968). Effects of contingency and contrast contexts on the cognition of words. A study of stereoscopic rivalry. *Scandinavian J. Psychology* **9**, 138–144.

Rommetveit, R., Berkley, M. and Brogger, J. (1968). Generation of words from stereoscopically presented non-word strings of letters. *Scandinavian J. Psychology* **9**, 150–156.

19. Meaning and Frequency in a Binocular Rivalry Situation*

J. KLEIVEN and R. ROMMETVEIT

Previous studies of binocular rivalry have focused upon effects of the meaning of rivalling strings of letters. Rommetveit *et al.* (1968a, 1968b) investigated the effect of various contexts on the outcome of the rivalry situation. When the meaning of one of the two rivalling strings of letters served to relate the string to the given context words, this string was seen more often than the other. Rommetveit and Kleiven (1968) replicated findings reported by Rommetveit *et al.* (1968) that choice of strategy in resolving binocular rivalry of letters depends upon the meaning of the strings of letters involved. Exposed to two words (meaningful strings), a person typically reported having seen one or the other of the two. Exposed to two non-words (meaningless strings), however, he frequently reported seeing a word "generated" by combining the two non-words. The meaning of the rivalling strings of letters determined what would be reported as seen.

In such studies, the importance of controlling factors not relevant to meaning is rather obvious. Thus, for example, Rommetveit and Kleiven (1968) put a great deal of effort into controlling purely structural or perceptual factors in their stimulus material. The present purpose is to investigate the effect of the frequency variable of the verbal-learning tradition (cf. Underwood and Schulz, 1960), relative to that of meaning. Two experimental hypotheses were tested:

(1) *The frequency hypothesis.* In a binocular rivalry situation, the more frequent of two rivalling strings of letters will tend to be seen.

(2) *The meaning hypothesis.* When a word is rivalling with a non-word, the word will tend to be seen.

* A more detailed report is available in Norwegian (Kleiven, 1969). The study is part of a research programme in psycholinguistics, supported by the Norwegian Research Council for Science and the Humanities. Published in *Scandinavian J. Psychology* (1970) **11**, 17–20.

Method

To assess the relative frequency of all three-letter combinations in Norwegian, a frequency count was undertaken with the "U-count" method of Underwood and Schulz (1960, p. 68), adapted to the possibilities of modern data processing. A total of about half a million words were counted by computer, using five sub-samples of about equal size: one novel, one textbook of music, one textbook of carpentry, and two samples of high-school compositions from different parts of the country.

The stimulus material was recorded on stereoscopic film, which was later run in the stereoscope. The letters were of the Gill Sans Light type, also used in earlier experiments. The stereoscope was built into a large black box, containing a movie projector which projected the image onto an opaque screen. The screen was viewed by the subject from the reverse side, through the glasses of an Engel stereoscope. The glasses were mounted in the opening of a narrowing tube protruding from the box. For control of illumination strength, two Polaroid filters were placed between the projector and the screen.

The subject was seated at the stereoscope in the dark room for about 15 min before the experiment started. He was then instructed to read aloud the words that would be shown, keeping in mind that some of the words would probably be unfamiliar to him, and to report whenever he was not quite sure of what he had seen.

The film started with a list of short familiar words, used for introducing method and apparatus to the subject. Then followed the 16 experimental items, interspersed in random order among 32 items containing short familiar words ("fillers") like the ones in the introductory list. Each experimental item consisted of two rivalling trigrams (three-letter combinations), of which one is at least three times as frequent as the other according to the count. All trigrams employed were normal and easily pronounceable letter sequences. There were four types of items:

(1) High-frequency word *vs* low-frequency word (HW/LW).
(2) High-frequency non-word *vs* low-frequency non-word (HN/LN).
(3) High-frequency word *vs* low-frequency non-word (HW/LN).
(4) High-frequency non-word *vs* low-frequency word (HN/LW).

Other features of the material, such as the randomization of structural factors, will be seen from Table I. Finally, 10 rivalry pairs of words were presented in order to assess eye dominance.

Before each item in all lists, the Norwegian word KLAR (ready) was shown for about 400 ms (10 frames at a film speed of 24 f/s), followed by a blank interval of equal length. Exposure time for each item was

TABLE I. Experimental stimulus items and their trigram frequencies.

Item type[a]	Item left/right	Frequencies left/right
HW/LW	dis/dit (haze/there)	474/52
	båt/bås (boat/stall)	232/1
	lus/lut (louse/lye)	49/414
	ost/oss /cheese/us)	150/623
HN/LN	ate/ase (—/—)	945/68
	pås/påt (—/—)	32/6
	gos/got (—/—)	1/19
	ønt/øns (—/—)	32/112
HW/LN	ert/err (pea/—)	1054/266
	når/nåt (when/—)	752/3
	døt/dør (—/door)	2/120
	bir/bit (—/bite)	5/38
HN/LW	jet/jer (jet/—)	47/587
	urt/utt (herb/—)	125/766
	fer/fet (—/fat)	486/66
	råt/rår (—/reigns)	54/7

[a] HW = High-frequency word.
LW = Low-frequency word.
HN = High-frequency non-word.
LN = Low-frequency non-word.

kept at about 40 ms (1 frame). After each item there was a longer blank interval, when the film was stopped while the subject reported what he had seen.

Subjects were students at the University of Oslo, 11 male and 13 female.

Results

The responses were divided into three categories:

HI responses. The high-frequency string was reported, without any symptoms of doubt or uncertainty.

LO responses. The low-frequency string was reported, without any symptoms of doubt or uncertainty.

O responses. All other responses, i.e. failure of reporting confidently either one of the two strings.

Table II gives the distribution of responses to the four types of items. A tendency to give more HI than LO responses is not statistically significant. Thus the general frequency hypothesis is not supported.

TABLE II. Distribution of responses for four experimental item types.

Item type	Response category[a]		
	HI	O	LO
High-frequency word *vs* low-frequency word (HW/LW)	32	49	15
High-frequency non-word *vs* low-frequency non-word (HN/LN)	22	16	58
High-frequency word *vs* low-frequency non-word (HW/LN)	57	11	28
High-frequency non-word *vs* low-frequency word (HN/LW)	20	35	41
Total:	131	111	142

[a] HI = High-frequency trigram reported as seen.
LO = Low-frequency trigram reported as seen.
O = Other responses.

On the whole, there was no tendency for high-frequency strings of letters to be reported more often than low-frequency ones. However, the distribution of responses is different for the four item types. Only the HW/LN items tended to give considerably more HI than LO responses, but this result is predictable also from the meaning hypothesis.

Two item types (HW/LN and HN/LW) consist of words rivalling with non-words. The HI and LO responses to these items may therefore be reclassified as word and non-word responses. In 92 cases (75%) of 123 such responses the word response was given. Of the eight items in question, seven gave more word than non-word responses. Under the null hypothesis—that half of the items would be expected in either direction—the probability of the outcome is 0·035 (Binomial Test). The meaning hypothesis is thus rather strongly supported by the data.

It may also be noted that item types give different amounts of O responses. When the types were compared two by two in fourfold tables (O responses *vs* all others), the Fisher Exact Probabilities Test always yielded a *p* of 0·04 or less. Thus, each item type produced an amount of O responses that is significantly different from that of any other item type.

The importance of meaning in this experiment may also be seen from the distribution of O responses. The item type HW/LW gave by far the smallest number of such responses. Among the 96 cases where words are rivalling, one or the other word was correctly identified in 81 cases, the rest being "other responses". Item type HN/LN, on the other hand, gave the greatest number of O responses. Among the 96 cases of rivalling non-words, one or the other was correctly identified in only 38 cases. When both rivalling strings of letters were words, one or the other was easier to identify correctly than when both were non-words. This finding fits well with the results of the tachistoscope experiments of Bjørgen (1968), who demonstrated that visual identification thresholds for letter sequences are predictable from the meaning of the sequences.

In conclusion, then, meaning is by far a more important variable than frequency in the binocular rivalry situation. Keeping frequency under control in such experiments seems not to be a matter of great importance.

References

Bjørgen, I. A. (1968). Visual duration thresholds; the part played by the exposure time for the single letters and the meaningfulness of the syllables. Unpublished manuscript, University of Trondheim.

Kleiven, J. (1969). Om frekvens og mening ved binokulær rivalisering. Unpublished dissertation, University of Oslo.

Rommetveit, R., Berkley, M. and Brøgger, J. (1968). Generation of words from stereoscopically presented non-word strings of letters. *Scandinavian J. Psychology* **9**, 150–156.

Rommetveit, R. and Kleiven, J. (1968). Word generation: a replication. *Scandinavian J. Psychology* **9**, 277–281.

Rommetveit, R., Toch, H. and Svendsen, D. (1968a). Effects of contingency and contrast contexts on the cognition of words. A study of stereoscopic rivalry. *Scandinavian J. Psychology* **9**, 138–144.

Rommetveit, R., Toch, H. and Svendsen, D. (1968b). Semantic, syntactic and associative context effects in a stereoscopic rivalry situation. *Scandinavian J. Psychology* **9**, 145–149.

Underwood, B. J. and Schulz, R. W. (1960). "Meaningfulness and verbal learning." Lippincott, Chicago.

20. Induced Semantic-associative States and Resolution of Binocular-rivalry Conflicts between Letters*

R. ROMMETVEIT and R. M. BLAKAR

When—under specific laboratory conditions—two different letters are competing for the same position in the visual field, a number of alternative perceptual strategies are possible. The two letters may be seen alternately or experienced as rivals for the same position. If not, only the left-eye or only the right-eye letter may be seen, or both letters may be experienced as positioned sequentially in either one or the other of two possible orders. A systematic survey of differential outcomes across systematically varied contextual arrangements of written material may hence yield insight into aspects of reading which are relatively inaccessible to introspection.

Consider, for instance, the two letters p and r as rivals embedded in three types of competing strings of letters: pop/por, shap/shar, and soup/sour. In accordance with previous experimental findings, an English-speaking fluent reader would be expected to adopt different strategies in the three different cases. In the first case he would most likely report seeing only pop, in the second sharp and in the third either soup or sour; i.e. he will as a rule resolve the conflict in such a way that a *word* is seen. Thus, Kleiven and Rommetveit (1970) found that a meaningful string of letters was identified more often than a competing non-word string of considerably higher frequency of occurrence in the language. Rommetveit *et al.* (1968) found that two competing non-word strings, each of length n, tended to be seen as a word of n + 1 letters whenever

* The study is part of a research programme in psycholinguistics, supported by the Norwegian Research Council for Science and the Humanities. Gunn Skartland assisted in conducting the experiment, and the final report was prepared while the first author was a fellow 1972–73 at Netherlands Institute for Advanced Study in the Humanities and the Social Sciences. Published in *Scandinavian J. Psychology* (1973) **14**, 185–194.

the two competing letters were legitimate neighbours in a word form, composed of the identical part of the two competing strings plus the two rivals. This phenomenon of word generation was replicated by Rommetveit and Kleiven (1968) under strict control of perceptual aspects of letter recognition.

Which one of two competing words will be identified, moreover, appears to be partly determined by induced semantic-associative states. Subjects would thus tend to see only the letter a or only the letter u of the two rivals a/u, depending upon whether the word towel or the word spoon had been shown immediately before or simultaneously with the rivalry pair soap/soup. Such context effects were explored for three types of semantic-associative linkages: *contrast* (warm–cold), *contingency* (towel–soap, spoon–soup), and *syntagmatic connections* (very–sweat, the–man). Contrast contexts had particularly strong effects when presented simultaneously with the rivalry pairs, whereas contingency contexts seemed to affect resolution more when appearing approx. 3·5 s before the rivalry pattern was shown (Rommetveit et al., 1968a,b).

The evidence indicating differentially optimal intervals between context and rivalry pair for the three types of contextual linkage is incomplete and rather inconclusive. Moreover, presumed differences between types of linkage are themselves in need of further clarification. A syntagmatic context effect resembles word generation in certain important aspects. The context word and the appropriate member of the rivalry pair constitute together a unit resembling a single composite word. Consider, for instance, the case when "the man" is reported in response to "the" plus "ran/man". The resultant English phrase "the man" corresponds in fact to a single composite word (*mannen*) in Norwegian. Previous explorations (Rommetveit and Turner, 1967) indicate that final decoding of such syntagmatically connected words under normal reading conditions is postponed until both of them have been seen. Choice of syntagmatically appropriate rival should hence occur most frequently when context and rivalry pair appear simultaneously.

Neither the contrast nor the contingency type is a linkage between neighbouring words constituting a phrase. For that reason, observed contrast and contingency effects cannot be attributed to the characteristic strategy of chunking segments into successively more inclusive meaningful units. The act of comprehending a single content word in isolation, however, can be conceived of as a complex chain of inter-related processes, expanding from a central region to successively more peripheral spheres of a topologically structured semantic-associative network (Rommetveit, 1972, pp. 71–73). Contrast linkages such as warm–cold must then be conceived of as located within the central region of each of the two words' semantic-associative networks. This implies that the very initial stage of comprehending "warm" involves cognition corresponding to whatever may be encoded in the word cold, and vice versa. A maximal context effect may therefore be expected when a rivalry pair such as cold/sold appears while the subject is still at a very early stage of comprehending "warm". Pure contingency linkages such as towel–soap, on the other hand, will appear in the semantic-associative maps as one of many possible pathways from the central to the more peripheral regions of the network constituting the entire meaning potential of the context word. That context word should hence affect resolutions of binocular rivalry most strongly when there is sufficient time for sequential associative activity, i.e. when appearing (relatively speaking) long before the rivalry pattern appears.

In previous experiments, efforts were also made to inquire into the phenomenal reality of the various kinds of resolution. As a rule, the subject was unable to give any coherent and satisfactory retrospective account of his own strategy. In the case of word generation, for instance, many subjects asserted with confidence that they had seen the word composed of $n + 1$ letters "out there"—when in fact they had generated the word spontaneously from two monocular strings of letters, each of length n. The issue of phenomenal reality is extremely complex, however. Reading is a highly overlearned and automatized skill, and a fluent reader would hardly be able to give a coherent introspective account of his performance under normal reading conditions; but what will happen in a laboratory setting if he knows in advance that letters will compete for the same position, and is asked explicitly to discover the rivalry? Will he then be capable of counteracting the effect of context words?

Experimental evidence bearing upon these questions may yield more insight into different types of contextual linkages and hypothesized semantic-associative states induced by context words. Thus, if contingency contexts affect resolution via activation of peripheral parts of the semantic-associative network of the context word, they should also be more transparent and hence more readily counteracted than contrast contexts. The latter, moreover, should be particularly resistant to voluntary control and inhibition under conditions of minimal time intervals between context and rivalry pair, and syntagmatic context effects should be particularly hard to counteract when context and rivalry pair appear simultaneously. This follows from what has already been hypothesized about type of context: i.e. that contingency linkages correspond to optional states at later stages of word comprehension, that contrast linkages correspond to non-optional states at the very early stage of decoding the context word, and that syntagmatic linkages correspond to acts of chunking neighbouring segments into more inclusive meaningful entities.

In summary, then, there is strong experimental evidence showing that binocular-rivalry conflicts between letters tend to be resolved in such a way that a word—and even a contextually appropriate word—is seen. More will hopefully be learned about the impact of semantic-associative states upon resolution by varying the type of linkage under conditions of different time intervals between context and rivalry pair, and by exploring to what extent different kinds of context effect can be counteracted when the subject knows that two letters will compete for the same position, and he is asked explicitly to try to identify the contextually inappropriate rival.

Method

Apparatus

The stereoscope employed is described in a previous report (Kleiven and Rommetveit, 1970). It was built into a large black box, containing a film projector which projected the image onto an opaque screen. The screen was viewed by the subject from the reverse side, through the glasses of an Engel stereoscope. The glasses were mounted in the opening of a narrowing tube protruding from the box. Two polaroid filters were placed between the projector and the screen for control of illumination.

Stimuli

The complete stimulus material for the experimental series of rivalry pairs is presented in Table I, with translations in English. The material was recorded on stereoscopic film. The letters were of the Gill-Sans-Light type used in previous experiments. The first 12 rivalry pairs in Table I contain six different pairs of competing letters, each pair appearing twice and in such a fashion that letter dominance and position are balanced. In order to identify the contextually appropriate rival, the subject must utilize the v of his left eye in VARM/TARM, but the t of his right eye in HAVET/HATET; the a of his right eye in SKUM/SKAM, but the u of his left eye in FULL/FALL; and so on. The two items at the end of the experimental series are word-generation pairs, i.e. monocular strings yielding a word if and only if the rivals g and r are experienced sequentially as rg.

Temporal sequence of rivalry pairs was always as in Table I, whereas contexts were presented in three different combinatorial schemes. The first scheme is indicated by asterisks in Table I. The second scheme followed the same diagonal pattern, the stereoscopic film being composed of the sequence FÆLT/FÆLT + VARM/TARM, ÆRE/ÆRE + SKUM/SKAM, and so on. The third scheme comprised all remaining combinations. The two word-generation pairs at the end of the sequence were in the

TABLE I. Stimulus material in Norwegian with translation in English.

Context			Rivalry pair
Contrast	Syntagmatic	Contingency	(left eye/right eye)
KALD*	FÆLT	OVN	VARM/TARM
cold	awfully	stove	warm/intestine
ÆRE	DIN	RØDME*	SKUM/SKAM
honor	your	blush	foam/shame
KRIG	MULIG*	FRIHET	FRED/FREM
war	possible	freedom	peace/forward
SULTEN*	GANSKE	MIDDAGSLUR	MITT/METT
hungry	rather	nap	my/satisfied
BILLIG	MEGET	PRIS*	DYR/DYD
cheap	very	price	expensive/virtue
SKITTEN	ALDELES*	SÅPE	RAN/REN
dirty	completely	soap	robbery/clean
ELSKET*	INTENST	FRYKTET	HAVET/HATET
loved	intensely	feared	the ocean/hated
EDRU	ALTFOR	SJANGLE*	FULL/FALL
sober	too	stagger	drunk/fall
LYS	SVÆRT*	SKUMMEL	DØRK/MØRK
light	very	dismal	deck/dark
STORM*	HELT	ANDAKT	STILLE/STELLE
storm	entirely	devotions	quiet(ness)/prepare
LIV	MANNENS	GRAV*	RØD/DØD
life	the man's	grave	red/death
DAG	LANG*	SOVE	NATT/NETT
day	long	sleep	night/net
GLEDE*	VARIG	TÅRE	SOR/SOG
joy	sustained	tear	SORG = grief
KJEMPE*	LITEN	KLOVN	DVEG/DVER
giant	small	clown	DVERG = dwarf

first scheme combined with contrast, in the second with syntagmatic, and in the third with contingency contexts.

All context words had been included as stimulus words in a free word-association task administered to 129 students enrolled in introductory psychology courses. In no single case was the contextually inappropriate member of the rivalry pair (i.e. TARM, SKUM, FREM, etc.) given as a response. Although every syntagmatic context word yielded a legitimate phrase (e.g. awfully warm) if and only if the appropriate member of the rivalry pair was chosen, the latter was never elicited as a free word-association response to its syntagmatic context. On the other hand, every contrast and every contingency linkage in Table I was also revealed as an associative connection in the free word-association task. On the average, contrast contexts elicited appropriate rival words in 47% of the cases, but only 16% for contingency contexts.

Directed word-association responses were also obtained for all contrast and contingency words, from 64 subjects. The appropriate member of the rivalry pair was given as "the opposite of" its contrast context in 85% of the cases. The rank-order correlation was 0·62 between the latter measure and associative strength as assessed by free word associations. Directed associations to contingency-context words were obtained with a sentence completion task, in which the requested associative linkage in each case was specified indirectly by means of a model sentence. For instance, the response to "grave" was elicited by:

The phenomenon "bed" goes together with "sleep".
The phenomenon "grave" goes together with . . .?

Under this condition contingency context elicited appropriate word in 44% of the cases, and the rank correlation with free word association was 0·69. A detailed description in English of the semantic-associative network in the stimulus material, explored by a set of directed-association tests, may be obtained from the authors.

Design and Procedure

Every context word was exposed for approx. 188 ms (3 frames of film at a speed of 16 frames per second), whereas the rivalry pair was shown for only 63 ms (1 frame). In one condition, context and rivalry pair were shown successively, with no blank frame between them, and with the context above the rivalry pair so as to avoid masking. The context word was thus experienced simultaneously with, but above, the rivalry pair. In two other conditions, the interval between context and rivalry pair was 1 and 4 s (16 and 72 blank frames), respectively.

Every combinational scheme of contexts and rivalry pairs was employed with each interval condition when the experimental task was defined (as in previous studies) by a request to report what is seen under conditions of brief exposure of written material (Task R). For Combination I (indicated by asterisks in Table I) a different set of instructions was employed as well, the subject being explicitly asked to try to discover and report the contextually inappropriate rival word (Task D). The complete design was therefore as shown in Table II, and 72 students, enrolled in introductory psychology and social science courses at the University of Oslo, served as subjects in the experiment.

Each subject was seated at the stereoscope in the dark room for about 15 min, and was then given a familiarization series of 10 words (same word on both eyes). He was asked to read each word aloud, and the word KLAR (ready) was presented for 625 ms (10 frames) before each task. In every condition the subject was asked to report what he actually saw, and encouraged to tell whenever he was uncertain about what he had seen. Before starting on the experimental series with Task R, he was told that two words would from then on appear after each ready signal. His task was to report both of them in the order in which they appeared, and he was requested not to read any one of them aloud until he had seen both.

Task D was introduced by an additional, careful demonstration of the rivalry as such and of the contextual relationships to be expected. The subject was shown on paper the three rivalry pairs FRISK/FROSK, STÅL/STOL, and VÅR/NÅR in conjunction with the contexts SYK/SYK, BORD/BORD and VAKKER/VAKKER. He was told that the series he was going to see consisted of such combinations, and that people under similar conditions tended to see only the context word and the contextually appropriate rival, namely SYK–FRISK (sick–healthy), BORD–

TABLE II. Number of subjects per experimental condition.

Context–rivalry interval	0 s			1 s			4 s		
Combination	I	II	III	I	II	III	I	II	III
Task R	6	6	6	6	6	6	6	6	6
Task D	6			6			6		

STOL (table–chair), and VAKKER–VÅR (beautiful–spring). Finally, he was explicitly asked to avoid such traps and try to identify, in each case, the entirely unrelated word, e.g. FROSK, STÅL, and NÅR (frog, steel, and when) in the examples he was shown. The information that letters would be competing, and the request for report of the contextually unrelated word, were repeated immediately before the experimental series started.

Results

A gross picture of context effect can be achieved simply by counting— for each particular combination of context type and interval—how often the contextually appropriate rival (and nothing else) was reported with confidence as seen. The results of such a count for Task R are presented in Table III. They show that the frequencies were particularly low for all three types of linkage when context and rivalry pattern were experienced simultaneously. For each type of linkage there was an increase in gross context effect when an interval of 1 s was introduced. For contrast and syntagmatic contexts, the effect decreased as the interval was increased from 1 s to 4 s, whereas contingency contexts affected resolution slightly more. These differences are small, however, and statistically insignificant.

It is also possible to examine, for each type of context, to what extent the pattern of effects remains the same across different intervals. Thus, all contrast linkages to the first 12 rivalry patterns in Table I were ranked with respect to their effects at intervals of 0, 1 and 4 s. A Rho of 0·87 was obtained between effects at intervals 0 and 1 s, indicating that contrast contexts affected resolution in much the same fashion, whether presented simultaneously with or one second prior to the rivalry pattern. A weaker, but still statistically significant correspondence (Rho = 0·53) was obtained for syntagmatic linkages at these

TABLE III. Mean number of rivalry pairs in which only the contextually appropriate word was seen (Task R).

| | Interval | | |
Type of linkage	0 s	1 s	4 s
Contrast	6·0	7·1	6·8
Syntagmatic	4·3	5·8	5·1
Contingency	5·3	6·1	6·6

intervals, whereas all remaining measures of correspondence across intervals gave insignificant coefficients ($p < 0.05$). The lowest measure (Rho = 0·28) was obtained between syntagmatic context effects at intervals 0 and 4 s under Task R.

Sequential positioning of rivalling letters was rarely experienced in response to the first 12 rivalry patterns. The g/r conflict in SOR/SOG and DVEG/DVER, on the other hand, was as a rule resolved as rg, even when the subject knew that two letters would be competing for the same position. Number of confident word generations in these cases are presented in Table IV.

TABLE IV. Number of word generations (g/r seen as rg) in response to the rivalry pairs SOR/SOG and DVEG/DVER.

| | | Interval | | |
Task	Type of linkage	0 s	1 s	4 s
D	Contrast	9	11	7
R	Contrast	10	8	12
R	Syntagmatic	4	12	10
R	Contingency	10	12	11

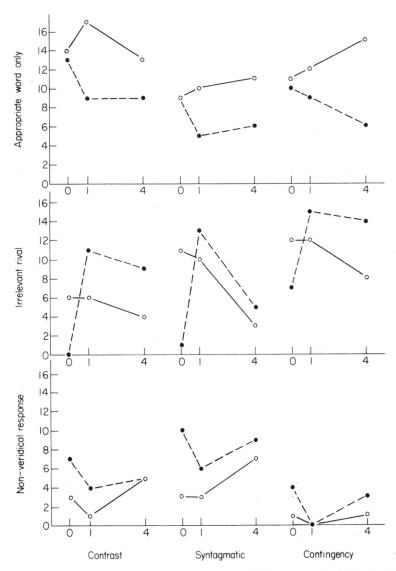

FIG. 1. Resolutions under conditions of Task R (solid lines) and Task D (broken lines).

Figure 1 permits a more detailed comparison of context effects under Task R (the traditional "report-what-is-seen") and Task D (deliberately trying to counteract context effect). Restricting the comparison to the combinatorial scheme indicated by asterisks in Table II, the contrast linkages involved are cold–warm, hungry–satisfied, loved–hated and storm–quietness (or rather: storm–calm weather); the syntagmatic connections are possible–peace, completely–clean, very–dark, and long–night; and the contingency items are blush–shame, price–expensive, stagger–drunk, and grave–death.

Number of possible solutions for each type of linkage at every interval condition is $4 \times 6 = 24$ (items × subjects). The upper diagrams show how many of the solutions were confident reports of seeing the contextually appropriate rival and nothing else. The middle diagrams represent reports of seeing the irrelevant rivalling letter, whether as part of the rival word only, as competing with the other rival, or as positioned before or after the latter. Together the upper and middle diagrams represent all veridical responses, i.e. all cases when the subject reported no letters other than those being shown, and when at least all letters of one or the other rivalry string were seen. The lower diagrams, on the other hand, give the number of non-veridical responses, reporting one or more letters that were not presented at all (guesses such as LIVET in response to HAVET/HATET; RULLE in response to FULL/FALL).

The most striking finding with reference to Fig. 1 is the complete failure of the subjects to discover the irrelevant rival, when directed to do so (Task D), in the case of contrast or syntagmatic context appearing simultaneously with rivalry pattern. They then reported seeing either the contextually appropriate word only or something which was not shown, or were unable to report anything at all. Performance improved greatly, however, at an interval of 1 s between context and rivalry pattern, but for syntagmatic linkages an interval of 4 s was not nearly as favourable.

The experiment was designed so that a general or individual bias, such as letter dominance (e.g. t seen more easily than v in v/t, or vice versa) or eye dominance (e.g. a preference for either right- or left-eye image) would favour the appropriate rival in one case and the irrelevant rival in the other. The null hypothesis of no context effect therefore implies that the contextually appropriate rival and its contextually irrelevant competitor should be seen equally often. An extremely simple, though statistically cautious measure of context effect may hence be derived by relating the two observed frequencies and considering their deviation from an expected 50/50 distribution (binomial test).

It will be seen from Table V that *contrast* contexts affected resolution significantly at each interval condition when the subject was instructed simply to report what he saw (Task R). *The effect was even stronger, but only under condition of simultaneous context, when instructed to try to counteract it* (Task D). In the case of *syntagmatic* linkages, the most unequivocal effect also appeared with Task D under condition of simultaneous context. In addition, there was an effect under the diametrically opposed condition (Task R and longest interval). For *contingency*

TABLE V. Comparing the frequencies of appropriate word only (numerator) and irrelevant letter (data as in Fig. 1).

Type of linkage	Task	Interval		
		0 s	1 s	4 s
Contrast	R	14/6[a]	17/6[b]	13/4[b]
	D	13/0[b]	9/11	9/9
Syntagmatic	R	9/11	10/10	11/3[b]
	D	9/1[b]	5/13	6/5
Contingency	R	11/12	12/10	15/8[a]
	D	10/7	9/13	6/14

[a] $p \leq 0.10$.
[b] $p \leq 0.05$; one-tailed binomial test.

linkages, the only evidence of context effect was also with Task R at longest interval. The value of p is in this case 0·105; but the frequencies of seeing only appropriate word (15) and *only* irrelevant rival (7) yielded $p = 0.067$.

In principle it should also be possible to evaluate response distributions under Task D with respect to deviation in the opposite direction, i.e. in terms of counteraction of context effect. Since, however, reports of both the rivals and of only the inappropriate one have been counted together in Table V, all ratios are in fact biased pro counteraction. Besides, Task D may create a response set in the same direction, i.e. a temptation *not to report* the appropriate rival even if it were seen. Examination of Task D distributions in Table V reveals, however, that there are only two out of 12 subconditions in which seeing the irrelevant rival and/or both rivals occurred significantly more often than seeing only the appropriate rival: syntagmatic linkage at 1 s interval (5/13), and contingency linkage at 4 s interval (6/14).

Main Findings

The results may now be summarized as follows.

Contrast contexts affected resolution of binocular-rivalry conflict, regardless of interval between context and rivalry pair, when the subject was simply asked to report what he saw (Task R). When asked to counteract such an effect (Task D) it disappeared, except when context and rivalry pair were presented simultaneously.

Syntagmatic contexts affected resolution under Task R only with an interval of 4 s between context and rivalry pair, and under Task D only when the context appeared 1 s before the rivalry pair.

Contingency context effects increased regularly with interval under Task R, but also became more susceptible to voluntary counteraction (Task D), as the interval between context and rivalry pair was increased from 0 via 1 to 4 s.

Discussion

Semantic-associative networks can be explored in a variety of ways: by free word associations (Deese, 1962), conditioning experiments (Luria and Vinogradova, 1959), word sorting tasks (Miller, 1969), and introspective accounts of sentence comprehension (Quillian, 1966). Some of the methods have yielded similar results, and the proposed maps of semantic-associative relations are perhaps interpreted most appropriately as attempts at representing, in "frozen" form, entire sets of interrelated conceptual-associative activities or word-meaning potentials (Rommetveit, 1972, pp. 64–70). Contextually appropriate resolution of binocular rivalry in the case of a contrast or contingency context would hence imply a match between particular meaning potentialities, activated at some stage of comprehending that particular context word and one of several possible perceptual organizations of another, genuinely ambiguous, pattern of letters appearing at that very instant.

Consider, first, pure contrast linkages such as cold–warm. Such pairs of opposites appear in maps of semantic-associative networks as close neighbours, whether distance is measured by word sorting or in terms of associative overlap (Rommetveit, 1972, p. 66). They are also linguistically complementary in the sense that only one of its members (the so-called unmarked word) is usually employed in questions. This implies—if we venture to make inferences from semantic-associative networks to abstract cognitive operations—that we are dealing with complementary, and temporarily inseparable, cognitive activities.

Relatively pure contingency linkages such as stagger–drunk, on the other hand, correspond to longer and far more complicated routes within semantic-associative maps. The two words are not complementary in the sense that, e.g. comprehending "stagger" is a *sine qua non* for understanding "drunk", and vice versa. Indeed, different paths may be employed, depending upon which of the two words is used as point of departure for associative thought. Such paths are also optional in the sense that "stagger" may or may not make one think of "drunk", depending upon particular contextual constraints upon word comprehension.

Thorough explorations of semantic-associative networks yield a very complex picture of mixed types of linkage and multiple pathways connecting pairs of elements. In the present study, perfect perceptual balance of rivalry patterns could be achieved only at the cost of purity of linkage type. It is very doubtful, e.g. whether the pair *storm–stille* (storm-calm weather) represents an unequivocal contrast linkage of precisely the same nature as cold–warm; and some conceptual interdependence, beyond the contingency exemplified by stagger–drunk, may well be involved in pairs such as price–expensive and grave–death.

With this reservation in mind we may now survey the obtained evidence, bearing upon the hypothesis that the two types of context affect resolution of binocular rivalry via induction of different semantic-associative states. Gross context effects were not very different under Task R. The data in Table III must, however, be evaluated in conjunction with measures of free word association. Contingency contexts affected resolution as strongly as contrast when the interval was increased to 4 s, despite the fact that average associative strength for the two sets of linkage was 16 and 47, respectively. Moreover, contrast effects were very similar under conditions of simultaneous presentation of context and rivalry pair as well as with an interval of 1 s—only stronger in the latter case, whereas the rank orders of the twelve contingency linkages with respect to impact upon resolution revealed considerable change as the interval was increased.

More conclusive evidence was encountered in the more detailed analysis of effects, employing the ratio of perceived appropriate to perceived irrelevant rival. On this basis, contingency context affected resolution to a significant extent only when appearing 4 s prior to the rivalry pair, which is the same condition under which the effect could be counteracted by voluntary effort. It is thus indicated that contingency contexts affect resolution via induction of optimal associative states at some later stage of a temporally extended process of word comprehension.

Contrast context, on the other hand, affected resolution most strongly when the subject tried to counteract the impact under simultaneous presentation. This finding may at first glance appear to be contrary to intuition. A voluntary effort to identify the irrelevant rival seems to induce a peculiar blind spot, of such a nature that the subject is blatantly incapable of seeing just what he is trying to identify.

The task of counteracting the effect of a particular context word implies, however, a strategy of elimination. The irrelevant rival cannot be identified unless the contextually appropriate one is discarded, and the latter cannot be identified until the context word has been clearly identified and comprehended. Thus, the subject who tries to avoid being trapped must attempt, first of all, to identify the trap itself, and hence delay his decision with respect to the rivalry pattern until he has comprehended fully the context word appearing above it. In the case of simultaneous presentation, this decision has to be made during the initial stage of comprehending the context word. Since the contrast corresponds to complementary and temporally inseparable aspects of the initial stage, he is then bound to be trapped—and even more so than a subject who is not on his guard against any trap. The latter may even try to make sense of the rivalry pattern before having identified the context, since the context word will be available as a visual image in immediate memory while he is inspecting the rivalry pattern. The apparently counter-intuitive outcome may hence be interpreted as particularly convincing evidence of the non-optional nature of contrast linkages, as such, and their hypothesized role at an initial stage of comprehending the context word.

A similar explanation seems plausible for the equally counter-intuitive effects of syntagmatic contexts when the subject tried to counteract them under simultaneous presentation. Unlike the "naive" subject engaged in Task R, he has to proceed sequentially in order to avoid being trapped. The brief exposure, however, does not allow completion of his sequential inference. The stimuli disappear while he is still in a state of indecision (cf. the large number of non-veridical responses) or at a stage when he has barely identified the very word he intends to avoid reporting.

Chunking of segments of written material is highly dependent upon spatial arrangements. Segments positioned as neighbours in a horizontal left-to-right sequence tend to combine into a phrase, whereas vertically neighbouring segments do not. The absence of syntagmatic context effect under Task R and context–rivalry intervals of 0 and 1 s may hence be attributed to lack of a strategy for chunking, since syntagmatic context effects have been demonstrated in previous experiments for sequential arrangements such as dark–hell/dark–tell (Rommetveit *et al.*, 1968b) and frm–house/fam–house (Rommetveit *et al.*, 1968).

The most puzzling finding, according to such a scheme of interpretation, pertains to the syntagmatic context effects under Task R and an interval of 4 s. There is rather strong circumstantial evidence, however, indicating that choice of syntagmatically appropriate rival at this interval is not due to the kind of immediate chunking which presumably is at work under simultaneous presentation. The first piece of evidence stems from the inter-conditions correlations reported. Moreover, an analysis of the fate of each of the four syntagmatic linkages included in the data of Fig. 1 and Table V, shows that their effects at interval 0, Task D were indeed different from those obtained at interval 4, Task R. By far the strongest effect under simultaneous presentation, Task D, pertains to the linkage ALDELES–REN (completely–clean), yielding a ratio of perceived-appropriate to perceived-inappropriate rival of 5/0, whereas its ratio was 2/1 at 4 s, Task R. The corresponding ratios for LANG–NATT (long–night), on the other hand, were 1/0 and 3/1.

Consider, first, the fact that nearly all subjects under simultaneous presentation and Task D were trapped by the long and difficult context word ALDELES (completely). This is what could be expected in view of what already has been said about the sequential inference inherent in Task D, provided that more time is required in order to identify ALDELES than for identification of any of the three remaining context words. An interval of 4 s, on the other hand, allows complete identification of the syntagmatic context word before the rivalry pattern appears. It may even permit reflective choice of appropriate rival, provided that the subject is not on his guard against such meaningful conditions. The strongest syntagmatic context effects under such conditions were obtained for the two linkages SVÆRT–MØRK (very–dark) and LANG–NATT (long–night), i.e. for linkages representing very familiar phrases. The effects may thus be outcomes of associative thought rather than products of perceptual chunking, and hence very different from those obtained under conditions of simultaneous presentation.

Syntagmatic context effects at the longest interval may in certain respects resemble contingency effects obtained under the same conditions. Identification of the appropriate rival may in both cases be facilitated by constructive search for meaningful relationships. We might also expect an increasing correspondence between associative strength, as measured by free word association, and context effect when the interval between context word and rivalry pair is increased, assuming that longer intervals will give room for more associative thought. All the syntagmatic linkages had zero associative strength. For contrast and contingency linkages at the various intervals, the rank correlations between associative strength and context effect were positive but insignificant. It may be noted, however, that for contingency linkages Rho increased from 0·05 with simultaneous presentation to 0·50 with 4-s interval. The latter value is nearly significant at the 5% level, suggesting that the expectation of increased associative thought is not entirely unwarranted in the case of contingency context words.

So far, nothing has been said about the last two rivalry pairs, SOR/SOG and DVEG/DVER. They were resolved by word generation in about 80% of the cases, and about equally often whether the subject had been informed about competing letters or not (Table IV). Frequency of confident word generation was thus markedly higher than for the same rivalry pairs under previous conditions of 200 ms exposure and no accompanying context word (Rommetveit and Kleiven, 1968). It should be kept in mind, however, that all subjects in the present study expected to identify words, whereas many non-word solutions were encountered in the previous study.

The readiness with which the subjects now switched from one strategy of resolution to another as soon as SOR/SOG was encountered, shows once more how perceptual operations are *embedded in* and *controlled by* superordinate cognitive activities. Indeed, these character-istics seem to be essential for fluent reading and speech comprehension (Rommetveit, 1972, pp. 164–175, 209–210).

Conclusion

The rivalry situation was employed in order to gain more insight into subtle mechanisms involved in fluent reading under normal conditions. Previous experiments has shown how resolution of rivalry conflicts is controlled by a superordinate request for meaning, and even for con-textually appropriate meaning. The present study indicates how the request can be specified further in terms of syntagmatic chunking and different semantic-associative states, induced by particular context words. The finding that, under certain conditions, a person was in-capable of identifying the contextually inappropriate rival, despite his deliberate attempt to do so, testifies to semantic-associative control of perceptual operations of a highly automatized and "intuitive" nature.

References

Deese, J. (1962). On the structure of associative meaning. *Psychological Review* **69**, 161–175.

Kleiven, J. and Rommetveit, R. (1970). Meaning and frequency in a binocular rivalry situation. *Scandinavian J. Psychology* **11**, 17–20.

Luria, A. R. and Vinogradova, O. S. (1959). An objective investigation of dynamic of semantic systems. *British J. Psychology* **50**, 59–105.

Miller, G. A. (1969). A psychological method to investigate verbal concepts. *J. Mathematical Psychology* **6**, 169–191.

Quillian, M. R. (1966). Semantic memory. Report No. 66–189, Project No. 8668, Air Force Cambridge Research Laboratories, Bedford, Massa-chusetts.

Rommetveit, R. (1972). "Språk, tanke og kommunikasjon." Universitets forlaget, Oslo.

Rommetveit, R., Berkley, M. and Brøgger, J. (1968). Generation of words from stereoscopically presented non-word strings of letters. *Scandinavian J. Psychology* **9**, 150–156.

Rommetveit, R. and Kleiven, J. (1968). Word generation: A replication. *Scandinavian J. Psychology* **9**, 277–281.

Rommetveit, R., Toch, H. and Svendsen, D. (1968a). Effects of contingency and contrast contexts on the cognition of words. A study of stereoscopic rivalry. *Scandinavian J. Psychology* **9**, 138–144.

Rommetveit, R., Toch, H. and Svendsen, D. (1968b). Semantic, syntactic, and associative context effects in a stereoscopic rivalry situation. *Scandinavian J. Psychology* **9**, 145–149.

Rommetveit, R. and Turner, E. A. (1967). A study of chunking in trans-mission of messages. *Lingua* **18**, 337–351.

21. The Acquisition of Sentence Voice and Reversibility*

E. A. TURNER and R. ROMMETVEIT

In 1953, Leopold reported that the passive-voice sentence tends to be late in development. In an observational study of pre-school children in Australia, Harwood (1959) found no occurrences of the true passive-voice form in the spontaneous speech of children with an average age of 5 years 8 months (12 700 spontaneous utterances were analysed). The past-participal form was used, but mostly in adjectival constructions of the form, "It's hurt" or "It's broken". Slobin (1964) however, reported finding occasional spontaneous productions of passive sentences in observations of seven and eight year olds' spontaneous speech.

In addition to these observational studies of language acquisition, several experimental studies focused on the acquisition of various grammatical structures including the passive voice. Cazden (1965) found that no child in a group of 12 children (28–38 months) from a Negro section of the Boston metropolitan area was able to imitate correctly the following passive sentence: "His hair has been cut". A form which was quite frequently substituted for this in the child's imitation was "hair been cut". Menyuk (1963) found that 14 out of 14 nursery school children could repeat the passive, while only five of these had been observed using this form. Fraser *et al.* (1963), using imitation, comprehension and production tasks, found that three year old children were correct only half of the time on their imitations of reversible passive-

* This study represents a portion of a dissertation submitted by E. A. Turner to the Graduate School of Cornell University in partial fulfilment of the requirements for the Ph.D. degree in child development, May, 1966. The research was conducted under National Science Foundation grant 6458 to R. Rommetveit at Cornell University. Preparation of this manuscript by E. A. Turner was supported by Carnegie Corporation of New York, grant B-3233, and National Institutes of General Medical Sciences, grant 5-T01-GM-01011, to Harvard University, Centre for Cognitive Studies, 1966–1967. Published in *Child Development* (1967) **38**, 649–660.

voice sentences. On tasks of comprehension and production, very few Ss responded correctly to the passive-voice sentences. On the production task, the passive-voice sentences ranked ninth out of 10 sentence problems, with only the problem of order of the indirect and direct object being more difficult ("He gave the boy the book"). Ammon (personal communication, 1965), in an experiment in which children were tested pre- and post-training on the use of grammatical forms, found that only three out of 28 four year old children were able to produce correctly *both* passive-sentence test items; six others produced one of the two passives correctly. In addition, in terms of improvement with training, it was found that the more difficult problems like the passive voice showed less improvement than problems which initially were found to be less difficult.

The present study hypothesizes that there are levels of sentence complexity, determined by both semantic and syntactic factors, and it attempts to investigate these levels in terms of active and passive, reversible and non-reversible sentences. The active-passive-voice contrast was chosen because the two forms differ primarily in terms of structural form, but not in terms of the general meaning of the sentence; that is, active- and passive-voice forms are equivalent but alternate vehicles or means of expressing the same content. When the same content is expressed in both voice forms, the differences between the two sentences (e.g. "The ball hit the boy" and "The boy was hit by the ball") are: (a) total number of words in the sentence, (b) word order or the relationship between the semantic "actor" and "acted-upon" elements and the syntactic "subject" and "object" elements; (c) the form of the verb used; and (d) transformational complexity in terms of Chomsky's grammar.

In order to define levels of sentence complexity, several assumptions were made. One assumption was that "semantic content" is "neutral" (Schlesinger, 1966) in grammatical form, but that it is most closely and most directly translatable into simple active, affirmative, declarative grammatical form with a word order of *actor-action-acted-upon* and/or *subject-verb-object*. Any word order which deviates from this order, for example, the passive-voice word order, is considered to be *more complex* and is, therefore, considered to contain more information, which places an additional load on processing (decoding, encoding, communicating accurately).

A second assumption relates to the semantic reversibility of the elements of the sentence. As suggested by Slobin (1964), the simplest semantic structure a sentence can have is one in which there can be no confusion as to the interpretation, one in which the actor and acted-upon cannot be interchanged and still produce a semantically consistent sentence. This type of sentence is termed a non-reversible sentence

(NR). A sentence in which different elements can be semantically interchanged, a reversible sentence (R), is considered to be more complex because correct and accurate processing involves dealing with the additional information of what is the actor and what is the acted-upon. In addition, it is assumed that voice and the reversibility factor similarly with verb tense so that within a given verb tense the simplest possible type of sentence is one with (a) basic *actor-action-acted-upon* word order and (b) non-reversible elements:

(1) *The car hit the tree* (non-reversible action, NRA).

(If either the *actor-action-acted-upon* word order or the non-reversibility of the semantic elements is changed, the sentence becomes more complex.)

(2) *The girl hits the boy* (reversible active, RA).

(3) *The tree is hit by the car* (non-reversible passive, NRP).

(Most complex of all would be the case where *actor-action-acted-upon* word order is reversed and the semantic elements are reversible or interchangeable.)

(4) *The boy is hit by the ball* (reversible passive, RP).

In the present experiment, an attempt was made to assess the development of these grammatical forms in terms of tasks of imitation, comprehension and production. These tasks were similar to the ones used in the Fraser *et al.* (1963) experiment. However, the procedures of the two experiments differ due to the use of only reversible sentences in the earlier experiment and the use of both non-reversible and reversible sentences in the present experiment. In accordance with the results of the Fraser *et al.* study, it was hypothesized that children would be able to imitate before they would be able to comprehend passive sentences and reversible sentences, and comprehend before they produce the same form. Table I presents a comparison of the tasks and task outputs used in the present experiment.

Methods

Subjects

The Ss were 48 children at each of five age levels. The five levels and mean ages per level were: nursery school (NS), 4·32 years; kindergarten (KG), 5·87 years; first grade (1st), 7·00 years; second grade (2nd), 8·11 years; and third grade (3rd), 9·00 years.

At each grade level, Ss were divided into four experimental groups of 12 Ss, six males and six females in each group. The KG through 3rd population came from a middle-lower-class to middle-class area in Ithaca, New York. The NS population tended to come from families of higher educational backgrounds than the older sample, as they were mostly children of the Cornell University staff.

TABLE I. Description of experimental tasks.

Task	Input	Hypothesized processing involved	Output
Imitation	1 sentence	Short-term memory Imitation or "parroting"	Sentence
Comprehension	2 sentences	Short-term memory Decoding: visual and verbal Matching: visual and verbal	Yes–no response
Production	2 sentences; 1 picture	Short-term memory Decoding: visual and verbal Matching: visual and verbal Delayed imitation	Sentence

Materials

The following sentences and corresponding pictures were used in the experiment:

NON-REVERSIBLE

(1) The grandmother washes the dishes
(2) The girl rides the pony
(3) The frog catches the fly
(4) The bird carries the branch
(5) The farmer drives the tractor
(6) The boys rake the leaves

REVERSIBLE

LIST A	LIST B
(1) The boy visits the doctor	(1) The doctor visits the boy
(2) The lamb chases the dog	(2) The dog chases the lamb
(3) The mother kisses the father	(3) The father kisses the mother
(4) The turkey follows the pig	(4) The pig follows the turkey
(5) The shell catches the crab	(5) The crab catches the shell .
(6) The class reads to the teacher	(6) The teacher reads to the class

Design

The four-group design used in this experiment is illustrated in Table II.

TABLE II. Experimental design.

Group 1	Group 2	Group 3	Group 4
Non-reversible *Active* "goat eats grass"	Non-reversible *Active* "goat eats grass"	Non-reversible *Passive* "grass eaten by goat"	Non-reversible *Passive* "grass eaten by goat"
Passive "pie is baked by cook"	*Passive* "pie is baked by cook"	*Active* "cook bakes pie"	*Active* "cook bakes pie"
Reversible "A" *Active* "boy hits ball" *Passive* "horse pulled by car"	Reversible "B" *Active* "ball hits boy" *Passive* "car pulled by horse"	Reversible "A" *Passive* "ball hit by boy" *Active* "car pulls horse"	Reversible "B" *Passive* "boy hit by ball" *Active* "horse pulls car"

The semantic elements or content of a reversible sentence were presented in a different form to each of the four groups. This was an attempt to control for the effects of a particular sentence structure on a specific content, as in some sentences one form of a reversible sentence might be easier than the other.

Procedure

Each child was given three types of tasks—imitation, comprehension and production. On each task, one of each of the four sentence types was presented to the S. The order of presentation of the sentence types on all tasks was:

(1) Non-reversible active (NRA)
(2) Non-reversible passive (NRP)
(3) Reversible active (RA)
(4) Reversible passive (RP)

Imitation Task.
One sentence of each of the four types was read to each child. Two sentences were read at a time, and the child was instructed to repeat the sentences after the E.

Comprehension
A single picture was placed in front of the child. The E said, "Here is a picture. I'm going to tell you two names. Only one name goes with

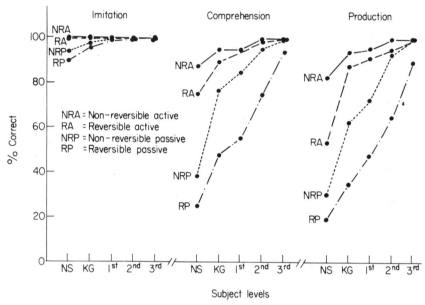

FIG. 1. Subject performance on sentence types in Imitation, Comprehension and Production tasks.

the picture. The other name doesn't go with the picture. I want you to tell me which name goes with the picture. One name is, "The frog catches the fly", and the other name is "The fly catches the frog". Only one name goes with the picture. Does the name "The fly catches the frog" go with the picture?" After the child responded, the E said, "Does the name, 'The frog catches the fly' go with the picture?" The correct name was randomly assigned to first and second position.

Production. This task paralleled the comprehension task, but the child was asked to produce or say the "right name", the "name that goes with the picture", instead of just saying "yes" or "no". Again the correct name was randomly assigned to the first versus second position.

Scoring

On the imitation task, a response was scored as correct if the sentence content, word order and morphological endings were the same or synonymous with the stimulus sentence. On the comprehension task, the child was credited with a correct response if he responded "yes" to the appropriate and correct name for a picture. On the production task, the criteria for a correct response were essentially the same as those on the imitation task. Any deviation in S's passive-voice sentence production from standard passive forms was recorded.

Results

A summary of the experimental data is presented in Fig. 1. A four-way analysis of variance (age level × voice × reversibility × task) with repeated measures was used (see Winer, 1962). All main effects were significant at the 0·001 level. Thus there was a significant tendency for scores to increase with age ($F = 53·08$, d.f. $= 4/35$, $p < 0·001$), for active-voice sentences to be responded to correctly more frequently than passive-voice sentences ($F = 146·30$, d.f. $= 1/35$, $p < 0·001$), for non-reversible sentences to be answered correctly more frequently than reversible sentences ($F = 35·75$, d.f. $= 1/35$, $p < 0·001$), and for scores to increase from the imitation task to the production task ($F = 82·64$, d.f. $= 1/35$, $p < 0·001$). All of the two-way interactions were found to be significant beyond the 0·01 level of significance, except the interaction between age level and sentence reversibility, which was significant at the 0·05 level. The three-way and four-way interactions were significant at the 0·05 level or beyond, except for the three-way interaction of age × reversibility × tasks, which was not significant.

The mean difference for the correct recall of active versus passive sentences was compared with the mean difference score for correct recall of non-reversible versus reversible sentences. The voice difference was found to be significantly greater than the reversibility difference ($t = 3·98$, d.f. $= 78$, $p < 0·001$).

The results of a multiple comparison breakdown (Newman-Keuls test used, see Winer, 1962) of the main effects of the experiment are presented in Table III. There was a significant increase in the number of correct responses with increasing age; each consecutive age level

TABLE III. Multiple comparisons.

Age levels (d.f. = 2/35)			Tasks (d.f. = 2/70)			Sentence types (d.f. = 2/35)		
Comparisons	q	p	Comparisons	q	p	Comparisons	q	p
NS < KG	10·15	0·01	I < C	21·35	0·01	NRA < RA	3·76	0·05
KG < 1st	3·04	0·05	C < P	6·61	0·01	RA < NRP	6·70	0·01
1st < 2nd	4·51	0·01	—	—	—	NRP < RP	11·65	0·01
2nd < 3rd	3·61	0·05	—	—	—	—	—	—

showed significant improvement. As shown in Fig. 1, these age differences did not hold for the imitation task, for even the NS level of Ss responded correctly.

In the analysis of the scores for the three experimental tasks, the comprehension task resulted in significantly more errors than the imitation task, and the production task resulted in more errors than the comprehension task. As Table IV shows, these differences among tasks were found at all age levels except 3rd, where a ceiling of perfect scores was approached. Table III shows that there were significant differences among the four sentence types. As predicted, the order of difficulty was: NRA < RA < NRP < RP. These differences were significant at the NS level, but tended to decrease in magnitude up to 3rd level, where none of the differences was significant.

TABLE IV. Multiple comparisons for sentence types and tasks at five age levels.

	NS		KG		1st		2nd		3rd	
	q	p	q	p	q	p	q	p	q	p
Sentence-type comparisons (d.f. = 2/35):										
NRA < RA	5·26	0·01	1·58	n.s.	0·79	n.s.	0·79	n.s.	0·00	n.s.
RA < NRP	8·24	0·01	5·00	0·01	3·42	0·05	0·52	n.s.	0·26	n.s.
NRP < RP	3·68	0·01	7·37	0·01	6·84	0·01	6·32	0·01	1·84	n.s.
Task comparisons (d.f. = 2/70):										
I < C	21·59	0·01	11·36	0·01	9·38	0·01	3·98	0·01	1·12	n.s.
C < P	5·11	0·01	3·98	0·01	3·10	0·05	1·98	n.s.	0·31	n.s.

Of the errors made, 398 or 94·5% involved the inversion of the actor and acted-upon elements (semantic reversals). Sixty-seven per cent of the semantic reversals occurred with the reversible sentences; however, 32·6% of the semantic reversal errors did occur on the non-reversible sentences. Although the semantic reversals occurred more frequently at the younger age levels, nine errors of this sort did occur at 3rd level. The differences in semantic reversal scores between consecutive grade levels were all significant (NS *vs* KG, $q = 9·01$, $p < 0·01$; KG *vs* 1st, $q = 2·59$, $p < 0·05$; 1st *vs* 2nd, $q = 3·61$, $p < 0·05$ and 2nd *vs* 3rd, $q = 3·04$, $p < 0·05$; with d.f. = 2/35 in all cases).

Another developmental pattern which occurred was a tendency for Ss' responses to become more consistent with increasing age. Consistency was defined as a regular pattern of responses; that is, if S answered a difficult task by sentence-type combination correctly, he most likely responded correctly to all easier combinations. The Ss were given a "plus" (+) in every cell of a matrix of tasks (3) by sentence-types (4) in which they gave a correct response and a "minus" (−) in every cell in which they gave an incorrect response. In terms of this method of scoring, a consistent pattern of responding was one in which there was no more than *one* sign change (from $+$ to $-$) in any row or column throughout the matrix. The number of Ss responding in a consistent manner increased with age. Correspondingly, there was a tendency for inconsistent and idiosyncratic response patterns to decrease with age. Inconsistent, idiosyncratic response patterns were response patterns which were not consistent (as defined above) and which were found only in *one* S's responses. Both trends were tested by the χ^2 statistic and found to be significant (consistent patterns, $\chi^2 = 22\cdot2$, d.f. $= 4$, $p < 0\cdot001$; inconsistent patterns, $\chi^2 = 12\cdot33$, d.f. $= 3$, $p < 0\cdot01$). In testing the inconsistent, idiosyncratic response trend, 3rd level was not included, as there was zero frequency in this cell.

Table V shows deviations in passive-voice sentences which Ss produced on the imitation and production tasks. From this table it is apparent that the deviations were primarily errors in the verb form or the use of colloquial forms in place of standard English passive forms. Errors of this type increased with age.

TABLE v. Deviations from standard passive-voice form on imitation and production tasks.

Deviations	Imitation					Production				
	NS	KG	1	2	3	NS	KG	1	2	3
Use of "to get" in place of auxiliary "to be"	3	1	1	0	0	18	15	12	5	4
Use of "been" in place of "is being"	3	4	4	1	0	13	10	7	5	6
Irregular past participles:										
"Ride"	1	1	1	0	0	—	—	—	—	—
"Rided"	13	4	4	1	0	—	—	—	—	—
"Visit"	3	4	0	0	0	—	—	—	—	—
"Catched"	—	—	—	—	—	13	11	7	2	2
"Readed"	—	—	—	—	—	16	11	4	2	2
"Droved"	—	—	—	—	—	4	6	2	0	0
"Drived"	—	—	—	—	—	10	11	3	3	1
"Drive"	—	—	—	—	—	3	2	1	0	0

Discussion

The results showed that significantly more errors were made in the processing of passive-voice sentences than in the processing of active-voice sentences on imitation, comprehension and production tasks; likewise, significantly more errors were made in the processing of reversible sentences than in the processing of non-reversible sentences. The voice factor was shown to have a significantly stronger effect than the reversibility factor. The actual order of difficulty—least difficult to most difficult—was: non-reversible active <reversible active <non-reversible passive <reversible passive. This contradicts the Miller and McKean (1964) hypothesis that difficulty in the processing of passive-voice sentences arises only if the actor and acted-upon elements are reversible.

These findings support the hypothesis that children have difficulty in processing a sentence form in which the semantic actor/acted-upon elements do not coincide with the grammatical subject/object elements and the hypotheses of Fraser *et al.* (1963) that young children tend to process the passive voice as the active voice, treating the passive markers *is*, *-ed* and *by* as if they are signs of some uncommon tense. The difficulty in the processing of the passive voice may be due to an additional load on the processing system which results from the child's having to take into account the distinction between the actor and subject elements, and between the acted-upon and object elements (i.e. having to differ-entiate the semantic and grammatical structures of an utterance). This distinction becomes particularly important in the reversible passive sentence because not only does not the actor coincide with the subject of the sentence and the acted-upon with the object, but the actor and acted-upon elements are semantically interchangeable. Therefore, in order to process this form correctly, the child must pay attention to the relationship between the grammatical structure and semantic structure and pay attention to which element is the actor and which the acted-upon.

The errors that were made on the comprehension and production tasks were, for the most part, semantic reversals or errors which involved the interchanging of the actor and acted-upon elements. The frequent occurrence of these errors on reversible sentences adds support to the interpretation given above. However, some semantic reversals (particularly at the younger age levels) occurred in the comprehension and production of non-reversible sentences too.

This tendency for semantic reversals to occur with non-reversible sentences might seem to be a bit puzzling. However, after having struggled to make up 24 reversible sentences with the vocabulary of a pre-school child, it became apparent to the authors that there is a relatively limited number of "actor + action + acted-upon" combina-tions which are *totally* reversible. Totally is stressed here, because there are many combinations in which the direction of the action *can* be reversed but in which the probability of the action occurring in one direction is far greater than the probability of it occurring in the other. For example, in the sentence, "The cat chased the mouse", the action is reversible, but the sentence, "The mouse chased the cat", is certainly less probable than the former form. This sentence probably would be considered less reversible than "The girls walked behind the boys", where the probability of either of the two possible forms would be relatively equal. Thus there seem to be degrees of reversibility. Within the non-reversible sentences, of course, there would be a similar continuum. This was actually suggested by some of the errors. For example, in several cases the following active sentences were produced. "The tractor drives the farmer", "The pony rides the girl" and "The branch carries the bird". At first this seemed somewhat startling because the children not only produced them but accepted these forms when produced by the experimenter with pictures available to the children against which to check the sentences. Upon closer examination, it becomes apparent that such sentences do actually border on being semantically acceptable English. For instance, "The pony rides the girl"—although it would probably be judged to be semantically anomalous by many adults—approximates one or more acceptable forms, "The pony gives the girl a ride" and "The pony carries the girl".

The tendency was strongest for the youngest age Ss. This finding suggests that younger children accept semantically anomalous sentences more frequently than older children do, which supports McNeill's (1965) results, which showed that children's recall scores for semantically anomalous and semantically consistent sentences differed less than adult scores. McNeill sees the process by which a child develops a semantic system, a system of dictionary entries for words, as involving a process of differentiation and refinement of semantic categories. The young child whose semantic markers or dictionary entries are not fully developed lacks some of the distinctions made by adults. Therefore he is more likely to accept and possibly to produce sentences which the adult would call anomalous.

The development and use of the passive voice may involve a similar process of refinement. In the young child's speech, the active form serves most purposes, and the child has no real need for the passive voice in order to express himself. It is not until, through a process of differentiation, the added pragmatic subtleties of de-emphasis of importance or interest in the actor become meaningful to the child that he might be thought of as *needing* the passive voice.

A developmental trend was apparent for the experimental tasks; the imitation task was found to be relatively easy for even the youngest Ss, the comprehension task was more difficult with the ceiling approached at 2nd level, and the production task was the most difficult with the ceiling being reached only at 3rd level. This was the same order of difficulty found by Fraser *et al.* (1963). However, it must be recognized that the order of difficulty of experimental tasks will depend on the specific experimental design and on what processes each task involves.

The specific processes hypothesized to be involved in the tasks of the present experiment are presented in Table I.

In the present experiment, the significant difference in experimental tasks was confounded, unfortunately, because the order of presentation of the tasks was fixed across all Ss and was imitation, comprehension, production, or from the simplest to the most difficult. Thus, the significant difference found might be attributed to a factor such as fatigue. However, the fatigue factor would seem to be rather unlikely as the experimental session lasted only about seven minutes. In addition, any effect of practice from the first to the last task would have tended to make the final task easier, which was not the case. Finally, Fraser et al. (1963) controlled for order of presentation and still found a marked effect due to tasks.

The descriptive findings of the types of verb forms used by Ss at all grade levels in the imitation and production of passive verb forms showed that the use of the colloquial passive ("to get" used as the auxiliary instead of "to be") tends to be relatively frequent, particularly among the younger Ss. As the passive-voice sentences which were presented to the child by the E used the standard English "to be" as the auxiliary, the possibility cannot be ruled out that some of the errors made in the processing of the passive voice resulted from the use of a passive verb form ("to be") which the children do not usually use, or which they use infrequently until they are taught it in school. Another area of difficulty within the passive voice was the past participle of the verb, particularly the past participle of irregular verbs. The lack of control for the use of irregular verbs may have affected the results.

References

Cazden, C. B. (1965). Environmental assistance to the child's acquisition of grammar. Unpublished doctoral dissertation, Harvard University.

Fraser, C., Bellugi, U. and Brown, R. (1963). Control of grammar in imitation, comprehension and production. *J. verbal Learning verbal Behavior* **2**, 121–135.

Harwood, F. W. (1959). Quantitative study of the speech of Australian children. *Language and Speech* **2**, 236–270.

Leopold, W. F. (1953). Patterning in children's language learning. *Language Learning* **5**, 1–14.

McNeill, D. (196). Development of the semantic system. Unpublished manuscript. Center for Cognitive Studies, Harvard University.

Menyuk, P. (1963). Syntactic structures in the language of children. *Child Development* **34**, 407–422.

Miller, G. A. and McKean, K. O. (1964). A chronometric study of some relations between sentences. *Quarterly Journal of experimental Psychology* **16**, 296–305.

Schlesinger, I. M. (1966). Effects of grammatical transformations. *In* "Sentence structure and the reading process". Technical Report no. 24, U.S. Office of Naval Research.

Slobin, D. I. (1964). Grammatical transformations in childhood-adulthood. Unpublished doctoral dissertation, Harvard University.

Winer, B. J. (1962). "Statistical principles in experimental design." McGraw-Hill, New York.

22. Experimental Manipulation of the Production of Active and Passive Voice in Children*

E. A. TURNER and R. ROMMETVEIT

The active-passive voice contrast in English is of interest primarily because the two forms can express the same denotative domain of events equally well and because they have "no equivocal differential functions with respect to communication patterns" (Rommetveit, 1967, p. 176). As the passive voice requires more words and is structurally more complex than the active voice, the question as to its function or role in the language arises. The fact that the passive voice allows for the deletion of the agent constituent of the message, and can be used when the agent is unknown or of little importance, suggests that the function of the passive voice may be a pragmatic one. The speaker may de-emphasize the agent element or conversely stress the object of the action by deletion of the agent or by relating the agent word to the final slot in the utterance and thereby reducing its order of importance. The idea that the first noun in a sentence is the most salient element in a setting has been suggested by Rommetveit (1965) and Carroll (1958). Carroll (1958) suggests that when a speaker reports an event he must select some element of the situation to be used as the subject of his utterance. Whether a sentence is active or passive in form is usually contingent upon the selection of the actor or acted-upon element of a situation as the subject of the sentence. Thus if the actor in a given situation is chosen as the subject of the sentence, the sentence will tend to be in the active voice; and conversely, if the acted-upon element is chosen as the subject, the sentence will be in the passive

* This study represents a portion of a dissertation submitted by E. A. Turner to the Graduate School of Cornell University in partial fulfilment of the requirements for the Ph.D. degree in child development, May, 1966. The research was conducted under National Science Foundation grant 6458 to the second author at Cornell University. Published in *Language and Speech* (1967) **10**, 169–180.

voice. In other words the most important or most salient stimulus element is encoded as the subject of the sentence. Slobin (1966) finds that deviations from standard simple active word order (agent-verb-object) are reported by most diarists as occurring when the object is psychologically the most important word. He cites a quotation from Leopold:

> On the whole, the words of Hildegard's brief sentences were arranged as in the standard languages (English and German). The utterances in which the word-order differed from that which the adult speaker considers normal were exceptional . . . the placement of the object in first position must be explained as due to the desire to give the "psychological subject", the item of dominating interest, an emphatic position.
>
> The latter is often the explanation for most examples of irregular word-order. It is often observed in child language. *My shoe brush* 1;10, if it meant "Brush my shoe", is exactly parallel. So is *Mama wake up* 1;10, *Mama* being the object, not a vocative: "I am going to wake up Mama". The imperative *coat button* and *nose blow* 1;11 are easily explained in the same manner (1949, p. 70).

Carroll (1958) carried out an experiment to test the effects of psychological "set" or "focus of attention" on the voice of sentences produced. High school students were presented with a short action event and then asked to describe the event. Four types of question were used to manipulate whether the focus of attention was the object of the action or the agent. When attention was directed to the object of the action, the first sentence in the subjects' descriptions of the situation tended to be in the passive voice; when the question directed attention to the agent of the action subjects tended to respond with active sentences.

The effect of focus of attention encoding has been further explored by Tannenbaum and Williams (1966). The differential foci of attention were extablished by the sequence of sentences preceding the task. The results showed that less time was required, other things being equal, when the subject was asked to describe the picture by an active sentence. When the preceding sentences had the acted-upon as the topic, however, subjects gave a passive sentence nearly as quickly as an active one. There was thus an unequivocal facilitation effect of the preceding context upon encoding performance. The conditions in this part of the experiment were identical as far as the structure of the preceding sentences was concerned. It was clear, therefore, that the set established had to do with content, with the relative saliency of the agent or object element of the situation. Purely syntactic sets (e.g. exposure to active *vs* passive constructions prior to the task) had some, but far less powerful, effect.

The present experiment consists of two different techniques for manipulating the set or focus of attention of the subject. The first technique used was a scanning technique. Scanning was defined as the sequence or temporal order in which the *actor* and *acted-upon* elements of a picture are seen. For example, a picture showing a boy hitting a ball could be exposed to a child in either an *actor–acted-upon* or an *acted-upon–actor* sequence by first revealing only part of the picture and then the remaining part. It was hypothesized that the form in which a child uttered a sentence could be manipulated by using such a scanning procedure. The greater the experimental control on the scanning, the greater the number of passive voice sentences was expected to be. When the *acted-upon* element was presented first, sentences were predicted to be in the active voice. However, as the active voice was considered to be a more basic form than the passive voice, it was predicted that there would be fewer sentences produced in the passive voice when the acted-upon was shown first than there would be active sentences produced when the actor was presented first. It was also hypothesized that fewer sentences would be produced in the passive voice in the case of the reversible picture than in the case of the non-reversible picture, because children would tend to invert or interchange actor and acted-upon in the reversible sentence in order to keep the sentence in the active voice. The fewest passive sentences were expected to be produced in the naming task where no attempt was made to manipulate the sentence voice; scanning was predicted to increase the number of passives produced; and controlled scanning, in which the subject was given a model in addition to the scanning, was predicted to elicit the greatest number of passive sentences.

The second technique paralleled Carroll's (1958) to some degree. In this case an attempt was made to manipulate the focus of attention through the question asked of the child when he described a picture. The predictions, based on Carroll's findings, were that subjects would tend to produce passive sentences to questions of "What happened to the (acted-upon)?" and "What was done to the (acted-upon)?" in this order; that the number of passive sentences produced in answer to these questions would tend to be much greater than in answer to the questions, "What did the (actor) do?" and "What happened?". With both methods it was hypothesized that the number of passive voice sentences would increase with age.

Methods

Experiment I. Name, Scanning and Controlled Scanning

Subjects

Forty-eight children, 24 males and females, at each of the following five age levels were used as subjects—nursery school (NS), kindergarten

(KG), first grade (1st), second grade (2nd) and third grade (3rd). At each grade level subjects were divided into four experimental groups of 12 each, six males and six females in each group. The KG through 3rd grade population came from a lower-middle to middle class area in Ithaca, New York. The NS population tended to come from families of higher educational backgrounds than the older sample as they were mostly children of Cornell University staff.

Materials
The following pictures were used:

NON-REVERSIBLE
(1) A bunny eating a carrot
(2) A mouse nibbling cheese
(3) A bee flying to a flower
(4) Santa Claus filling a stocking
(5) A goat eating grass
(6) A chicken laying an egg

REVERSIBLE

Form A	Form B
(1) A bear hugging a monkey	(1) A monkey hugging a bear
(2) A cow licking a calf	(2) A calf licking a cow
(3) A turtle following a snake	(3) A snake following a turtle
(4) A duck pulling a boat	(4) A boat pulling a duck
(5) A lion watching a tiger	(5) A tiger watching a lion
(6) Boys chasing some girls	(6) Girls chasing some boys

Design
Since four reversible sentence form-picture combinations were used in Experiment I (reversible form A, actor presented first; reversible form B, actor presented first; reversible form A, acted-upon presented first; reversible form B, acted-upon presented first), subjects were divided into four groups. The examples in Table I illustrate the four group design for Experiment 1.

Procedure
Naming (natural scanning). The child was shown a picture and asked to give it a name. Two reversible and two non-reversible pictures were used for each group.

Scanning (without verbal model). A picture was gradually drawn past a cellophane window in a cardboard frame. In some cases the *actor* appeared first and in some cases the *acted-upon* appeared first. The child was told that the picture was going to be drawn very slowly from behind the screen and that his task was to start naming the picture as soon as part of it appeared. In order to discourage the child from merely naming each object in the picture, the child was told that he should give the picture a name which would tell "what was happening in the picture".

TABLE I. Design of Experiment I.

	Group 1	Group 2	Group 3	Group 4
(A) Naming				
Non-reversible	"bunny eating carrot"	"bunny eating carrot"	"bunny eating carrot"	"bunny eating carrot"
Reversible	"bear hugs monkey"	"monkey hugs bear"	"bear hugs monkey"	"monkey hugs bear"
(B) Scanning and controlled scanning				
Non-reversible	(a) *Actor first* "*bee* visits flower"	(a) *Actor first* "*bee* visits flower"	(a) *Acted-upon first* "bee visits *flower*"	(a) *Acted-upon first* "bee visits *flower*"
	(b) *Acted-upon first* "Santa fills *stocking*"	(b) *Acted-upon first* "Santa fills *stocking*"	(b) *Actor first* "*Santa* fills stocking"	(b) *Actor first* "*Santa* fills stocking"
Reversible "A"	(a) *Actor first* "*Turtle* follows snake"	Reversible "B" (a) *Actor first* "*Snake* follows turtle"	Reversible "A" (a) *Acted-upon first* "Turtle follows *snake*"	Reversible "B" (a) *Acted-upon first* "Snake follows *turtle*"
	(b) *Acted-upon first* "duck pulls *boat*"	(b) *Acted-upon first* "boat pulls *duck*"	(b) *Actor first* "*duck* pulls boat"	(b) *Actor first* "*boat* pulls duck"

Controlled scanning (with verbal model). This condition was essentially the same as the Scanning Condition with the addition of a verbal model. The experimenter showed the child two examples: one in which the acted-upon element was presented first with a passive sentence used to describe the picture and the other in which the actor was presented first with an active sentence used to describe the picture.

Experiment II. Question Answering

Subjects

Twenty-four children, 12 males and 12 females, were tested at each of the following grade levels: KG, 1st, 2nd and 3rd grade. This sample of children came from a rural school (Danby Elementary School) just outside of the Ithaca City Limits, but nevertheless was in the same general area as the one where the children were in the sample tested in Experiment I.

Materials

The following pictures were used in this experiment:

NON-REVERSIBLE

(1) The bunny eating a carrot
(2) The farmer driving a tractor
(3) The chicken laying an egg
(4) The nurse pushing a baby carriage
(5) The bird carrying a branch
(6) The mailman delivering a letter
(7) The goat eating the grass
(8) The bee visiting the flower
(9) The mouse eating the cheese
(10) The girl riding the pony
(11) The grandfather smoking the pipe
(12) The frog catching the fly

REVERSIBLE

(1) The boy hitting the ball
(2) The father kissing the mother
(3) The horse pulling the car
(4) The squirrel biting the cat
(5) The lion watching the tiger
(6) The crab catching the shell
(7) The duck pulling the boat
(8) The pig following the turkey
(9) The mother cow licking the baby cow
(10) The turtle following the snake
(11) The bear hugging the monkey
(12) The dog chasing the lamb

Design

The experiment was divided into four conditions on the basis of four questions asked of the subjects:

(1) "What is (the actor) doing?"
(2) "What is happening in the picture?"
(3) "What is being done to (the acted-upon)?"
(4) "What is happening to the (acted-upon)?"

The 24 sentences were divided into four arbitrary groups, each with three reversible sentences and three non-reversible sentences. When the four groups of sentences were matched with the four conditions (questions) the result was 24 permutations. Each permutation was presented to one subject at each grade level. This was an attempt to control for any interaction between sentence and condition.

Procedure
Each child was shown 24 pictures; each question (condition) was applied to six pictures (three reversible and three non-reversible). The experimenter placed a picture in front of the child and said, "I'm going to show you a picture in which you will see an X ($X = actor$ in Conditions 1 and 2; $X = acted$ $upon$ in Conditions 3 and 4) like this one (pointing to the picture of the X). Watch carefully so that you can tell me . . .

Condition 1. "What X (actor) is doing? X is doing something. Can you tell me what X is doing? Here is the picture. What is X doing? The X is . . . (experimenter waits for child's response).

Condition 2. "What is happening in the picture? Something is happening. Can you tell me what it is? Here is the picture. What is happening? The X is . . ."

Condition 3. "What is being done to the X (acted-upon)? Something is being done to the X. Can you tell me what is being done to the X? Here is the picture. What is being done to the X? The X is . . ."

Condition 4. "What is happening to X? Something is happening to X. Can you tell me what it is? Here is the picture. What is happening to X? The X is . . ."

Pre-test showed that it was necessary to add "The X is . . ." at the end of the questions, because there were only four passive voice sentences produced out of 120 sentence-answers when this prompt was left out.

Scoring
Sentences were scored as active sentences if the active voice word order and active voice morphological endings were used; sentences were scored as passive sentences if the passive voice word order and passive voice morphological endings were used. A semantic reversal was scored whenever *actor* and *acted-upon* elements shown in the pictures were interchanged.

Results

Table II shows the number of passive sentences produced at each grade level for both reversible and non-reversible sentences on all experimental tasks of Experiment I.

A three-way analysis of variance showed that the effects of grade level ($F = 33 \cdot 19$, d.f. $= 4/8$, $p < 0 \cdot 001$), tasks ($F = 11 \cdot 39$, d.f. $= 2/8$, $p < 0 \cdot 01$), and sentence reversibility ($F = 15 \cdot 86$, d.f. $= 1/4$, $p < 0 \cdot 05$) were all significant. The interaction between grades and tasks was found to be significant ($F = 24 \cdot 57$, d.f. $= 8/8$, $p < 0 \cdot 001$), as was the interaction between tasks and reversibility ($F = 19 \cdot 04$, d.f. $= 2/8$, $p < 0 \cdot 01$). The interaction between grades and reversibility was not significant ($F = 2 \cdot 24$, d.f. $= 4/8$, n.s.). In the analysis of the number of passive voice sentences produced on the three experimental tasks, it was found that significantly more passive voice sentences were produced on the Scanning task than on the Naming task ($t = 3 \cdot 55$, d.f. $= 18$, $p < 0 \cdot 01$) and significantly more passive voice sentences were produced on the Controlled Scanning task than on the Scanning task ($t = 3 \cdot 92$, d.f. $= 18$, $p < 0 \cdot 01$). There was also a significant increase in the number of passive voice sentences produced with an increase in age for both reversible pictures ($\chi^2 = 29 \cdot 85$, d.f. $= 4$, $p < 0 \cdot 001$) and non-reversible pictures ($\chi^2 = 42 \cdot 88$, d.f. $= 4$, $p < 0 \cdot 001$). At the 3rd grade level, 90% of the subjects produced passive sentences for non-reversible pictures and 67% produced passive sentences for reversible pictures. The tendency

TABLE II. Number of passive sentences produced in Experiments I and II.

	Grade levels				
	NS	KG	1st	2nd	3rd
Experiment I					
Naming (total picture presented)					
Non-reversible picture	2	1	1	2	0
Reversible picture	2	2	1	0	1
Scanning (acted-upon presented first)					
Non-reversible picture	2	3	5	6	10
Reversible picture	2	2	2	2	5
Controlled Scanning (acted-upon presented first)					
Non-reversible picture	11	14	29	38	43
Reversible picture	5	6	13	20	36
Experiment II					
Condition 3					
Non-reversible picture	—	39	41	57	64
Reversible picture	—	40	51	50	60
Condition 4					
Non-reversible picture	—	43	51	48	65
Reversible picture	—	35	45	57	64

for the number of passive sentences produced in the Controlled Scanning task to increase with age was found to be related to an increase in the number of subjects who received perfect scores on imitation, comprehension and production tasks of an earlier experiment (Turner and Rommetveit, 1967). The number of subjects at each grade level who had perfect scores on the imitation, comprehension and production tasks in the earlier experiment and who produced passive voice sentences on the Controlled Scanning task increased with age ($\chi^2 = 29.55$, d.f. $= 63$, $p < 0.001$, NS level being excluded because of zero frequency). These subjects accounted for 64·44% of the passive voice sentences produced on the Controlled Scanning task.

Of the four experimental conditions of Experiment II, Conditions 1 and 2 elicited *only* active sentences (as predicted). Table II shows the number of passive sentences elicited by Conditions 3 and 4 at each grade level for both reversible and non-reversible sentences. The difference in the number of passive sentences elicited by Conditions 1 and 2 *vs* Conditions 3 and 4 was highly significant ($p < 0.001$) at each of the four grade levels—KG ($t = 10.46$, d.f. $= 23$), 1st ($t = 21.22$, d.f. $= 23$), 2nd ($t = 23.90$, d.f. $= 23$) and 3rd ($t = 82.81$, d.f. $= 23$). From Table II it is apparent that no difference was found between the general categories of reversible and non-reversible pictures. In fact the total number of passive sentences produced for each of these picture types was very nearly the same (408 and 402 for non-reversible and reversible pictures respectively).

A three-way (grades by conditions by sentences) analysis of variance of the number of passive sentences produced was carried out for Conditions 3 and 4. The main effect of subject grade levels was significant at the 0·005 level ($F = 5.48$, d.f. $= 3/69$); there was no significance for either conditions ($F = 0.01$, d.f. $= 1/69$, *n.s.*) or sentences ($F = 1.17$, d.f. $= 23/69$, *n.s.*). The only two-way interaction which was found to be significant was the interaction between grade levels and sentences ($F = 5.53$, d.f. $= 695/69$, $p < 0.005$). The total number of passive sentences produced for each picture at each of the four grade levels and the ranks for these total scores within each grade level are presented in Table III. This table shows different numbers of passive sentences were produced across age levels for the different pictures used. In an attempt to see whether there was any consistency to the patterns of total number of passive sentences produced to different pictures, a Friedman two-way analysis of variance of ranks was carried out. The ranks for each picture within each grade level are shown in Table III. The tendency for different pictures to elicit different numbers of passive sentences was found to be consistent across ages ($\chi^2_r = 38.97$, d.f. $= 23$, $p < 0.02$).

Table IV shows the types of errors made in the production of passive sentences for both Experiments I and II. The colloquial form of the

TABLE III. Number of passive sentences produced for each picture and score rankings within grade levels.

	No. of passives				Ranks			
	Grades				Grades			
PICTURE	KG	1	2	3	KG	1	2	3
		(N=12)				(N=12)		
(A) NON-REVERSIBLE								
(1) Mouse eating cheese	8	11	9	11	18·0	22·5	11·5	10·5
(2) Girl riding pony	7	8	11	12	11·5	12·0	20·0	18·5
(3) Nurse pushing carriage	7	12	9	11	11·5	24·0	11·5	10·5
(4) Bunny eating carrot	7	7	11	12	11·5	9·0	21·0	18·5
(5) Bird carrying branch	8	7	8	12	18·0	19·0	11·0	18·5
(6) Goat eating grass	8	10	9	12	18·0	19·5	11·5	18·5
(7) Farmer driving tractor	2	6	8	12	2·5	5·5	7·0	18·5
(8) Frog catching fly	7	6	10	12	11·5	5·5	16·5	18·5
(9) Mailman delivering letter	10	8	9	9	24·0	12·0	11·5	4·5
(10) Chicken laying egg	5	6	7	10	5·5	5·5	4·5	7·0
(11) Bee visiting flower	5	4	6	4	5·5	2·5	3·0	1·0
(12) Grandfather smoking pipe	8	7	8	12	18·0	9·0	7·0	18·5
(B) REVERSIBLE								
(1) Boy hitting ball	7	11	11	11	11·5	22·5	21·0	10·5
(2) Dog chasing lamb	7	9	11	12	11·5	12·5	21·0	18·5
(3) Lion watching tiger	1	1	3	6	1·0	1·0	1·0	2·0
(4) Father kissing mother	9	10	10	10	22·5	19·5	11·5	18·5
(5) Squirrel biting cat	4	8	7	7	4·0	12·0	4·5	3·0
(6) Turtle following snake	2	9	10	10	2·5	12·5	16·5	7·0
(7) Crab biting shell	9	6	10	12	22·5	5·5	16·5	18·5
(8) Pig following turkey	6	4	4	9	7·5	2·5	2·0	4·5
(9) Bear hugging monkey	8	9	9	12	18·0	12·5	11·5	18·5
(10) Horse pulling car	6	9	12	12	7·5	12·5	24·0	18·5
(11) Duck pulling boat	8	10	9	11	19·0	18·5	11·5	10·5
(12) Cow licking calf	8	10	11	12	18·0	19·5	21·0	18·5

passive, e.g. "The carrot's *getting* eaten by the rabbit", using the auxiliary "to get" in place of some form of "to be" occurred more frequently in Experiment II in sentences produced in answer to the question, "What is happening to the carrot" (Condition 4) than in answer to the question "What is being done to the carrot?" (Condition 3). The difference in the total number of "getting's" produced in these two conditions was significant ($t = 5·53$, d.f. $= 125$, $p < 0·005$).

Discussion

The results of Experiment I showed some evidence for the support of the hypothesis that the voice in which a sentence is produced can be

TABLE IV. Types of errors made in passive voice sentences.

ERRORS	GRADE LEVELS				
	NS	KG	1st	2nd	3rd
(1) Use of "to get" as an auxiliary verb in place of "to be"					
Experiment I	10	19	18	19	22
Experiment II	—	63	51	49	28
(2) Use of "been" in place of "is being"					
Experiment I	12	9	11	13	9
Experiment II	—	25	17	9	5
(3) Incorrect past participles					
(a) eated, aten, ate, ated, eat					
Experiment I	15	15	16	12	5
Experiment II	—	14	14	7	4
(b) drived, drove, droved, droven					
Experiment II	—	8	10	5	1
(c) rided, rode, roden, roded					
Experiment II	—	6	6	3	1
(d) took, tooken					
Experiment II	—	2	4	2	0
(e) sitted, sit, is sat					
Experiment I	5	15	8	3	0
(f) throwed, bited, holded, gived, flied, smoken					
Experiment II	—	9	10	4	0
(4) Semantic reversals					
Experiment I	3	4	6	2	10
Experiment II	—	5	7	5	2

controlled by manipulating the direction (actor or acted-upon first) in which a picture is visually scanned. However, the only significant trend for the number of passives produced to increase with age was found on the Controlled Scanning task which was the most structured experimental task. This suggests that the failure to find a significant increase with age in the number of passive sentences produced on the Scanning task might have been a result of the lack of structure or control of the experimental situation. In other words, the task was not structured enough to elicit the passive voice sentences effectively. This problem is faced generally in experiments involving speech production where an attempt is made to structure the situation to the degree that the response can be elicited without actually telling the subject the exact response that is desired.

The finding that 64·44% of the passives produced on the Controlled Scanning task came from subjects who received perfect scores on the imitation, comprehension and production tasks of an earlier experiment (Turner and Rommetveit, 1967), and that the number of these subjects increased with age suggests that manipulation of the voice in which a sentence is produced cannot be carried out effectively until a child has exhibited "control" (ability to respond correctly on tasks assessing imitation, comprehension and production skills) of the grammatical form.

In Experiment II no difference was found between reversible and non-reversible pictures in the number of passive sentences elicited through questioning. This suggests that in a structured situation in which a subject is encoding a specific observable event into language it does not matter whether the actor and acted-upon elements of the event are potentially reversible or not. The confusion as to what element is the actor and which is the acted-upon, which becomes an issue when the stimulus is entirely verbal, is absent. The subject can encode his sentence while visually checking the actual direction of the action in the physical world. Difficulty in processing reversible sentences might tend to arise when the task involves verbal encoding in the absence of observable, physical events or when the task involves both visual and verbal decoding in addition to the encoding of a response, verbal or otherwise.

Although the main effect of sentence content was not found to be significant, the interaction between sentence content and grade level was found to be significant. Also, there was a significant consistent pattern across ages in the number of passive voice sentences elicited for the various sentence contents. Thus perhaps an interaction between syntax and semantics may have been operant, affecting the ease with which a given sentence could be put into the passive voice.

The passive voice sentences which were produced in the present experiments tended to be of the colloquial English form in which the auxiliary verb "to get" is used in place of the standard English auxiliary "to be". In Experiment I the child was given an example or model for his passive voice sentence production; in Experiment II he was not given a model answer. The frequency of the use of "getting" was lower in Experiment I than in Experiment II. This suggests that the child was influenced by the form of the adult model. There was further evidence for this hypothesis as a subject tended to vacillate between using the auxiliary verb "to get" and "to be", depending on the question asked. The child tended to respond more frequently with the standard English form of the verb "to be" when this form was used in the question asked of the child (Condition 3); when "to be" was not used in the question, the child tended to use the colloquial form of the passive auxiliary verb "to get" (Condition 4). Thus it might be that the inability of young children to produce the passive voice successfully in an experimental task is due, in part, to the use of the standard English form "to be" in the stimulus material. The standard form may be acquired later than the colloquial form because the colloquial form occurs more frequently in everyday speech and the standard is not emphasized until the child attends school.

References

Carroll, J. B. (1958). Process and content in psycholinguistics. *In* "Current Trends in Psychology". Pittsburgh Press, Pittsburgh.

Leopold, W. F. (1949). "Speech development of a bilingual child." Northwestern University Press, Evanston.

Rommetveit, R. (1965). Personal communication. Cornell University.

Rommetveit, R. (1967). "Words, meanings, and messages." Academic Press and Universitetsforlaget, New York, London and Oslo.

Slobin, D. I. (1966). Early grammatical development in several languages, with special attention to Soviet research. Unpublished manuscript. University of California, Berkeley.

Tannenbaum, P. and Williams, F. (1966). The effects of relative focus upon production of active and passive sentences. Unpublished manuscript, University of Wisconsin.

Turner, E. A. and Rommetveit, R. (1967). The acquisition of sentence voice and reversibility. *Child Development* **38,** 649–660.

23. Focus of Attention in Recall of Active and Passive Sentences*

E. A. TURNER and R. ROMMETVEIT

In English the active-passive voice contrast offers two equivalent ways of expressing a given semantic content. The difference between the two voices seems to be primarily a pragmatic distinction. When a speaker reports an event, he must select some element of the denotative domain of events as the sentence subject. Carroll (1958) suggests that the speaker selects the most salient element of an extralinguistic situation as the subject of a sentence. If the *actor* in a given situation is the most salient element, a sentence will tend to be in the active voice; and, conversely, if the *acted-upon* element is the most salient, the sentence will tend to be in the passive voice. A recent experiment by Segal and Martin (1965) tends to confirm Carroll's (1958) hypothesis. In this experiment, the subject of the sentence was rated as the most important element, whether the subject element corresponded to either the *actor* or *acted-upon* element in the denotative domain of events (i.e. whether the sentence was active or passive in voice).

Prentice (1966) found that increasing response strength, or salience of the first noun in a sentence affects the ease of learning. When the first noun, the subject, is made most salient, the sentence is learned more easily than when the second noun, the object, is made most salient. Thus the active-voice sentence was learned more easily when the actor was most salient than when the acted-upon element was most salient;

* This study represents a portion of a dissertation submitted by the senior author to the Graduate School of Cornell University in partial fulfilment of the requirements for the Ph.D. degree in child development, May, 1966. The research was conducted under National Science Foundation grant 6458 to the second author at Cornell University. Preparation of this manuscript by the senior author was supported by Carnegie Corporation of New York, grant B-3233, and National Institutes of General Medical Sciences, grant 5-T01-GM-01011 to Harvard University Centre for Cognitive Studies, 1966–1967. Published in *J. Verbal Learning Verbal Behaviour* (1968) **7**, 543–548.

and the passive-voice sentence was learned more easily when the acted-upon element was most salient than when the actor was most salient.

In the present memory experiment, it was hypothesized that the focus of one's attention during the storing or retrieving of sentences, or both, may influence the choice of a sentence subject in recall. Pictures of the actor, the acted-upon, and the total sentence content were used in an attempt to manipulate the child's focus of attention on a particular aspect of the sentence content, both at the time of sentence storage and at the time of sentence retrieval. All of the various storage-retrieval picture combinations were used with both active and passive sentences. In general, it was hypothesized that when the picture on which the child focused his attention was congruent with the subject of the stimulus sentence, correct recall would be facilitated; on the other hand, when the picture focused on was incongruent with the subject (but congruent with the object) of the stimulus sentence, there would be a tendency for transformations in sentence voice to occur in recall such that the subject of the sentence recalled would be congruent with the pictured element. Thus the actor and total pictures were hypothesized to facilitate recall of active sentences and transformations of passive sentences to the active voice, while the acted-upon pictures were hypothesized to facilitate the recall of passive sentences and transformations from active to passive voice. As the active voice has been found to occur more frequently in children's descriptive usage (Turner and Rommetveit, 1967b) than the passive voice, it was predicted that there would be more transformations from passive to active voice than vice versa and that the total number of active sentences would exceed the number of passive sentences produced in recall.

Method

Subjects

Forty-eight children, 24 males and 24 females, at each of the following five grade levels were used as Ss: Nursery School (NS), Kindergarten (KG), first grade (1st), second grade (2nd) and third grade (3rd). At each grade level, Ss were divided into four experimental groups of 12 Ss, six males and six females in each group. Each group was presented with a different form of the stimulus materials.

Stimulus Materials

A total of 48 sentences, or 12 different sentences of each of the following four types, was presented to each S:

(1) Non-reversible Active (NRA): Active sentences in which actor and acted-upon elements are not interchangeable ("The bunny was eating the carrot").

(2) Reversible Active (RA): Active sentences in which actor and acted-upon elements are interchangeable ("The mommy was kissing the daddy" or "The daddy was kissing the mommy").

(3) Non-reversible Passive (NRP): Passive sentences in which the actor and acted-upon elements are not interchangeable ("The carrot was eaten by the bunny").

(4) Reversible Passive (RP): Passive sentences in which actor and acted-upon elements are interchangeable ("The daddy was kissed by the mommy" or "The mommy was kissed by the daddy").

One sentence of each of the four sentence types—NRA, RA, NRP and RP—was randomly paired with each of 12 storage-retrieval picture combinations. The picture that was presented at the time of sentence storage was either a picture of the actor element, the acted-upon element, the total sentence content, or was merely a blank card; the same type of pictures was used at the time of sentence retrieval, with the exception that no blank cards were used. Pre-testing had shown that, with few exceptions, Ss were unable to recall the stimulus sentence when a blank card was presented at the time of recall. Therefore, this condition was eliminated from the experiment.

Design

The four-group design was necessary in order to control for the form in which any reversible sentence content was expressed. For example, the three words, "mommy", "kiss", "daddy" could be used to make four different sentences: (a) "The mommy kisses the daddy". (b) "The daddy kisses the mommy". (c) "The daddy is kissed by the mommy". (d) "The mommy is kissed by the daddy".

Each group was presented with a different form of the reversible sentences. As there are only two forms, one active form and one passive form, for a given non-reversible sentence, two groups received the same form of the non-reversible sentences.

Although the sentences were randomly paired with storage-retrieval picture combinations, the pairings were the same for all Ss within a group. The random order of presentation of the 48 sentences and corresponding pictures combinations was also held constant within a group. The number of pictures presented as a set on one trial was varied for the different age levels in order to keep the frequency of errors relatively constant for all grade levels. Pre-testing showed that the error level could be kept in the 50–60% range by dividing the 48 pictures into sets of eight for the NS level, sets of 12 for the KG Ss, sets of 16 for the 1st grade, and sets of 24 for the 3rd grade. As there was no way to divide the 48 pictures into sets of 20 for the 2nd grade, they were divided up as follows: 12 pictures, then 16 pictures, and finally 20 pictures in the last set. This division was pre-tested and the frequency of errors was not significantly greater than that of the other grades.

Procedure

The S was shown storage pictures, one set at a time. The sentence that corresponded to a given picture was read as the picture was shown. When E had finished presenting all the sentences in one set, the retrieval pictures corresponding to this set of sentences were presented. The S was then asked to recall the sentences that corresponded to the retrieval pictures in front of him. When one set was completed in this way, E went on to the next set of sentences and the procedure was repeated until all sentences had been presented.

Scoring

A response was scored as correct if the sentence content was the same as that of the stimulus sentence and if the grammatical form given by S had the word order and morphological endings appropriate to the voice of the stimulus sentence. A sentence was scored as a grammatical transformation if the content of the recalled form was the same as that of the stimulus sentence, but the grammatical voice of the sentence was the *opposite* of the voice of the stimulus sentence. For example, if the sentence, "The carrot was being eaten by the bunny", was recalled as "The bunny was eating the carrot", S would be scored with a transformation to the active voice. In instances where S interchanged the actor and acted-upon elements of a sentence, the recalled form was scored as a semantic reversal. For example, the reversible sentence, "The boys were chased by the girls" might be recalled with actor and acted-upon elements interchanged as "The girls were chased by the boys". When actor and acted-upon elements were interchanged and the sentence was recalled in the opposite voice, it was scored as a transformed semantic reversal.

Results

The four groups, or four forms of the stimulus materials, were not found to be significantly different in terms of either the number of sentences correctly recalled or transformed. In addition, no effect was found for sentence content or order of presentation for a specific picture combination (storage and retrieval pictures).

A summary of the correct score results for the experimental variables (Grades, Sentence Reversibility, Sentence Voice, Storage Pictures and Retrieval Pictures) is presented in Table I. As the variance due to Grades was only significant when the NS level was included, $F(4, 35) = 17.76$, $p < 0.001$, and as an attempt had been made (and was successful for the older Ss) to equate Grades on task difficulty, the NS level was excluded from the further analyses.

TABLE I. Summary of percentage of correct recall scores for different grades and sentence types.

Grades	Non-reversible sentences		Reversible sentences	
	Active	Passive	Active	Passive
Nursery school	43·53	19·10	36·28	18·40
Kindergarten	50·35	30·73	41·67	23·44
First grade	51·22	29·86	43·06	23·96
Second grade	51·74	32·12	40·97	25·00
Third grade	52·08	31·08	42·71	24·30

The data were analysed by a repeated-measures analysis of variance (cf. Winer, 1962). The results strongly supported the hypothesis that focus of attention on Storage and Retrieval Pictures affects the voice in which sentences are recalled. In analysis of correct scores, the main effect of Retrieval Picture was significant, $F(2, 56) = 347.51$, $p < 0.001$, while the effect of Storage Picture was not. The predicted differential effect of the actor, acted-upon, and total pictures was evident from the significant Sentence Voice by Retrieval Picture Interaction, $F(2, 56) = 996.43$, $p < 0.001$. As shown in Fig. 1a, when the original stimulus sentence was in the active voice, both actor and total pictures significantly facilitated correct recall over the acted-upon picture at the time of sentence retrieval, $q(3, 56) = 6.98$, $p < 0.001$ and $q(2, 56) = 10.67$, $p < 0.001$ (Newman-Keuls method of multiple comparisons; cf. Winer, 1962); in contrast, when the original sentence was in the passive voice, the acted-upon element facilitated recall over the actor and total picture cues, $q(2, 56) = 6.12$, $p < 0.001$ and $q(3, 56) = 4.53$, $p < 0.001$, respectively. Although the main effect of Storage Picture was not significant, the Voice by Storage Picture interaction was significant, $F(3, 84) = 21.83$, $p < 0.001$, as was the Storage Picture by Retrieval Picture interaction, $F(6, 168) = 8.57$, $p < 0.001$. In general, the differential effects of storage pictures on the recall of active and passive sentences were the same as those mentioned above for retrieval picture.

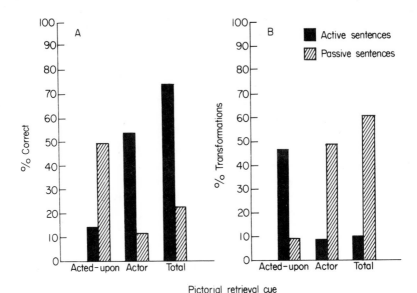

Pictorial retrieval cue

FIG. 1. Summary of Sentence Voice × Retrieval Picture Interaction.

However, the differential effects of storage picture were less marked. In the interaction of Storage Picture by Retrieval Picture (see Table II), recall was consistently better for the total retrieval picture than for either the partial actor or acted-upon retrieval pictures $q(2, 56) = 3\cdot01$, $p < 0\cdot05$, and $q(3, 56) = 3\cdot87$, $p < 0\cdot01$. The Storage Picture by Retrieval picture interaction between partial pictures—actor and acted-upon pictures—was such that recall was better if Ss were shown one of the partial pictures on storage and a *different* one on retrieval, than if S saw the *same* partial picture both at the time of storage and retrieval.

The analysis of variance showed that more active sentences were produced in recall than passive sentences, $F(1, 28) = 903\cdot07$, $p < 0\cdot001$.

TABLE II. Relations between storage and retrieval pictures in terms of percentage of sentences correctly recalled.

| | Retrieval picture | | | | | |
| | Actor | | Acted-upon | | Total picture | |
Storage picture	Active	Passive	Active	Passive	Active	Passive
Blank	51·04	8·85	9·38	44·79	74·22	19·27
Actor	50·26	8·07	15·36	51·56	75·26	17·19
Acted-upon	55·99	13·02	10·16	46·09	63·02	32·81
Total picture	57·03	14·32	16·40	52·34	83·29	22·14

Also, more non-reversible sentences were correctly recalled than reversible sentences, $F(1, 28) = 141 \cdot 23$, $p < 0 \cdot 01$. Finally, the Sentence Reversibility by Retrieval Picture interaction was significant, $F(2, 56) = 4 \cdot 81$, $p < 0 \cdot 05$. A further analysis of correct scores showed that the non-reversible sentences were recalled significantly better than the reversible sentences in the case of the actor, $F(1, 35) = 27 \cdot 94$, $p < 0 \cdot 001$, and the acted-upon retrieval pictures, $F(1, 35) = 17 \cdot 69$, $p < 0 \cdot 001$; however, the superiority of the nonreversible sentence was not found in the case of the total retrieval picture.

In general, the results of the analysis of the transformation scores were the same as those for the correct score. In the case of the transformation scores, of course, as shown in Fig. 1b, the actor and total retrieval pictures tended to facilitate the transformation of passive sentences to the active voice in recall, and the acted-upon picture tended to facilitate transformations from active to passive voice. In contrast to the results of correct scores, in the results of transformation scores the main effect of Storage Picture was found to be significant, $F(3, 84) = 5 \cdot 29$, $p < 0 \cdot 001$.

The frequency of both semantic reversal and transformed semantic reversal errors was relatively constant across age groups beyond the NS level. Of the 776 semantic reversals and transformed semantic reversals, 559 or 72% were such that the first noun in the sentence produced by the S was the element pictured in the retrieval picture. For example, when the retrieval picture was a picture of *boys*, Ss tended to recall the sentence, "The girls chased the boys" as "The boys chased the girls", if they failed to recall the sentence correctly.

In 754 or 29% of the passive-voice sentences produced by the Ss in this experiment, the colloquial form of the auxiliary verb was used; more specifically, the form "to get" ("The cheese was *getting* eaten by the mouse") was used in place of the standard auxiliary verb form "To be" ("The cheese was being eaten by the mouse"). The use of the colloquial form occurred at all grade levels, but was most frequent at the KG level. In addition, in 18·6% of the passive-voice sentences the child used an incorrect form of the past participle.

Discussion

The results supported the primary hypothesis that the focus of one's attention at the time of sentence storage and at the time of retrieval can influence the voice in which a sentence is recalled. When the retrieval picture was congruent with the subject of the original stimulus sentence or when the total extralinguistic situation was pictured, correct recall was facilitated; on the other hand, when the retrieval picture was not congruent with the subject of the original stimulus sentence, sentences tended to be transformed to the opposite voice in recall.

More specifically, when the *actor* or *total picture* is presented as a retrieval cue, active sentences tended to be recalled correctly and passive sentences tended to be transformed into the active voice in recall; when the *acted-upon* picture is presented, active voice sentences tended to be transformed into the passive voice and passive sentences tended to be recalled correctly (see Fig. 1). The frequency of active-voice sentences in recall was greater than that of passive-voice sentences, as was predicted.

Although the main effect of Storage Picture was only significant in the analysis of transformation scores, there was additional evidence that storage pictures do affect the voice in which a sentence is recalled. It would seem that the stronger Retrieval Picture effect tended to suppress the effect of focus of attention at the time of the storing of sentences. A condition in which a blank card is presented at the time of sentence retrieval would have provided more clear-cut information with regard to the effects of storage pictures. However, as mentioned earlier, this condition was not used in the experiment because pre-testing had shown that Ss were unable to remember the sentences for which there were no pictures. The effect of storage cue might better be tested with an experiment in which storage cues are varied but in which free recall without pictures is used.

In general, it was found that both correct and transformation scores were higher when both elements (*actor* and *acted-upon*) were presented as memory aids, one at the time of storage and the other at the time of recall, than when the same element was presented both times. This suggests that Ss made use of both storage and retrieval pictures and that the more information presented pictorially, the better were the recall scores.

The main effects of Sentence Reversibility and Voice were both found to be significant. As we reported in an earlier experiment (Turner and Rommetveit, 1967b), the effect of reversibility tended to disappear when S encoded a sentence from a specific, entirely observable event; this was the case when the total picture was presented for sentence retrieval. When the total picture was presented in contrast to the presentation of the actor or acted-upon element alone, the S was given a complete set of visual stimuli from which to encode his verbal response. There could be no confusion as to which element was the actor and which was the acted-upon, because the visual representation supplied all necessary information and the memory load was all but eliminated. As a result the difference between reversible and non-reversible sentences disappeared.

Sentences produced when the total picture is presented at the time of recall are difficult to evaluate. The S may have recalled the stimulus sentence, at least in terms of the content, or he may have merely described the picture in front of him. An earlier study (Turner and Rommetveit, 1967b) provides some evidence to show that children use the active voice almost exclusively when describing pictures. Therefore, it would seem that the passive-voice sentences produced in response to a total picture at the time of recall are evidence for the effect of the experimental manipulation.

When the total picture was not present at the time of recall of a reversible sentence, a large number of semantic reversal errors were made. These errors tended to support the focus-of-attention hypothesis inasmuch as 72% of these errors were such that the noun pictured last (the Retrieval Picture) tended to be the first noun in the sentence recalled by the child. Thus the most salient semantic element, whether the actor or the acted-upon element, tended to become the subject of the sentence.

The tendency to use the colloquial passive verb form was apparent at all age levels but was strongest at the KG level. This finding supports the hypothesis that the use of "to be" in place of the colloquial "to get" tends to be learned after the child attends school and not so much from everyday speech (see Turner and Rommetveit, 1967a, 1967b). Again, there were a number of errors in the production of irregular past participal verb forms. This corroborates the suggestion that one of the areas of difficulty and one of the major differences between the active and passive voice sentence is the verb form.

References

Carroll, J. B. (1958). Process and content in psycholinguistics. *In* "Current Trends in Psychology". Pittsburgh Press, Pittsburgh.

Prentice, J. L. (1966). Response strength of single words as an influence in sentence behavior. *J. verbal Learning verbal Behavior* **5**, 429–433.

Segal, E. M. and Martin, D. R. (1966). The influence of transformational history on the importance of words in sentences. Paper presented to Psychonomic Society, October, 1966.

Turner, E. A. and Rommetveit, R. (1967a). The acquisition of sentence voice and reversibility. *Child Development* **38**, 649–660.

Turner, E. A. and Rommetveit, R. (1967b). Experimental manipulation of the production of active and passive voice in children. *Language and Speech* **10**, 169–180.

Winer, B. J. L. "Statistical Principles in Experimental Design." McGraw-Hill, New York.

24. Unrepresentativeness of Studies on Memory of Verbal Material*

R. M. BLAKAR

Students taking introductory courses in psychology at the University of Oslo in 1969 were asked to write an essay on memory as part of their examination. A content analysis (Blakar, 1972) showed that most of the students tried to relate what they had learned about memory from their textbooks (chiefly Hilgard and Atkinson, 1967) to experience from everyday life, but that they did not succeed very well in the attempt.

What is it, then, that makes the concepts and empirical findings on memory presented by psychologists so difficult to integrate with everyday experience? An examination of the dominant traditions in the study of memory reveals that the stimulus material is (a) particularistic or atomistic (dots, numbers, letters, nonsense syllables, words, single sentences) and very seldom presented within relevant contexts; (b) often so-called meaningless in the tradition after Ebbinghaus; and (c) usually presented or repeated more than once. These characteristics are not independent. Thus, very often the stimulus material appears "meaningless" because it is presented out of relevant contexts, or it may become so in the course of many presentations (Blakar and Rommetveit, 1971a). Mention should, of course, be made of the rather unique position of Bartlett as one of the few who "violates" these unwritten "rules" for the game of studying memory.

Kvale (1971) has made a content analysis of all the 67 experiments on memory reported in Vol. 7 (1968) of the *Journal of Verbal Learning and Verbal Behavior*. His findings as regards types of stimulus material used are in line with points a and b of the characterization above (cf. Table I). Yet, outside the laboratory one is very seldom requested to process "meaningless" material. Equally infrequently is anything presented more than once in exactly the same form. It may be suspected, therefore, that many of the theoretical problems traditionally focused

* Published in *Scandinavian J. Psychology* (1973) **14**, 9–11.

upon in the research on memory are created artificially in and by these experimental settings.

As Brunswik (1949) argues, the artificial untying of variables that experimental designs allow is often needed to get new insights. No doubt, the contributions of Ebbinghaus were made possible through such experiments. Even though almost a century has passed, the nonsense syllable is nevertheless still cultivated in ever more refined experimental designs. The difficulty of relating the laboratory findings to everyday experience suggests that the representativeness or "ecological generality" of the dominant traditions need to be questioned.

TABLE I. 67 experiments on memory[a] classified according to type of stimulus material used.

Type of stimulus material	Experiments	
	n	%
Nonsense syllables	19	24
Lists of letters	7	9
Lists of numbers	11	14
Lists of words	32	41
Sentences	8	10
Figures	1	1
Pictures	1	1
Total	79[b]	100

[a] Reported in *J. verbal Learning and verbal Behavior* (1968) Vol. 7. Data from Kvale (1971).
[b] Total number is larger than 67 because more than one type of stimulus material were used in some experiments.

An Experiment

The issue may be illustrated by a simple experiment with a group of seven beginning students of psychology (Blakar, 1970). Three different lists of nine three-letter syllables were constructed of the same 27 letters, arranged in List 1 in nine nonsense trigrams, and in List 2 in nine three-letter well-known words (Norwegian). In List 3 the nine words of List 2 were arranged in a meaningful Norwegian sentence, which in English could read: No it was a boy who beat me.

List 1. NEV OSI DIL NAT GOM ITE TUS REG MET
List 2. SLO DET EIN TIL NEI VAR SOM GUT MEG
List 3. NEI DET VAR EIN GUT SOM SLO TIL MEG

The subjects were told that three lists of nine three-letter syllables would be presented, and they were asked to write down what they remembered just after each list had been presented. Lists 1, 2 and 3, in that order, were then read in a monotonous voice, with one trigram each second.

The results were as expected from common sense. List 3 was recalled perfectly by all subjects, reproducing the nine trigrams (words) in the exact order. The recall of List 2 was quite good, while List 1 was poorly reproduced. Mean number of letters recalled was 27, 23 and 10, respectively.

The same 27 letters were obviously processed differently in the three contexts of this experiment. By using "meaningless" stimulus material, or material out of relevant context, the risk is therefore run of studying memory stripped of one of its most effective means: the rules for grasping and organizing meaning.

There are findings, moreover, which suggest that different strategies are at work when verbal material are presented many times rather than only once (point c above). Blakar and Rommetveit (1971a, 1971b) showed that the retrieval of the content of a sentence may be at least as good when the sentence is presented only once in a more natural context (picture context), as when presented five times and each time repeated orally by the subject. In this connection it should be mentioned that it adds further to the unrepresentativeness of experimental research on memory that usually only verbatim recall is counted, while such recall is seldom required in everyday life.

Finally, the unrepresentativeness of the still dominating traditions may be illustrated by relating the findings of Kvale (cf. Table I) to the results from the above experiment. No doubt, the meaningful sentence (List 3) is the condition most representative of everyday life, and the nonsense syllables (List 1) the most unrepresentative, while List 2 of unconnected words falls somewhere in between. Figure 1 presents the

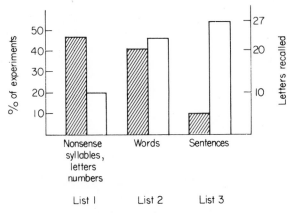

FIG. 1. Relative frequency of experiments on memory, using different types of stimulus material (filled columns) and mean number of letters recalled under corresponding stimulus conditions (Lists 1–3) in present experiment (unfilled columns). (See *J. verbal Learning verbal Behavior* (1968) Vol. 7.)

recall of the 27 letters in these contexts (unfilled columns) together with the relative frequency of experiments using corresponding stimulus material (filled columns). It will be seen that the more unrepresentative types of stimulus material, yielding poor recall, were cultivated intensively in research as of 1968, while the opposite held for material yielding very good recall.

This state of affairs brings to mind a comment by the editor to the third volume of "Psychology: A Study of a Science": "Almost all contributors to Volume 3 stress the need for significant observational analysis of behavior under 'natural' conditions" (Koch, 1959, p. 750); and with reference to "the normally staid area of rote learning" Asch concludes (1968, p. 214): "In the course of a relatively brief period a number of the most basic assumptions in the field have been brought into question. So elementary are the points at issue that one cannot help asking whether the foundations of this intensively cultivated part of psychology are at all secure".

References

Asch, S. E. (1968). The doctrinal tyranny of associationism: or what is wrong with rote learning. *In* "Verbal behavior and general theory". (T. R. Dixon and D. L. Horton, Eds) pp. 214–228. Prentice-Hall, Englewood Cliffs, New Jersey.

Blakar, R. M. (1970). Konteksteffektar i språkleg kommunikasjon. Unpublished thesis, University of Oslo.

Blakar, R. M. (1972). Ein innhaldsanalyse av eksamensoppgaver til grunnfag. *Impuls* **1,** 41–46.

Blakar, R. M. and Rommetveit, R. (1971a). Processing of utterances in contexts versus rote learning of sentences: Some pilot studies and a design for an experiment. *In* "Social contexts of messages". (E. A. Carswell and R. Rommetveit, Eds) pp. 57–66. Academic Press, London and New York.

Blakar, R. M. and Rommetveit, R. (1971b). Processing of utterances in contexts versus rote learning of sentences: A progress report. Unpublished manuscript, Institute of Psychology, University of Oslo.

Brunswick, E. (1949). "Systematic and representative design of psychological experiments." University of California Press, Berkeley and Los Angeles.

Hilgard, E. R. and Atkinson, R. C. (1967). "Introduction to Psychology." Harcourt Brace Jovanovich, New York.

Koch, S. (Ed.) (1959). Epilogue. *In* "Psychology: A study of a science". Vol. 3, pp. 729–788. McGraw-Hill, New York.

Kvale, S. (1971). Fenomenologi og eksperimentell forskning. *In* "Psykologi och praxis". (A. Johansson and M. Johansson, Eds) Bo Cavefors Bokförlag, Stockholm.

25. A Study of "Chunking" in Transmission of Messages*

R. ROMMETVEIT and E. A. TURNER

The purpose of the present paper† is to explore some effects of particular word groupings or word orders on reception and retention of linguistically mediated messages. The problems under investigation are related to linguistic enquiries into word groups and to psychological and psycholinguistic studies of "chunking".

In modern linguistics the method of sentence structure analysis employed has been, for the most part, immediate constituent analysis. By this method, the sentence or its content is gradually parsed into smaller and smaller groups of words, until one finally arrives at a string of morphemes. A sentence is, thus; represented by a hierarchical structure with the subject noun phrase and the predicate verb phrase as its two major constituents and with morphemes as its ultimate constituents. Immediate constituent analysis stresses proximity of words as a factor in uncovering important and significant word groups. This has resulted in some problems and awkward analyses in cases in which non-adjacent words obviously seem to form a group.

A more thorough and functional analysis of word groups which takes both syntax and semantics into account is that of Reichling (1963)‡ and Uhlenbeck.§ Some word groups have been shown to be so cohesive that they behave like single words in many respects. The word group

* The authors are indebted to Dr. J. Nadler for advice and assistance in the statistical analysis of the data. Published in *Lingua* (1967) **18**, 337–351.

† The study was conducted at Cornell University under N. S. F. Grant 6458 in 1965 and initial analyses were carried out during the summer of 1965 at the Centre for Cognitive Studies, Harvard University. The study was written up at the Centre for Advanced Study in the Behavioural Sciences, Stanford, California, in 1966.

‡ See, for instance, Reichling's discussion of the word group "noun with definite article".

§ See Uhlenbeck's discussion of word groups (1962, 1964) and his analysis of noun + noun groups in Substantief + substantief in Modern Algemeen Nederlands (1966).

consisting of "definite article + noun" in English is one of them. The group "the boy" thus corresponds to the single word "guten" in Norwegian. What in English is achieved by a separate word ("the") is achieved in Norwegian by a suffix ("-en"). Experimental confirmation (see Johnson, 1965) of the cohesiveness of the "definite article + noun" group has shown that once the definite article is recalled correctly, the noun is recalled also. Uhlenbeck also argues, for instance, that a parsing of a noun phrase such as "the old man" first into "the" + noun phrase and secondly parsing of the noun phrase into adjective + noun is unwarranted in terms of the semantic processes involved. "The" is by virtue of its semantic value attached directly to the noun, as much as the adjective is attached to the noun. Hence, the phrase should, according to Reichling's and Uhlenbeck's theory, be represented as "the   old   man" rather than "the   old   man".

Further evidence of the complexity of sentence structure and word groups when both syntax and semantics is taken into account is revealed in an example given by van Holk (1962): "The birds are preening their feathers". Once one has arrived at "preening", there is a strong compulsion in the selection of the object-noun "feathers". Insertion of another word would probably result in a more unusual sentence. In this sentence, there are obvious connections between "preening" and "feathers", "birds" and "preening", and "birds" and "feathers". This example suggests that connections exist between words in a sentence which are not revealed on any level of immediate constituent analysis. It is thus apparent that Reichling and Uhlenbeck do not view syntax as establishing relationships between meaningless or structural forms, but as serving to connect meanings in one way or another in an utterance. Thus syntax is the vehicle by which meanings of individual elements are combined into a semantic connection. "And so the function of all syntactic means is in the last resort a semantic one" (see Reichling, 1961).

The mechanism of "chunking" as a psychological phenomenon was first explicitly described and analysed by G. A. Miller (1956). A characteristic feature of information processing in a variety of settings is an organization of discrete elements into higher-order units or "chunks". A person who is familiar with both the binary and the decimal number system can thus instantaneously recode elements of one system into the other. A string such as 10100–01001–01010–00100 is immediately perceived as the decimal chunks 20–9–10–4. Instead of assimilating and retaining a sequence of 20 elements, a person can accomplish the same thing by organizing the stimulus input into four numbers and retaining these four numbers. As immediate memory is relatively fixed with respect to the total number of elements or "chunks" which can be assimilated or memorized at one time (approximately seven), this ability to recombine elements into larger and larger chunks increases the total amount of information which can be processed at one time. Thus chunking helps to expand the immediate memory span far beyond the limits set by an individual's capacity of approximately seven discrete elements.

Miller (1962a) has pointed out that some sort of chunking must be operant in speech production and in the perception of speech, and hence in organization of strings of words into word groups. As a speaker–hearer is encoding or decoding an average of four to five syllables per second (Pollack and Pickett, 1964) for a relatively long period of time, it seems evident that some grouping or chunking of the stimulus is necessary for efficient processing. Miller (1962b) suggests that the hearer probably segments the "ongoing flow of sound" into chunks which have some semantic reality or representation, namely into words and groups of words. Since words themselves can be uttered at a rate of two to three per second, it would seem that some sort of higher order or hierarchical grouping is essential for the speaker-hearer. Thus it is possible that words are grouped and regrouped into larger syntactic-semantic units. In this way, as Miller (1962) expresses it, we are allowed to make our perceptual decisions about what we are hearing at a slower and more comfortable rate.

A model of speech *encoding* which is based on a hierarchical structure such as that just described is Yngve's (1960, 1964) depth model. In essence, the model is based on the hypothesis that as we speak, we incur commitments to finish some units in certain ways. The commitment, furthermore, is assessed in terms of chunks of words which have to be stored in immediate memory. When a speaker starts to utter a phrase such as "very clear pictures", he has committed himself, in a way, to the whole word group "very clear pictures", i.e. he has planned, in general, *what* he wants to express, if not specifically *how* he is going to express it. If the final output or product of the encoding process is to be a complete grammatical utterance (which is not always the case in spontaneous speech by any means), such as "The very clear pictures appeared on the screen", the speaker actually has three commitments when he first utters "very"—he has committed himself to some adjective, to a noun completing the noun phrase, and to a verb phrase so as to form a complete sentence. Thus although the more complex a sentence is, the more commitments incurred by the speaker, it is more economic to think of the speaker's planning or generation process in this way than as involving single words planned in advance and uttered one by one. Hence Yngve's hypothesis of sentence encoding is such that the speaker can encode or plan the overall structure of a sentence and then encode what he wants to express in terms of segments or groups without having to plan the entire structure of his utterance ahead of time.

Yngve suggests that the English language is so designed that it seldomly involves more than seven commitments at any given time. This is thought to result from the fact that the greater the number of commitments, the greater the load on the speaker's short-term memory. And short-term memory, as discussed above, seems to be able to handle only about seven items at one time. Regressive or left-branching phrase structures tend to put the greatest load on memory. For example, the more the speaker elaborates the subject noun phrase ("Very clear newly painted modern American watercolour pictures"), the more probable it is that he will fail to remember what and how he wanted to express himself or where he was in the generation or encoding process. However, the speaker is generally able to go back and re-phrase his utterance using similar lexical items, but different constructions which do not tax the short-term memory so much.

The three words "very clear pictures", presented in the example above, form a pre-integrated response unit according to Johnson's (1965) analysis of sentence encoding. In addition, this pre-integrated response can be combined with others into larger units. Thus it is suggested that there is a hierarchy of pre-integrated response units involved in the generation of a sentence. This is closely related to Miller *et al.* (1960) idea of a hierarchy of plans which are pre-integrated units controlling the execution of a behavioural sequence or a series of movements or processes. Johnson tested his hypothesis concerning the pre-integrated response unit in an experiment by measuring the probability that an entire phrase is recalled correctly when at least one word is recalled correctly, and measuring so-called transitional error probability. The latter is the probability that a word in the sentence is incorrectly recalled given that the preceding word is correctly recalled. It was found that there was a high degree of dependence among words in a phrase and that—although existing at the start of the learning process—this dependency increased with learning. The subject in the sentence learning experiment will frequently be able to reproduce the whole phrase "very clear picture" without recalling "appeared", whereas the probabilities of remembering "very" without "clear" and "clear" without "picture" are low. For the most part, the transitional error probabilities supported a phrase structure analysis of the sentences with the most errors being made *between* phrases and the fewest *within* phrases. There were a few slight discrepancies between transitional error probabilities and the hierarchical structure of the sentence as described in the phrase structure analysis.

An improvement in the match between the phrase structure of the sentences and the transitional error probabilities was found when the model was altered slightly. Nodes in the phrase structure diagrams were assumed to represent "successively more inclusive encoding units", and the process of sentence generation was thought of as involving a series of encoding steps and not word-to-word links. Thus, instead of sentence generation being thought of as a set of associations between pre-integrated response sequences, it seems more likely that they are between encoding steps.

These hierarchical models argue against word-by-word sequential dependencies and support the notion of word groupings in language encoding. Although a similar hierarchical process is probably involved in the decoding of sentences, syntactic-semantic and temporal patterns may make for certain asymmetries between encoding and decoding which perhaps can be best explicated by left-branching patterns such as "very clear pictures". *What is going to be said* by means of the whole string has to be decided when "very" is spoken; *what was said* cannot be decided until "pictures" has been heard. The speaker may *pre*-integrate what he is uttering, but the hearer must postpone decoding or the integrating of the word elements in a sequence until he has reached the end of a syntactic-semantic group (*post*-integration). Another way of comparing production and comprehension is in terms of the strain on short-term memory. As the speaker is relieved of the load upon his short-term memory, the hearer's load increases. "Very" cannot be fully interpreted until "clear" is heard; "very clear", furthermore, requires the additional word "pictures" in order to be fully decoded. It is interesting to note that this post-integration or delayed decoding process was formulated in Europe some thirty years ago by Stenzel (1934) and Reichling (1935). Uhlenbeck (1963) calls this process the *principle of sustained memory* which "holds that a certain number of elements following one another linearly, may remain unconnected and (may be) kept present, until an element or elements appearing in the utterance much later can be connected with them" (1963, p. 13).

In the following discussion, the results of two small experiments related to potential grouping or chunking processes in the reception of linguistic material are presented. In the first exploratory experiment, subjects were college students. The subjects' task was to proof-read typewritten material in which a number of deliberate typographical errors has been made. A number of unrelated sentences were presented consecutively in small booklets, and the subjects were requested to proceed page by page, reading carefully and correcting every error in such a way that the entire sentence made sense.

There were three versions of booklets. A given sentence with a typing error would be read in three different spatial settings by three different subjects, namely, *broken up between two pages in two different ways* (breaking points 1 and 2, as shown below) and *consecutively on one line of a page* (breaking point 3). Two of the sentences were as follows:

(I) "People were far$_1$ more$_2$ l—ely there$_3$"
(II) "The judge was just$_1$ -hen$_2$ passing the sentence$_3$"

In sentence I there were three major possibilities of correcting the error: "*lonely*", "*lively*" and "*likely*". For sentence II, either "*then*" or "*when*" would do. We might therefore see whether and to what extent the *enforced break* positions 1 and 2 affected the resolution of the ambiguous typing error-problem. The findings for the two sentences above were as follows: When the break appeared at location 2, the problem was solved in the same way as when the whole sentence appeared on the same page. The break at location 1, on the other hand, gave a different pattern of resolutions in both cases.

For sentence I, more than two-thirds of our subjects put in "lonely" when there was no break or a break at location 2, whereas less than half the subjects did so when the interruption appeared at location 1. What happened with sentence II when split up at location 1 was a considerable increase of "when"–solutions. Externally induced "coding stations" between "far" and "more" and between "just" and "-hen" thus appeared to be more at variance with internally determined coding stations than stops after "far more" and "just -hen", respectively.

Consider first sentence I when broken up at location 1. The subject is reading the string "People were far . . ." with a set to assess its entire meaning before proceeding to the next page. The word "far" is then dwelt on in a situation when nothing is yet fully known about subsequent words. Meaning potentialities such as those indicated by the contrast "far"–"near" and related syntagmatic potentialities such as "far-away" may hence be evoked. And precisely such associative-syntagmatic processes, which will *not* be actualized when "far" is perceived in the context "far more", may account for the fact that an interruption immediately after "far" makes for a different resolution of the typing error problem than either a stop at location 1 or no stop at all.

Sentence II, furthermore, is genuinely ambiguous: The word string "just" may be processed either as an adjective meaning "exercising justice" or as an adverb "just", as in "just now", "just then". An externally induced stop immediately after "just" affects the choice between these two alternatives in favour of the former.

If we conceive of the decoding process as proceeding by jumps or chunks, i.e. from "were" to "l—ely" or "there" in sentence I, some of the possible interpretative paths at location 1 will then be skipped. The referential and associative word meanings which would lead into various interpretative paths (such as "far . . . away") are probably not evoked at all. The implication of this "skip-path" model of sentence decoding is hence that the initial element in left-branching structures such as "far" in "far more lonely" is not fully decoded until "more" or even "lonely" is received.

In a second study, we tried to find out how different word orders and other aspects of linguistic form affected comprehension and storage of specific messages. The non-linguistic entities of the communication setting in this study were specific entities such as curves, squares and numerals inscribed in circles. Every item was described in terms of a set of pairs of binary adjectives such as "ascending"/ "descending", "filled"/"empty" and "peripheral"/"central". Each of the descriptive adjectives was explained to the subject and/or explicated by simple visual demonstration prior to the experimental task. For each item, furthermore, there were two different linguistic descriptions, A and B. The A version always had the adjectives prior to the noun (pre-position), the B version had at least *some* adjectives in post-position.

The following is a sample of the descriptions:

(1A) "A leftward, jaggedly descending broken *curve*".
(1B) "A jagged, broken *curve* descending leftward".
(2A) "A small, filled and tilted *square*".
(2B) "A *square*, small, filled and tilted".
(3A) "An encircled and peripherally located two-digit *numeral*".
(3B) "A *numeral* of two digits in a circle at a peripheral location".

Altogether there were eight separate items: three resembling item 1 (curve, path, line), three resembling item 2 (square, triangle, arrow), and two resembling item 3 (numeral and word). The sequence of descriptions was spoken distinctly and slowly. The total time taken to present one of the eight items was 3·5 to 4·0 s. Pauses of 3·0 s duration separated the descriptions of the different items. Precisely the same speed and equally long pauses between items were observed for both sequence A and sequence B. Both sequences were presented with natural prosodic patterns. An additional variation which was used in this experiment was to present sequence B without a natural prosodic pattern, in an entirely monotonous form. This variation was also spoken at the same rate as the other versions. Hence, we had three different tape-recorded versions, respectively: sequence A, with natural intonation; sequence B, with natural intonation; and sequence B, with monotonous pattern (B').

The experimental task was introduced as a test of short-term memory. The subject was first informed about the nature of the task by a pre-test: After having listened to a verbal description of a *spiral* he was asked to *identify that particular spiral among 16 different spirals on a* "*target sheet*". (The actual target sheet for item 1 above is presented in Fig. 1, with a cross next to the correct choice.) The subject was then

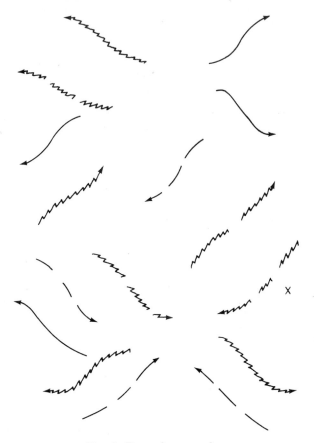

Fig. 1. Example target sheet.

asked to listen carefully to all eight descriptions for the particular purpose of later on identifying each particular item among many similar items. After having listened to the entire sequence, he was given the eight target sheets in a fixed order. For each sheet, he was asked to single out which item had been described. His next task was to reproduce, for each noun in the sequence (such as *"curve"*, *"square"*, *"numeral"*) the remaining part of the verbal description. We also added a fourth condition, in which the subject *first* was asked to give all verbal reproductions of the eight items and *afterwards* to identify each item on the target sheet. This reversal of tasks, however, did not have any significant effect on the retention measures.

The major demand upon the subject was thus to decode and retain in memory eight different complex messages. Retention, for each separate attribute of each separate item, was assessed according to the following criteria: (1) correct non-verbal identification of the attribute,

(2) correct verbal reproduction, (3) no reproduction of the word for the attribute in any context where it does not belong.

This means, more specifically, that a subject would not be judged as having retained the property "leftward" for item 1 unless he had picked one of the leftward-pointing curves in Fig. 1 and also given back the word *"leftward"* when reproducing the description of *"curve"*. Even it he had succeeded in both these tasks, however, he might be judged as having *not* retained the property. This would be the case if and only if he *also* reproduced the word "leftward" in conjunction with some noun to which it had *not* been *connected* (such as *"path"* or *"line"*).

Notice that the eight items could be confused very easily: there were continuous lines and broken curves, horizontal paths and vertical lines, etc. The measure of retention described above can hence most appropriately be interpreted as a measure of retention and *preservation of boundaries between the eight separate items* during decoding of the tape-recorded descriptions and subsequent storage in memory. And the major purpose of the enquiry was hence an illumination of the impact of *linguistic forms* (version A and the two prosodic variants of B) upon decoding and storage.

Since all properties were binary, the overall retention can be assessed in terms of bits of information. The *overall results* show, first of all, that retention is best when adjectives appear in pre-position, that is, when all descriptive adjectives precede the item which they are describing. The omission of natural prosodic features, on the other hand, had only negligible effects in this particular setting. Those who had listened to version A, gave back, on the average, 15·3 bits, whereas the corresponding results for the natural and the monotonous variants of version B, respectively, were 13·4 and 12·7 bits. This difference between form A on the one hand and form B on the other, however, stems almost exclusively from items of type 1. In fact, almost identical results were obtained for type 2A and 2B and for 3A and 3B items, respectively, whereas the recall of items of type 1 was far superior when given in form A. It became clear, furthermore, that adverb-adjective constructions such as "jaggedly descending" did not serve to glue the two attributes together any more than constructions in which both attributes were encoded by adjectives one or more word positions apart.

The subjects, who were undergraduate students at Cornell University, were also asked to report whether they formed visual images of the items when listening to the descriptions. It appeared that this was very frequently the case with items such as the *square* (item 2), but extremely seldom for items such as *curve* (item 1). Three-bits items such as the square and the numeral were very well and equally well-recalled under all conditions. It appeared to be the case, furthermore, that *post-position of adjectives then facilitated visualization*: filledness and tiltedness could more easily yield immediate visual impression when it was already known that the attributes pertained to a *square*.

The findings are thus not unequivocal: the lack of significant differences between the different conditions in recall of the easy items (types 2 and 3) may be partly due to the fact that they were too easy and partly to the fact that pre-position of adjectives for those particular items facilitated visual imagery. The inclusion of adverb-adjective constructions and change of order among modifiers further complicates the interpretation.

The consistent and statistically significant* superiority of version A over version B for four-bits items such as item 1, however, can hardly be accounted for in any other way than by an examination of some particular linguistic features of the two versions. Let us now see what happened to the curve in Fig. 1 when it was linguistically encoded by 1A and 1B. Consider, in particular, the two attributes *leftward* and *descending* which appear in post-position in version B: *both of them* were retained by *only 2 out of the 28 subjects* who listened to the natural intonation variant of form B, but by *14 out of 27 subjects* in the A-condition. Moreover, retention of these attributes was actually poorer for those who received the natural than for those who listened to the monotonous variant of form B.

All the three items of type 1 have all four modifiers before the noun in version A. In version B, on the other hand, there are always two modifiers after the noun (. . . "descending leftward", . . . "winding smoothly"), the first of which is always the *present participle of a verb*. The unique feature of this latter version is thus a patterning of the initial part of the description into a relatively autonomous word group. The listener has the opportunity for a full decoding when the noun is heard. The first part of 1B, for instance, is "*A jagged, broken curve*". This string may be fully decoded, and the continuation ". . . *descending leftward*" may then be decoded as a verb phrase, e.g. as conveying *what happens* to the particular curve *already described*. In 1A, on the other hand, none of the adjectives can be fully decoded until "*curve*" is heard. The words "*leftward*" and "*descending*", even though one word position apart, must accordingly both be kept in storage and decoded jointly when the whole description of the item has been heard.

We may hence conceive of forms of 1A and 1B as providing different "*decoding stations*". In form 1A there is only one possible coding station, namely after "curve". This means, more specifically, that the listener has to store all four adjectives and postpone final decoding until they can be integrated into one chunk. In form 1B, on the other hand, there are at least two coding stations involved: the listener may first group

---

* An analysis of variance was carried out and showed this difference to be significant at the 0·005 level.

together *"jagged, broken curve"*. Moreover, the next pair *"descending leftward"* appears to conform more to a right-branching paradigm than the sequence *"leftward . . . descending"*. The decoding process in case 1B, therefore, may proceed when the chunk *"jagged, broken curve"* has been formed, in a cumulative way such that first "descending" and then "leftward" are attached to the already established semantic entity at each successive stage. The two hypothesized different decoding patterns may hence be depicted as follows:

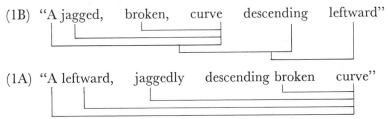

(1B) "A jagged,   broken,   curve   descending   leftward"

(1A) "A leftward,   jaggedly   descending broken   curve"

In case 1B, we have a major chunking of the first four words, of precisely the same type as the final (and only) chunking in case 1A. The last two words, however, are decoded separately and then attached, not to "curve" directly, but *to the chunk or word group of which "curve" constitutes an ingredient.*

This interpretation is in agreement with our previous discussion of decoding, i.e. that *chunking* and *decision concerning what has been said* are intimately related to the formation of word groups. It is also in agreement with Johnson's (1965) hypothesis that connections are apparently established, *not* between contiguous words as such but between semantic-syntactic entities irrespective of whether they are *words* or *word-groups*. This explains why form 1B shows so little *cohesion* as measured by the retention test: the focal word "curve", which is also given as the prompt word in the verbal recall task, is first of all part of the chunk *"jagged, broken curve"* and has actually no *direct* linkage to the subsequent *"descending leftward"*. The fact that the loss of these last two attributes is even more pronounced for the natural intonational variant than for the monotonous variant of 1B provides additional support for this view. A natural prosodic pattern will further enhance a separate grouping of *"jagged, broken curve"* and *". . . descending leftward"*. If the loss of the last two attributes is largely due to the particular pattern of decoding we have suggested above, it would therefore be greatest when the natural prosodic pattern is preserved.

Recent psycholinguistic enquiries into syntactic processes have, to a large extent, made use of tasks such as learning and recall of lists of entirely unrelated sentences.* A unique feature of such a sentence-

* This is the case in Mehler and Miller's study (1964) of syntactic transformations and see also Johnson's study (1965).

learning context is a detachment of the utterance from the message level of communication. The sentence is then no longer a linguistic tool, but an entity which, by virtue of the instructions from the experimenter, demands attention in its own right. As it is overlearned, attention is more and more focused upon otherwise subordinate aspects. This means, more specifically, that strategies of scanning for word order, etc. may be operant in the sentence-learning experiment which bear little resemblance at all to processes we encounter in non-experimental settings of comprehension and recall of linguistically mediated messages.

An important feature of the present study in comparison to many sentence-learning and -retention experiments is the *set for message reception*. This feature may perhaps partly explain why the violation of a normal prosodic pattern did not have significant overall effects: the subjects were already optimally geared toward comprehension and message reception. They knew that they would be asked to identify the items with respect to every attribute described. This optimal set on the part of the subjects and *the lack of difference* between two prosodic variants of form B, however, make the difference between forms 1A and 1B even more remarkable. In 1A, "*leftward*" and "*descending*" are linked to "*curve*" by *attribution*. In 1B, on the other hand, "*descending leftward*" is an *apposition*. In our study, we used pre-versus *post*-position in order to achieve the two types of linkages between modifiers and nouns. As Seiler (1960) has demonstrated, however, there are a variety of other means by which the same two types of linkages can be established. It remains to be seen, therefore, whether superior cohesiveness of *attribute + noun-groups* (as compared to *apposition + noun-groups*) holds when the two types of construction are achieved by means other than word order.

References

van Holk, A. (1962). Referential and attitudinal constructions. *Lingua* **11**, 181.

Johnson, N. F. (1965). The psychological reality of phrase structure rules. *J. verbal Learning verbal Behavior* **4**, 469–475.

Mehler, J. and Miller, G. A. (1964). Retroactive interference in the recall of simple sentences. *British J. Psychology* **55**, 295–301.

Miller, G. A. (1956). The magical number seven plus or minus two: some limits on our capacity for information processing. *Psychological Review* **63**, 81–97.

Miller, G. A. (1962a). Decision units in the perception of speech. *IRE Transformational Information Theory* IT–**8**, 81–83.

Miller, G. A. (1962b). Some psychological studies of grammar. *American Psychologist* **17**, 748–762.

Pollack, I. and Pickett, J. M. (1964). Intelligibility of excerpts from fluent speech: auditory versus structural context. *J. verbal Learning verbal Behavior* **3**, 79–84.

Reichling, A. (1935). "Het Woord." F. F. Berkhoūt, Nijmegen.

Reichling, A. (1961). Principles and methods of syntax: cryptanalytic formalism. *Lingua* **10**, 1–17

Reichling, A. (1963). Das problem der bedeutung in der sprachwissenschaft. *Innsbrucker Beitrage zur Kulturwissenschaft* Sonder 19, Innsbruck.

Seiler, H. (1960). "Relativsatz, Attribut und Apposition." Otto Harrassowitz, Wiesbaden.

Stenzel, J. (1934). "Philosophie der Sprache."

Uhlenbeck, E. M. (1962). De beginselen van het syntactisch onderzoek. *In* "Taalonderzoek van ouze tijd". pp. 18–37.

Uhlenbeck, E. M. (1963). An appraisal of transformational theory. *Lingua* **12**, 1–18.

Uhlenbeck, E. M. (1964). Betekenis en syntaxis. *Forum der Lettern*, pp. 67–82.

Uhlenbeck, E. M. (1966). Een begin van syntactische beschrijving. *De nieuwe taalgids* **59**, 291–301.

Yngve, V. H. (1960). A model and an hypothesis for language structure. *Proceedings American Philosophical Society* **104**, 444–466.

Yngve, V. H. (1964). Implications of mechanical translation research. *Proceedings American Philosophical Society* **108**, 275–281.

26. Context Effects and Coding Stations in Sentence Processing*

R. M. BLAKAR

The process of comprehending an utterance is influenced by the situational non-verbal context in which it is embedded, by what is said before, and by what is expected to be said and subsequently is said. Moreover, the sentence itself is made up of elements in such a way that one element is embedded in another (letters, words, phrases), and so that elements at the same level interact and influence each other (Rommetveit, 1968, 1971). This study explores such influences within a single sentence.

At certain points during the process of comprehension, the listener or reader seems able to decide what he has heard or read up to that point. Miller (1962) and Rommetveit (1968) label them coding stations, since they are critical points of time at which the receiver can decode rather safely and thus get the content or message. Using a technique developed by Rommetveit (1968), an attempt was made to locate such critical decision points and to get some ideas about what goes on at these points, in particular whether contextual influences are at work (Blakar, 1970).

Procedure

The subjects, serving in three separate groups, received a booklet of five pages (Group A) or only three of the pages: no. 1, 3, 5 (Group B), or 2, 4, 5 (Group C). The groups consisted respectively of six, five and five students of psychology assigned randomly. The five pages contained these typewritten texts (in Norwegian):

(1) En ele-ant
(2) En ele-ant herre -ikk

* Published in *Scandinavian J. Psychology* (1973) **14**, 103–105.

(3) En ele-ant herre -ikk til
(4) En ele-ant herre -ikk til oppdrag å le-e
(5) En ele-ant herre -ikk til oppdrag å le-e hele arrangementet

The completed sentence of page 5 could read in English: An elegant man got as task to lead the whole arrangement.

The subjects were told that each page would give a sentence or part of a sentence, but that there would be typing errors indicated by a dash (—). Their task was to correct each error by inserting one letter only for each dash, and then to complete the sentence.

Results

The corrections of all the typing errors in the different contexts are given in Table I. Take as an example the corrections of the typing error *-ikk*. In the context *En ele-ant herre -ikk* (p. 2), six subjects corrected to *g* (*gikk*/went) and five to *f* (*fikk*/got), with no other letters proposed.

TABLE I. Type and number of corrections of errors in five different contexts (pages 1–5).

Page in booklet	Subjects per page	Groups	Typing error (—)		
			ele-ant	*-ikk*	*le-e*
1	11	A, B	elegant (4) elefant (7)		
2	11	A, C	elegant (11)	fikk (5) gikk (6)	
3	11	A, B	elegant (9) elefant (2)	fikk (1) gikk (10)	
4	11	A, C	elegant (11)	fikk (11)	lede (3) lese (4) leve (3) levere (1)[a]
5	16	A, B, C	elegant (14) elefant (2)	fikk (16)	lede (16)

[a] This subject actually violated the instructions by inserting more than one letter.

In the context *En ele-ant herre -ikk til* (p. 3), 10 subjects corrected to *g* (*gikk*/went), and one to *f* (*fikk*/got). On page 4 with *En ele-ant herre -ikk til oppdrag å le-e*, all 11 subjects correcting this page inserted *f* (*fikk*/got). And when the whole sentence (p. 5) was given as context, all 16 subjects inserted *f* (*fikk*/got).

Interpretations and Discussion

Context Effects

From the corrections it may be inferred how the subject, from the context available at each point, interpreted the missing "letter". In discussing the different aspects of context effects revealed in the results, the corrections of *-ikk* serves again as an example.

First of all it can be seen that the corrections are influenced by far wider contexts than the sequence of letters of which the missing "letter" itself is a part. More interesting, however, is the finding that extending the context perceived does not represent a passive enlargement, but an active process, where every new part being included in the context seems to influence the element focused upon. Thus, there was a high degree of uncertainty of choice between f and g in the context given on page 2. When the context was extended with *til* (as) only (p. 3), this uncertainty nearly disappeared, 10 of 11 subjects deciding upon g. When the context was extended further, however, all the subjects decided upon f. That the mere preposition *til* (as) influenced the f/g rivalry in quite another way than *til oppdrag* (as task), demonstrates how subtle the active interaction may be between different elements within a sentence. (One subject's explanation of his correction actually points to such interaction: "Since it is an elegant man and not merely a man, it is more plausible that he goes there or there rather than that he gets so or so.")—As a point of clarity for the reader who does not know Norwegian, the Norwegian preposition *til* sometimes has to be translated "as", as in "got as task", and sometimes "to", as in "went to town".

The active re-structuring reflected in the corrections of this error, demonstrates how the post-context also influences the decoding of what has come before (Lashley, 1951). It can be seen, moreover, that language comprehension is an ever back-and-forward-going process; the context prior to the element processed (at the moment) creates particular expectations about what comes next, and subsequent context gives corrections backward about interpretations that might have seemed reasonable at earlier points of time.

Extending the context usually seems to help the receiver to decode adequately. Two subjects, however, went on making "a wrong correction" even when it resulted in a crazy sentence (their corrections of *ele-ant*). This shows how the context may fix an interpretation of an element in such a rigid way that a re-interpretation may be very difficult, even when the extended context falsifies that earlier interpretation. Both subjects reported afterwards that they had found *En elefant herre* (An elefant man) crazy or amusing. They had been unable,

however, to get any other meaningful word than *elefant* (elefant) out of
ele-ant (cf. Luchins and Luchins, 1950).

In analysing the context effects reflected in the corrections of the
typing error *-ikk*, it was pointed out that an uncertainty existed as to
the choice between *f* and *g* in the context given on page 2. In fact, the
subject may have been uncertain about the meaning of the phrase or
sentence as a whole. Such an uncertainty may be reflected, however,
in his difficulty of choosing between *fikk* (got) and *gikk* (went) on the
word level, and between *f* and *g* on the letter level, thus illustrating
how a complex verbal unit such as a sentence is made up of elements
within elements on different levels (cf. Rommetveit, 1968, 1971).

Coding Stations

At some of the coding points introduced artificially by the booklet, the
subjects seemed to be able to decode adequately as regards the sentence
as a whole, at others not. When forced to correct *-ikk* between *-ikk* and
til (p. 2), almost total uncertainty between *g* and *f* seems to have pre-
vailed. This point, therefore, is obviously an inadequate point for
decoding. The subject has to postpone decoding until he has more
(sufficient) relevant context. Between *til* (as) and *oppdrag* (task) on p. 3,
he seems to have sufficient cues for choosing; the conclusion, however,
being inadequate as regards what follows. Given *-ikk til oppdrag*, even
though it is not known what "The elegant man" mentioned in the
sentence is going to (*le-e* may give these Norwegian verbs: *lede*/lead,
leke/play, *lene*/lean, *lese*/read, *lete*/seek, and *leve*/live), everybody decides
upon *f* (*fikk*/got). After *oppdrag* (task) the subject seems to have sufficient
relevant context to decide about this particular error.

Three different types of coding point appear to be exemplified by
the experiment: (a) Coding points where the lack of context results in
almost total uncertainty in choosing between two or more divergent
interpretations. (b) Coding points where no or little uncertainty seems
to exist, but where the decoding or interpretation is inadequate or
misleading as regards what follows. (c) Coding points where no or
little uncertainty seems to exist, and where the decoding is adequate as
regards what follows.—The difference between inadequate (a and b)
and adequate (c) coding stations seems, therefore, to be the varying
access they allow to relevant contexts. Coding stations may be said,
therefore, to be critical points of time at which the receiver's decisions
regarding contextual influences are reflected.

The experimental technique used is a very artificial one, and the
analysis does not imply that the process of comprehending utterances
under more natural conditions goes on like this ("--" may represent
noise): When the listener has heard *En elegant herre -ikk*, he says to

himself that "It may be f ($fikk$) or g ($gikk$), I don't know". Then he hears *til* and decides that it must have been g. But then he hears *oppdrag*, and he gets the "aha-experience" that it was not g but f. In natural communication, of course, the listener postpones decoding until he has heard the whole sentence; or may be, depending on the length and complexity of the sentence (Yngve, 1960) and the capacity of his short-term memory (Miller, 1956), he decodes at adequate coding stations within the sentence, such as after *-ikk til oppdrag*. It should also be noted, however, that splitting up a sentence—as was done in the booklet—may detect many potential context effects, of which only a few may occur under natural conditions.

References

Blakar, R. M. (1970). Konteksteffektar i språkleg kommunikasjon. Unpublished thesis, University of Oslo.

Lashley, K. S. (1951). The problem of serial order in behavior. *In* "Cerebral mechanisms in behavior". (L. A. Jeffress, Ed.) pp. 112–136. John Wiley and Sons, New York.

Luchins, A. S. and Luchins, E. H. (1950). New experimental attempts at preventing mechanization in problem solving. *J. general Psychology* **42**, 279–297.

Miller, G. A. (1956). The magical number seven plus or minus two: Some limits on our capacity for information processing. *Psychological Review* **63**, 81–97.

Miller, G. A. (1962). Some psychological studies of grammar. *American Psychologist* **17**, 748–762.

Rommetveit, R. (1968). "Words, meanings and messages." Academic Press and Universitetsforlaget, London, New York and Oslo.

Rommetveit, R. (1971). On concepts of hierarchical structures and micro-analysis of language and thought. *In* "Hierarchical models in the study of cognition". (G. Eckblad, Ed.) pp. 34–46, 64–77. Unpublished compendium, Department of Psychology, University of Bergen.

Yngve, V. H. (1960). A model and a hypothesis for language structure. *Proceedings American Philosophical Society* **104**, 444–446.

27. Word Order, Message Structure and Recall*

A. H. WOLD

Introduction

All events—also language events—take place in real time and have thus *a temporal dimension*. This is an obvious fact, but nevertheless one that has not received due attention in recent studies of language. Definite symptoms of detemporalization may be found in studies of language and psycholinguistics influenced by Chomsky (Rommetveit, 1974; Wold, 1978).

One set of problems that necessarily attracts attention when the dimension of time is given consideration, are problems concerning *temporal sequence of information*. Why is one specific sequence chosen by the sender, and how do alternative sequences affect the receiver? In what follows, the latter part of the question will be explored.

In this short article, the many ramifications of these issues can only be suggested, however. A rough outline of a theoretical frame within which the problem may be discussed, will first be presented. Some experiments exploring effects of variations in word order will then be sketched. In order to account for the experimental results, the concept of *message structure* has been found useful, and this concept will therefore be introduced towards the end of this presentation.

The theoretical position adopted, as well as the experiments, are spelled out in a much more thorough fashion in my book "Decoding Oral Language" (1978), and the interested reader is referred to this book for more information.

* This paper was prepared for this book.

An Outline of a Theoretical Frame

It is in the opinion of this author that a proper understanding of language requires both a *social-psychological* and an *individual-processing* perspective. Language is primarily used for communication, and it is necessary to understand how it is used as a mean to make something shared between sender and receiver. An explicit social-psychological approach to language is adopted by Rommetveit (1972a, b, c, 1974) and my work is clearly influenced by his discussions of language.

The aim of communication serves to *constrain* and *direct* language processing. The information has nevertheless to be processed by individuals, and language processing is thus also influenced by capacity limitations on the part of the individual as well as by more specific individual strategies.

In this short article, however, one of the perspectives—the social-psychological one—is given priority. The individual processing perspective should be added to complete the picture. In Wold (1978) the latter perspective is pursued with particular emphasis upon *memory processes*. The concept of "depth or levels of processing" (Craik and Lockhart, 1972; Craik, 1973) is central in that discussion. Issues concerning language on the one hand and issues concerning memory on the other have earlier been discussed with rather few attempts towards cross-references (Fillenbaum, 1971, 1973). To pursue the relationship between "depth of processing" and language processing represents one possible approach to a simultaneous focus on both areas.

The generality and importance of *the dimension of time* was stated rather programmatically in the introduction. The structure of language is to a great extent given in temporal patterns because of the primary oral character of natural language. Such a fact emphasizes the necessity to take temporality into consideration when language and communication are considered. One consequence of this position is an attempt to focus on language *processing* as such rather than on the *output* of processing.

This may at first glance appear as a consequence derived primarily from the individual processing point of view. A focus on the dimension of time also has a more clear social-psychological implication, however, in that attention is geared toward the more abstract sequence in which what is initially intersubjectively shared becomes expanded and/or modified. The concept of message structure to be introduced later copes precisely with this latter aspect of temporality.

The importance attributed to the dimension of time also clearly reflects the conception of word meaning adopted. The meaning of a word is in this article conceived of as *open* and susceptible to contextual modifications. It is also *dynamic* in the sense of being only *partially determined* and therefore susceptible to still further modification or enrichment as more information is presented. Since what is said *now* is influenced by what was said *earlier* and may also possibly be modified by what is *still to come*, attention must be paid to the time dimension.

The conception of word meaning suggested here is at variance with the predominant conceptions in the Chomskian tradition where word meaning is conceived of as much more fixed or invariable. Such conceptions seem logically to justify less concern with the dimension of time and constitute part of the detemporalization characterizing their approach to language.

Experiments

The experiments were performed to explore how different sequences of information affects the receiver. Descriptions like the following were used as stimulus material:

(I) A SECRETARY WHO IS SEVERE, COOL, EXTRAORDINARY, BEAUTIFUL, PLEASANT

(II) A SECRETARY WHO IS PLEASANT, BEAUTIFUL, EXTRAORDINARY, COOL, SEVERE

(III) A SEVERE, COOL, EXTRAORDINARY, BEAUTIFUL, PLEASANT SECRETARY

(IV) A PLEASANT, BEAUTIFUL, EXTRAORDINARY, COOL, SEVERE SECRETARY

The same noun and adjectives are used in descriptions I, II, III and IV. What varies is the sequence in which this information is presented. The main variation concerns the position of the noun. The noun is presented before the qualifying adjectives in forms I and II. In forms III and IV, on the other hand, the presentation of the noun is postponed until every adjective is given.

The position of the noun is supposed to influence the decoding process. Forms with noun first (I and II) may be said to allow for a cumulative strategy in which every successive adjective is decoded immediately so as to yield a modified impression of the secretary at each successive stage. This means, for example, that as soon as SEVERE is heard, the latter may immediately be decoded and serve to modify the impression generated by SECRETARY.

Forms with a noun at the end (III and IV), on the other hand, make for a postponement of decoding of adjectives. This is the case because what is made known by each adjective remains largely undetermined until it is known what sort of entity it describes. When only A SEVERE, COOL . . . is heard, it is impossible for the listener to know what is referred to. It might as well be, e.g. the weather or some style of architecture as a person. The meaning of SEVERE and COOL will be somewhat different in the three cases, and final decoding of adjectives has therefore to be postponed until the noun is heard.

The reversal of the sequence of adjectives connects these experiments to the impression formation tradition. Explorations of effects of alternative order of information have been a main and recurrent theme within this tradition (e.g. Asch, 1946; Anderson and Barrios, 1961; Anderson and Hubert, 1963; Luchins, 1966a, b; Anderson, 1968; Margulis et al., 1971). The implications of the present experiments for impression formation will not be spelled out here, however. The interested reader is once more referred to Wold (1978).

The experiments were performed with groups of students serving as subjects. Each group heard six descriptions of either form I–II–III or IV. Their tasks were to form impressions of the things described and also to try to remember the descriptions presented. The impression formation ratings were to be given immediately after each description was heard, while the recall task was postponed until every one of the six descriptions were presented. The more exact procedure varied between different sets of experiment. Intentional as well as incidental recall were tried out, and both adjectives and nouns functioned as prompt words. In what follows only the most outstanding result from the recall tasks is given consideration, whereas performance on the impression formation task is not discussed at all.

When the noun is used as prompt word, the adjectives from descriptions with noun first are recalled about twice as well as adjectives from descriptions with the noun at the end. This result is supported by results from a modified replication performed in Belgium with soldiers with low educational background as subjects (Jaspars et al., 1971) and also by the results from the experiments by Katagiri (1969) and Skjerve (1971). This difference in recall-performance implies that *the change in the temporal ordering of information makes for different decoding strategies.*

Message Structure

The difference between descriptions has been spelled out as that between descriptions presenting *the noun* ahead of a series of *adjectives* as compared to those presenting *the adjectives* first and *the noun* at the end. The experimental results seem thus to show the superiority of the *Noun-Adjective* sequence over the *Adjective-Noun* sequence. These results raise one important question. Are the experimental results due to specific psychological characteristics of *noun* and *adjectives* or should they be explained by *the functional relationship* between these word groups in the present descriptions? The latter alternative seems the most reasonable one to this author.

The noun and the adjectives within the description might be considered instances of what has been called *free* and *bound* information respectively (Rommetveit, 1972c, 1974). The superiority of recall in descriptions with noun first might thus tentatively be considered as one example of a more general rule stating the superiority of pre-position of free information. Findings from an experiment using sentences as stimulus material performed by this author (Wold, 1978) support such a view. The results of an experiment by Bransford and Johnson (1973) may also be explained within the same theoretical frame.

But what is actually meant by the concept of free and bound information? Only a very brief explanation can be offered here. Some few comments on the more inclusive notion of message structure will also be included. For an expanded discussion the reader should consult Rommetveit (1974) and Wold (1978).

The concepts of free and bound information are primarily to be understood within the framework of *language use*. They apply to communication, to the sending and receiving of messages, and to *prerequisites for making something known to another person*. These concepts are, furthermore, based upon the assumption that different parts of an utterance function in different ways. *The free information* may be defined as that part of the entire information which provides the background, or the necessary information for processing of other parts. The other parts, then, convey *bound information*. In our descriptions, therefore, the noun (for example: SECRETARY) serves as free information. Thus, what is conveyed by SEVERE cannot be fully determined unless it is taken for granted that a secretary is being described.

Free and bound information are to be understood as rather general concepts. They pertain to different kinds of information, non-verbal as well as verbal, and are of a relative character. Information which at one point functions as bound information may later on, as communication procedes, come to constitute part of the common background information—the free information.

The specific *pattern* of free and bound information has been called *message structure* by Rommetveit. One force of this concept is that it seems to capture the abstract temporal aspect of communication—the sequence in which what is initially intersubjectively shared becomes expanded and/or modified. This aspect, as well as the more concrete sequencing of elements of information, have to be taken into account when we try to understand language in actual communication settings and with due attention towards the dimension of time.

References

Anderson, N. H. (1968). Application of a linear-serial model to a personality-impression task using serial presentation. *J. Personality Social Psychology* **10**, 354–362.

Anderson, N. H. and Barrios, A. A. (1961). Primacy effects in personality impression formation. *J. Abnormal Social Psychology* **63**, 346–350.

Anderson, N. H. and Hubert, S. (1963). Effects of concomitant verbal recall on order effects in personality impression formation. *J. verbal Learning verbal Behavior* **2**, 379–391.

Asch, S. E. (1946). Forming impression of personality. *J. Abnormal Social Psychology* **41**, 258–290.

Bransford, I. D. and Johnson, M. K. (1973). Considerations of some problems of comprehension. *In* "Visual information processing". (W. G. Chase, Ed.) pp. 383–438. Academic Press, New York and London.

Craik, F. I. M. (1973). A "levels of analysis" view of memory. *In* "Communication and affect. Language and thought". (P. Pliner, L. Kramer and T. Alloway, Eds) pp. 45–65. Academic Press, New York and London.

Craik, F. I. M. and Lockhart, R. S. (1972). Levels of processing: A framework for memory research. *J. verbal Learning verbal Behavior* **11**, 671–684.

Fillenbaum, S. (1971). Psycholinguistics. *Annual Review Psychology* **22**, 251–308.

Fillenbaum, S. (1973). "Syntactic factors in memory?" Mouton, The Hague.

Jaspars, J., Rommetveit, R., Cook, M., Havelka, N., Henry, P., Herkner, W., Pêcheux, M. and Peeters, G. (1971). Order effects in impression formation: A psycholinguistic approach. *In* "Social Context of Messages". (E. A. Carswell and R. Rommetveit, Eds) pp. 109–125. Academic Press, London and New York.

Katagiri, A. (1969). Decoding strategies and linguistic form: verbal learning applications. Unpublished manuscript, University of California.

Luchins, A. S. (1966a). Primacy-recency in impression formation. *In* "The order of presentation in persuasion". (C. I. Hovland, Ed.) 3rd edn, pp. 33–61. Yale University Press, New Haven, and London.

Luchins, A. S. (1966b). Experimental attempts to minimize the impact of first impressions. *In* "The order of presentation in persuasion". (C. I. Hovland, Ed.) 3rd edn, pp. 62–75, Yale University Press, New Haven and London.

Margulis, S. T., Costanzo, P. R. and Klein, A. C. (1971). Impression change and favorableness of first impressions: A study of population and of commitment effects. *Psychonomic Science* **22**, 318–320.

Rommetveit, R. (1972a). Language games, deep syntactic structures, and hermeneutic circles. *In* "The context of social psychology: A critical assessment". (J. Israel and H. Tajfel, Eds) pp. 212–252. Academic Press, London and New York.

Rommetveit, R. (1972b). Deep structure of sentences versus message structure. Some critical remarks on current paradigms, and suggestions of an alternative approach. *Norwegian J. Linguistic* **26**, 3–22.

Rommetveit, R. (1972c). "Språk, tanke og kommunikasjon. Ei innføring i språkpsykologi og psykolingvistikk." Universitetsforlaget, Oslo.

Rommetveit, R. (1974). "On message structure. A framework for the study of language and communication." John Wiley and Sons, London.

Skjerve, J. (1971). Word sequence and recall. In "Social contexts of messages". (E. A. Carswell and R. Rommetveit, Eds) pp. 139–142. Academic Press, London and New York.

H. Wold, A. (1978). "Decoding Oral Language." Academic Press, London and New York.

28. Utterances *in vacuo* and in Contexts

An experimental and theoretical exploration of some interrelationships between what is heard and what is seen or imagined *

R. M. BLAKAR and R. ROMMETVEIT

Theoretical Background

Psycholinguistic research inspired by Chomsky's provoking and penetrating analyses of language structure has been characterized by a firm decision to find out what language IS before exploring questions of PURPOSE AND USE. Chomsky claims (1968, p. 62): "If we hope to understand human language and the psychological capacities on which it rests, we must first ask what it is, not how or for what purposes it is used". Psychologists sharing such a hope have thus adopted a traditionally linguistic research strategy of examining utterances *in vacuo*, assuming that models of linguistic performance as INDIVIDUAL INFORMATION PROCESSING which emerge from such studies can later on be expanded to account for language processing embedded in complex HUMAN COMMUNICATION. They thereby seem to endorse a widely shared view, to which Moscovici (1972, p. 61) has strongly objected, that ". . . social behaviour is . . . considered in the same way as any other kind of behaviour, the only difference being that social behaviour is supposed to include superimposed social characteristics". Such a view implies that language behaviour in principle can be explained—even though possibly only in a very remote future—by adding auxiliary theorems to a general model of individual linguistic competence.

No knowledge of linguistic competence, however, can be assessed

* This study is part of a research programme supported by the Norwegian Research Council for Science and the Humanities. Gunn Skartland assisted in conducting the experiment. The final report was prepared while R. Rommetveit was a fellow at Netherlands Institute for Advanced Study in the Humanities and Social Sciences 1972–73. Published in *International J. Psycholinguistics* (1975) **4**, 5–32.

without resort to some form of language use. Consider the case of the
UTTERANCE *IN VACUO,* i.e. all psycholinguistic studies of perception,
comprehension and recall of unrelated written or tape-recorded sentences. The setting in such experiments resembles in certain important
respects the peculiar situation of the virgin Mary when she was given a
message from God about the miracle that was going to take place.
Comprehending what was said without being able to decode the
message it conveyed, she "preserved the words in her heart". The
words were thus comprehended and stored as MESSAGE POTENTIAL(S) in
the hope that future events might provide a context for decoding what
God had intended to make known.

A subject encountering an utterance *in vacuo* is in a similar situation.
The psycholinguist who has dreamt up the utterance has no intention
of making anything known to the subject at all. Language use is hence
completely detached from message transmission. The subject, of course,
knows the game; if he is a good subject, he will try to comprehend what
is said or written and preserve the words in his mind in expectation of a
request for reproduction. In this respect, his language use resembles that
of an uninformed liaison person who, himself deprived of every contextual clue as to what is being made known, is requested to reproduce
what he has heard to somebody else. In order to do so, he may resort
to particular strategies that are hardly ever adopted under other conditions of language use. He may succeed by ROTE LEARNING, or he may
try to INVENT SOME PLAUSIBLE CONTEXTUAL BACKGROUND for what he
hears. On other occasions he may deliberately try to decode what he
heard IN TERMS OF AN ABSTRACT COGNITIVE REPRESENTATION OF SOME
ENTIRELY AUTONOMOUS EVENT OR COMPOSITE STATE OF AFFAIRS, and thus
provide the psycholinguist with evidence for the psychological reality
of AUTONOMOUS DEEP SENTENCE STRUCTURES.

It has been argued that such research on utterances *in vacuo* has
developed a theory of linguistic competence in which language is
stripped of its essential social and temporal aspects. A radical reorientation has been proposed by Rommetveit (1972a, b, c). The main focus
within this alternative approach is upon the utterance as embedded in
an ACT OF COMMUNICATION, and problems concerning LANGUAGE AND
CONTEXT (Slama-Cazacu, 1961) are hence considered to be of central
theoretical significance. Encoding and decoding are considered complementary activities, within such a framework, and our aim is to explore
what language IS when it is USED FOR THE PURPOSE OF MAKING SOMETHING
KNOWN. The act of speech implies tacit contracts between speaker and
listener which deal with a temporally shared social world. What is made
known can only expand the domain of such a shared social world if it is
nested onto what is already assumed, by the speaker and listener, to be
the case. Any particular utterance in its specific context can in principle

be analysed as a complex equation, containing ENTITIES THAT ARE UNKNOWN TO THE LISTENER PRIOR TO THE ACT OF SPEECH as well as presumably SHARED KNOWLEDGE which allows for identification of those novel entities. Its MESSAGE STRUCTURE can be explored as the formula for its solution, i.e. as a particular pattern of nesting novel information onto whatever is assumed to be the case by both participants at any particular phase of the communication act.

Previous exploratory studies have shown how decoding and recall are affected by discrepancies between message structure and temporal organization. Wold (1971), examining recall of utterances *in vacuo*, varied word order in lists of descriptions, each description consisting of one noun and five adjectives. Different temporal organizations were examined, e.g.

(1A) *A secretary who is severe, cool, extraordinary, beautiful, pleasant,*
     versus
(1B) *A severe, cool, extraordinary, beautiful, pleasant secretary.*

Final decoding of adjectives is in such a case nested to decoding of the noun, i.e. what is made known by *severe* cannot be fully identified until the listener knows whether severeness is being attributed to some climate, an act of legislation, or some person, for example. Twice as much was recalled under conditions of word order type A, with correspondence between temporal organization and message structure. Similar though less striking results were also obtained in an impression formation experiment by Jaspars *et al.* (1971) and by Wold in a second study (referred to in Rommetveit, 1972a). She examined recall of adjectives inserted in full sentences under systematic variation of temporal organization, such as the following:

(2A) *That the examinations went well, was pleasant, noteworthy, and encouraging,*
     versus
(2B) *It was pleasant, noteworthy, and encouraging that the examinations went well.*

Attempts have also been made to assess message structure across extralinguistically mediated and verbal components of communication. Rommetveit *et al.* (1971) conducted an experiment in which pictures were presented as ready signals for the utterances to be recalled. The relationships between the picture and utterance were of two kinds. Half of them resembled:

(3A) Picture of hand knocking at a door, followed by: *"It is a pity she was not at home"*.

The other half were similar to:

(3B) Picture of a large and derelict house, followed by: "*There was not enough gain from the production*".

The picture portrayed in each case aspects of a plausible extralinguistic condition for uttering what immediately followed. The first type of linkage, however, resembles the pattern of intralinguistic nesting in (1A) and (2A): what is seen provides a contextual background for what is subsequently heard. The second type of linkage, however, represents a case of discrepancy between message structure and temporal organization similar to those of (1B) and (2B): the picture as such does not allow for any unequivocal identification of the house with respect to its function or use. What is said makes sense if and only if the house is experienced as a factory or an industrial building of some sort. What is heard imposes particular contraints upon the listener's categorization of what he saw IMMEDIATELY BEFORE the utterance.

Recall was in the latter experiment assessed by various methods. Retrieval under conditions in which the utterances had been experienced in meaningful pictorial contexts was compared with performance under identical experimental conditions except for the fact that those meaningful pictorial contexts were replaced by pictures of arbitrary geometrical forms. This comparison showed that Type 3A pictures, which portrayed aspects of plausible extralinguistic conditions and which in some way served to constrain what was constrained verbally, had a particularly strong effect by facilitating recall.

The experiment discussed in this paper aims at a further exploration of message structure across extralinguistically mediated and verbal components of communication. Our basis is once more the EXAMINATION OF THE UTTERANCE *IN VACUO*, i.e. of comprehension and recall under conditions when unrelated utterances are listened to with the explicit goal of being able to reproduce them at a later time. This general condition of use will be materialized in three different versions. In a baseline condition, each utterance will be heard only once, and geometrical forms will serve as ready signals; in the second condition, such arbitrary signals will be replaced by meaningful pictorial contexts; in the third condition, the same set of utterances will be employed in a rote leaning task.

The three conditions will be compared with respect to recall and mode of organization of what was heard. We shall compare alternative means of facilitating retention, means such as REPEATED EXPOSURE TO THE UTTERANCE *IN VACUO* as opposed to ADDING A MEANINGFUL PICTORIAL CONTEXT. In addition, we shall hopefully collect some evidence bearing upon the more general and complex issue of WHAT LANGUAGE IS under different CONDITIONS OF USE. The condition in which meaningful pictorial contexts serve as ready signals may actually be conceived of as A CARTOON MOVIE SIMULATION OF NATURAL COMMUNICATION SETTINGS. The listener's situation resembles that of a witness who, having been explicitly asked in advance to report what he hears, overhears a fragment of discourse in a real life situation. Something is then MADE KNOWN to him by the utterance in the sense that comprehension implies expansion and/or modification of whatever cognitive representation of that situation he had beforehand. The utterance conveys no message addressed directly TO THE EXPERIMENTAL SUBJECT. Its message structure is nevertheless partly revealed to him via its linkage to the visually portrayed extralinguistic condition for uttering it.

The utterance *in vacuo*, being devoid of such a message structure, mediates only some MESSAGE POTENTIAL. The experimenter's request for subsequent reproduction may induce a medium-bound strategy of comprehension and retention; while listening to the utterance *in vacuo*, the subject can do no more than try to comprehend and "preserve the words". Nothing more is made known by repeating the utterance. Repeated exposure with no opportunity for cognitive afterwork serve only to further enhance such a medium-bound strategy. If, on the other hand, something is MADE KNOWN by the utterance when experienced in a meaningful pictorial context, OR in a contextual frame dreamt up by the subject himself, decoding must by definition imply some emancipation of that "something" from the particular linguistic medium by which it is made known. The context thus allows for a shift of intention from medium to message, i.e. language use on the part of the listener will resemble use in real life situations where he quite frequently recalls WHAT was made known without being able to remember HOW it was said. In view of what has been maintained about the difference between message transmission and reproduction of some message potential, we shall hence expect qualitatively different performances in response to identical requests for retrieval in the three conditions. Since the latter actually represents experimentally induced variations of "how and for what purposes" language is used, we shall try to explore some researchable aspects of the extremely intriguing issue of essence and use.

The Experiment

Stimulus Material

The experiment was conducted at the University of Oslo, where students from introductory psychology classes served as subjects. Two separate sets of utterances were employed, sets A and B (see Table I). The eight utterances within set A were modified Norwegian translations of the Dutch utterances used in a similar study done at the University of Louvain (see Rommetveit *et al.*, 1971, p. 39); the pictorial contexts were also adopted from the Louvain study. Context and utterance were supposed to be linked so as to preserve congruence between temporal order and message structure in half of the cases (IIA, IIIA, VA and VIIIA). In the other half of the cases (IA, IVA, VIA and VIIA), the linkage was supposed to cause a discrepancy between the two factors. This distinction has previously been referred to as PRESUPPOSITION versus IMPLICATION (Rommetveit *et al.*, 1971; Blakar and Rommetveit 1971).

Another set of eight Norwegian utterances was constructed in such a way that they could be meaningfully related to pictures in this same set. Each picture served as a ready signal for two separate utterances, one from set A and the other from set B. If it served as a contextual background for what was made known by the utterance from set A, however, its linkage to the utterance from set B should be such that the latter should serve mainly as a means for deciding what was made known by the picture, and vice versa. For set B, congruency between temporal order and message structure was thus our aim for combinations IB, IVB, VIB and VIIB, whereas combinations IIB, IIIB, VB and VIIIB were supposed to represent cases of discrepancy. The very same eight SENTENCE BEGINNINGS (indicated by [/] for each sentence in Table I) were employed in both sets of utterances. As far as essential semantic aspects are concerned, these eight beginnings can in fact be reduced to only four, since THEY ARE PAIRWISE SYNONYMOUS. What is encoded in the first part of the utterance is INSUFFICIENCY (*insufficient* in IA and VB; *not enough* in VIA and IIB); REGRET (*pity* in VA and IB; *shame* in IIA and VIB); PROBABILITY (probably in IIIA and VIIB; *very likely* in VIIIA and IVB); and FREQUENCY (*all the time* in IVA and IIIB; *always* in VIIA and VIIIB).

Design and Procedures

The two different sets of utterances were employed in recall tasks identical to those of the Louvain study: The subject was simply asked to listen to the sets carefully and try to reproduce each of them immediately afterwards as accurately as possible. The whole sequence of eight utterances was presented using a tape-recorder which was synchronized with an automatic slide projector. A slide was projected on a screen in front of the subject for 4 s as the signal for attention, informing the subject that the next utterance would follow immediately. The interval between ready signals was kept constant at 8 s. The order of presentation is shown in Table I.

In one condition, the ready signals were the drawings described in Table I, in another condition they were randomly chosen drawings of geometrical forms (a triangle, a square, etc.). The instructions for

TABLE I. Stimulus material: Pictorial context (roman numeral) and corresponding set A and set B utterance with the content clue (CC) used to prompt retrieval.

I: *Drawing of a withering plant.*
(A) "There were insufficient / water and heat". ("Det var ikke tilstrekkelig / vann og varme") CC: "moisture" ("væske")
(B) "It was a pity / that it was not decorating as it was before". ("Det var leit / at den ikke pyntet opp som før".) CC: "previously" ("tidligere")

II: *Drawing of a train leaving a station.*
(A) "It was a shame / that she did not get there in time with the letter". ("Det var trist / at hun ikke kom tidsnok med brevet".) CC: "too late" ("for sent")
(B) "There were not enough / concessions for electric power". ("Det var ikke nok / bevilgninger til elektrisk drift".) CC: "grants" ("løyvinger")

III: *Drawing of a luxurious car.*
(A) "Probably / he will have problems with the installments". ("Antakeligvis / vil han ha problemer med avdragene".) CC: "the payments" ("nedbetalingen")
(B) "All the time / the consumers want new models". ("Ustanselig / vil det kjøpende publikum ha nye modeller".) CC: "the customers" ("kundene")

IV: *Drawing of a table with a candle, a book and a glass on it.*
(A) "All the time / there are breakdowns in the electricity". ("Ustanselig / er det kluss med elektisitetsforsyningen".) CC: Literally translated: "conduction of the (electric) current" ("strømtilførsel")
(B) "Very likely / she will be having a nice time without company". ("Etter alt å dømme / skal hun hygge seg uten selskap".) CC: "alone" ("alene")

V: *Drawing of a hand knocking at a door.*
(A) "It was a pity / that she was not at home that morning". ("Det var leit / at hun ikke var hjemme den formiddagen".) CC: "away" ("borte")
(B) "There were (an) insufficient / (number of) telephones in that area". ("Det var ikke tilstrekkelig / telefonapparater i det strøket".) CC: "the district" ("distriktet")

VI: *Drawing of a tumbledown building.*
(A) "There was not enough / profit from the production". ("Der var ikke nok / utbytte av driften".) CC: "gain" ("avkastning")
(B) "It was a shame / that the repair work had not been started" ("Det var trist / at reparasjonen ikke ble satt igang".) CC: "the restoration" ("istandsettingen")

VII: *Drawing of a man knocking in a ceiling with a stick.*
(A) "Always / there is somebody making noise upstairs". ("Uavlatelig / er det noen som lager støy ovenpå".) CC: "bustling" ("bråker")
(B) "Probably / it will become quiet upstairs". ("Antakeligvis / blir det stille ovenpå".) CC: "calm" ("rolig")

VIII: *Drawing of a man with a fishing rod.*
(A) "Very likely / the line will break". ("Etter alt å dømme / kommer snøret til å gå i stykker".) CC: "be torn" ("slites")
(B) "Always / some people get fed up with city life". ("Uavlatelig / blir enkelte lei bylivet".) CC: "tired of" ("trett av").

---

listening and retrieval were tape-recorded and identical for both sets of utterances and both types of ready signals. Retrieval was assessed after all eight utterances had been heard and two different prompting methods had been employed. Half of all subjects in each condition were given the sentence beginnings at random and were asked to complete them. This subcondition will be referred to as SENTENCE COMPLETION (SC). The other half were given the content clues in Table I one by one, also in random order. The latter subcondition will be referred to as retrieval by CONTENT CLUE (CC). In the conditions where pictorial contexts had served as ready signals, an additional recall task was performed after retrieval of what had been heard. Each utterance was then presented in written form, and the subject was asked to describe, in as much detail and with as much accuracy as possible, what he had seen on the screen immediately before he heard that utterance.

For utterance set A, a rote learning task was conducted as well. The eight utterances were again heard from tape, each of them five times in a row, at intervals of 3 s during which the subject repeated the utterance aloud. When every utterance had been heard AND repeated by the subject five times, recall was tested. Retrieval for half of the subjects was then prompted by sentence beginnings (SC), for the other half by content clues (CC). Order of retrieval for the rote condition, however, was the same as that of presentation.

The complete design was as outlined in Table II. Five male and five female students were assigned to each of the ten subconditions. Six of the combination possibilities were left unexplored, however, and subsequent analysis of data will be restricted so as to provide answers to only a few important questions. The design allows, first of all, for an analysis of variance of retrieval performances strictly analogous to that of the Louvain study. Disregarding the rote learning condition for the moment, we can examine whether systematic variations with respect to recall can be attributed to the NATURE OF THE READY SIGNALS (meaningful pictorial contexts, P; versus vacuous signals, V), to the RETRIEVAL METHOD (SC versus CC) or, within the pictorial context condition, to the TWO TYPES OF PICTURE-UTTERANCE LINKAGE (picture "background" for each utterance versus the reverse relationship). Such an analysis of variance can be performed separately for set A (the two first columns in Table II) and for set B (the fifth and sixth columns in Table II).

For set A, moreover, comparisons can be made among the following: retrieval after one exposure of each utterance in a pictorial context (P), after one exposure of each utterance *in vacuo* (V), and after five exposures AND repetitions in a rote learning situation (R). Qualitative differences between conditions should be particularly transparent in SEMANTICALLY APPROPRIATE MISMATCHES of sentence beginnings and

TABLE II. Experimental design and distribution of subjects across subconditions.

Utterances		Set A				Set B			
No. of exposures		One		Five (+five)		One		Five (+five)	
Retrieval		SC	CC	SC	CC	SC	CC	SC	CC
Setting	Pictorial context	10	10			10	10		
	In vacuo	10	10	10	10	10	10		

sentence endings in the sentence completion task, for example, in a tendency to complete *It was a shame* . . . with the last part of the utterance that on the tape had the beginning *It was a pity* . . . . The effect of pictorial contexts and type of picture-utterance linkage can also, since every picture was employed in presumedly different ways in conjunction with its set A and its set B utterance, be further explored by comparing its effect upon retrieval under those two different conditions. Hopefully, more can be learned ultimately about the ways in which pictorially and verbally mediated information merge in message decoding, by comparing responses made to the request for an accurate description of a given picture by subjects who experienced it in connection with two entirely different utterances, in one case as an extralinguistic condition for an utterance within set A, in the other case an utterance within set B.

Results

Every utterance employed in the study can be broken down into three main semantic components, one encoded in its beginning and two of them in its ending (see the original Norwegian versions in Table I). Two of the three components were used to prompt retrieval. The only recall measure allowing for comparison of performance between the two retrieval conditions was reproduction of the third component, for example, *heat* in utterance IA, *not decorating* in IB, *letter* in IIA, and so on. This third component could be reproduced in the form of the exact word(s) that had been heard on the tape, or re-encoded in an unequivocally synonymous form. The data presented in Tables III and IV and in Fig. 1 are based upon SEMANTICALLY APPROPRIATE RECALL. A score of 1 was assigned for retrieval of the third semantic component, irrespective of whether it had been given back verbatim or in a synonymous form. Every case of semantically appropriate mismatch of sen-

TABLE III. Analysis of variance, Set A.

Source	d.f.	Ss	MS	F	P
C (context, P/V)	1	12·1	12·1	4·51	0·05
R (retrieval SC/CC)	1	0·9	0·9	0·34	—
C × R	1	0·4	0·4	0·15	—
s.w. (CR)	36	96·6	2·68	—	—
L (linkage type)	1	0·05	0·05	0·025	—
C × L	1	0·2	0·2	0·1	—
R × L	1	0·2	0·2	0·1	—
C × R × L	1	0·45	0·45	0·23	—
s.w. (CR) L	36	71·4	1·98	—	—

TABLE IV. Analysis of variance, Set B.

Source	d.f.	Ss	MS	F	P
C	1	21·02	21·02	8·58	0·01
R	1	50·62	50·62	20·66	0·01
C × R	1	3·03	3·03	1·24	—
s.w. (CR)	36	88·10	2·45	—	—
L	1	2·82	2·82	0·99	—
C × L	1	0·10	0·10	0·047	—
R × L	1	0·28	0·28	0·13	—
C × R × L	1	0·45	0·45	0·21	—
s.w. (CR) L	36	76·90	2·14	—	—

tence beginning and sentence ending was coded as a case of INCORRECT RECALL and assigned a score of 0.

The analysis of variance of semantically correct retrieval in Tables III and IV is analogous to that of the Louvain study, but yields somewhat different results. The main effect of PICTORIAL CONTEXTS is duplicated, i.e. significantly more of what was heard was retrieved when meaningful pictorial contexts served as ready signals. For set B there is a strong main effect of RETRIEVAL CONDITION, the content clue being far superior to the sentence beginning as a prompt. There is no evidence, however, that the two presumably different TYPES OF LINKAGE between picture and utterance affected retrieval differently. Such evidence was revealed in the Louvain experiment in significant effect of interaction of CONTEXT × LINKAGE TYPE and CONTEXT × LINKAGE TYPE × RETRIEVAL. As Tables III and IV show, these interaction effects were negligible in the present study. Pictures facilitated retention to the same extent, irrespective of a presupposed type of linkage between pictorial context and utterance.

Average gain in retention due to pictorial context is visualized by

Fig. 1, in which retrieval performance for set A, after rote learning (R), is presented for comparison as well. Adopting performance after one exposure of the utterance *in vacuo* (V) as our baseline, we find that nearly twice as much was retrieved when the utterance was heard only once, but in a meaningful pictorial context (P). This holds true for three out of the four subconditions, whereas the gain due to pictorial contexts was somewhat smaller when content clues were employed to prompt retrieval of set A. MORE WAS GAINED BY ADDING ONE PICTURE (P) THAN BY FIVE EXPOSURES AND REPETITIONS OF THE UTTERANCE *IN VACUO* (R). The order of achievements in Fig. 1 is P> R> V. When each of the eight utterances within set A is examined individually, five of them conform precisely to that order. Two more fit the modified pattern P ≥ R ≥ V, and we are left with only one clear-cut exception. The latter is utterance VIIA (see Table I), which was actually *more accurately* recalled when presented *in vacuo* than in its pictorial context.

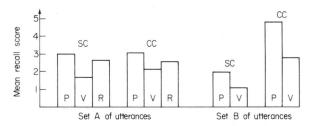

FIG. 1. Mean recall performance for the utterances in pictorial contexts (P), *in vacuo* (V), and in rote learning task (R) when retrieval was prompted by sentence completion (SC) and by content clue (CC).

Maximum recall score is eight. Correct retrieval, as defined by the coding criteria on which the means in Fig. 1 are based, is a very difficult task, and the overall impact of pictorial contexts should be measured against what was gained by TEN REPETITIONS OF THE UTTERANCE *IN VACUO* (five from tape and five by the subject himself). WHAT was gained in the rote learning session can only be fully understood by more detailed analysis of different kinds of error during retrieval. Such a detailed analysis for set A sentence completion is presented in Table V. The latter allows for an assessment of SEMANTICALLY APPROPRIATE RECALL, disregarding match or mismatch between sentence beginning and sentence ending. If we disregard all error of mismatching due to pairs of synonyms (e.g. to mixing up *insufficient* and *not enough*, etc.), the two upper rows of Table V may both be considered as containing only instances of correct retrieval. The revised means for the three conditions are for P, $(30+31) \div 10 = 6 \cdot 1$; for V, $(17+18) \div 10 = 3 \cdot 5$; and for R, $(27+7) \div 10 = 3 \cdot 4$. Considering how much of WHAT WAS MADE KNOWN was retrieved by the utterances in set A performances in the sentence

TABLE V. Distribution of performances in sentence completion (SC) of utterances in pictorial contexts (P), *in vacuo* (V) and in rote learning task (R).

	Conditions		
Coupling of sentence beginning and ending	P	V	R
Semantically correct match	30	17	27
Semantically correct mismatch	31	18	7
Semantically incorrect mismatch	4	4	5
"non-veridical" ending	5	16	23
None, no response	10	25	18

completion task show that nearly twice as much was recalled when a pictorial context had been provided. Ten repetitions of the utterance *in vacuo*, on the other hand, merely served TO REDUCE THE PROBABILITY OF THE SEMANTICALLY APPROPRIATE MISMATCH BETWEEN SENTENCE BEGINNING AND SENTENCE ENDING; that is, REPETITION THUS ONLY ENHANCED RETENTION OF THE EXACT WORDS.

The impact of pictorial context upon retrieval of utterances can also be examined picture by picture. This can be done by an inspection of Table VI, in which performances from the two retrieval conditions have been collapsed. The number in each cell is P–V, i.e. HOW MANY MORE SUBJECTS RECALLED THE THIRD SEMANTIC COMPONENT OF THAT PARTICULAR UTTERANCE WHEN A PICTURE SERVED AS A READY SIGNAL. Every cell representing a linkage in which the picture was supposed to serve as a contextual background for what was heard is marked with an asterisk. Table VI thus specifies the main effect of context from Tables III and IV and shows that picture VII stands out as an exceptional case. This picture elicits poorer recall in conjunction with the utterance from set A, but makes for a striking improvement when combined with the utterance from set B. As expected from the analysis of variance in Tables III and IV, pictures have on the whole clearly facilitated recall regardless of type of linkage with the utterance. The

TABLE VI. Gain in retrieval of the third semantic component of the utterance due to presence of pictorial context (see Table I).

	Pictorial context							
Utterance	I	II	III	IV	V	VI	VII	VIII
A	5	1*	6*	6	3*	1	÷3	3*
B	4*	6	3	2*	0	2*	8*	4

average gain is $29 \div 20 = 1 \cdot 85$ for cells marked with asterisks and $22 \div 20 = 1 \cdot 1$ for all cases supposed to represent discrepancy between message structure and temporal order.

Finally, all 40 descriptions of each picture obtained as responses to the final recall task were examined by a judge. His task was to decide, exclusively on the basis of HOW THE SUBJECT DESCRIBED WHAT HE HAD SEEN, whether he had experienced that picture in conjunction with utterance A or B. The results of this blind coding of the potential retroactive impact of what was heard upon what had been seen are presented in Table VII.

TABLE VII. Impact of utterance upon recall of picture: No. of correct identifications of utterance by a judge for all 40 reproductions and for those 20 he felt most sure about.

N	Picture							
	I	II	III	IV	V	VI	VII	VIII
40	20	34	22	30	17	24	20	22
20	10	19	15	19	10	15	5	12

Theoretical Significance and Some Implications for Further Research

Researchable Aspects of Issues Concerning Language Essence and Conditions of Use

In our attempts at assessing the theoretical significance of these results, two important observations should be kept in mind: (1) the subjects in all subconditions listened to the utterances with the goal of trying to reproduce them as accurately as possible, and (2) the conditions P and V were identical except for what appeared on the slides, as ready signals. What was induced by meaningful pictorial contexts, moreover, was something more than what can be conveyed by verbal descriptions of those contexts. This had been clearly revealed in the Louvain study, by adding a condition in which the slides portraying pictorial contexts were replaced by slides with concise and pregnant descriptions of the same contexts. Retrieval under the latter condition was no better than for utterances *in vacuo*, for example when arbitrary geometrical forms served as ready signals.

The difference with respect to CONDITION OF USE between P and V must hence be explained along the lines suggested in our theoretical introduction—the picture appears to serve as a cartoon movie type simulation of aspects of an extralinguistic condition for uttering what is heard immediately afterwards. The subject's cognition of that extra-linguistic condition necessarily provides some message structure for what he hears. He listens to the utterance with the explicit aim of reproducing it later on but is incapable of decoding what he hears as an entity separate from what he has just seen. The moment the utter-ance is coupled with the visually portrayed situation, comprehension can no longer be disentangled from the issue of what more is MADE KNOWN about that situation.

The results presented in Tables III and IV and in Fig. 1 testify to the unequivocal and strong effect of pictorial contexts upon retrieval of utterances. The expectation of increased emancipation from particular linguistic form, moreover, is fully confirmed by the data on semantically appropriate mismatch in Table V. Let us now focus only on set A and compare the three conditions P, V and R using one exposure of the utterance *in vacuo* (V) as a baseline condition for examining TWO DIFFERENT MEANS OF ENHANCING RETRIEVAL.

Figure 1 shows that the rank order between conditions was P> R> V, and only one out of the eight utterances in set A was found to deviate from this pattern. With respect to purely quantitative aspects, the results are quite unequivocal. Retrieval was improved by adding a pictorial context as well as by massed repetitions of the utterance, but more was gained by presenting one meaningful pictorial context prior to the utterance rather than by repeating it ten times in a row. If conditions are rank ordered in terms of decreasing frequencies of semantically appropiate mismatch, however, the order is P> V> R. Massed repetitions of the utterance thus lead to a significant decrease in absolute frequency of mismatch, whereas the addition of a meaning-ful pictorial context has a striking effect in precisely the opposite direction. Having heard an utterance in conjunction with its visually portrayed context, the subject usually recalls afterwards WHAT was made known at the beginning of that utterance without remembering HOW it was made known. In fact, his choice between pairwise synony-mous beginnings is no more accurate than chance.

We may still argue that language use in all subconditions was kept constant, since THE TASK HAD BEEN DEFINED AS ACCURATE REPRODUCTION. But do we not, by such a stubborn insistence to leave problems of use aside, adopt the policy of the ostrich attempting to escape difficulties by hiding his head in the sand? How can we, in view of the unequivocal qualitative differences revealed in Table V, avoid recognizing the experimenter-centred fallacy inherent in such an operational definition of use?

The moment we start considering use from the point of view of OUR SUBJECT and what he recalled afterwards, we are immediately encoun-tering the issue of WHAT was decoded and retrieved. What has been added by a meaningful pictorial context is in fact the *here* of the spatial-temporal-personal co-ordinates of an act of communication (see Fig. 2). However fragmentary and incomplete, that *here* allows for some cognitive representation of an event or a state of affairs so that something can be MADE KNOWN by what is heard. The difference in language use

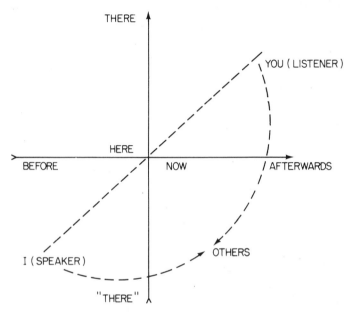

FIG. 2. The spatial-temporal-personal co-ordinates of an act of speech.

between *our* subject and the subject in the rote learning experiment can thus most appropriately be described as MESSAGE RECEPTION AND RETRIEVAL OF WHAT WAS MADE KNOWN versus COMPREHENSION OF SOME MESSAGE POTENTIAL AND REPRODUCTION OF THE WORDS IN WHICH IT WAS ENCODED.

So far, we have considered the conditions P and R as DEVIATIONS FROM V. But what do we actually know about our baseline condition V? Let us now ponder this issue by reversing our approach, i.e. for example, exploring language use on the part of the subject when an utterance is heard *IN VACUO* AND ONLY ONCE in the light of what happens when a PICTORIAL CONTEXT IS ADDED and under condition of MASSED REPETITIONS.

Ebbinghaus' (1895) pioneer work on nonsense syllables has been followed up by thousands of investigations aimed at an assessment of the NATURE AND DEGREES OF MEANINGFULNESS. One might expect that psycholinguists deciding to examine comprehension and recall of sentences in isolation would be concerned with somewhat similar issues of

relative autonomy of sentence categories, or the extent to which contextual frames would be provided by the listener himself. Yet no
systematic research has been conducted along such lines. A survey of
sentences used by psycholinguists in settings of the *in vacuo* utterance
type reveals a wide variety of sentences, apparently constructed *ad hoc*
for the purpose of exploring performance aspects of particular structural
features.

It will be remembered that the interval between ready signals in
conditions P and V was kept constant at 8 s, whereas the subjects in R
each time were given only 3 s to repeat the utterance aloud before
hearing it from the tape again. This implies that if we compare only V
and R, CONSIDERABLY MORE TIME WAS AVAILABLE IN CONDITION V FOR
CONTINUOUS COGNITIVE AFTERWORK ON WHAT HAD BEEN HEARD. The
short interval in condition R had in fact been introduced after systematic pretests (Blakar and Rommetveit, 1971). The latter had shown that
time available for cognitive afterwork was indeed a very important
factor. They indicate, moreover, that such cognitive afterwork in part
takes the form of an active organization of what is heard within whatever is available in memory and imagination as potential contextual
frames. A *he*, a *there*, or even A PROPER NAME may thus serve as a tag to
a more or less vividly imagined situation.

With these casuistic observations and the data from Table V in mind,
we can no longer safely describe condition V as a baseline case of an
utterance *in vacuo*. If we do, we shall once more commit the sin of
experiment-centred description of what is going on, and we shall in fact
proceed as if our subject does not make use of his creative cognitive
capacities in spite of evidence to the contrary. The most plausible single
explanation of the high frequency of semantically appropriate mismatch
under condition V is thus a very simple one? The subject was not given
a ready-made visually portrayed *here* for what he heard, but he was
provided with time enough to provide some contextual frame of his
own—at least in some cases and with some degree of success. He tries to
preserve and reproduce what he hears by PRETENDING THAT SOMETHING
IS MADE KNOWN by the utterance, and he therefore quite often remembers WHAT was made known without remembering HOW, unlike the
subject in the rote learning situation.

The analogy between the early research on nonsense syllables and
recent research on the utterance *in vacuo* should thus be seriously considered. Ebbinghaus resorted to apparently nonsensical trigrams in
order to study retention detached from the intricacy of pre-established
meaningful connections. Psycholinguists resort to isolated sentences in
order to study language processing detached from the intricacy of
extralinguistic conditions. But, alas, the subject seems in both cases to
bring with him to the experimental situation what the scientist initially

intended to leave out: what is left vacuous BY THE EXPERIMENTER is in part filled with products of his subject's meaning-creating capacity. Within the verbal learning tradition initiated by Ebbinghaus, we have witnessed a marked shift of focus of research interest. What initially was considered a troublesome source of error soon became a topic for investigation of great interest *per se*. Psycholinguists, however, have so far behaved more like the man who had lost his money in a very dark place but went on searching for it in some other place where the street was illuminated. They tend to cling firmly to their operational and experimenter-centred notion of the utterance *in vacuo*, considering issues of language use such as those raised in the present paper as AT BEST a legitimate topic for philosophers with metaphysical inclinations.

We fully agree that issues of language use are complex, but we have tried to show that some aspects of them can be explored experimentally. The prospect of more insight into language processing appears to be very slim unless we once and for all abandon the idea of assessing linguistic performance as an entity detached from extralinguistic conditions. This does not imply that we shall have to start preparing an inventory of "contextual dispositional properties" of utterances corresponding to indices of meaningfulness of trigrams in verbal learning tasks. There are other ways of exploring how subjects fill in what is left vacuous by the experimenter.

A word of caution should immediately be added: linguistic competence is assumed to be of an intuitive nature and we have every reason to believe that the same holds true for the capacity to provide some contextual frame for an utterance in isolation. Little can be learned about such frames by asking the subject for a retrospective account of what happened at the moment that he listened to the isolated utterance. Hopefully, more can be learned by having him reflect upon a ready-made set of potential contextual frames for that utterance and indicate which one—if any of them—comes close to what he feels he had in mind. WHAT he had in mind may vary from a vividly imagined particular scene of action to a vague presupposition concerning the kind of the discourse in which the utterance may have been embedded. Whatever cognitions serve to fill in the contextual vacuum, they will most likely serve as transient backgrounds rather than as sustained foci of intention during comprehension of the utterance.

Relative autonomy of utterances may upon closer examination in many cases, turn out to be primarily an issue of STANDARD OR CONVENTIONAL CONTEXTUAL FRAMES. Utterances conveying generic statements, for instance, will often invite the listener to presuppose some more or less well-defined domain of discourse. An utterance such as *One and one make one*, it may be argued, can be considered autonomous and as conveying a false statement, provided that the listener fills in the contextual vacuum with the widely shared contextual frame of elementary arithmetic. Unfortunately, however, listeners do not always conform to such an expectation. They often immediately decode what they hear as a praise of the institution of marriage or as a vigorous protest against square-headed reasoning. Sometimes the utterance may even be interpreted as making known what happens when two rivers merge into one. A structurally and lexicographically very similar utterance such as *Twenty-three and fifty-four make seventy-seven*, on the other hand, will be decoded as conveying a true statement within a context of arithmetic discourse.

Suppose, however, that we were able to select utterances in such a way that our subjects most likely would fill in the contextual vacuum with the very same conventional frame. If so, we are still left in a state of ignorance concerning the impact of that particular frame upon decoding and retention. Our primary interest may pertain to linguistically defined structural features. For example, we may want to explore how constructions of the form *It is . . . that* $+ S_2$ are comprehended and organized in long term memory, and we make sure that we present utterances that are unequivocally experienced as conveying statements concerning, for example, economic issues. This implies, *eo ipso*, that we shall have to be concerned with that which the subjects ASSUME TO BE THE CASE in respect to those issues in order to decide WHAT IS MADE KNOWN TO THEM by the utterances. We may otherwise easily arrive at rather arbitrary conclusions concerning the impact of form. The utterance which appears in the slot *It is . . . that* will most likely behave differently in long-term memory depending upon whether it is occupied by the word *usual* or *unusual*, as in: *It is . . . that increased salaries lead to increased prices*. The subject will in this case tend to remember more easily what is *unusual*, literally as well as IN THE SENSE OF DENYING SOMETHING THAT HE FIRMLY EXPECTED TO BE THE CASE (see Wearing, 1970).

In order to steer clear of such complications, one may resort to utterances describing unique events or states of affairs of which the subject in the experiment could not possibly know nor presuppose anything in advance. Whatever is made known in such a case, one may argue, must be structured in terms of intrinsic (and most likely "deep") properties of the sentence as such. Examples of such sentences are *John is eager to please* and *John is easy to please*; *John* is said to be the subject of the first sentence but the object of the latter, in terms of their deep structures (Miller and McNeill, 1969). Another example is *The clever young thief was severely sentenced by the rather grim-faced judge*, of which it has been maintained (Osgood, 1963, p. 750) that . . . *judge* is the real topic of the sentence.

Such attempts at explicating what a presumedly autonomous sentence in some more profound or "real" sense IS, testify to considerable conceptual confusion. This confusion seems to stem from a confounding of concepts from transformational grammar, categorical grammar and propositional logic in an otherwise PSYCHOLOGICAL ANALYSIS of what is made known. (See Rommetveit, 1972b, c.) Consider, for instance, the claim that *judge* is the REAL topic of the sentence about the clever young thief. IF NOTHING ELSE IS KNOWN, and if we begin another sentence with the pronoun *He . . .*, the latter will necessarily refer to *the thief*. There is some message structure inherent in the utterance as such; its passive voice may in fact be said to imply a proposal for a contract concerning the sustained topic of discourse, contrary to Osgood's claim. In addition, the utterance contains patterns of nesting of what is made known. *The . . . thief*, for instance, commits the listener to play the game of assuming that some thief has already been unequivocally identified. Therefore, the definite article serves the function of "eine Als-bekannt-Setzung" in a communication act (Reichling, 1963). What is made known by *young*, moreover, cannot be fully decoded unless *thief* (or, rather, e.g. *person* in contrast to, e.g. *culture*) is presupposed. And the thief's *youth* is not made known in the same way as what is encoded in *was severely sentenced*. The former (his youth) is presented as part of a shared social reality, as something already assumed to be the case by both encoder and decoder, when the fact that he was sentenced is made known.

An utterance *in vacuo* can at best be examined with respect to inherent message structure of the kind suggested above, for instance under conditions resembling a situation when a person listens to THE OPENING SENTENCE OF A NOVEL. As soon as some extralinguistic or verbal context is provided, however, entirely different structures may emerge. Thus in the example above, even the grim-faced look of the judge can be made the significant novelty, depending upon what is already assumed to be the case and which question (overtly or tacitly) is being asked. WHAT is made known and how it is made known, however, will most likely remain UNKNOWN to the psycholinguist who insists on catching it in nets developed by grammarians and logicians for entirely different purposes.

On Message Structure Across Extralinguistic and Linguistic Components of What is Made Known

Our expectation that pictorial context would affect retrieval of the utterance to different degrees, depending upon whether the linkage between picture and utterance provided for congruity or discrepancy between message structure and temporal order, was not clearly confirmed in the present study. The negative findings (see Tables III, IV and VI) thus stand out in contrast to the strong effects of type of linkage existing in the Louvain study.

We have already dwelt with the issue of cognitive afterwork in our comparison between the conditions V and R, arguing that subjects tend to fill in the contextual vacuum with some general setting or frame of their own. The necessity for afterwork, however, is by no means entirely eliminated by providing them with pictorial contexts. The difference between our two presumedly different kinds of linkage may be in fact further explicated in terms of HOW MUCH and WHICH KIND OF cognitive afterwork is required in order to relate the picture and utterance to form a meaningfully organized entity. In pre-tests, subjects were given all 16 combinations of Table I and asked to indicate how the picture and the utterance in each particular case were related. Their accounts appeared to indicate two somewhat different strategies of organization. For linkages supposed to represent congruity between message structure and temporal order, they tended to express the relationship as a SEQUENTIAL CONNECTION (IB: *One sees the withering plant, and then regrets that it has lost its beauty*; IIA: *The train leaves the station, and she has not yet arrived there . . .*). For linkages supposed to represent discrepancy, the utterance was most often interpreted as an explanation of aspects of what had been seen (IA: *The plant was dying because of lack of water and heat*; IIB: *The train had a steam engine since funds were not available for change . . .*). The latter *because of*-organization seems to represent a more heavy taxation of the subject's capacity for creativity and rapid reinterpretation than the simple sequential arrangement of what was seen and what was said.

The fact that our subjects in the Louvain study did not profit very much from pictures that were "explained by" subsequent utterances may be due to the fact that they were far less experienced in the kind of cognitive afterwork required in order to organize such combinations meaningfully. The Louvain subjects were soldiers with an average of only one-and-a-half years of lower education beyond the elementary school level (see Rommetveit *et al.*, 1971, p. 38). The Oslo subjects were equally homogeneous, but represented a strikingly superior level with respect to educational background. It is possible, therefore, that the latter in most cases managed to restore congruity between message structure and temporal order by quickly reorganizing what was jointly made known by picture and utterance AS A CAUSAL CONNECTION.

Their organization of what was seen and what was heard into meaningful entities, moreover, is reflected in somewhat different descriptions of the same picture, depending upon whether it was followed by utterances A or B (see Table VII). Such systematic differences, however, were only clearly revealed for some pictures. Thus, *the steam* arising from the train was as a rule only recalled when picture II had served as a ready signal for the utterance about scarcity of funds for electricity. The tumbledown building would hardly ever be labelled *factory* unless picture VI had been followed by the utterance about insufficient profit.

In order to assess the theoretical significance of the data in Table VII, two additional observations must be considered. First of all, correct identification was generally based upon symptoms of explanatory or causal relationships such as those described above. This means, for example, that the judge would actively infer that picture VI had been followed by utterance A if the word *factory* had been used in describing it, and he would guess at utterance B for all descriptions which did not contain symptoms of that and similar kinds. Secondly, additional tests had been conducted in advance in which some subjects saw only the pictures, other subjects were shown the pictures in conjunction with the utterances of set A, and still others saw the same pictures in conjunction with set B. Under these conditions, however, they were asked to pay attention to each picture so as to be able to give a detailed and accurate description of it immediately afterwards, and no request was made for reproductions of what they had heard. The resultant descriptions of pictures were then examined by the same judge whose performance is presented in Table VII. His attempts at identifying which utterance had been heard in conjunction with the picture were under these conditions in no single case significantly better than chance.

The data on RECALL OF PICTURES in the present study thus indicate that the linkages between pictorial context and utterance actually were of two somewhat different kinds, even though the kind of linkage did not affect retrieval of WHAT WAS HEARD in any consistent and systematic fashion and even though subjects managed to be unaffected by what they heard under conditions where they were deliberately trying to do so. Symptoms of retroactive modification of whatever THE PICTURE conveyed *in vacuo*, were observed mainly for linkages in which the utterance was supposed to serve as a background for what was seen. Success at identifying the utterance on the basis of its impact upon recall of picture, however, varies from picture to picture. It is almost perfect for picture II, but actually inferior to chance performance in the case of picture VII (see Table VII).

The latter stands out as an exception in two respects: (1) it actually made for poorer recall of what was heard when combined with its utterance from set A, and (2), it was itself recalled in such a way that the judge tended to infer that it had been experienced in connection with utterance A when in fact it had served as a ready signal for utterance B. What is even more remarkable is its strikingly different impact upon retrieval of what was heard in the two cases (see Table VI) and we shall at this point examine what may have happened with the combinations VIIA and VIIB somewhat more in detail.

The pictorial context is simply a drawing of a man knocking in a ceiling with a stick. This picture is in one condition followed by utterance A: *Always there is somebody making noise upstairs*, in another by utterance B: *Probably it will become quiet upstairs*. The act depicted is in both cases clearly related to what is heard afterwards as an action ELICITED BY and INTENDED TO PUT AN END TO THE NOISE, a noise which is MADE KNOWN by utterance A and IMPLIED by utterance B. Whatever "disambiguation" of picture VII is caused by utterance A and utterance B, the resultant interpretation should be essentially the same. This implies, in effect, that the judge must be deprived of such DIFFERENTIAL symptoms of retroactive modification as the word *steam* in recall of picture II and the word *factory* in recall of picture VI.

The linkage VIIA, however, appears to be rather complex. The utterance has the form of a generic statement. For example, it is maintained that some state of affairs (noise upstairs) occurs regularly or with high frequency. This may serve to explain the particular action of the man with the stick. But linkage VIIB, conforms very closely to the simpler pattern where WHAT IS SEEN PROVIDES THE SCENE FOR WHAT IS HEARD and the latter serves to make known an opinion concerning WHAT MAY HAPPEN NEXT IN THAT PARTICULAR SETTING. The strikingly different effect of the very same picture upon retrieval of the two different utterances thus testifies to two different message structures across linguistic and non-linguistic components of what was made known in the two cases.

The necessity of exploring pictorial context and utterance jointly was, in the Louvain study as well as in the present experiment, also indicated by INTRUSIONS FROM WHAT HAD BEEN SEEN IN RETRIEVAL OF WHAT HAD BEEN HEARD. Such intrusions are in some cases easily identified, as for instance when *to the station* is added to what was heard about coming too late in IIB. Similar productive errors of retrieval, however, occur even when the utterances are heard *in vacuo*, and they may then yield some clues as to what kind of contextual backgrounds the subject himself had provided in order to assess what was made known.

Systematic research on contexts and message structure is of recent date and, for that reason, of a very exploratory nature. The prospect of further progress, however, should also be evaluated in the light of recent linguistic research in which systematic attempts are made at disentangling SEMANTIC CONSTRAINTS AND POTENTIALITIES INHERENT IN THE SENTENCE AS SUCH (in this paper vaguely referred to as "message potential") from WHAT IS INFERRED OR IMAGINED ON THE BASIS OF PRESUPPOSED EXTRALINGUISTIC CONDITIONS (Uhlenbeck, 1971, pp. 135–157). Hopefully, such inquiries and experimental research on extralinguistic aspects of message transmission will converge with respect to basic conclusions.

The mere possibility of examining message structure across pictures and words also offers some hope for researchers in their search for a conceptual framework applicable to extremely complex and important practical issues of multi-channel communication such as analysis of various T.V. programmes and with a variety of more or less precisely defined goals and APPLICATION OF AUDIO-VISUAL AIDS for different educational purposes. The issue of congruity versus discrepancy between message structure and temporal order, moreover, appears to be an issue of the utmost practical significance in the education of mentally retarded children. A very brief sketch of a single case may illuminate HOW and WHY.

A major obstacle to progress was, in this particular case, the child's inability to comprehend even very simple verbal instructions. He was consequently often deprived of the opportunity for "learning by doing", since the teacher simply did not manage to make known to him which sequence of actions he was supposed to perform. The task might be, for instance, simply to push a tiny car on the table in front of him with a pencil located some distance from it. The teacher would then say, pointing at the car and then at the pencil: "Push that car with this pencil"; the child did nothing. It turned out that the teacher could convey to the child what he was supposed to do by carefully rearranging his words. When the teacher said: "With this pencil push that car", the child immediately understood and did what he was told to do.

We may hesitate to consider the correspondence between word order and sequential properties of the performance that the teacher described as a case of congruity between temporal organization and MESSAGE STRUCTURE. The problems appear to be of essentially the same nature as those discussed in the introductory part of this article, however, and such problems constitute the major and perpetually recurring difficulty in the construction of combined pictorial and verbal instructional materials for the mentally retarded. Making things known to the mentally retarded child is only possible in terms of a progressive expansion and modification of the very restricted perceptual and social reality of the child himself, a reality which is not at all shared by his teacher. The concept of message structure may prove particularly useful in such a situation for two reasons: By definition, it implies that verbally mediated messages are anchored in extralinguistic conditions, and it offers the embryo of a formula for assessing patterns of sequential nesting of novelties in whatever is being MADE KNOWN.

References

Blakar, R. M. and Rommetveit, R. (1971). Processing of utterances in contexts versus rote learning of sentences. *In* "Social Contexts of Messages". (E. A. Carswell and R. Rommetveit, Eds) Academic Press, London and New York.

Chomsky, N. (1968). "Language and Mind." Harcourt Brace Jovanovich, New York.

Ebbinghaus, H. (1895). "Memory." Translation by H. A. Ruger and C. E. Bussenius (1913). Teachers College, New York.

Jaspars, J., Rommetveit, R., Cook, M., Havelka, N., Henry, P., Herkner, W., Pêcheux, M. and Peeters, G. (1971). Order effects in impression formation: A Psycholinguistic approach. In "Social Contexts of Messages". (E. A. Carswell and R. Rommetveit, Eds) Academic Press, London and New York.

Miller, G. A. and McNeill, D. (1969). Psycholinguistics. In "Handbook of Social Psychology". (G. Lindzey and E. A. Aronson, Eds) Vol. III. Addison-Wesley, Reading, Massachusetts.

Moscovici, S. (1972). Society and theory in social psychology. In "The Context of Social Psychology: A Critical Assessment". (J. Israel and H. Tajfel, Eds) Academic Press, London and New York.

Osgood, C. E. (1963). On understanding and creating sentences. American Psychologist 18, 735–751.

Reichling, A. (1963). Das problem der bedetung in der Sprachwissenschaft. Innsbrucker Beitrage zur Kulturwissenschaft Sonderheft, 19.

Rommetveit, R., Cook, M., Havelka, M., Henry, P., Herkner, W., Pêcheux, M. and Peeters, G. (1971). Processing of utterances in contexts. In "Social Contexts of Messages". (E. A. Carswell and R. Rommetveit, Eds). Academic Press, London and New York.

Rommetveit, R. (1972a). "Språk, tanke og kommunikasjon." Universitetsforlaget, Oslo.

Rommetveit, R. (1972b). Language games, deep syntactic structures and hermeneutic circles. In "The Context of Social Psychology: A Critical Assessment". (J. Israel and H. Tajfel, Eds) Academic Press, London and New York.

Rommetveit, R. (1972c). Deep sentence structure versus message structure: Some critical remarks on current paradigms, and suggestions for an alternative approach. Norwegian J. Linguistics 26, 3–22.

Slama-Cazacu, T. (1961). "Language et contexte." Mouton, The Hague.

Uhlenbeck, E. M. (1972). "Critical comments on Transformational-Generative Grammar 1962–1972." Smits, The Hague.

Wearing, A. J. (1970). The storage of complex sentences. J. verbal Learning verbal Behavior 9, 21–29.

Wold, A. H. (1971). Impression formation: A psycholinguistic approach. In "Social Contexts of Messages". (E. A. Carswell and R. Rommetveit, Eds) Academic Press, London and New York.

29. Verbal Communication and Social Influence

A theoretical framework and some reflections
concerning implications for public education on
drugs and drug abuse*

R. ROMMETVEIT

In a way, I interpreted the invitation to contribute to this symposium as a challenge. We have come together to mobilize insights and experiences from a wide variety of research areas in a joint attempt at coping with very serious and urgent problems of human welfare and social action. Some years of research within the fields of psycholinguistics and verbal communication, however, have left me with a rather modest crop of well established and practically applicable knowledge. So much energy has recently been invested in a search for psychological manifestations of abstract linguistic structures, and so few studies have dealt with message transmission and social influence in complex social situations such as those encountered in social action and planning of information campaigns on drug abuse. It was with some reluctance and anxiety, therefore, that I accepted the challenge to try to convey some ideas which, even though developed in a sheltered sphere of academic laboratory experimentation and speculation, may be of some relevance to the important practical issues of this symposium.

I shall, first of all, try to outline a very general but somewhat fragmentary theoretical framework for analysis of communication when verbal message transmission is embedded in complex situations of interpersonal interaction. In trying to elucidate more specific implications of this framework, I shall then attempt to refer to problems encountered in mass media communication to actual and potential drug addicts. Finally, some of the ideas of potential relevance will be

* Published in "Communication and Drug Abuse" (1970) (F. A. Wittenborn, F. P. Smith and S. A. Wittenborn, Eds) pp. 68–78. Charles Thomas, Springfield.

summarized in terms of a number of questions in connection with planning of public education on drugs and drug abuse.

Verbal and Non-verbal Components of Communication: A tentative theoretical framework

The point of departure for any analysis of verbal communication has to be what might be called *the temporal-spatial-directional co-ordinates* of the communicative act. In the case of spoken language, these co-ordinates are defined in terms of the *time* at which the act of speech takes place, its *location*, and the reciprocal identification of *speaker and listener* (Hockett, 1963). A psychological analysis of the communication process, however, has to transcend the precise assessment of the *"now"*, the *"here"* and the *"I—you"* of the communication process in terms of exact time and location of speech and proper names of speaker and listener. The subjectively established "now", for instance, will have very different denotative extensions depending upon whether the discourse concerns, e.g. departure of a plane the listener is supposed to board or a historical survey of juvenile delinquency. The "here" of the act of speech, moreover, may be tagged onto the whole United States or a corner of this particular room, depending upon whether we are oriented toward the topic of drug abuse in different countries or toward the issues of where coffee is going to be served. The "I", finally, may pertain to my role as an adult educator and member of the Establishment or to my more or less idiosyncratically defined personal identity, depending upon whether I am addressing young people I do not know or a very good friend.

Which message is being transmitted by words, whether spoken or written, is thus to a very large extent determined by the more inclusive communication setting in which they are embedded and by tacit presuppositions on the part of the participants in the communication process. Consider, for instance, the simple utterance "Here are too few seats" in two different contexts of speaker-hearer interaction:

> The speaker is in either case a political candidate who has rented a room for a campaign meeting, and the utterance occurs shortly before the meeting starts. The hearer, however, is in one case the janitor who is standing in front of the closet where extra chairs are stored. In the other case, the utterance is made in response to a telephone call from the speaker's wife who is eager to know whether her husband has attracted a large crowd.
>
> The message conveyed in the speaker-to-janitor context is a directive or a command. The janitor understands immediately that the speaker wants him to bring some more seats. The presuppositions involve in this

case a master-to-servant relationship between the two participants in the communicative act. The utterance conveys its message by virtue of this role relationship, the location of the janitor during the act of speech, etc. These features of the communication setting constitute a frame within which the utterance fits in as a fragment.

The integration of the utterance in the situation may under such conditions be so perfect that the receiver can hardly tell which components of the message were mediated verbally and which were not. If we ask the janitor what the speaker said, he may very well respond: "He told me to bring more seats." The wife, on the other hand, may rush from the telephone and tell her children: "Daddy has attracted a large crowd tonight." And such spontaneous recodings of the same utterance suggest that transmission has been successful in both cases: The linguistic medium has brought about correspondence between intended and received message by virtue of its embeddedness in pre-established relationships between sender and receiver and other features of the communication setting. (Rommetveit, 1968, p. 50.)

A somewhat more detailed analysis of the subtle interaction of linguistic and extralinguistic components of the communication process is attempted in Fig. 1. We assume, in this case, a shared domain of objects and events (including, of course, persons, the speaker and the listener, legal sanctions, drugs, etc.) as an ultimate prerequisite for message transmission. Verbal message transmission is then broken down into a process of encoding and a complementary process of decoding. Encoding, moreover, is being controlled by the speaker's intention to make something known, his subjective cognitive representation of the

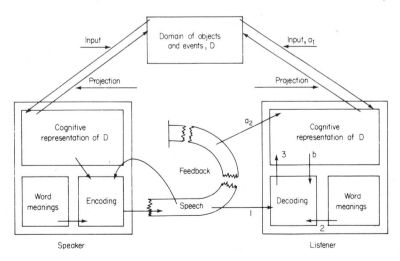

Fig. 1. Linguistic and non-linguistic constituents of messages (Rommetveit, 1968, p. 193).

objects and events he wants to speak about and his acquired linguistic competence. The latter consists in part of what may be called acquired word meanings, but also in his capacity to anticipate potential discrepancies with respect to word meaning between speaker and listener which may induce loss or distortion of information. Encoding implies thus always a component of *anticipatory decoding*, i.e. a taking the role of the receiver of the message. This anticipatory activity is brought to our attention when we, in response to our own speech and prior to any symptom of misunderstanding on the part of the listener, feel that we fail to reach him and therefore try to rephrase what we just tried to say. The process of decoding, finally, is depicted as involving *the listener's* subjective cognitive representations and word meanings. An intention of making known something about the real world which the listener has *not* experienced himself is then achieved if decoding results in a representation which, if projected onto the shared external domain of objects and events, corresponds to the input which the speaker wanted to make known.

Non-linguistic components of the situation will, according to this model, enter an otherwise verbally mediated process of message transmission in a number of different ways. We have, first of all, simple cases of quasi-predication in which, e.g. the topic of discourse is induced by a convergence of attention in a shared visual field. We may for instance both be watching a television commercial on tranquillizers. A one-word utterance such as "Bad!" is then sufficient in order to convey my attitude toward that commercial. Secondly, we have the so-called purely deictic or pointing elements of language (such as demonstratives, time and place pronouns, tense of verbs, etc.) by which shared elements defined in terms of the subjectively established temporal-spatial-directional co-ordinates are introduced. A "this" serves to introduce into the message whatever happens to be attended to at the moment, be it a dish of food in front of the listener (arrow a_1) or the problem of drug abuse legislation mentioned a moment ago (arrow a_2).

There is, however, a deictic aspect attached to every content word as well. Words such as "narcotics", "drugs", "dependence" or "abuse" are by no means devoid of shared and lexicographically defined reference. They are in actual usage, however, more or less ambiguous, and their ambiguity is reflected in *interpersonal differences* of interpretation as well as considerable variations with respect to semantic contributions across *different social situations* (Naess, 1933). Which cognitions are being triggered by them in any particular case will therefore to a considerable extent be determined by the communication setting in which they are embedded and by tacit presuppositions on the part of the participants in the communication process. Decoding of such words seems to proceed as indicated by arrows a_1–b–2–3 in Fig. 1, i.e. the recipient's orientation toward and subjective experience with the *referent* will significantly affect what is being transmitted via the *word*.

Experimental studies have shown that comprehension and retention of the verbally mediated message is enhanced when the listener is provided with a fairly unequivocal image of the non-linguistic context in which the utterance is embedded (Blakar and Rommetveit, 1971; Rommetveit *et al.*, 1971). The same series of studies aim also at an exploration of the ways in which *what is being said affects the listener's interpretation of the situation* in which the utterance is embedded. A visually presented somewhat ambiguous scene may be immediately disambiguated in different ways, depending upon what is being said in response to that scene. I may be driving with a friend who, as we are passing a derelict building, says to me: "There was not enough profit from the production". This utterance makes sense to me if, and only if, I accept the tacit presupposition that the building is an abandoned factory, and the building is consequently immediately cognized as such.

The speaker is in such cases imposing his own particular interpretation of the situation upon the listener, since none of the other possible interpretations makes for comprehension of what is being said. The impact of the verbally mediated message is thus by no means restricted to its manifest content but must often be sought in tacit presuppositions and implications with respect to aspects of the domain of objects and events *which are not mentioned at all*. The relation between the overt verbal communication and the extralinguistic, socially defined situation in which it is embedded is thus a bidirectional one: Tacit presuppositions concerning the extralinguistic context will partly determine what can be conveyed by verbal elements, and what is being said may to a considerable extent serve to structure (or restructure) the entire communication setting.

Recently developed programmes for content analysis (Henry, 1971; Pêcheux, 1969) aim at revealing what has been referred to as "conditions of production of discourse". The latter include the speaker's tacit presuppositions concerning particular role relationships involved, his assumptions concerning credibility attributed to him by the listener, assumed psychological distance between the two participants in the communication process, and so forth. Studies by Moscovici and Plon (1966) show how purely syntactic characteristics of language vary with specific physically manipulated aspects of the communication setting such as whether two participants in a discussion are talking to each other face to face, side by side, or back to back. The latter two experimental conditions seemed to induce experienced distance and a style of speech resembling that of written language. General syntactic and stylistic features are thus cues by which the receiver of the message may be informed about the sender's underlying attitude. *How* something is being said (or written) may, when the "I-you" relationship of the communication process have not yet been unequivocally defined, serve to establish such important parameters as psychological distance.

In summary, then, recent theoretical and empirical explorations indicate that we have to transcend manifest content and venture to undertake a thorough analysis of the social setting in which a given verbal communication is embedded, including the network of tacit presupposition which to a considerable degree determines its latent message and potential social influence. Wittgenstein (1961, p. 200) conceives of predication as an abstract semiotic form: What is being made known by the spoken or written word can be identified neither by means of a syntactic-semantic analysis nor by a traditional logic analysis of the utterance *in vacuo*. The predicate of a communicative act, even in a very narrow sense, has to be assessed in terms of what is novel and what was already presupposed. An immediate and frequently overlooked impact seems to reside in the recipient's tacit acceptance or reflective rejection of the presupposition underlying what is being said. *How* it is said (or written), moreover, may affect important parameters of interpersonal communication such as credibility and experienced psychological distance.

Illustrations from Verbal Communication on Drugs and Drug Abuse

It follows from what has been said above that a thorough analysis of the immediate communication setting should be the initial step in any search for potential long-range effects of verbal communication with respect to drugs such as change of attitudes and conduct. The critical issues will be very different, for instance, as we pass from one category of communication settings to another. At the one extreme we encounter the ex-addict face-to-face with a single addict or potential addict; at the other we have the public educator on the television screen addressing a nationwide and heterogeneous audience. In the first case we envisage the possibility of a shared world of experiences and presuppositions due to common fate. The face-to-face situation allows also in principle for an intuitive *and* reflective assessment of the recipient's entire life situation, and it allows the communicator to try to re-structure the setting in response to immediate feedback from the recipient. In doing so, moreover, he has at his disposal a rich repertoire of non-verbal behaviours and paralinguistic responses by which he may convey, e.g. empathy and induce credibility.

The educator on the screen is deprived of some of these privileges. He is the victim of the power and the inbuilt weakness of the mass medium, in which language is detached from its original setting of physical proximity and two-way interaction between speaker and listener and yet, in order to affect the listener, dependent upon a subjectively established "now-here-I-and-you" frame of *experienced* proximity. We shall in what follows explore some of the problems that are bound to arise in such situations.

Some very serious problems are encountered the moment we ask the simple question of *who is being addressed*. A traditional demographical description of the population of potential receivers may be a helpful first step in exploring these problems. Such a description, however, will in many cases confirm our suspicion that the public educator who makes use of the mass media is up against an almost hopeless task. The Establishment, the addict, the potential addict, and other categories of potential receivers represent a wide variety of backgrounds, personal experiences and ideologies with respect to the topic. They, the receivers, have the power to switch off and on the stream of verbalization. An investigation of pre-established attitudes and basic orientations, moreover, will most likely disclose subjective orientations toward the sender in his role as public educator varying from submission and complete faith to militant rejection and lack of confidence.

This picture is in part a reflection of power conflicts and existing ambiguities and ambivalences with respect to drug and drug abuse in our part of the world. Christie and Bruun (1968) consider also the disturbing terminological confusion in the field from this angle. A survey of the key words employed in public communication leaves them with an image resembling a psychedelic picture. "The words . . . are as many as 'pebbles on the beach': alcohol—alcoholism, drug—drug dependence, excessive drinkers, symptomatic drinkers, addiction, habituation, narcotics, use, abuse, chemicals, stuff, mind-expanding substance, sickness, sin, crime, treatment, punishment, help, and so on" (p. 1). It is quite obvious that the educator's selection among such words will serve to define his own position and in part determine which category of potential receivers will respond with faith and acceptance and which categories will reject him or switch him off.

Some ambiguities and ambivalences of terminology can be traced back to institutional ambiguities and ambivalences in our society. Words about drugs and drug abuse are, after all, fragments of a much more inclusive picture of conduct, legislation and medical practice. The drug addict has in our societies for a long time been located in the strange two men's land of the criminal *and* the sick (Aubert, 1958). This means that he is being exposed to the language of the criminal law, with its underlying assumptions concerning *voluntary control of* and *responsibility for conduct*, and at the same time to a natural science language of *causation of sickness*. The by far most significant novel development is the open rebellion against the legal as well as the medical definitions of drug abuse; the labelling of non-legalized drugs as "mind-expanding substance" marks a very powerful attempt at redefining the strange two men's land as the land of a young generation which deliberately rejects the present society's conventions and constraints in favour of an entirely new style of life.

Christie and Bruun (1968) argue that the existing *vagueness* in terminology—at least in the Scandinavian countries—serves to disguise inconsistencies in legislation and institutional practice. Such inconsistences are brought to our attention when we examine words and combinations of words such as "alcohol", "drugs", "narcotics", "use", "abuse" and "dependence". Alcohol and the barbiturates, for instance, appear to be equivalent in most respects, except that one is generally accepted for pleasures while the other is not. In spite of that, however, we have a complete organizational and conceptual split between alcohol and drugs. Christie and Bruun comment upon these facts as follows (1968, p. 3):

> To stress the resemblance between alcohol and drugs could interfere both with pleasures and other functions of alcohol in society. At the same time, it might also have some bad consequences in the fight against drugs. If the commonly used substance alcohol is a drug, then the horror-connotations around drugs might be substantially reduced—so let us keep them separate to the utmost content.

The public educator will hence encounter a series of dilemmas. He wants to reach the potential addict. But if he addresses himself to the latter with the presupposition that he shares the institutionalized values, he will alienate those who rebel. With the increased frequency of experience with drugs among young people, moreover, he has to consider his own message as second-hand information compared to the recipient's own private experience and observations of friends and agemates who are using drugs. The impact of verbal generalizations appears in general to be very weak as compared to relevant inductive evidence (Abelson and Kanouse, 1966). A generic assertion concerning the danger of drugs may still have the intended impact in an audience of young people from a law-abiding and puritan society with nearly no drug abuse, whereas the very same assertion may have an entirely different effect upon a group of young people who have tried smoking marijuana themselves and know others who use it regularly. An indiscriminate warning against drugs may in the latter case primarily reduce credibility. Subsequent very accurate descriptions of particularly serious effects of specific drugs may hence be distrusted, and an initial desire to experiment with "mind-expanding stuff" may actually be strengthened by an expectation of disconfirming "hypocritical propaganda".

The only possible way out of such dilemmas seems to be a so-called "neutral" and more precise language, and this is also the approach proposed by Christie and Bruun. This is by no means an easy way, however. Increased precision may first of all, as Christie and Bruun suggested, serve to disclose inconsistencies and "hypocrisies" inherent in the present penalty system. The public educator may therefore possibly be forced into a choice between a precise, neutral language with explicit rejection of some parts of the existing institutional practice *and* the present terminological ambiguities with acceptance of the practice. "Neutrality", moreover, is extremely difficult to define in these matters, and even more difficult to achieve. No programme of education can exclude private human experiences and social consequences in connection with drugs. Attempts at increased neutrality imply attempts at maximally value-free representations of such experiences and consequences. Talking about experiences as if they were entirely deprived of human values, however, is hardly the way to reach those potential addicts who claim that their use of drugs is part of a mode of living which can only be comprehended "from within", with full recognition of the existential freedom and as yet unexplored boundaries of human experiences. Increased precision and neutralization of the language of drugs and drug abuse may hence signal "Entfremdung" and thereby induce increased distance between sender and receiver when the latter happens to conceive of himself as a rebel against a dehumanized society in the hands of a hypocritical Establishment.

Questions in Connection with Public Education on Drugs and Drug Abuse via Mass Media

What emerges out of our tentative model of verbal communication and subsequent excursions into public communication on drug abuse may perhaps best be summarized in terms of some questions to be seriously considered when programmes of education via mass media are being planned. What is known about the spectrum of different backgrounds and presuppositions concerning drugs on the part of the recipients of the communication? Which—if any—position with respect to socially controversial issues is explicitly adopted? If none, which position is tacitly implied in terms of choice of key vocabulary and form of presentation? Who is being addressed by any particular part of the programme? What is being presupposed in terms of own experience with drugs and/or personal contact with users of drugs on the part of the recipient of communication? How does a given programme deal with different but interrelated subgoals such as breaking down barriers of communication, establishing credibility and transmission of information? Can the dilemmas due to ambiguities inherent in our social institutions and conflicting attitudes on the part of different categories of receivers be avoided by a deliberate neutralization and increased precision of the core terminology in the field? What do we know about potential consequences of such a strategy? Will it make people more aware of inconsistencies inherent in our present institutions dealing with sale, prescription and legal sanctions? Will it reduce the chance of reaching those potential addicts who experience their use of drugs in a subjective context of a novel and revolutionary mode of life?

The questions above may perhaps not even touch upon some of the most important practical issues, and they are certainly not inclusive. They are merely scattered illustrations converging in a plea for deliberate expansion of the scope of enquiries into communication and drug abuse far beyond the world of narrowly defined "facts" and manifest content of verbal communications.

References

Abelson, R. P. and Kanouse, D. E. (1966). Subjective acceptance of verbal generalizations. *In* "Cognitive Consistency". (S. Feldman, Ed.) Academic Press, New York and London.

Aubert, V. (1958). Legal justice and mental health. *Psychiatry* **21,** 101–113.

Blakar, R. M. and Rommetveit, R. (1971). Processing of utterances in contexts versus rote learning of sentences: Some pilot studies and a design for an experiment. *In* "Social Contexts of Messages". (E. A. Carswell and R. Rommetveit, Eds) Academic Press, London and New York.

Christie, N. and Bruun, K. (1968). The conceptual framework. Paper presented at the 28th International Congress on Alcohol and Alcoholism, Washington, D.C., September 15–20.

Henry, P. (1971). On processing of language in context and referents of messages. *In* "Social Contexts of Messages". (E. A. Carswell and R. Rommetveit, Eds) Academic Press, London and New York.

Hockett, C. F. (1963). The problems of universals of language. *In* "Universals of Language". (F. J. Greenberg, Ed.) M.I.T. Press, Cambridge.

Moscovici, S. and Plon, M. (1966). Les situations colloques: Observations theoretiques et experimentales. *Bulletin Psychology* **19,** 702–722.

Naess, A. (1933). "Interpretation and Preciseness." Jacob Dybwad, Oslo.

Pêcheux, M. (1969). "Vers l'analyse automatique du discours." Dunod, Paris.

Rommetveit, R. (1968). "Words, Meanings and Messages." Academic Press and Universitetsforlaget, New York, London and Oslo.

Rommetveit, R., Cook, M., Havelka, N., Henry, P., Herkner, W., Pêcheux, M. and Peeters, G. (1971). *In* "Social Contexts of Messages". (E. A. Carswell and R. Rommetveit, Eds) Academic Press, London and New York.

Wittgenstein, L. (1961). "Note Books". (G. H. von Wright and G. E. M. Anscomb, Eds) Harper and Row, New York.

30. Verbal Communications and Intensity of Delivery*

J. KLEIVEN

In several communication situations, e.g. listening to a TV debate, a speech, or a lecture, people's comments frequently focus on the speaker's physical appearance, his language, or his way of speaking. This may perhaps indicate that the spectators have been less preoccupied with what the speaker was saying than with the person himself and how he performed. Such a reaction, of course, is rarely intended by the speaker, and is hardly conducive to success in communicating a message. The present experiment attempts to study the effect of certain variations in speaker behaviour on the listener's focus of attention, and to see if a shift of attention away from the verbal message influences retention of the message.

In a review of message factors in attitude change, McGuire (1969, pp. 207–208) discusses briefly a variable called intensity of delivery. In persuasive communications, he holds:

> We might expect the more dynamic, intense presentation to be more effective in that it would better hold the receiver's attention, indicate more clearly what the point was, and cause greater yielding because of its more vivid presentation. On the other hand, we might expect it to be less effective in that the receiver would perceive it as more propagandistic and intending to persuade and hence discount its arguments somewhat.

He finds it difficult to anticipate "which of these opposite effects will be the more powerful in those several studies which define the delivery style only in general terms or in terms of judges' ratings where the criteria are not explicit".

The dilemma referred to might be avoided, however, by a reformu-

* This study was supported by the Norwegian Research Council for Science and the Humanities. Published in *Scandinavian J. Psychology* (1973) **14**, 111–113.

lation of the problem, without necessarily resorting to more specific or explicit terms or measures. If intensity of delivery is extended in both directions beyond the relatively small range conventionally employed in these studies, it may well be that both effects are operative, but in different parts of the scale. At low intensities, any increase in intensity of delivery may be beneficial, e.g. by increasing the listener's attention. At high intensities, on the other hand, a reverse effect may appear, e.g. if the listener discounts unduly propagandistic messages. Thus, the relationship between intensity of delivery and effectiveness of communication may be curvilinear, in that both very high and very low intensity of delivery are ineffective. The formal similarity with the model of Janis (1967) for analysing effects of emotional appeals, will be noted.

It seemed reasonable to suppose that attention to the message would be greatly reduced at either end of the scale. When intensity of delivery is very high or low, the listener's attention may be diverted from the verbal message, as such, to the speaker and his behaviour, while at moderate levels it may be directed primarily to what is being said; hence more would be learned and remembered at moderate than at extreme levels of delivery.

In line with the view of human communication as a multi-channel process (see, e.g. Argyle, 1969; Ekman, 1965), it seemed possible to vary the intensity of delivery by non-verbal means, such as gestures and facial expressions, and by a variety of paralinguistic cues, such as strength and pitch of voice, speech rate, etc. without altering the verbal message itself.

On this basis it was hypothesized that there would be a curvilinear relationship between the intensity of delivery and the listener's degree of attention to the verbal message itself, and hence between the intensity of delivery and the speaker's success in transmitting the verbal message.

Method

Stimulus Material

Five staged interviews were video-taped, each portraying a situation where a male person is asked by another to give his opinion on the question of Norway entering the European Economic Community (EEC)—a topic under lively debate at the time (April, 1971). The two roles were played by the same persons, the interviewer by the author and the interviewee by a professional actor, and the verbal dialogue was identical in all five cases. Physical setting and camera techniques were also kept constant. The interviewer always played a very minor part, mainly prompting the other to proceed, and he was not in the picture during most of the time.

Under three of the conditions (Low Normal, Normal and High Normal), care was taken to stay well within the range of what most observers would accept as normal behaviour in a television interview. In the Normal condition, the actor tried to be as persuasive as possible; he argued quite slowly and carefully, looking at the interviewer most of the time and using a normal volume of voice. In the Low Normal condition, he was obviously milder and quieter, a bit slower, and he used a greater number of hesitations and pauses. In the High Normal condition, he was more fluent and forceful than in the Normal, using a stronger voice, less pausing, and a slightly higher speech rate, besides a few hand gestures. In all these cases, gross differences in non-verbal behaviour were avoided, differentiation being obtained mainly through the use of such paralinguistic techniques as voice volume, speech rate and hesitation.

The more extreme cases employed a wider repertoire of non-verbal techniques. In the Low condition, the actor appeared visibly disinterested in the topic. He proceeded at a very slow rate, with long and frequent pauses, and with a flat and quiet voice. He spent most of his time looking around and away from the interviewer—even down into his own lap for extended periods. In the High condition, he looked obviously angry and excited after the first few words, and used a loud, strong voice at a fairly rapid rate. He was not sitting quietly, but kept looking around, and he used a clenched fist to underscore several of his points.

Subjects

Norwegian high school students around age 15 served as unpaid subjects, one class of about 20 students (about half of each sex) for each experimental condition. The five classes were very similar with respect to social background and school achievement.

Procedure

Each class was told that they would first be watching a TV interview, and then asked to fill in a questionnaire about it at once. The questionnaire was very simple, and the subjects were requested to write their names on the front page.

Two recall tasks were administered in the order indicated:

(1) On this page, you will give a short description of the television interview. Write here:

(2) In the interview, several arguments against Norwegian EEC membership were used. Write down as many of these as you can recall.

A recognition task followed, consisting of a check-list of 25 arguments about the EEC. The subjects were instructed to mark the 10 arguments on the list which had actually been used in the interview.

Finally, the subjects were asked to state briefly their personal opinion on the EEC issue.

Five minutes were allowed for completing each of the recall tasks, and three minutes for the recognition task.

The questionnaire also included similar recall and recognition measures of information about the person interviewed, but they need not concern us here.

Ratings

The responses to the recall tasks were rated by two independent judges, who knew neither the design nor the purpose of the experiment. They rated all responses to one task before proceeding to the next. The first task—description of the interview—was to be rated according to "the relative weight the description puts on the person and the informational content" of the interview, using a five-point scale as follows:

(1) Strongly biased toward describing the person.
(2) Slightly biased toward describing the person.
(3) Equal weight on person and content.
(4) Slightly biased toward informational content.
(5) Strongly biased toward informational content.

Before rating the responses to the second task, the judges were given a complete list of the arguments actually used in the interview. They were instructed to give a subjective estimate as to how well (from 0 to 100%) the arguments in the subject's description did cover the complete list.

Results

"Free" Recall of the Interview

The scores of the two raters of these descriptions gave $r = 0.80$, indicating satisfactory reliability. Using the mean of the two scores for each subject, the five group results are given in Table I. A one-way analysis of variance gave $F = 8.8964$, $p = 0.00003$; and t tests yielded significant differences ($p < 0.05$) between group 3 (Normal) and groups 1 (Low) and 5 (High). In addition, group 1 differed significantly from groups 2, 4 and 5. Thus, both high and low intensity of presentation yielded descriptions biased toward person information, while medium levels gave more argument-biased descriptions of the interview.

TABLE I. Mean ratings on the "free" recall task, low score indicating person-biased and high score argument-biased description of the interview.

Intensity of delivery	N	M	S.D.
High	24	3·8	1·3
High normal	20	4·1	1·2
Normal	23	4·5	0·8
Low normal	18	4·0	1·2
Low	17	2·4	1·4

Recall of Arguments

The reliability of ratings for recall was also considered satisfactory $(r = 0·76)$. One-way analysis of variance gave $p = 0·35$; nor did any two groups differ significantly.

Recognition of Arguments

One-way analysis of variance of the percentage of correct responses gave $p = 0·51$, and there was no significant difference between any two groups.

Concluding Remarks

Having replicated the experiment six months later (October, 1971) and obtained essentially the same results as above, it is clear that one of the measures employed was strongly affected by the staged variations in intensity of delivery; the ratings of the free descriptions show that subjects wrote relatively more about the informational content of the interview under conditions of medium levels of intensity than under the more extreme conditions.

It seems reasonable to accept the descriptions as an indication of how the interview was experienced by the subjects. If a subject describes the interview almost exclusively in terms of what was being said (as most subjects did in the Normal condition), it may be inferred that the content was most important to him, and hence what he attended to while listening. Conversely, if a description is centered around the interviewee's behaviour, it may be inferred that the subject paid relatively more attention to the person and how he acted. Hence the ratings of descriptions suggest that either a very forceful or a very subdued delivery may serve to shift the listener's attention away from what the speaker is saying. Nevertheless—and contrary to expectation—the speaker's success in transmitting the verbal message appears to be independent of mode of presentation under the conditions of this experiment.

It is likely, however, that the verbal message used was rather familiar and easy to follow for the subjects. This may be one reason why the shift of attention did not affect retention, and further research is being planned to check the possibility.

References

Argyle, M. (1969). "Social interaction." Atherton, New York.

Ekman, P. (1965). Communication through nonverbal behavior: A source of information about an interpersonal relationship. *In* "Affect, cognition, and personality". (S. S. Tomkins and C. E. Izard, Eds) Springer, New York.

Janis, I. L. (1967). Effects of fear arousal on attitude change. *In* "Advances in experimental social psychology". (L. Berkowitz, Ed.) Vol. 3. Academic Press, London and New York.

McGuire, W. L. (1969). The nature of attitudes and attitude change. *In* "Handbook of social psychology". (G. Lindzey and E. Aronson, Eds) Vol. 3. Addison-Wesley, Reading, Massachusetts.

31. Social Stereotypes Elicited by Linguistic Differences—Descriptive and Evaluative Aspects*

J. KLEIVEN

Lambert *et al.* (1960) have developed an experimental paradigm—the matched-guise technique—to show that language differences elicit stereotyped evaluations of speakers belonging to different linguistic-cultural groups. When listening to tape recordings of four bilingual speakers, who all read the same passage once in French and once in English, subjects were strongly influenced by the language used when making personality ratings of the readers. Adult English-speaking subjects—who were kept unaware of the fact that each speaker appeared twice—rated the speakers in their English guise more favourably than in their French guise on such traits as intelligence, dependability, ambition and character. And somewhat surprisingly, French-speaking subjects showed the same bias on several traits, i.e. evaluating a speaker more favourably in his English guise.

This technique has later been used in a number of studies of the social significance of different languages, since it "appears to reveal judges' more private reactions to the contrasting group than direct questionnaires do" (Lambert, 1967, p. 94; Lambert *et al.*, 1965). Lambert (1967) discussed these results in terms of a general evaluational bias in favour of the majority language of the community in question.

In Great Britain, rather similar results have been obtained by Cheyne (1970) and Giles (1971) in studies of evaluations of "Standard"

* This study was supported by the Norwegian Research Council for Science and the Humanities. *Reports from the Institute of Psychology*, University of Bergen (1974) No. 8, 1–8. Stencilled report.

The author is greatly indebted to Per Gjerde and Bjørn Ellertsen for their competent and enthusiastic assistance in all practical matters. Thanks are also due to the Bergen school authorities for granting us permission to use students from Rå and Dragefjellet secondary schools as subjects in the experiment.

English and certain regional accents. Other studies (Labov *et al.*, 1968; Bourhis *et al.*, 1973) have produced an apparently discrepant finding: minority group members evaluate speakers of the minority language more highly.

Discussing the results from a series of scales in terms of a general evaluational bias may be misleading, however, since rather similar descriptive facts may be quite differently evaluated and labelled by in- and out-group. Although French Canadians may rate the English-speaking guise as, e.g. more ambitious and intelligent and having more "character" when forced to use such scales, this need not imply a favourable evaluation of these traits. Perhaps scale labels with similar informational content but negative evaluational aspect would have been more representative of the minority group's views of the majority, e.g. pretentious, cunning and rigid. The evaluational implications of responses to certain scales could thus easily be misjudged: a minority group may agree that the majority is more "ambitious" in a purely descriptive way—without sharing the positive evaluation of this trait.

A preliminary study (Kleiven, 1972) has suggested that rather strong social stereotypes exist in the Bergen region of Norway. People from the city itself and people from the rural vicinity were viewed by Bergen students as belonging to two different social categories—"bergenser" and "stril"—two groups of people who use slightly different dialects. When asked to think about "what opinion most people at home would have", both students from Bergen and students from other places in Norway rated the "bergenser" as, e.g. more self-sufficient, snobbish, frivolous, enthusiastic and ambitious than his rural neighbour. The "stril" was seen as, e.g. more religious, stable, poor, stupid and quiet.

The main purpose of the present study is to see if such stereotyped impressions will be elicited by the relatively small differences between the urban and the rural dialects—through the use of the matched-guise technique. In an attempt to minimize the confounding of evaluative and descriptive aspects of scales, however, scales were used that would include both positive and negative evaluations of both groups.

Method

Stimulus Material

Tape recordings were made of four fluently bidialectal individuals reading the same letter to the editor from a local newspaper. Two male and two female voices were used for the "experimental" recordings, each voice reading the passage once in Bergen city dialect and once in a dialect from Fana—a rural area geographically very close to the city.

The two recordings of each speaker were made as similar as possible in terms of duration, speech rate, pauses and vocal quality. The resulting eight recordings were interspersed in an approximated random order among 10 "filler" recordings of different voices—recordings of five voices from Bergen and five voices from Fana reading the same passage. Each pair of matched voices was separated as much as possible, and the first of these recordings appeared as the third voice on the tape. All recordings were between $1\frac{1}{2}$ and 2 min long.

Rating Scales

From a set of seven-point scales which had been tried out in a preliminary study (Kleiven, 1972), 15 were selected for use in the present experiment. The scales are given in Table I. Twelve of the scales had previously yielded statistically significant differences between the judgements of "bergenser" and "stril" groups. The remaining three scales (nos 2, 6 and 23) had yielded significant interaction effects

TABLE I. Mean ratings of "bergenser" and "stril" guises.

Scales	"bergenser"	"stril"
(1) uttrykksfull/tam (expressive/tame)	3·7	3·9
(2) normal/rar (normal/strange)	3·6	3·8
(3) sneversynt/tolerant (narrow-minded/tolerant)	3·6	3·9
(4) ærgjerrig/likegyldig (ambitious/indifferent)	4·0	4·0
(5) overlegen/grei (haughty/straightforward)	3·9	4·4
(6) vulgær/fin (vulgar/fine)	4·2	4·1
(7) dum/klok (stupid/wise)	4·1	4·0
(8) reservert/åpen (reserved/open)	4·7	4·6
(9) affektert/uaffektert (affected/unaffected)	4·2	4·3
(10) ung/eldre (young/older)	3·1	3·3
(11) snobbete/usnobbete (snobbish/unsnobbish)	4·2	4·7
(12) usikker/sjølgod (unsure/self-satisfied)	4·7	4·4
(13) real/lunefull (straight/capricious)	3·4	3·4
(14) moderne/umoderne (modern/unmodern)	3·6	4·4
(15) ekte/tilgjort (genuine/affected)	3·4	3·2

between judged groups and subjects' background: i.e. data from Bergen subjects yielded other group differences than did the data from other subjects. As mentioned above, care was taken to include adjective pairs that would imply both negative and positive judgements of both groups. The final set of scales were given in a small booklet containing the instructions, and with one page of scales for each of the 18 recordings on the tape.

Subjects

Two classes of high school students were used, one from Bergen and one from Fana. Students were representative of the dialects concerned, and were about 14 years old. The Bergen sample included 11 boys and 16 girls, and the Fana sample 12 boys and 11 girls.

Procedure

The subjects were first asked to write their name and class on the front page, and then turn to the next page, where the instructions were given. The experimenter also read aloud the instructions, in which the subjects were first reminded of the common tendency to judge the personalities of speakers heard over the telephone or the radio, and then asked to use the rating scales to evaluate the voices on the tape. An example of how to use a seven-point scale was shown on the blackboard. The subjects were instructed to put a check *in the margin* of the page if a scale was felt not to be appropriate. A two minute time limit for rating each voice was introduced, and the first two voices were used as practice runs. After each, an opportunity was given to ask questions. When all questions had been answered, the subjects were reminded of the time limit, and the remaining 16 voices were rated.

Results

For each subject, the mean of his four ratings of each dialect was used as a score. The means of these scores are given in Table I. Two-way analyses of variance were carried out on all scales, the first factor being urban *vs* rural subjects, and the second being urban *vs* rural dialect guises. The results of the analyses are summarized in Table II.

The statistically significant main effect on the first factor that was obtained on scales 1 and 10 is not immediately relevant to our concerns—it shows that the two subject groups used these scales differently. On the second factor, significant main effects were obtained on scales 5, 10, 11, 12 and 14. Table I shows this to mean that the Bergen city guises were seen as more haughty, snobbish and self-sufficient than their rural counterparts, and that the rural guises also were rated as older and less modern. No significant interaction effects between the two factors were obtained, indicating that the observed guise differences were similar for the two groups of judges.

Discussion

The data clearly show that different social stereotypes were elicited by the two dialects. On five out of 15 scales, voices with a Bergen city

TABLE II. F-values obtained in analyses of variance on mean ratings of "bergenser" and "stril" guises made by subjects from two dialect areas.

Scale no.	Subject's dialect (A) d.f. = 1·48	Guise (B) d.f. = 1·48	Interaction (A × B) d.f. = 1·48
(1)	12·368[a]	2·257	0·122
(2)	1·577	1·386	1·116
(3)	0·591	3·240	0·276
(4)	0·021	0·116	0·078
(5)	2·152	10·582[a]	1·969
(6)	2·602	0·470	0·564
(7)	3·920	0·182	0·004
(8)	0·429	0·298	0·514
(9)	0·942	0·272	0·152
(10)	9·765[a]	8·024[a]	0·633
(11)	3·413	8·512[a]	1·316
(12)	1·048	10·524[a]	0·097
(13)	2·561	0·186	0·321
(14)	2·598	60·762[b]	0·114
(15)	0·766	1·397	0·974

[a] $p < 0.01$.
[b] $p < 0.001$.

dialect were rated as significantly different from voices with a rural Fana dialect. This may have important consequences for the people concerned: When using these dialects one obviously runs the risk of being stereotyped in rather definite ways. It may also be noted, however, that since the dialects concerned are sufficiently similar to enable most people to do some switching between the two, the speaker here has an opportunity of manipulating other people's impression of himself. Through choice of dialect, one may determine which stereotypes will be elicited (cf. Blom and Gumperz, 1971).

The differences obtained in the present study are consistent with previous results, but are generally weaker and less consistent than what was suggested by the preliminary study of the scales (Kleiven, 1972). It seems likely, however, that the former procedure of asking subjects "what opinion most people at home would have" about the two groups may have rather strong demand characteristics, leading to exaggerated differences in judgements. Another reason for expecting a weaker effect in the present study, is that subjects' attention to the characteristics of the voices may yield information that will counteract the stereotypes concerned. Although a "bergenser" will generally be stereotyped as, e.g. rather expressive and affected, the voices in the present experiment may in fact have other characteristics, so that these aspects of the stereotypes are overruled by the factual information. A recent article by Delia (1972) may also lend some support to this hypothesis, demonstrating that although dialect-cued stereotypes do influence first impressions rather strongly, they may later yield to other types of information.

In contrast to previous studies, no clear evaluative preference for one group was apparent. The urban voices were closer to the favourable end of some scales, the rural voices on others. Since the present scales were selected with the explicit intention of permitting both negative and positive evaluations of both groups, this may suggest that choice of scales is a critical factor in the evaluations obtained in studies of this type. It may be noted that Peabody (1967) recommends that a distinction be maintained between evaluative and descriptive aspects of judgements. A later study (Peabody, 1968) shows that different ethnic groups in the Phillipines tended to agree about the descriptive, factual characteristics of each group, but to disagree about the evaluation of each other. Although not directly addressed to this point, the present study may suggest that the distinction between evaluative and descriptive aspects should be considered also when selecting scales for matched-guise studies. Since subjects in earlier studies may have responded to the descriptive aspects of scales without necessarily agreeing about the evaluative aspect, discussing the results of these studies in terms of a general evaluative bias may be misleading.

References

Blom, J. P. and Gumperz, J. J. (1972). Social meaning in linguistic structures: Code-switching in Norway. In "Directions in Sociolinguistics: The Ethnography of Communication". (J. J. Gumperz and D. Hymes, Eds) Holt, Rinehart and Winston, New York.

Bourhis, R. Y., Giles, H. and Tajfel, H. (1973). Language as a determinant of Welsh identity. European J. Social Psychology 3, (4), 447–460.

Cheyne, W. M. (1970). Stereotyped reactions to speakers with Scottish and English regional accents. British J. social clinical Psychology 9, 77–79.

Delia, J. G. (1972). Dialects and the effects of stereotypes in interpersonal attraction and cognitive processes in impression formation. Quarterly J. Speech 58, (3), 258–297.

Giles, H. (1971). Patterns of evaluation to R. P., South Welsh and Somerset accented speech. British J. social clinical Psychology 10, 280–281.

Kleiven, J. (1972). Some stereotypes attached to social groups in the Bergen region—a preliminary study. Reports from the Institute of Psychology, University of Bergen, No. 8.

Labov, W., Cohen, P., Robins, C. and Lweis, J. (1968). "A study of the Nonstandard English of Negro and Puerto Rican speakers in New York City." Final Report, Cooperative Research Project No. 3288, Vols I and II. Office of Education, Washington, D.C.

Lambert, W. E. (1967). A social psychology of bilingualism. *J. social issues* **23,** 91–109.

Lambert, W. E., Hodgson, R. C., Gardner, R. C. and Fillenbaum, S. (1960). Evaluational reactions to spoken languages. *J. Abnormal Social Psychology* **60,** 44–51.

Lambert, W. E., Anisfeld, M. and Yeni-Komshian, G. (1963). Evaluational reactions of Jewish and Arab adolescents to dialect and language variations *J. Personality Social Psychology* **2,** 84–90.

Peabody, D. (1967). Trait inferences. Evaluative and descriptive aspects. *J. Personality Social Psychology* **7,** (Whole No. 644).

Peabody, D. (1968). Group judgment in the Phillipines: Evaluative and descriptive aspects. *J. Personality Social Psychology* **10,** 290–300.

32. How Sex Roles are Represented, Reflected and Conserved in the Norwegian Language*

R. M. BLAKAR

Introduction

As part of a series of analyses of "language as a means of social power" (Blakar, 1971, 1972a, b, collected in Blakar, 1973) a systematic analysis of some aspects of the complicated "social reality—language" relationship had to be undertaken. We wanted to test the hypothesis that language is *not* a neutral tool, but in its conceptualization of the "reality" represents the *perspective(s)* and *interest(s)* of the ones in power. With regard to Norwegian, such a point of view could have been illustrated by analysing how the language as such *represents* the perspective(s) and interests(s) of, e.g. urban people as opposed to rural people, of employers as opposed to workers, of grown-ups as opposed to children, etc. However, we chose to analyse *if* and eventually *how* Norwegian, in our male dominated society, represented men's perspectives and interests at the expense of women.

Naturally such an analysis is primarily of interest to those who speak Norwegian. Moreover, it is difficult, not to say impossible, to translate such an analysis into another language. A "translation" would almost automatically imply conducting a similar analysis on that second language. On the other hand, some of the findings and conclusions reached through our analysis may be of more general interest, from a linguistic as well as a social perspective. This is even more so, since

* The author is indebted to Ragnar Rommetveit, Colin Fraser, Hilde Eileen Nafstad, Ivana Markova, Jacob Mey and Harriet Holter for useful comments and suggestions. The research upon which the present paper is based was supported by Norwegian Research Council for Science and the Humanities on grant B. 60.01–85. Published in *Acta Sociologica* (1975) **14**, 515–534.

there has recently become a more serious interest in exploring "sexism in language" (cf. Lakoff's (1973) analysis of "sexism in English").

Approaches and Methods

The following quotation from Lakoff (1973, p. 57) gives a representative idea of the problems she focused on as well as the approaches she chose:

> . . . the problem of women and the English language: the way in which women prejudice the case against themselves by their use of language. But it is at least as true that others—as well as women themselves—make matters so by the way in which they refer to women. Often a word that may be used of both men and women (and perhaps of things as well) when applied to women, assumes a special meaning that, by implication rather than outright assertion, is derogatory to women as a group.

In other words, Lakoff devoted her paper to two different analyses, one of *how* women talk English, and one of *how* women are talked about in English. In our study of Norwegian, only the last of the two analyses was performed. While Lakoff posed the very open question "how women are talked about in English", we asked the more restricted one "how is the female sex role (as compared to the male sex role) *represented* in Norwegian". This implies that while Lakoff was free to analyse what may be called "sexism in (verbal) interaction", we restricted ourselves to an analysis of "sexism in the tool (the language) itself". On this background it is interesting that we reached very much the same conclusions.

Lakoff's description of her methodical approach is fairly representative for me as well: "The data on which I am basing my claims have been gathered mainly by introspection: I have examined my own speech and that of my acquaintances, and have used my own intuition in analysing it". (Lakoff, 1973, p. 46.) However, the analysis of the two words "mann" (man) and "kvinne" (woman) was conducted on the basis of more systematically collected data. In this analysis more thorough empirical data, such as word associations and sentence completion tasks were used together with dictionaries. Furthermore, the language in newspapers, advertising, cartoons and other forms of written Norwegian was analysed with respect to sex role representation.*

---

* A particular aid in collecting such data in a systematic way, was a computer programme which could search for particular sequences of letters, and print out the context in which they appeared. In our case the key words searched for were "kvinne" and "mann". I am grateful to Hans Olav Egede-Larsen for his kindness in allowing me to use his programme.

Findings and Conclusions

The main findings may be subsumed under four headings, all of direct relevance to the mutual interaction between *social reality* and *language*: (1) A systematic mapping of the sex roles as represented in the language exposed a very clear, if somewhat exaggerated picture of sex role distribution in Norway. The perspectives and interests represented in and expressed by the language proved to be at the woman's expense. (2) The analysis revealed that language as such in various ways exerts *resistance* against social change of the type that the women's liberation movement represents. (3) Furthermore, it illustrated how the sex role pattern is transmitted to new generations *via* the language. (4) Taking the above findings as a point of departure, strategies were outlined for *how* language could be changed into a tool in the fight for social change, i.e. in the women's liberation movement. In this somewhat summary presentation, the analysis and findings will be presented and discussed in relation to each one of these four headings.

Of course, these four findings are not independent, but in different ways interrelated. Naturally, the resistance of the language against women's emancipation follows more or less by implication from the finding that our language is a man's language. Much the same holds as regards the fact that the sex role pattern is transmitted via the language.

Two reservations have to be made, however. First, it will *not* be maintained that language is the only factor, not even the main one, in conserving our male dominated society with its oppression of women. It will be shown, however, that language is *one* of these factors, and a factor very often neglected and overlooked, thereby being extremely underestimated. Secondly, it will *not* be maintained that the language represents the main tool in the women's liberation movement. However, it will be argued that, exploited in a more systematic and reflective way than is the case today, language may represent *one* of the effective tools.

The Sex Roles as Represented in Norwegian: A comparison between the words "mann" (man) and "kvinne" (woman)

If Norway had been a society characterized by equality between the two sexes, and if this status of equality had been reflected in the language, an analysis of the two words "mann" (man) and "kvinne" (woman) should reveal no *other differences* than the ones *directly* dependent upon sex. However, an analysis reveals immediately that the two words are *dissimilar* in many other respects as well. For example, "mann" seems to imply higher status than "kvinne". In Norwegian many social roles having a higher status are labelled ". . . -mann", even though the position can be held by women. Examples are "for*mann*" (chairman), "fylkes*mann*" (district governor), "statsjeneste*mann*" (civil servant), etc. Even if we take a neutral field, such as sport, we find "mål*mann*" (goal keeper) and "anker*mann*" (anchor man) on female teams as well. Metaphorical use of language may be particularly revealing in showing *how* different the two words are with respect to status (high–low), emotionally (positive–negative), etc. An illustrative example is the following often used expressions: (a) "*mannen* i huset" (the man of the house/home) and (b) "*kvinna* i huset" (the woman of the house/home). Such metaphorical expressions do not have a precise meaning, but while (a) seems to refer to the one being the authority of the family, (b) gives associations in direction of somebody making it nice and comfortable.

Long lists of such examples testifying to a strong degree of sexism in Norwegian could easily be given. However, we wish to tie our analysis of "language–social reality" more closely to theory. In our analysis of the words "mann" and "kvinne", we wish to take Rommetveit's (1968, 1972a) model of word processing as our point of departure. In theoretical as well as empirical analyses Rommetveit has shown that in processing a word, three different components or processes are elicited; a referential, an associative and an emotive component. In our analysis we wanted to cover all three components. In this way we will not run the risk of being accused of merely having picked examples to fit our hypothesis (cf. footnote on p. 410).

According to this programme a standard Norwegian dictionary* was first examined as regards the meaning of "mann" and "kvinne". The lists of synonyms given differed in a lot of ways. Most striking was the fact that many more synonyms were given to "kvinne", particularly very many *negative* and *derogatory* synonyms. (It is a pity that such lists of synonyms are totally impossible to translate, but my impression is that dictionaries of English show a parallel tendency.) A few observations may be worth mentioning, just to give an idea of the differences. "Mor" (mother) is given in the list of synonyms to or explanations of "kvinne", while "far" (father) is *not* given to "mann". "Person" (person) and "personlighet" (personality) were given to "mann", but *not* to "kvinne". Moreover, "arbeider" (worker) was given to "mann" while no corresponding term was given to "kvinne".

In a standardization of word associations in Norway (Håseth, 1968) "mann" as well as "kvinne" were included in the list of stimulus words (a Norwegian translation of the Kent-Rosanoff list of words). It was possible, therefore, to compare the associations given to these two words by a representative Norwegian sample. The associations elicited tell us

* "Norsk Synonymordbok" (1970) Gyldendal, Oslo.

a lot about how men and women are conceived of (Blakar, 1972c). Thus, "arbeid" (work), "arbeidskar" (worker), and even "karriere" (career) were given as responses to "mann", but *not* to "kvinne". On the other hand "sex" (sex), "sexy" (sexy), and "seng" (bed) were all elicited by "kvinne", but *not* by "mann". Furthermore, many more answered "barn" (child/children) and "mor" (mother) to "kvinne", than "barn" (child/children) and "far" (father) to "mann". This observation is consistent with the fact that "mor" (mother) was given in the list of synonyms to "kvinne". Among other things, these responses indicate that "kvinne" seems to imply "mother and mistress", while "mann" seems to imply "somebody doing a job". And, in the dictionary "elskerinne" (mistress) was actually given in the list of synonyms to "kvinne", while "elsker" (lover) was *not* given to "mann".

In order to explore the emotive component of the two words more systematically, the semantic differential (Osgood *et al.*, 1957) was applied. The words "mann" and "kvinne" were presented as key words together with a list of other words, and rated on 29 seven-point scales. Nothing was said about sex roles; only the standard instruction as presented by Osgood *et al.* was used. "Kvinne" and "mann" were rated significantly* differently on the following scales: (In all the cases "kvinne" is closer than "mann" to the first mentioned pole of the scale.) *myk-hard* (soft-hard)**, *varm-kald* (warm-cold)**, *følsom-følelsesløs* (sensitive-insensitive/unfeeling)**, *farlig-ufarlig* (dangerous-not dangerous)**, *usikker-sikker* (insecure-secure)*, *spennende-kjedelig* (exciting-boring)*, *tiltrekkende-frastøtende* (attractive-repellant)*, *søt-sur* (sweet-sour)**, *rund-kantet* (round-angular)**, *lett-tung* (light-heavy)**, *liten-stor* (small-big)**, *ren-skitten* (clean-dirty)**, *åpen-lukket* (open-closed)**†. It is worth noting that there was almost no difference as regards *how* the male and the female subjects rated "mann" and "kvinne" on the various scales. In other words, men and women conceive of and understand themselves through the very same language, and this seems to be a language representing and expressing the man's interest(s) and perspective(s).

Studies of words *in isolation* may be misleading, and one has to be extremely careful when interpreting and generalizing (Rommetveit, 1968, 1972a; Rommetveit and Blakar, 1973; Blakar, 1970). To get a first check on our findings on the word level, sentence completion and sentence sorting tasks were applied. (Of course, all the problems related

* Levels of significance: **0·01, *0·05.

† On the other hand, it is worth noting that "mann" and "kvinne" were not significantly (0·05) different as regards: *dum-klok* (stupid-wise), *svak-sterk* (weak-strong), *våt-tørr* (wet-dry), *edru-full* (sober-drunk), *fattig-rik* (poor-rich), *stygg-pen* (ugly-handsome), *optimistisk—pessimistisk* (optimistic-pessimistic), *upraktisk-praktisk* (impractical-practical), *nyttig-unyttig* (useful-useless), *passiv-aktiv* (passive-active), *god-dårlig* (good-bad), *økonomisk-uøkonomisk* (economical-uneconomical).

to studying linguistic units in isolation or out of relevant contexts are *not* solved merely by expanding the scope from words in isolation to words in sentences (cf. Rommetveit, 1968, 1972a,b; Blakar and Rommetveit, 1975).) The findings from the different methods were similar, and consistent with what would be predicted from the analysis of "mann" and "kvinne" above. Therefore, only one of the tasks will briefly be described:

Fifty sentences of the type "Det var en mann/en kvinne som . . ." (There was a man/a woman who . . .) was given to the subjects. They were asked to sort the sentences, putting 10 in each of the following five categories: (1) Absolutely most reasonable with "kvinne", (2) More reasonable with "kvinne", (3) Equally reasonable with "mann" as with "kvinne", (4) More reasonable with "mann", and (5) Absolutely most reasonable with "mann". Each sentence was given a score of 1 when put in category (1), a score of 2 when put in category (2), etc. With 10 subjects, five male and five female students participating, the score could vary from 10 to 50, with a "neutral point" at 30.

The scores on some of the sentences will show that the differences revealed in the analysis of the words "mann" and "kvinne" in isolation, are *activated* or actually *"played upon"* when the two words are exposed in the context of a sentence. The sentences with the highest scores, i.e. the most typical for "mann", were: ". . . som reparerte bilen" (. . . who repaired the car), which scored 49, and ". . . some kjørte i fylla" (. . . who was driving while drunk), which scored 48. While the sentences with lowest scores, i.e. the most typical for "kvinne", were: ". . . som kjøpte symaskin" (. . . who bought a sewing machine), which scored 14, and ". . . som vasket trappa" (. . . who washed the staircase), which also scored 14. And, around the "neutral" point, ". . . som arbeidet i hagen" (. . . who worked in the garden) scored exactly 30. A more detailed inspection of the sentences sorted, reveals a lot of interesting aspects about the use of the words "mann" and "kvinne". For example, ". . . som hadde svært god lønn" (. . . who earned a very high wage) scored very high (46), while ". . . som hadde svært dårlig lønn" (. . . who earned a very low wage) scored very low (17). It is a bit funny to note that ". . . som drakk øl" (. . . who drank beer) scored very high (44), while ". . . some drakk sherry" (. . . who drank sherry) scored very low (17). It is also interesting that the activity of washing itself seems not to be dependent *only* upon sex, because while ". . . som vasket trappa" (. . . who washed the staircase) got the lowest score (14) of all the 50 sentences, ". . . som vasket bilen" (. . . who washed the car), on the other hand, scored very high (45). And, let it be mentioned that while ". . . som utførte mordet" (. . . who murdered) got a very high score (45), ". . . som ble myrdet" (. . . who was murdered) got a relatively low score (22).

The above analyses have given us a fair idea of the *definitions*, or more adequate, the *meaning potentials*, we keep in mind while using the words "mann" and "kvinne". The differences between the two definitions are highlighted by an examination of the following two pairs of words:

"kvinne" (woman)—*"yrkeskvinne"* (a woman employed outside her own home)

"mann" (man)—*"yrkesmann"* (a man employed outside his own home)

Of these four easily comprehensible Norwegian words, a single one, namely "yrkes*mann*" seems to be strange or even impermissible in Norwegian. Something seems to be fundamentally wrong with this constructed word. The word "mann", as opposed to the word "kvinne", seems somehow *by definition* (cf. the analysis above) to imply being employed outside the home. (In linguistic terminology one might say that "mann" is unmarked while "kvinne" is marked as regards this aspect.) When the word "mann" is used, it seems almost to be implied that the one referred to has a job. The constructed word "yrkes*mann*" represents, therefore, *a totally redundant construction in Norwegian*. If the meaning of words are represented with circles, "being employed outside the home" would be included *within* the circle ("meaning potential", cf. Rommetveit, 1968, 1972a) of "mann", but be *outside* the circle of "kvinne" (cf. also the dictionary and the word associations above). When a woman is employed outside the home, this has to be made *explicit*, e.g. by introducing the composed word "yrkes*kvinne*". As will be seen later this may have fundamental implications for boys and girls growing up to become men and women.

Provocatively, it may be concluded that in Norwegian the words "kvinne" (woman) and "kvinneleg" (female) imply nothing but *"ikkje-mann"* (*non*-man), while it is "mann" (man) that means something. (Again, linguists might say that "kvinne" is marked and "mann" unmarked.) This is clearly reflected in expressions such as "kvinneleg formann" (female chairman), "kvinneleg drosjesjåfør" (female taxi driver), "kvinneleg lege" (female doctor), etc. If nothing is said about the sex, the tacit presupposition in Norwegian (and English?) seems to be that the person in focus is a man. If "formann" (chairman), "sjef" (chief), or "drosjesjåfør" (taxi driver) are used with no specification of sex, it is automatically conceived of and interpreted as referring to a man. If it is a woman, it has to be explicitly stated. This conclusion corresponds nicely to the well-known fact that the poles in a contrast pair may be marked or unmarked.

The very same type of sexism as we have demonstrated on the word level, seems to pervade our whole language. For example, our system of address and presentation seems to imply that it is always the man who holds the actual position or title. Suppose that Mr Hansen is a professor. His wife may then—in Norway—be presented and addressed as "fru professor Hansen" (Mrs Professor Hansen), and it is unlikely that this will be misunderstood in the direction that *she* is the professor. However, suppose that Mrs Hansen is a professor. It is then totally improbable that Mr Hansen will be presented or addressed as "herr professor Hansen" (Mr Professor Hansen). Such a presentation would also result in the misunderstanding that *he* is the professor. Our system of presentation and address is all about the man. The woman is merely presented as an item more or less incidentally attached to the man. This point is made extremely clear by Norsk Lysningsblad (the official Norwegian gazette containing announcements of marriage, etc.) where the husband is consistently presented *with* title, whereas the wife is merely presented as "hustru" (wife).

Somebody may prefer to argue that the above analysis has not at all revealed any *sexism* in the (Norwegian) language. The analysis has only demonstrated that the language, as a tool, is developed so as to function most adequately in society as it is, namely male dominated. This argument may at first seem to be convincing. However, for one thing, the language proved not only to reflect the sex roles in the surrounding society, but the differences and the downgrading of the women were even exaggerated. Secondly, the language—as we will see—functions so as to *resist* change toward greater equality, thereby contributing to "keep women in the kitchen".

Resistance of Language to Social Change

In two different but interrelated ways language may exert resistance to basic social change of the type that the women's liberation movement represents. Firstly, the language structure itself represents a conserving factor. Language is constructed by and during earlier generations. Hence, the language reflects and represents the conditions—social and psychological as well as material—of "earlier times". Secondly, new or recent linguistic constructs may actually delay social change, e.g. by concealing or veiling the "real" situation. This last fact is related to the complex power distribution in society, i.e. who is powerful enough to have their linguistic and conceptual proposals generally accepted (Blakar, 1973).

The analysis above has suggested *how* the language is a main factor in defining, and, thereby in oppressing and downgrading women. As soon as women try to occupy any of the man's traditional privileged positions, the language seems to exert resistance. The language "lacks terms for a female . . .", "a female . . . sounds amusing", etc.

This preserving aspect of language may seem obvious. It may be of more surprise that recently created linguistic terms or labels may actually work in the very same direction. An illustrative example (from Norwegian) will be presented and discussed in some detail. Our society is hierarchical, and as regards the two sexes, the proportion of women is smaller toward the top than toward the bottom. This is also reflected in the language, e.g. in titles and labels. Two random examples are "stortings*mann*" (Deputy to the Norwegian Parliament) and "vaske-*kone*" (charwoman or washwoman), where the first has high status and the last low status. The slowly increasing development toward greater equality has brought a few women into the Norwegian parliament (Storting), and a few men have got washing jobs. Of course, these changes had to be reflected in the language. Logically seen, this change could have been taken into account in three different ways:

(1) "-mann" and "-kone" could have been given extended meaning, so that the words "stortings*mann*" and "vaske*kone*" could be used irrespective of sex. This is the case with, e.g. "for*mann*" (chairman) and "mål*mann*" (goal keeper), which are used irrespective of sex.

(2) As a consequence following directly from this development, the words "stortings*kvinne*" and "vaske*mann*" respectively could have been introduced. The first one of these two has actually been used to a certain extent, while the last one has not been used at all. As we will see, this might have been the most adequate solution as far as equality between the sexes is regarded.

(3) By means of new labels *not* containing "-mann" and/or "-kone", thereby being neutral as regards sex. This third alternative has actually been the chosen solution, and the recently constructed words "stortingsrepresentant" (parliamentary representative) and "reingjerings-hjelp" (cleaning assistant) have been introduced.

This solution apparently is neutral as regards sex, since "-mann" and "-kone" have been replaced by the neutral "-*representant*" (representative) and "-*hjelp*" (assistant). Nevertheless, these new linguistic constructions have actually had a veiling effect. Firstly, the situation is that only very few women have yet been elected to the Norwegian Parliament (Storting) and relatively few men have got washing jobs. But *because* we are now talking about "-representant" and "-hjelp", and not about "-mann" and "-kone", the unequal distribution is *not* as easily detectable any longer. Secondly—and this is even more serious, and illustrates the powerful conserving effect of language in general— the neutral label "-representant" has been absorbed in the linguistic system, and has become more and more closely associated with *men*. Since it is not labelled "-mann" any more, it is easy to overlook this discriminatory state. A brief quotation from a Norwegian newspaper will show how strong and pervasive this veiling effect actually is: "Yesterday Parliament was assembled for the first time after vacation. The representatives, even some of their wives, met in the corridors...".* From this quotation it becomes obvious that "-representant" (representative) has already lost its apparent neutrality, since the members *have wives*.

Transmitting the Sex Roles to New Generations

Language reflects, represents and conserves social reality. Furthermore, language plays an active role in transmitting social reality to new generations (Berger and Luckman, 1967). The sex roles are transmitted both directly and indirectly *via* language and language use.

A short story from everyday life in Norway will illustrate the *direct* linguistic influence: A mother came along with her two children, a little girl of six and a young shaver of two or three. The little girl is long, thin and ungainly, as is often the case at that age, while the boy is short and chubby. An elderly lady, meeting them, compliments the children in the following way: "for ein stor, kraftig kar". (What a big, strong boy.) "For ei nett og pen lita jente". (What a nice, pretty little girl.) The mother as well as the children seem to be very well satisfied. For one who happened to be standing nearby, there is a striking discrepancy between the children observed and what is said about them. The compliments given seem *not* at all to be influenced by the actual children, but rather to represent (appreciative) linguistic constructions or stereotypes. Such compliments—compliments often reflect ideals—surely influence and shape the children.

The *indirect* influence is not equally obvious. Generally, it can be maintained that we grow into a culture or a society, e.g. the Norwegian male dominated society, by learning the actual language. However, let us try to exemplify the influence exerted by this mechanism too. The young boy knows that he is going to become "*mann*". We have seen that to be "mann" implies a lot of different functions or aspects, among other things "å ha eit yrke" (to be employed outside the home). While "learning" the language, particularly the word "mann", the young boy realizes that *he has to get a job*. On this point he seems to be left with no choice. Realizing this, naturally, involves a very strong intrinsic motivation to qualify oneself for a proper job.

The situation faced by the young girl on exactly this point is a very different one. She knows that she will become "kvinne". To be "kvinne"

* In Norwegian: "I går var Stortinget samlet for første gang etter ferien. Representantene, ja til og med noen av deres fruer, møttes i korridorene . . ." From "Dagbladet" October 3rd, 1970.

implies a lot of different aspects and functions. But, as we have seen "kvinne" does *not* imply "å ha eit yrke" (to be employed outside the home). Contrary to the young boy, the young girl—implicitly or explicitly—has to make *a choice* as to whether or not she is going to have a job, i.e. is going to become "yrkeskvinne" (to be employed outside the home).

One can easily imagine how the mere fact that the definition of "mann" but *not* of "kvinne" implies "å ha eit yrke", *may* influence the development from boy to man and from girl to woman. Analogous reasoning may, of course, be made as regards all other aspects where the words "mann" and "kvinne" differ.

However, on this point a word of warning may be needed. What is discriminating against the women is *not* the linguistic labels as such, but the (social) reality which is conceived of, and hence preserved and transferred, by the language. And, we share the programmatic position stated by Lakoff (1973, p. 73) when she is claiming that: "Linguistic imbalances are worthy of study *because they bring into sharper focus* real-word imbalances and inequities. They are *clues* that some external situation need changing . . ." (my italics).

Language—A Possible Ally in the Women's Liberation Movement

From the women's point of view, this analysis may have revealed language as a barrier almost impossible to surmount on the road toward equality. It may be added that the influence of language can have been so strong and pervasive only because most people *have been unaware of it*. Therefore, a very important first step in getting rid of or at least in reducing the influential sexism in language is just to make people be aware of and reflect upon the actual state of affairs.

Having analysed sexism in the Norwegian language along the lines illustrated above (Blakar, 1971, 1973), we have tried to point out *how* language and language use could possibly be changed into an ally of those who want social change, leading to greater equality. Two strategies have been outlined. One is to be used at the present stage in order to reveal the sexism implicit in the language. (The present analysis is itself an example of this strategy.) The main techniques proposed are: (1) Every time the language is used discriminatorily against women— either by yourself or by somebody else—to question and make explicit the premises for this particular use of language. For example, when using or hearing the word "yrkeskvinne", the question should be posed *why* such a discriminatory term is used. (2) To *reverse* the actual language use. This technique is extremely powerful in making people aware of the linguistic oppression of the women. This reversal can be accomplished, e.g. by consistently talking about "a male chairman", "a male doctor", "a male taxi driver", etc., thereby revealing the discriminatory aspect implicit in such common expressions as "a female chairman", "a female doctor", "a female taxi driver", etc. Furthermore, a lot of eyeopeners such as "masculinist" (feminist), "charman" (charwoman), "houseman" (housewife), etc. may be constructed and used.*

This first strategy has as a consequence that the sex dimension is foregrounded all the time. This may actually be necessary in order to counteract the conservative influence exerted by the language in this case. A further strategy intended to reduce excessive focusing on the sex dimension has hence more of a long-term purpose. This strategy is to create linguistic labels which are neutral as regards sex. However, on this point we have to be on our guard, not to be trapped as was the case with the apparently neutral term "stortingsrepresentant". Before this strategy can be effectively used, we have to get closer to a state of true equality (cf. the two reservations made on p. 411). In attaining this state, the techniques proposed above may hopefully represent an effective tool.

Concluding Remarks

If we now leave the concrete topic of our analysis, we will see that two points of more general theoretical interest can be made on the basis of this and similar analyses. First, the very subtle two-way interaction between language and social reality has been thoroughly illustrated. One might even suspect that penetrating analysis of single words will tell fascinating stories about *how* the social reality surrounding us is conceived of. Secondly, we have got a demonstration of the general rule that whenever possibly divergent or rival interests and perspectives may be represented and expressed in language, the interests and perspectives of those in power (in our case men) will dominate at the expense of the weaker ones (in our case women).

References

Bem, S. L. and Bem, D. J. (1970). We are all nonconscious sexists. *Psychology Today* **4**, no. 6.
Berger, P. L. and Luckmann, T. (1967). "The Social Construction of Reality." Anchor Books, Doubleday, New York.
Blakar, R. M. (1970). Konteksteffektar i språkleg kommunikasjon. Unpublished thesis, University of Oslo.

* Bem and Bem (1970) have applied a somewhat related strategy when they try to reveal the discrimination implicit in so-called "liberal" men's attitudes.

Blakar, R. M. (1971). Kan mannssamfunnet sprengast utan språkrevolusjon? *Syn og Segn* **77**, 550–561.

Blakar, R. M. (1972a). Språket som maktmiddel eller avsendaren som aktiv skapar. *Tidsskrift for samfunnsforskning* **13**, 199–222.

Blakar, R. M. (1972b). Det voldtatte "fjøsspråket" eller jenta som kom "fra Benklærnes i Lobenet". *Mål og Makt* **2**, no. 3/4, 2–13.

Blakar, R. M. (1972c). Om ordassosiasjons-forsøk som metode og innfallsport til språkpsykologisk innsikt. *Working Papers in Linguistics from Oslo* **1**, no. 3, 65–92.

Blakar, R. M. (1973). "Språk er makt." Pax forlag, Oslo.

Blakar, R. M. and Rommetveit, R. (1974). Utterances *in vacuo* and in contexts: An experimental and theoretical exploration of some interrelationships between what is heard and what is seen or imagined. *International J. Psycholinguistics*.

Håseth, K. J. (1968). "Norske ordassosiasjons-normer." Universitetsforlaget, Oslo.

Lakoff, R. (1973). Language and woman's place. *Language in society* **2**, 45–80.

Osgood, C. E., Suci, G. J. and Tannenbaum, P. H. (1957). "The measurement of meaning." University of Illinois Press, Urbana.

Rommetveit, R. (1968). "Words, meanings and messages." Academic Press and Universitetsforlaget, New York, London and Oslo.

Rommetveit, R. (1972a). "Språk, tanke og kommunikasjon." Universitetsforlaget, Oslo.

Rommetveit, R. (1972b). Deep structure of sentences versus message structure: Some critical remarks to current paradigms, and suggestions for an alternative approach. *Norwegian J. Linguistics* **26**, 3–22.

Rommetveit, R. and Blakar, R. M. (1973). Induced semantic-associative states and resolution of binocular rivalry conflicts between letters, *Scandinavian J. Psychology* **14**, 185–194.

33. Communication Efficiency in Couples With and Without a Schizophrenic Offspring*

H. A. SØLVBERG and R. M. BLAKAR

Since the early 1950s, there has been a fundamental change in attitudes to schizophrenia, and psychopathology in general. There has been an increasing tendency to see schizophrenia as a product of interaction/communication in the family and close environment instead of a purely genetically determined phenomenon.

One of the earliest, but still one of the most theoretically sound and explicit redefinitions of psychopathology in terms of communication, is the book "Communication: The Social Matrix of Psychiatry" by Ruesch and Bateson (1951). Here they hold that "psychopathology is defined in terms of disturbances of communication" (p. 79). They admit that this may come as a surprise, but argue that:

> ... if the reader cares to open a textbook on psychiatry and to read about the manic-depressive or the schizophrenic psychosis, for example, he is likely to find terms such as "illusions", "delusions", "hallucinations", "flight of ideas", "dissociation", "mental retardation", "elation", "withdrawal", and many others, *which refer specifically to disturbances of communication* (our italics); they imply either that perception is distorted or that expression—that is, transmission—is unintelligible (1951, pp. 79–80).

* The authors are indebted to Fritz Johannessen, Jay Haley, Maureen Hultberg, Hilde Eileen Nafstad, Ragnar Rommetveit and Kjell Raaheim for valuable comments on an earlier version of this paper. This research has been supported by the Norwegian Council of Social Science and the Humanities on grants B. 60.01-85 and B. 60.01-100 given to R. M. Blakar.

We are grateful to the Dikemark Hospital in Oslo for their kind co-operation regarding the subjects. Published in *Family Process* (1975) **14**, 515–534.

The position taken by Ruesch and Bateson in 1951 was obviously a programmatic one, but their programme grew out of systematic analysis of human communication in its broadest sense. Almost a decade later Haley, in retrospect, described the change of perspective that took place in the study of schizophrenia throughout the 1950s in the following way:

A transition would seem to have taken place in the study of schizophrenia; from the early idea that the difficulty in these families was caused by the schizophrenic member, to the idea that they contained a pathogenic mother, to the discovery that the father was inadequate, to the current emphasis upon all three family members involved *in a pathological system of interaction* (our italics) (1959, p. 358).

As is often the case, such a scientific redefinition or re-orientation was followed by enthusiasm and optimism. Much research was initiated and various theories were developed. (For a review, cf. Mishler and Waxler, 1965; Framo, 1972; Sølvberg, 1974). Recently, a more critical and rather pessimistic mood has become dominant in the field. Even some of the "pioneers", those who were closely associated with this movement have recently expressed scepticism and criticism (e.g. Haley in Framo, 1972). Having reviewed the research conducted on schizophrenia and communication, Haley is forced to conclude:

. . . if we judge the exploratory research done to date by severe methodological criteria, one can only conclude that the evidence for a difference between the normal family and a family containing a patient is no more than indicative. This does not mean that schizophrenia is not produced by a type of family, nor does it mean that a family with a schizophrenic is grossly different from the average family. It means *that sufficient reliable evidence of a difference has yet to be provided. The methodology for providing that evidence is still being devised* (our italics) (in Framo, 1972, p. 35).

We agree that Haley is correct in his conclusion that "the methodology still has to be devised". But we want to emphasize that this lack of adequate methods is merely a reflection of the striking lack of explicit theory on communication in this field (cf. Blakar, 1975a, b). We have earlier (Blakar, 1974) claimed that in the eagerness to redefine schizophrenia in terms of communication in the family and close environment, researchers and theorists have almost forgotten to define communication. In plain words, there has been a tendency to explain one mystery (schizophrenia) by another mystery (communication or, more accurately, deviant or pathological communication). On reviewing the literature on this subject, one is struck by the amount of knowledge available about schizophrenia, whereas that on communication—normal as well as deviant—is rather limited. In much of this literature you will find that concepts such as "communication", "interaction", "co-operation", etc. are all mixed up and used *without* being defined.

Worse still, the concepts are frequently employed as though they are completely unproblematic and everyone would know and agree upon what "normal communication" is or implies. Even the best and so-called "authoritative" expositions of the idea of communication in relation to schizophrenia (and psychopathology in general) strike one as vague and inexplicit in their use of the concept of communication as an analytic tool. For example, in the very interesting, and in many ways clarifying book *"Pragmatics of Human Communication"*, by Watzlawick *et al.* (1967) communication appears to be "defined" so broadly that it may encompass *all* human behaviour. With the aim in mind of "devising a methodology for providing that evidence", it is necessary to operate with a far more stringent and explicit use of the concept of "communication". In developing adequate methods in this field, one cannot rely exclusively on one's knowledge of, and insights into, schizophrenia and psychopathology, but one has to take into account and capitalize on *general* theory of communication as well (cf. Blakar, 1975b).

The purpose of the present paper is twofold. Primarily, our aim is to make a methodological contribution to the field by introducing a new experimental method. By employing this particular method, we thus intend to make a preliminary attempt at bridging the far too wide gap between the study of schizophrenia and the psychology of language and communication (cf. Brown, 1973). The second aim is to add to the still only "indicative evidence" that there are qualitative differences with respect to communication patterns between "normal" families and families including a schizophrenic member.

The Method and Its Background

In an effort to identify and describe the *prerequisites for communication*, we developed a rather particular experimental method (Blakar, 1973). The method was derived directly from the social-cognitive theory of communication as developed by Rommetveit (1968, 1972). The ideas behind the method were further inspired by various studies of communicational breakdowns, especially those typical for children (e.g. Piagetian studies on egocentrism), but also analyses of "usual" misunderstandings and how they occur (e.g. Ichheiser, 1970; Garfinkel, 1972).

The idea behind the method was simple in the extreme but very difficult to carry out in practice. The fundamental idea was to try to create a communication situation in which one of the pre-conditions for (successful) communication was *not* satisfied. If you were able to create such a situation, you would be able to study, at least: (a) the impact of that particular variable on communication; (b) the potential "missing" requirements or preconditions to which the subjects would attribute the resultant communicational difficulties; and (c) what the subjects actually do in order to try to "improve" their communication when it goes astray.

Maybe the most basic precondition for successful communication to take place at all is that the participants have "a *shared social reality*", a common "here-and-now" within which exchange of messages can take place (Rommetveit, 1968, 1972; Blakar and Rommetveit, 1975; Blakar, 1975a).

From what has already been said, an ideal experimental situation would then be one in which two (or more) participants communicate with each other *under the belief* that they are "in the same situation" (i.e. have a common definition of the situation's "here-and-now") but in which they are in fact in different situations. In other words, we should try to create a situation in which each participant speaks and understands what is said on the basis of his own particular situation and *falsely believes* that the other speaks and understands on the basis of that very same situation (cf. everyday quarrels and misunderstandings).

A great deal of effort was expended in developing an experimental situation that "worked", i.e. a situation in which the subjects would communicate for a reasonable period of time without suspecting something awry (see Blakar, 1972, 1973). The final design, however, is simple and seems quite natural. Two persons, A and B, are each given a map of a relatively complicated network of roads and streets in a town centre. On A's map two routes are marked in with arrows: one short and straightforward (the practice route) and another longer and more complicated (the experimental route). On B's map no route is marked in. A's task is then to explain to B the two routes, first the simple one, then the longer and more complicated one. B will then, with A's explanations, try to find the way through town to the predetermined endpoint. B can ask questions, ask A to repeat explanations or to explain in other ways, etc. The experimental manipulation is, of course, that the two maps are not identical. There is an extra street added on B's map. So no matter how adequately A explains, no matter how carefully B carries out his instructions, B is bound to go wrong. The difference between the two maps has significance only for the complicated route; the practice route is straightforward for both.

In constructing the maps, two problems in particular were difficult to surmount: (a) to make the maps different, yet sufficiently alike so that the subjects would not realize the difference *before* it had a chance to influence their communication; (b) to make the design "fool-proof" so that everyone was bound to go wrong and get into communicational difficulties, whatever type of explanation (strategy) they chose.

The practice route was included for three reasons: (a) to get the subjects used to the situation; (b) to strengthen their confidence in the maps; and (c) to obtain a sample of their communication in the same kind of situation, but unaffected by our experimental manipulation (a "before-and-after" design). The two participants sit at opposite ends of a table with two low screens hiding their maps from each other. The screens are low enough for them to see each other and have natural eye contact (cf. Moscovici, 1967; Argyle, 1969). Everything said is tape-

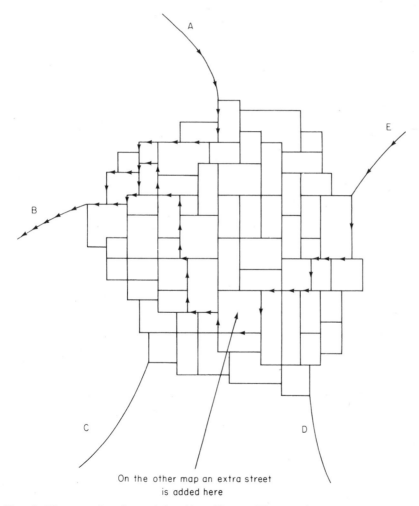

On the other map an extra street
is added here

Fig. 1. The map that the explainer/the wife gets. The practice route is marked with double arrows.

recorded, and for certain analyses the tape must be transcribed afterwards. For a more detailed presentation of the method and its theoretical backgrounds, see Blakar (1973).

The Clinical Application of the Method

A study using students as subjects (Blakar, 1972, 1973) convinced us that the experimental manipulation was successful. The most interesting observations from this first study were: (a) It took an average of 18 min from the start on the experimental route before any doubt as to the credibility of the maps was expressed. During this time the subjects communicated under the false assumption that they were

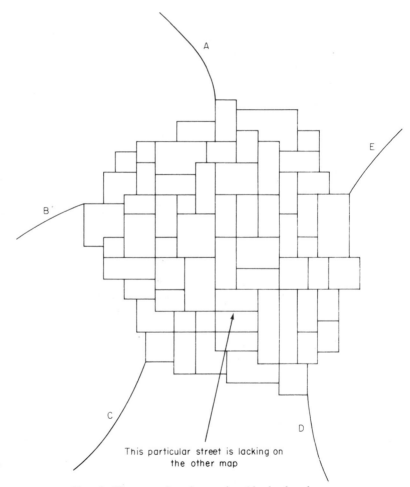

This particular street is lacking on
the other map

FIG. 2. The map that the receiver/the husband gets.

sharing the same situation (the same "here"). (b) Moreover, the situation proved successful in throwing light on: (1) how the subjects "diagnosed" their communication difficulties; and (2) what kind of "therapeutic" tools they had at their disposal in order to repair and improve their communication. The experimental situation appeared to make great demands upon the subjects' powers of flexibility and ability to modify their communication patterns and also upon their capacity to decentrate and see things from the other's perspective.

It was the latter findings in particular that led to the idea that the method could possibly be used to illuminate communication deficiences in families with schizophrenic members. We might then start from Haley's review of current research. He concludes:

> If we accept the findings of the research reported here and assuming it is sound, evidence is accumulating to support the idea that a family with a patient member is different from an "average" family. As individuals, the family members do not appear different according to the usual character and personality criteria. Similarly, evidence is slight that family structure, when conceived in terms of role assignment or dominance, is different in normal and abnormal families. On process measurements there is some indication of difference: Abnormal families appear to have more conflict, to have different coalition patterns, and to show more inflexibility in repeating patterns and behavior. *The most sound findings would seem to be in the outcome area: When faced with a task on which they must cooperate, abnormal family members seem to communicate their preferences less successfully, require more activity and take longer to get the task done* (our italics) (Haley, in Framo, 1972, p. 35).

Our method was invented precisely in order to make possible more detailed analyses and descriptions of the processes in "the outcome area" in terms of more general theory of communication. Communication difficulties were bound to emerge. Concepts such as attribution (how and to what the induced communicational difficulties are attributed), the ability to decentrate and take the perspective of the other, the capability to endorse, maintain and revise interactional contracts, etc. would consequently become of central significance in the analysis. The present method would thus enable us hopefully to draw upon theorists within general psychology such as Heider, 1958; Mead, 1934; Piaget, 1926; Rommetveit, 1972, 1974; and others in our description of the deviant communication in abnormal families.

In this first exploratory study we chose—both for theoretical and practical reasons—to concentrate on the parent dyad. Obviously, that is the core dyad in establishing the milieu into which the child is born and within which he later grows into a healthy or pathological person. Moreover, we did not want to include the patient himself in this very first study in which the method itself was to be tried out.

Since the communication task given each couple is in principle unsolvable, we had to decide beforehand the criteria for terminating the experimental session:

(1) The task would be considered successfully finished as soon as the error was correctly localized and identified.

(2) The task would also be considered resolved if and when the route was correctly reconstructed to the point of the error and one or both of the subjects insisted that the maps were not identical and hence that there was no point in going on. (In this connection it has to be emphasized that the experimenter was instructed to neglect all suggestions that something might be wrong and give the impression as long as possible that everything was as it should be.) (See Blakar, 1973, p. 418).

(3) Furthermore, if no solution according to criteria one or two was reached within 40 min, the communication task would be brought to an end. The subjects would then be shown the discrepancy between the maps and told that the task was in reality unsolvable. The 40 min limit was chosen on the basis of earlier experiments (Blakar, 1973) and pre-tests with married couples of the same age and social background as the subjects to be.

(4) Finally, it was decided that if the task should cause the couple too much emotional upset, the experimenter should stop and reveal the introduced error to them.

In order to simplify comparison between various couples, the distribution of the two differential maps to the spouses had to be standardized. In order to counteract culturally determined male dominance, we gave the map with the routes marked in to the wives so that the husbands had to follow the directives and explanations of their wives.

The Sample and the Administration of the Experimental Procedure

A very important issue in the exploratory study was to establish two comparable groups, one consisting of parents *with* schizophrenic offspring (Group S) and one matched control group *without* (Group N). During this exploratory research we chose to limit ourselves to small but heavily controlled and strictly matched groups.

First we concentrated on establishing Group S. We decided to accept the definition of schizophrenia generally held within Norwegian psychiatry, i.e. according to Kraepelin. Our point of departure was that the reference person in Group S had been diagnosed as being a schizophrenic at a psychiatric institution and that the diagnosis should be established beyond doubt. The use of the diagnostic category entailed that all reference persons would be over 15 years old. We put the upper age limit at 30, and within this range we sought the youngest possible reference persons to ensure that they had not been separated from their families for too long.

To establish Group S was a long and laborious process. A large number of potential reference persons were dropped because either the parents were too old, one or both parents were dead or had mental or somatic ailments, or because the reference person had been brought up by foster parents. Others were dropped because the respective therapists considered the mental state of the parents so labile that they would not expose them to the possible strain of this type of research.

Having scanned our pool of potential subjects, we ended up with eight reference persons and parent couples who satisfied our criteria. Of these eight, we managed to get five to participate. One couple was dropped because the two of them never managed to speak enough to each other to agree on an appointment. The remaining two couples who dropped out refused point blank at the first request on the telephone.

In the final Group S, age ranged from 48 to 58 with an average of 52. The couples had been married for 22 to 29 years with an average of 25 years, and all lived in the Oslo area. In respect to education, income and living conditions, the group represented a heterogenous sample. Average number of children in the family was three, with a range of one to four. All the couples appeared to be normally well-adapted, and no one in the family, apart from the patient, had demonstrated any deviant behaviour that had resulted in contact with either treatment or penal institutions. Four of the five reference persons were male.

Having established Group S, much effort was put into establishing a matching Group N. Variables such as age, number of years of marriage, education, employment, social group, annual income, domicile, living conditions, number of children and their sex and age, were all matched. Thus the age of the parents in Group N ranged from 45 to 57 years with an average of 51, and the couples had been married 24 to 27 years, an average of 25 years. (For further details on the matching, see Sølvberg, 1974, pp. 62–67). Group N therefore represented a "normal group" in the sense that they constituted comparable, ordinary Oslo couples *without* problems that had led themselves or their children into contact with treatment or penal institutions. Nothing else is implied by "normality" in this case.

Hypotheses

Since the primary purpose of the present study was methodological, our hypotheses bearing upon the differences between Group S and

Group N couples were not very refined. The following rather general hypotheses may in fact be considered tentative conclusions based upon a review of the literature in accordance with Haley's views (see quotation above):

(I) Couples from Group S will communicate less efficiently than those from Group N if the co-operation situation is vague and complicated, requiring a critical evaluation and change in patterns of communication. In other words, the Group S couples will have *more problems* and use *longer time* in solving the experimental route where the error is introduced.

(II) Couples from Group S will manage equally as well as couples from Group N if the co-operation situation is plain and simple in the sense that no readjustment is required from their usual pattern of communication or co-operation. In other words, no difference in time spent on the training route will be expected.

(III) Qualitative differences in the communication between Group S and Group N couples will be revealed, and such differences are expected whether the communication situation is simple or difficult. It is expected, moreover, that such qualitative differences observed in communication on the simple training route will shed some light on why Group S communication fails when the situation is more demanding.

Results

All the couples, as also all the same-sex student dyads that had participated in the earlier experiment (Blakar, 1973), became involved in the task. The experimenter had no particular problems getting them to grasp the instructions and start on the training route, although some of the couples put some pressure on the experimenter to structure the situation more.

Let us start by examining some quantitative measures bearing upon efficiency in solving the communication task. None of the couples seemed to face serious problems on the training route. The actual time spent, however, ranging from 2 min 2 s to 9 min 56 s, indicates that the task and situation were not equally simple for all of them. If we compare the two experimental groups, we find that Group S used 4 min 50 s in mean (ranging from 2 min 9 s to 9 min 56 s), while Group N used 4 min 57 s in mean (ranging from 2 min 2 s to 8 min 52 s). Actually, this is very close to the student dyads, with a mean of 4 min 27 s on the training route (1973). Until then, all the student dyads we had run had solved the induced communication conflict according to criteria one or two above, and *within* the 40 min limit. However, only six out of the 10 parent couples managed to solve the communication conflict according to criteria one or two. Four of the 10 couples went on for more than 40 min, and were consequently stopped and shown the discrepancy between the maps. None of the couples was stopped because of criterion four above—thus, on the experimental route the 10 couples divided themselves into two sub-groups: six solvers and four non-solvers, and the crucial question is how the Group S and the Group N couples were distributed over these sub-groups. While all five Group N couples solved the induced communication conflict, only one of the Group S couples managed to do it. All four non-solvers were thus Group S couples.

As a curiosity only, it may be mentioned that we learned afterwards that the one Group S couple that had managed to solve the communication conflict was the only one of the five that had been given some family therapy in connection with the treatment of their hospitalized daughter.

Thus, on the training route where no conflict is induced and hence no critical evaluation and readjustment of communication strategy is required, Group S parents performed as well as Group N parents, and actually on a par with the younger and more highly educated student dyads. However, when a discrepancy with respect to premises is induced, most Group S parents failed.

Further Analysis and Findings

The primary aim of the present study was methodological, and the data presented already suggest that our method is worth the investment of more effort in further elaboration and refinement. Further qualitative analysis, however, was performed at this first stage of the research. Three types of analysis were conducted in order to further identify differences and similarities in communication between the two groups of couples:

(1) The tapes were blind-scored by a communication-oriented student trained in clinical psychology.

(2) A detailed analysis (on utterance level) of the organization of the communication was carried out.

(3) The emotional climate was assessed on a set of five-point scales.

Clinical Analysis of Communication

In order to get (a) some sort of a clinical "validation" of the differences revealed by the mere time measures, and (b) a more global and qualitative description of the communication patterns, a student trained in clinical psychology was given the 10 recordings and the following instruction:

> These tapes record what took place when ten parent couples were presented with a standardized cooperation task. Five couples are parents of a person diagnosed as schizophrenic. The other five couples have offspring with no obvious form of psychopathology. You may listen to each of the ten tapes as many times as you want, and then give a short description of each couple and what takes place between them. Then tell which of the recordings you believe to be of the schizophrenic's parents and which are not.

On the basis of her *clinical evaluation*, she correctly identified four couples who she felt sure belonged to Group S. In the communication of the other six she found no particular characteristics which, according to her clinical knowledge, would lead her to classify them as belonging to Group S. When forced to guess at the last Group S couple, she was incorrect, but she stressed that she was in severe doubt. For what this finding may be worth, it suggests that potential pathological characteristics of communication are highlighted in this situation to such an extent that they can be identified fairly easily by a clinical psychologist. In comparison, the extensive notes on how each couple appeared to the experimenter *outside* the experimental setting revealed no systematic differences between Group S and Group N couples. They all appeared to him (also trained in clinical psychology) to be normal, well-adjusted, middle-age couples (cf. Sølvberg, 1973, pp. I–VIII).

A closer examination of the scorer's descriptions of the communication pattern shows that the Group S couples (as compared to the Group N couples) were characterized by (a) more rigidity (in explanation strategy, in role distribution, etc.); (b) less ability and/or willingness to listen to, and take into account, what the other said; (c) a more imprecise and diffuse language (imprecise definitions, concepts, etc.); and (d) more "pleasing" and/or pseudo-agreement in situations in which the erroneous maps had made them lose each other.

Utterance Analysis of Communication

The categorization system that was developed and applied in order to analyse the organization (on utterance level) of the communication represents a preliminary attempt to bridge the gap between the communication-oriented studies on schizophrenia and general theory of language and communication. Our categorization system as applied in this study was immature and very laborious, and the more promising aspects of it are now being further developed and refined in ongoing studies (see below). Hence we will not present it in any detail here, but will outline it only to the extent that may be indicated by some of the most interesting of our preliminary findings.

Every single utterance—as well as every sequence of two and two utterances—were classified with respect to some formal and some content aspects. For practical as well as theoretical reasons, the training route was chosen. For practical considerations, the couples spent much less time on the training route, and such an analysis is extremely time-consuming. Theoretically, if any qualitative differences were found on the training route, where the two types of couples had been equally efficient and where they had not been influenced by our experimental manipulation, these (eventual) qualitative differences could hopefully shed some light on why the Group S couples failed when the communication conflict was induced.

Our detailed analysis of the utterances on the training route revealed various differences between the two groups, of which only the three most significant will be presented briefly and commented upon:

(a) Every utterance was classified as being either *active* (in the meaning that it was initiated by the person himself) or *reactive* (in the meaning that it represented a reaction to something the other had said or done). When we examined the distribution of active utterances within each couple, we noted that the Group S wives tended to have a larger proportion than the Group N wives. Four of the five Group S wives had more active utterances than their respective husbands, whereas three of the five Group N husbands had more than their respective wives. This tendency toward "marital skew" in the schizophrenic family (cf. Lidz, 1963), however, becomes much clearer if all "questions" and "comments" are excluded from the active utterances, so that one is left with "directives" only ("go there and there", "do so and so", etc.). In all five group S couples, the wife gave many more such active directives (on the average, almost twice as many as the husbands), whereas in the Group N couples the distribution between the spouses was much more equal (in three couples the husband gave more, and in two the wife gave more such active directives).

(b) The active utterances, furthermore, were classified in "directives", "questions", and "comments". Comments again were classified as being either *task-relevant* (comments that could be of help in solving the task) and *task-irrelevant* (comments that were judged to be entirely irrelevant from the point of view of solving the communication task). First, at group level the Group N couples used many more comments (almost twice as many) as the Group S couples, but there was some overlap. However, if the distribution of task-relevant and task-irrelevant comments within each couple is inspected, it is found that a much larger proportion of the comments in the Group S couples were task-irrelevant (a mean of 57% of the comments were irrelevant) as compared to the Group N couples (in mean 19% of the comments were irrelevant). And, with respect to the total number of relevant comments, there were on the average three times as many in Group N as in Group S couples.

This finding is of particular theoretical interest in that relevant comments may reflect a capacity and willingness on the behalf of the spouses *to decentrate* (e.g. one describe to the other how it looks on the map where he or she is) and thereby re-establish a shared here-and-now within which meaningful communication can take place (cf. the theoretical framework briefly outlined above).

(c) Furthermore, for every active utterance elicited by either member of the couple, the reaction of the other was classified as being *adequate* (confirmation, disconfirmation, relevant answer or question, etc.) or *inadequate* (in particular, ignoring and no response). In Group S, a larger proportion (an average of 36%) of the active utterances were ignored by the other as compared to Group N (an average of 21%). And, there is almost no overlap between the two groups with the exception of one Group S couple whose extremely few active utterances were ignored. But this couple can obviously be characterized as pseudo-mutual, as described by Wynne and collaborators (1958).

The Emotional Climate

The emotional climate was assessed on five-point scales (from "very much" to "very little") of the following type: "To what extent is the interaction characterized by warmth (openness, confidence, helplessness, intimacy, mutual respect, etc.)?" All 10 couples were scored by two students of psychology. This scoring procedure did not reveal any differences between the two groups. Analyses of variance (2 groups × 2 raters) did not show more significant differences than would be expected by chance (cf. Bakan, 1967). The reasons for this may be many—apart from the obvious one that there may really be no such differences. (A possible counter argument against this latter hypothesis is the fact that in the above analysis a student of clinical psychology easily picked out four of the five Group S couples.) Of the other possible reasons: Our two student raters were not well enough trained to detect more subtle differences, and on a lot of variables the interscore reliability was too low. (However, separate analyses for each of the two raters did not give any more significant group differences.) Furthermore, on many of the variables all 10 couples scored either very high or very low, so that no differences could possibly be demonstrated. With respect to the method as such, it is promising that all 10 couples scored high on "To what extent is their interaction characterized by involvement?" Regarding this particular analysis, the evidence thus seems to be inconclusive.

Emergence of New Questions

Our results are in line with earlier findings and conclusions (cf., e.g. Haley's conclusion (Haley, in Framo, 1972), and "marital skew" as described by Lidz (1963)) at the same time that many intriguing new questions emerged from the above analyses. Instead of presenting the preliminary findings in any more detail, some of the questions and some of the observations upon which these questions are based, will be outlined. These questions are at present the subject of further research:

(1) Do Group S couples have a more egocentric and less decentrated communication? In other words, are Group S spouses less able and/or willing to take the perspective, and speak on the premises of, the other? For instance, utterances such as ". . . and then you go up *there*", ". . . and from *here* you take a right" when "here" and "there" respectively could obviously not be known to the other— were rather frequently observed in the Group S couples.

(2) Are Group S couples less able and/or willing to endorse (and adhere to) contracts that regulate and monitor the various aspects of their communication (e.g. role distribution, strategy of explanation)? Few contractual proposals were found (regarding, for example, language use, explanation strategy). Furthermore, many cases were observed in which implicitly or explicitly endorsed contracts were broken or ignored.

(3) Do Group S couples show less ability and/or willingness to attribute (adequately or inadequately) their communicative difficulties to any potential causes? The Group S couples could apparently return to the starting point again and again without any (overt, explicit) attempt to attribute their communicative difficulties to anything.

These were some of the most significant questions that emerged from this exploratory research. All these questions are formulated within a framework dissimilar to that usually employed in the study of schizophrenia. The formulations are inspired by the theoretical work of people such as Heider, Mead, Piaget, Rommetveit, etc. (see above). More systematic research has to be carried out in order to settle these questions. But the mere posing of them may represent a contribution in the direction of describing (and hence in part explaining) schizophrenia within the framework of general social-cognitive theory of language and communication.

Ongoing and Planned Expansions

Throughout the present paper, the exploratory and preliminary character of the present study and findings have been emphasized.

Following is a brief outline of the continuation studies planned for the future and a discussion of some critical questions that have to be posed on the basis of the work reported thus far.

A first objection is that our samples, even though very well matched, are too small. Hence, both Group S and Group N are now being enlarged.

An even more critical objection would be that the demand characteristics of the experimental situation are different for the two groups of couples, so that our findings may represent mere tautologies (cf. Haley, in Framo, 1972). However, the results of two studies just completed applying the same method make this explanation very unlikely, or at least insufficient.

In the first (Alve and Hultberg, 1974) it was found that parents of borderline patients showed a communication pattern different from *both* Group N and Group S. In the other (Wikran, 1974), parents having a child with a serious heart disease showed communication behaviour identical to the Group N couples, whereas parents having an asthmatic child either managed just as well as the Group N couples (two-thirds of them) or they did extremely badly, demonstrating a communication pattern unlike all the other groups studied so far (one-third of them). If the differences found could be accounted for by different demand characteristics of the experimental situation, all the various "pathological" couples should have behaved more or less similarly; at least such systematic groups differences would not be expected.

If we want to explore the relation between the communication pattern of the parents and the schizophrenic state, either as to etiology or maintenance, it will not be sufficient to study the communication of the parents only. Jacobsen and Pettersen (1974) placed the parents *and* the daughter (in half the cases schizophrenic, in half normal) in our communication situation, and the parents were asked to explain the routes to their daughter. Their findings testified to the existence of equally strong group differences as we have found in the present study.*

Another serious weakness of the present study is the lack of relevant analytic tools by means of which the potential qualitative differences may be assessed. Therefore, in ongoing research much effort is being put into developing relevant scoring and categorizing systems. Whereas the exploratory, clinical application of the method presented above took the work of the Palo Alto group as a point of departure, we have found that in developing and elaborating scoring procedures very much can be gained from the more systematic clinical work carried out by the research groups organized by Lidz and Wynne. Alve and Hultberg

* All these studies are in Norwegian in the form of unpublished theses from the University of Oslo, but reports in English are being prepared in co-operation with R. M. Blakar.

(1974) have developed a system by which *the attributional process* in the couples' communication can be described. Jacobsen and Pettersen (1974) have refined the analysis of *egocentrism in communication*, and Moberget and Reer (in preparation) are developing a systematic scoring system regarding *the contractual aspect*. Endresen (in preparation) is developing a model describing the critical stages or phases at which the various couples fail to solve the communication conflict, as compared to those who successfully solve it.*

References

Alve, S. and Hultberg, M. (1974). Kommunikasjonssvikt hos Foreldre til Borderline Pasienter. Unpublished thesis, University of Oslo.

Argyle, M. (1969). "Social Interaction." Methuen, Atherton.

Bakan, D. (1967). "On Method." Jossey-Bass, San Francisco.

Blakar, R. M. (1972). "Ein Eksperimentell Situasjon til Studiet av Kommunikasjon: Bakgrunn, Utvikling og Nokre Problemstillingar." Mimeographed by Institute of Psychology, University of Oslo.

Blakar, R. M. (1973). An experimental method for inquiring into communication. *European J. social Psychology* 3, 415–425.

Blakar, R. M. (1974). Schizofreni og Kommunikasjon: Foreløpig Presentasjon av ei Eksperimentell Tilnaerming. *Nordisk Psykiatrisk Tidsskrift* 28, 239–248.

Blakar, R. M. (1975a). "Human Communication—an Ever-Changing Contract Embedded in Social Contexts." Mimeographed by Institute of Psychology, University of Oslo.

Blakar, R. M. (1975b). "Kommunikasjon og Psykopatologi." Mimeographed by Institute of Psychology, University of Oslo.

Blakar, R. M. and Rommetveit, R. (1975). Utterances *in vacuo* and in contexts: An experimental and theoretical exploration of some interrelationships between what is heard and what is seen or imagined. *International J. Psycholinguistics*, 4, 5–32.

Brown, R. (1973). Schizophrenia, language and reality. *American Psychologist* 28, 395–403.

Framo, J. L. (Ed.) (1972). "A Dialogue Between Family Researchers and Family Therapists." Springer, New York.

Garfinkel, H. (Ed.) (1972). Studies of the routine grounds of everyday

---

* There are also other ongoing expansions, but they are not as closely connected to the present study: Lagerløv and Stokstad (unpublished thesis) found that high-anxiety, same-sex student dyads did much worse on the experimental route than low-anxiety student dyads, while they did equally well on the simple training route. Fætten and Østvold (in preparation?) are studying the communication of couples in which the wife is hysteric. Dahle (in preparation?) compares the communication of couples with differential class, as well as rural and urban, backgrounds. Brisendal (in preparation) is making an inquiry into the subjects' experience of the communication conflict they are facing in this experimental situation.

activities. *In* "Studies in Social Interaction". (D. Sudnow, Ed.) The Free Press, New York.

Haley, J. (1959). The Family of the Schizophrenic: A Model System. *J. Nervous Mental Disorder* **129,** 357–374.

Heider, F. (1958). "The Psychology of Interpersonal Relations." Wiley, New York.

Ichheiser, G. (1970). "Appearances and Realities. Misunderstandings in Human Relations." Jossey-Bass, San Francisco.

Jacobsen, S. M. and Pettersen, R. B. (1974). Kommunikasjon og Samarbeide i den Schizofrenes Familie. Unpublished thesis, University of Oslo.

Lagerløv, T. and Stokstad, S. J. (1974). Angst og Kommunikasjon. Unpublished thesis, University of Oslo.

Lidz, T. (1963). "The Family and Human Adaptation." International University Press, New York.

Mead, G. H. (1934). "Mind, Self and Society." University of Chicago Press, Chicago.

Mishler, E. G. and Waxler, N. E. (1965). Family interaction processes and schizophrenia: A review of current theories. *Merrill-Palmer Quarterly of Behavior and Development* **11,** 269–315.

Moscovici, S. (1967). Communication processing and the properties of language. *In* "Advances in Experimental Social Psychology". (L. Berkowitz, Ed.) Academic Press, New York and London.

Piaget, J. (1926). "The Language and Thought of the Child." Harcourt Brace Jovanovich, New York.

Rommetveit, R. (1968). "Words, Meanings and Messages." Academic Press and Universitetsforlaget, New York, London and Oslo.

Rommetveit, R. (1972). "Språk, Tanke og Kommunikasjon." Universitetsforlaget, Oslo.

Rommetveit, R. (1974). "On Message Structure." Wiley, London.

Ruesch, J. and Bateson, G. (1951). "Communication: The Social Matrix of Psychiatry." Norton, New York.

Sølvberg, H. A. (1974). Kommunikasjon og Samarbeide Mellom den Schizofrenes Foreldre. Unpublished thesis, University of Oslo.

Watzlawick, P., Beavin, J. H. and Jackson, D. D. (1967). "Pragmatics of Human Communication." Norton, New York.

Wikran, R. J. (1974). Kommunikasjon og Samarbeide Mellom Astma-Barnets Foreldre. Unpublished thesis, University of Oslo.

Wynne, L., Ryckoff, I., Day, J. and Hirsch, S. (1958). Pseudo-Mutuality in the family relations of schizophrenics. *Psychiatry* **21,** 205–220.

34. Anxiety, Rigidity and Communication

An experimental approach*

S. J. STOKSTAD, T. LAGERLØV and
R. M. BLAKAR

Introduction

Recourse to a communication perspective and application of communication theory has recently become more and more popular within a wide range of disciplines. Almost everything—*from* the sale success of a particular product *to* a psychotic breakdown—has been explained in terms of communication. The explanatory value of the main part of this communication oriented research, however, is for at least two reasons questionable. The concept of communication itself has, first of all, frequently remained *undefined* and been used in vague and implicit manners. As a consequence, one is left with a somewhat paradoxical situation where a researcher who knows a lot about a phenomenon (e.g. schizophrenia) is "explaining" this phenomenon by means of another phenomenon (communication, or more adequately, deviant communication) about which he seems to know far less (cf. Blakar, 1974b; Sølvberg and Blakar, 1975).

Secondly, there has been a tendency within this type of research to think *only* in terms of systems and functions and almost totally ignore individual characteristics or dispositions of the people constituting the interactional system. But it is questionable to talk about "senders" and "receivers" within a "system" *without* taking into account, e.g. each *individual sender's/receiver's ability* to decentrate and take the perspective of the other, *personal characteristics* such as rigidity versus flexibility, level

* The authors are indebted to Hilde Eileen Nafstad, Ragnar Rommetveit, Kjell Raaheim, Per Schioldberg and Astri Heen Wold for valuable comments on an earlier version of this paper. This study was supported by the Norwegian Research Council for Science and the Humanities on grants B.60.01-85 and B.60-01-100 given to R. M. Blakar. Published in an internal stencilled report series "Informasjonsbulletin frå Kommunikasjons-og Psykopatologi-prosjektet" (1976) No. 3.

of anxiety, etc. We are of course fully aware of the fact that a person's rigidity, anxiety and egocentrism, etc. vary over different social situations (e.g. Mischel, 1968, 1973). But to take this to mean that, since "the person is influenced by the social situation", personality and personal dispositions should be disregarded, would be as dangerous as the blindness regarding social variables that has characterized the dominant traditions within individually oriented psychology. (For an illustrative example, see Ichheiser's (1970) comments on Freud.)

A pragmatic solution would be in this dilemma, rather than arguing for a social or an individual psychology, to make clear at each stage of research from which perspective, the social or the individual, one is exploring the variable in focus. Thus the individually oriented psychologist would have to make explicit what is presupposed of social character in his concepts and theory, and correspondingly, the social psychologist should make clear what he presupposes as regards personality (cf. Blakar, 1974a). The interaction between individual characteristics and social settings (e.g. actual communication situations) should hence be brought into the focus of research.

A field in which the communication perspective has been particularly influential and generated promising research is in the study of psychopathology. Since Ruesch and Bateson in 1951 programmatically redefined psychopathology "in terms of deficiencies of communication", there has been an ever increasing tendency to adopt a basic communication/interaction perspective on psychopathology. (For reviews, see e.g. Mishler and Waxler, 1965, Riskin and Faunce, 1972.) In hardly any other field would one expect ignorance of the above mentioned problems to be so vital, however. (How is it possible to analyse, say, a schizophrenic breakdown *without* having explicit rules for how to disentangle social and individual variables within the family system?) As one might expect, the optimism that characterized this field in the 1960s (cf. Handel, 1967, Mishler and Waxler, 1965) has therefore been replaced by a more pessimistic and critical attitude (Haley, 1972, Riskin and Faunce, 1972, Jacobsen and Pettersen, 1974). The lack of progress has been ascribed to lack of adequate methods (Haley, 1972) or of "intermediate concepts", connecting observable data to superordinate concepts, such as "double bind", "marital skism & marital skew", "pseudomutuality", to mention a few of the most well known, used in theorizing about families with deviant members (Riskin and Faunce, 1972). Riskin and Faunce as well as Haley are pointing at essential weaknesses. These issues, however, are in our opinion both merely reflections of another even more basic deficiency, namely that the concept of communication has remained vague and undefined (Blakar, 1975a). A particular problem in studies of interaction in families with psychopathological members, is to decide what should be ascribed to the familial communication and what to the individual members' abilities and personal dispositions. This problem is clearly reflected in the following quotation from Haley's recent attempt to assess what has been found out about pathological families:*

> If we accept the findings of the research reported here and assuming it is sound, evidence is accumulating to support the idea that family with a patient member is different from an "average" family. As individuals, the family members do not appear different according to the usual character and personality criteria. Similarly, evidence is slight that family structure, when conceived in terms of role assignment or dominance, is different in normal and abnormal families. On process measurements there is some indication of difference: Abnormal families appear to have more conflict, to have different coalition patterns, and to show more inflexibility in repeating patterns of behaviour. The most sound findings would seem to be in the outcome area: when faced with a task on which they must cooperate, abnormal family members seem to communicate their preferences less successfully, require more activity and take longer to get the task done (Haley, 1973, p. 35).

An empirical approach to these issues may take place along the following lines: Given a communication situation (e.g. a co-operation task) in which differences (e.g. efficiency/inefficiency in getting the task done) between "normal" and "pathological" families are demonstrated, *then* interaction between "normal" subjects with *varying* personal dispositions (for example high versus low anxiety) ought to be studied in *the very same* co-operation task. Such parallel research, even though revealing very little concerning causality, may be useful in disentangling social (e.g. familial communication) and personal (e.g. anxiety) aspects (cf. Blakar, 1975b).

Having created an experimental communication situation (Blakar, 1973) in which clear cut differences between the pattern of communication in families with and without psychopathological members have been demonstrated (Sølvberg and Blakar, 1975), we chose in the present study to study the influence of anxiety upon communication in the very same situation.

Anxiety and Communication

We follow Rommetveit (1972, 1974) in defining communication as *to make common* (communicare). Thus the purpose of the present study is

---

* This quotation is *not* chosen because it gives a generally accepted assessment of the field, but because the problems in focus are very well illustrated. For example, Theodore Lidz (personal communication) disagrees with the conclusions drawn by Haley.

to examine how different levels of anxiety affect the process by which two (or more) people *make something known to each other.*

It may be hypothesized that level of anxiety will affect some basic pre-conditions for successful communication, of which only a few will be exemplified here. A certain capacity for decentration and ability and willingness to take the perspective of the other is one such pre-condition. It is not unlikely, however, that a high anxiety person will stick more to his own perspective and be less open to take the perspective of the other. And when communication runs into trouble (quarrels, misunderstandings, etc.) a certain degree of flexibility is particularly needed. It may be hypothesized (see below) that high anxiety then will result in rigidity.

Even though we have found no studies relating level of anxiety *directly* to communication (e.g. efficiency of communication), a number of studies seem to show that level of anxiety affects various aspects of communication such as speech. For example, "speech disturbance ratio" (frequency of unfinished sentences, repetitions, stuttering, slips of the tongue, omissions, etc.) was thus by Mahl (1956) found to be highest in anxiety filled phases of therapeutic sessions. Similar findings are reported by Boomer and Goodrich (1961), and Kasl and Mahl (1965). Gynter (1957), moreover, demonstrated that anxiety (measured on a Welch A-scale) and an ego-involving stress-instruction influenced what she called "the communication efficiency" in that it caused the subjects to omit a higher number of irrelevant as compared to relevant utterances in an interview situation.

Studies of this kind are problematic for two reasons: First, they do not bear upon communication or interaction as such, but merely on various aspects of the individual's speech. Secondly, it is difficult to ensure independent operationalization of speech/communication variables and anxiety measures. Hence, in the present study effort was taken to ensure that *level of anxiety* and *communication* would be conceptualized and operationalized within different frameworks (*intra*personal versus *inter*personal). Anxiety was accordingly measured by the widely used and standardized personality inventory M.M.P.I., via Taylor's Manifest Anxiety Scale (MAS) (Taylor, 1953).

As suggested above, one may imagine various ways in which anxiety influences communication, and high/low anxiety will also affect the very emotional climate of the communication process. The main hypothesis of the present study will be elaborated by means of the intermediate concept of "rigidity". Before we proceed to the hypothesis, however, the communication task and the theoretical rationale behind the operationalization of communication efficiency has to be presented.

The Method, Its Background and Earlier Applications

In an effort to identify and describe some *prerequisites for communication*, a particular experimental method was developed (Blakar, 1973). The method was derived from the social-cognitive theory of communication as developed by Rommetveit (1968, 1972). The ideas behind the method were further inspired by various studies of communication breakdowns, especially those typical for children (e.g. Piagetian studies on egocentrism), but also analyses of "usual" misunderstandings and how they occur (e.g. Ichheiser, 1970, Garfinkel, 1972).

The idea behind the method was simple in the extreme, but very difficult to carry out in practice. The fundamental idea was to try to create a communication situation where one of the pre-conditions for (successful) communication would *not* be satisfied. If one is able to create such a situation, one would be able to assess: (1) the impact of that particular variable on communication, (2) the potential "missing requirements" or pre-conditions to which the subjects would attribute the resultant communicational difficulties, and (3) what the subjects actually do in order to try to "improve" their communication when it goes astray.

Maybe the most basic pre-condition required for successful communication to take place at all, is that the participants have "a *shared social reality*", a common "here-and-now" within which exchange of messages can take place (Rommetveit, 1972, 1974, Blakar and Rommetveit, 1975, Blakar, 1975c). An ideal experimental situation would thus be one where two (or more) participants communicate with each other under the belief that they are "in the same situation" (i.e. have a common definition of the situation's "here" and "now"), whereas they are in fact in *different* situations. In other words, we should try to create a situation where each participant speaks and understands what is said on the basis of his own particular interpretation of the situation and falsely *believes* that the other (others) speaks and understands on the basis of that same interpretation as well (cf. everyday quarrels and misunderstandings).

This is not the place to tire the reader with all the toil we encountered in developing an experimental situation that "worked", i.e. a situation where the subjects would communicate for a reasonable period of time *without* suspecting something awry (see Blakar, 1972, 1973). The final design, however, is simple and seems quite natural. Two persons, A and B, are each given a map of a relatively complicated network of roads and streets in a town centre. On A's map two routes are marked in with arrows: One short and straightforward (the practice route) and another longer and more complicated one (the experimental route). On B's map no route is marked in.

A's task is to explain to B the two routes, first the simple one, then the longer and more complicated route. With A's explanations, B then has to try to find the way through town to the pre-determined end point. B may ask questions, ask A to repeat explanations, or to explain in other ways, etc. The experimental manipulation is simply that the two maps are not identical. There is an extra street added on B's map. So, no matter how adequately A explains, no matter how carefully B carries out his instructions, B is bound to go wrong. The difference between the two maps has implication only for the complicated route however, the practice route being identical for both.

Since the communication task given to each dyad is in principle unsolvable, the criteria for terminating the experimental session had to be decided upon in beforehand: (1) The task would be considered as successfully finished as soon as the error was correctly localized and identified. (2) The task would also be considered resolved if and when the route was correctly reconstructed to the point of the error, and one or both of the subjects insisted that the maps were not identical, and hence that there was no point in going on. (In this connection it should be emphasized that the experimenter was instructed to neglect all suggestions that something might be wrong and give the impression that everything was OK as long as possible, see Blakar, 1973, p. 418). (3) Furthermore, if no solution according to criteria (1) and/or (2) was reached within 40 min, the communication task would be brought to an end. The subjects then would be shown the discrepancy between the maps and told that the task was in fact unsolvable. The 40 min limit was chosen on the basis of earlier experiments (Blakar, 1973).

The practice route was included for three reasons: (1) To get the subjects used to the situation, (2) to strengthen their confidence in the maps, and (3) to obtain a sample of their communication in the same kind of situation, but *un*affected by the experimental manipulation (a "before-after" design). The two participants are seated at opposite ends of a table, with two low screens hiding their maps from each other. The screens are low enough for the subjects to see each other and to have natural eye contact (cf. Moscovici, 1967, Argyle, 1969). Everything said is tape-recorded, and for certain analyses the tape must be transcribed afterwards. (For a more detailed presentation of the method and its theoretical background, see Blakar, 1973).

A first study in which students served as subjects (Blakar, 1972, 1973) convinced us that the experimental manipulation was successful. The most interesting observations from this first study were: (1) It took an average of 18 min from the start on the experimental route *before* any doubt as to the credibility of the maps was expressed. During this time the subjects communicated under the false assumption that they were sharing the *same* situation (the same "here"). (2) Moreover, the situation proved successful in throwing light on (a) how the subjects "diagnosed" their communicational difficulties, and (b) what kind of "therapeutic" tools they had at their disposal in order to repair and improve their communication. The experimental situation also appeared to make great demands upon the subjects' flexibility and ability to modify their communication patterns, and also upon their capacity to decentrate and see things from the other's perspective.

It was the latter findings in particular that led to the idea that the method could be used to illuminate communication deficiencies in families with members with psychopathology. (For a rationale of this clinical application of the method, see Blakar, 1974b). In a first exploratory study (Sølvberg and Blakar, 1975) 10 couples, five *with* and five *without* a schizophrenic offspring, were run through this particular communication situation. As far as efficiency of communication was concerned, the two groups did equally well (and just as well as the younger and higher educated students in the earlier experiment) on the simple training route, where no critical evaluation and re-adjustment of one's communication is required. However, on the experimental route, where the induced communication conflict requires a critical evaluation and re-adjustment of one's communicative strategy, the couples with schizophrenic children did significantly worse than the control group. Whereas all five Group N couples resolved the task according to criteria (1) or (2) above, four of the five Group S couples did *not* manage to do so. The induced error had therefore to be revealed to them by the experimenter when more than 40 min had elapsed (Sølvberg and Blakar, 1975).

Rigidity as the Link between Anxiety and Inefficiency of Communication

It has been suggested (p. 444) that (level of) anxiety may influence communication in various ways. The specific hypothesis to be tested in the present study is that *high anxiety persons will show more rigidity, which in turn will result in less efficient communication.*

Several studies indicate a relation between anxiety and certain features of the individual's cognitive functioning, thus anxiety seems to lead to rigidity (Ainsworth, 1958, Pilisuk, 1963, Beier, 1965). As to rigidity, two issues of direct relevance to the present study have been discussed. First, it has been asked whether the various manifestations of rigidity might be explained by *one underlying rigidity factor*. But already in the discussion of the authoritarian personality in the early 1950s, it was demonstrated that rigidity is a multidimensional concept, and hence has to be specified in each concrete study (Brown, 1953). In the present study a discrepancy between the two participants with respect to premises is induced, and it is hypothesized that rigidity will be reflected in resistance against giving up and revising the premises on which the individual is communicating. Rigid persons (or persons who develop rigidity in the communication situation) will hence need longer *time* in resolving the induced communication conflict.

Secondly, there is still the unsettled issue as to whether rigidity is a *situationally induced state* or a more stable *personality trait*. Different positions are taken by Luchins (1951), who on the basis of a series of problem-solving experiments concludes that rigidity is a situationally induced state, and Rokeach (1960) and Rubenowitz (1963, 1970) who claim that rigidity is a more or less stable personality characteristic.

In accordance with our general introductory comments, rigidity was therefore induced in two different manners in the present study. The "personality aspect" of it was assessed by selection of subjects, in that the person's level of anxiety was varied. In addition, different instructions were used to induce different levels of stress on the subjects in the experimental situation.*

TABLE I.

		Instruction:	
		Standard instruction	Stress instruction
Level of anxiety:	High anxiety		
	Low anxiety		

The final experimental design therefore included the following four different experimental conditions (see Table I) where an equal number of male and female dyads were run in each of the four conditions.

* Whereas the standard instructions merely present the task to the subjects (cf. Blakar, 1973, for a verbatim presentation of the standard instructions), the stress instruction is intended to put a heavy pressure on the subjects in order to co-operate efficiently and quickly. In addition to the mere presentation of the task as with the standard instructions, the impression was given that the task represented a standardized test on the ability to co-operate. And, it was explicitly added that people normally used 2–3 min on the simple route and about 10 min on the more complex route. It was even said that "students such as you are almost always quicker than that".

Subjects

A total of 155 undergraduate students, aged 19–21 years, 87 females and 68 males were tested on MAS. Average score on MAS was 18·43 (18·37 for the men, 18·48 for the women). The standard error was 7·68 (8·31 for the men, 7·15 for the women).

A split half reliability correlation of 0·88 was found (Spearman-Brown's method, Guilford, 1965). The highest and lowest scores on MAS were selected for the communication experiment. In order to get two extreme groups from our pool of 155 subjects, the number of dyads was restricted to 24 (six in each experimental condition). The final high anxiety group scored from 25–43, whereas the low anxiety group scored from 2–12.* The 24 dyads,† each consisting of either *two high scorers* or *two low scorers*, were run in randomized order and the experimenter did not know their scores on MAS.

Hypotheses

The following hypotheses were put forward:

(I) On the training route, where no conflict is induced between the premises which the subjects already have been given about the maps and what later will prove to be the case, the anxiety level will not produce differences in solution time (i.e. in development of rigidity). On the experimental route, however, where such a conflict will arise, the anxiety level will produce differences, so that the high anxiety dyads will develop more rigidity and need longer time.

(II) On the training route, the standard versus stress instruction conditions will not produce differences in solution time (i.e. in development of rigidity). On the experimental route, however, these conditions will cause differences such that those given the stress instruction will develop more rigidity and need longer time.

(III) On the training route, there will be no interaction effect between anxiety and instruction conditions as regards solution time (i.e. development of rigidity). On the experimental route there will be such an interaction effect.

* Since we start with extreme groups, the regression effect has to be taken into consideration (McNemar, 1962). The "true" values calculated on the basis of the reliability coefficient are 3·97–12·77 and 24·71–40·05 for the low and high anxiety groups respectively. Both groups are almost exclusively recruited from the highest respective lowest quarter of our pool of subjects.

† A total of 29 dyads were run through the experimental communication situation. One dyad was rejected because one of the participants did not master Norwegian well enough, and another because one of the participants proved to be 26 years old. Three dyads were rejected because they applied particular explanatory strategies that took them through the experimental route *without* the induced error causing any trouble, and thus these dyads *did not* face any communication conflict.

Results

A first crucial observation was that all subjects became involved and seemed highly motivated to solve the two tasks (cf. footnote to Table III), and the experimenter had no particular problems in making them grasp the instructions and start on the practice route.

All the 24 dyads managed the practice route without too much trouble (4 min 45 s in mean), but the variation in time used (from 1 min 9 s to 17 min 10 s) indicates that the task was not equally simple for all of them. These results are almost identical with those obtained in earlier experiments with student subjects in the same communication situation (Blakar, 1973).

To test for the possible effect of (level of) anxiety and (type of) instruction on communication in the simple situation, an analysis of variance was conducted. Neither main effects nor interaction effects proved significant.

On the experimental route, 17 dyads managed to resolve the induced communication conflict according to criteria (1) and/or (2), whereas seven dyads did not, and hence were shown the induced error by the experimenter when more than 40 min had elapsed. In Table IIa and b is given the distribution of solvers/non-solvers over the four experimental conditions.

TABLE IIA and B. Distribution of solvers/non-solvers over the various experimental conditions.

	Solvers	Non-solvers	Total		Solvers	Non-solvers	Total
Low anxiety	12	0	12	Standard instruction	8	4	12
High anxiety	5	7	12	Stress instruction	9	3	12
Total	17	7	24	Total	17	7	24

The effect of (level of) anxiety on communication in this conflict situation is testified to in that all the seven non-solvers were among the high anxiety dyads. However, no effect of the stress instruction is revealed by this rough measure (solvers versus non-solvers). Analysis of variance on time used on the experimental route* showed that the effect of anxiety upon communication in the conflict situation was significant: $F(1 \cdot 23) = 13 \cdot 68$, $p < 0 \cdot 01$. No effect of type of stress

* In the analysis of variance the seven non-solvers were all given a time of 40 min.

instruction was found, however. Nor was there any significant inter-action between (level of) anxiety and (type of) instruction.

We were thus correct in our expectations that neither (level of) anxiety nor (type of) instruction would influence the efficiency of communication in a simple situation where no critical evaluation and re-adjustment of communication is required. Furthermore, we were correct in our hypothesis that high anxiety would lead to rigidity and inefficient communication when the situation became complex in such a way that critical evaluation and re-adjustment of the communicative strategy was required. Our expectation that the stress instruction would also lead to rigidity and inefficient communication in the conflict communication situation, was not confirmed. It is possible though that our "stress instruction" was not a successful manipulation. Logically, there are two different alternative explanations: Either the stress instruction was not really experienced as stressing, or the situation itself (with the standard instruction) may have been so stressing, that the "stress instruction" did not make any difference at all. The hypothesis about the impact of situationally induced stress should therefore not be rejected on the basis of the present study only.

In order to explore the effect of anxiety upon communication some-what further, two different qualitative analyses were conducted:

(1) An analysis of the (level of) precision in the dyads' verbal explana-tions.

(2) An analysis of the emotional climate of the interaction.

The rationale for analysis of level of precision resides in previous studies (cf. above) indicating a relationship between anxiety and various verbal skills. We wanted to explore, therefore, whether the observed differences could be explained by different degree of precision in the verbal explanations, or if (level of) anxiety affected more basic aspects of communication.

Degree of precision may be defined differently. In the present com-munication situation precision of explanations was operationalized along the following dimensions: To what extent was an explanatory utterance precise with respect to the critical categories (1) distance, (2) direction and (3) localization on the map. A certain degree of precision with respect to all these three aspects is required if the task is to be successfully accomplished. The dyads' verbal interaction on the experimental route *from* they started *until* they reached the point of the induced error the first time, was scored. Every dyad was scored inde-pendently by two trained scorers, and each utterance was given a score (from 1 to 4) according to its degree of precision in relation to the three critical dimensions mentioned above. On the basis of these scores, the 24 dyads were rank ordered from 1 to 24 according to degree of precision. Interscorer reliability on this final rank order was 0·85.

To test the possible effect of (degree of) precision upon efficiency of communication, the rank order correlation between time used on the two routes and precision, was calculated. No significant correlation was found between time used and degree of precision, neither on the practice route (rho = −0·18) nor on the experimental route (rho = 0·17). The differences in communication efficiency can therefore hardly be explained as being due to differences in verbal precision in the explanations.

In order to assess the emotional interaction climate of the various dyads, two scorers were given tape-recordings of the 24 practice routes and the 24 experimental routes in random order and asked to rate the interaction on 12 seven-point scales of the type "co-operative-competitive" (see Table III). All scales with interscorer reliability lower than

TABLE III. The twelve scales used to assess the emotional interaction climate, as well as the interscorer reliability co-efficients.

		Interscorer reliability	
Scales		Practice route	Experimental route
samarbeidende (co-operative)	konkurrerende —— (competitive)	0·33	0·88
sikker (sure)	usikker —— (unsure)	0·71	0·86
formell (formal)	uformell —— (informal)	0·40	0·46
fredelig (peaceful)	aggressiv —— (aggressive)	0·51	0·77
strukturert (structured)	ustrukturert —— (instructured)	0·87	0·80
anspent (tense)	avslappet —— (relaxed)	0·57	0·62
tolerant (tolerant)	intolerant —— (intolerant)	0·24	0·81
engasjert (involved)	uengasjert —— (uninvolved)	0·15	0·00[a]
tillit (confident)	mistillit —— (inconfident)	0·38	0·85
alvorlig (serious)	humoristisk —— (humorous)	0·55	0·83
rigid (rigid)	fleksibel —— (flexible)	0·31	0·81
varm (warm)	kjølig —— (cool)	0·08	0·71

[a] From the point of view of the method, it is worth reporting that all the dyads scored relatively high on involvement.

0·70, were rejected. We were thus left with nine reliable scales on the experimental route, and only two on the shorter practice route.

A factor analysis of the ratings of the experimental route on the nine reliable scales revealed two factors, explaining 67% and 16% of the total variance respectively. Factor I correlated highest with the scales tolerant/intolerant, confident/inconfident and flexible/rigid. Factor I thus seems to reveal something about openness/closedness regarding what is to be made known or exchanged in the dyads. We therefore labelled factor I a *"rigidity factor"*. The two scales correlating highest with factor II were humorous/serious and warm/cool. Factor II was therefore labelled an *"emotional tone factor"*.

An analysis of variance conducted on the reliable scales and the two factors (see Table IV) revealed no influence of any of the experimental manipulations on the practice route. On the experimental route, however, the communication of the high anxiety dyads was significantly different from that of the low anxiety dyads on eight of the nine scales

TABLE IV. Summary of analyses of variance on scales and factors on the communication on the practice route and the experimental route respectively.

		Source					
		(level of) anxiety		(type of) instruction		Interaction	
Situation	Scale/Factor	F	p	F	p	F	p
Practice route	(2) sure–unsure	0·00	—	0·52	—	0·52	—
	(4) structured-unstructured	0·08	—	0·60	—	0·46	—
	(1) co-operative–competitive	10·99	0·01	4·33	—	2·62	—
	(2) sure-unsure	163·21	0·01	0·02	—	0·62	—
	(3) peaceful–aggressive	4·60	0·05	3·25	—	0·59	—
	(4) structured-unstructured	16·76	0·01	0·42	—	0·42	—
Experimental	(5) tolerant-intolerant	14·73	0·01	1·76	—	0·35	—
route	(6) confident–inconfident	13·62	0·01	2·64	—	0·78	—
	(7) serious-humorous	0·06	—	0·72	—	1·19	—
	(8) rigid–flexible	29·73	0·01	3·50	—	1·12	—
	(9) warm–cool	3·64	—	0·83	—	5·01	0·05
	Factor I	42·75	0·01	1·59	—	0·23	—
	Factor II	0·06	—	1·44	—	2·05	—

and factor I. The high anxiety dyads were significantly more rigid (factor I) than the low anxiety dyads, but no such difference was found with respect to factor II. The different instruction conditions did not influence communication significantly in any of the two tasks as rated on any of the scales or factors.

Concluding Remarks

Two more general theoretical comments may be made on the basis of the present study. First, it demonstrated the possible substantial contributions of studies conducted on the general formula: How does the personal disposition X influence communication?

Secondly, the present study did so by revealing a significant effect of anxiety upon communication. The influence was reflected in efficiency as well as in ratings of emotional climate of the communication process. However, this particular effect was dependent upon situational factors, so that the influence was merely exposed in a complex conflict situation, and not in a simple and straightforward situation. A person's behaviour in a social situation can, therefore *neither* be explained exclusively by a trait or disposition theory *nor* by situational factors (situationism). We have instead *to specify under which social situation conditions a particular personal disposition will be influent.*

References

Ainsworth, L. H. (1958). Rigidity, insecurity and stress. *J. Abnormal Social Psychology* **56**, 67–75.

Argyle, M. (1969). "Social Interaction." Methuen, Atherton.

Beier, E. G. (1951). The effect of induced anxiety on flexibility of intellectual functioning. *Psychological Monographs* **65**, no. 9.

Blakar, R. M. (1970). Konteksteffektar i språkleg kommunikasjon. Thesis, University of Oslo.

Blakar, R. M. (1972). Ein eksperimentell situasjon til studiet av kommunikasjon: Bakgrunn, utvikling og nokre problemstillingar. Stencilled report. Institute of Psychology, University of Oslo.

Blakar, R. M. (1973). An experimental method for inquiring into communication. *European J. Social Psychology* **3**, 415–425.

Blakar, R. M. (1974a). Distinguishing social and individual psychology. *Scandinavian J. Psychology* **15**, 241–243.

Blakar, R. M. (1974b). Schizofreni og kommunikasjon: Førebels presentasjon av ei eksperimentell tilnærming. *Nordisk Psykiatrisk Tidsskrift* **28**, 239–248.

Blakar, R. M. (1975a). Psykopatologi og kommunikasjon: Arbeidsrapport frå ein eksperimentserie. Stencilled report. Institute of Psychology, University of Oslo.

Blakar, R. M. (1975b). Schizofreni og kommunikasjon: Vidare-føring av vår eksperimentelle tilnærming. *Tidsskrift Norsk Psykologforening* **12**, no. 8, 16–25.

Blakar, R. M. (1975c). Human Communication—an ever changing contract embedded in Social Contexts. Stencilled report. Institute of Psychology, University of Oslo.

Blakar, R. M. (1975d). Double-bind teorien: Ei kritisk vurdering. *Tidsskrift Norsk Psykologforening* **12**, no. 12, 13–26.

Blakar, R. M. and Rommetveit, R. (1975). Utterances *in vacuo* and in contexts: An experimental and theoretical exploration of some inter-relationships between what is heard and what is seen or imagined. *International J. Psycholinguistics* **4**, 5–32.

Boomer, D. S. and Goodrich, D. W. (1961). Speech disturbance and judged anxiety. *J. Consulting Psychology* **25**, 160–164.

Brown, R. (1953). A determinant of the relationship between rigidity and authoritarianism. *J. Abnormal Social Psychology* **48**, 469–476.

Garfinkel, H. (1972). Studies of the routine grounds of every-day activities. *In* "Studies in Social Interaction". (D. Sudnow, Ed.) The Free Press, New York.

Guildford, J. P. (1956). "Fundamental Statistics in Psychology and Education." McGraw-Hill, New York.

Gynther, R. H. (1957). The effects of anxiety and situational stress on communicative efficiency. *J. Abnormal Social Psychology* **54**, 274–276.

Haley, J. (1972). Critical overview of present status of family interaction research. *In* "A dialogue between family researchers and family therapists". (J. L. Framo, Ed.) Springer, New York.

Handel, G. (Ed.) (1967). "The psychological interior of the family." George Allen and Unwin Ltd., London.

Ichheiser, G. (1970). "Appearances and realities. Misunderstanding in Human Relations." Josey-Bass, San Francisco.

Jacobsen, S. M. and Pettersen, R. B. (1974). Kommunikasjon og samarbeid i den schizofrenes familie. Thesis, University of Oslo.

Kasl, S. V. and Mahl, G. F. (1965). The relationships of disturbances and hesitations in spontaneous speech of anxiety. *J. Personality Social Psychology* **1**, 425–433.

Luchins, A. S. (1942). Mechanization in problem solving: the effect of einstellung. *Psychological Monographs* **54**.

McNemar, Q. (1962). "Psychological Statistics." Wiley, New York.

Mahl, G. F. (1956). Disturbances and silences in the patient's speech in psychotherapy. *J. Abnormal Social Psychology* **53**, 1–15.

Mischel, W. (1968). "Personality and assessment." Wiley, New York.

Mischel, W. (1973). On the empirical dilemmas of psycho-dynamic approaches: Issues and alternatives. *J. Abnormal Social Psychology* **82**, 335–344.

Mishler, E. G. and Waxler, N. E. (1965). Family interaction processes and schizophrenia: A review of current theories. *Merrill-Palmer Quarterly of Behavior and Development* **11**, 269–315.

Moberget, O. and Reer, Ø. (1975). Kommunikasjon og psykopatologi: En empirisk-teoretisk analyse med vekt på begrepsmessig og metodologisk avklaring. Theses, University of Oslo.

Moscovici, S. (1967). Communication processing and the properties of language. *In* "Advances in Experimental Social Psychology". Vol. 3. (L. Berkowitz, Ed.) Academic Press, New York and London.

Pilisuk, M. (1963). Anxiety, self-acceptance, and open-mindedness. *J. Clinical Psychology* **19**, 388–391.

Riskin, J. and Faunce, E. E. (1972). An evaluative review of family interaction research. *Family Process* **11**, 365–455.

Rokeach, M. (1960). "The open and closed Mind." Basic Books, New York.

Rommetveit, R. (1968). "Words, Meanings and Messages." Academic Press and Universitetsforlaget, New York, London and Oslo.

Rommetveit, R. (1972). "Språk, tanke og kommunikasjon." Universitetsforlaget, Oslo.

Rommetveit, R. (1974). "On message structure." Wiley, Chichester.

Rubenowitz, R. (1963). "Emotional Flexibility-Rigidity as a Comprehensive Dimension of Mind." Acta Psychologica, Stockholm.

Rubenowitz, R. (1970). "Personlighetspsykologi." Bokförlaget Aldus/ Bonniers, Stockholm.

Ruesch, J. and Bateson, G. (1951). "Communication: The Social Matrix of Psychiatry." Norton, New York.

Sølvberg, H. A. and Blakar, R. M. (1975). Communication efficiency in families with and without a schizophrenic offspring. *Family Process* **14**, 515–534.

Taylor, J. A. (1953). A personality scale of manifest anxiety. *J. Abnormal Social Psychology* **48**, 285–290.

35. On the Relationship between Children's Mastery of Piagetian Cognitive Operations and their Semantic Competence*

R. ROMMETVEIT

The very ambitious aim of this article is to convince you that certain significant modifications of assumptions are required in the Genevan approach to children's language and thought. In order to achieve such a highly ambitious aim, however, I shall adopt a rather cautious strategy. The point of departure for my critique will thus be some observations of children's achievements in very simple communication tasks.

The latter are all tasks of *identifying reference* (Strawson, 1969). The child is simply asked to identify one particular target object located within a specific referential domain of similar objects. The target object is made known to the child by means of an unequivocal *identifying description* of it, either immediately *before* or *after* he is shown the referential domain (see Fig. 1). Lack of intersubjectivity is hence revealed if the child points out some object other than the one referred to by the adult.

Some of the kinds of tasks we tried out are indicated in Table I. The referential domain would for instance be six circles, presented in one

* The data reported in this paper were collected by a team of students and teachers under the direction of Karsten Hundeide and R. Rommetveit at the University of Oslo in 1975, and we are particularly grateful to Ingegerd Lindström for her assistance in the project. A first version of the paper was presented at the Stirling Conference on the Psychology of Language, June, 1976, at the University of Stirling, Scotland.

Later a part of the paper was presented at the Danish Speech and Hearing Association annual meeting 1977, Nyborg Strand, Nyborg, Denmark. Published in *Nordisk Tidsskrift Logopedi og Foniatri* (1977) **2,** 107–117.

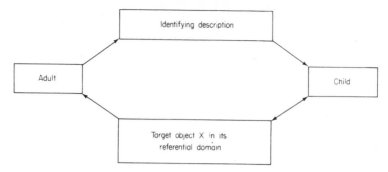

FIG. 1. Structure of task of identifying reference.

of the four spatial arrangements shown in Cells 1 to 4, and the child would be asked to point out:

(1) "the one of the WHITE circles that is SECOND LARGEST".*

TABLE I. Some referential domains in tasks of identifying reference.

Spatial distribution of		Type of cross-classification		
Attribute I (dichotomous)	Attribute II (graded)	A x B	(A₂+B) x A₂	A₁ x A₃
Separated	Ordered	Cell 1	Cell 5	Cell 9
	Random	Cell 2	Cell 6	Cell 10
Mixed	Ordered	Cell 3	Cell 7	Cell 11
	Random	Cell 4	Cell 8	Cell 12

Correct identification of the target object presupposes in this case mastery of *cross-classification* and *ordering*. Notice, however, how different purely spatial arrangements of the same six objects may affect ease of identification. There are thus quite a few children at the age of six and seven years who are perfectly capable of pointing out the target object in Cell 1, yet unable to do so when it is encountered in Cell 3. Their errors in the latter case, moreover, are all of the same kind: They point out the second largest of ALL circles rather than the second largest one of the WHITE circles only.

* In Norwegian: "den av de HVITE rundingene som er NEST STØRST".

This error is thus clearly due to *diffusion of the domain of the ordering operation*. Children who hit the target object in Cell 1 but fail to identify it in Cell 3, will therefore succeed *also in the latter task* if the same target object is verbally described as:

(1′) "the one of the WHITE circles that is SECOND SMALLEST".

This identifying description merely implies a reversal of the direction of ordering, starting from the SMALLEST one and proceeding from right to left. The second smallest of ALL circles is BLACK, however. The child will hence—even though initially engaged in ordering ALL six circles—immediately discover the error with respect to colour and proceed one step further to the left.

Let us now briefly reconsider the task of identifying "*the one of the* WHITE *circles that is* SECOND LARGEST" in Cell 3 of Table I. What is required, in terms of Piagetian cognitive operations, in order to solve it? The child must obviously be able to cross-classify and order objects and, in addition, be capable of restricting his ordering operation to one particular subset of the referential domain while attending to the entire set of objects. Mastery of *cross-classification, ordering* and *class inclusion* is hence apparently required in order for the child to establish inter-subjectivity on adult premises. And this will be the case in all the variants of tasks we shall consider next.

Consider, first, an alternative identifying description of the target object in Cell 3. The child is now, immediately before he is shown the drawing of objects, asked to point out:

(1A) "the one of the SNOWBALLS that is SECOND LARGEST".

Some children who fail when the white objects are described as WHITE CIRCLES are now able to solve the task. What is achieved by verbal categorization of the subset as SNOWBALLS is thus an effect comparable to that obtained by spatial separation of the two subsets in Cell 1: The white objects are apparently *mentally set apart* from all others in such a way that ordering of the entire set is prevented. So far, the tasks have involved classification of objects with respect to colour and size. The latter are *orthogonal attributes* in the sense that (a) the sensory-motor mechanisms involved in identification of one of them is totally unrelated to those involved in the other and (b) they are referred to by distinctively different words. But let us now see what happens in otherwise—as far as Piagetian cognitive operations are concerned—formally identical tasks in which objects have to be cross-classified with respect to intimately *related attributes*. Consider, for instance, a referential domain such as the one indicated in Cell 11 in Table I and a request to point out:

(2) "the one of the SHORT MEN who has the SECOND LARGEST way to the house".*

The crucial attributes are in this case SHORT as applied to body height and LONG as applied to horizontal distance, and simultaneous attendance to two different variants of length is hence required in order to identify the target object: The child must attend to length *qua* body height (A1) while ordering length *qua* horizontal distance (A2) in order to select the appropriate subset of distances to be ordered.

It is hardly surprising, therefore, that even eight and a half year old children who have no difficulties whatsoever in identifying *"the one of the* WHITE CIRCLES *that is* SECOND LARGEST" in Cell 3 fail when asked to point out *"the one of the* SHORT MEN *who has the* SECOND LONGEST *way to the house"* in Cell 11. Diffusion of the domain of ordering may also in this case, however, be counteracted by purely verbal means. We may for instance, immediately before we show the drawing, ask the child to point out:

(2A) "the one of the BOYS who has the SECOND LONGEST way to the house".

The child will then simply take it for granted that the drawing contains BOYS at the moment he starts inspecting it. What has been *said* serves as a basis for making sense of what is *seen* in such a way that the SHORT objects are mentally set apart as a more discrete and autonomous subset than what appears to be the case if they are verbally described as SHORT MEN. The otherwise very salient perceptual feature height (vertical length) is attended to merely as a means of identifying those BOYS and—once that identification has been performed—of secondary concern.

Imagine, next, that we put skirts on the three short creatures in Cell 11 and move the whole drawing into Cell 7. The two subsets to be kept apart for ordering purposes will now differ with respect to two attributes, and cross-classification will be of type $(A_1 + B) \times A_2$. Cell 7 is consequently inhabited by tall males and short females, and the target object may be verbally described as *"the one of the* LADIES *who has the* SECOND LONGEST *way to the house"*. An alternative referential domain for a task of type $(A_1 + B) \times A_2$ may for instance be *long black-clothed and short white-clothed men* approaching the top of a mountain, whereas an additional variant of type $A_1 \times A_2$ is produced by placing *short and tall firemen at different vertical positions on a ladder*.

---

* In Norwegian: "den av de KORTE MENNENE som har NEST LENGST veg til huset". Body height is in Norwegian expressed optionally by the two adjective pairs KORT/ LANG (SHORT/LONG) and LÅG/HOG (LOW/HIGH). The former pair refers to horizontal distance as well.

Let us now consider eight and a half year old children's achievements on five such tasks of identifying reference (see Table II). These five tasks are identical as far as taxation of formally defined Piagetian operations is concerned. Each identifying description is of the general form: "the one of the (attribute I) that is second (attribute II)" and identification of the target object presupposes therefore in every case mastery of cross-classification and ordering. The purely spatial arrangement of objects is for every task such, moreover, that *diffusion of the domain of the ordering operation leads to failure.*

TABLE II. Success ($+$) and failure ($-$) by eight and a half year old children on five tasks of identifying reference.

Task	Verbal identification					
	Pre-			Post-		
	−	+	N	−	+	N
(1) A × B WHITE DOGS—SECOND BIGGEST	3	18	21	2	16	18
(2) (A₁+B) × A₂ LADIES—SECOND LONGEST WAY	4	17	21	4	14	18
(3) (A₁+B) × A₂ BLACK-CLOTHED MEN—SECOND LONGEST WAY	13	8	21	6	12	18
(4) A₁ × A₂ HIGH MEN—SECOND SHORTEST WAY	14	7	21	7	11	18
(5) A₁ × A₂ LOW FIREMEN—SECOND HIGHEST ON LADDER	18	3	21	7	11	18

The children were pupils of an elementary school in an upper middle class district near Oslo. There were 39 children who completed all five tasks, 21 of them under conditions of verbal pre-identification and the remaining 18 under conditions of verbal post-identification of the target object. And Table II may thus in principle be read as a story about what happens to formally defined operations of thought when such operations are imbued with content and encountered in systematically varied contexts of communication.

Notice, first of all, that nearly all children succeed in task 1, whereas nearly all of them fail in task 5 when the target object is verbally described immediately before they are shown the referential domain. It turns out, moreover, that 19 out of the 21 individual patterns of success and failure under conditions of verbal pre-identification conform to a strictly ascending order of difficulty from task 1 to 5. Level of difficulty is thus clearly *not* unequivocally determined by the invariant logical structure of the tasks, but intimately linked to variant semantic and communicative aspects. And Table II may consequently, from the point of view of Piaget's theoretical framework, possibly be interpreted as portraying tasks representing different levels of resistance to the same operative structures and hence as a specification of what he conveniently refers to as "décalage horizontal".

His very notion of "décalage horizontal", however, seems to be based on the assumption that operations ". . . play an indispensible role in logic . . ." and are at the same time also ". . . actual psychological activities . . .", whereas language is composed of "conventional signifiers" and "the index of what has become conscious" (see Piaget, 1957, p. 7; Piaget, 1951, p. 93 and Piaget and Inhelder, 1966, p. 69). Mastery of Piagetian operations of thought is accordingly revealed in *syntactic competence* and mastery of *"operator-like words"*, whereas ". . . other lexical items (e.g. long, short, thin, thick, high, low) are far less closely linked to operativity" (see Sinclair-de-Zwart, 1972, p. 275). As Furth (1970, p. 251) points out, the child's semantic competence is thus according to Piaget's assumptions *by definition* nearly devoid of operative aspects. Verbal communication is consequently in Piagetian experiments conceived of as a necessary, though unobtrusive and rather insignificant, component of an interaction aiming at diagnosis of operations of thought. Intersubjectivity is taken for granted on the assumption (Olson, 1970, p. 264) that ". . . words specify an intended referent relative to the set of alternatives from which it must be differentiated".

This is true, however, of every single identifying description included in tasks 1 to 5 in Table II, and there is no doubt that all our eight and a half year old children in a certain sense "understand" every word of each of the five instructions. Even task 5 is thus immediately solved by all of them under conditions of verbal post-identification *if the three short firemen are set apart from the tall ones on a separate ladder* (see Cell 9 of Table I). We might hence, in accordance with Piaget's and Sinclair-de-Zwart's approach to language and thought, conclude that 18 out of 21 children "comprehend" all words involved in verbal pre-identification of the target object in task 5, yet fail to master the "operations of thought" required in actual identification of it.

Such an interpretation, however, seems absurd in view of our data. Ease of identification of the target objects is, first of all, in every single task determined in an interplay between *what is seen* and *what is said about it*. It is true, moreover, that the tasks are identical as far as taxation of formally defined Piagetian operations is concerned. Whether the child will attain intersubjectivity on adult premises, though, is dependent upon which pictorially presented entities have to be kept apart, which contracts concerning categorization are embedded in the adult's identifying description of them, and—thirdly—upon what can be taken for granted by the child when something else is made known. Success in some of our tasks of identifying reference under conditions of verbal pre-identification is thus dependent upon a level of *operative semantic competence* far beyond the level required in conventional assessment of word comprehension.

The level of operative semantic competence required in task 5, for instance, may be tentatively specified as a capacity to cope simultaneously with two intimately related, though distinctively different, variants of LOW/HIGH. There is no doubt, moreover, that the two expressions LADIES and BLACK-CLOTHED men both are "understood" by all our eight and a half year old children. The fact remains, though, that only one of them (LADIES) serves to set the referent mentally apart in such a way that a majority of the children can withstand diffusion of the domain of the ordering operation. We are accordingly once more forced to recognize *a regulative function of words* beyond what is involved in passive comprehension (Luria, 1961).

Which operations of thought can be performed on a given referential domain is thus clearly dependent upon our capacity to structure that domain in terms of discrete, though orderly related elements. Such structuring, moreover, is achieved by attribution of meaning and categorization of perceptual units which make them stand out as discrete, meaningful and familiar entities. And this is precisely the reason why some seven year old Norwegian children can immediately point out the target object in Cell 3 of Table I when it is called a SNOWBALL but fail to do so if it is described as a WHITE CIRCLE.

Consider, next, the significant difference between conditions of verbal pre- and post-identification in performances on task 5 in Table II. What is made known by the expressions "LOW FIREMEN" and "SECOND HIGHEST on the ladder" may, when said about visibly available firemen at different vertical positions, be immediately "disambiguated" in terms of particular perceptual features of the referential domain. Correct identification of the target object when it is verbally described immediately before it is seen, on the other hand, is contingent upon mastery of abstract drafts of contracts concerning categorization in anticipation of contextually determined specific elaborations of them. The negligible time interval between the identifying description of the target object and exposure to the referential domain may therefore, at a certain developmental stage of semantic competence, be of crucial importance.

This appeared also to be the case with seven year old children's mastery of the adjectives HEAVY/LIGHT in a task requiring simple cross-classification. The referential domain consisted of four men at work. These four men represented all possible combinations of being *heavily built* versus *slim* and *putting stamps on envelopes* versus *carrying big sacks*, and the child was simply asked to point out "*the* HEAVY *man with a* LIGHT *work*". Identification of the target object turned out to be no problem at all for our eight and a half year old children, and even 22 out of 27 children in the seven years group succeeded when they were watching the drawing of the four men while listening to the identifying description. More than half of them failed, however, when the target object was described immediately before they were shown the drawing.

An expression such as LIGHT WORK is thus at a certain stage of language acquisition apparently immediately understood when bound to an experientially taken-for-granted referential domain of some men putting stamps on envelopes and others carrying big sacks, yet incomprehensible in the linguistic context "HEAVY MAN with LIGHT WORK" if no such referential domain can be taken for granted at that very moment. The child's partial mastery of the word is therefore perhaps most plausibly described as not yet fully decentred, but *bound to* particular experiential contingencies. What is involved in mastery of the antonyms HEAVY/LIGHT at the level of adult operative semantic competence, on the other hand, seems to be a very abstract draft of a contract that in specific acts of verbal communication can be elaborated into reciprocally endorsed contracts concerning categorization of WORK, MEALS, TAXES and DUTIES as well as of HUMAN BODIES and STONES.

Some of these categorizations may be considered instances of "literal", other of "metaphorical" use. The expressions HEAVY STONE, HEAVY WORK and HEAVY DUTY may thus be said to mirror an extrapolation from an initially narrow and sensory-motorically anchored referential domain to successively less "tangible", though "actual" human realities. The same may be said about distinctively different elaborations of BIG/SMALL, however, as a topic of discourse such as *size of particular material objects* is replaced by, e.g. *numerical value*. Increased operativity—which by Piaget and his associates is dogmatically and exclusively attributed to thought—is thus an essential aspect of the child's developing *semantic competence* as well as of his intimately related expanding *knowledge of the world*.

Operative semantic competence is in our simple communication tasks revealed in the child's attempt to grasp a "social" (i.e. talked-about) reality and convert it back into the visually portrayed "actual" reality referred to by the adult. And verbal pre- versus post-identification constitute different conditions for such conversion. The white objects in Cell 3 of Table I may thus stand out as a particularly familiar and discrete set if the child takes it for granted that they are SNOWBALLS the moment he gets to see them. What is said about SHORT men and LONG ways in connection with Cell 11 of Table I, on the other hand, may hardly be fully understood at all unless the child *at that moment* can take it for granted that it is said about those particular visible creatures approaching that house. Whether verbal pre- or post-identification provide an optimal condition for intersubjectivity can hence only be decided via a systematic analysis of message structure and, more specifically, by a careful analysis of patterns of dependencies between *what is seen* and *what is said about it* in each particular case of identifying reference (Rommetveit, 1974 and 1977).

Piaget's claim that logical operations of thought are "actual psychological activities" and his programmatic denial of operative aspects of language make for a peculiar "negative rationalism". This is reflected in a general strategy for assessment of children's cognitive development: The child's thought is explicated in terms of deviations from some fully formalized logical calculus, and conceptual development is assessed as an approximation to scientifically elaborated conceptual frameworks.

These are perfectly legitimate strategies, of immediate diagnostic relevance in educational settings aiming narrowly and precisely at mastery of those very calculi and conceptual frameworks. The resultant psychological knowledge is bound to be of a negative nature, though, in the sense that our initial ignorance of the child's mind is being replaced by knowledge of its shortcomings relative to superimposed, formal models. Suppose, for instance, that we want to make use of the five tasks and the two different conditions of communication in Table II for diagnostic purposes. What, precisely, would a given particular individual pattern of successes and failures then tell us? Would it be possible at all to assess mastery of Piagetian operations *as such*, without specifying what kind of *knowledge of the world* and which *level of operative semantic* competence *were required*? And what should we say about a child who behaves "logically" toward white and black circles if and only if the former are being *talked about* as SNOWBALLS?

Similar questions have already been raised, although from slightly different theoretical and empirical backgrounds, by Smedslund (1970), Wason and Johnson-Laird (1973), and others. Smedslund is in a recent paper particularly concerned with Piaget's faith in the psychological reality of logical operations and his failure to recognize the circular relation between understanding and logic in psychological diagnostics. And he concludes (Smedslund, 1976, p. 6):

> In so far as Piagetian psychologists focus on logicality as a variable . . .
> and give only peripheral attention to the problem of determining
> children's understanding of instructions and situations, I think they
> are making an epistemological error and are out of step with everyday
> life as well as with all useful psychological practice.

References

Furth, H. G. (1970). On language and knowing in Piaget's developmental theory. *Human Development* **13,** 241–257.

Luria, A. N. (1961). "The Role of Speech in Regulation of Normal and Abnormal Behaviour." Pergamon Press, Oxford.

Olson, D. (1970). Language and thought. Aspects of a cognitive theory of semantics. *Psychological Review* **77**, 257–273.

Piaget, J. (1951). "Judgment and Reasoning in the Child." Routledge and Kegan Paul, London.

Piaget, J. (1957). "Logic and Psychology." Basic Books, New York.

Piaget, J. and Inhelder, B. (1966). "La Psychologie de L'enfant." Presses Universitaires de France, Paris.

Rommetveit, R. (1974). "On Message Structure. A Framework for the Study of Language and Communication." Wiley, Chichester.

Rommetveit, R. (1977). On Piagetian cognitive operations, semantic competence, and message structure in adult-child communication. *In* "The Social Context of Language". (I. Markova, Ed.) Wiley, Chichester.

Sinclair-de-Zwart, H. (1972). Developmental psycholinguistics. *In* "Language in Thinking". (P. Adams, Ed.) pp. 226–276. Penguin Books, Harmondsworth.

Smedslund, J. (1970). Circular relation between understanding and logic. *Scandinavian J. Psychology* **11**, 218–219.

Smedslund, J. (1976). Piaget's psychology in practice. Stencilled report, Institute of Psychology, University of Oslo.

Strawson, P. F. (1969). "Individuals." Methuen, London.

Wason, P. C. and Johnson-Laird, P. N. (1972). "The Psychology of Reasoning: Structure and Content." Batsford, London.